The
German
Air Force

1933-1945
An Anatomy of Failure

Matthew Cooper

JANE'S

LONDON · NEW YORK · SYDNEY

First published in the United Kingdom in 1981 by
Jane's Publishing Company Limited
238 City Road, London EC1V 2PU

ISBN 07106 0071 2

Published in the United States of America in 1981 by
Jane's Publishing Incorporated
730 Fifth Avenue
New York
N.Y. 10019

ISBN 0 531 03733 9

Maps: Alec Spark

Typesetting by Method Limited
Woodford Green, Essex

Printed in Great Britain by
Mackays of Chatham Limited

Contents

Introduction   i

Unit Designations   iv

Equivalent Officer Ranks   v

I.   THE HIGH COMMAND   1

II.   THE STRATEGIC BASE   34

III.   THE ONSET OF WAR   61

IV.   THE EARLY CAMPAIGNS   97

V.   THE ONSLAUGHT AGAINST BRITAIN   121

VI.   BLITZ AND COUNTER-ATTACK   164

VII.   THE MEDITERRANEAN   195

VIII.   THE ATTACK ON THE SOVIET UNION   218

IX.   THE CRISIS   259

X.   1943 – YEAR OF DEFEAT   287

XI.   1944 – THE BEGINNING OF THE END   320

XII.   THE END   358

Conclusion   377

Appendix: German Military Aviation, 1919-1933   379

Notes   390

Select Bibliography   396

Index   400

List of Maps

Battle of Britain   137
Battle of the Atlantic, 1941   177
Organisation of the Reich's Defence Against Night Raids,
    late 1942   189
The Mediterranean   202
Operational Areas of Commands, summer 1942   261
Forces under Luftflotte 3, 6th June 1944   334

Photographs follow pages 150 and 278

Introduction

'Our job was to piece together the bodies for burial. It was a difficult business, as there were often many bits missing altogether. We had no means of knowing if a certain leg belonged to a particular body, or if a head was once attached to any of the various limbs and torsos arranged in neat rows in front of us. . . . The stench was so awful that we hurried to complete the task, and often bodies only half complete were put into coffins. On one occasion, I remember, a joker gave one body four arms, and that was how it was buried. . . . The relatives knew nothing about this sort of thing, of course.' So wrote a citizen of Cologne of an aspect of the Second World War which sprang directly from the failure of the Luftwaffe in the sky over Germany. His experience was not unique, and was shared by countless millions on both sides of the conflict. In Europe and the Soviet Union alone, it is estimated that total casualties, military as well as civilian, from air warfare was in excess of one million dead and two million seriously injured. In this, the German Air Force played a major part.

Little more will be written in this book of the effect of air warfare on human beings: instead, its strategic causes and consequences will be analysed. But nevertheless, this is a work which, in the words of one historian of the Luftwaffe, Professor Richard Suchenwirth, stems not from 'any affection for militarism, but rather from the realisation of the extent to which freedom and the greatness and fate of a people are dependent upon military decisions; of how many brave soldiers and people behind the front are affected by good or bad leadership in time of war'.

The German Air Force was a failure. No amount of description of its early successes, or the feats of its pilots and field commanders, should be allowed to obscure that fact. Indeed, the seeds of its defeat were being sown even while it was proceeding from victory to victory in Poland, Scandinavia, and France and Flanders, against enemies that were substantially inferior both in equipment and tactics. By 1941, the weaknesses with which the Air Force had begun the war were well in evidence; the loss of superiority in the air was the result, and with it, failure at the three fronts and over the Reich. Although this alone did not bring about the defeat of Hitler's Germany, it was an essential precondition. Indeed, the Luftwaffe's failure was the most important single factor which led to the downfall of the Third Reich; it alone did not allow the Soviets to enter Berlin or the Western Allies to reach the Elbe in April 1945,

i

but it certainly hastened their arrival.

Had the Luftwaffe been capable of fulfilling the tasks given it by Hitler, the course of the war would have been very different, with Britain, in all probability, subjected to German rule, and the Mediterranean, together with Persian oil, under Axis domination. The United States of America would then have found it very difficult to enter the war against Germany, and the Soviet Union would have faced the undivided might of the whole Wehrmacht. But a reverse in the skies over south-east England in the summer of 1940, made worse by failure over Malta in the following two years, together with a deepening commitment in the Soviet Union, made defeat inevitable. Time, in the guise of a quick victory, the Luftwaffe's most precious ally, had been sacrificed, and the enemy was allowed to develop their air forces to a point where the Germans could not hope to match them. Loss of the initiative in the air was the result, and by the autumn of 1944, although air warfare was by then the single most dominant feature of the war, the Luftwaffe had ceased to be a factor of any importance. Defeat had turned into oblivion.

In my analysis of that failure, I concentrate on the strategic development of the Luftwaffe, and only so far as they bear upon that have I taken tactical or technical details into account. The feats of individual pilots, or of units, are seldom mentioned, even though they were among the finest in the history of military endeavour. All this has been done too well in many other books to call for any contribution here. Indeed, this work deals solely with the one remaining area of the Luftwaffe that has been poorly served by historians. For not since 1946 has any book appeared which covers both comprehensively and in detail the strategic development of the German Air Force from 1933 to 1945. It is this gap in the history of the Second World War which I have tried to fill. It is an enormous subject, and much has had to be excluded in order to produce a book concise enough to be published. For example, the political course of Göring's career is seldom mentioned, as are those aspects of the Luftwaffe that were peripheral to its main taks of prosecuting air warfare: the anti-aircraft units with the armies, the paratroopers and the ground troops.

The writing of this book has led me to question many of the premises on which historians have based their judgement of the Luftwaffe. While it cannot be called a radical reappraisal, I hope that it serves as a useful re-evaluation. For, all too often, the development of the German Air Force is seen from the vantage point of hindsight to the exclusion of all else. But decisions which to post-war man might appear wrong, were often seen in a very different light at the time in which they were made. Thus, the Luftwaffe's judgements concerning dive-bombing and heavy bombers here receive a more sympathetic treatment than is usual, as does its decisions regarding the development of new aircraft types during the war. Even Udet, usually the *bête noir* of the Luftwaffe's historians, bears much less blame than is usually ascribed to him. In the book I have touched on a theme which particularly interests me: namely, that the practice of Blitzkrieg as has been popularly understood since the war is, at the very least, misleading. The use of the Luftwaffe to support the Army has been described with this in mind, and it is interesting to note that the German Air Force did not come to concentrate on those types of operations which have traditionally been associated with Blitzkrieg until the victorious Blitzkrieg campaigns were a thing of the past. Hitler's abuse of his responsibility not only as head of state but as the Supreme Commander of the German Armed Forces also comes under scrutiny. His actions, above all else, led to the failure of the Luftwaffe, just as they did for the Army. I have also spent much space in the book analysing the Battle of Britain, which I consider to have been of crucial importance. I differ from the usual interpretations of the Battle in my belief that the Luftwaffe not only *could* have won the battle but *should* have won it, at least as far as gaining air superiority over south-east England. Even the RAF's radar was, I believe, more of an ally to the Germans than a disadvantage.

I should like to thank those who have helped me in the writing of this book: Miss Elaine Austin, whose patience in reading my manuscript was matched only by the perspicacity of her suggestions; Alex Vanags-Baginskis, whose generous use of his own time and his considerable knowledge of the technical aspects of the Luftwaffe has saved me from many a *faux pas*; James Lucas of the Imperial War Museum; Brian L. Davis for his help in obtaining the uniform reproduced on the jacket; Michael Stevens of Jane's; Anthony Shadrake of King's College, London; Dora Clarke, of the House of Commons Library; and Clare Pearson.

Because many of the Luftwaffe's records were destroyed at the end of the war, and because many standards of classification concerning aircraft types, battle strengths and losses have been used since 1945, there are no universally recognised figures which represent the Luftwaffe's development in these areas. During the Battle of Britain, for example, the RAF often claimed, in good faith, the destruction of three times the number of German aircraft than was actually the case. Moreover, aircraft classification tables are often at variance one with another. With this in mind, I have taken care to keep to the same classifications throughout the book. Experts may well disagree on certain, if not many, points, but it should be remembered that the importance of the figures given here lies not in their specific accuracy, but in the underlying historical trends to which they point. Finally it should be mentioned that owing to the frequent use of German terms it has been decided not to italicise them, as is normal practice.

Matthew Cooper
December 1980

Unit Designations

As there are no accurate equivalents, this book has kept the original Luftwaffe unit designations which are explained below.

The basic operational unit in the Luftwaffe was the *Gruppe*. Depending on the aircraft type (fighters, bombers, reconnaissance, coastal aviation) a *Gruppe* could comprise three to four *Staffeln* of nine to 16 aircraft each. Including its *Stab* (Staff Flight) of three to four machines a *Gruppe* had an establishment strength of 30 to 68 aircraft. However, the actual strength was often below the establishment, particularly during the last year of the war.

Certain *Gruppen* were formed as, and remained, independent formations. Their basic functions were indicated by an abbreviation, thus: Aufkl.Gr. (*Aufklärungsgruppe*) = reconnaissance; FAGr. (*Fernaufklärungs-*) = long-range reconnaissance; JGr. (*Jagd-*) = day fighters; KGr. (*Kampf-*) = bombers; Kü.Fl.Gr. (*Küstenflieger-*) = coastal aviation; NAGr. (*Nahaufklärungs-*) = short-range reconnaissance; NJGr. (*Nachtjagd-*) = night fighters; and, before 1943, KGr.z.b.V. (*Kampfgruppe zur besonderen Verwendung*, or KGr. 'for special duties'), indicating an often temporary transport *Gruppe* of varying strength.

A *Geschwader* had a nominal strength of three to four *Gruppen* plus a *Stab*. As in the case of *Gruppen*, the establishment strength depended on the type of aircraft and the basic role, and could vary from 120 to over 200 aircraft. The actual strength was usually lower, being affected by such factors as combat losses, delayed replacements and (quite often) lack of matériel and aircrews in the first place. As with *Gruppen*, the basic function was indicated by an abbreviated prefix, thus: JG (*Jagdgeschwader*) = day fighters; KG (*Kampf-*) = bombers; NJG (*Nachtjagd-*) = night fighters; SG (*Schlacht-*) = close support; St.G (*Stuka-*) = dive bombers (before October 1943); TG (*Transport-*) (after October 1943); and ZG (*Zerstörer-*) = heavy fighters.

The *Gruppen* within a *Geschwader* were indicated by Roman numerals before the unit designation and the *Staffeln* – by Arabic numerals. Thus I/KG 4 = I *Gruppe* of KG 4; 9./KG 55 = 9.*Staffel* of KG 55 (part of III/KG 55).

Equivalent Officer Ranks

Luftwaffe	**RAF**	**USAAF**
Generalfeldmarschall	Marshal of the RAF	General (five star)
Generaloberst	Air Chief Marshal	General (four star)
General der Flieger	Air Marshal	Lieutenant General
Generalleutnant	Air Vice Marshal	Major General
Oberst	Group Captain	Colonel
Oberstleutnant	Wing Commander	Lieutenant Colonel
Major	Squadron Leader	Major
Hauptmann	Flight Lieutenant	Captain
Oberleutnant	Flying Officer	First Lieutenant
Leutnant	Pilot Officer	Second Lieutenant

1

The High Command

On 11th November 1918, the First World War was brought to a close. On that day the Imperial German Flying Service possessed an authorised strength of 2,709 aircraft. It had fought a long war, honourably and well, during which its airmen had shot down no fewer than 7,425 enemy aeroplanes. On 21st January 1919, the Service was demobilised; its commanding general, Ernst von Hoeppner, told his men that they had 'established an outstanding record at the front, a record whose brilliance increased further as the war progressed.'[1] In March, the new Reichsheer that emerged from the old defeated Imperial Army still retained a number of air units; but these were short-lived. On 10th January 1920, they were disbanded in accordance with the provisions of the Versailles Treaty, Article 198 of which stated that 'Germany is forbidden to maintain either land-based or naval air forces'. Article 202 requested that all existing military aircraft be surrendered to the victorious Allies, and, as a result, Germany either destroyed or handed over no fewer than 15,000 aircraft, 28,000 aero-engines and sixteen airships, and dismantled one million square metres of hangars. This was intended to be the end of German military aviation; yet, within twenty years, a German air force was again at war, the strongest in Europe and destined to win devastating victories over its enemies. It was a story of success with few equals, a success so great as to obscure those inherent weaknesses which were to bring about its downfall in war.

These weaknesses were several. In part they stemmed from the Air Force's high command, in which discord predominated, and from the decisions it took both before and during the war. But, in the main, they were the result of Hitler's choice, made in 1939, to risk a major war before Germany's armed forces were prepared for it. The Air Force, in particular, was ill-equipped for a conflict that involved any commitment greater than one short-lived campaign at a time. Before the invasion of Poland, it had undergone only six and a half years of full-scale development, just four and a half of which were untrammelled by any need to preserve secrecy. For, in the twelve years until Hitler's assumption of power in 1933, the Versailles Treaty had been successful in its aim. Despite all attempts to circumvent the restrictions, German military capability remained severely limited, and military aviation was quite inadequate, both in extent and preparation, to form any but the barest skeleton on which to place flesh in the future. The foundations on which the National Socialists had to build a new air force were meagre indeed.*

Certainly, Germany's new leaders were not entirely without some legacy. In particular, several types of aircraft had been developed that were to form the initial front-line strength of the new force: the Ju 52 transport-bomber, the Do 11 bomber, the Ar 64 and He 51 fighters, the He 45 and He 46 reconnaissance aircraft, and He 5, HD 38 and Do 15 Wal seaplanes, all of which compared not unfavourably with their counterparts abroad. However, that alone did not compose an air force, for which in Germany in 1933 there was neither a suitable command structure nor the personnel and material available. For, during the years of the Weimar Republic, little had been spent on clandestine military aviation. Despite a recognition of its potential among officers in both the Army and the Navy, only some 170,000,000 Reichsmarks were made available for all aspects of secret air rearmament over the seven years from 1926 to 1932, quite insufficient to produce a fighting force of any significance. Despite the establishment of an air base in the Soviet Union, at Lipetsk, the institution of the civilian Luftfahrt Verband (Aviation League) and commercial flying schools and glider clubs, through which military training was secretly undertaken, and the formation of the airline Deutsche Luft Hansa and commercial companies such as Severa GmbH, all of which were used to overcome the Versailles restrictions, German military aviation was in a poor condition by the end of 1932. In the Reichswehr, there were only 550 pilots and 180 observers, while the military flying units were few and scattered among a number of different agencies. They comprised just five bomber, three fighter, five reconnaissance, and two seaplane Staffeln, and one air-towing Staffel, which, together with reserves, amounted to some 250 aircraft of indifferent quality, many of which were convertable civilian machines to be used only in emergencies. In addition, two Army transport companies provided a small pool of mechanics.

Just as important was the lamentable condition into which the once-significant German aircraft industry had fallen. Not only was it extremely small, having an output of just 0.2 per cent of total German industrial production, of which only a fraction was military machines, but it also required considerable state support in order to survive. On 4th April, the Army's Air Inspectorate reported that the aircraft industry was incapable of producing more than 100 military aircraft a month after nine months of mobilisation, whereas plans called for an output of 300 within six months. Much, then, had to be done. The magnitude of the task that lay ahead for Germany's new leaders is shown by a comparison between their inheritance and the force at their disposal by the autumn of 1939. The sixteen Staffeln had grown to 302; the 730 flying personnel to 20,000; and the 250 aircraft to 3,500, the quality of which was far superior to their predecessors.

Such was the position of German military aviation when Hitler became

---

*See Appendix for a brief history of German military aviation from 1919 to 1933.

Reich's Chancellor on 30th January 1933. Undaunted, he and his colleagues immediately set about greatly strengthening the air force as part of their plans for general rearmament. On 3rd February, Hitler appointed his close political aide, Hermann Göring, to the new post of Reichskommisar für den Luftverkehr (Reich Commissioner for Air Traffic), giving him control of civil aviation which till then had been the responsibility of the Transport Ministry. The military establishment was alarmed; the generals were aware that the newly appointed Commissioner would not content himself with civil aviation. They moved with speed. A military counterpart to the new civilian organisation was deemed necessary, one to supervise all developments in the Army and Navy and which was firmly under the control of the Defence Ministry. On 8th February, General Werner von Blomberg, the Defence Minister, merged the aviation offices of the two services, and on 1st April the Luftschutzamt (Air Defence Office) came into being. This fully centralised the operations, administration, research and development of military aviation, and replaced the previously chaotic structure whereby responsibility had been divided among no fewer than eight departments, as well as partly shared with the Transport Ministry. The chief of the Luftschutzamt, Colonel Eberhard Bohnstedt, was referred to by the Army Commander, von Hammerstein, as 'the stupidest clot I could find in my General Staff'.[2] But however low a priority aviation might have been within military circles, the aim of the new office was clear: to foster the development of an air force not as a new, independent service under Göring's control, but as an integral part of the existing armed services.

But the military's efforts to retain their autonomy in this field were short-lived. On 28th March, Göring was nominated Reichsminister für Luftfahrt (Minister for Aviation), and on 5th May the new Reichsluftfahrtministerium (RLM – State Air Ministry) was instituted. A former director of the national airline, Erhard Milch, was made Staatssekretär (Secretary of State) and served as Göring's deputy. On 15th May, following Hitler's order, agreed to by President von Hindenburg (who, until his death in 1934, was Supreme Commander of the Armed Forces), the Luftschutzamt was incorporated within the Ministry. The first step towards the creation of a new German Air Force as an independent service had been taken. Henceforth, the pace of aerial rearmament was greatly accelerated, entailing a quantitative and qualitative jump that indicated a complete change of policy by the German leadership.

For a long time, however, their efforts were hampered by the necessity of preserving secrecy, and it was possible to establish new formations only as civilian training units. In the spring of 1933, the Flying School Command was instituted, with the purpose of preparing for the creation of training schools and of supervising military instruction given in the commercial organisations, such as German Sport Aviation Ltd. On 1st April 1934, it was transformed into the Inspectorate for Flying Schools (Inspektion der Fliegerschulen). At the same time, the training of reserve fliers was given to the supervision of another Inspectorate, the Inspektion der Fliegerreserve. By the summer of 1934, no fewer than thirty-two schools were available for flying training. The structure of the new Air Force, too, was developed. In December 1933, fifteen regional air offices were instituted, and, on 1st April 1934, Germany was divided into five Luftkreiskommandos (District Air Commands), whose geographical areas corresponded to two or more Army Wehrkreise (Defence Districts). For purposes of camouflage, they were known as Gehobene Luftämte (Higher Air Offices). A new command was also created for naval flying units. On the same date, too, Fliegerdivision 1 was instituted in Berlin, under Colonel Hugo Sperrle, a First World War flier who also held the office of Kommandeur der Aviation Heeresflieger (Commander of Army Aviation). Then, too, the first fighter unit was instituted, Jagdgruppe 132, based at Döberitz near Berlin. It was commanded by Major Robert Ritter von Greim, and was formed of three Jagdstaffeln equipped with Ar 65 and He 51 biplanes.

By the beginning of 1935, the new Air Force possessed twenty Staffeln and 11,000 officers and men. Of its 1,800 aircraft in service, 370 were bombers (Do 11s, Do 23s, and Ju 86s), 450 were Ju 52s, 250 were fighters (Ar 64s, Ar 65s, and He 51s,), 590 were reconnaissance aircraft (He 45s and He 46s), and 120 were seaplanes. In addition, threre were some 30,000 men in the Deutscher Luftsport Verband (DLV or German Air Sport League), instituted on 23rd March 1933 to incorporate all private flying clubs so as to lay the foundation for standardised pre-military flight training. The aero-industry, too, had expanded considerably; the floor space of the airframe manufacturers had risen from 30,000 square metres in 1933 to 231,000 square metres by 1935, and the total value of production in 1934 was nearly five-fold that of 1933. By March 1935, no fewer than 2,500 new aircraft had been delivered to the armed services since Hitler had become Reich's Chancellor. It was a bold expansion. But it was to be as nothing compared with what was to come.

On 26th February 1935, Hitler signed the decree, effective from 1st March, which officially established an Air Force to be the third service of the German Armed Forces, with a status equal to that of the Army and the Navy. On 10th March, a suspicious world was told that the Reich indeed already possessed such a force, known as the Reichsluftwaffe (this name never found favour, and it soon came to be known as simply the Luftwaffe). In an interview with a British newspaper correspondent, Göring declared: 'in the extension of our national defence, it was necessary, as we repeatedly told the world, to take care of defence in the air. As far as that is concerned, I restricted myself to those measures absolutely necessary. The guiding line of my actions was not the creation of an aggressive force which would threaten other nations, but merely the completion of military aviation which would be strong enough to repel, at any time, attacks on Germany.'[3] The new Oberbefehlshaber der Luftwaffe (Commander-in-Chief) ended with the assurance: 'The German Air Force is just as passionately permeated with the will to defend the

Fatherland to the last, as it is convinced, on the other hand, that it will never be employed to threaten the peace of other nations.' On the 16th, Hitler confirmed that Germany was rearming; in fulfilment of Article 22 of the National Socialist Programme, he announced that Germany would no longer be bound by the Versailles restrictions.

Secrecy was over. The real purpose of service establishments throughout Germany became known. Thus the Höhenflugzentrale des deutschen Flugwetterdienstes (High Altitude Flight Centre of the German Aviation Weather Service) at Lechfeld was revealed as the Kampffliegerschule und Fliegerschützenlehrgang (Bomber and Air Gunner Instruction Course) which, in reality, it had always been. At the same time, the personnel of the new air force replaced their civilian insignia with the emblem of the Luftwaffe (appropriately enough a swooping eagle with a swastika held firmly in its claws), the aeroplanes in service were given military markings, and all pretence was finally done away with. On 14th March, I Gruppe/JG 132 was re-established as Jagdgeschwader Richthofen in memory of past glories; a few days later, on the 16th, the same unit flew over Berlin in a demonstration of strength on the occasion of Hitler's declaration of rearmament. From this time on, Germany's armed strength was to be kept continually in the forefront of public attention.

The command to which the new Air Force had been entrusted was a complex one, both in personalities and organisation, and its history makes sorry reading. The structure of the Air Ministry (RLM) was, at first, unwieldy. Divided into two parts, sometimes antagonistic, the one military, under Bohnstedt, the other civilian, under Milch, it was united only in the person of Göring as Minister. This was clearly inconsistent with the co-ordination of all the various aviation agencies necessary to develop a new air force, especially as Göring's many political and state responsibilities prevented him from attending to his duties adequately. On 1st September 1933, a major reorganisation of the RLM gave it the unity required. Milch was made Göring's deputy in all matters, military as well as civilian, and was put in charge of all the Ministry's various offices. Thus, unity of command and co-ordination of effort was ensured. Subordinate to Göring and Milch were the seven principal offices of the RLM. The most important was the Air Command Office (Luftkommandoamt), responsible for air strategy, preparations for mobilisation, drawing up operational specifications for aircraft and equipment, training, and budgetary planning. In addition, its Inspectorates oversaw the development of particular arms of service. In short, the Air Command Office was the Luftwaffe's equivalent to the Army's General Staff. All other Air Force matters were dealt with by the Administrative Office (Luftwaffenverwaltungsamt), the Personnel Office (Luftwaffenpersonalamt), the Technical Office (Technisches Amt), and the Supply Office (Nachschubamt). Civil aviation was dealt with by the General Office (Allgemeines

Amt), while the Central Department (Zentralabteilung) handled all questions internal to the Ministry and its establishments.

To staff the RLM , 200 officers were transferred from the Army in 1933. In the main, their selection appears to have been arbitrary; all those who were included on the 'pilots' roster' (those who, at any time, had completed flight training) were automatically assigned to Göring's new empire, together with a small number of General Staff officers, amounting to some forty in all. These were specifically appointed with the particular aim of providing first-class officers to guide the development of the new force; for von Blomberg and others were concerned that it should be commanded by able men dedicated to sound military traditions, and with an understanding of basic Army requirements. The dangers inherent in the development of a force under Göring, whose appointment was the result simply of political considerations, and of Milch, a civilian of strong mind and independent views, were to be guarded against.

Central to von Blomberg's plan was a newcomer to aviation, Colonel Hans Jürgen Stumpff, Chief of the Air Personnel Office, who placed the few military commanders at his disposal with special care. Five out of the six offices of the Ministry were headed by highly qualified, middle-ranking officers: apart from Stumpff himself, there were Colonel Walther Wever, chief of the Air Command Office; Colonel Wilhelm Wimmer, chief of the Technical Office (and the only army officer who was not General Staff trained but who had served in the Air Inspectorate); Colonel Albert Kesselring, chief of the Administration Office; Captain (Navy) Rudolf Wenninger, chief of the Central Branch; Ministerialdirektor Wilhelm Fisch, chief of the General Air Office, an able administrator, was the only civilian. A major omission from the RLM, however, was Ernst Brandenburg, a renowned First World War bomber pilot who had played a large part in developing aviation during the Weimar Republic; his strong personality and obvious dislike of Göring made him quite unacceptable, and the new Luftwaffe was forced to do without his considerable experience and talents.

Many of the men such as Kesselring and Wever whom Stumpff placed in key positions had no experience of aviation, but to compensate for this he ensured that they had able General Staff aides from the Army, many of whom were well versed in flying. The most prominent of the Reichswehr officers whom von Blomberg made available to the RLM were Colonels Helmut Felmy, Nikolaus Maier, Ernst Müller, Hugo Sperrle, Helmut Wilberg and Ludwig Wolff; Lieutenant-Colonels Hans Geisler, Fritz Loeb, Max von Pohl, Wilhelm Speidel and Dietrich Volkmann; Majors Paul Deichmann, Josef Kammhuber, Hans Jeschonnek, Wolfram von Richthofen, Herhudt von Rohden, Kurt Student, and Otto Hoffmann von Waldau; and Captains Andreas Nielsen, Hermann Plocher, Josef Schmid and Hans Seidemann. Some of them, such as Felmy, Jeschonnek and Student, had been involved in aviation for some time, Felmy and Jeschonnek in the Army's Air Inspectorate and Student in the Ordnance Office, but others were quite ignorant of aviation. They were, however, quick to learn. During the later expansion of the Air Force, these officers quickly rose to high positions, and dominated the Luftwaffe officer corps until the end of the war. In addition, the RLM was given permission by von Blomberg to recruit former General Staff officers unable to fly and who were then on the reserve list. A number were appointed to senior positions in the regional administration of the Air Force, and men such as Generals Karl Eberth, Hans Halm, Leonhard Kaupisch, Karl Schweckhard and Edmund Wachenfeld, the first commanders of the various Luftkreise (Territorial Air Commands) undertook much important work.

In its early days, the high command of the new Air Force, then, had much to recommend it. Supported by a highly able and industrious body of serving officers, the two top men in the ministry, Göring and Milch, could function well. In them, the infant air force was particularly fortunate. Given the political and economic realities of Germany in the early 1930s, it is arguable that no better men could have been found to fill the posts of Minister of Aviation and Secretary of State, and that, given their personalities, they could not have been supported by a better man than Wever as Chief of the all-important Air Command Office. However, as time was to tell, it was a fragile partnership, one that, after two years, was to dissolve into the disharmony and discord which, for the rest of its existence, was to characterise the Luftwaffe's high command.

Hermann Wilhelm Göring was born in Rosenheim, Bavaria, in 1893, the youngest son of a judge and colonial administrator whose energies had led him to produce nine children by two wives. After a robust childhood, Göring entered the Imperial Army in fulfilment of his sole ambition, and became a lieutenant in 1914. His service as an infantry officer, however, was short-lived. Within months he was confined to hospital with rheumatism, during which time he heard that his friend, Lieutenant Bruno Lörzer, was attending a pilot training course. Göring immediately applied to join him, and, when he was rejected by his regimental commanding officer, simply disregarded orders and went to Darmstadt to join his comrade, who took him as an observer on a number of flights. Disobedience had its reward; Göring not only gained the Iron Cross First Class but, after learning to fly at his own expense, he avoided serious punishment and succeeded in transferring to the Air Service. By July 1918, Göring, a captain and a fighter ace with the Pour le Mérite, Prussia's highest military decoration, and twenty kills to his credit, became commander of Jagdgeschwader 1, the famous 'Red Knight' unit of Baron von Richthofen.

Germany's defeat in the war was a personal tragedy for the young Göring. Embittered, and hating the Weimar Republic, he earned his living flying in Scandinavia. There, he fell in love with the beautiful and romantic Swedish Baroness, Karin von Gantzow, who, returning his affection, divorced her husband, renounced all claim to her son, and, in February 1922, married the debonair flier in Munich. There, in November of that year, Göring saw Hitler for the first time, and fell completely under his spell. After offering his services to the new National Socialist Party, Göring was made head of its stormtroops (Sturmabteilungen-SA) in March 1923, in which post he was wounded during the abortive putsch in Munich on 9th November. To avoid arrest, he fled abroad with his wife, spending time in Austria, Italy and Sweden, where he became a business agent for several aircraft companies. At the end of 1927, Göring returned to Germany, renewed his old political contacts, and, in the Reichstag elections of May 1928, won one of the twelve NSDAP seats. In his new position, the former fighter ace received considerable fees as a consultant to Lufthansa and other firms. In turn, he lent his support to demands for the expansion of aviation within the Reich.

Göring was useful to Hitler, who used him to offset political rivals in the Party such as Julius Streicher and Gregor Strasser. Furthermore, Göring was accepted by high society, and numbered among his acquaintances the German Crown Prince Friedrich August von Hohenzollern, Prince Philip of Hesse, the President of the Reich's Bank, Dr Hjalmar Schacht, and the industrialist, Fritz Thyssen. After the elections in 1930, in which the National Socialists made impressive gains, Göring was even invited by President von Hindenburg to his ancestral estate. His impressive bearing and war record, his ease of manner and diplomatic skill, as well as the vigour of his public speaking, made him an ideal figure for the Party as it emerged into prominence. In 1931, Göring became President of the Reichstag, and by the following year he was regarded as the most important man in the Party after Hitler. In May 1933, he was made Prussian Minister of the Interior, a position of influence which, a few weeks later, was to give him both control of the Prussian security services (including the Gestapo) and political power as Minister-President of Prussia. The accumulation of high offices was to continue through the early years of the Third Reich. In addition to his responsibilities for aviation, Prussia and the Reichstag, and his influence in political affairs, Göring was made Reich's Forest-Master and Hunting-Master in July 1934, duties which gave him much pleasure, and, in October 1936, he was appointed chief of the Four Year Plan for economic self-sufficiency in the event of war. For two months in 1937-1938, he was even entrusted with the duties of Minister for Economics. In September 1941, he became Hitler's nominated successor. Ironically, however, by that time his influence with the Führer was on the wane.

Göring's distinctive character, combined with his importance in the Party, and his multifarious interests and duties, were immensely beneficial to the German Air Force during the early years of its development. There can be no doubt that he viewed the building of the Luftwaffe as his main mission in life. He regarded it as *his* air force, and *his* achievement. Pompous and bombastic though Göring was in extolling its (and, therefore his) virtues, his obsession was not allied to any desire for hard, continuous work. Therefore he granted much independence to his subordinates. The amateur did not interfere with the professionals, Kesselring remembered: 'In . . . Hermann Göring, the Luftwaffe had a former flying officer, a National Socialist, and a generous man as its Commander-in-Chief. He required a great deal from us generals in the Reich's Air Ministry, but he gave us complete freedom of action and shielded us from all political criticism. In my long years as a soldier, I have never been so free of outside influences and so able to act independently as during this early period of Luftwaffe development. . . .'[4] Indeed, although all decisions were taken in the name of Göring, it is impossible to point to a single major conclusion arrived at by the RLM affecting the Luftwaffe's development before the war that was influenced by him against the advice of his subordinates. However, that distance from everyday responsibility which Göring preserved, while a benefit in the first few years of the Air Force's existence, was later to prove fatal to the cohesion of its Command.

If Göring made little contribution to the discussions of the RLM, he was strong in his advocacy of the Luftwaffe's cause within the councils of the Reich. Here, his value lay. His ability to gain immediate access to the Führer, and the latter's respect for his views on matters of aviation, however unsuitable they were, proved an invaluable asset in the struggle for the Reich's limited financial and economic resources during rearmament, an asset which neither von Blomberg nor the commanders-in-chief of the other two services possessed. His appointment as head of the Four Year Plan was also to have important consequences for the Luftwaffe. Without Göring's wider responsibilities, the Air Force would have been denied a valuable promoter of its interests. But while his advantages as Commander-in-Chief of the Luftwaffe were derived from his position within the Reich, his defects, which only seriously revealed themselves after 1936, stemmed directly from his character.

Göring was an enigma. He was as much the stuff of which heroes are made as are villains. He was a remarkable combination of contradictions; for every strength could be found a corresponding weakness of equal prominence. Only his ambition remained untrammelled by its opposite. He was both energetic and lazy; realistic and romantic; brutal and kind; brave and cowardly; refined and coarse; intelligent, vain, humourous and ruthless by turns, an inspiration to some, an object of ridicule and detestation to others. He loved beauty, nature and domesticity, wealth, glory and power. Natural in the company of friends, he could turn at once to become a consummate actor, revelling in the image he created of himself as an 'Iron Man'. But, although Göring may have hoped himself to be such, in reality he was very different. His health was poor, and he tired easily. His physician during the war, Dr von Ondarza, stated that he was: 'an unusually tall and very fat man. He needed large quantities of liquid, not alcohol. His heart had never been too good, nor was his circulation entirely in order. He had attacks during which his heart seemed to be galloping and his pulse varied between 100 and 220. There must also have been some weakness of the cardiac muscle. His blood pressure was subject to fluctuation, but was not the reason for his feeling of fatigue.'[5] In addition, Göring was, for a time, addicted to morphine. But physical debilities apart, Göring lacked, too, the mental attributes of an 'Iron Man'.

He could be a poor judge of character; incapable of taking ruthless decisions where the capabilities of a friend and subordinate were in question, and quite unable to apply himself in any purposeful manner. Such defects were to become glaringly obvious to many within the Luftwaffe high command after the first few years of his leadership.

Below Göring, came Milch, the Secretary of State of the RLM. He gave to Hitler's intentions and his chief's ambitions the foundation without which neither would have succeeded. In his citation for Milch's promotion to Field Marshal in 1940, Göring justly credited him 'with outstanding merit in the formation of the German Air Force'.[6] For such a part he was well qualified. Born in Wilhelmshaven in 1892, the adopted son of a pharmacist in the Navy, he was commissioned into an artillery regiment in 1911. After seeing action on the Eastern Front, he transferred to the Flying Service in 1915 as an aerial observer and photographer, in which role he served on the Western Front. In 1918 he was promoted captain, and was accepted for the General Staff; but, although he could not fly, he was given instead command of a reconnaissance Gruppe and, for the last month of the war, of a field replacement fighter Gruppe. Until 1920, Milch served in the Prussian air police on the Polish border, and then went into civil aviation, soon gaining a high reputation. In 1926, he became one of the three directors of the new national airline, Deutsche Luft Hansa (later known just as Lufthansa), and was the key figure in establishing an efficient air network throughout the Reich.

In Lufthansa, Milch's vitality, appetite for work and business-like approach to life bore fruit. In spite of the fact that he himself could not fly, he mastered the technology of aviation and developed his gift for administration, so that he soon became the most important director on the airline's board. Although not a member of the National Socialist Party, he was clearly sympathetic to at least some of its aims, and readily placed aircraft at the disposal of Hitler. Milch's reputation, together with the value of his personal contacts with a number of National Socialists, made him the obvious choice for the post of Secretary of State, a post which, despite its importance, he was at first reluctant to take. After a year in office, Göring, impressed by Milch's qualities, asked Hitler to nominate the Secretary of State his successor in the event of his death. It was an act of generosity he was later to regret.

Despite his success, Milch felt, like so many ambitious men, insecure. Outspoken and arrogant though he could be, he was also personally highly sensitive. Courteous to officers of inferior rank, Milch would allow his tongue unbridled licence when dealing with those who might threaten his position. He was not averse to making serious, even wild, accusations and threats. General Kreipe, a future Chief of the Luftwaffe General Staff, remarked that 'In his judgements he was too irresponsible and excessively sharp. He placed no check upon his insolent manner', while Göring was aware that 'At every meeting, the Field Marshal [Milch] speaks of executions by firing squad. . . .'[7] While indulging in such talk, Milch would also lapse into self-contradictions, giving rise to severe doubts about his veracity. Furthermore, he seemed to need constant reassurance; his preference for men who supported rather than contradicted him became too prominent. For a military leader with his responsibilities, subordinates with constructive critical ability would have been more appropriate.

But apart from his vulnerability, Milch was a first-class administrator with a quick and perceptive mind, high intelligence, an ability to make fast decisions, and a capacity for hard work and devotion to duty. He was, too, utterly ruthless in the pursuit of his aims. For example, he did not balk at making theats and using police action to remove the anti-Nazi Professor Hugo Junkers from control of his near bankrupt firm in late 1933, largely because of his views against rearmament, and replace him by Dr Heinrich Koppenberg as General Manager of the firm in which the Air Ministry also took a controlling financial interest. Milch's greatest asset was that, recognising Göring's limitations, he was quite prepared to make use of his many talents in creating an air force without waiting for instructions from above. Of him, Kesselring wrote: 'Milch was, next to Göring, the decisive personality, and, despite his youth, proved to be extraordinarily useful in the establishment of the Luftwaffe'.[8]

The third man in the new Air Force's triumvirate was Walther Wever, described by all who knew him as a general of genius. Born in 1887 in the province of Posen, he joined the infantry as an officer-candidate in 1905. In 1915, after front-line service on the Western Front, he was promoted captain and entered the General Staff. His reputation grew, and in late 1917 he was posted to the staff of von Hindenburg and Ludendorff. After the war, Wever remained in the service as a member of the Troop Office. In 1930, he was promoted lieutenant-colonel, and later took over control of the Training Branch, and on 1st September 1933, he became chief of the Air Command Office. Wever's attitude to his new task was summed up after the war by General Andreas Nielsen, a General Staff officer in the RLM:

> Greeting his new assignment with enthusiasm, Wever devoted his full attention to the new mission with typical zeal. His quick intelligence, his remarkable receptiveness towards the developments of modern technology, and his vast store of military experience soon enabled him to grasp the fundamental concepts of his mission. He worked untiringly to exploit the unusually favourable circumstances provided by the time in order to create a military instrument equal to the other Armed Forces branches for the defence of the nation. He was quick to realize that the chance given him was a unique one, and that he might take advantage of all the available national and economic resources in creating a new and unique force.[9]

Unable to fly when appointed to the Air Command Office, Wever at once began training, and at the age of forty-six earned his pilot's licence and became a good aviator. He lost no opportunity to visit units by air, when, over coffee and cake, which he often took with him, he would talk over problems and policies with even the most junior of officers. Indeed, in the art of dealing with people, Wever was a master. Not only did he get on well with Göring, who would hear not a word said against him, but also with Milch, despite occasional differences of opinion. With them, his exemplary tact and willingness to remain in the background paid great dividends; but, more than that, they understood good material when they saw it, and fully recognised his qualities. As Milch was to eulogise after the war: 'He [Wever] was the most significant of the officers taken over from the Army. If he had remained in the Army he would have reached the highest positions there as well. He possessed not only tremendous professional ability, but also great personal qualities. He was the only General Staff Chief since the end of World War 1 who came close to Moltke. Wever, not Beck! [The Army Chief of Staff]'[10]

Such were the three men who, in late 1933, became the leaders of Germany's new air force. In the three years in which they were to work together, they laid the foundations of a Luftwaffe which was to dominate the skies over the Continent of Europe. It was a remarkable achievement. However, the triumvirate, powerful combination though it was, still depended upon one another man: Adolf Hitler. His views on aviation, on its nature and its importance in rearmament, were vital. Without his concurrence and active support for their proposals, little could have been achieved. However, in those early days, all four men were in broad agreement as to what was required for Germany's Air Force.

Hitler, although knowing little of the technicalities of aviation, and speaking seldom on the subject, nevertheless possessed, in common with most men of his generation, a great belief in the potential of air power. As a corporal in the trenches, he had seen the aircraft circling above the front lines, and had known of their military value; as an intelligent man he was aware of the great and impressive strides that were being made in the field of aviation, of Lindberg's solo crossing of the Atlantic in 1927, of the trans-oceanic flights of the giant German seaplane Do X, and of the considerable advances in speed and range that were being demonstrated daily. As a politician and military enthusiast, he was familiar with the prophets of air power, who predicted the future of war in terms of fleets of aircraft and mass destruction by bombing. Indeed, Hitler fully appreciated the value of aviation to himself as leader of a growing national party. As the years went by, although he never really enjoyed flying, he made increasing use of aircraft. 'Hitler über Deutschland' (Hitler over Germany) became a catch-phrase of the 1932 presidential election, during which he visited forty-six cities and towns in twenty days by means of a chartered Lufthansa aircraft. Thus, by the time he came to power, the aeroplane was regarded by Hitler as an essential element of modern life, as much in political organisation as in military power. To control the great Eurasian land mass, which was his aim, armies and navies were not enough; an air force was essential, not only to safeguard the armies at the front and the industries at home from aerial attack, but also to destroy the enemy in pre-emptive strikes, to paralyse his war-effort. To Hitler, the importance of having a strong air force was axiomatic, a necessary precondition for a strong Germany. His ideas may not have been profound, but they were firmly held, and in the early days served only to benefit the Luftwaffe.

Until the middle of 1936, then, the high command of the new Luftwaffe worked well. Its personalities were suited to planning the development of a new force, and, in the process, a harmonious, dynamic and effective relationship was built up between them. However, on 3rd June, an event occurred which signalled the end of the RLM as it then was: Wever was killed when an aeroplane, which he himself was piloting, crashed. It was a major loss to the Luftwaffe. Göring wept like a child when he heard the news, and, at the funeral oration, told his listeners: 'In Wever, the Army gave me its best. From day to day, as our work brought us together, I realised that I had been given the best of them all'.[11] Gone, not only was an able General Staff officer and far-sighted strategic thinker, but also a man whose personality promoted effective working relationships within the RLM. His death was to further a series of events which, in less than three years, led to the virtual breakdown of the Luftwaffe's command.

Wever's end came at a time when relations between Göring and Milch were becoming distinctly cool. The Minister was resentful of the Secretary of State, whose success at his work was widely recognised; Göring, the vainglorious egocentric, for whom the creation of the Luftwaffe was a personal fulfilment, must have flinched when he heard Hitler declare in public: 'Two names are ineradicably linked with the birth of our Luftwaffe – Göring and Milch'.[12] The Minister would not tolerate such a sharing of honours. Furthermore, the close ties that existed between Milch and the National Socialist Party, the party in which Göring regarded himself as second in importance only to Hitler, gave the Minister more reason for suspicion. Milch clearly enjoyed the trust of Hitler, whom he knew how to flatter. On occasions, the Führer would turn to Göring when some difficult problem was posed for solution, and say 'Milch will handle it; that is what he is good at'.[13] The prominent personalities of the Reich, men such as Himmler, Goebbels, Hess and von Blomberg, all of whom had Hitler's ear, were frequent guests at Milch's home. In order to keep himself closely allied with, and informed about, the Party, Milch even appointed a high Party official to a prominent position in the RLM as his special-duty staff assistant. Such connections by one so able and industrious could prove dangerous to the indolent Göring in the internecine atmosphere of the Third Reich.

Göring's resentment of Milch, fuelled by his own self-doubt and insecurity among the Luftwaffe professionals, began to reveal itself towards the end of 1935, at first in petty ways. No longer was the Secretary of State invited as a guest at the Minister's hunting lodge, or to share his foreign holidays, and he came to be omitted from his Christmas list. Even Frau Milch suffered; when a

Luftwaffe brooch, designed by Göring, received wide circulation, she was not among the recipients. Personal dislike showed itself in abuse at work, so much so that in November 1936 Milch offered his resignation, and, when it was refused, he motioned towards his revolver and indicated that there were other ways out of the situation. Göring took to interviewing Milch's subordinates without his presence, and instructing them not to inform the Secretary of State that he had done so, even when the matter discussed was important. On one occasion in 1936, Göring even involved the Chief of the RLM Central Office, General von Witzendorff, who 'lost' a letter proving that the Minister had asked Milch to stand in for him to take the salute from the first bomber unit that went to Spain. This gave Göring the excuse for berating Milch for acting as if he himself were the Minister and Commander-in-Chief and then lying to cover up his much-vaunted ambition. Early in February the following year, 1937, when Milch fell ill with appendicitis, Göring showed little sympathy, and, when Milch returned to work, left Berlin for the Alps without even bothering to see him. Roughly two and a half months were to pass before the two men met again.

By mid-1936, then, Göring had come both to resent and to fear Milch. He saw how Hitler was concentrating ever more power into his own hands, leaving to his ministers and party officials empty panoply, and realised that the time might come when he would tire of them altogether. Certainly, in the immediate aftermath of the Blomberg-Fritsch crisis of January 1937, when the commanders of the Wehrmacht and the Army were forced from office, in no small way due to Göring's scheming, the Führer gave no more influence to his political companions, and the Luftwaffe Commander was denied the prize which he so earnestly desired: the post of Commander-in-Chief of the Wehrmacht. That, Hitler took for himself. It was not too fanciful to imagine that, one day, an all-powerful Führer would give hard work and expertise its due, banish Göring from his, by then, empty titles, and make Milch the Minister and Commander-in-Chief. This fear was not allayed by the fact that Göring was aware that, in close circles, Milch would occasionally refer to himself as 'The Minister'. 'Trees should be lopped in good time' was a German proverb, and Göring sought to fulfil it.

But how to curb Milch? The Secretary of State's good connections with the highest men of Party and Reich, coupled with his obvious competence and success in his job, precluded any coup undertaken without good reason. As General Paul Deichmann wrote: 'During this critical period there were rumours in Göring's immediate circle to the effect that he would have liked very much to rid himself of his State Secretary, but that Milch had been shrewd enough to convince the Nazi Party that he was needed in his position as a counterbalance to Göring, whose unwarranted extravagances were beginning to make him unpopular.'[14] If Milch's dismissal were impossible (and there is no reason to believe that Göring thought it even desirable, recognising, as he did, his Secretary of State's undoubted capabilities), then the only alternative was to curtail his powers. In this, Göring was fortunate, for at the same time that he was growing tired of Milch, so too were others within the RLM.

Most men have their Achilles heel. Von Blomberg, the Wehrmacht Commander, had derived his from marrying, far beneath his status, a former prostitute turned typist; von Fritsch, the Army Commander, acquired his partly from his concept of honour and the proper conduct of a German officer, and partly from the accident of fate that a lying blackmailer should have found an army captain, a certain von Frisch, in a homosexual act. By comparison, Milch's Achilles heel was considerably more commonplace. At one time, in 1933, Göring, together with many others, had no doubt thought him a half Jew. That would have been enough to have brought about Milch's resignation in accordance with the legal provisions of the 'Aryan Paragraph', whereby Jews were not allowed to hold positions in public service or the armed forces. However, a confidential enquiry was undertaken which revealed that Milch's father was unquestionably Aryan, if not the man married to his mother! Tragic though the revelation was to Milch, it proved him beyond doubt to be free of the 'Jewish bacillus', although some of his colleagues continued to believe that his blood was so tainted. But if Milch was neither Jewish, nor immoral, nor inefficient, neither was he an experienced soldier. Here lay his weakness.

By 1937, Milch was no longer simply a first-class civil servant administering an air ministry with skill and foresight; he was, perforce, a military commander. He had left the German Army in 1919 after nine years' service, during which time he had gained the rank of captain and, although not a flier, the command of a fighter Gruppe for the last five weeks of the war. After that, he acquired no more military experience until, in 1933, he was made deputy to the leader of the emerging Air Force, with the rank of colonel in the Army. By 1936, he was a General der Flieger. Not only had he missed nearly thirteen years of military service, during which time he would have held important staff posts, but he was also several years younger than his more experienced subordinates, such as Wever and Kesselring. He had gained an advantage in rank of nearly twenty years over his fellow Luftwaffe officers. But in their eyes at least, he was at a considerable disadvantage in terms of military experience. By 1936, it was openly alleged that, with Wever to deal with strategic and tactical matters, and with competent men running the Technical and Personnel Offices, there was now no longer any need for Milch's presence in the Luftwaffe. It was proposed that he should be confined to civil aviation. These allegations continued after Wever's death. Milch, aware of the murmuring about his unsuitability, sought to end them by applying himself ceaselessly to work. He was firm in the conviction that, as permanent deputy to the Minister and Commander-in-Chief, he had a duty to be deputy in all matters – the more so since he had to compensate for Göring's idleness. But the more Milch attempted to master the military art, the more he interfered, and the more he was resented. The more he was resented, the more arrogant and high handed he became, and this, in turn, made him the more unpalatable to his military rivals.

This Achilles heel was more imagined than real. Milch's considerable abilities, his interest in military affairs, and his willingness to leave Wever to work relatively undisturbed, ensured that the Secretary of State's efficiency did not suffer from his lack of a General Staff and higher-command training. Certainly, Wever did not find it difficult to establish good relations with Milch, and he appears to have made no complaint about the situation. As Milch remembered after the war: 'When Wever was there, everything functioned properly', while Kesselring agreed that 'It was an excellent marriage'.[15] However, what matters so often is not what exists in reality, as what exists within the minds of men. Göring's rise, the service officers could appreciate: he was, after all, Hitler's deputy and an air ace. But Milch was different. Middle-class, a man who had made his name in commercial enterprises (even if in aviation) in the 1920s, he was essentially a civilian. If the Luftwaffe were headed by a man deficient in military experience, his second-in-command should not lack it also, or so it was argued. Göring's indolence was acceptable, since it allowed the soldiers to get on with their work as they knew best. Milch's hard, intelligent work was another matter; it betokened unwanted and, in their minds, unwarranted interference. As the Luftwaffe continued to grow, the military became increasingly intolerant. With Wever gone, their dissatisfaction had its chance to be felt.

The new Chief of the Air Command Office in June 1936, Albert Kesselring, the former head of the Air Administration Office, was born in 1885, near Bayreuth. He entered the Army in 1904, where he received training as a balloon observer, and during the First World War he served as an adjutant and on the General Staff, in 1919 becoming a captain. During his service in the Reichswehr, he continued to show his capacity for loyalty, hard work, and quick comprehension of problems. An early admirer of the National Socialist regime, Kesselring won the respect even of Adolf Hitler, a man not noted for his warmth towards the military, a respect which was to last to the end of the war. He brought with him the same dedication to work, close connections with field units, and good relations with his colleagues and subordinates that were evident in his predecessor, whose work he was quite content to continue. As he wrote not long after his new assignment: 'Because of his [Wever's] genius, I have not had to look for new ways, but was able to continue where he stopped. This also led to the rapid establishment of an atmosphere of confidence among myself, the individual branches of the General Staff, and the various Inspectorates. I was very fortunate in having the support of outstandingly well-qualified officers, and this made my work a pleasure'.[16]

For all his qualities, Kesselring lacked one, the willingness to remain subordinate, that was essential to maintain good relations with Milch. He was, above all else, a professional officer, whose respect for civilian 'meddling' in service matters was scant. His broad smile and amiable manner belied a complete confidence in his own capabilities and an inherent desire to lead. He was a man who had no intention of limiting himself merely to fulfilling the directives of superiors, especially those whose military experience he saw as inferior to his own. His new position, therefore, brought him immediately into conflict with Milch. He refused to accept the Secretary of State's interference in matters he regarded as the exclusive preserve of the military. The first clash came soon after his new appointment, when Milch demanded that a court-martial be held on Hans Jeschonnek, the commander of Training Gruppe Greifswald because of serious aircraft crashes at the station. Kesselring would have none of it, and firmly defended the commander, who was not prosecuted. On another occasion, Kesselring even accused Milch of high treason for having disclosed too much of the Luftwaffe's strength and intentions during a visit to Britain.

In addition to their resentment of Milch, the officers within the RLM possessed another, and sounder, argument for a reorganisation of the Ministry that would diminish the responsibility of the Secretary of State. The existing system was no doubt appropriate to the situation in 1933, when Germany possessed only a handful of military aircraft, and when aerial rearmament, being illegal, was liable to bring about foreign intervention, but matters had changed considerably since then. In March 1935, the existence of the Luftwaffe had been declared openly to the world, and the RLM had become, in practice if not in name, the high command of a national air force, which, by 1938, was to be the largest in Europe.

Thus, there developed in 1934 and 1935 a considerable number of Air Force officers who advocated the establishment of a Luftwaffe General Staff within the RLM comparable with that in the Army High Command, and which would have full responsibility for the operational development of the service. They were particularly concerned by the drawbacks caused by the lack of General Staff training of Luftwaffe officers experienced when dealing with their counterparts from the Army and Navy. Not only were the representatives of the Air Force younger in age and lower in rank, but they had none of that aura traditionally possessed by General Staff officers, with their distinctive red piping and trouser stripes. Their feeling of inferiority was further exacerbated by the distain displayed by officers of the older services towards those of the new, especially by men, such as Beck, Chief of the Army General Staff, who were sceptical of the claims made for air power. Thus, it was deemed necessary to equate the status and influence of the Luftwaffe with that of the other two branches of the Wehrmacht. The creation of a Luftwaffe General Staff was seen to be, in part, the answer. Furthermore, as Stumpff realised, the existence of an élite body within the Air Force, with its distinctive uniform and preferential consideration for promotion, would act as a strong inducement for outstanding leaders among the troop units to attempt the transfer to command staffs. The training received there to qualify for service on the General Staff would further ensure that only those men would be chosen who revealed the necessary knowledge, intelligence and leadership for higher command, qualities which decorations and promotion earned in the field could not always adequately measure.

Wever, at first, had been unenthusiastic about the creation of a General Staff, fearing that the development of an élite group within the Luftwaffe would jeopardise the unity of the heterogeneous officer corps. However, in 1935, conceding the arguments of his fellow officers, he agreed, his decision being influenced by the establishment of the Air War and Air Technical Academies from which a new generation of trained General Staff officers would emerge. Furthermore, the Air Command Office, of which he was chief, was in most respects a General Staff by another name. Its duties were to issue orders concerning the command, organisation, training, and armament of the Luftwaffe to all other offices of the RLM, the Troop Commands and the Inspectorates at the behest of the Minister or the Secretary of State, as well as the preparation of operational instructions. It therefore exerted a great deal of influence over the development of the Air Force. As Kesselring remembered: 'From the very beginning it was recognized as a prince among peers, and its position as a Ministry office permitted it to exercise a decisive influence on the entire field of aviation and on the function of command over the Air Force troops.'[17]

However sound the military reasons for the establishment of a General Staff, it was vigorously opposed by Milch and his supporters, the civil servants, officers recruited from the commercial airlines and even by members of Göring's circle. They knew that the creation of such a body would lead to a decrease in their own influence, that it would emerge, in line with all General Staffs, as the sole operational adviser to the Commander-in-Chief, a position that would render it supreme during a period of rearmament and war. The arguments they marshalled against its establishment were many, but they generally played upon Göring's suspicion, often manifested, of any élite, highly professional band of men whose expertise might undermine his own authority. However, this fear was in large part allayed by the extremely good relations which the Minister enjoyed with Wever, and his respect for the latter's personal integrity and efficiency. Göring was further persuaded by the military arguments for the establishment of a General Staff, no doubt believing that his own status would be enhanced by the existence of such a prestigious institution under his command. Finally, the fact that Milch's own position would be undermined by such a creation, no doubt appealed to Göring. His mind made up, on 1st August the Luftwaffe General Staff was instituted. Wever having been killed two months previously, its first chief was Kesselring.

The new General Staff was simply a new title for the old Air Command Office. Nothing else had changed, except perhaps an enhancement in the prestige of the men who now wore its distinctive uniform. Milch remained permanent deputy to Göring, and the required reorganisation that would displace him from his dominant position was yet to come; until then, the creation of the General Staff had only served to strengthen the Secretary of State's resolve to remain supreme within the Ministry. Relations between Milch and Kesselring worsened, to such an extent that, after less than a year had passed, the Chief of the General Staff requested that he be relieved of his post. Kesselring remembered:

> The disagreements, of an official as well as personal nature, between myself and my superior, State Secretary Milch, were the motivating factor in my requesting to be relieved of my assignment. I requested that I be either transferred to service with a troop unit or permitted to resign. . . . As State Secretary, Milch remained Göring's deputy in the Ministry. I felt the deepest respect for Milch as a man of ability, a skilled discussion partner, an outstanding organizer, and an untiring worker, and I was sincerely pleased that the feeling of mutual confidence typical of the early period was gradually restored under my successor.[18]

Kesselring was transferred to become commander of Luftkreis III based at Dresden, and was succeeded, on 30th May 1937, by the Chief of the Personnel Office, General Hans Jürgen Stumpff. Born in 1889, in Pomerania, Stumpff had entered the Army in 1907, ending the First World War as a captain in the General Staff. His post-war service in the Reichsheer was competent, although not brilliant, and in 1933 he was transferred to the RLM as a colonel. As head of the Luftwaffe's Personnel Office, Stumpff's reputation grew; his success in building up the numbers and quality of the new force's personnel was remarkable. He was not fitted for the post of Chief of the General Staff, and made no pretence of wanting it, but realising that as a congenial, skilled administrator, he was a perfect stop-gap until a more suitable candidate could be found, he accepted it. Stumpff was not, however, the first choice. Before his appointment, Göring had discussed with von Blomberg the possibility of acquiring an officer from the Army for the post. General Franz Halder, then Deputy-Chief of the Army General Staff (and its future head) was offered it, but refused, von Blomberg commenting that no man could be ordered to face the prospect of working with a man as difficult as Milch. Alfred Jodl, later Chief of Operations in the Armed Forces High Command, was also given the chance to serve in the Luftwaffe, but he, too, declined. Thus, Stumpff was called from the job he so much enjoyed and placed in the middle of the battle for command of the Luftwaffe. His place as head of the Personnel Office was taken by Colonel Robert Ritter von Greim, a fighter pilot of the First World War and holder of the Pour le Mérite. Born in 1892, he had risen to command a Fighter Gruppe by the end of the war. After 1918 he saw service in the Freikorps. He then gave flying exhibitions, studied law and became manager of commercial air training centres, as well as organiser of the Cantonese Air Force. In 1934, he re-entered the Wehrmacht, and became first commander of the new Richthofen Fighter Gruppe, following this by the posts of Inspector of Fighters and Dive Bombers and Inspector of Equipment. His influence in the new Air Force was considerable, and he was thought of as an upright, decent man, well fitted for his new responsibilities in the Personnel Office.

Stumpff's new position as Chief of the General Staff was a difficult one. Not only had he to follow the strong personalities of Wever and Kesselring, but he also inherited the unfortunate conflict with Milch. Three days after his appointment, however, on 2nd June 1937, a reorganisation of the RLM intended to solve the problem was introduced by Göring. He announced: 'Now that the construction of the Luftwaffe has reached its provisional conclusion, I intend to apply to the Luftwaffe's structure a form relevant to command problems in war as well as in peace.'[19] From then on, Göring would be in sole charge, without a permanent deputy. The Chief of the General Staff was given unfettered control of the General Staff, seven of the ten Inspectorates and the two Academies, while the Secretary of State was left with the remaining offices of the RLM (the General Air Office, the Technical Office, the Administration Office, the Supply Office, the Personnel Office, the Central Branch and three Inspectorates). The Chief of the General Staff was made equal in status with the Secretary of State. In some respects, however, he was more influential, since the General Staff retained the authority to issue orders to the other sections of the RLM in matters concerning mobilisation, operations, training, armament and supply. On all these questions, the Chief of the General Staff was to report directly to Göring, and was required only to keep the Secretary of State informed of decisions taken. If the latter's views differed from those of the Chief of the General Staff, his sole recourse was to make representations to the Minister. Only when Göring was away from work through illness or leave was Milch to act as his deputy. A few weeks later, Milch's position was further underminded when the Chiefs of the Personnel Office and the Technical Office were allowed to report directly to the Minister. As Deichmann wrote, 'objectively considered, the first round of the battle went to the Chief of the General Staff'.[20]

By mid-1937, Milch had, therefore, been ousted from his position of supremacy. It was the first move in the creation of a situation which was to bedevil the future development of the Luftwaffe: a lack of coherent leadership. At the time, Milch warned Göring: 'You are ruining the Air Force this way. Somebody has to be in charge of everything. If I don't do it, then you will have to . . . but you won't!' Upon being reassured by Göring that he would henceforth exercise the responsibilities of his command, Milch replied 'I don't believe it. I request that I be relieved of my post'. Göring's answer was straightforward: 'Look here, Milch, I'm not demoting you because you've failed, but because you've succeeded too well. The Party keeps telling me that it's Milch who does all the work. And . . . I won't stand for that'.[21] Milch's request was refused; for all his jealousy, Göring could not afford to lose such a valuable aide. He no doubt recognised that Milch possessed the qualities necessary for the supervision of the Luftwaffe which he himself lacked completely: energy, perseverance, industry and steadiness. Nor did the Minister wish to become the captive of the General Staff. 'Divide and Rule' was the cornerstone of his Führer's approach to politics; so, too, would it be Göring's. By the end of the year, matters had reached such a state between the two men, that Milch again felt forced to offer his resignation. Göring refused him. Milch responded by telling his Minister that if he was not allowed to resign, there was nothing he could do except commit suicide.

The reorganisation of 2nd June 1937 failed to solve the discord between the Secretary of State and the Chief of the General Staff. Indeed the rivalry became worse, for there now existed a power vacuum at the very top of the Luftwaffe command which each sought to fill. Subsequent reorganisations before the war provided no solution. Lack of co-operation continued. Milch advocated the establishment of an office of Chief of Air Defence, to combine the Administration, Personnel, Supply and General Air Offices as well as the Central Department as a counterbalance to the General Staff, and the creation of a post of Inspector-General, which would oversee all ofices within the RLM, including the General Staff, and thus be the 'eyes and ears' of the Minister. Unity of command would be restored, presumably under Milch himself. Stumpff would have none of this. However, as time went on he himself became increasingly concerned at the organisational chaos within the Ministry. In a letter dated 6th December 1937, he wrote: 'Instead of one command agency we now have two. An absolute chaos of orders and directives has been the inevitable result'.[22] Of the period, General Nielsen, then in the Personnel Office, wrote: 'Inasmuch as the Secretary of State and the offices under his direction were also responsible for many important missions closely allied with the military establishment (technological development, administration . . .), it was obvious that continual friction was bound to result in complete paralysis of the command function sooner or later'.[23] Another, Deichmann, wrote:'In my capacity as Chief of Branch I, which at that time included the group responsible for establishing tactical-technological requirements, I soon had the impression that, from the date of Stumpff's appointment on, the technical sections (which were directly subordinate to the State Secretary, and not to the Chief of the General Staff) were actively resisting any attempt at cooperation with the General Staff'.[24]

Something clearly had to happen. In late 1937, Stumpff took the initiative, and proposed that he, as Chief of the General Staff, should again place himself under the direction of the Secretary of State as the sole representative of the Minister. In return, the General Staff was to be recognised as the only agency of command within the RLM, even during peace-time when preparations for war were involved. It was a brave proposal, and one that, given Milch's continued presence and unyielding opposition, had to be made. On 18th January 1938, Göring ordered a major reorganisation of the RLM and a revision of the responsibilities of its top officials. The Secretary of State and his staff were incorporated into the Office of the Minister (Ministerialamt, which had been created on 1st December 1937 to help Göring master his responsibilities), and Milch thus became, in fact if not in name, his representative in all matters. The Chief of the General Staff was nominated the Minister's chief of operations and principal adviser on all questions pertaining to combat readiness, leadership, organisation and training. The offices of the Chief of Air Defence and the Inspector-General (in charge of the ten Inspectors) were instituted, and these, together with the Chiefs of the Personnel and Technical Offices (General Ernst Udet had replaced Wimmer as the head of the latter), were all made directly subordinate to the Minister. Milch took on the function of Inspector-General, and General Otto Günther Rüdel, a fifty-five-year-old staff officer who had had much experience in air defence and was Inspector of Anti-Aircraft Artillery, became Chief of Air Defence.

This reorganisation, while in theory strengthening Milch's position and restoring unity to the Luftwaffe's Command, in reality further weakened both. Only the position of the Chief of the General Staff was improved, his role as the sole operational advisor, whether through Milch or not, being recognised. Milch was left without any RLM offices to control directly (the Inspectorates remained subordinate to the General Staff, although the Inspectors themselves were responsible to Milch) and was rendered substantially impotent, being dependent solely on the cooperation of the other office chiefs. They, being responsible to Göring, could, if they so desired, easily by-pass his deputy, and were charged only with keeping him informed of all policy decisions. Only when his Minister was absent, would Milch possess the executive power he so desired. Nor was Göring's habitual inability to devote himself to ministerial work any particular asset to Milch; instead of dealing directly with the Secretary of State, the RLM chiefs would get on with their own tasks as best they thought fit. Thus, in place of the one centre of power under Göring that had existed before June 1937 (Milch), or the two that had existed after that first reorganisation (Milch and Stumpff), there were, after January 1938, no fewer than five (Milch, Stumpff, Udet, Rüdel and von Greim), of which three (Milch, Stumpff, and Udet) were pre-eminent. The Luftwaffe was, in truth, leaderless.

It soon became apparent that this new organisation could not be maintained even in peace-time, let alone in war. Misunderstandings and disagreements continued between the Secretary of State and the Chief of the General Staff, exacerbated by the curious arrangement over the Inspectorates (a decision worthy of Solomon if ever there was one), while the other offices also fought to preserve their newly won autonomy. It was thought necessary that the command of the Luftwaffe be brought into line with those of the other two services, and that it be prepared for the evacuation of its operational sections from Berlin in the event of war. Thus, on 1st February 1939, a new, and final, reorganisation took place, based on a plan drawn up by Hans Jeschonnek, then Chief of Operations in the General Staff. The Luftwaffe's command apparatus was separated from the rest of the Ministry by removing the General Staff from the organisation of the RLM itself. The Chief of the General Staff, who, from 1st February, was Jeschonnek (who retained his position as Chief of Operations) was made responsible solely to the Commander-in-Chief, and had only to inform the Secretary of State about operational matters after they had been discussed with Göring. Should any disagreement then arise, Milch had the right to be present at the resulting conference between Jeschonnek and Göring. All those sections within the General Staff that were not directly concerned with the conduct of military operations were detached and placed in the RLM under the Secretary of State.

The General Staff lost its direct influence over training and communications, but this was thought necessary in order to achieve both an effective, coherent and tightly knit organisation for the general Staff, and its detachment from the Ministry. As a result, two new offices were created within the RLM, the Office of Signal Communications, under General Martini, and the Office of Training under General Kühl (who possessed the fourteen Inspectorates under his control), to add to those already existing: the Office for Air Defence, the Central Branch (re-organised out of the Air Defence Office), and the newly created Office of the Chief of Lutwaffe Supply and Procurement under Udet (which combined the old Technical Office with a number of other agencies). Milch, as Inspector-General, was given the right to inspect all Ministry agencies and troops in the field, and was confirmed as Göring's deputy, should he be required to fulfil that function in case of illness or absence. Stumpff, the new Chief of the Air Defence Office, was, ironically, appointed Milch's deputy. The Chief of the Personnel Office was made directly responsible to Göring for officer appointments and promotions, but in all other matters came under Milch's supervision, as did the Chiefs of Signals, Training, Air Defence and Supply and Procurement. Such was the organisation of the Luftwaffe's command at the outbreak of war, one which did nothing to diminish the disunity that had come to dominate the counsels of the Air Force.

Of all the men who, in the year of the outbreak of war, had come to lead the German Air Force, the most important should have been Hans Jeschonnek, the prodigy of the Luftwaffe, who, at the age of thirty-nine, became Chief of its General Staff. He was then fifteen years younger than any previous German Chief of General Staff, whether Army or Air Force, had been. It was a tragedy he did not live up to expectations. Of him, Kesselring remembered:'During the war years, the most impressive personality among the Chiefs of the General Staff was Generaloberst Jeschonnek . . . an unusually intelligent and energetic person. Even Jeschonnek, however, was not strong enough to oppose Göring successfully (occasionally he did succeed in opposing Hitler) in matters of decisive importance. A very definite lack of harmony brought effective co-ordination to a standstill'.[25]

Born in 1898 in Hohensalza, East Prussia, the son of an assistant secondary school master, Jeschonnek volunteered for war service in the infantry at the age of fifteen and a half. In 1917, he became a fighter pilot, downing two enemy aircraft, and after the Armistice transferred to the Border Patrol. In the 1920s, as a cavalry officer, he served under Student in the Inspectorate for Arms and Equipment, and then entered the General Staff, working for Felmy in the Air Inspectorate. There, his intelligence and quickness impressed all who met him, and on 2nd February 1933, with the creation of the RLM, he was made adjutant to Milch. In 1934, he became a captain in a bomber unit, being promoted to major the following year. In October 1936, he assumed command of Lehrgruppe III, his influence on the development of Luftwaffe training procedures becoming considerable. In April 1937, he was promoted lieutenant colonel. He then entered the RLM, and on 1st February 1938 became Chief of the Operations Staff of the General Staff, later that year attaining the rank of colonel. Jeschonnek's career had been spectacular; his success in his various posts, impressive. Their variety and, for his youth, their importance reveal that he was being groomed to be Wever's eventual successor, and was thus being provided with the means to improve his military experience and demonstrate his ability. Thus it was, on 1st February 1939, that he became Chief of the General Staff with, as from 14th August, the rank of Generalmajor (on 1st March 1942, at the age of forty-two, he was to become the youngest Generaloberst in the Wehrmacht). His rise, indeed, was meteoric.

Jeschonnek was noted for his keen intelligence, quickness of comprehension, diligence, and ability to give rapid, concise orders. Abstemious, comptemptuous of frippery and unwarranted luxury, he personified the dedicated professional soldier both in bearing and manner of living. Pleasure, culture, and his family took second place to his duties, and religion found no place in his scheme of things. Even his great ambition seems to have been directed more towards the success of his service than himself. Outside his professional life, Jeschonnek's only other strong interest was politics. He was a dedicated National Socialist. He worked energetically to fulfil the goals of the new Reich, and thereby typified the young, aggressive military-political activist, unshakeably loyal to the Führer, that Hitler and the Party leadership found so inspiring.

However, Jeschonnek had his faults. He had climbed too high too soon; his intelligence had outstripped his maturity. Brilliant though he was with facts and concepts, his ability to handle people was limited – a severe handicap for a Chief of the General Staff, the more so for one who was forced to exist in the atmosphere of suspicion, jealousy, and dislike that permeated the high command of the Luftwaffe. All around him, Jeschonnek found generals senior to him in age, rank, and service, many of whom were strong-willed and not above going directly to Göring with their requests. The pressures which men such as Sperrle and von Richthofen, among the foremost of the Luftwaffe's field commanders could put on the young Chief of the General Staff were considerable, and he often found their demands irresistible. As a result, he tended to prefer the company of younger officers and to seek their opinions, rather than those of the older generation. During the war he was to show a marked preference for the young 'aces', such as Galland, Mölders and Baumbach, who always found him approachable. But, brilliant though they were, and however well they kept him informed about matters in the field commands, they too lacked the full maturity necessary in order to make sound, balanced decisions that were required of a Chief of the General Staff. Jeschonnek disliked social events, and was free and easy only with a small group of intimates. With subordinates he was often brusque and reserved, bitingly sarcastic, and, on occasions, surprisingly dictatorial. He lacked Wever's and Kesselring's gift of inspiring all those with whom they came in contact; there was too much of the cold intellectual professional soldier in him for that. He was unable to be the great mentor, or father, of his General Staff, or, in the wider sense, of his force that has characterised the great General Staff leaders in German history, men such as von Moltke, von Schlieffen, Beck, Wever and even Halder.

Unfortunate for the Luftwaffe, too, was Jeschonnek's inability either to control his dilettante chief, Göring, or to work harmoniously with his partner, Milch. Despite his early close association with the Secretary of State, who was seven years older than he, the two men had become alienated. Two incidents in particular had contributed to this. In 1934, when they were together, an SA officer had flagged them down to ask if they would transport a wounded storm-trooper to hospital. Milch took one look at the injured man, and ordered that, owing to severe skull injuries, he should not be moved until medical aid arrived. Upon their return to the Ministry, Jeschonnek denounced his superior for refusing to assist a storm-trooper in distress (at the time there was severe tension between the Armed Services and the SA), and persisted in the allegation even when the SA officer concerned bore out the truth of Milch's statement. Shortly after, Jeschonnek was moved to a bomber Gruppe. A second confrontation took place two years later, when Jeschonnek was commanding his Lehrgruppe. Milch later remembered the incident:

> One day I received a report from the Training Geschwader that an airplane had crashed on the water; the machine had got out of control in a low dive over the sea. The next day two more machines, with their crews, were reported missing for the same reason. I requested copies of the orders and in them I read the following sentence: 'In practising low-altitude flight, the pilot should make certain that the propeller tips touch the water.' It was reported to me that the comment 'Anyone who doesn't do it this way is a coward!' was added orally. I now faced the decision of whether or not to initiate court martial proceedings against Jeschonnek. I decided against it, however, and gave him a severe reprimand instead. From this moment on, he was my deadly enemy.[26]

Jeschonnek never forgave Milch, and allowed enmity to influence his whole attitude in the future.

For his part, Milch no doubt resented the young Jeschonnek, seeing in his obvious intelligence and ability a threat to his own position. Indeed, he expressed the conviction that Göring had made Jeschonnek Chief of the General Staff for that very purpose. Rivalry and dissension intensified. Milch, together with Udet, took care to see that the General Staff should have no part in taking decisions on technical matters, thus rendering it incapable of ensuring that its armament requirements, especially in new aircraft, were met. The only way to circumvent Milch's obstruction was for the Chief of the General Staff to go direct to Göring, but this, because of the latter's inadequacies as a leader, involved considerable difficulty and was rarely successful. Göring did nothing to end the feud between his two major subordinates; indeed, hoping that friction between the two would keep them from joining forces against himself, he appears to have encouraged it. This enmity was further compounded by the new structure for the General Staff which Jeschonnek proposed, and inherited, in 1939, and which caused it to lose a great deal of influence on several important aspects of military development. Branch III of the General Staff, in charge of training, had largely been stripped of its function when all weapon inspectorates and training schools were transferred to the new Chief of Training (responsible to Milch) and its duties were limited to issuing general guidelines in consultation with Kühl's office. Branch VII (signal communications) had also been transferred from the General Staff to Milch's domain, although its chief, Martini, continued to co-operate in every way with his former colleagues. Branch VI (armaments) was rendered virtually impotent by Milch's refusal to treat the General Staff as a body with any relevant views on the subject of weapons and equipment, which came within his realm.

Jeschonnek's relations with his Commander-in-Chief were likewise disastrous, but for different reasons. Initially Göring welcomed his appointment, believing it was easier to work with younger men, less set in their ways, than with older, more experienced, officers, many of whom were his seniors in age. However, Jeschonnek was no man to handle his chief's moods, and he soon instilled into Göring a sense of insecurity which made the Commander-in-Chief hesitate to consult his Chief of General Staff. Important decisions would be made without Jeschonnek being asked for his opinion, and this led to serious disagreements between the two men. Jeschonnek simply could not handle Göring, and, as time progressed, became the scapegoat on whom the Commander-in-Chief could vent his frustrations. Thus, unable to ally himself with those around him, even with his own deputy, Quartermaster-General Hans Georg von Seidel, Jeschonnek became increasingly isolated from the centres of power, and during the war witnessed the office of the Chief of the General Staff degenerate simply into that of an adviser to the Commander-in-Chief on operational matters.

So did Göring become estranged from both his Secretary of State and his Chief of the General Staff, an estrangement which, because of his position, caused a further centre of power to grow up around him. As he himself was quite incapable of providing either the dedication or the expertise for his job of commanding the Luftwaffe, he came to rely on an 'inner circle' of advisers. As with Hitler, there grew around Göring a very influential group of old comrades and friends who were well rewarded for their loyalty. They had his ear, and could enter his presence at any time. Foremost among them were

Generals Bodenschatz, Lörzer and Keller, together with Secretary of State Paul Körner, an old Party friend and Göring's deputy in Prussia. Karl Bodenschatz, a Bavarian, a professional soldier, and a wartime comrade of Göring, became the Minister's Adjutant in 1933, at the age of forty-three. After a brief flirtation with a field command (that of the new Richthofen Fighter Group), he became chief of the Ministerial Office in December 1937. In 1939, he was also appointed Liaison Officer between Göring and the Führer at his Headquarters. Bruno Lörzer, born in 1891 in Berlin, was also a wartime fighter pilot, a comrade of Göring, and a winner of the Pour le Mérite, who, in the 1920s, was active in civil aviation, during which time he organised the Lithuanian Air Force. He had good Party connections, his brother being the first Gauleiter of Braunschweig. In 1933, he was appointed President of the German Air Sports League, and, in 1935, he was made National Air Sport Leader. In 1937, as a Generalmajor, he was placed in command of Fliegerdivision 2. Alfred Keller had been a First World War pilot who pursued civil aviation in the 1920s, becoming head of training at the German Transport Aviation School at Braunschweig. In 1934, he joined the Air Force with the rank of colonel. After service in the RLM, he was appointed in 1935 to command Luftkreis IV, by the outbreak of war becoming a General der Flieger and commander of a Luftgau (Air Administrative Area). None of these men possessed a great understanding of the intricacies of modern war, and they all shared a dislike of Milch and Jeschonnek, their rivals for influence. It was a dislike that was fully returned, and the two men individually were forced to add to their many problems the struggle against the prejudices of this 'inner circle'.

Apart from Göring, Milch and Jeschonnek, there was one other major centre of influence in the high command of the Luftwaffe when war began: Ernst Udet. Although the most colourful personality of the German Air Force, Udet was quite unsuited to the post of Chief of Supply and Procurement which he held, a post essential to the Luftwaffe's ability to wage war successfully. He was a man of externals, and possessed none of that inner self-discipline so necessary for high command. Lacking any petty self-importance, Udet nevertheless tended towards the aggrandisement of himself in other people's eyes. A brilliant fighter ace and stunt-pilot, a movie-maker, a bonvivant of Bohemian bent, a crack shot, a gifted cartoonist, a fine story-teller and humourist, Udet lacked the maturity and patience to concentrate on building permanent relationships, whether in the services, business, marriage or politics. He left the Army after four years, his aircraft business after five, and his marriage lasted an even briefer period. He could never evince any interest in matters of State, even when National Socialism, with which he came to have some sympathy, reigned supreme. Brave, charming, even captivating, Udet was the personification of the dilettante. In his position, this was to prove fatal. As the Luftwaffe judge-advocate wrote of him after his death: 'He had none of the qualities needed for a high office. Above all he lacked real knowledge, he lacked moral rectitude and he lacked a sense of responsibility'.[27]

Born in 1896, the son of a wealthy businessman, Udet was a flying enthusiast from his earliest days. Joining the infantry in 1914, he transferred to the Air Service the following year, to become Germany's second-highest-scoring fighter ace, with sixty-two victories and a Pour le Mérite to his name. His feats were legendary. The end of the war found him commander of the 4th Staffel of the Jagdgeschwader Richthofen under Göring. Disinclined to remain in the Army, where he would be unable to fly, he resigned in 1919, and two years later established a small aircraft factory. In 1926 he left the business and took up flying for a profession, undertaking flights from Antarctica to Africa for film companies. His stunt-flying was remarkable, and was exemplified by his ability to pick up pocket handkerchiefs on the ground by means of a hook fastened on a wing-tip. When the National Socialists gained power, it was unthinkable that their propaganda-minded leaders would pass by such a man, even though at that time he revealed no sympathy for their cause. In 1934, Göring and Lörzer, both his war-time comrades, persuaded him to accept the honorary post of vice-commander of the German Air Sports League. His interest in aviation, especially in the concept of the dive-bomber, together with his reputation ensured that he was not to be excluded from the development of Germany's new air force. On 1st June 1935, as a result of a joint decision between Milch, Wever and Stumpff, he entered the Luftwaffe with the rank of colonel. He had been reluctant to do so, and was finally persuaded only because the Air Force would buy two American Curtiss biplanes he wanted very much but could not afford.

On 10th February 1936, Udet succeeded his friend, von Greim, to the post of Inspector of Fighters and Dive Bombers. He was in his element, and it was unfortunate both for him and the Air Force that there he did not remain. But the Führer had other ideas. As Milch remembered:

> Hitler quite properly saw in Udet one of Germany's greatest pilots. Unfortunately, he also saw in him, quite erroneously, one of Germany's greatest technical experts in the field of aviation. Bowing to necessity, Göring appointed Udet to the post of Chief of the Technical Office. This was surely not easy for him, for he and Udet had been on anything but good terms for the past decades. . . . It goes without saying that I voiced a number of objective reservations, but I do not believe that Göring made any attempt to understand these. For him the important thing was to enhance his own position with Hitler.[28]

On 9th June 1936, Udet became Chief of the Technical Office in succession to Wimmer. It was a major responsibility, his first in ten years, for which he had neither the training nor the temperament required. He, like Göring, was an amateur. Professional military service, regular hours, definite duties, consistency, coolness, dedication to matters which he might find boring – all these, and more, were not only new but alien to him. He had to compete for limited raw materials in a period of major rearmament, in which two other services were actively engaged in far-reaching expansions. He had to deal with soldiers, politicians, economists, businessmen and designers, in a harsh world where new industrial interests were mushrooming around the birth of the air force, where, in an environment of breath-taking development, there was little or no time for reflection or for correcting mistakes. A wrong decision could have its impact five to seven years after it was taken, and result not only in the production of a poor aircraft but in the dislocation of the entire development of the Air Force.

A talent for dedicated leadership and attention to detail was vital, a talent which became even more essential after 1st February 1939, when the new office of Generalluftzeugmeister (General Aircraft Master) was instituted. Udet, by then a Generalleutnant, came to be not only head of the Technical Office, but also of a number of other offices relating to the supply and production of the aircraft and equipment for the Air Force. Having been given immense administrative and budgetary power (in 1939, his budget reached some 5.4 billion Reichsmarks) it came to be he, with the ultimate, but virtually nominal approval of Göring, who determined the numbers and type of aircraft with which the Luftwaffe was to wage war. It was a daunting responsibility, for which Udet was sadly unfitted.

Moreover, Udet had not the good fortune to be served by an able deputy. Early on, he lost Wolfram von Richthofen, his head of development, who went to Spain as chief of staff of the Condor Legion, and Fritz Loeb, his production chief, who was appointed by Göring to head an important office within the Four Year Plan. Udet's Chief of Staff, Colonel August Ploch, was, like his chief, incapable of the task he had to perform, and his adjutant, Colonel Max Pendele, was competent as far as his duties required, but was not, overall, a highly effective adviser. Udet, therefore, came to rely increasingly upon his senior engineers, one of whom, Leading Chief Engineer Rulof Lucht, at thirty-four, was quite incapable of making an independent evaluation of technical problems (even Udet's understanding was regarded as more profound). The other, Günther Tschersich, head of Technical Planning, managed to acquire great influence over his chief, but placed his interest in the development of aircraft at the expense of their procurement. Moreover, in April 1938, during a reorganisation of the Technical Office, Udet lost his personal staff who had proved highly effective in coping with a large variety of problems, and who brought only the most difficult matters to their chief. Foolishly, Udet rejected the offer made by Jeschonnek for the permanent assignment of four or five able General Staff officers. It was a decision, arrived at through suspicion, he later regretted.

Thus, without an effective deputy, Udet soon found himself alone and at sea. The results were disastrous. When he took over the Technical Office it consisted of just four departments, logically divided into research, development, procurement and internal administration and budget. Its structure was horizontal, testing and manufacture being on an equal level, and each of the departments dealt with all the various types and models of aircraft. The Office was efficient, and, in co-operation with the General Staff, had been responsible for fine work that was to give the Luftwaffe three bombers (the Ju 86, the He 111, the Do 17), one dive bomber (the Ju 87), the possibility of two four-engined bombers (the Do 19 and Ju 89), as well as two fighters (the Bf 109 and Bf 110). However, on 1st April 1938, a reorganisation of the Technical Office changed its structure completely. Instead of the four departments there were thirteen; instead of the structure being horizontal, it was vertical (engines, airframes, signal and navigation equipment, testing, technical planning etc). Udet's staff gone, he was forced to deal with the thirteen departments single handed. For a busy man neither suited nor experienced in routine or bureaucracy, the result was fatal. Departmental chiefs soon had to wait for several months to see their chief.

Clearly, a simplification of the Technical Office's new structure was much required; but, instead, less than a year later, on 1st February 1939, the opposite was to occur. Then, with the creation of the gigantic office of the Generalluftzeugmeister, Udet was made responsible for not only the thirteen departments of the Technical Office but also a further nine, as well as five testing stations, an industrial section and a supply office (taken from the Air Defence Office). No fewer than twenty-six departmental chiefs were now responsible to Udet (even Milch had never had more than four). For this, he was quite unfitted. However, he continued to preside over an office in which, as the Luftwaffe's top legal officer later reported, 'Internally, everyone was working against everyone else.'[29] In the face of such discord, Udet was helpless. As Colonel Werner Baumbach, a famous bomber pilot who was warm in his liking for Udet, admitted:

> . . . it was not in him, in face of the eternal dissension in the departments of the Ministry, to force his ideas on the Engineer Generals, fighting and intriguing for power and our industry and economy. . . . The Technical Office soon became a department in which the Engineer Generals did pretty much what they liked. At a time when revolutionary discoveries, especially with regard to armament and the effect of jet and rocket propulsion on speed, had been made, and were clamouring for materialisation, the personal vanity of the leading men in the Luftwaffe made them eye each other with suspicion and quarrel over silly questions of authority.[30]

Lacking a competent deputy, sufficient personal staff, a harmonious, sensible, organisation, and the will to attend to detailed work other than in the field of aircraft development, Udet simply went through the motions of running his empire. Göring stated in 1943: 'If only I could understand what Udet was thinking of. He made a complete chaos out of our entire Luftwaffe programme.'[31]

If Udet could not manage his own office, nor could he the tangled, even vicious, personal relationships within the RLM. He and Jeschonnek were like chalk and cheese; they never got on, the Chief of the General Staff being quite open in his contempt for the dilettante Generalluftzeugmeister. For his part, Udet did not trouble to hide his dislike for the whole idea of an élite General Staff. With Milch, matters were different. At the beginning, he and Udet were good friends, and Udet even taught him to fly. Then, Udet used to ask the Secretary of State, at that time his chief, for advice, which was willingly given. Their relationship, Ploch remembered, was 'like father and son'.[32] Milch was clearly relieved that he was still able to exercise his influence over air armament. However, the seeds of discord were sown in late 1936, when Udet prepared a major production plan (No.4) in direct consultation with Göring, without reference to Milch. The Secretary of State felt slighted. When, in 1938, the Chief of the Technical Office was made responsible only to Göring, relations cooled significantly. Milch, aware that the shift in power had been aimed at him, was suspicious of all who had benefited, including Udet. No doubt he suspected that the reorganisation was brought about, in part, at Udet's instigation. At the same time, Udet failed to keep the Secretary of State fully informed of what was happening within his domain, and energetically defended his privilege of direct access to Göring. He, in his turn, became suspicious of Milch. Deprived of the Secretary of State's advice, Udet turned increasingly to his subordinates, and, because of their antipathy towards Milch (arising, no doubt, from their desire to increase their own influence), this further alienated the two men. Later, Milch was to describe Tscherisch and Ploch as 'Udet's evil spirits'.[33]

The final break between Milch and Udet came with the latter's acceptance of the post of Generalluftzeugmeister, to the responsibilities of which the Secretary of State felt himself eminently more suited (as, indeed, he was). Although, by the new reorganisation of the RLM, Milch was again nominally Udet's superior, he remained largely excluded from aeroplane and equipment design, production and procurement, the most important elements of any armed service so highly dependent upon technology and industrial production as an air force. Bodenschatz remembers that Milch was so embittered that he was willing to let Udet 'fend for himself'[34] and take the full brunt of the consequences, which, he had no doubt, would be dire.

In such a manner did those responsible for the technical development of the Luftwaffe become divorced from those in whose hands lay its operations. The inter-relationship between strategy and armament, so fundamental to modern armed forces, was thereby put in jeopardy. Tension between the Generalluftzeugmeister's empire and the General Staff, between Udet and Jeschonnek, was exacerbated by Milch, who, deprived of all but nominal responsibility for air armament, was determined to see that his rival, the Chief of the General Staff, possessed none either. The close relationship that had existed between the Technical Office and the General Staff before Udet's stewardship, a relationship which Kesselring described as 'a vital factor in the creating from nothing, of an effective Luftwaffe',[35] was gone. Moreover, the co-ordination between the military and the engineers that had existed within

the Technical Office under Wimmer, was absent within the Generalluftzeugmeisteramt under Udet (as, indeed, was even proper co-ordination
between engineers). As General Nielsen wrote:

> It seems certain that many of the decisions made by Udet and Milch
> would have been different if their advisers had not been purely
> technical people but rather military men with General Staff training
> and with sufficient understanding of technological developments to
> coordinate them fully with military requirements. Weapons develop-
> ment and armament are matters of the greatest importance to the
> commitment of a technical force during wartime. The failure of
> military leaders to retain their influence in these matters is tanta-
> mount to their renouncing any voice in the decisions concerning the
> weapons with which they are to fight.[36]

Udet's relationship too with Göring, the only man who was in a position to
keep a check on his decisions, brought little good to the Luftwaffe. Comrades
in war they might have been, but not good friends. During their service
together, there had been evident some distance between them, a rift which
increased after the war when Udet and not Göring was elected chairman of
the Richthofen Veterans' Association. Moreover, Udet challenged the
authenticity of some of Göring's 'kill' claims, and, quietly, had him excluded
from the Association. When Hitler expressed his desire for Udet to hold a
major office in the new Air Force, Göring was far from pleased, although he
may have seen the appointment as a means of silencing the ace who,
annoyingly, had the ear of the Führer on aviation matters. Certainly, Udet
was to be of advantage to Göring in helping him to keep the Secretary of State
out of armament and procurement matters completely. This, Göring did
despite his misgivings about Udet's capabilities. When Udet was made
Generalluftzeugmeister, Göring bemoaned: 'What are we going to do with
Udet? He just isn't doing the job.'[37] But the Minister did not help him; indeed
by giving Udet new responsibilities he ensured that he would not be able to
cope even with his initial ones. Nor was Göring the man to give any advice to
his subordinate, and, when the two men came together for conferences, they
rarely discussed official business. They usually reminisced over old times, or
talked about hunting; as Göring admitted, work was scrupulously avoided.

Indeed, Göring was singularly adept at shunning work, even when the
various reorganisations of the RLM thrust considerably more responsibility
on his shoulders. His laziness increased, and he took only a sporadic interest in
affairs. He asked for little advice, except from his intimate circle, and, once his
mind was made up, tolerated no contradiction. His method of working, Milch
remembered, seemed to lie in scribbling little notes 'usually in a different book
every day, without anybody being able to see the point of it all, since he
invariably forgot or distorted what had been under discussion'.[38] The type of
leadership which he provided, is well exemplified by the following story.
During a conference with the Führer in 1937, a Luftwaffe officer mentioned

that Germany did not possess a single up-to-date bomb. Hitler, who had just heard Göring extol the virtues of his bomber fleet, was understandably surprised. Several days later, he sent for his Luftwaffe commander and his senior officers and proposed that, as a provisional solution, the bombers could drop oxygen and acetylene cylinders filled with explosives. One of the officers present pointed out that their aerodynamic properties would be poor, and that they could not be armed properly. Hitler was annoyed, but before he could give vent Göring interjected: 'My Führer, may I express my thanks for this wonderful solution! I must admit that none of us could have thought of such an ingenious idea! You, and you alone, have saved the situation. Good Lord, to think we are all such dumb-bells! I shall never be able to forgive myself.'[39] Needless to say, not a single bomber unit was equipped with the cylinders. The story, though amusing, is a sad comment on the leadership of the Air Force.

The state in which the Luftwaffe's command found itself by the outbreak of war was not a happy one. It was dominated by four men, Göring, Milch, Jeschonnek and Udet, all of whom lacked the qualities and experience necessary for high command; three of them were, essentially, civilians, and two were quite unsuited for any office of high military responsibility. All found co-operation with others difficult, and all were fired by personal animosity to one or more of their colleagues. They were united only by their loyalty to Hitler. Thus, the high command of the Luftwaffe was composed of four centres of power, none of which co-operated with the others, and was united in title only by a Minister and Commander-in-Chief, a man who provided no leadership worthy of the name.

II

The Strategic Base

In 1933, the architects of the Luftwaffe lacked both a strategy and the material resources on which to build a new air force. Of the two, the former was the more important. For strategy forms the basis of any armed service; it is the element which gives coherence, form, and direction to what would otherwise be a haphazard collection of men and equipment. Simply, it may be defined as the art of applying military means to fulfil the ends of policy. Basic though this is, however, in 1933 in the field of military aviation Germany possessed neither the means nor any concept of their application, let alone a policy to fulfil. The three elements in strategy (policy, means, and application) interact one with another, but, of them, policy can be regarded as the most important, for only when that is established can the means and their application be considered. If, for example, the policy were to be primarily the destruction of the enemy's cities and industrial centres, then a heavy bomber force would be required. If it is the support of the Army in the field, then a medium and light bomber force would be called for. If it were to be solely the defence of the homeland from air attack, a strong fighter force would be of primary concern. If, however, the policy were to be a combination of all three, a balanced air force would be required, to include an appropriate number of all three types. Once the policy is decided upon, the most difficult part of the process begins. Then, the high command of an armed force has to determine the means (i.e. for the Luftwaffe, the type of aircraft and their quantity) and their application (i.e. operational employment). At this point, one other factor has to be taken into account, one so fundamental and pervasive that it can either limit the attainment, or, indeed, necessitate a complete change of policy: it is the availability of resources, whether in terms of finance, raw materials, technology or manpower. Thus, a policy which requires the development of a heavy bomber fleet, would be impossible of fulfilment if the nation, short of financial and material resources, is unable to produce sufficient aircraft, lacks the technology to design them, or cannot train enough crews to fly them. Economic reality can prove far stronger in influencing the final outcome of strategy than either military theory or political aims, coming to determine the nature of an armed force just as surely as does service doctrine. Of the truth of this, the Luftwaffe is a prime example.

In May 1933, the month the RLM was instituted, the first study for the development of a German air force was produced which took account of the changed political circumstances within the Reich. Till then, plans had been modest, calling for an air force of some 1,000 aircraft, including reserves, by 1938. With the advent of Hitler as Reich Chancellor, however, such a modest expansion immediately became irrelevant. Requested by Milch, the new study was the work of Dr Robert Knauss, Lufthansa's traffic manager, an aviation theorist and a future commander of the Air War Academy. In common with previous planners, such as Felmy, he argued that, since modern states were particularly vulnerable to dislocation and destruction by aerial bombardment, air power was destined to become a weapon of decisive strategic importance. During the difficult period of rearmament, Knauss continued, an effective air force would deter foreign interference until the Wehrmacht as a whole was fully developed. By the creation of a bomber force of some 400 aircraft, at the mere cost of building two battleships or raising five divisions, Germany could secure herself from any interference from France, Czechoslovakia, or Poland. A defensive air force, based on fighter interceptors, was regarded as inadequate; attack, based on bombers, was considered the best means of defence. Thus was born the idea of the Risiko Flotte, the 'Risk Fleet' described by Göring in 1939 as the only means by which Germany had been able to 'ensure further rearmament and prepare the way for the Führer to proclaim the resumption of the universal draft'.[1] From the beginning, a purely defensive strategy, based primarily on fighter interceptors, was rejected.

Milch was in complete agreement with Knauss's proposals, as also were Hitler and Göring, and the three men immediately adopted the concept of the 'risk fleet'. In mid-June 1933, Milch revealed his plan to achieve an air force of 600 front-line aircraft by late 1935, of which two-thirds would be bombers. This was approved by Göring and von Blomberg on the 27th. A month later, on 25th July, Milch ordered that measures be taken 'to make it impossible for foreign powers to prove actual violations of our existing foreign commitments [i.e. the Versailles Treaty]', and to prevent them 'from deriving any clear picture of the rate of growth, or of the actual size and organisation of the air force we are founding'.[2] Not long afterwards, Bohnstedt, Chief of the Luftschutzamt, sadly out of touch with his master's wishes, submitted plans for the future Luftwaffe: two hundred aircraft, of which only twelve would be bombers! Bohnstedt was amazed to hear that the State Secretary had 600 aeroplanes in mind, and he could only protest: 'But this is terrible, poor Germany!'[3] Bohnstedt was, much to his own relief, retired on 31st August, when a reorganisation of the RLM came into effect. There was no room for caution in the new Luftwaffe.

Almost the moment it was produced, Milch's plan was regarded as insufficient. Even the Army Command wished for more; General Wilhelm Adam, Chief of the Truppenamt, requested more reconnaissance Staffeln (an increase from twelve to sixteen) and stipulated that the six fighter Staffeln should be employed in the defence of the field armies. Further aircraft would have to be found for shielding the Reich. In September, a new aircraft production plan for the forthcoming two years was introduced, nearly doubling the previous figures, but even this was soon seen to be quite inadequate. In January 1934, a new plan, the 'Rhineland Programme', envisaged the production of 3,715 aircraft by the end of 1935, but by July this requirement had been increased even further, to 4,021 aeroplanes by September 1935. By July of that year, it was anticipated that the Reich's factories would be turning out 293 military aircraft a month. It was a bold plan, when it is considered that, in 1933, Germany's aircraft factories had produced an average of only thirty-one machines a month.

The 'Rhineland Programme' represented a balance between the need to establish a 'risk fleet' and to build up an air force from nothing. Thus, 1,760 training aircraft were ordered, in addition to 822 bombers (the Do 11, Do 13 and Ju 52) fifty-one dive bombers (the He 50) and 590 reconnaissance aeroplanes (the He 45 and He 46). In line with the anticipated requirements of a deterrent force, only 245 fighters (the Ar 64, Ar 65, and He 51) were ordered. The Navy was to have 149 machines, and these, together with the 394 liaison and miscellaneous aircraft, were to constitute the total air force available to the Reich. In addition, the basis for the future beyond 1935 was laid; three types of bomber, the Do 17, the He 111, and the Ju 86 were programmed to enter service. By 1935, during which year German military aircraft production continued to rise to reach 3,183 aeroplanes, progress of the 'Rhineland Programme' was so good that, on 1st January, Milch ordered a new plan to achieve a total of 9,853 aircraft by 1st October 1936. This, however, was outdated by October 1935, when a new programme, Production Plan No. 1, was drawn up: by 1st April 1936, the German aircraft industry was expected to have produced no fewer than 11,158 serviceable machines since 1933. Of these, 462 were to go to the Navy, 6,876 were to be non-combat aircraft such as trainers and transports, and 3,820 were to be either bombers, fighters, or for reconnaissance. Still, the emphasis was placed on bombers: 1,849 in all, compared with 970 fighters. It was not long, however, before Production Plan No. 1 was superseded, in March, July and October of 1936 by Plans Nos. 2, 3 and 4 respectively, which not only raised the number of aircraft required by 1st April 1936 to 12,309, but also incorporated many new models that were to be introduced by 31st March 1938. By then, the Luftwaffe was expected to possess no less than 18,000 aircraft, made up of eighty models and variants.

Numbers of aircraft alone, however, do not make an air force. Just as important is the composition of that force. By their adoption of a 'risk fleet', Germany's military leaders had emphasised the importance of attack and, therefore, the employment of the bomber, and had rejected a defence that was solely responsive to enemy action, and thus the employment of the fighter, to secondary importance. Also significant was the type of bomber on which the Luftwaffe was to be based. All this involved not only a judgement of the operational role which air power was expected to fulfil, but also the establishment of certain political and economic priorities during the period of rearmament. It was the nature of these considerations, as much as the theories of military aviation, which determined the character and, to a large extent, the progress of the German Air Force before and during the Second World War.

Behind the concept of the 'risk fleet' lay a strong belief in the destructive power of bomber forces, a belief held by politicians, military experts and public alike. In the 1920s, an Italian general, Giulio Douhet, had predicted: 'War will be waged essentially against the unarmed populations of the cities and great industrial centres'. His words were destined to have considerable impact upon informed and general opinion in Europe and North America. He continued: 'A complete breakdown of the social structure cannot but take place in a country subjected to this kind of merciless pounding. . . . The time would soon come when, to put an end to the horror and suffering, the peoples themselves, driven by the instinct of self-preservation, would rise up and demand an end to the war – this, before their army and navy had time to mobilise at all.'[4] What manner of war would achieve this? The answer was simple: air power. It was, Douhet asserted in his book, *The Command of the Air* (first published in 1921 and revised in 1927), a 'brutal but inescapable' conclusion 'that in the face of the technical development of aviation today, in case of war the strongest army we can deploy . . . and the strongest navy we can dispose on our seas, will prove no effective defence against determined efforts to bomb our cities'.[5] Protection was impossible: the use of anti-aircraft guns would merely be a 'waste of energy and resources',[6] and the numbers of aircraft needed to defend every possible target would be so great as to render them quite unobtainable by even the most advanced industrial nations. Air forces could only be used in the offensive, to win command of the air and then to attack 'industrial and commercial establishments; important buildings, private and public; transportation arteries and centres; and certain designated areas of civilian population. . . .'[7] In order to achieve this, the guiding principle of bombing would be the complete destruction of the objective in one attack. The air offensive would be short but decisive. 'No-one can deny that, today, an aeroplane can carry a ton of bombs from Paris to London. Neither can it be denied that 1,000 tons of explosive, incendiary and poison gas bombs dropped on Paris or London could destroy these cities, the hearts of France and England. . . . It will be an inhuman, an atrocious, performance; but these are the facts'.[8]

This concept of the use of air power, as a 'weapon of decision' in its own right, had its roots in the First World War and, specifically, in the 103 German air raids over south-east England, in which 269 tons of bombs were dropped. Undertaken by Zeppelin airships and Gotha twin-engined bombers and resulting in 1,413 deaths, these had made a considerable impression at the time. To the Allied press and propaganda machine, they had been yet one further example in a long saga of Teutonic barbarity, this time with its wanton and indiscriminate destruction of private property and killing of innocent civilians regardless of their age or sex. To the military, however, they represented something more ominous: a revolution in war. In August 1917, Field Marshal Jan Smuts reported to the British War Cabinet that 'The day may not be far off when aerial operations, with their devastation of enemy land and destruction of industrial and populous centres on a vast scale, may become the principal operation of war, to which the older forms of military and naval operations may become subordinate'. Smuts was particularly impressed by the German raid on London on 16th July 1917, in which some 150 people had been killed and more than 350 injured for the loss of not a single bomber, despite the activities of ninety British fighters. It was proof, Smuts wrote, that an air force could become 'an independent means of war operations'.[9] The British straightway formed a force of bombers which, for a few weeks at the end of the war, operated against military and industrial targets inside Germany.

On the basis of the effects of the bombing in 1917 and 1918, it was estimated after the war that a ton of high explosive dropped on a city would produce fifty casualties. It was widely accepted that, in any future conflict, one person in twenty-five would either be killed or wounded by enemy action from the air. In Britain, it was declared that, in the first raid, no less than 600,000 Londoners would be killed and 1,200,000 wounded. After reports of air raids on Barcelona and Guernica during the Spanish Civil War, and on Nanking during the Sino-Japanese War, it was feared that a figure of seventy-two casualties per ton of explosive would be more realistic. More terrible, however, was the prospect of the use of poison gas dropped from the air. The populations of whole cities, it was argued, could be wiped out within hours by relatively small bomber fleets. Armageddon was truly round the corner, or so it was believed.

As a result, numerous studies and works of fiction appeared during the 1930s, predicting the course of a future war in which air power would predominate. One organisation, the 'Hands Off Britain Air League', warned the public: 'England awake! Why wait for a bomber to leave Berlin at 4 o'clock and wipe out London at 8. London can be bombed, battered and broken within a few hours', the League declared: 'Today what matters most is mastery of the air. . . . Mr Baldwin says: "The bomber will get through any defence you can visualise today." '.[10] Theoretical works, written by men such as Billy Mitchell, Alexander de Seversky, and Camille Rougeron, supported such dire predictions, and books such as *Invasion from the Air, War upon Women, Chaos, Air Reprisal, Menace,* and *Empty Victory* appeared on bookstalls, containing scenes of devastated cities, mutilated survivors and the destruction of millions of people of all ages and both sexes after only a few days, or even hours of war, the result of thousand-bomber raids and the deliberate use of poison gas. *The Gas War of 1940*, published in 1931, was typical. Its author, S. Southwold, writing under the pen-name 'Miles', envisaged a world war that bore only certain superficial resemblances to what was to come eight years later: 'Poland was attacked from the air, and its bloody ruins occupied by tanks. Alsace and Lorraine were invaded after punishment from a German air fleet that left alive a mere handful of their people'. Such destruction was spread across the world. The fate of London was typical: 'And then, in a moment, the lights of London vanished. . . . And in the dark streets the burned and wounded, bewildered and panic-stricken, fought and struggled like beasts, scrambling over dead and dying alike, until they fell and were in turn trodden underfoot by the ever-increasing multitude around them.' The moral of it all was, according to 'Miles', that 'Man has created a peril which he must at all costs avoid. That peril is the perfection of instruments of destruction'.[11] In Germany, too, there appeared similar works. Authors such as Dr Robert Knauss (*Der Luftkrieg, 1936*) Franz Hermann (*Die Erde im Flammen*) and Ernst Ohlinger (*Bomben auf Kohlenstadt*) envisaged the wars of the future in terms of wholesale and immediate death and destruction, with the air arm being the decisive instrument of power. This, too, was the view of a number of Army officers. As Colonel Wilhelm Wimmer of the Reichswehr Technical Office wrote in February 1932, there was 'not the least doubt that, in the future, the only nations to have anything to say will be those that possess powerful air fleets built around an aeroplane that can, day or night, strike fear into the hearts of the enemy population'.[12]

Established military opinion in Germany took much notice of men such as Douhet and their predictions for the future. Indeed, their principles lay at the basis of the employment of the Risk Fleet. However, the standard regulations for the conduct of air warfare, the *Luftkriegführung* (Conduct of Air War) prepared by General Helmut Wilberg, Commander of the Air War Academy, under the supervision of Wever and first issued in 1936, looked beyond the role of the Luftwaffe simply as a deterrent force. It did, however, still base the Air Force's strategy on offence rather than defence, as exemplified by the fact that, of the 280 paragraphs in the regulations, only thirty-five were devoted to the latter. The principle that offence is the best means of defence was to be the main guarantor of German air space in the event of war. Moreover. it was to be an offensive undertaken by all three armed services in conjunction. As the *Luftkriegführung* stated: 'The mission of the Wehrmacht in war is to break the will of the enemy. The will of a nation finds its strongest expression in that nation's armed forces. Defeat of the enemy armed forces is the primary objective in war. . . . The mission of the Luftwaffe is to serve this purpose by conducting air warfare as part of the overall pattern for the conduct of the war'.[13] Here, German doctrine departed from the view of Douhet and the apostles of air power as the sole 'arm of decision'. There was to be no attempt to bring about a victory by the Luftwaffe's efforts alone. To rely solely on an instrument of war as novel as an air force was a gamble that no nation was prepared to take in the 1930s; nor, indeed, was it a luxury they could afford if, at the same time, they wished to build up their conventional land and sea forces. Therefore, the emerging Luftwaffe was not destined to adopt a revolutionary strategy; on the contrary, it was made clear that, for the time being at least, the Air Force was to co-ordinate its operations with those of the other two services.

However, the extent of the Luftwaffe's strategic basis should not be misunderstood. Certainly, because the Army was by far the larger and the more important, the prime task of the Air Force would be to support its manoeuvres. Air superiority would be gained as a preliminary to the successful prosecution of any campaign. This would not only allow the subsequent uninhibited use of air power, but would also prevent the enemy air force from interfering with the ground troops. The Army's operations would then be aided by air attacks on the enemy's headquarters, communications, and reserves, helping to paralyse his armies in the field. In addition, some strikes could be undertaken on his strong points in or near his front line. Such a strategy might have been expected, for the senior officers who were responsible for drawing up its premises had spent their adult life in the Army (a very few in the Navy), and were imbued with the German military tradition. But this was not to be the whole extent of the Luftwaffe's activities. Although the advocates of massive aerial bombardments against populations were openly rebuffed, the *Luftkriegführung* stipulating that it was 'absolutely forbidden' to attack cities 'for the purpose of terrorising the civilian population',[14] this did not limit the Air Force solely to the support of the troops in the field. The airmen realised the potential value of the weapon in their control, and recognised the importance of operations against the enemy's sources of power: his war industries. As the *Luftkriegführung* noted: 'By combat action against the enemy's sources of military power and by interrupting the flow of power from those sources to the front, it endeavours to paralyze the enemy's military forces. Warfare in enemy territory is not directed exclusively against the operational forces and their bases. It is also directed against the logistical services and the production centres of the hostile air force, and thus becomes a battle for the sources of military power.'[15] The authors of the *Luftkriegführung* also recognised that 'Air power carries the war right into the heart of the enemy country from the moment war breaks out' and '. . . strikes at the very root of the enemy's fighting power and the people's will to resist'.[16] Indeed, if the war on the ground yielded inconclusive results, and stalemate ensued, then might the Luftwaffe be 'the only means to bring about a decision. In such a case, the primary condition of success would be a complete shift of emphasis to the conduct of air warfare, at the expense of all other means of warfare'.[17]

Nor should the nature of the Luftwaffe's support for the Army be mistaken. The combination of tank and dive-bomber in attack has become an established part of the myth of Blitzkrieg, the revolutionary strategy which German Armed Forces were supposed to have practised in the first half of the Second World War. In 1940, an anonymous British staff officer wrote: 'German dive-bombers . . . have proved . . . irresistible in conjunction with tanks in this campaign',[18] while, after the war, the famous military theorist and historian, Sir Basil Liddell Hart, spoke of the campaign in Poland as one in which the Poles were 'quickly disintegrated by a small tank force in conjunction with a superior air force, which put into practice a novel technique'.[19] It was the combination of tank and dive-bomber which, according to accepted belief, gave to the panzer formations added power, and made Blitzkrieg irresistible. This impression of German air power coincided directly with the arguments put forward by the proponents of the use of tanks the 1920s and 1930s. As early as 1919, General J.F.C. Fuller envisaged an important role for aircraft which would help to bring about the paralysis of the enemy, and in 1926 Liddell Hart stipulated that dive-bombers should replace artillery in supporting tank attacks. He wrote: 'the best chance of penetrating an enemy's front lies in an armoured force's combination of smoke, supporting fire, and synchronised air attack'.[20] German experience in the First World War seemed to confirm this. In July 1917, the first ground attack accompanied by supporting aircraft took place in the coastal area of Flanders; infantry of the German 4th Army were accompanied by a light bomber squadron during the assault. The results were impressive, as much through the effect on enemy morale as through the impact of fire-power from the air. The German High Command thereupon decided to adapt its escort Staffeln (established in 1916 to provide protection for reconnaissance units) to ground-support (Schlachtstaffeln). They proved particularly valuable during the March-April 1918 offensives, representing a highly effective force which could be brought, at short notice, to support an advance by destroying the enemy's artillery positions, bases and reserves, and even by inducing panic among his front-line troops. By November 1918, the German Air Force had no fewer than thirty-eight Schlachtstaffeln, totalling 228 aircraft, which were among some of the last units to be disbanded as a result of the Versailles Treaty.

After 1918, a number of German soldiers and theorists recognised the value of air support for ground operations. A few believed that the aeroplane was the natural ally of the tank. General Heinz Guderian described his vision thus: 'Panzer divisions and supporting air squadrons will thrust deep into enemy territory, the aeroplanes paving a way for the tank, ensuring that not only are the enemy's strongpoints neutralised but that his reserves are prevented from intervening in the battle. . . . Air transport will enable the mechanised forces to continue their drive with unrelenting momentum over ranges hitherto unheard of.'[21] However, this theory was not one officially espoused by the Wehrmacht. Although, as the *Luftkriegführung* made clear, the German Air Force was designed for co-operation with the ground forces, and was not viewed as an independent force in Douhetian terms, this did not necessarily mean that its aeroplanes would be used in the direct support of ground operations, attacking strong-points in the line of advance, as desired by the armour enthusiasts. Indeed, that was to be the exception rather than the rule. The German military establishment, aviators as well as soldiers, believed that it had been the static conditions of the First World War which had required the use of thirty-eight ground-attack Staffeln, and that, in future, modern weapons, including aeroplanes, would render them unnecessary. Furthermore, post-war experiments had pointed to problems inherent in such operations, including high losses and poor accuracy. Thus, although experience gained in the Spanish Civil War had shown that even out-dated fighter aeroplanes could achieve considerable results interfering in ground combat, it was generally held that, owing to the limited resources of the Air Force, indirect air-support for the Army, against the enemy's reserves, communications, main headquarters and so on, would yield greater benefits.

The *Luftkriegführung*, then, specifically guarded against much use of 'direct' co-operation of air with ground forces. This was, in general, to be confined to defensive measures, including action against enemy aeroplanes that were attacking German troops. It stated: 'Direct co-operation with, and direct support of, the Army are missions primarily of those units of the Air Force which are allocated to, and assigned under, the Army for purposes of reconnaissance and air-defence.'[22] Furthermore, the use of the bomber and ground-attack forces in close support was specifically discounted as of little significance: 'In close co-operation with the ground forces . . . air units, and particularly the bomber units, frequently will be unable to find targets against which they could bring their full striking power to bear, and through the destruction of which they could effectively support the army.'[23] Indeed, in the 1940 version of the *Luftkriegführung*, which declared that 'Strong forces of the Air Force can be committed to participate in critically important battles on the ground',[24] it was specifically stated that, as a rule, direct support for the front line was 'unlikely to produce results commensurate with the effort expended, although such action might be required in special circumstances'.[25] To reinforce this statement, it was noted: 'Air action within the range of friendly artillery fire is only justifiable in cases where the artillery is unable fully to accomplish its mission'.[26] Instead of direct support for the advancing units against targets such as enemy strong-points and forward troop positions, the Luftwaffe would be used primarily in their 'indirect' support. 'It is sounder practice', the 1936 version of the *Luftkriegführung* declared, 'to commit these [air] units against distant targets, the destruction or neutralisation of which can exercise a decisive influence on the combat operations of the Army . . .'[27] The targets would be headquarters, rearward troop concentrations, lines of communications, supply depots and military installations of a like nature. This applied equally to both dive-bombers and horizontal-attack aircraft.

The general attitude of the Army was to regard the Air Force as an umbrella to protect it from enemy interference by air and, as far as possible, to prevent enemy troop movements from menacing its flanks or deploying ahead to counter the grand encircling movements of the attack. It did not cause the military establishment to modify its approach to strategy; the role of air power was simply to allow the manoeuvres of the ground forces as much freedom as possible. As a result, many historians and even German Air Force officers have argued that the Luftwaffe's employment was not 'strategic' but merely 'tactical'. But this is a misnomer. The employment of any armed force as a whole can never be regarded as merely 'tactical'; it is always 'strategic'. Moreover, the Luftwaffe's support of the ground forces during campaigns was on such a scale that it cannot be described as 'tactical'. Although the Luftwaffe was not designed to win a war through its efforts alone (nor indeed, in the conditions of the Twentieth Century, was the Army), it was built at enormous cost in order to make a major contribution to victory. Its strategic basis was not only to allow the Army's traditional manoeuvres to be undertaken with greater success than ever before, but also to extend the method of war, so that the defeat of the enemy could be brought about to a significant degree by activities in the air independent of action on the ground. The employment of the Luftwaffe in such a manner was destined to have a considerable impact on the course of the Second World War.

The strategic policy of the Luftwaffe dictated the structure of its organisation. Had its operations been regarded as primarily independent of the Army, a vertical structure would have been adopted, whereby each type of aircraft fulfilling an individual function, whether bomber, ground-attack, maritime or fighter, was organised and commanded separately. Then, the Luftwaffe would have instituted a Bomber Command, a Fighter Command (or a Home Defence Command) and a Close-Support Command, so as to coordinate most effectively the equipment, personnel, training, tactical development and operations of each arm. However, since the support of ground troops was the primary consideration, support which entailed the concerted action of bombers, dive-bombers, fighters, transports and reconnaissance aircraft, territorially-based, mixed commands were needed, to be both flexible and mobile, so that they could be adapted to the activities of the army groups or armies to whose support they were assigned. Thus, in 1935, the six Gehobene Luftämter (Higher Air Offices), which had been instituted the year before to coordinate the development of the infant Air Force throughout Germany, were reorganised into Luftkreise (Air Districts), with borders similar to those of the Army's Wehrkreise (Defence Districts). On 1st April 1937, a seventh Luftkreis was added. These commands were directly subordinate to the RLM, and, between them, coordinated all the air and ground units within the Luftwaffe. Responsible to the commander of a Luftkreis were the Höherer Fliegerkommandeur in charge of all air units (this post did not exist in Luftkreis I, and in Luftkreis VI it was called the Führer der Luft and was tactically subordinate to the Navy), the Höherer Flakkommandeur, commanding all anti-aircraft units, two or three Luftgaukommandos, responsible for the ground organisation, supply and replacement of the operational units within the Luftkreise, and various signals and training units.

On 1st April 1938, this command structure was reorganised, great emphasis being placed on mobility and flexibility of operation, and identity with Army operational commands. From the seven Luftkreise, three

Luftwaffengruppenkommandos (Luftwaffe Group Commands), were instituted, together with three other, lesser, commands: Luftwaffenkommando See (its air units being under tactical control of the Navy), Luftwaffenkommando Ostpreussen (East Prussia, which was then separated from the rest of Germany by the Polish Corridor), and Luftwaffenkommando Österreich (Austria, which had just been incorporated into the Reich). Subordinate to these commands were the air units, reorganised on 1st August into Fliegerdivisionen (there were initially five of these), Luftgaue (of which, on 1st July, ten were organised to cover Germany), and the usual communication, training and anti-aircraft units. The final reorganisation came on 1st April 1939, when Luftwaffengruppenkommandos, 1, 2 and 3 were retitled Luftflotten 1, 2 and 3, and Luftwaffenkommando Österreich was raised to the status of Luftflotte 4. Luftwaffenkommando Ostpreussen was made subordinate to Luftflotte 1, and Luftwaffenkommando See was abolished, its responsibilities being taken over by the General der Luftwaffe beim Oberbefehlshaber der Marine und Befehlshaber der Marineflieger-verbände (Luftwaffe General with the Commander-in-Chief of the Navy, and Commander of Naval Air Units). A similar command (that of the Luftwaffe General with the Commander-in-Chief of the Army) known after 1st March 1939 as the Commander of the Army Air Units and Luftwaffe General with the Army Commander-in-Chief (Befehlshaber der Heeresfliegerverbände und General der Luftwaffe beim Oberbefehlshaber des Heeres), was responsible for the reconnaissance units under the tactical control of the Army.

Within each of the four Luftflotten, the administrative work was undertaken by two or three Luftgaue, and the operational tasks were performed by one or two Fliegerdivisionen (after February 1940 most were known as Fliegerkorps). The front-line strength of a Luftflotte could vary enormously, from 200 or 300 aircraft to a maximum of 1,250, depending on its operational requirements, as could that of a Fliegerdivision, from 200 to 750 aircraft. The Fliegerdivisonen were formed by a number of Geschwader, which, nominally, comprised three Gruppen, the basic flying unit of the Luftwaffe, each consisting of thirty aircraft usually based at one airfield. There was a further sub-division into Staffeln, three of which formed a Gruppe.

The strategic policy of the Luftwaffe once decided upon, it was necessary to develop the various aircraft to carry it out. The selection was crucial, for upon a few types would depend the fortunes of the German Air Force. As Wever stated: 'Perhaps in no other arm of service is the mutual dependence of tactics and technology and their interdependence so great as in the Luftwaffe'.[28] Two agencies were theoretically responsible for the choice of aircraft: the General Staff and the Technical Office. Co-operation between them was, initially, seen as essential. The General Staff began the process, by drawing up tactical-technical specifications for aeroplane types, based on likely operational requirements. These were passed on to the Technical Office in the form of a directive. There, the technical implications were studied, and the conclusions then passed on to the aircraft industry as research and development contracts. Competing designs were submitted to the Technical Office, and the most promising were chosen for the construction of full-size mockups. After their evaluation, contracts were issued for prototypes, which were extensively tested by both the aircraft company and the Technical Office. As a result, modifications usually amounted to between five and twenty thousand, and covered all parts of the aircraft. A pre-production series of the chosen aircraft was then field-tested by units of the Lehrdivision (Training Division), and a close interest in the process was taken by the General Staff. Alterations resulting from this process could be as high as 70,000. The final decision as to the aeroplane's suitability was then made by the Commander-in-Chief, after hearing the opinions of the General Staff and the Technical Office. Finally, estimates of the number of the aircraft required were submitted to the manufacturers by the Technical Office as part of its procurement programme. The whole process usually took between four and five years. After 1937, as has been seen, the close co-operation between the two offices, so essential to the Luftwaffe's development, broke down.

The General Staff (or until 1936, the Air Command Office), was faced with a difficult problem in its choice of aircraft. Clearly, an air force whose prime role was to aid the progress of the Army required reconnaissance aircraft to provide adequate intelligence, bombers for close and medium support and to attack targets far behind the front line; fighters, as primarily defensive machines, were to take a secondary role. But what were to be the specifications of the bombers? Were they to be high or low level in operation, dive or horizontal in attack, capable of carrying a light bomb-load over a long range, or a heavier over a shorter? Of what should their defensive armament consist? What should be the total number of bombers, and the proportions of the various types to the whole? Should, indeed, a long-range heavy bomber be developed? This was virgin territory, for, apart from some minor efforts in the years 1914-18, no bomber force had been tried and tested in war according to the precepts of either Douhet or the *Luftkriegführung*. Matters were not helped by the speed at which aircraft technology was developing; by the end of the decade following 1929, for example, the speed, range, and bomb-load of bombers had more than doubled. Furthermore, there was little leeway for error. It was reckoned that, by 1940, the maintenance of peace beyond the forthcoming ten years could, at best, be regarded as dubious; indeed, preparedness for war by 1943 was the assumption on which the Luftwaffe leaders based their plans. Thus, from 1933, there was enough time to develop and produce only two or, with luck, three generations of aircraft.

In 1933, the Air Ministry had inherited little that could be a guide to its future needs. The bombers already in existence were either the medium Do 11s, Do 23s and the Ju 52s or the light He 45s, and all were being built under the 'Rhineland Programme' and Production Plan No. 1. Until the mid-

1930s, the main offensive power of the Luftwaffe was destined to lie in the employment of twin-engined medium bombers, together with a few light bombers. Both the Do 11 and its successor, the Do 23 (which began to replace the former in the autumn of 1935), achieved a top speed at sea level of 161 mph and carried a bomb-load of 2,205 lb (just over a ton), the Do 23 possessing a radius of action of 420 miles compared with the 298 miles of the Do 11. The Ju 52, a lumbering bomber-transport, had a radius of 310 miles and a top speed of 172 mph at 3,000 ft., and could carry 3,300 lb of bombs. All these aeroplanes were far from satisfactory, in part because of the low quality of the work in the factories. The Dorniers had poor manoeuvrability and speed, not to mention flying characteristics that could be positively lethal (their wings had a propensity to whip in bumpy weather conditions), while the Junkers was never regarded as more than a stop-gap. In December 1934, the Technical Office even went so far as to consider halting output until new prototypes were ready for series production some eighteen months later. This was a desperate solution born of a desperate situation, and was not put into practice; instead, output of the obsolete machines continued. Indeed, throughout the Luftwaffe's existence, production plans were bedevilled by countless delays, some even of years, owing to the unpredictable nature of aircraft development, and made worse, as will be seen, by decisions taken by the RLM.

In 1934, the Technical Office issued specifications for a medium bomber with a top speed of 215 mph, a radius of 600 miles, and a bomb-load of 2,200 lb. Its airframe had also to be suitable for use as a civilian transport. The three aircraft accepted by the RLM under these specifications were the He 111, the Do 17, and Ju 86, which entered service in late 1936 or early 1937. Two, the He 111 and the Do 17, were to form the basic offensive force of the Luftwaffe in the first year of war, and one, the He 111, was to continue in service as a bomber until mid-1944. However, on their appearance, all three possessed serious limitations. The Ju 86, for a time the Luftwaffe's standard bomber until it was phased out in 1938, was erratic in performance because of its diesel engines, and carried a small bomb-load of 1,760 lb. The slowest of the three, capable of a top speed of only 202 mph at 9,840 ft it, however, had the greatest radius of action: 350 miles. The He 111, destined to become the major work-horse of the German Air Force in the first few years of the war, began life with many problems before it settled down to become a popular, serviceable aircraft, easy to handle. Its capabilities, however, were never outstanding. The He 111B-2, which entered service in late 1936, possessed a top speed of 230 mph at 13,120 ft, a radius of 250 miles, and a maximum bomb-load of 3,307 lb (a smaller bomb-load would allow extra fuel to be carried, and the range thereby extended). By the outbreak of hostilities in 1939, most Luftwaffe bomber units were equipped with the P-4 version of the He 111; when loaded, it was capable of a maximum speed of 230 mph at 16,400 ft, and had a radius of action of 500 miles with 2,000 lb of bombs. Its maximum bomb-load was 4,410 lb. Its defensive fire-power, consisting of three machine guns, was poor, but it was also well-provided with some 600 pounds of steel plate as protection for the crew.

The Do 17, known as the 'Flying Pencil' because of its shape, was initially designed as a commercial transport, but came to exemplify the theory, prevalent in the 1930s but later to be proved fallacious, that bombers could possess sufficient speed to elude intercepting fighters. Its introduction, and its success during the Spanish Civil War, initiated the German trend towards high-powered, medium, versatile bombers, which could also be used for long-range reconnaissance. Indeed, so confident were some within the RLM that the speed of the Do 17 was its major defence, that proposals were made to give it no defensive armament whatsoever. That idea was, fortunately for the crews, overridden. The first prototype of the aeroplane was flown in the autumn of 1934, and the Do 17M-1 entered service in early 1937, at a time when it was twenty-five miles an hour faster than the most advanced enemy fighter. Reliable, versatile and popular, it possessed a top speed of 255 mph at 13,120 ft, a radius of 310 miles with a maximum bomb-load of 2,205 lb, together with three machine guns. An improved, later, version, the Do 17Z-2, with which the Luftwaffe began the war, possessed a smaller radius of action, 205 miles with 2,205 lb of bombs (its maximum load), because it carried an extra crew member (a total of four) and more defensive armament (up to eight machine-guns) and equipment.

Disappointment with these three medium bombers was prevalent among senior Luftwaffe commanders. None was considered to possess all the attributes required of a standard attack aircraft. The search for such a machine continued. Fortunately, a solution was at hand. During the winter manoeuvres of 1933-1934, the RLM had detected a need for a heavily-armed, close-support aircraft, whose small bomb-load facilitated a high speed. In May 1934, the Technical Office issued specifications for a multi-purpose, high-altitude, long-range reconnaissance aircraft that could also adopt the role of bomber. It was given fourth priority in development, after the heavy bomber, the dive-bomber, and the medium bomber. In June, new specifications were issued calling for a Kampfzerstörer (Battle Destroyer), which was to have a top speed of 240 mph, a radius of 600 miles, and was to be heavily armed and capable of night-flying. From this were developed the Focke-Wulf 57 and the Henschel 124. The Technical Office, however, was not satisfied, realising that to combine the functions of fast bomber, heavy fighter, and reconnaissance aircraft was impracticable. In early 1935, it issued new specifications which called for three different aeroplanes: a heavy fighter (later to be the twin-engined Bf 110), a fast reconnaissance bomber (the Do 17 already under development), and a fast bomber (known as the Schnell-bomber). The specifications for the Schnellbomber, reaffirmed and expanded in February 1936, called for a lightly armed (one machine-gun) aircraft, with a crew of three, possessing a normal and a maximum bomb-load of 1,100 lb and 1,765 lb respectively, a top speed of 310 mph, a radius of 750 miles, an excellent rate of climb, and capable of operating from short, rough runways.

Three firms submitted prototypes, Henschel, Messerschmitt and Junkers, and in December 1937 the Technical Office chose the Ju 88. Early the following year, the aircraft was programmed to become the successor to the He 111 and the standard bomber of the Luftwaffe.

The Ju 88 promised to be a fine aircraft. In March 1939, one of the first prototypes established a new 621 miles closed-circuit record by carrying a 4,409 lb payload at an average speed of 321.25 mph. Much was expected of this so-called 'Wonder-Bomber'. However, high hopes were to be shattered; it was later to be referred to by Göring as 'the product of a pig-sty', and by Milch as 'a flying barn door'. The trouble stemmed from a decision made by the RLM in December 1936, that the Ju 88, till then envisaged as a 'horizontal bomber', should be given the capability to dive-bomb.

The German preoccupation with dive-bombing had its origins in the First World War, with the employment of Schlachtstaffeln to support the front-line troops. This interest was maintained by the Reichswehr and the aircraft designers (who produced the K 47 and the He 50, both dive-bombers), and by 1933 the Inspectorate for Aircraft Equipment and the Technical Office had evolved specifications for the development of a standard dive-bomber. A two-stage programme was envisaged, the first calling for a single-seat biplane suitable for rapid development, and the second for a more-advanced, two-seater monoplane. Confirmation of this plan, if confirmation were needed, came from outside Reichswehr circles when, in September 1933, Udet, then a civilian, flew a Curtiss Hawk dive-bomber (with which he had been impressed at the 1931 Cleveland Air Races) in the United States. By that time he had already persuaded Göring and Milch to buy two for evaluation by the Technical Office, and was even prepared to enter the Air Force on condition that they did so. In November, the aeroplanes arrived in Germany. One crashed at Tempelhof with a jammed elevator, but the other was displayed to great effect by Udet before a gathering of senior officers at Rechlin in December 1933. Göring was delighted by what he saw; his blessing given, the Sturzbomberprogramme (Dive-Bomber Programme) was approved and specifications for the first stage were issued.

In 1935, two biplane prototypes appeared, the Fieseler 98 and the Henschel 123. The latter immediately proved its ascendancy, and by the summer of 1936 the Luftwaffe was in receipt of the first production models. The Hs 123A-1 possessed a maximum speed of 212 mph at 3,940 ft., a radius of 275 miles, and a bomb-load of four 110 lb bombs and two containers of anti-personnel bombs. It was capable of diving at angles exceeding eighty degrees. Operational experience was to show that the Hs 123 was more properly employed as a Schlachtflugzeug (close-support aircraft), taking a direct part in landbattles, strafing enemy troops, destroying anti-tank guns, machine-gun posts and the like. For this it was well-suited, being able to absorb more anti-aircraft fire than any other Luftwaffe aircraft and still keep on flying. The Sturzkampflugzeuge (Dive-bombers or Stukas), however, were initially envisaged as supporters of the ground forces in an indirect role, confining their activities to targets behind the front lines.

Work was begun by Junkers on the second phase of the Sturzbomber-programm in late 1933, although the Technical Office did not issue its specifications until January 1935, specifications which, in large part, arose from manoeuvres in which bombers were used in close support of tanks and infantry. Three months later, in April, the first prototype of the Ju 87 appeared, an evil, predatory looking machine, to be followed, some time later, by its rivals, the Arado 81, the Heinkel 118, and the Blohm und Voss Ha 137. The Ju 87, however, was clearly ahead of its competitors, and by early 1937 the first of its type had reached the flying units. The Ju 87B-1, with which the Luftwaffe entered the war, was a two-seater capable of a maximum speed of 232 mph at 13,500 ft, a radius of 185 miles, and of carrying a bomb-load of 1,102 lb and three machine-guns. A serviceable aircraft, simple to maintain and employ, the Ju 87 was to prove effective in the hands of expert pilots, who, in dives of eighty degrees to within 2,300 ft from the ground, could deliver a bomb with an accuracy of less than thirty yards. Even average pilots could achieve a twenty-five per cent success rate in hitting their targets, a far higher proportion than that attained in conventional, horizontal-attack bombers. Mishaps could occur; pilots might black out and lose control when diving and, on one occasion during training in 1939, low cloud caused a whole formation to be late in pulling out from a dive and many simply ploughed straight into the ground. But, for all that, it was, within the specifications laid down, an effective dive-bomber whose reputation has survived the war and whose name is synonymous with the concept, however erroneous, of Blitzkrieg.

Sceptics of dive-bombing remained during the pre-war years, foremost among whom was von Richthofen who, as a field-commander, was to become a brilliant practitioner of ground support. On 9th June 1936, he even submitted a memorandum advocating the discontinuance of the Ju 87; the following day, however, Udet was appointed Chief of the Technical Office, and development continued. Indeed, the former flying ace did all he could to help perfect his 'baby', even inventing special whistles to attach to the bombs, the terrifying sound of which was designed to induce fear and panic in those under bombardment. In this, the so-called Trumpets of Jericho were remarkably effective. But there was far more to the dive-bomber than just the enthusiasm of Udet, for whom the skill and daring required to pilot such an aircraft were compelling. The adoption of dive-bombing was, as Jeschonnek saw, an ideal solution to the bomber problem after 1937. On this issue both the Chief of the General Staff and the Head of the Technical Office were in complete agreement, a rare event which serves to emphasise the importance attached to the concept.

Before the war, the German Air Force lacked an effective bomb-sight capable of dropping high explosives on targets as small as military installations and troop concentrations. The standard Görz Visier 219 sight was inaccurate, and it needed much practice to achieve passable results even in area bombardment (which was not intended to form the main part of the Luftwaffe's operations). The improved telescopic bomb-sights, the Lotfe 7 and 7D, were still only experimental. Thus, in 1938, even well-qualified bomber crews could achieve only a two per cent bombing accuracy in high level, horizontal attacks (up to 13,500 ft), and twelve to twenty-five per cent accuracy in low level attacks against targets of between 165 to 330 ft. in radius, during which time the aircraft were vulnerable to anti-aircraft fire. To make matters worse, the bomb-load of the German bombers was low, only four 550 lb bombs being carried by the Do 17 and six by the He 111. Thus, if the target were to be completely destroyed, the only way to compensate for inaccuracy would be to employ large numbers of aircraft flying in close formation, a method that was not only wasteful of limited resources (in terms both of the numbers of bombers and the amount of fuel available), but would also leave the bombers vulnerable to enemy action. How much better would it be if the destruction of a target could be achieved by one aircraft instead of ten. Such was the forceful logic behind the adoption of dive-bombing by the Luftwaffe: it provided a way of achieving maximum offensive power with minimum resources. As the Luftwaffe General Staff announced in the spring of 1938: 'The emphasis in offensive bombardment has clearly shifted from area to pin-point bombardment'.[29] Such, indeed, was the theory. As an interim solution it had much force, as the victories in the early war years were to show; but, given the state of technical development in the 1930s, as a principle of air warfare it was to be disastrous.

The disadvantages of the dive-bombers were apparent to some even before the outbreak of the war. General Marquardt later wrote that the Luftwaffe General Staff 'did not understand the basic principle of aircraft development, namely that those qualities ought to be emphasised which serve to make the aircraft different from all other military vehicles, in other words those attributes which enable it to overcome the obstacles of distance and time and so to achieve its maximum effect. . . . In the dive-bomber, it is precisely these attributes which are sacrificed, because it must utilize brakes to reduce its attacking speed, and because, in order to be able to release its bombs from a relatively low altitude in the interests of maximum accuracy, it is forced to descend into the effective range of enemy anti-aircraft artillery fire'.[30] The Ju 87 proved to be particularly vulnerable during its attack, not only to anti-aircraft guns but also to enemy fighters, especially when just pulling out of a dive. However, the difficulties of the Ju 87 were as nothing compared to those of the Ju 88.

The early expectations for the Ju 88 'Wonder Bomber' were of the highest. A fast aircraft, capable of deep penetration into enemy territory with over two tons of bombs, was promised. In April 1939, Göring boasted to Mussolini that the Ju 88 had 'such a long range that it could be used to attack not only England herself, but also could branch out towards the West, to bombard the ships approaching England from the Atlantic'.[31] On the basis of the success of the first prototypes in March 1938, it was anticipated that the Ju 88 would become the standard offensive aircraft of the Luftwaffe. In June, September and October, there appeared the first Ju 88 prototypes which incorporated the dive-bombing capabilities ordered nearly two years previously. For a twin-engined aircraft to be capable of diving, a far more robust construction was required than for horizontal bombing; modifications to the engine and the addition of dive-brakes were also necessary. These changes involved a significant increase in weight, so that the Ju 88 could not rely on its speed to outdistance fighters. When additional armament and a man to operate it were deemed necessary, more weight was added. Thus, the final production model of the aeroplane was significantly different from its initial conception. The Ju 88A-1, which came into service in September 1939, had a crew of four (originally to be three), a top speed, when loaded, of 258 mph at 18,050 ft (once intended to be 310 mph), and a range of 550 miles with 2,000 lb of bombs (initially to be 775 miles and promising to be more). When it carried its maximum bomb-load of 3,800 lb (under two tons) cruising at around 190 mph, its radius was cut down to just 250 miles. Tests had shown, however, that, in capable hands, the Ju 88 could place fifty per cent of its bombs within a target area fifty metres in diameter.

Further complications arose from the insistence of Göring, Udet and Jeschonnek that, to fulfil its schedule, the Ju 88 be mass-produced even before all testing on the prototypes had been undertaken. The 25,000 changes that were to be introduced as a result of the dive-bombing requirement were by no means complete when, on 30th September 1938, Göring gave Dr Koppenberg, the general-manager of Junkers, the instruction to create 'in the shortest possible time a mighty armada of Ju 88 bombers'.[32] In fulfilment of his instruction, Koppenberg was empowered to take all measures necessary to guarantee the early series production of the Ju 88 in the greatest quantities possible. However, as Heinrich Hertel, a prominent engineer, remembered, he was unable to achieve this, and 'on the contrary, his intervention did much to hamper the Luftwaffe in meeting scheduled goals for equipping flying units'.[33] Milch was uneasy, fearing that the aeroplane was not going to come up to expectations. He was correct. Not only was its performance worse than originally intended (for example, there were complaints during the early years of the war that it was slower than the He 111), but the design of a dive-bombing capability, together with the forcing of the pace of development before testing had been completed, caused delays of almost a year in the final production, resulting in severe dislocation to the Luftwaffe's entire procurement programme. Teething troubles experienced by the Ju 88A-1 model continued until they were phased out of service.

In a more developed form, however, the later Ju 88 versions were a far better proposition and, although demanding of their pilots, became most efficient weapons in capable hands. Eventually, the Ju 88 of various marks became the most widely built twin-engined German warplane (over 15,000 produced), fulfilling such diverse roles as horizontal and dive bomber, long-range reconaissance, torpedo-bomber, night fighter and heavy Zerstörer.

Fighters, though they did not form the basis of the new Luftwaffe, nevertheless had two roles to play: one, regarded as the lesser in importance, was, with the aid of anti-aircraft artillery, to defend the Reich from air attack, and the other was to afford the bombers passage free from enemy interception. Their choice posed fewer problems than did that of the bombers, but the consequences of a wrong decision were to be just as harmful to the Luftwaffe's prospects in war, if not more so. The search for a new generation of fighters began in late 1933, to replace biplanes such as the Ar 68 and He 51, aircraft that were armed with two 7.9 mm machine guns and capable of top speeds of only 208 mph and 205 mph and radii of 155 and 177 miles respectively. In their place, the RLM wanted a monoplane armed with two 7.9 mm machine guns capable of improved rates of roll and turn, good dive and spinning behaviour, and greater power and range. Four aircraft companies vied with one another for this lucrative contract, the Bayerische Flugzeugwerke (in July 1936 to be renamed Messerschmitt GmbH) Arado, Heinkel and Focke-Wulf. In the autumn of 1936, the fighter designed by Professor Willi Messerschmitt of the Bayerische Flugzeugwerke AG (Bavarian Aircraft Works) the Bf 109, was chosen by the RLM. It easily outclassed the Ar 80 and FW 159 prototypes, and, in the air, had the edge over the He 112, although the latter was easier to handle on the ground. Although Milch personally disliked Messerschmitt, his aeroplane was favoured by Göring, Udet and von Greim. Production factors also preferred the Bf 109, it being cheaper and easier to build than the He 112 owing to the new system of fuselage construction employed, in which one bulkhead and one section of skin were formed simultaneously from the same sheet of metal. Moreover, at the time, Heinkel was heavily involved with other aircraft projects, and the RLM was fearful that a major contract for a fighter might interfere with the mass production of the He 111. Although small-scale manufacture of the He 112 continued, the Bf 109 was accepted as the standard fighter for the Luftwaffe, and in the spring of 1937 the first service models arrived at the flying units. By the outbreak of war, this machine was to be the main Luftwaffe fighter. It was destined to serve throughout the conflict, and to win for itself the reputation of being among the top three fighters of the period. Certainly in 1939, the Bf 109E, which was then the standard type in service, was marginally superior to the best fighter that any other nation could put in the air. The E-1, introduced in spring 1939, was armed with four 7.9 mm machine guns, and was capable of a top speed of 342 mph at at 13,120 ft, a service ceiling of 34,450 ft and an initial climb rate of 3,050 ft per minute. The E-3 version, introduced several months later, was heavier armed, possessing two 20 mm cannon and two 7.9 mm machine guns. It was to prove a formidable warplane.

However, the Bf 109 had one serious limitation: its range. A small, single-engine aircraft with capacity for only eighty-eight gallons of fuel, its radius of action, with allowance for combat, was some 125 miles. It could remain in the sky for only one and a half hours. Thus, it could neither accompany bombers on long-range missions, nor maintain standing patrols far from its base in order to intercept enemy aircraft away from their targets. These roles had to be fulfilled by the larger, twin-engine machine known by the Germans as a Zerstörer (Destroyer), a type of aircraft which originated during the First World War. In June 1934, the RLM issued its first specifications for an updated version of the Kampfzerstörer, a twin-engine, three-seat monoplane, heavily-armed, possessing high speed and an all-weather capability, to serve as a heavy fighter, a fast reconnaissance aircraft, and a fast bomber. Within the RLM, there was much scepticism about such a multi-purpose machine. It was pointed out that the Kampfzerstörer would, of necessity, be a compromise between the requirements of speed and manoeuvrability and those of long-range and fire-power. It was argued that the weight and size of such an aircraft would surely result in a slow and unwieldy warplane. And so it would. However, three firms submitted prototypes: Henschel, the Hs 124, Focke-Wulf, the FW 57, and the Bavarian Aircraft Works, the Bf 110.

But, in the spring of 1935, before even prototypes could be assembled, the Kampfzerstörer concept was discarded, and three individual aircraft types were chosen to fulfil the three main roles previously intended to be undertaken by one aeroplane (the fast bomber role was taken by the Ju 88, and the reconnaissance bomber by the Do 17). The Bf 110 was, henceforth, to be regarded simply as a Zerstörer, a long-range fighter. The specifications from the RLM were now altered. Heavily-armed and with two engines, the machine was to have a crew of two, a top speed of between 350 and 370 mph, a flight duration of three hours, and an all-weather capability. Its manoeuvrability and speed were to be equal to those of the best single-engined fighters, although its rate of climb, its service ceiling and take-off and landing characteristics would be slightly inferior. In May 1936, the first prototype was flown, and, early in 1937, it was chosen to be the Luftwaffe's long-range fighter. Production was ordered to begin without delay, and, after another year of testing and modification, during which time it received new engines, the first Bf 110 was delivered to a service unit in mid-1938.

Although the Bf 110 was later to become an effective night-fighter, it proved incapable of adequately fulfilling its role as a Zerstörer. The Bf 110C-1, with which the Luftwaffe began the war, was, on paper, a formidable machine. Seating two or three crew-members, possessing two 20 mm cannon and five 7.9 mm machine guns, it was capable of a maximum speed of 336 mph at 19,685 ft and a radius of 280 miles. While it was the best twin-engined fighter then in service with any air force, it was so heavy that it was easily out-manoeuvred by single-engined fighters. As an interceptor of bombers, the Bf 110 was effective; as a long-range escort, when combat with enemy interceptors was necessary, it was a failure. The compromise between fire-power and range on the one hand, and speed and manoeuvrability on the other, had proved unworkable.

Although the failings of the Bf 110 were to become particularly noticeable in war, they had not escaped the notice of the RLM even in peace-time. Its performance, which was below that of a single-engine fighter, and its range, which fell far short of expectations, caused the Technical Office to hold back on mass production; only the Czechoslovakian crisis of 1938 prompted an order of around 1,000. Even before the first service Bf 110 was off the production line, Messerschmitt had been asked to consider its successor. Again, specifications were issued which called for a twin-engined, multi-purpose, aircraft with higher performance and capable of fulfilling the roles of long-range fighter, fast reconnaissance and ground-attack. However, it was to have a radius of 620 miles, with half an hour for combat as well, more than double that of its predecessor. Moreover, it, like the Ju 87 and the Ju 88, was to be capable of dive-bombing. In the summer of 1938, shortly after the Bavarian Aircraft Works had been renamed Messerschmitt AG, with the Professor as its Chairman and Managing Director, the plans were submitted to the RLM. The Technical Office accepted them, allocating the designation Messerschmitt (Me) 210 to the new aircraft. Confidence in the designer's abilities were such that, before even the first prototype was completed, let alone tests begun, the RLM placed an option on 1,000 production machines. It was anticipated that the first aircraft would reach the Luftwaffe in mid-1941, and become the multi-purpose replacement for the Bf 110, the Ju 87 and the Hs 123.

On 5th September 1939, the prototype of the Me 210 made its first flight, which was successful only in as much as it managed to land intact. Its instability and extremely unsatisfactory handling characteristics were thought to lie in the twin fin and rudder tail assembly, and, without informing the RLM, Messerschmitt had it replaced by a large, centrally mounted, fin and rudder. This achieved little improvement in performance, however; the aircraft remained unstable and unpredictable, a particularly dangerous aspect of which was its tendency to whip into a spin at high angles of attack. But this lack of promise did not deter preparations for series production, and, by mid-1940, without any solution to the Me 210's shortcomings in sight, the first airframes were under assembly. The progressive phasing out of the Bf 110 had already been ordered. Reliance upon the Me 210 was total. This was, however, to be fatal. In 1942, Göring was to lament that on his tombstone should be etched the words: 'He would have lived longer had the Me 210 not been built'.[34]

While, as a heavy fighter, the Me 210 was planned to be supreme, as a ground-attack aircraft it was to have the support of a purpose-built machine, relatively small but heavily armed and armoured, intended solely for the direct support of the ground forces. In April 1937, the Technical Office issued somewhat vague specifications to four manufacturers, and received sub-missions by the following October. Two were accepted for further development, the Henschel 129 and the Focke-Wulf 189 (an adaptation of the reconnaissance aircraft). In the spring of 1939, the Hs 129 prototype was first flown, the FW 189 being regarded as a back-up programme in case Henschel's machine failed. In the event, it did not, but poor handling characteristics and low priority in development were to ensure that, not until May 1942, was it to reach the front-line.

But it was not simply combat aircraft that formed the Luftwaffe's strength. Reconnaissance machines were a particularly important part of its order of battle, and, in September 1939, amounted to roughly one-seventh of its total of front-line aircraft. They were regarded as the 'eyes' of the Army and Air Force, providing valuable information about the strength of the enemy, his strong-points and movements. The gaining of accurate intelligence has always been regarded as of the highest importance in warfare, and the German Armed Forces of the 1930s and 1940s did not fail in this respect, at least in the early war years. For long-range work, reliance was initially placed upon the He 45, a biplane capable of a radius of action of 370 miles and a top speed of 180 mph. Production of this machine was stopped in 1936, and its role taken over by the Do 17. In the mid-1930s, short-range reconnaissance was the task of the He 46, a strutted monoplane, capable of a maximum speed of 161 mph and a radius of 307 miles. Long obsolete, manufacture of the machine was ended in 1936. The replacement of the He 46 posed some problems for the Technical Office, but in the late summer of 1937 it chose the Hs 126, the B-1 version of which had a maximum speed of 221 mph and a radius of action of 224 miles. All the Luftwaffe's reconnaissance aircraft were armed, and could carry bombs on their missions.

Because of the length of time involved in the design, testing, and production of advanced combat aircraft, the Luftwaffe began to think about replacements for its intended main types even before the war started. In the autumn of 1937, active consideration was given to a successor to the Bf 109. Both Messerschmitt and Heinkel submitted proposals, which were awarded the designations Me 209 and He 100 respectively. The Me 209 bore no similarity to its predecessor, and was designed initially with the idea of producing a high-speed, record-breaking aircraft. Prototypes of both flew in 1938, the Heinkel machine showing the better promise. Both won world speed records, the He 100 in June 1938 and the Me 209 in April 1939. However, it was another machine altogether that caught the attention of the RLM. In the spring of 1938, Focke-Wulf had been invited to submit its proposals for a fighter, later to be known as the FW 190. Its design won the favour of the Generalluftzeugmeisteramt for several reasons. First, it held great promise for the performance of the final production model; second, it was the product of the designer Kurt Tank, who was held in great esteem by the Air Ministry; and third, it was fitted with a novel air-cooled engine. This latter point proved to be of considerable importance, since the demand for conventional liquid-cooled engines was high and was destined to get even higher, thus placing a considerable burden on the aircraft industry's ability to produce sufficient numbers. The RLM's choice proved to be a sound one. By the middle of 1941, when the fighter was ready for issue to front-line units, the FW 190A-1 approached a top speed of 390 mph (410 mph for the short period of a minute), and was superior at low altitudes to the existing Bf 109 versions, as well as possessing better manoeuvrability and landing characteristics. However, the new fighter suffered more than the usual share of teething troubles, particularly regarding engine cooling, and at one point it was nearly dropped from the production programme altogether. Only drastic measures and modifications saved it, but the engine cooling problem was never completely solved. Nor were bombers neglected. In July 1939, specifications for 'Bomber B' were issued, designed to take the concept of the medium bomber a significant step forward. The new machine had to possess a radius of action of 1,115 miles (sufficient to encompass the entire British Isles), a maximum speed of 373 mph, which compared favourably with the speed of contemporary fighters, and a bomb-load of 4,400 lb. No dive-bombing capability was requested; instead, it was to fly and attack from high altitudes. Defensive armament was to be primarily remote-controlled (necessitating pressurised crew accommodation). In July the following year, the General-luftzeugmeisteramt was presented with four proposals, from Arado, Dornier, Focke-Wulf and Junkers. Two were chosen, the FW 191 and the Ju 288, and development continued.

For the defence of the Reich from air attack, great faith was placed in the efficacy of anti-aircraft guns, which, in 1935, came under the control of the Luftwaffe. It was expected that artillery alone would prove sufficient to deal with any raiders which might invade German air space in the event of war, and no reliance was made for the provision of large fighter forces for the purpose. Nor was there any attempt to develop a specially designed night fighter for the interception of enemy bombers. Night fighting would be undertaken by Bf 109s and the obsolete Ar 68Es, biplanes capable of a top speed of only 208 mph, and not until the summer of 1939 were a few Staffeln earmarked for such purposes. The men of the Flak service (Fliegerabwehr-kanone – anti-aircraft cannon) were considered an elite body, and in 1939, before mobilisation, numbered 107,000. When the war broke out they deployed 2,600 heavy guns and 6,700 light and medium guns, together with 3,000 searchlights, under the overall direction of the Chief of Air Defence, General Rüdel, and the Inspector of Flak Artillery, General Alfred Haubold. Operational control of the various Flak units was exercised by the Luftgaue, which came under the various Luftflotten. The guns consisted of the light 20 mm with an effective range of about 5,000 ft, the 3.7 cm with a practical ceiling of 6,000 ft, and the highly effective 8.8 cm with a range of between 9,000 and 32,000 ft. Heavier guns, the 10.5 cm and 12.8 cm Flak were under development.

Most of these guns were deployed either around large cities, such as Berlin or Hamburg, and vulnerable targets in the Ruhr, or in the Western Air Defence Zone, running along the Western frontier. It extended for about 375 miles along the Rhine, at the rear of the Army's West Wall, from the Dutch border as far north as Münster then to Mannheim, from there to Lake

Constance, and thence along the right bank of the Rhine bordering on Switzerland. The zone depth was about twelve and a half miles in the northern area, from twenty-five to twenty-eight miles between Wesel and Cologne, and about sixty-two miles south and south-east of Koblenz (including the Flak defences around Mainz, Mannheim, and Stuttgart). In addition to providing extra protection for the Rhine-Westphalian industrial district and for the chemical and heavy industries along the middle and upper Rhine, the Zone was designed to form as unbroken barrage of fire, while at the same time presenting an advance belt of operations for the areas and targets situated further to the east. Enemy aircraft, weakened by continuous losses while flying over the Zone, were to be forced to climb to their maximum altitude (and into areas of poor visibility) in order to escape defensive fire. On the other hand, German planes returning from missions over enemy territory were to find protection against pursuing enemy fighters once they had crossed the Reich's border. By September 1939, the Flak artillery arm had 245 reinforced concrete positions in the Zone, and a continuous belt of searchlights behind and between them. It was hoped that the Zone, when fully manned by 250 batteries with 788 pieces of heavy artillery and 576 pieces of light artillery, would provide a three-fold over-lapping field of fire cover at an altitude of 23,000 ft. Considering the flying speeds at that time, this meant that every enemy aircraft would be exposed to five minutes of continuous fire by three batteries, assuring a concentration of about 600 rounds of ammunition on each raider. By such means it was hoped to preserve the integrity of German air space. Göring expressed his conviction thus in August 1939: 'I have convinced myself of the measures taken to protect the Ruhr against air attack. . . . We will not expose the Ruhr to a single bomb dropped by enemy aircraft'.[35]

However, the Flak defences suffered from considerable shortcomings. The sighting and plotting of the raiders had to be undertaken by sound and by sight, both of which were notoriously inadequate in times of darkness or cloud cover. Altitude, speed and direction all had to be determined exactly in order to set the guns. But this information could only be provided by the reflection of radio waves from the airframe of the aircraft back to a transmitting and measuring apparatus on the ground: a radar. By the beginning of the war, Germany had undertaken much valuable research into the problem, and had eight 'Freya' radar stations in action, capable of detecting enemy aircraft up to ninety-three miles away. But they only covered a short strip of German coastline between the frontiers of Holland and Denmark, and served simply to give early warning of the approach of raiders towards the Reich's borders. They were of no use in the laying of guns. Much work still remained to be done. But even were a comprehensive radar system created, the Flak had still to hit the target, and this was extremely problematic since the accuracy of the heavy guns fell off by fifty per cent every 5,000 ft above 15,000 ft. A barrage of shells was required, but this, too, had its difficulties. As a British anti-aircraft expert, Professor A.V. Hill, wrote about the problems: 'One cubic mile of space contains 5,500,000,000 cubic yards. The lethal zone of a 3.7-in AA shell [the British counterpart to the 8.8 cm Flak] is only a few thousand cubic yards and exists for only one-fiftieth of a second. The idea of a "barrage" of shells is nonsense. The word ought to be dropped; it gives a false impression. Nothing but aimed fire is any use.'[36] Thus, the expenditure of only 600 shells for each raider would avail the Germans nothing; as the early years of the war were to show, an average of some 3,400 heavy artillery shells were fired for each enemy aircraft brought down over Germany. Thus until an invulnerable air defence system could be created, the danger to Germany from the air could only be met fully by an attack against the enemy's air force at the very beginning of hostilities.

In the mid and late 1930s, at the time that major decisions were being made concerning the Luftwaffe's strategy, events far from Berlin appeared to be confirming their validity. In the sky over Spain, the German Air Force reassured itself that the technical course on which it had embarked was right. Indeed, one of the foremost reasons for Germany's intervention in the civil war in Spain, between the nationalists under General Franco and the Republicans, was to test its new military equipment. As Göring remembered in the dock at Nuremberg: 'When the Civil War broke out in Spain, Franco sent a call for help to Germany and asked for support, particularly in the air. Franco with his troops were stationed in Africa and . . . he could not get his troops across, as the fleet was in the hands of the Communists. . . . The decisive factor was, first of all, to get his troops in Spain. . . . The Führer thought the matter over. I urged him to give support under all circumstances; firstly, to prevent the further spread of Communism; secondly, to test my young Luftwaffe in this or that technical respect.'[37]

The saga of the Reich's intervention in Spain began on 25th July 1936, when German and Spanish emissaries arrived in Berlin to request military assistance for the Nationalist cause. After a brief consultation with Göring and von Blomberg, Hitler agreed to the request, and, on the 26th, the Luftwaffe set up Sonderstab W under General Wilberg to control the operation. On 27th July, twenty Ju 52 transports were flown to Spain by Lufthansa personnel and Luftwaffe volunteers, to be followed on the 28th by six He 51 fighters and twenty 20 mm anti-aircraft guns transported by sea. So began an intervention that was to last until April 1939. Immediately, the Ju 52s were used to transfer Nationalist troops from Morocco to Spain, and by 11th October no less than 13,500 men and 594,400 lb of war material had been transported by the Germans in what was the first large-scale airlift operation in history. During this, two of the Ju 52s were refitted as bombers so as to attack an enemy cruiser that was firing at the airlift. On 14th August, in the first bombing attack ever undertaken by the Luftwaffe, the ship was forced to retire, having twice been hit from a height of 1,500 ft. As Hitler remarked in 1942, 'Franco ought to erect a monument to the glory of the

Ju 52. It is this aircraft that the Spanish revolution has to thank for its victory'.[38]

On 1st November, the German force, then standing at 4,500 men, was given to the command of General Sperrle and became known as the Legion Condor. It continued to grow, and by January 1937 numbered some 6,000 volunteers. The men were interchanged at regular intervals so that as many Luftwaffe pilots and crews as possible could gain combat experience. At first, the Legion consisted of a command staff, a bomber Gruppe (forty-eight Ju 52s divided into four Staffeln), a fighter Gruppe (forty-eight He 51s in four Staffeln), a reconnaissance Staffel (twelve He 70s), two Ketten (subsections of a Staffel) each of He 123s and He 112s, four heavy anti-aircraft gun batteries (sixteen 8.8 cm guns) and two light batteries (eight 20 mm guns), together with various signals, meteorological, medical and supply units. However, in aircraft the Legion was markedly inferior to the best of its opponents. Because of its slowness, lack of manoeuvrability, inadequate communications and dispersed crew, the Ju 52 made a poor bomber, while the He 51 was no match for the Russian I-15 and I-16 fighters possessed by the Republicans. The poor reports sent back to Berlin by the newly established special combat reporting team and by Sperrle's chief of staff, Freiherr von Richthofen, the former head of development in the Technical Office, ensured that during 1937 the Legion Condor was re-equipped with the latest German models. By the autumn of 1938, when the Legion, since November 1937 under General Volkmann, was at its peak, it possessed forty He 111s, five Do 17s, three Ju 87s, forty-five Bf 109s, four He 45s, and eight He 59s, together with eight batteries of heavy and light anti-aircraft guns. This force experienced considerable success. The He 111s and Ju 87s proved themselves extremely valuable in their different roles, while the Bf 109B, C and D fighters were superior to all opposition except the I-16s. The Legion, supported by the 146 Spanish and 134 Italian aircraft, established command of the air; it shot down in aerial combat no less than 277 enemy aircraft, and a further fifty-eight by anti-aircraft fire, and provided much valuable support for the Nationalist ground forces, for the loss of 500 men killed, with 3,000 wounded and ninety-six aircraft destroyed (forty through enemy action). The cost of the Legion was some 354 million Reichsmarks.

Of all the events of the Spanish Civil War, it was the bombing of Guernica, in April 1937, which was most publicised and raised the greatest outcry. It was regarded as confirmation not only of German ruthlessness but also of the efficiency of the bomber. Attacked by He 111s and Ju 52s, the centre of Guernica, thirty kilometres behind the front line, was destroyed, some 1,600 people killed and 900 wounded (estimates vary wildly, from 100 to 6,000!). However, far more significant for the Luftwaffe was an air attack which took place a few days earlier, at the end of March. Then, nine He 51 fighters, each armed with six 10 kilogram bombs, made a low level attack, at a height of some 500 ft, on fortified enemy positions along the northern front, with considerable success. The soldiers, terrified by the German aircraft, fled.

Lessons such as this had considerable influence on the Luftwaffe's planning. They confirmed that the concepts of strategy and tactics which had been developed from theory and in manoeuvres in Germany, were basically sound. It was proved that bombers were extremely effective when used against enemy troop concentrations, strong-points, and lines of communication. General Wolfram von Richthofen, who became the last commander of the Legion on 1st November 1938, was particularly concerned to promote the closest liaison between air and ground forces. He instituted a system whereby air controllers were sent into the forward battle-zones to direct air strikes from the ground. The importance of good ground-to-air communication was noted, as was the need for highly accurate maps and aids to quick target identification.

Moreover, the efficacy of dive-bombing by the Ju 87s as compared with the far more inaccurate high-level attacks of the He 111s, was revealed. The success of the Heinkel bomber was found to lie more in low-level, high speed runs against targets, and this vindicated the view that a 'wonder-bomber' along the lines of the Ju 88 was required, even more so because it would have the capacity to dive-bomb. A high degree of invulnerability from enemy fighters as well as greater accuracy was thought to be promised by such a machine. As regards fighters, the Air Ministry's idea of their offensive and defensive use was confirmed: the Bf 109s were excellent weapons against enemy bombers and good defence for friendly formations. A system of tactics was worked out for the fighters, based on practical experience, which gave the best compromise between concentration of fire power and flexibility. When they came to be used in future campaigns, they were found to be greatly superior to the tactics then in use by Germany's enemies. Furthermore, owing to the surprisingly high resistance to damage shown by bombers, it was decided that heavier and better-grouped weapons were needed in fighters, and 20 mm cannons were provided for the Bf 109s. However, the short range of the aircraft was seen to be a disadvantage, and greater emphasis was placed upon the production of the twin-engined, long-range fighters, the Bf 110s. Thus, with their belief in Army support and dive-bombing confirmed, and their commitment to the development of the 'wonder-bomber' and the heavy fighter vindicated, the Luftwaffe's leadership proceeded towards war in full confidence that they had found both the means and the application to fulfil the ends of policy. All that remained was to develop a long-range heavy bomber – if, indeed, such a machine were required.

III

The Onset of War

Until 1937, the industrial base necessary for the creation of a new German Air Force had flourished. Money had proved no object; as Göring said in October 1935. 'There is no ceiling on the credit for the financing of rearmament.'[1] In three years from mid-1933, the aircraft industry had increased its output from 0.2 per cent to 1.6 per cent of German industrial production (which itself had nearly doubled), to become the Reich's fourteenth largest industrial sector, employing some 125,000 people. In four years, the floor-space capacity of the airframe manufacturers rose from 30,000 to 1,001,000 square metres. By November 1936, the Air Force had accepted into service no fewer than 8,778 aircraft since the National Socialists had gained power, forty-five more than planned. But such a meteoric growth was not to continue. The year 1937 witnessed a dramatic slowing in the rate of expansion, and in 1938 there was even a slight decrease in the number of aeroplanes produced. Several factors were responsible for this, such as the necessary retooling for new models and unforeseen technical delays in aero-development, but by far the most important was the state of Germany's economy.

Until the invasion of Poland, the Third Reich spent some sixty-four billion Reichsmarks on rearmament, roughly one seventh of its gross national product, and of that some forty per cent went towards the development of the Luftwaffe, a high proportion of the total. This was at a time when the other two Services were also expanding, the Army's manpower, for example, by over seven hundred per cent in seven years. Because of lack of resources, however, the Army was to be committed to battle ill-prepared to meet the demanding conditions of modern, mobile warfare. Only fourteen of its 103 divisions were fully motorised, the rest being dependent on their soldiers' feet and on some 450,000 horses. The standard weapon was a rifle based on a design first drawn up in 1898, a fact which reflected on the quality of other equipment. Severe shortages were common; for example, half the divisions had neither machine-pistols, light or medium mortars, 2 cm anti-aircraft guns, nor heavy infantry guns, while ammunition was seventy per cent short of requirement. If such were the condition of the main service on which the fortunes of the Reich relied, how would the other two fare?

Competition for resources was acute, and nowhere more so than for the raw materials on which the Reich's armaments depended, materials such as iron and steel, zinc, copper, aluminium, manganese, tungsten, tin, rubber and oil.

Shortages in these were felt as early as 1934, when a lack of foreign exchange prevented the Reich from importing its greatly expanding requirement. In response, the RLM with some success encouraged manufacturers to simplify their needs for such materials; airframe factories, for example, reduced from eighteen to nine the number of light metals used in manufacture. The position, however, continued to deteriorate, and, in December 1936, because of poor deliveries of raw materials, the Technical Office was forced to give new combat aircraft the highest priority in production over all other types. Of the 4,500 tons of aluminium required each month for aircraft manufacture, only half was available. As Jodl was to note in his diary on 4th February 1937, 'The phrase: "Money is an unimportant factor" has become true. . . . The main part is the raw materials.'[2]

This shortage led to a crisis of confidence within the political and economic leadership of Germany. The coalition of big-business, the military and the National Socialists dissolved. Some, the most powerful, led by Hitler, Göring, senior Party officials and a number of industrialists, wanted not only to continue but to accelerate the pace of rearmament, while others, led by Hjalmar Schacht, the Finance Minister, von Blomberg, the Defence Minister, and Kerrl, Special Minister for Economic Affairs, wished for a significant cutback. Whatever the arguments, none could dispute the facts: a rapid depletion in foreign exchange (the deficit in mid-1936 was half a billion Reichsmarks) brought about by a low level of exports caused by the production of armaments rather than merchandise, had resulted in an increasing shortage of raw materials. Germany simply had not the money with which to pay for them. Foreign exchange could only be earned by producing consumer goods instead of armaments, and exporting them. This, however, would in turn threaten the whole pace of rearmament, and, politically, was regarded as unacceptable by the more ardent National Socialists.

Hitler's answer to this dilemma was to introduce the Four Year Plan. Initiated on 16th October 1936, it was designed to make the German economy, particularly agriculture, invulnerable in any crisis, most important of all in war, and as self sufficient as possible, while at the same time maintaining the nation's massive construction programmes and continuing with rearmament unabated. No cut in consumer spending could be contemplated; the Reich's leaders were too mindful of their popularity for that! On the industrial side, synthetic substitutes for raw materials were to be developed and produced (for example, synthetic oil and rubber through the hydrogenation of coal); all the potential for extracting raw materials within the Reich was to be exploited (such as the low-grade iron-ore in the Salzgitter area); and a consortium was to be set up to handle the low-grade ores. Controlling agencies for imports and exports were to be instituted, which would also stock-pile raw materials, rationalise industry, and improve agriculture. By means of a government investment over four years of three billion Reichsmarks in the synthetic-products industries, Hitler hoped to save half a billion Reichsmarks in foreign exchange, and, by 1939, to reach a position whereby all the oil and half the rubber and iron ore required for Germany's mobilisation plan would be met by the Reich itself. The man appointed to head the Four Year Plan was none other than the Führer's self-proclaimed 'faithful paladin', Hermann Göring.

Göring, as Special Representative of the Führer for the Four Year Plan, undoubtedly used his position to favour the Air Force at the expense of the Army and Navy. Von Blomberg believed that the actions he took in his new office even threatened the unified direction of the Wehrmacht. One of his first decisions was to direct labour to the aircraft factories, where it was much needed, and to give the Luftwaffe preferential treatment in the allocation of raw materials and money. Despite this, the Air Force continued to suffer from shortages. On 4th January 1937, when a plan for the peace-time mobilisation of the aviation industry was presented to Göring, he was told that his hopes for the future were quite unrealistic. The shortage of construction steel was especially severe, and was forcing the industry to defer the purchase of capital equipment for the retooling needed for the production of a new generation of aircraft. Matters did not improve during the year. The annual output of steel remained at around 19,800,000 metric tons, while the system of allocation became chaotic; no priorities were laid down and no overall economic direction was attempted. Throughout the summer of 1937, the steel shortage increased. The effect on the Air Force was considerable. On 4th June 1937, the Quartermaster-General of the Luftwaffe reported to Jeschonnek:

> The annual allocation of steel had to be reduced from 290,000 to 180,000 tons, 48,000 of which had been earmarked for the expansion of production facilities. The allotment of 63,000 tons per year for Flak artillery pieces was reduced to 30,000 tons, resulting in a bottleneck in the vital conversion from machine-guns to 2 cm Flak artillery pieces. Instead of 80,000 tons per year, only 41,000 could be spared for Flak artillery ammunition, and, instead of 18,000 tons for bombs per year, only 2,000 was allocated. . . . The allotment for motor vehicle production was curtailed from 47,000 tons per annum to 22,000 tons, thereby reducing the Flak artillery batteries to a state of immobility. Twenty-three medium aircraft fuel columns had to be disbanded, a dangerous omen with respect to the refuelling of airfields not equipped with railway spurs or underground tanks.[3]

The shortage became so severe that, of the 1,800,000 tons of steel produced each month, the Armed Services requested 750,000 tons and received just 300,000 tons.

At the same time as economic circumstances began to bear heavily on the Reich's capacity to produce armaments, the guiding figure of Milch was removed from a position of decisive influence over the selection and production of aircraft. The death of Wever, the succession of Kesselring, the appointment of Udet, the coolness of Göring, together with the ascendency of the industrialists such as Heinkel, Messerschmitt and Koppenberg, all combined to cause the control of aerial rearmament to slip away from the Secretary of State. Centralisation was gone; dissension intensified, as the General Staff, the Technical Office, Göring, Milch and the manufacturers vied to fill the vacuum. In the end, none did. Confusion and chaos took the place of consistent policy. As General Reidenbach, one of Udet's assistants, commented after the war, 'The case of Koppenberg showed in a shocking manner how much dilettantism, coercion, and improvisation became a pattern with us. . . .'[4] Firms tried to build all types of aircraft, from trainers to bombers, and resisted the attempts by the RLM to make them specialise. In 1938, for example, the Heinkel concern had the He 111 under large-scale production, together with eleven other aircraft either in limited production or in prototype form, of which only three were to see operational service. Economic and technological problems were made worse by the constantly changing programmes emanating from the Technical Office, which, in its turn, was reacting to the ever-changing tactical-technical specifications of the General Staff. Co-operation between the two was minimal. This was not an environment which was calculated to produce sound decisions regarding the future armament of the Luftwaffe. As Baumbach wrote: 'What the German Air Force . . . lacked was the co-ordinating expert, the military-cum-scientific head.'[5]

The decision as to whether to develop a heavy bomber, capable of long-range operations independent of the requirements of the Army, must be viewed against this background. It was one that had been long in the making. Indeed, as early as 1927, the Reichsheer had drawn up technical specifications for a four-engined night bomber, and in 1932 the Reichswehr's armament plans for the period 1933 to 1938 included the development of a heavy-bomber fleet. In July 1932, new tactical and technical specifications were issued for a heavy bomber with a radius of 776 miles, and a bomb load of 2,400 lb, specifications which were revised upwards and reissued on 1st February 1933. Finally, work on the project was begun by Dornier and Junkers. The use of large bombers continued to be recommended during the early years of National Socialist government. In May 1933, Dr Knauss's memorandum, which advocated the principle of the 'risk fleet', called for the creation of a heavy bomber force, although quite what the specifications were to be was not made clear. Göring agreed with Knauss's proposals, which accorded with his own limited views on aerial warfare. He had, of course, read Douhet and the advocates of air power, and had agreed with their arguments; but, nonetheless, he appears not to have possessed any profound, coherent ideas on the future role of heavy bombers. Like Hitler, he saw the Luftwaffe in bald terms of power and prestige, measured by the number of aircraft rather than by their quality. The precise nature of the Air Force he left to others to decide, and was content to concur with their views, provided that the fastest possible build-up of air strength was not compromised thereby.

Wever, however, was of different calibre. His thoughts on the strategy to be adopted by the Luftwaffe recognised that air power could, alone, be decisive in warfare. He was in general agreement with the strategic concepts then being propounded throughout Europe. As he wrote: '. . . in a war of the future, the destruction of the armed forces will be of primary importance. This can mean the destruction of the enemy air force, army, and navy, and of the source of supply of the enemy's forces, the armament industry. . . . Only the nation with strong bomber forces at its disposal can expect decisive action by its air force.'[6] Wever's strategic views became even clearer to the observers of the war games at Salzbrünn in the spring of 1936, simulating a hypothetical conflict between Germany and Czechoslovakia. The plans called for the early achievement of air superiority and the support of army operations during a breakthrough of the Czech border fortifications; but, at the last minute, Wever also included a large-scale attack by the Luftwaffe on the most important political and military targets in, and around, Prague. By means of a 'Douhetian' mission intended to bring about panic, chaos and despair, the enemy was to be made aware of the uselessness of further resistance, and a quick conclusion to hostilities would thereby be achieved.

Wever believed that the Reich should concentrate first on creating an air force which could protect Germany and deter foreign aggression while the rearmament programme was under way. At the same time, the armed forces should gear themselves towards war with the Soviet Union. Wever, who had distinct leanings towards the National Socialist government, had read and noted Hitler's *Mein Kampf* and his statements of policy. Time and again, the Führer had stated that he did not want war with either Britain or France, and that he only wished to deter those countries from attacking Germany. The British Empire he regarded as a part of the world order, and Britain as the Reich's natural ally. As for France, he was even prepared to renounce Alsace-Lorraine permanently, if by that he could avoid war. There was only one enemy which Germany had to take seriously: the Soviet Union. The aggressive urges of the Slavs, inflamed by Jewish-inspired Bolshevism, had to be dealt with at some time in the future, and for this the Luftwaffe should prepare itself. Wever therefore concluded that a long-range, heavy bomber was required, with a range great enough to penetrate deep into the vast spaces of the Soviet Union.

The Army authorities, however, became less enthusiastic about the development of such an aircraft, seeing no need for a machine that was designed to operate independently of the ground forces. They argued that development of a heavy bomber would take at least three years before production could even begin; that the capacity of the aircraft industry was so limited that this would leave little surplus for other types of aeroplane; and, that, even were a long-range bomber force to be created, there would be no role for it. The foreign policy of the Reich as laid down by Hitler meant that only Poland and France were potential enemies for the foreseeable future, and these countries could be dealt with effectively by short-range, medium bombers. Even for a campaign in Russia, it was believed that the Luftwaffe's aircraft, operating from forward bases and keeping up with the pace of the advance, had sufficient range to perform their task. It was argued that, given the need for rapid rearmament with limited resources, air power should be designed for the support of ground operations; anything else was a waste. But, despite the Army's rejection of a heavy bomber, the senior officers of the Air Ministry remained firm in their advocacy. Wever, Wimmer, Deichmann and Felmy all emphasised the importance of independent operations as well as of army-support, and Milch looked towards the development of a bomber that could fly around Britain from its base in Germany. While they continued with light and medium bomber programmes, they nevertheless aimed for the future production of a fast, long-range bomber with a heavy bomb-load that was able to operate at high altitudes. As Deichmann, at one time Chief of Operations in the General Staff, argued:

> Even at that early date, the Luftwaffe General Staff was firmly convinced that the standard bomber of the future would have to be a long-range machine. . . . Information received from abroad as well as the views of a number of recognized engineers indicated clearly that the performance of the four-engine bomber was expected to be so far superior to that attainable by a twin-engine machine that the four-engine aircraft would certainly develop into the air weapon of the future. I emphasized that the four-engine bomber was capable of a far greater flight range than could ever be developed for its twin-engine counterpart, and that the presumably remote targets involved in any future war could be reached only by a four-engine bomber. I continued, explaining that a four-engine bomber was capable of attaining a sufficiently high service altitude to keep it safely out of the range of anti-aircraft artillery fire; its considerably greater carrying capacity would permit it to carry not only a greater number of bombs, but also heavier armour plating and more and better airborne armaments. Its higher speed would help to reduce its vulnerability to attack by enemy fighter aircraft.[7]

Thus, the creation of a heavy-bomber force was regarded as the culmination of a mature, well-balanced, and effective air force. However, the technology required was formidable: a new aeronautical design, super-charged engines, pressurised cabins, electronic bombing systems, and long-range radio and navigational equipment would have to be developed, and their reliability assured. At the earliest, the heavy bomber would not be ready in sufficient numbers until the very late 1930s, but that would be time enough for use in a future war, so the planners then believed.

By May 1934, the year in which the Americans began to design two heavy bombers, one of which became the Boeing B-17, the projected German machine, known within the Air Ministry as the 'Uralbomber' in expectation of its range and possible target, had been given first priority in the Air Force's development programme. This called for a mock-up version of the machine to be completed by the end of June, prototypes to emerge by July 1935, and large-scale production to begin in 1938. On 1st January 1935, a comprehensive production plan issued by Milch included, for the first time, the scheduling of seven prototypes of a heavy bomber, known as the Langstrecken-Grossbomber. Late in 1936, Dornier and Junkers had produced their prototypes ready for flight tests, the Do 19 and the Ju 89, equipped with four 600-700 hp engines. The Do 19 was capable of a top speed of 196 mph, a radius of 494 miles and a bomb-load of 6,600 lb; the Ju 89 could achieve a top speed of 242 mph, and carry 8,800 lb of bombs over a similar radius. These were specifications markedly better than those possessed by any other German bombers, either in production or in prospect, and bore some resemblance to the standard four-engined RAF bombers of the forthcoming war: the Stirling, Halifax and Lancaster, which appeared in 1941 and 1942. But possession of the Dorniers and Junkers, however, gave no satisfaction to the Luftwaffe command, and they were regarded as quite unsuitable; seven months earlier, on 17th April, new specifications had been issued, under the signature of Wever, nearly doubling both the speed and the range of the required heavy bomber, and thus rendering the two prototypes obsolete even before they had appeared.

It might have been possible to develop the Do 19 and Ju 89 prototypes further, using the more powerful class of engine capable of 1,000 hp then under development, and to have built bombers which, although not up to the specifications of 17th April 1936, nevertheless were suitable for operating over long-ranges. For example, it was believed possible to increase the Do 19's top speed to 230 mph and its radius to 620 miles. But this was not to be so. In June, the replacement of Wever by Kesselring and of Wimmer by Udet, brought about a decisive change in the key personnel of the Luftwaffe. Both newcomers advocated the continuance and extension of the Air Force's ground-support role, and argued against the creation of a bomber force along Douhetian lines. Their reasoning was sound. Germany, they argued, required an effective air force, which, in nine years, had to be raised from virtually nothing, to be ready for major operations in 1942. The design and production of good aircraft was obviously essential to this process, and in both these areas it was considered that the heavy bomber was simply not a feasible proposition.

The technical progress involved in the development of the Air Force was considerable, and it was accepted that German airframe and aero-engine manufacturers had much to learn from experience before truly serviceable products could be designed and delivered in adequate quantities. The problems of design inherent in the creation of a long-range heavy bomber were huge, and it was regarded as highly questionable whether they would be overcome in time. Even if they were, production of such a machine in sufficient quantities was held to be quite impossible. The economy or, more specifically, the raw material allocation to the Luftwaffe, simply would not allow it. If the creation of a well-balanced Luftwaffe were not to be sacrificed on the altar of the long-range bomber, training, reconnaissance, maritime and fighter aircraft would continue to consume some sixty per cent of the aircraft industry's productive capacity, leaving only forty per cent for bombers. If this ratio of sixty:forty continued (and there was evidence to indicate that the output of fighters, especially long-range types, would have to be increased to provide escorts for the heavy bombers), it was calculated that it would mean the creation of a force of between four and five hundred four-engined bombers by 1942, instead of roughly two and a half times that number of twin-engined machines. As it was then argued, and as experience was to show, five hundred bombers with a rate of serviceability of seventy per cent or less were simply not sufficient to form an effective force for use over any extended length of time. Further problems would arise from the major retooling of the aircraft industry required by the change from medium to heavy bombers, causing a disruption that would temporarily result in a decrease in output. Indeed, in the period 1936 to 1939, the industry was already experiencing just such a process, with the retooling necessary for the second generation of the Luftwaffe's aircraft. Moreover, even the making of machinery that would be needed to build the heavy bombers was impracticable, since that itself involved a fairly heavy consumption of scarce raw materials.

Shortage of fuel, too, militated further against the heavy bombers. Each machine would need an average of six tons of fuel for an operation, which, allowing for six missions per month, and two for training, would mean an average monthly fuel consumption for 500 heavy bombers of some 24,000 tons (roughly one third of Germany's monthly aviation fuel production in 1940). Added to this, it would have been difficult, certainly in the short term, to train the crews to fly the heavy bombers; some 3,500 men, not including reserves and replacements, would be required for 500 aircraft to sustain successful, continual operations. Thus, as Kesselring argued some years after the end of the war, 'Even if the role of the Luftwaffe had been viewed as a strategic [independent] one, and a well-thought-out production programme devised to cover it, by 1939 there would still have been no strategic Luftwaffe of any significance'.[8]

With compelling reasons against the creation of a four-engined heavy bomber, Kesselring, Udet and Milch decided that further development of the first generation of heavy bombers was unjustified, especially in view of the specifications issued in April 1936. So, on 26th October, the new development programme for the Luftwaffe indicated that no further Do 19s or Ju 89s were to be built. Six months later, they were placed last in the Luftwaffe's list of equipment priorities, and on 29th April 1937, Göring upon advice stopped further development of the two prototypes. He even expressed the opinion that the Technical Office should not have commissioned heavy bombers without first seeking his approval on such an important matter (although he had, in fact, been briefed on the subject in the winter of 1934, characteristically indicating neither dissent nor assent). Henceforth, the prototypes were to be used solely for tests relating to a more advanced long-range aircraft (in particular, the Ju 89 formed the basis of the Ju 90 heavy transport), and the Reich's production was to concentrate on smaller, twin-engined, bombers.

This decision was corroborated by Jeschonnek when, in early 1938, he became Chief of Operations in the General Staff. Deichmann remembered:

> Colonel Jeschonnek . . . reminded me that I myself had written a memorandum concerning the conduct of strategic air warfare in which I had stated that the important thing was to destroy the vital part of a target, using the smallest possible number of aircraft and bombs. In illustration of this point, I had pointed out that a single direct hit in the boiler house of a large industrial plant could paralyse it completely. Further I had stated that such pin-point bombing was impossible from an aircraft flying horizontally at high altitude; what we needed was a dive-bomber, which could approach the target closely and in comparative safety. He went on to say that we now had what we needed in the Ju 88. At this point I called his attention to the fact that the really important targets in any future war would probably lie considerably farther away, and that, as far as I knew, the Ju 88 did not possess the necessary flight range. Besides, no aircraft built chiefly for diving performance was capable of developing the speed needed to escape attack by enemy fighter aircraft. Hereupon Colonel Jeschonnek refused to discuss the matter with me any further, stating that all my arguments were based on theoretical speculation. He, on the other hand, as the former Commanding Officer of the Training Wing, had had practical experience with the Ju 88, and he felt that it was the most suitable model to serve as the standard bomber of the Luftwaffe![9]

The ending of the Do 19 and Ju 89 programmes in April 1937 did not, however, conclude the Luftwaffe's interest in developing larger bombers. In March 1937, the General Staff proposed that two Geschwader, one each of He 111s and Ju 86s, should be converted to have a long-range capacity by the fitting of additional fuel tanks. In addition, the Technical Office began to show an interest in an improved Do 17, and framed technical specifications calling for a larger, heavier load-carrying aircraft with a greater radius of action, which became the Do 217. Classified as a heavy bomber, with a capability of dive-bombing, the first prototype was flown in August 1938. Poor flying characteristics were experienced, largely because of the requirements for diving, and, after some delay, in the summer of 1939 the RLM allowed Dornier temporarily to waive this specification. This became permanent in the summer of 1941 after further tests had shown the impracticability of diving. In late 1940, the Do 217 bomber was being produced in fairly small quantities, the E-2 version being capable of a maximum speed of 320 mph at 17,060 ft, a radius of 450 miles with 2,000 lb of bombs and a maximum bomb-load of 8,818 lb over a shorter range.

However, the Do 217 was never intended to become a major warplane, and at the same time as interest was being shown in it, the Technical Office unofficially assigned to the Heinkel concern a development study for an entirely new heavy bomber. Early in 1938, Udet issued specifications for such a machine arising out of the General Staff requirements issued in 1936, which called for an aircraft capable of carrying 4,410 lb of bombs, and a radius of over 1,000 miles, with a top speed of 310 mph. In the late spring, Heinkel submitted its proposal, Projekt 1041. A mock-up was completed in November, and a year later the Technical Office ordered six prototypes of the bomber, by then known as the He 177.

Enthusiasm for the He 177 was not great. Many were unsure whether it should be built at all. As Udet remarked to Heinkel:

> It's possible that Jeschonnek and the General Staff may not even have any use for it. None of them think that we'll be going to war with England. . . . Before it was decided to concentrate all our efforts on the twin-engine, five-bomber programme the "Iron Man" . . . discussed things thoroughly with the Führer. A war against England is completely out of the question. If anything happens at all, it will be a conflict with Poland or Czechoslovakia. The Führer will never let us in for a conflict which might take us beyond the confines of the Continent. Consequently, it will suffice for any potential conflict if we have a medium bomber with relatively limited range and relatively low bomb-carrying capacity, but with a high degree of diving accuracy, in short, the new Ju 88. And, with the means at our disposal, we can build as many of these as the Führer wants. At the same time, it will impress England and France sufficiently, so that they will leave us alone in any case. We shall continue to develop the He 177 as an experimental aircraft, perhaps as a long-range aircraft for the Navy.[10]

Thus, the RLM was luke-warm towards the project; it saw no compelling reason why the resources of the aircraft industry, already over-burdened, should be further stretched by a serious development of a heavy bomber that would oust or cut back existing programmes which, themselves, were constantly being rationalised because of shortages. Moreover, it should also be remembered that, at this time, when the potential of the Ju 88 was so highly regarded, the need for another bomber was not readily perceived. It was not until July 1939, by which time war with Britain had become a distinct possibility, that the RLM urged Heinkel to hasten the construction of a prototype, and placed an order for twenty He 177 pre-production models.

To meet its technical requirements, the He 177 was designed with a number of special features, foremost among which were its engines. To achieve a top speed of over 300 mph, some 4,000 hp would have to be generated; as no 2,000 hp engines were then available (and there were to be none until towards the end of the war), four 1,000 hp units would be required.

However, as so many engines would inhibit manoeuvrability and increase drag, a solution was found, as in the experimental He 119, whereby the two independent 1,000 hp engines were coupled together on each wing to drive one propeller, thereby achieving all the advantages of a twin-engined aeroplane over a four-engined, but with no reduction of power. Although a fine idea in theory, it proved unworkable in practice; when tested, this coupling arrangement was soon found to be unreliable. Overheating and a tendency to catch fire in mid-air were the most spectacular of the faults. Moreover, the trials of the first prototype proved disappointing, its speed being nearly fifty mph below that demanded by the specifications. On 19th November 1938, Heinkel accordingly asked the Technical Office for permission to end the experiment and, instead, provide the aircraft with four separate engines. This was refused: the He 177 had to have a dive-bombing capability, and dive-bombers could not operate with more than two propellers.

In fact, the dive-bombing requirement had only been added by the RLM as an after-thought. When, in the spring of 1938, Udet and Jeschonnek had seen the mock-up of the He 177, they had requested a four-engine construction, only to defer to Heinkel's current enthusiasm for the coupling arrangement. A few months later, the Technical Office, with the agreement of the General Staff, requested that the He 177 be capable of an angle of dive of sixty per cent. When Udet remarked to Heinkel that 'The He 177 must be made capable of diving at all costs', the aircraft manufacturer replied, 'You can't make a dive-bomber out of an aircraft that size'. To this, Udet responded 'For all practical purposes it's a twin-engine aircraft. If the twin-engined Ju 88 can dive, why shouldn't the He 177?'[11]

The insistence upon dive-bombing ensured that the He 177 had to be provided with coupled engines, the result of which soon earned it the nickname of the Luftwaffenfeuerzeug (Luftwaffe's Lighter). A considerable strengthening of its structure was required to withstand the very great stresses it would experience as it pulled out of the dive. The first, non-diving, He 177 prototype had a weight of 30,247 lb; by the time the He 177 saw service, this had increased by almost one third, to 39,771 lb. As with the Ju 88, speed and manoeuvrability were sacrificed to provide for the ability to dive-bomb. Certainly, the first production version of the aircraft, the He 177A-1-R1, fulfilled the Technical Office's specifications; it carried a crew of five, and possessed a maximum speed of 303 mph at 19,030 ft. It was capable of a radius of action of 1,200 miles carrying a bomb-load of 2,000 lb (its maximum was 12,000 lb). But, in reality, the He 177 was unserviceable. Of this, more is written later. Suffice to mention that, during tests, almost fifty prototypes either burst into flames or broke apart during dives. By September 1942, only thirty-three He 177A-1s had been accepted for service, and, of these, only two were still operational.

The Luftwaffe's inability to secure the production of an effective long-range heavy bomber has widely been regarded as a major set-back. After the war, Milch admitted that 'this is one of the reasons for the failure of the air offensive against Britain and for the Luftwaffe's inability to provide adequate protection for Germany's submarines at sea'.[12] It has been argued that a German bombing offensive aimed at the enemy's shipping lanes, communications and centres of industry would have been highly effective. As it was, however, the Germans dropped on Britain just three per cent of the tonnage of high explosive the Allies deposited on the Reich. The Luftwaffe's Ju 88A-1 could carry only 2,000 lb over a radius of 550 miles, or 3,380 lb over 250 miles. In contrast, the RAF Avro Lancaster could carry 4,000 lb of bombs over a radius of 875 miles, and could reach the Reich by night, with minimum defensive armament, with 8,500 lb. The American B-17, the only four-engined bomber in the west to be in service at the beginning of the war, could carry 2,000 lb of bombs over a 900 mile radius, and reach the Reich, by day, with 3,500 lb. The B-29 'Superfortress', introduced in 1944, but, in fact, never used over Germany, could carry no less than 20,000 lb of bombs (the laden weight of a Ju 88A-1), and 12,000 lb over a radius of 1,625 miles.

Nonetheless, the lack of a highly costly long-range bomber fleet may well not in itself have been as detrimental to the Luftwaffe as many historians have argued. Leaving aside the contentious question of whether the bombing of an enemy's economy was a cost-effective method of waging war given the high rate of inaccuracy experienced in the first years of the war, it is probable that, even had the Reich possessed large numbers of a heavy bomber equal to the American B-17 (something that was quite impossible by the outbreak of the war in 1939), the German Air Force would have proved unable to operate them effectively due to one factor: the lack of a suitable long-range escort fighter. Owing to the inadequacies of the Bf 110 and the failings of the Me 210, the Luftwaffe simply did not possess such a machine. As experience was to reveal, without the accompanying Mustang and Thunderbolt fighters, the Allied daylight raids in 1944 would not have been possible; by night, early war-time navigation and bombing aids were unsuited to all else except the area bombardment of cities, and that turned out to be an occupation as fruitless as it was violent.

Thus, against the United Kingdom, a long-range, unescorted bomber force would, in all probability, have failed, whether it had operated by day or night; only against the Soviet Union, which lacked an effective air defence, would it have had some chance of achieving any significant success. By mid-1941, when the invasion of the Soviet Union took place, and when bombers might have succeeded in penetrating deeply into enemy territory without sustaining unacceptable casualties, not only was the Luftwaffe not expected to possess a long-range bomber fleet, but only one nation in Europe did, the USSR, and then it consisted of just 100 obsolescent machines (the TB-3s) with a handful of modern types (Pe 8s) coming into operations. Nor did the Americans have large numbers of B-17s in service. Not until 1943 did the Allied heavy bomber raids on Germany really begin to take effect, by night, and by that time the Reich may be considered to have lost the war – and to have lost it on the ground. Certainly the slow-moving Ju 89 and Do 19, which could have been operational by 1939, would not have been so efficacious as the Allied heavy bombers, even had they been available in sufficient numbers. As for a maritime role, it is difficult to envisage a heavy, high-altitude aircraft, such as the Lancaster or Superfortress, being well employed bombing targets as small as merchant ships. In that role, too, a smaller bomber such as the Ju 88 would prove far more effective.

But even were heavy bombers, suitably escorted, the potential asset to the Reich that many argue they might have been, the decision to discontinue development of the Do 19 and Ju 89 in 1937 was sound. The technological and economic limitations of the time simply did not permit the development of a heavy bomber force in addition to the creation, from nothing, of a well-balanced air force whose primary role was to support the Army in its operations. Such a support was to prove highly valuable in the war and, arguably, for the resources employed was far more effective than heavy bombing of the enemy's homeland. Had the second generation of heavy bomber, the He 177, been developed without its fatal requirement to dive-bomb, its introduction into service in large numbers may well have been possible; but even then it would not have been ready in sufficient force until more than two years after war had broken out, at a time when German air superiority was on the wane. Then, because of the failings of the Bf 110 and Me 210, the He 177 would have been left to fend for itself over enemy territory without the support of a long-range fighter. Over Britain, certainly, it would not have lasted long in daylight, and at night it would have been incapable of the accuracy necessary to fulfil its role. Thus, in order for the Luftwaffe to meet its political goal of massive rearmament in as short a time as possible, to fulfil its primary role of support for the Army, to plan its aircraft in line with its technological capabilities, and, above all, to adjust its production programmes to economic reality, it was forced to recognise that it could not have a heavy bomber force until mid-1942. In the event, it was not to have one at all. It must remain a matter for conjecture whether this was the loss that historians have alleged it to be.

The heady optimism that prevailed in Luftwaffe circles in the first years of its existence from 1933 to 1936, during which time the yearly production of military aircraft increased from 372 to 5,112, had evaporated by 1938. By then it was realised that not even Göring, in his new capacity as head of the Four Year Plan, could shield the Air Force from the severely debilitating shortage of raw materials. The first indication came in November 1936, when, in the interest of production and supply, it was decided to concentrate on the Bf 109 and Bf 110 as the only fighters to equip the Luftwaffe. No capacity for the parallel production of similar types would be provided for; the Air Force would, for the next five years, stand or fall by the efficacy of these two machines. In the case of the Bf 109, the gamble was sound; the

Bf 110, however, was another matter.

At this time, the Luftwaffe's commander remained undaunted, stimulated, no doubt, by his Führer, whose expansionist policy had been reiterated at a meeting of senior military commanders as late as 5th November 1936, to whom it was stated that Germany would have to begin her outward movement by 1943 at the latest. On 2nd December, Göring ordered that, at the beginning of the new year, all aircraft manufacturers were to operate at the pace required by the plans for mobilisation. Money was no object, for, as the Minister pointed out, although 'peace until 1941 is desirable . . . we cannot know whether there will be implications before. We are already in a state of war; it is only that no shot is being fired so far'.[13] However, to achieve greater output, Göring accepted that fewer models could be produced. For example, all proposals for developing a range of fighters to fill four distinct roles were dropped. On the 16th, the Technical Office announced that it had decided to discontinue development of nine aircraft, and a cutback in models under production was considered a few days later. But Göring's hope that the output of aircraft should run at mobilisation rate, was soon proved to be unrealistic. In March 1937, a new production plan, No.5, was introduced, which called for a lower monthly output than its predecessor, and extended the conclusion of the programme from 31st March to 1st October 1938. By that date, it was expected that, since 1933, 18,620 aircraft would have been accepted by the Luftwaffe, whereas plan No.4 had envisaged 18,000 six months earlier. The ratio of fighters to bombers was also altered, from 1:3 to 1:2, reflecting a growing concern with the capabilities of foreign air forces, both to attack the Reich and to intercept its bombers. To avoid sharp cutbacks in the aircraft industry's manpower caused by the drop in monthly output, and the reduction in the number of model types, the new plan accelerated the rate of conversion to new machines and increased the number of development contracts.

Further trimming of the Luftwaffe's plans was to follow. On 29th April 1938, the Ju 86 programme was curtailed, to no-one's disappointment since the aircraft had little to recommend it. In June, the Technical Office reported that the rate of new production was only ten per cent of the planned level of increase. It extended the delivery date for some aircraft and reduced purchases. A new production plan, issued later that month, foresaw a cut of some 430 aircraft and a further extension of the terminal date, to 31st March 1939. For the first time, the RLM planned for an interruption in the steady increase of the aircraft industry's output. Workers were even to be laid off.

Further standardisation measures were introduced. In July 1937, after a conference with industrial leaders, the RLM committed itself to shorten testing procedures, to reduce the number of changes requested, to make do with fewer models and their variants as well as types of equipment, and to run longer production series. The principle of 'communality', i.e. the unification of many types of function (bomber, fighter etc) in one aircraft, such as the Me 210, was pursued with greater vigour. This idea involved the adoption of a standard airframe that could be put to several uses by the addition of different engines and equipment. However, these attempts to speed and simplify aircraft development had some unfortunate consequences. Haste in field testing caused faults to be included in the final production series, which not only resulted in a slow-down of output but also in expensive and time-consuming corrections. At the same time, the planners and designers became unduly cautious, preferring to choose existing methods and types rather than to search for fresh solutions. The pressure to produce as much as possible, in as short a time as possible, was not conducive to the building of a well-balanced air force, in which quality was not sacrificed to attain quantity.

In September 1937, Production Plan No.6 was issued, which concentrated on still fewer models with longer production runs. The key aeroplanes were to be the He 111 (1,202 to be built), the Do 17 (1,319), the Bf 109 (1,535), the Bf 110 (520) and the Ju 87 (499). On 30th October 1937, Milch reported to Göring that, because of shortages, the Luftwaffe production target would have to be revised downwards by twenty-five per cent; for the anti-aircraft artillery programme, the reduction would have to be in the order of seventy-five per cent, and the civil defence programme would be cut totally, in so far as the use of steel was concerned.

The new year, 1938, brought no immediate improvement. The preliminary budget request from the RLM for the financial year 1938-1939 was 6.1 billion Reichsmarks, but the Finance Ministry would allow it only 4.5 billion. Further sharp cutbacks were envisaged, with more lay-offs in the aircraft industry. Under such constraints, Production Plan No.7 was introduced in March, to run until 30th June 1939. A still further decline in monthly production was foreseen, so that the extension by three months of the terminal date of the previous plan resulted in an increase of only 489 aeroplanes in the final total. The average monthly production under Plan 7 would be 455.8 aircraft (compared with the planned output of some 1,179 a month during the 'mobilisation' which Göring had envisaged in December 1936). On this basis, the Luftwaffe would be entirely re-equipped with the new models of aircraft by the spring of 1940. Prominent among these would be the Ju 88, production of which was planned to have entirely replaced that of He 111s and Do 17s by October 1939. The total Luftwaffe strength by April 1940 was estimated to be 10,380 aircraft, of which 2,620 would be bombers, 973 dive-bombers, 3,048 fighters, 2,048 transports, and 1,727 reconnaissance machines.

In the spring of 1938, the Luftwaffe's problems were temporarily eased. The seizure of Austria in March lessened the severity of the continuing crisis in foreign exchange. Austria possessed an estimated 230 million Reichsmarks in reserves and seventy-five million in unminted gold and clearing accounts, whereas Germany had only 90 million; it also added to the Reich's industrial capacity, in particular in raw materials such as iron-ore, coal, and electric energy. In addition, imports of iron and minerals from Spain, which had been increasing since 1937, were of benefit. The looming Czech crisis, which, it was feared, might result in a major war, also had its effect. The Wehrmacht's spending for the year increased from the planned eleven billion Reichsmarks to fourteen billion, of which the Luftwaffe would get its fair share. On 8th July, Göring addressed major aircraft industrialists at his country estate, Karinhall, and told them that, in the face of war, the petty problems of the industry were irrelevant and must be solved. He wanted mass production of fewer models in larger series, the furtherance of development programmes in high-altitude and rocket engines, and long-range bombers. Factories should be placed on a war-footing. On 11th July, the Luftwaffe began preparations for the attack on Czechoslovakia, code-named 'Case Green'. Previous concerns now thrown to the wind, the RLM produced Production Plan No.8 on 15th August 1938, to run until 1st April 1940. Whereas Plan No.6 had called for the production of 2,055 fighters and 2,521 bombers in 18 months, No.8 envisaged 3,744 and 3,060 respectively. Ambitious though this was, it still had to cope with reality: by October, for example, the Luftwaffe was short of 366,000 tons of steel, most of it allocated for factory expansion. In 1938, the Reich's aircraft factories produced 5,235 military machines, 371 fewer than in the previous year, monthly output falling from an average of 467 machines to 436. Not until May 1939 did production reach the level of March 1937. Indeed, it has been estimated that, had reality matched the optimism of 1934 and 1935, an average output of 1,200 aircraft a month would have been reached by 1939, almost double the actual number in that year. Instead, it took until February 1942 to meet that estimate.

The Czechoslovakian crisis in the autumn of 1938 had a profound effect on Hitler and the Reich's leaders. On 21st April, a month after he had successfully incorporated Austria into 'Greater Germany', Hitler asked OKW to draw up a plan for the invasion of Czechoslovakia, a small country, but not insignificant militarily. As he explained, it lay in a vital strategic position, close to the heart of the Reich, which could be used as a base for Soviet forces when the final reckoning with Bolshevism came. Its menace should be removed. Nevertheless, because of world opinion, Hitler rejected the idea of an unprovoked attack, and instead preferred punitive action based on a trumped-up incident for which the Czechs could be held responsible. The plan, drawn up by OKW, was ready for Hitler's signature on 20th May. It opened with the words: 'It is not my intention to smash Czechoslovakia by military action in the immediate future, without provocation....'[13] However, plans were soon overtaken by events. On that same day, 20th May, the Czech government, alarmed at rumours of a German attack, ordered a partial mobilisation of its armed forces. The British and French governments warned Germany of the possibility of a general war should Czechoslovakia be invaded, while France and the Soviet Union reaffirmed their promise of immediate support for the Czechs. Outraged rather than frightened at such reactions, and unwilling to accept any loss of prestige, Hitler took a fateful decision: to solve the Czechoslovakian issue that same year, even at the risk of a European war. The plan for the invasion was recast, and, on 28th May, Hitler gave his signature to the new, and last, version of 'Case Green'. Its first sentence ran: 'It is my unalterable decision to smash Czechoslovakia by military means, in the near future'.[14]

The date set for the attack was 1st October, and the political basis for such action was carefully prepared. Hitler demanded the incorporation into the Reich of the Sudetenland (that part of Czechoslovakia in which the ethnic German population was the majority), and issued an ultimatum to that effect on 26th September. It was to expire at two o'clock on the afternoon of the 28th. Hitler announced to the British ambassador on the 27th: 'I am prepared for every eventuality. It is Tuesday today, and by next Monday we shall be at war.'[15] In Berlin, massed armour paraded down the Wilhelmstrasse, and in London trenches were dug. The Czechs massed a well-trained, 800,000 man field-army behind strong defences; the French partially mobilised to become capable of placing sixty-five divisions to face twelve of the Germans on their frontier; the British mobilised their fleet; the Soviets stated they would honour their treaty obligations. The Italians, Germany's only ally, did nothing. Hitler was faced with the real possibility of a war on two fronts. With his troops outnumbered by those of France and Czechoslovakia alone by two to one, and his own people, at best, apathetic to war, he cannot have been happy with the prospect. But, just as Europe teetered on the edge of a general war, fate presented the Führer with the means not only to avoid almost certain failure, but also to gain at least part of what he demanded, with the prospect of the rest to come. The governments of France and Britain were still not convinced of the necessity for war, and, through the mediation of Mussolini, Hitler was persuaded to accept Chamberlain's proposal for a four-power conference on the Czechoslovak question. The meeting of the four leaders, Hitler, Mussolini, Chamberlain, and Daladier, which took place at Munich on 29th September 1938, resulted in the total acceptance of the Führer's demands. On 1st October, German troops marched, unopposed, into the Sudetenland. It had, however, been a close run thing.

On 14th October, two weeks after the Munich conference, Hitler announced a major new armament programme. Never again did he intend to be made to fear the consequences of his actions as he had done before Munich. Pride of place was reserved for the Luftwaffe, and top priority was given to its five-fold expansion in preparation for the possibility of a war on two fronts. By early November, the General Staff had estimated that, in practice, this meant the production of 45,700 aircraft by the spring of 1942, to give the Luftwaffe a force of some 10,300 in operational units, with 8,200 in reserve. These were to be employed in fifty-eight bomber Geschwader (Ju 88s and He 177s), sixteen long range fighter Geschwader (Me 210s and Bf 110s) sixteen fighter Geschwader (Bf 109s), and eight dive-bomber Geschwader, as well as considerable numbers of recce aircraft. The cost was estimated to be sixty billion Reichsmarks, roughly the amount spent between 1933 and 1939 on all military rearmament. A draft production plan, No.9, issued by the Technical Office on 15th November, elaborated on the General Staff's requirements, and called for the construction, by 31st March 1942, of 703 He 177s; 7,327

Ju 88s; 900 Do 17s; 2,000 He 111s; 2,002 Ju 87s; 3,320 Bf 110s; and 4,331 Bf 109s. Subsequently, these figures were reduced, but not substantially.

On 15th November also, Göring and Milch discussed the need to increase the Luftwaffe's training capacity and to plan future operations against Great Britain. The RLM immediately began preliminary feasibility studies into the latter proposal. Emphasis was also placed on the construction of air bases and the development of long-range bombers and fighter-escorts to undertake missions over England and beyond, out into the Atlantic. A note of urgency had already been sounded when, on 24th October, Göring told Milch that the Luftwaffe's ground units had to be fully motorised in order to be able to follow the army's advance and move air bases into occupied territories nearer to England. Two days later, a conference of senior officers at Karinhall had discussed the requirements for an air war against the United Kingdom, at which the establishment of at least 500 long-range bombers by 1942 was proposed, together with the development of armour-piercing bombs of 2,500 lb for use against shipping. Jeschonnek was to repeat these plans at a conference with naval officers one month later, at which, again, the common enemy was clearly recognised as Great Britain.

But however enthusiastic the leadership might be for the expansion of the Luftwaffe, considerable doubts were manifested as to Germany's ability to undertake anything so ambitious as Hitler's scheme. The Technical Office agreed that in theory, given the proper investment, the aircraft industry could cope with the new requirements, but feared that, in practice, such an expansion was impossible for lack of resources. Moreover, because of difficulties in development, there would be a substantial delay before the Ju 88, He 177 and Me 210 appeared. The He 177, for example, was not planned to enter service until 1942, and only by mid-1943 would 500 heavy bombers be available. But most important of all considerations, the raw materials and foreign exchange required would be so considerable as to be quite unobtainable; the fuel supply alone for the planned air force would require importing no less than eighty-five per cent of the existing world production of aviation fuel. A more realistic programme was drawn up by Colonel Josef Kammhuber, chief of the RLM Organisation Division, which cut Hitler's requirements by roughly two-thirds. Both Milch and Stumpff thought this to be feasible, and proposed its adoption until a solution had been found for the problems inherent in the Führer's aims, if that were at all possible. On 28th November, the heads of the RLM met, without Göring, to decide what to do. Milch outlined the problem, reminding those present that even Production Plan No.5, introduced in March 1937, was still far from completion, and ended by recommending Kammhuber's plan. Everyone was in agreement, except Jeschonnek, who declared 'I am opposed! Gentlemen, in my view it is our duty to support the Führer and not work against him.'[16] Milch, unable to dismiss the opinion of one so influential, took him to Göring, to whom they both explained their contrary views. The Field Marshal, anxious not to disagree with his Führer, sided with Jeschonnek, and Milch returned to the conference to announce that it was Göring's decision that, even if Hitler's programme could not be carried out, every departmental chief would have to do his utmost to see that as much as possible was achieved. Kammhuber demanded to know from where the resources were to come; he received no answer.

The dilemma in which the Luftwaffe's leaders found themselves, placed between Hitler's demands and economic reality, was resolved in a manner that was fast becoming standard practice in a nation where political aims were so often divorced from their means of fulfilment. On 13th December 1938, a meeting of the senior officers of the three services was convened to discuss the problems and allocations of Hitler's new armament programme. Göring and Milch presented their case to the Army and Navy chiefs, based on a report drawn up by the Technical Office a few days previously. The aircraft industry could produce 43,000 aeroplanes by 1st April 1942 (the General Staff wanted 45,700), of which 10,900 would be bomb carriers (7,700 of which would be He 177s and Ju 88s) and 7,500 fighters (Bf 109s, Bf 110s and Me 210s). Aviation fuel production would have to increase from the current 38,000 cubic metres a month to 300,000 cubic metres, and an extra 6.6 million cubic metres of storage tank space would be required to reach the planned total of 10.3 million cubic metres. Simply to transport the fuel, the Luftwaffe would need 9,000 railway wagons, 7,500 more than those already in use. To service the five-fold expansion, iron and steel allocations to the aircraft industry would have to increase three-fold (from 100,000 tons in 1938 to 290,000 tons in 1941), aluminium would have to nearly double (4,800 tons to 8,900 tons), copper would have to treble, wood quadruple and explosives for aerial armament increase from 1,000 tons annually to 23,000 tons. The production of anti-aircraft guns, too, would have to more than double. Labour in the industrial and construction centres would take roughly forty-five per cent of the Reich's reserves by 1940. The other military leaders were, understandably, alarmed, especially as they had their own massive armament programmes to consider. They refused to grant the Luftwaffe the priority that it required, with the result that, while the Führer's programme was openly subscribed to, in practice the means to fulfil it were not granted. No reaction was forthcoming from the RLM. Hitler was not to be told, and there is no evidence that anyone ever attempted to do so.

In addition to the immense strains placed upon the material resources of the Luftwaffe, Hitler's call for a five-fold expansion caused considerable dislocation to the training programme of the men who were to fly the large numbers of aircraft required. In the autumn of 1938, there were only three bomber pilot, one naval pilot and one fighter pilot training schools in existence, and no plans were made to create new ones. As General Deichmann, Chief of Staff to the new Chief of Training, an office instituted during the final reorganisation of the RLM in January 1939, wrote: 'When the office was first created, the Chief of Training prepared a report for the Chief of the General Staff and requested authorization for new pilot training schools. The General Staff refused his request, stating that all technical resources were being wholly utilized in the activation of new front units'.[17] The Chief of Training, unaided by Jeschonnek since his office had been transferred to Milch's domain, was forced to enlist the help of the NSFK (the National Socialist Flying Corps which, in April 1937, had replaced the DLV); their schools, based on club-lines, were scattered throughout Germany, and each used its own methods. Even front-line Gruppen commanders were forced to accept the task of training replacements at the same time as bringing their units to combat-readiness. So short were technicians and materials in this period of feverish expansion, that the Chief of Training could not even provide an altitude chamber for crew-testing or aero-medical research. Of the consequences of all this, Milch was to state at Nuremberg:

> We had just sufficient personnel replacements for a comparatively small Luftwaffe at that time. The lack of personnel replacement was the greatest handicap of all in building up the Luftwaffe. The whole question of time limits, etc., depended on the training of personnel. It was the personnel question which regulated the pace. It was possible to build planes more rapidly, but it was not possible to expedite the training of the crews. . . . Pilots and technical personnel are of no use unless thoroughly trained. It is much worse to have half-trained personnel than no personnel at all.[18]

Thus, Hitler's programme foundered. Caught between economic and military reality and political irresponsibility, between the demands of the General Staff and the inabilities of the Technical and Training Offices, the goals of the five-fold expansion simply faded away, leaving the Luftwaffe to develop much as had already been planned. The only result was that there was some acceleration in the build-up of planned units and in production schedules, resulting in more haste than was proper in the creation of any armed force. Programmes became one thing; actual development quite another. As Kammhuber realised, the Luftwaffe was 'drifting'.[19]

Problems with the Luftwaffe's programme were to continue. On 24th January 1939, Production Plan No.10 was issued, which took account of delays in the He 177 and Ju 88 programmes, and thus necessitated extensions in the service of the He 111s and Do 17s. The final total of aircraft to be produced, however, remained the same. Further delays took their toll, and, on 1st April, just a few days after Czechoslovakia had been completely occupied, and the Memel had been placed under the Reich's rule, without any interference from the rest of the world, a new Production Plan, No.11, was issued. This set more realistic goals than its predecessor, to be achieved in the following three years. Only 7,748 bombers were required for service (some 2,500 less than in Plan 10), of which just 4,419 would be He 177s and Ju 88s, and the number of fighters was also reduced to 5,859, of which 3,881 would be

Bf 109s and the rest Bf 110s and Me 210s. However, within a very short time even this revision was seen to be far too ambitious. On 12th April, nine days after Hitler had ordered military preparations against Poland, the Technical Office reported that only forty per cent of the bombs and explosives quota could be met, while, on 5th May, Milch warned Göring that, because of serious raw material shortages, aircraft production might also have to be cut by thirty or forty per cent. A shortage of labour further exacerbated the situation. On the same day, Jeschonnek, newly appointed Chief of the General Staff, warned Luftwaffe field commanders that, because of a fall in output, half the active units could not be brought up to full strength. On 12th May, the Quartermaster-General announced that there would be severe shortages in supplies of aircraft parts, especially radios, instruments, fuel and munitions, and, on the 15th, it was reported that the Luftwaffe only possessed a 2.8 month reserve of fuel.

By prodigious efforts, the airframe industry managed to keep to its production schedules, but deliveries from engine and auxiliary equipment manufacturers were anywhere between three and thirty-seven per cent behind schedule. The whole aircraft industry was hampered by a shortage of labour and the continuous lack of raw material. A series of reports from the RLM in June revealed that, despite a rise in quotas, the industry still received only seventy per cent of its requirement of iron and steel, seventy-three per cent of aluminium, forty-five per cent of wood, thirty per cent of copper, and thirty-one per cent of nickel. The production of anti-aircraft guns was particularly low and, on 16th June, the Quartermaster-General warned that, if the situation did not improve, the Air Force would be short of one hundred gun batteries by April 1940. As a result, in July 1939, Production Plan No.12 was drawn up, with a further reduction of some twenty per cent in production goals.

An improvement in the output of anti-aircraft guns was relatively easy to secure. When the threat of war grew during the summer of 1939, Hitler became concerned lest a successful enemy aerial bombardment of the Reich might damage his popularity with the people. He granted permission to raise the production of 8.8 cm and 10.5 cm heavy guns from forty a month to 150, and requested a speedier development of the 12.8 cm and 15 cm guns. To accelerate the aircraft programme proved much more difficult. The Ju 88 was still giving trouble, and, on 22nd July, Udet reported that a further delay of three months would be unavoidable; production could begin in nine months, and by April 1943 it was expected that some 5,000 of the aircraft would have been delivered. However, until then, a bomber 'gap' would occur in 1940, as the He 111s and Do 17s were phased out to be replaced by an insufficient number of Ju 88s. This proved the final straw for Göring. Alarmed both by this and by the cumulative effect of all previous reports on the parlous state of the development programme, on 5th August, as the final preparations for the invasion of Poland were being made, the Field Marshal called Milch, Udet and Jeschonnek to attend him on his yacht, *Karin II*, to discuss a new programme.

Concerned by the prospect of a general European war, the outbreak of which was viewed in terms of years not months (even at this late stage, 1942 was still the key date in the minds of the Luftwaffe planners, rather than September 1939), Göring proposed that greater emphasis be placed on offensive power. A force of 4,300 bombers should be formed by 1st April 1941 (of which over half would be Ju 88s), with 670 in reserve, and a total of 5,000 He 177s would be produced by 1st April 1943. To achieve this accelerated programme, the Luftwaffe would have to concentrate on the development of only four types of aeroplane, the He 177, Ju 88, Me 210 and Bf 109; to facilitate this, aircraft such as the Hs 129 and the FW 189 would have to be removed from the programme altogether, while others were to be cut back, such as the Ju 87, Hs 126 and Ju 52. Simplification of production and multi-purpose utilisation of only a few models were the solutions which Göring and the Technical Office agreed would enable the Luftwaffe to be prepared for a major war. To fulfil this demand, the Technical Office drew up Production Plan No.13. It was, however, in vain, as was Plan No.14, which even then was under consideration. Events moved too fast, and, by 3rd September, Germany was involved in a major European war. Production Plan No.11 was still in force, with the aircraft industry turning out some 700 aircraft a month. By a directive dated 12th September, Udet ordered a considerable reduction in all development projects, and a concentration on the Bf 109, Me 210, He 177 and Ju 88 – the logical and final conclusion to a process that had been developing since the autumn of 1936. On just four combat aircraft, the fortunes of the Luftwaffe were to be based.

To create an effective military force, it is essential that it be based on sound technical and military decisions and not on political expediency or the speed of events on the international scene. War should only be contemplated when the means to wage it are fully prepared. This, however, Hitler, with his fascination for numerical strength and his obsession with foreign expansion, proved quite unable to comprehend. He viewed ultimate political influence in terms of military might, which he assessed solely as numbers of men under arms, tanks, guns and aeroplanes, regardless of their quality. As Göring admitted, the most important factor in the creation of the Luftwaffe was 'to impress Hitler, and to enable Hitler, in turn, to impress the world'.[20] Consequently, constant pressure was exerted on the wiser counsels within the RLM to increase the size of the Luftwaffe with all possible speed; in justification, Göring would often remark: 'The Führer will not ask how big the bombers are, but only how many there are'.[21]

This policy undoubtedly achieved considerable successes for Hitler from 1935 to September 1939. Fear of the Luftwaffe's capability, whether real or imaginary it mattered little, was a major factor influencing the decisions of the Reich's enemies. To achieve this, Germany's aerial strength was deliberately magnified. At air shows, at National Socialist rallies, and even at the 1936 Olympics, the Luftwaffe took every opportunity to show off its equipment. Such propaganda was especially important during the visits of foreign politicians and military officials. For example, in August 1938, during a visit of a delegation from the French Air Force, headed by General Vuillemin, every effort was made to exaggerate the Luftwaffe's strength. On one occasion, every fighter in Germany was flown to one airfield in southern Germany, where Vuillemin's aeroplane was scheduled to make a casual stop. On another, the French general was 'buzzed' by an He 100 fighter at full speed, and was informed that the third production line for such machines was about to be started up (in reality, only a handful were ever manufactured). The gullibility of foreigners never ceased to surprise the Germans. Even as early as fifteen days after the existence of a German Air Force had been proclaimed in March 1935, the British Foreign Secretary, Sir John Simon, was prepared to believe Hitler's boast that the Luftwaffe was already the size of the RAF. It was, but only if unarmed trainers were counted as front-line combat aircraft.

In contrast with such manoeuvring, German aviation had real technological achievements to its credit. At the International Flying Meeting in Zurich in July 1937, for example, a specially modified Bf 109 won the climb and dive competition, and a 'boosted' Do 17, in which Milch was the co-pilot, won the Alpine Fly-around, proving itself faster than any foreign fighter taking part (the RAF did not participate). In November, the Bf 109 achieved a new world speed record, which was superseded in June 1938 by an He 100 flown by Udet. Two more world speed records were established in March and April 1939 by the He 100 and Me 209, the last reaching a top speed of 469.22mph. Moreover, in order to deceive the world into thinking that the Luftwaffe actually had these aircraft in service, the Me 209 was known publicly as the Me 109R. The He 100 was involved in the deception then being practiced to make it appear as if the He 112 was also within the Air Force's order of battle, the record-breaking aircraft being known as 'He 112U'. Later, the handful of He 100Ds built were given the spurious designation 'He 113', and succeeded in misleading Allied intelligence for several years. In 1939, too, Heinkel set eight world seaplane records with an He 115, then about to enter service. An aviation industry that could develop such aircraft, and a service that could fly them, could not fail to arouse respect.

Moreover, in Germany's several acts of expansion during the 1930s, the Luftwaffe played a not undistinguished part. During the occupation of the Rhineland in March 1935, it had deployed only two Gruppen, one of dive-bombers, the other of fighters (whose guns were not sighted), both of which had been in existence for only a short time and were not of high quality. Great reliance was placed on bluff, and the few Staffeln were moved from airfield to airfield, repainting their insignia each time, so as to convey the impression of greater force than in reality existed. In the Spanish Civil War, the Condor Legion took a major and much publicised role, and revealed to the world the efficiency of the Luftwaffe's new weapons. In March 1938, with less than forty-eight hours notice, the Air Force contributed over 400 aircraft, mainly He 111s, Ju 86s and Ju 52s, to the annexation of Austria, and flew 2,000 fully-equipped troops to Vienna. Fighters and reconnaissance aircraft accompanied the German soldiers on the march, while bombers dropped leaflets over the Austrian capital. Moreover, the Air Force had played its part in the negotiations preceding the *Anschluss*. It was not a mere accident, nor could it be attributed solely to his martial expression, that Hitler kept General Sperrle, commander of Luftwaffenkommando 3, near during the luncheon given on 12th February in honour of the Austrian Chancellor, Dr Kurt Schuschnigg. For the fifty-three-year-old Hugo Sperrle, in reality a good-hearted man despite his harsh, almost brutal features, represented the German Luftwaffe, a force which was already a tangible factor in military planning, capable of inspiring both respect and fear. Shortly after Schuschnigg's visit, the German Army and Luftwaffe gave demonstrations along the Bavarian-Austrian border to draw attention to the importance of the agreements reached at Berchtesgaden. These demonstrations were repeated during the critical days following Schuschnigg's announcement that a plebiscite would be held concerning the incorporation of Austria into the Reich, and continued until his final resignation on 11th March 1938.

It was during the Sudeten crisis in the autumn of 1938 that the German Air Force was to prove its greatest value in peace-time. Just as the Wehrmacht was in danger of getting embroiled in a war on two fronts, for which it was ill-prepared, the Reich's enemies drew back from the brink and, at the Munich conference, gave Hitler what he demanded: the Sudetenland. This was not because they thought that thereby, they would fulfil the dictator's appetite for new territories, nor because they feared defeat at the hands of the German Army; it was due primarily to their fear of German air power. On 23rd September 1938, at the height of the tension over the Sudetenland, when war appeared imminent, the United States' Ambassador in London, Joseph Kennedy, cabled the following to Washington:

> I feel certain that German air strength is greater than that of all other European countries combined, and that she is constantly increasing her margin of leadership. I believe that the German factories are now capable of producing in the vicinity of 20,000 aircraft every year. Her actual production is difficult to estimate. The most reliable reports that I have obtained vary from 500 to 800 planes per month. . . . Germany now has the means of destroying London, Paris and Prague if she wishes to do so. . . . England and France are far too weak in the air to protect themselves.[22]

The words were those of Colonel Charles Lindbergh, the famous and influential American aviator, who, like Kennedy, was an advocate of 'America First', wishing to keep the USA out of Europe's troubles. His belief in the formidable power of the German Air Force was total, and this both echoed and fuelled the fears of politicians and soldiers throughout Europe. A few weeks earlier, General Vuillemin had declared upon his return from Germany that, in the event of war, the French Air Force would be destroyed in fifteen days, a view shared by the French politicians. War was unthinkable.

The British were hardly less pessimistic. On 5th April 1938, Air Chief Marshal Newall wrote to the Secretary of State for Air, the Earl of Swinton: 'We are at the present moment temporarily in a position of immense strategical inferiority to Germany. In my belief we are today in no position to resist any demand by Germany, and if we attempted to do so I believe we should be defeated by the knock-out blow. . . . '[23] In July, the Air Staff estimated that, provided the weather was good, the Luftwaffe could drop a daily average of 600 tons of bombs on Britain during the first few weeks of an assault, causing at least 20,000 casualties in each raid. Churchill's warnings, given since 1934 of the menace of German air power, were at last heeded. Malcolm Macdonald, Minister for the Colonies, believed that war 'would mean the massacre of women and children in the streets of London. No Government can possibly risk a war when our defences are in so farcical a condition'.[24] On 20th September, General Ismay, Secretary to the Committee of Imperial Defence and the Chiefs of Staff Sub-Committee, concluded that, by preventing war breaking out over Czechoslovakia, Britain could build up her air defences, and within a year, would have substantially reduced Germany's 'only chance of a rapid decision'.[25] At that time, neither the military chiefs nor the politicians believed that support of Czechoslovakia was worth the risk of war. At Munich, therefore, Hitler's demand for the incorporation of the Sudetenland into the Reich was met by the British and French leaders, and on 1st October, when German troops crossed the Czech border, supported by nearly 500 aircraft, they found no opposition. The Sudetenland was occupied, followed in April the next year by the rest of Czechoslovakia. Not a finger was raised to prevent it. As Göring put it in a speech on 1st March 1939: 'Our worried enemies found themselves faced with the fact that Germany possessed the mightiest air force in the world. There can be no doubt that this fear has helped to restrain such warmongers from war; they could not block the peace-loving statesman's road to our Führer and a fair understanding'.[26] More neutral commentators thought differently; as one wrote: 'It is blackmail which rules Europe today, and nothing else: blackmail made possible only by the existence of air power'.[27]

Indeed, the actual strength of the Luftwaffe was formidable at the time of Munich, and was more than a match for the combined French, British and Czech air forces. On 1st August 1938, the Luftwaffe's front-line units consisted of 2,928 aeroplanes, of which 1,284 were bombers, 207 dive-bombers, 173 ground-attack aircraft, and 643 fighters. The British had 640 bombers and 566 fighters, the French 859 bombers and fighters, and the Czechs 566 front-line aircraft of both classes. At that time, the total German monthly production of aircraft was more than double that of the Allies combined. However, this force was far from the awesome dealer in death and destruction that its enemies feared. Of the 2,928 aircraft, only 1,669 (fifty seven per cent) were operational; serviceability was low because of the inferior nature of their equipment. Of the 1,284 bombers (including Do 17 bomber-reconnaissance aircraft) 235 were the obsolescent Ju 86s, and the rest were early versions of the Do 17 (479) and the He 111 (510); although they were as good, and often better, than their counterparts in Europe, their performance was inferior to the models with which the Luftwaffe was to be equipped a year later. Certainly, such a force was not capable of delivering anything approaching 600 tons of bombs on Britain daily from their bases far away in Germany, or even from northern France and Belgium should those areas be occupied: moreover, quite irrespective of losses from enemy action, the high rate of unserviceability during operations would have still further reduced its capacity. In the quality of its fighters too, the Luftwaffe was significantly less well-equipped at the time of Munich than it was to be a year later; of the 643 at its disposal, only a few were Bf 110s, and less than half were Bf 109s; these, being early production types, were less formidable than those with which the German Air Force was to begin the war.

Indeed, as regards comparative strength, the British and French Air Forces lost rather than gained by the 'year of grace' that the Munich agreement had given them. By 31st August 1939, the Luftwaffe possessed a front-line strength of 4,093 aircraft, of which seventy-five per cent, 3,070, were capable of immediate action – more than double the previous year's total. Never again was it to have such a high percentage of serviceable aircraft. Of the total, 1,176 were bombers, 406 dive-bombers and 1,179 fighters. Owing to the Luftwaffe's planned introduction of newer types, all were of a quality significantly better than those of the previous year. Moreover, the extra twelve months had been put to good use as regards training. The Reich's enemies, lacking the benefit of a long-term production programme coming to fruition, had by no means improved sufficiently to offset the Luftwaffe's advance, let alone to reach even a level of equality. Moreover, they had lost support from Czechoslovakia's air force, which, in March, had largely been made over to the German occupiers, many aircraft being used later. Thus, against the Luftwaffe's 4,093 front-line aircraft, the British could muster 1,660 aeroplanes (536 bombers, 608 fighters, ninety-six reconnaissance machines, 216 coastal and 304 Fleet Air Arm aircraft), and the French 1,735 (463 bombers, 634 fighters, 444 reconnaissance machines, and 194 belonging to the navy), a total of 3,395, not including a further thousand held in their colonies overseas. Whereas a year previously, the Luftwaffe was barely numerically superior to its enemies, by September 1939 its strength was almost double theirs. Only in the state of the British air defences was the German position weakened. By September 1939, a majority of the RAF fighter squadrons had been re-equipped with Hurricanes and Spitfires, the anti-aircraft gun units had been greatly expanded, radar had covered most of southern and eastern England, and aircraft production was well on the way to surpassing German output.

Moreover, German aircraft and their equipment were generally superior in quality to those of their opponents. Significantly outclassing anything the French could put in the air, with the exception of the few Dewoitine D 520 fighters, the Luftwaffe's machines were also superior to those of the RAF. In 1939, no European nation possessed a heavy bomber comparable to the US four-engined B-17, and thus the delays in producing the He 177 were not then regarded to be as serious as they were later. The He 111s, Do 17s and Ju 88s were marginally better than the Wellingtons, Hampdens and Whitleys of RAF Bomber Command and could outstrip two-thirds of the foreign fighters. The Bf 109E was considered to be superior to the British Hurricane fighter, and, arguably, had the edge over the Spitfire; as a heavy fighter, the Bf 110 was greatly superior to the Blenheim both in performance and armament. The RAF had no counterpart to the Ju 87, although the French had a far less effective machine, the LN 411. Only in bombs and in gun-mountings were the Germans technically inferior, the former having worse ballistic characteristics (being designed for ease of production) than those of their enemies, and the latter being driven by hand instead of by power.

On the basis of such comparisons, it is not surprising that optimism prevailed in the counsels of the Luftwaffe. On 2nd May 1939, Colonel Beppo Schmid, Chief of the Air Intelligence Office of the General Staff, submitted his report entitled 'The Air Situation in Europe'. It stressed the relative superiority of the German Air Force, which had made possible the peaceful conclusion of the Sudetenland crisis, and argued that the dominance of Germany in the air was the decisive factor in the inferiority felt by the Allies. The British were believed to possess 5,545 aircraft, of which 3,600 were in the United Kingdom, the rest being scattered throughout the Empire; only some twenty per cent were first-class machines. The tactics and training of the RAF were regarded as primitive, and the British Army's few anti-aircraft artillery units were seen in no better light. In addition, British aerial rearmament would not be completed until after 1940, and even then the bomber fleet would remain outdated. The French, with their estimated 4,650 aircraft, were in an even worse position, although by mid-1940 they would be re-equipped with modern fighters and heavy anti-aircraft guns equal in quality to those of the Germans. Of the Italians, their aircraft were obsolete and their industry incapable of achieving a renewal. The Soviet Union, possessing an estimated 6,000 aircraft, was considered a major power, but only one-third of their machines were of modern type. The rest of the European states, Schmid's report dismissed as unimportant. Ten days later, on the 12th, the Luftwaffe Quartermater-General issued his report entitled 'Air Armament of the Western Powers'. In the year from 1st April 1939, he estimated that Great Britain would build 3,730 war planes, France 2,450, and the USA 2,700, a total of 8,880 compared with Germany's 9,192. However, a note of warning was sounded: while the Reich might outnumber its potential enemies in production, in terms of front-line strength the gap would be severely narrowed. On 1st March 1939, the British and French between them were estimated to possess 2,010 first-class machines, whereas by 1st April 1940 they would have 6,400. Closely following the Quartermaster-General's report, came one from the Technical Office, dated 13th May, which, like its predecessors, was optimistic about the present strength of the Luftwaffe vis-à-vis its enemies, both in terms of quantity and quality.

However, in all these reports there lay a note of warning: the relative superiority of the German Air Force would decline in a few years to a point where its technological and numerical advantage might be lost. As Jeschonnek warned in his report on the last major Luftwaffe manoeuvres before the war, too much reliance could not be placed on the continuance of the Air Force's technological superiority over its opponents. It might be momentary, lasting at best only six months before the enemy could match or outclass it. As the Luftwaffe's leaders recognised, all depended on the continued expansion of the Reich's aircraft industry and, more important, on the acceptance into service, on time and in sufficient numbers, of the new aircraft, the Ju 88, He 177 and Me 210 on which the Luftwaffe was to base its offensive capabilities in the early to mid-1940s. By the spring of 1939, not one Ju 88 had reached an operational unit, despite the fact that, as long ago as 1936, it had been planned to introduce the machine in late 1938. The He 177 was still scheduled for late 1940, and the Me 210 for mid-1941.

The need for these aircraft was emphasised in the studies undertaken in 1938 and 1939 regarding a possible air war against Great Britain. In the middle of the Sudeten crisis, on 23rd August 1938, Felmy, commander of Luftwaffengruppenkommando 2, and his staff were instructed to study the possibilities of an attack against Britain. Their conclusions, reported on 27th September, were pessimistic. Because of the limited range of both German bombers and fighters, advance airfields in Belgium and Holland would be necessary before any full-scale attack could be mounted. Attention was drawn in particular to the drawbacks of the He 111. Felmy noted: 'With our present available resources, only a harassing effect can be counted upon. Whether this can lead to the attrition of the British will to fight depends in part upon imponderable and, in any case, unforeseeable factors. . . . A war of annihilation against England appears to be out of the question with the resources thus far available'.[28] It was even proposed to convert four-engined civilian aeroplanes such as the four-engined FW 200 and the Ju 90 into bombers. This idea was dropped in favour of waiting until the He 177 arrived in sufficient numbers in 1942, although, in the event, a number of FW 200 were converted into long-range maritime reconnaissance and bomber aircraft, with some success. Further studies were undertaken in 1939 concerning separate attacks on France (Studie Rot), Poland (Studie Grün) and Great Britain (Studie Blau). For the latter, Felmy again submitted a report in which he stated that 'The armament, state of training, and strength of the Luftflotte 2 cannot bring about a decision in a war against England within a short time in the year 1939'.[29] All depended on the development of the Luftwaffe to the standard envisaged in the various production programmes that had been drawn up over the preceding years, production programmes that would end by mid-1942. Then, it was believed, the Luftwaffe would have the right aeroplanes in large enough numbers to wage a major European war.

In the spring of 1939, the RLM saw no reason why peace would not hold until these aircraft should make their appearance in sufficient quantities. In an optimistic report, dated 16th March, the RLM outlined its major development projects. Heinkel reported steady progress with the He 177, and was planning a new fighter. Junkers was working on an up-dating of the Ju 88, to be known as the Ju 188, and was developing a new medium bomber, the Ju 288, and a new transport aircraft, the Ju 252. Messerschmitt had the Me 210 and Me 261 (a long-range, fast aircraft of unspecified role) under construction, and was experimenting with a fast fighter, the Me 209. Focke-Wulf was engaged in developing the FW 190 fighter, the FW 187 heavy fighter, and the FW 191 bomber, Henschel a ground attack aircraft, the Hs 129, and a high altitude bomber, the Hs 130, and Arado the Ar 240 multi-purpose aircraft. Engine development, too, which had proved such a problem in previous years, was proceeding apace, and even jet engines were being built. On 30th June 1939, the He 176, the world's first rocket-powered aircraft, was flown, followed two months later by the He 178, the world's first jet. Heinkel was undertaking development of the He 280 jet fighter, while Messerschmitt was already under contract from the RLM for an experimental jet, the Me 262, the engines for which were to be built by Junkers.

On 3rd July 1939, the words of the RLM report of 16th March came to life at the Luftwaffe's experimental testing station at Rechlin. There, the latest innovations were shown to Hitler in a display, the prime purpose of which was to win his support for the provision of economic resources to fulfil the Luftwaffe's five-fold expansion programme. The Führer saw the new Ju 88, the Bf 110, the Me 209, and He 100, and a mock-up of the Me 262, as well as an air-to-ground missile, an early warning radar, a pressurised high-altitude cabin, a powerful 30 mm cannon, rocket-assisted take-offs, and much else besides. Most of the equipment had still to be developed further, but Hitler was impressed nonetheless. So, indeed, was Göring, who, as a result ordered on the 20th that even if it involved cutting production of other models, the Ju 88 programme should be speeded up to achieve a total of at least 5,000 machines by April 1943. Because of what he saw at the display, Göring remarked in May 1942, 'The Führer reached the most serious decisions'.[30] (i.e. the decision to invade Poland and risk a major European war). Whether this were so, is open to doubt. General Schmid remembered Hitler at Rechlin as saying: 'I haven't succeeded in achieving my political objectives in Europe by peaceful means. . . . We are going to get a war'.[31] Milch, on the other hand, asserted that the Führer had declared he did not want a general war, and was only bluffing with the armaments at his disposal. In all probability, the Führer said both; contradiction never worried him. Certainly, however, he placed great reliance upon his Air Force.

How much Hitler knew in 1939 of the Luftwaffe's weaknesses, it is impossible to tell. Milch asserts that he warned him at Rechlin not to expect too much of the weapons he saw displayed, as it would be some years before they were in operation. A few weeks earlier, on 8th June, Milch and Udet had even gone to see Rudolf Hess, the Deputy Führer, to impress upon him the dire results of the critical shortages in raw materials, but there is no evidence to suggest either that Hess passed this on to the Führer, or that, if he did, anything was done about it. Nor is there any reason to assume that Hitler was shown any of the pessimistic studies produced by Felmy. Göring, who was the only Luftwaffe leader with direct access to Hitler, does not appear to have given any indication that his Air Force was other than in a high state of preparedness. Indeed, it is questionable whether he himself thought other-wise. An indication that he was living in a world of dreams comes from his attitude to the Ju 88 project, and his remark, made in 1942, when he complained that the inventions he had seen at Rechlin had not materialised in front-line service: 'Do you know, I once witnessed a display before the war at Rechlin, compared with which I can only say what bunglers all our professional magicians are! Because the world has never before, and never will again see the like of which was conjured up. . . . at Rechlin'.[32] Jeschonnek, who was not entirely content with the existing situation, did not urge Göring to warn Hitler, and, by his acceptance of the five-fold expansion, made every attempt to carry out his Führer's wishes. Certainly, failings on the part of the Luftwaffe were not to deter Hitler from embarking upon further foreign expansion.

Exactly when Hitler decided upon war with Poland, it is impossible to say. His top secret directive issued to the service chiefs on 3rd April 1939 cannot be held as a final decision. It was more in the way of a precaution. It opened with the words: 'The present attitude of Poland [over the German demand for the return of Danzig and the 'Polish Corridor' to the Reich] requires . . . the initiation of military preparations to remove, if necessary, any threat from this direction whatsoever.'[33] Military plans were to be drawn up so that an attack could take place at any time from 1st September. On 23rd May, Hitler personally outlined his intentions to a group of senior officers from all three services, including Göring, Milch and Jeschonnek. 'Further successes can no longer be attained without the shedding of blood. . . . Danzig is not the subject of the dispute at all. It is a question of expanding our living space in the East. There is no question of sparing Poland, and we are left with the decision to attack Poland at the first suitable opportunity. We cannot expect a repetition of the Czech affair. There will be war. Our task is to isolate Poland.'[34] Should Britain and France stand in her way, they too would be 'smashed'. The general impression left upon Hitler's listeners, was that, while he was not actively pursuing the path of a general European war, he was aware that one might be inevitable in the future. It was, they believed, his way of warning them not to be complacent about rearmament.

While war with Poland might be regarded as inevitable in 1939, or 1940 at the latest, the spreading of the conflict throughout Europe was considered by the Luftwaffe's leaders to be highly unlikely. The vast majority of Germany's generals and politicians believed that, as with Czechoslovakia, Poland would stand alone, unaided by her allies. Indeed, Hitler, the victor of so many foreign gambles, had constantly asserted that he would never become involved in a war on two fronts; he had even declared that he would not become embroiled in a world war for the sake of Danzig or the Corridor. When Hitler met his senior officers on 22nd August, he told them that Germany had no other choice but to act, and concluded with the words 'Whoever has pondered over this world order knows that its meaning lies in the success of the best by means of force. . . .'[35] Even then, when Britain and France were clearly allying themselves with Poland's cause, many believed that there would be an eleventh hour settlement, leaving Poland isolated and vulnerable to invasion while peace would be maintained in the rest of Europe.

The Luftwaffe leaders were no exception to this general credulity. Göring was dead against war, and, believing in the genius of his Führer to effect a peaceful victory, he contrived to operate in his normal lazy manner, taking a long summer holiday on his yacht, and accepting with little concern the usual reports of delays in the Ju 88 and He 177 programmes. Not until August did he bestir himself. Others within the RLM were even more sanguine than Göring, believing that no major war would come until 1942. All their plans hinged on that assumption – plans which, despite the hectic international activity during the first seven months of 1939, had not changed. The preparations for the invasion of Poland, known as 'Case White', were regarded as simply another move in a long line extending back to the military reoccupation of the Rhineland in 1936. Since then, there had been Case Red, plans for a two-front war against France and Czechoslovakia, Case Green, plans for the attack on Czechoslovakia, and a number of variations on these two deployments, none of which were undertaken. It was believed that, like the others, Case White would not result in a general conflagration. As Kesselring later admitted 'We had complete confidence in [Göring], and we knew that he was the only person who had a decisive influence on Adolf Hitler. In that way we knew, since we also knew his peaceful attitude, that we were perfectly secure, and we relied on it'.[36] Certainly, the RLM showed no signs of active preparation for a major war until the beginning of August, when political events finally demanded it.

Indeed, it seems that, only a week before the invasion of Poland, Hitler himself did not expect the outbreak of a general European war. He remarked: 'As neither France nor Britain can achieve any decisive successes in the West, and as Germany, as a result of the agreement with Russia [signed on 22nd August], will have her forces free in the East after the defeat of Poland, as air supremacy is undoubtedly on our side, I do not shrink from solving the Eastern question even at the risk of complications in the West.'[37] These were hardly the words of a man believing he was unleashing a world war. But the Führer was mistaken. On 25th August, Great Britain gave her guarantee to defend Poland's territorial integrity; France followed suit. As the British

Prime Minister had warned in March, '. . . no greater mistake could be made than to suppose that, because it believes war to be a senseless and a cruel thing, this nation has so lost its fibre that it will not take part to the utmost of its power in resisting such a challenge [as the attempt to dominate the world by force], if ever it is made'.[38] Undeterred, on 28th August Hitler decided upon war, even if there was the risk that it should be on two fronts. On the 30th, the order for attack was issued, and at 4.35 a.m. on 1st September the Luftwaffe dropped the first bombs of the Second World War. Two days later, Germany was at war with France and Britain; a general European conflict had begun.

For the German Air Force, war had come too soon. As Milch was later to admit at Nuremberg: 'The few years between 1935 and 1939' were insufficient for any soldier in any country to build an air force equal to the task with which we were faced from 1939 on'.[39] According to Kesselring, to have expected an effective armed service to have been raised within that time would have been 'insanity'.[40] It is true to say, however, that after 1939, the longer Hitler waited before making territorial demands, the more the Reich's enemies would be likely to reach a level of armament that, if combined, would remove most of Germany's numerical superiority. But this was a development of which the military authorities were fully aware. The presumptions of the RLM reports of May 1939, concerning the relative air strengths of the major nations, were echoed by the Economic Office of the Wehrmacht High Command. Its chief, Colonel Georg Thomas, made a series of speeches in the first half of 1939 which emphasised that Germany had two choices: either to embark upon a quick war almost immediately, when her military advantage would still remain, or to replan her rearmament policy completely in order to prepare for a long war sometime during the 1940s. Thomas, rightly, preferred the latter solution. Quantitatively superior to its enemies, the Wehrmacht might have been, but all three of its services suffered from serious disabilities – disabilities which made full-scale war a hazardous undertaking before rearmament had been completed. The Army, for example, was so short of motor vehicles and spare parts that, early in 1940, it was forced to undergo a demotorisation programme that would increase still further its already considerable dependence on the horse. Likewise with the Luftwaffe; however numerically and qualitatively superior it might be to its enemies, it was simply not in a fit condition to risk embarking upon a major war that might last for years rather than months. But, because of Hitler's decision, that is precisely what it had to do.

On 31st August 1939, the day before war broke out, the Luftwaffe possessed 3,374 combat aircraft (bombers, fighters and reconnaissance machines), together with 552 transport aeroplanes and 167 seaplanes, of which seventy-five per cent were serviceable (in front line units, this was ninety per cent). The combat aircraft were divided among four Luftflotten in seven Fliegerdivisionen (Nos.1 to 6 and the Lehrdivision, instituted in 1938 to test new aircraft models at troop level). The breakdown by types was:

257 Do 17   long-range reconnaissance
275 Hs 126 ⎫
 67 He 46 ⎬ 356 short-range reconnaissance
 14 He 45 ⎭
400 He 111H ⎫
349 He 111P │
 38 He 111E │
212 Do 17Z ⎬ 1,176 bombers
119 Do 17E │
 40 Do 17M │
 18 Ju 88   ⎭
40 Hs 123   ground attack
366 Ju 87   dive-bombers
 68 Bf 110C ⎫
 27 Bf 110D ⎬ 95 twin-engined fighters
 36 Bf 109C ⎫
389 Bf 109D │
631 Bf 109E ⎬ 1,084 single-engine fighters
 28 Ar 68   ⎭
552 Ju 52 transports
167 seaplanes (He 60, He 59, He 115, Do 18)

In addition, the Luftwaffe possessed a small reserve, varying between ten and twenty-five per cent of front-line strength, according to types, some 2,500 training aircraft, and 500 operational types used for operational training. Before mobilisation, the Luftwaffe's personnel strength was some 373,000 men, of whom 208,000 were in the flying and airborne units (1,500 were paratroops) 107,000 in anti-aircraft artillery (to operate 2,600 heavy and 6,700 medium and light guns, and 3,000 searchlights) and 58,000 in signals; the number of pilots was just five per cent of total strength, at some 20,000. After mobilisation, the Air Force possessed no less than 1,300,000 men, an increase of nearly three hundred and fifty per cent.

Impressive machine though the Luftwaffe might have appeared to be in the autumn of 1939, it nevertheless possessed severe weaknesses. Its front-line strength of 4,093 aircraft was but one sixth of the total planned for the autumn of 1942, the date by which the Luftwaffe's leaders aimed at being prepared for war. Moreover, the quality of the aircraft would by then have been considerably superior. Thus, instead of 1,158 Do 17s and He 111s, the German Air Force would have had 7,700 He 177s and Ju 88s, and instead of 1,179 Bf 109s and Bf 110s, no less than 7,500 improved versions of those machines, together with the Me 210. Although economic reality may well have shown these plans to be over-optimistic, had even half these figures been realised, the Luftwaffe's order of battle would have been considerably improved, both in quantity and quality. But in September 1939, not only was the German Air Force well below its planned strength, but also it was not even prepared for action based on the limited numbers it already possessed. The flying units were still in the process of being formed, as is shown by the fact that, of the thirteen Kampfgeschwader in existence, only thirty of their full strength of thirty-nine Gruppen were formed (no more than there had been since November 1938). The rest of the Luftwaffe's formations found themselves in a similar situation: the five Stukageschwader possessed only nine of their fifteen Gruppen, the fourteen Jagdgeschwader had only eighteen of their forty-two Gruppen, and the six Zerstörergeschwader just ten of their twenty-seven. Moreover, the composition of the much-vaunted Zerstörer-geschwader was far from ideal, only ninety-five Bf 110s being available (insufficient for one full-strength Geschwader), their other 313 aircraft being Bf 109s. In night-fighting, the Luftwaffe was almost entirely deficient, possessing just two Staffeln of Ar 68 biplanes and plans only for the raising of three more, two of Bf 109s and one of Bf 110s, all without any special night-flying equipment. In its transport aircraft, too, the Luftwaffe was sadly lacking, even though it possessed over 500 Ju 52s. Only one Geschwader (some 150 aircraft) was specifically allocated to transport duties with the parachute and air-landing forces, and many of the rest were used by the Luftwaffe's training schools. To obtain sufficient transports to support the movement of the Luftwaffe's air and ground units during a campaign, there was no alternative but to raid the Training Command's resources, at both short term and, owing to battle casualties, longer-term cost to the output of well-trained crews to cater for battle losses as well as expansion.

For the future, there was much to be concerned about. Of the four types of aircraft on which the Luftwaffe was to base its offensive strength, only one, the Bf 109, was in service and had proved its capabilities. Of the others, the Ju 88 had still to make its appearance one year late in front-line units (although eighteen of the machines were officially listed as being in the Air Force's front-line strength as at 31st August) and, owing in large part to its severe teething troubles, was not to see service in significant numbers for some time; by February 1940, for example, of the forty Kampfgruppen in existence, only three were equipped with Ju 88s. The introduction of both the He 177 and the Me 210 was far off, and the troubles being experienced with their development did not inspire optimism for their combat efficacy. As a result, over a third of the bomber force was incapable of carrying more than a ton of bombs over a radius of more than 205 miles, and the rest could, at best, manage a ton over 550 miles. By contrast, the He 177 was expected to carry a ton over 1,200 miles or three tons over a shorter distance. Moreover, the speed of the existing medium bombers was lower than that of the new generation of fighters being produced by Germany's enemies, and, to make matters worse, they lacked an effective escort fighter, the Bf 110 being insufficient both in speed and manoeuvrability. The ground-attack aircraft, the Hs 123, was an obsolete biplane, and the Ju 87 dive-bomber too slow for safety, so that both could operate only when Germany had superiority in the air over the target area. Thus, with the exception of its single-engined fighter, the Bf 109, the Luftwaffe was forced to embark upon a major war equipped with machines which it regarded as unsuitable, and with no prospect of the replacement of most of them within two years.

The flying units were plagued by other weaknesses, such as poor bomb-sights and a lack of communication between bombers and their fighter escorts; but the shortage of bombs and fuel was the most prominent. Stocks of bombs were estimated to last for only four weeks' combat, and despite representations to Hitler, there was little prospect of any improvement. The Führer had said, 'Nobody inquires whether I have any bombs or ammunition, it is the number of aircraft and guns that count',[41] and the Luftwaffe had gone without. Even more serious was the shortage of aviation fuel, stocks of which were only some 690,000 cubic metres in mid-August, sufficient for just under four months of war, and, of these, only 420,000 cubic metres were fit for use owing to a shortage of ethyl fluid. The inadequacies in material were matched by inadequacies in pilots. The effort needed to develop an air force from virtually nothing, and to comply with Hitler's expansion programme, left little time or resources for an extensive pilot training scheme. Thus, at the beginning of the war, although the Luftwaffe possessed no less than 3,960 fully qualified front-line aircraft crews, there was a shortage of 173 crews and 139 fighter pilots. While no aircraft was prevented from flying because of this lack (due to the rate of aircraft unserviceability, which from ten per cent in front-line units at the outbreak of war soon grew to twenty to twenty-five per cent), it did mean that there were no reserve crews to make good the losses in action. Just as serious, were the often inadequate standards achieved. Regarding the general state of training, Jeschonnek stated that he was concerned at the slow progress being made 'with the further development of tactics. The fault lies with the lack of fully experienced formations to push development forward. The Luftwaffe Lehrdivision cannot cope with the problem unaided.' To this, General von Pohl added: 'Let us hope, then, that we don't get the wrong ideas. We must face up to the fact that we have to fight with moderately well trained formations.'[42]

At the outbreak of the Second World War, then, the resources of the Luftwaffe in material and personnel dictated to a significant degree the strategy which its leaders were forced to pursue. To a large extent, however, reality directly coincided with theory, and the Air Force, despite all its deficiencies, proved itself fully capable of giving adequate support to the Army's operations in one campaign after another. Certainly, the Luftwaffe was quite unfit to wage independent, 'Douhetian', operations against an enemy's homeland, and the most it could hope to achieve on its own was aerial ascendancy over an enemy's air defences. It was also ill-prepared to meet a determined air offensive against the Reich, although the probability of such an event in 1939 was remote. But for neither of these roles had the RLM prepared, and, apart from its plans to create a bomber force to blockade Britain's sea-lanes, there is no evidence to suggest that it believed its operations should be totally independent of those of the Army. The Luftwaffe generals recognised as well as did their Army counterparts that victory could only be guaranteed by the physical occupation of their enemy's territory, and that that could best be achieved by the support of the ground forces.

But what the commitment of the German Air Force to battle two and a half years too early did achieve, was to dictate the pace of events in every campaign in which it was to fight. Speed would be the essence of operations, not simply because this was the best way of defeating the enemy, but because it was the only means by which the Luftwaffe could avoid defeat. Lacking both the material and the men for a prolonged war on one front, let alone on two, the Luftwaffe was forced to concentrate all its resources in the support of the Army to help it to gain victory in the shortest possible time. Any distraction from this would be detrimental to the Luftwaffe's interests, for it did not even possess an aircraft industry that was capable of replacing high losses in sustained operations. Thus, action against the enemy's war economy, or the aerial defence of the Reich, would have to take second place to the support of the ground-forces, while long-term plans for the development of the Air Force would have to be sacrificed for short-term gains. As Jeschonnek realised shortly before the invasion of Poland: 'We must conduct a short war; everything must therefore be thrown into action at the outset.'[43] The Luftwaffe high command was, therefore, committed, whether it liked it or not, to that gamble as basic to its war-time strategy. Because war came upon it too soon, the German Air Force had no alternative but to follow such a course, dangerous though it was, and fatal though it proved to be.

IV

The Early Campaigns

Immediately before the campaign against Poland, Göring issued his first order-of-the-day of the war. It read:

> I have done my best, in the past few years, to make our Luftwaffe the largest and most powerful in the world. The creation of the Greater German Reich has been made possible largely by the strength and constant readiness of the Air Force. Born of the spirit of the German airmen in the first World War, inspired by faith in our Führer and Commander-in-Chief – thus stands the German Air Force to-day, ready to carry out every command of the Führer with lightning speed and undreamed-of might.[1]

Three weeks later, when Poland's armed forces lay shattered by one of the quickest campaigns known to history, Göring's words were shown correct. As the German high command noted about the actions of the air units in its official report: 'In close co-operation with the Army . . . their death defying valour saved the Army a vast number of casualties and contributed materially to ultimate victory'.[2]

The first, and major, task of the Luftwaffe during the invasion of Poland had been the destruction of the Polish Air Force. The importance of this mission was emphasised by the *Luftkriegführung*, which stated: 'Combat action against enemy air forces must be taken from the very beginning of a war. Neutralisation of enemy air power weakens the whole military power of the enemy, and serves to protect the friendly forces, the civilian population and the homeland. It also releases the offensive friendly air units for the execution of other missions which are of vital importance'.[3] This view was reaffirmed by Jeschonnek who, drawing on the lessons gained from war games in June 1939, stated: 'The damage which can be inflicted on a hostile army [from the air] in the first two days of war is in no way proportionate to the damage an enemy air force can inflict if it remains completely operable'.[4] Indeed, it was the Luftwaffe's view that action against opposing air forces was not only a precondition to the support of the ground forces, but an integral part of such support.

Fortunately for the Luftwaffe, the enemy air force which it had to destroy was neither large nor particularly effective. Of the 800 aircraft it possessed, only some 463 could be regarded as front-line combat machines ready for action. The 270 bombers, mostly PZL P-23 Karas, were considerably inferior to their German counterparts, although the new PZL P-37Bs compared favourably with the Do 17s. The 277 fighters were such, Kesselring remembered, as to claim 'respect'.[5] However, the PZL, P-7As and P-11Cs, though sturdy, were obsolete, and no match for the Bf 109s. Against this meagre force, the Luftwaffe disposed 1,939 aircraft, of which some ten per cent were unserviceable on the day war broke out. Of these 648 were bombers, 219 dive-bombers, thirty ground-attack aircraft, 210 fighters, and 474 reconnaissance aeroplanes and transports, divided between two Luftflotten, commanded respectively by Generals Albert Kesselring and Alexander Löhr, a fifty-four-year-old Austrian who had been head of the Austrian Air Force. In addition, the Luftwaffe's high command kept 133 reconnaissance and transport machines directly under its control, the Army maintained 288 reconnaissance and communication aircraft, and the fighter defence units in eastern Germany had 216 Bf 109s. Kesselring's Luftflotte I consisted of Fliegerdivision 7 under General Ulrich Grauert, the Lehrdivision under General Förster, and the East Prussia Command under General Wilhelm Wimmer, and was committed to the northern sector of operations; Löhr's Luftflotte 4, allocated to the south, was made up of Fliegerdivision 2 under General Bruno Lörzer and the Special Purposes Air Command under General Wolfram von Richthofen.

According to the official pronouncements coming from OKW, the world was led to believe that the Polish Air Force was effectively destroyed within the first forty-eight hours of the campaign. On 1st September, the German Armed Forces High Command reported: 'Today, the Luftwaffe, in repeated, powerful attacks, bombarded and destroyed military emplacements on numerous Polish aerodromes . . . [and] succeeded in establishing its air supremacy over Poland'.[6] The following day, OKW announced: 'Successes achieved today justify the conclusion that the strength of the Polish Air Force has been more seriously impaired. The Luftwaffe now dominates the whole of Poland and is free to undertake other tasks for the protection of the Reich'.[7] Such sentiments were repeated on the 3rd. Indeed, the Luftwaffe had made a determined effort to destroy its rival. On the first day, despite the poor weather which inhibited operations, widespread destruction was caused at the airfields of Cracow, Lvov, Radom, Vilna, Lublin, Warsaw and many others. Even aircraft factories in the Polish capital were bombed. But, as the Luftwaffe commanders asked themselves, where was the Polish Air Force? Except for a brief appearance over Warsaw, and for the burnt out skeletons of a few machines caught on the ground, the enemy aircraft had, as Kesselring wrote, 'To a large extent . . . remained unseen'.[8] The Luftwaffe high command was worried, and, that night, ordered: '. . . the whereabouts of the Polish bombers shall be located . . . pending [which] . . . our own bomber units will remain on the ground in readiness for immediate attack'.[9] The General Staff was warned that the Poles, having withdrawn their machines to camouflaged bases, were preparing for a counter-attack; to prevent that, the

Luftwaffe was to keep a large part of its bomber force inactive in readiness for an assault on those bases. Until the enemy aeroplanes had been accounted for, support for the ground forces would continue to take second priority.

The 2nd September, then, saw a continued attack on the Polish airfields. Much material destruction was recorded, but, again, the Polish bomber force could not be located on the ground. As one Polish officer, Major Kalinowski, wrote: 'The German Luftwaffe did exactly what we expected. It attacked our airfields and tried to wipe out our aircraft on the ground. In retrospect, it seems quite naïve of the Germans to have believed that, during the preceding days of high political tension, and with their own obviously aggressive intentions, we would leave our units sitting at their peace-time bases. The fact of the matter is that, by 31st August, not a single serviceable aeroplane remained on them'.[10] Thus, the Polish Air Force survived the initial onslaught, to remain in action until the beginning of the second week of the campaign, and to account for 126 German aircraft, as well as drop 200 tons of bombs. Moreover, the Polish bomber force was able to attack the German Army's spearheads on a number of occasions. However, technical and numerical inferiority was soon to tell, and Polish aerial activity, never very great, diminished daily. In the first five days of fighting, no fewer than 116 Polish fighters were destroyed in aerial combat. Particularly damaging was the Luftwaffe's destruction of the enemy's lines of communications, which had the effect of paralysing his command and of inhibiting the supply of his Air Force as much as of his Army. Kalinowski wrote: 'The turning point was 8th September. The supply situation had become hopeless. More and more of our aircraft became unusable. There were no spare parts. Just a few bombers continued operating until the 16th'.[11] On the 17th, after it had lost over 330 machines, the Polish Air Force received orders to withdraw its remaining aeroplanes to Romania, and 116 later landed there.

However, whatever the position of the Polish Air Force, by the 3rd the Luftwaffe believed it to pose no threat; the full support of ground operations could begin. Not that Luftwaffe units had been inactive in this respect since the beginning of the campaign. At dawn on the 1st, one Gruppe of the Hs 123s in von Richthofen's command undertook the first direct support operation of the war, with considerable success, attacking entrenched Polish soldiers at the village of Panki just over the border. Flying in support of 10th Army, the strongest and most important of the five armies in the campaign, the Hs 123s flew up to ten sorties a day, keeping close to the advance of the mechanised XIV Corps. Experience was to teach the pilots that it was not the armament of their biplanes which had the greatest effect on the enemy troops, but the sound their engines made at certain revolutions. It was found that an airscrew speed of 1,800 rpm made a noise similar to heavy machine gun fire, inspiring terror amongst men and animals alike. Such a tactic was particularly effective in dispersing advancing or retreating columns. Ironically, when such a noise was made, it proved impossible to fire the aircraft's machine guns, as they were designed to fire through the airscrews rotating at lower speeds.

In its support role, the Luftwaffe was extremely effective. General von Reichenau, Commander of 10th Army in the south, wrote to von Richthofen:

> I should like to express my sincere thanks and grateful appreciation to you and to the units under your command for the effective support rendered to the Tenth Army during the battle of Sochaczew. I myself was a witness on several occasions to the extreme effectiveness and accuracy of the operations carried out by your units. It is my personal conviction that our victory could not have been so complete without the support of the Luftwaffe.[12]

Indirect support of the ground troops predominated over direct support by a ratio of five to four. In the first five days, no less than 4,806 sorties were made against targets such as railway junctions, highways and military depots, compared with 3,746 against enemy batteries, strong-points and positions. A General Staff study later revealed that, as a result of attacks against the railways, the Poles were able to bring into action only thirty-seven infantry divisions of the forty-five they had mobilised, eleven of the sixteen cavalry brigades and seven of the border guard brigades. During the battle of the Radom Pocket, the Luftwaffe halted all rail and road traffic in northern and eastern Poland, and thereby frustrated Polish efforts to muster a counter-attack force at Kielce. By 8th September, all movement on the major routes Poznan-Kutno-Warsaw, Crakow-Radom-Deblin and Crakov-Tarnov-Lvov had been halted. Continuous harassment from the air and the destruction of vital bridges also prevented an orderly retreat by Polish forces, and the establishment of a line of resistance west of the Vistula. The Commander of the Polish Poznan Army, General Kutrzeba, recorded the effects of air bombardment:

> Towards 1000 hours the enemy commenced vigorous air attacks against the bridges of Vitkovice. In point of the number of aircraft committed, the severity of the individual strikes, and the acrobatic daring displayed, the [enemy air operation] represented a record. Every movement, every troop concentration, and all march routes were taken under annihilating fire from the air. . . . It was Hell come to Earth. The bridges were destroyed, the fords were blocked, the anti-aircraft and part of the other artillery forces were annihilated. . . . Continuation of the battle would have been nothing but a matter of holding out, and to have remained in position would have posed the imminent threat that the German air forces would have turned the whole place into a graveyard, since anti-aircraft defences in any form were completely lacking.[13]

Indeed, it was the efforts of the Luftwaffe that were primarily instrumental in preventing the Poznan Army from inflicting damaging wounds on the rear of the German 8th and 10th Armies during their advance on Warsaw. By the 19th, the battle for the Poznan Army was over, and 170,000 Polish soldiers were taken into captivity. Such had been the success of the Luftwaffe, and the speed of operations on the ground, that on 12th September the withdrawal of air units to the West began, sixteen days before the campaign was over.

But before the fighting ended, the Luftwaffe was to undertake one, final, decisive act: the bombing of Warsaw. Military targets such as aircraft factories within the boundaries of the Polish capital had been attacked from the beginning of the war, but the Luftwaffe had made no attempt to undertake the destruction of the city; indeed, the indiscriminate killing of civilians, so earnestly advocated by Douhet and his disciples, was specifically forbidden in German orders. On 2nd September, for example, the General Staff called for an attack on Warsaw's military targets only, and stipulated that they were to be spared 'if situated in heavily populated areas'.[14] By the 16th, Warsaw was encircled by the Germans, and was declared a 'fortress' by the Poles. No less than 100,000 Polish troops erected barricades and prepared themselves for hard fighting in street battles. A German officer went to the Polish military governor to persuade him to capitulate, but was not received. Leaflet raids over the capital were mounted on five separate days, exhorting the inhabitants to spare themselves senseless sacrifice by yielding. On four further occasions, the Polish military leaders were asked to surrender the city. An air attack scheduled for the 17th was cancelled when the Poles announced that they would send an emissary to negotiate the evacuation of the civilian population. The negotiator did not appear. On that same day, the Russians invaded eastern Poland, aiming to reach Warsaw by 3rd October, in fulfilment of their non-aggression pact with the Germans, which called for a partition of Poland along the Narev, Vistula and San rivers. Hitler, desirous of having a frontier further east, along the river Bug, ordered that Warsaw was to be in German hands as soon as possible. Thus, on the 25th, more than 400 bomb-carriers dropped 500 tons of high explosive and seventy-two tons of incendiary bombs on selected military targets on the western part of the city for the better part of a day, accompanied by artillery fire and ground attack. It was a remarkably amateur affair when compared with the bombardments that were to come later in the war. Part of the bomber force consisted of thirty Ju 52s laden with incendiary bombs, which the crews threw out of the side doors with coal shovels. The Army generals were furious at the bombing, since the resulting fires and smoke merely masked the targets at which their artillery wished to shoot. Hitler, however, insisted that the attack should continue. The following day, the commander of Warsaw sued for terms, and early on the 28th the capital of Poland surrendered. About this, and other events, the French Air Attaché in Warsaw, General Armengaud, reported: 'I must emphasise that operations by the German Air Force have been in conformity with the rules of warfare'.[15]

The campaign in Poland was, by any standards, a considerable success for German arms. Soldiers and airmen alike had performed well. In twenty-eight days, the Luftwaffe had lost 285 aircraft destroyed and 279 damaged (a quarter of which would be repaired and returned to the front-line units) and

539 airmen had been either killed, wounded or missing. In return, the Polish Air Force had been smashed, and the German Army's operations made substantially easier. The generals who had led the Luftwaffe units were content with the result. Löhr stated that 'The Luftwaffe was to operate for the first time in world history as an independent arm. Thereby it was to open up new aspects of a strategy which, in its principles, had remained unaltered throughout the course of history'.[16] Kesselring regarded the campaign as 'the touchstone of the potentialities of the German Air Force, and an apprenticeship of special significance'.[17] But, nevertheless, the victory had been won over a markedly inferior opponent; as Göring was to admit in 1943: 'There was no *tour de force* there.'

The experiences of the Luftwaffe, both in the Spanish Civil War and in Poland, served to convince its leaders that their strategic principles were valid. Certainly, the destruction of the enemy air force, even one so small as that of the Poles, had proved more difficult than originally imagined, and, equally as surely, co-ordination between the requirements of the ground forces and the employment of the air units had to be improved; but, overall, there was no reason to change the basis on which the Luftwaffe had fought. Von Richthofen's use of the Air Liaison Detachments (Luftnachrichten-verbindungstruppe), which were sent into the front-line with the Army's spearhead units, had proved invaluable: requests for air support could thereby be radioed directly to his headquarters, without having to go through the time-consuming network of front-line to division to corps to Luftflotte and back down to Fliegerdivision, and decisions concerning air attack would be decided on the spot. Moreover, air liaison officers could suggest to field commanders that air strikes were both suitable and available in a given situation, something of which Army officers were then not always aware. The efficacy of the dive-bomber had been proved, even though it had operated with little or no enemy interference, and the He 111s and Do 17s had also shown their worth in support operations. Mistakes had been made; on one occasion, for example, dive-bombers had destroyed bridges over the Vistula just as a German armoured division was about to cross them. But such incidents were rare, and both the Army and the Luftwaffe emerged from the campaign convinced of the value of air support. As the OKW's verdict on events in Poland stated: 'In closest cooperation with the Army, bombers and dive-bombers repeatedly attacked block-houses, batteries, massed troops, units on the march, troops detraining etc. Their death-defying valour saved the Army a vast number of casualties and contributed materially to ultimate victory.'[18] Even Germany's enemies were strong in their praise for the Luftwaffe's feats. General Armengaud believed that the Luftwaffe's role in the Polish campaign had been 'the most decisive because the defenders' manoeuvrability was frustrated, and because the command is made blind and cannot get its orders through'.[19] The effectiveness of the Luftwaffe was also referred to by French Intelligence, which believed that the wide-ranging air strikes 'resulted in almost complete paralysis of the Polish High Command, which was incapable either of completing mobilisation or concentration, delivering supplies, or executing any kind of co-ordinated manoeuvre'. This was a verdict upheld throughout the world.

On 27th September, the day on which Warsaw capitulated, Hitler addressed his service chiefs at the Reich Chancellery. He had decided to exploit the momentum of Germany's victory and attack in the West before the Anglo-French forces were ready. The military leaders, including Göring, were aghast. The Wehrmacht was simply not prepared for such a campaign. The Luftwaffe, for example, was extremely short of bombs, stocks of which would be exhausted within the first two weeks of fighting. Demands on the armament industries from the other two services were such that not until 12th October would Hitler allow any increase in the output of bombs, by which time it was clear that the Allies had rejected his offers of peace. Then, he ordered that adequate stocks be established, and Milch was given powers to organise an urgent programme of manufacture. Because of shortages of steel, which, for the Armed Services, were of the order of 600,000 tons a month, concrete bombs filled with shrapnel were even produced, so greedy was the Luftwaffe for the munitions of war.

But, heeding neither the arguments of his generals nor the anxieties of his ally, Italy, the Führer set his mind firmly on attack. He wanted to bring the conflict to an end while Germany's military advantage was at its height; he believed that every month of inactivity would see a relative decline in German strength vis-à-vis the Allies. As Hitler had told his generals on 23rd November: 'My decision is unchangeable. I shall attack France and England at the most favourable and quickest moment. Breach of the neutrality of Belgium and Holland is meaningless. No one will question that when we have won. . . . Without attack, the war is not to be ended victoriously.'[20] The dictator, however, shrank from recognising that he had unleashed a second world war. In January, he authorised the Navy to refer to the war as 'der englische Krieg', and decided that the campaigns in Poland and in the West would be known to history as the 'Great German War of Liberation'. He was confident of success. As he had assured the Italian Ambassador, '1940 will bring us victory'.[21] His troops in the West, two million of them, were ready to occupy northern France, Belgium and Holland; only the weather could keep them from attacking.

The plan for Hitler's invasion of the West, code-named 'Yellow', had been drawn up in October 1939. An attack, originally scheduled to begin on 12th November, would be mounted through Belgium to occupy northern France (Holland was later included by means of a Führer Directive). Poor weather, however, caused its postponement, much to the relief of the generals. On 9th November, 'A' day was re-scheduled for the 19th; on the 13th it was put off to the 22nd; on the 16th it was set for the 26th; on the 20th for 3rd December; and on 27th November for 9th December. Poor meteorological reports from the Luftwaffe were the reason. Patiently, the generals waited for the code-word 'Rhine' to be flashed to their headquarters as the signal for the attack; instead they received only 'Elbe' (withhold attack). And so it went on during the severe winter of 1939-40, 'A' day being put off from 9th December to the 11th, then to the 17th, and then 1st January 1940. Finally, on 27th December, the invasion was set for an unspecified date between the 9th and 14th January, a period when Hitler hoped for clear, if cold, weather, frozen ground, strong ice, and good flying conditions. Should poor weather then prevail, the operation would have to be postponed until after the thaw, to the spring.

On the afternoon of 10th January, Hitler and his OKW chiefs met Halder, Chief of the Army General Staff, to discuss the forthcoming invasion. The Luftwaffe meteorologists had forecast ten to fourteen days of clear winter weather, and the invasion was, therefore, set to begin at fifteen minutes before dawn on 17th January. During the preceding four or five days, the Luftwaffe would undertake heavy bombing raids on French air force installations. That evening, OKH sent warning signals to all the troop commands: the invasion was on. Hitler's confidence was high. However, shortly before midday the following day, the 11th, news reached the Führer in Berlin which caused him considerable consternation. Just a few hours before the meeting at which the time of the invasion had been fixed, a light aeroplane carrying highly secret documents about Plan Yellow had crash-landed in Belgium near Mechelen-sur-Meuse, twelve miles north of Maastricht. As Hitler shouted to Jodl, 'It's things like this that can lose us the war!'[22] The following day, Jodly wrote in his diary: 'If the enemy is in possession of all the files, the situation is catastrophic'.[23]

This was the so-called Mechelen incident, which, many historians allege, caused the final postponement of the invasion until May, and thereby allowed the formulation of a new plan of operations immeasurably superior to that planned for January, which the Anglo-French forces were prepared to meet. Thus, so the argument runs, the Germans were assured of victory. Even generals closely connected with the incident have agreed that this was so. After the war, General Kurt Student, commander of the airborne forces, stated that, after hearing of the loss of the plans, Hitler 'at first . . . wanted to strike immediately, but fortunately refrained – and decided to drop the original plan entirely. This was replaced by the Manstein plan'.[24] General Warlimont, Jodl's deputy in OKW, also stated that Hitler decided to change Plan Yellow, and that this was 'chiefly due to the air accident'.[25] The generals, however, were mistaken. The Mechelen incident had no such effect: Plan Yellow would have been postponed and the plan altered even had that incident not taken place.

The story of the incident is as follows. A Major Helmut Reinberger had been detailed as a liaison officer to the staff of a transport unit (Ju 52s), part of Fliegerdivision 7 under Student, to help prepare the plans for airborne landings in Holland and Belgium. He was on his way, by rail, to a conference in Cologne at the headquarters of 22 Air Landing Division (an Army formation), carrying the operational instructions of Luftflotte 2 for the invasion, which intimated that an offensive was near, and also details of an airborne attack between the Meuse and Sambre rivers. Congested railway traffic in the Ruhr area caused him to break his journey at Münster, where, on the evening of 9th January, he stayed at the officers' mess. There, he came across a Major Hönmanns, commandant of the nearby airfield at Lodden-heide. Hönmanns had been a pilot during the First World War, and had since then retained much pleasure in flying. On this particular occasion, he was also anxious to visit his wife in Cologne, Reinberger's destination. So he offered Reinberger a lift in an aeroplane. The parachute officer knew that it was forbidden to carry secret orders and maps by air, but his impatience to be in Cologne was too great. The offer was accepted, and the two men set off the following morning in a Bf 108 Taifun (Typhoon) courier aeroplane.

After taking off, Hönmanns lost his way in thick cloud, set his course too far to the west, and then accidentally shut off the fuel supply of his aeroplane (a type which he had flown only once before). The engine stopped, and the aircraft had to make a forced landing. At first the two officers thought they were near the river Rhine, but they soon realised that it was the Meuse, and that they were inside Belgian territory. Reinberger began to destroy his papers by setting fire to them, but Belgian soldiers got to him before they were burnt. The two Majors were then taken to the local police headquarters, where Reinberger's second attempt to burn the documents, this time by throwing them into a stove in the room in which he was being interrogated, was frustrated by a Belgian officer, who thrust his hand into the fire to retrieve the smouldering fragments. The two officers went into Belgian detention and then captivity, ending the war as prisoners in Canada. Ironically, just as the plane was making its forced landing, Milch was receiving a high decoration from the Belgian Ambassador!

Information of this incident reached Berlin through diplomatic channels the following morning, and was immediately relayed to the Reich Chancellery. Hitler, not unnaturally, was furious with the Luftwaffe, and this upset Göring. Kesselring remembered that 'Never before or afterwards did I see Göring so down in the dumps, and that is saying something with Göring's temperament'.[26] The Luftwaffe Commander later recorded: 'The Führer rebuked me frightfully, as the Commander-in-Chief of the unfortunate courier, for having allowed a major part of our western mobilisation, and the very fact of such German plans, to be betrayed. Look what a ghastly burden on my nerves it is to know that in the Führer's view my Luftwaffe officers have thrown this, the German people's mortal struggle, into jeopardy'.[27] In response to his Führer's anger, Göring dismissed the commander of the two Majors, General Felmy, commander of Luftflotte 2 (replacing him with Kesselring) and removed his chief of staff, Colonel Josef Kammhuber (later to be in charge of night fighters, and a future head of the new German air force after the war) to a bomber group in Bavaria. On his wife's suggestion, the

Luftwaffe Commander also consulted a clairvoyant, who assured him that the documents had been destroyed; this news was straightway told to Hitler, and confirmed what the dictator already believed. After the Mechelen incident, the Belgian newspapers, with only one exception, had reported that the German officers had managed to destroy their documents. No doubt this was inspired by Belgian Intelligence. On the 12th, General Wenninger, the German military attaché in Brussels, notified OKW that the two Majors (whom he had interviewed in captivity) had assured him that they had destroyed all plans apart from a few insignificant pieces (they were, in fact, three parts burnt). This report he presented in person to Hitler the following day. As Jodl put in his diary: 'Result: Dispatch case burned for certain'.[28] The Führer was relieved for, as Jodl had impressed upon him, had the plans fallen into enemy hands, the situation would have been serious indeed: German intentions would have been thoroughly known.

The Mechelen incident, then, did not deter Hitler from his course. At 3.15 p.m. on the 11th, even before he knew whether the plans had been destroyed, he remained cool and confirmed his decision to launch the invasion. It was not until 1.00 p.m. on the 13th, after his interview with Wenninger, that he ordered the attack to be cancelled, and then it was simply because a weather report had indicated that there would be heavy fog between the 16th and 19th. The invasion was postponed, yet again, this time to the 20th. But the meteorological prospects grew worse; a thaw was on its way. On the afternoon of the 16th, the Führer finally called off the offensive until the spring.

The Mechelen incident affected neither the commencement nor the cancellation of the invasion, nor the nature of the plan after the final postponement. By the 16th, it was clear to the Germans that the Allies knew about their plans, and that Major Reinberger's documents had not been fully destroyed. The German military attaché in the Hague reported that, on the night of the 10th, the King of the Belgians had had a long telephone conversation with the Queen of Holland. On the 11th, the Belgians had passed on copies of the remnants to the English, French and Dutch; the Allied armies were put on the alert, and, on the afternoon of the 14th, Gamelin, the French Commander-in-Chief, moved more divisions up to the Belgian frontier. That same day, a French cavalry column entered Luxembourg. It was decided not to enter Belgium before the invasion, for there was still the fear, felt especially by the Belgians, that the Mechelen documents might be a 'plant' designed to distract the Allies from the intended area of assault. The Belgians did not mobilise, but Belgian defences were improved, and the frontier barriers with France were removed to permit passage should it be needed. The Allies were ready, but there was no alarm. As Gamelin wrote 'The information gathered from the German airmen did not, as far as I was concerned, have any influence on our decisions! Plan D [to meet the German invaders] was to remain unaltered'.[29] As Churchill noted in his war history, 'In spite of all the German major's papers, no fresh action of any kind was taken by the Allies or the threatened States'.[30]

German intelligence noted the Allies' preparations. Furthermore, they had broken the Belgian codes, and much could be gleaned from that. On the evening of the 13th, the Belgian military attaché in Berlin had warned Brussels that the invasion would begin the next day. On the 17th, the Belgian Foreign Minister, Paul-Henri Spaak, sent for the German ambassador to Brussels and told him, as the latter reported to Berlin, that 'the plane which made an emergency landing on 10th January had put into Belgian hands a document of the most extraordinary and serious nature, which contained clear proof of an intention to attack. It was not just an operations plan, but an attack order worked out in every detail, in which only the time remained to be inserted'.[31] The Germans were not quite sure whether Spaak was bluffing, but his story did agree with the facts as they had by then come to know them. However, even though it appeared that the Mechelen incident had revealed far more than at first was supposed, little was done to alter the basic nature of Plan Yellow. On the 16th, Hitler told Jodl that he was going to put the entire operation on 'a new basis' so as to ensure 'secrecy and surprise'.[32] This did not entail a complete revision of the plan. Instead, it meant that the four-day alert (known to the Allies) would be abandoned, and the troops given only twenty-four hours in which to deploy into their final dispositions along the frontier. On 20th January, at a conference between Hitler, Göring, von Brauchitsch, Halder, Jeschonnek, Keitel, Jodl and a few others, at which the Führer reiterated his demand for strict military security, the 'new basis' was confirmed. In addition, the period between the decision to attack and the invasion was shortened to just three days. Thus, it was hoped, the enemy would be caught off guard (expecting as he was a four-day warning period), and surprise ensured. A final version of the OKH plan of 29th October 1939, incorporating these charges, was produced on 30th January. On this plan, issued twenty days after Major Reinberger had made his forced landing, the Wehrmacht was prepared to invade the West in the spring. The Mechelen incident had done nothing to alter the strategic basis of Plan Yellow.

However, the incident was to have one major, and lasting, impact on the German conduct not just of the campaign in the West but of the entire war. It came at a time when Hitler was already concerned about lax security; two lesser incidents, also involving Luftwaffe personnel, had previously been brought to his attention. In one, an officer had dropped a dispatch case from a moving train, and, in the other, an adjutant of a Luftflotte had lost a file of secret documents. But those were as nothing to what had happened at Mechelen. As a direct result, on the 15th, Hitler issued his 'Basic Order No. 1' on security, and stipulated that it be displayed on posters in every military headquarters. Henceforth, no-one was to be given any classified information that was not directly relevant to his job, and, even then, he was not to be told earlier, or more, than was absolutely necessary. The order read:

1. No agency or officer will receive any information pertaining to a classified project unless it is absolutely necessary, for reasons of duty,

that they obtain such information.

2. No agency or officer will receive more detailed information regarding a classified project than is strictly necessary to permit them to carry out their assigned missions in connection with it.

3. No agency or officer will receive any information pertaining to a classified project prior to the last possible moment consistent with effective performance of their work on that project.

4. This directive expressly forbids the automatic forwarding of orders, whose secrecy is of prime importance, in accordance with established distribution lists.[33]

While, at first glance, this order might appear simply a desirable security measure, its consequences were disastrous. As General Nielsen wrote after the war:

Because of this directive, no one in a position of military responsibility was ever informed of the ultimate aims of the Führer, and no one – not even the members of the Armed Forces High Command – was given access to sufficient information to construct an accurate picture of the over-all situation. No military leader, whether he be a member of the General Staff or in charge of some other important military function, can fulfil his mission effectively unless he is informed of the ultimate objectives of the political leader and is familiar with the over-all situation. Otherwise he is like a hen who pecks about in the dark and occasionally manages to find a grain of corn.[34]

Such was the result of the Mechelen incident.

Before Hitler could put into operation Plan Yellow, his interest in the West broadened to take account of Norway and Denmark. On 2nd September, he had declared the inviolability of Norway, so long as it was not infringed by a third power; yet, on 13th December, he ordered OKW to investigate how best to seize that country. This was a precautionary measure taken because of the growing Allied interest shown in blocking shipments of Swedish iron ore, which came through Norway, shipments vital to German production. On 6th January 1940, the British Foreign Secretary, Lord Halifax, declared that Britain would prevent German merchantmen from using Norwegian territorial waters, even if this meant that the Royal Navy would have to conduct operations within them. A month later the Allies decided to land four divisions in early spring at the important Norwegian port of Narvik, and to proceed from there to occupy the Swedish iron mines of Gallivare and thus gain access to airfields from which to operate against the Reich. Although this was unknown to the Germans, sufficient was clear to make it imperative that they moved fast to forestall probable Allied interference.

By the middle of January, OKW had finished its preliminary investigations, and had proposed that the matter be taken further by a group headed by Milch, with a naval officer as his chief of staff and an operations officer from the Army. The plan would be code-named Auster (Oyster). Hitler, however, would have none of that. The group, which held its only meeting on 14th January, was disbanded, the Führer fearing, in the light of the Mechelen incident, that his Air Force was quite incapable of guarding secrets; instead, he placed the responsibility for planning with the OKW, and on the 27th issued a directive stating that the operations in Scandinavia would be carried out under his 'immediate and personal influence'.[35] The OKW planning staff, however, proved incapable of undertaking the organisation for such a complicated combined operation as 'Weserübung' (as it was then code-named), and, on 21st February, a corps headquarters, XXI under General von Falkenhorst, was detached from the Army and made responsible to OKW for the planning of the invasion of Denmark and Norway. In addition to his army corps, von Falkenhorst was to have all the Luftwaffe units assigned to the invasion consolidated in General Hans Geisler's Fliegerkorps X, under his control. Göring, ever conscious of his prerogatives, reacted strongly to this and, after a short but sharp battle, the Luftwaffe was allowed to retain control over its units. Requests for air support were to be transmitted from Falkenhorst to the Luftwaffe General Staff whenever necessary. Göring's success in preserving his autonomy was in stark contrast to the failure of the Army leaders, whose bitterness at the passing of XXI Corps from their control to OKW found no outward expression.

On 20th March, Fliegerkorps X issued its operational plan. While the Army occupied Denmark and Norway, the combat units of the Luftwaffe were to give demonstrations of strength so as to force the peaceful submission of the people and governments. Only if there was resistance was action to be taken. In contrast to the psychological role assigned to the bombers and fighters, the Ju 52s were to support the Army by carrying airborne infantry and paratroops to certain points in Denmark and Norway. There was some element of risk from the small Norwegian air force, based largely on Oslo, and from the RAF. However, it was hoped that the Norwegian aeroplanes would be destroyed on the ground, and that the RAF, based far away in Scotland, would not appear before midday on the first day of the invasion, by which time it could be dealt with by the fighters and anti-aircraft artillery already established on occupied airfields. After the initial invasion, the main task of the Luftwaffe would be to frustrate any landing attempts made by the Allies, and to maintain supplies and replacements for the German troops. For this, the force allocated to Geisler consisted of some 1,000 aircraft, evenly divided between combat and transport units. Medium bombers, mainly He 111s, predominated over the Ju 87 dive-bombers (290 compared with forty) since only they had the necessary range to operate freely over Norway and its approach waters. In addition, Fliegerkorps X had thirty Bf 109s and seventy Bf 110s, forty reconnaissance and thirty coastal aircraft, and five hundred transports, mainly Ju 52s, but with a few Ju 90s and FW 200Bs (civil aircraft), together with two Ju 89 heavy bomber prototypes. Of the transport aircraft, some 340 were taken from pilot training schools to be used to land men and equipment once the airfields had been secured. The 160 Ju 52s of Flieger-divison 7 would ferry the paratroops and air-landing troops to their targets.

The Germans managed to forestall the Allied invasion of Norway. At 0500 hours on 9th April, Operation Weserübung opened according to plan, with the crossing of the Danish frontier by land forces and with seaborne landings on Danish islands and in Norwegian ports. In Denmark, air operations began ninety minutes later, with paratroop drops at the two Aalborg airfields, followed by infantry borne by Ju 52s. The airfields fell with ease, one of them to a handful of Bf 110s, and the whole of Denmark was in German hands within the day. In Norway, however, matters were different. There, the seaborne landings at the ports had been followed three and a half hours later by Bf 110 attacks on Stavanger-Sola and Oslo-Fornebu airfields, which were soon occupied by paratroops and airborne infantry (the Oslo airfield had been captured by the Bf 110s due to an opportune crash by one of them, and to bad weather causing the non-appearance of the paratroops). Further airfields were occupied, and the Norwegian air force, with the exception of nine Gladiator biplanes, was destroyed on the ground. These few remaining aircraft, however, posed little threat, and were shot down before the day was out. But Norwegian resistance was far from over. It was to take a further two months before the campaign was finally won.

Opposition from the Norwegian Army was strong, and was bolstered by three Allied landings between 15th and 19th April. The situation became so tense that Hitler suffered from his first panic of the war, even ordering the evacuation of the vital port of Narvik until persuaded otherwise by the OKW's Chief of Operations, General Jodl. To meet the opposition on the ground and to prevent British ships from landing their cargoes in Norway, Fliegerkorps X was strengthened. At the peak of the fighting in early May, the number of medium bombers had increased by seventy, Ju 87s by ten, Bf 109s by twenty, reconnaissance aeroplanes by twenty, and maritime by ninety, to bring the grand total of combat aircraft to 710. At the same time, the transport arm had been considerably reduced, being progressively with-drawn to Germany to prepare for the forthcoming campaign in the West. They had, however, performed stirling service during Operation Weserübung; no less than 3,018 transport sorties had been flown, during which 29,280 soldiers and airmen, 2,376 tons of supplies and 259,300 gallons of petrol were flown to strategic points in Norway. The commitment of the Luftwaffe to the Norwegian campaign, having been greater than expected, had necessitated a higher command than a Fliegerkorps. Thus, on 15th April, the headquarters of Luftflotte 5 was established at Hamburg, to exercise command over Norway, and on the 24th it was moved to Oslo. The temporary commander was Milch, who retained his office as Secretary of State. He entered upon his new task with vigour. He encouraged the development of new airfields, and increased to the fullest possible extent the operational sorties of his force.

Milch was to prove a particularly strong commander during the crisis at Narvik, when even von Falkenhorst was countenancing withdrawal. There, the value of air support, whether by transport or bomber, had again been proved, and had shown itself to be a major factor in the German victory. Of particular significance for the future, was the air action against the enemy navies. This began as early as 8th April, when the British Home Fleet was attacked off Bergen by eighty-eight bombers. One destroyer was sunk, three cruisers were damaged by near misses, and a battleship received a direct hit. On the 17th, a Royal Navy cruiser was heavily damaged. But of far more importance for the outcome of the campaign was the operation mounted by Fliegerkorps X on the Allied landings at Namsos and Andalsnes. Begun on the 20th with 150 bombers and sixty Ju 87s, the attack was so intense that it prevented strong formations of supplies from being landed to reinforce the troops already on Norwegian soil, and thus ensured the failure of the enemy's plans. As the British Commander at Namos commented: 'I see little chance of carrying out decisive, or indeed any, operations, unless enemy air activity is considerably restricted'.[36] Without such actions on the part of the Air Force, it is no exaggeration to state that the German offensive might well have ended in failure. As General Jodl wrote in his official report: 'The Luftwaffe proved to be the decisive factor in the success of the operation. It bore the main burden of the fight against the enemy fleet, which was numerically far superior to our Navy. . . . The Air Force has provided proof, decisive for future developments, that no fleet, however strong it may be, can operate in the long run within the close effective range of an enemy air force'.[39]

While fighting continued in Norway, the Germans began their invasion of the West. The plan which they put into operation was very different from that on which they had been prepared to base their calculations for success a few months previously. Instead of a frontal attack which pushed through Belgium and northern France to the Channel coast, the German Army was to mount a strong left hook through the Ardennes by General von Rundstedt's Army Group A, at a point where the Allies were weakest and least expecting attack. To the north, a frontal assault would be undertaken by General von Bock's Army Group B, and to the south, General von Leeb's Army Group C would cover the Maginot Line. The decisive attack would take place in the centre, where von Rundstedt's Army Group, spearheaded by strong panzer forces, would cross the Meuse at Sedan and move westwards to reach the Channel at the mouth of the Somme. There it would be in an excellent position to attack the rear of the main enemy forces that were engaging Army Group B, and to encircle and destroy them.

In support of this plan of operations, the Luftwaffe had two priorities, arrived at both from pre-war theory and from experience gained in Poland. Hitler's guide-lines laid down in October 1939 stated: '. . . it will be the

Luftwaffe's task not only to destroy or at least put out of action enemy air forces, but also primarily to hinder or prevent the enemy High Command from putting its decisions into effect'.[38] Around 4,000 aircraft were allocated to the attack, divided between two Luftflotten. In the north, Kesselring's Luftflotte 2 supported Army Group B, and consisted of Fliegerkorps I, IV, and VIII, Fliegerdivision 7 (air landing), and Fliegerdivision 9, employed in a maritime role, under Generals Grauert, Kurt Pflugbeil, von Richthofen, Kurt Student and Joachim Coeler respectively. To the south, Sperrle's Luftflotte 3 supported both Army Group B and C, and was composed of Fliegerkorps II and V under Generals Lörzer and von Greim, which had the major share of the fourteen Kampfgeschwader employed in the West. Between them, the two Luftflotten deployed 1,120 He 111s, Do 17s and Ju 88s, 324 Ju 87s, 42 Hs 123s. 1,106 Bf 109s, and 248 Bf 110s, together with some 600 reconnaissance aircraft and 500 transports. To meet this force, the French, British, Dutch and Belgians possessed between them a total of 1,151 fighters, two thirds of which were slower than the machines they were supposed to intercept, and 1,045 bombers and ground-attack aircraft. In Britain, the RAF possessed a further 1,200 combat aircraft, but the majority of these would have to be retained for home defence. None of the French fighters could rival the Bf 109E. The Bloch 152, the Morane-Saulnier 406 and the Curtiss 75A Hawk were from fifty to seventy-five mph slower than their German counterparts, and the new Dewoitine 520, although only fifteen mph slower, were few in number.

True to form, the Luftwaffe began the campaign with a heavy assault on the enemy air forces. At first light on 10th May, more than 300 Heinkels and Dorniers from six Geschwader attacked twenty-two airfields in Holland, Belgium and northern France. By the evening, the Dutch Air Force was rendered impotent, and in the following days was never able to put into the sky more than twelve aeroplanes to meet the invader. The plight of the Belgian Air Force was similar, while the French squadrons also fared badly. Indeed, on the first day only the British escaped serious damage on the ground, with just one squadron of eighteen Blenheims totally incapacitated after the day's onslaught was over. But the following days were to exact their toll. By the end of the 12th, the RAF had lost half of its aircraft on the Continent, while the French Armée de l'Air in the north had suffered a similar proportion of casualties. German fighters and anti-aircraft fire proved highly effective in inhibiting Allied offensive operations. On 10th May, for example, thirty-two RAF Fairey Battles were sent against German columns; thirteen were shot down, and the rest damaged. Of the six Blenheims sent against Wallhaven airfield, five were destroyed by Bf 110s. The next day, seven out of eight Battles were shot down when attacking German infantry in Luxembourg, and so the saga continued. In the first forty-eight hours, the bomber strength of the RAF Advanced Striking Force was reduced from 135 to seventy-five aircraft. On 20th May, as the Allied armies were facing defeat in northern France and Flanders, the RAF flew its last aircraft back to

England. Only sixty-six out of the 261 fighters originally based on the Continent, returned.

The daily OKW reports chronicled the demise of the Allied air forces. On 10th May, no less than seventy-two aerodromes were bombed, and between 300 and 400 aircraft destroyed on the ground. The next day, a further 300 enemy aeroplanes were estimated to have been eliminated, followed by 320 on the 12th, 150 on the 13th, 200 on the 14th, 98 on the 15th, 59 on the 16th, 108 on the 17th, 147 on the 18th, 143 on the 19th, 47 on the 20th, and 120 on the 21st (a total of over 2,000). Exaggerated though these figures may have been (the OKW reports claimed a total of 3,391 enemy aircraft destroyed), they give some indication of the overwhelming success enjoyed by the Luftwaffe. By the end of the campaign, the French, Belgian and Dutch air forces had been totally destroyed, and the RAF had lost 474 fighters, 334 bombers, and 46 seaplanes, just under one half of their total front-line aircraft (1,873) in both the United Kingdom and the Continent at the start of the campaign. Against this, the Luftwaffe lost some 1,130 aircraft of all types, 539 of them in the first six days of operations.

On the northern sector of the Western Front, the Luftwaffe's support for the ground forces began audaciously.Even as the bombers were searching out the enemy's air force, the Ju 52s were busy ferrying paratroops and air landing troops to their targets in Holland and Belgium. It was expected that Dutch resistance would be especially severe behind the Meuse and Yssel rivers, and in the area north of Rotterdam, known as 'Fortress Holland' and that in Belgium the attacking forces would encounter fierce opposition from the fortified areas along the line of the Meuse and Albert Canal, which hinged on Fort Emael, north of Liège. Speed of operation was vital to the Germans, and all checks to the advance of Army Group B had to be eliminated. Action from the air was considered the most feasible. For this, the Germans relied on the existing airborne forces, which comprised five battalions (4,500 men) of parachute troops and one Army infantry division (12,000 men) capable of being air-lifted into battle. Some of these had seen action before. During the occupation of Norway in April, a parachute battalion had been employed to seize two airfields and drops were made at Narvik, to reinforce beleaguered troops, and at Donbas, to prevent Norwegian and Allied units from joining forces. During the occupation of Denmark, a company was used to capture a bridge between two islands and to neutralise a coastal battery on another. In the attack in the West, however, these forces were used to greater effect. In Holland, four parachute battalions and one air-landing regiment captured three vital bridges so as to prevent the flooding of the lowlands and to allow the advancing German Army unhindered progress, and also seized four aerodromes. At the same time, another parachute battalion and two air-landing regiments attempted to take The Hague, but failed. In Belgium, a spectacular action by sixty paratroops borne by gliders took the vital fortress of Eben Emael, and over 400 others captured two bridges over the Albert Canal to allow the German Army to sweep into Belgium. But however successful these operations were, they were undertaken at considerable loss to the Luftwaffe. Of the 430 Ju 52s engaged, 109 were destroyed or so badly damaged as to be rendered unfit for action again, while a further fifty-three were repairable. One Geschwader, for example, lost ninety per cent of its aircraft during landing attempts in The Hague area. Such losses, suffered by aircraft and crews the majority of which had been temporarily assigned from the Luftwaffe's flying schools, had a severe impact on the level of training, especially of bomber crews. A marked reduction in the acceptances of new crews into front-line units was the result.

By 13th May, opposition in Holland was almost over, with the exception of the Dutch forces who were holding Rotterdam, and who could effectively bar any further German advance to the north. Time was of the essence to the Wehrmacht; a check here, and the thrust through Belgium and northern France would be deprived of its full impact. Furthermore, it was feared that British landings in Holland were imminent, which would threaten the flank of von Bock's advance. Therefore, in the evening of the 13th, General von Küchler, commander of 18th Army in Holland, ordered that resistance at Rotterdam be broken by an armoured attack on the morrow. To precede this, artillery fire and aerial bombardment would paralyse the enemy's defence. The bombers were to drop their load within a triangle to the north of the Meuse bridges, in the old town, where it was known that the enemy had established one of its major zones of resistance. The operation was not intended to induce surrender through terror, but simply to aid the progress of the ground forces in their attack. As von Küchler stipulated, 'all means to prevent unnecessary bloodshed among the Dutch population'[39] were to be used, and no incendiary bombs would be dropped. Indeed, beforehand, an attempt would be made to persuade the Dutch authorities to surrender, and emissaries were sent immediately to Rotterdam with that aim.

However, the Dutch commandant saw no reason to surrender at once, and the German demand was answered evasively. But some time after 1.00 p.m. on the 14th, the German commander in charge of the attack, General Schmidt, sent a radio message to Luftflotte 2: 'Attack postponed owing to parley'. Negotiations were not over. The aerial bombardment, scheduled for 3.00 p.m., was to be called off. Unfortunately, this message arrived three quarters of an hour too late for the attacking Kampfgeschwader; its He 111s were already over the Dutch border, just as the talks were coming to a head. All attempts to contact the aircraft in the air failed. However, to meet a situation such as this, the Germans had instituted a system whereby red Very lights shot from the Meuse island would signal that the attack had been called off. The men on the ground could only hope that the aircrews would see the lights through the mist, smoke and anti-aircraft fire that was over Rotterdam. As it was, only one of the two attacking formations of the Kampfgerchwader saw the flares, and turned away in time; the other, comprising fifty-seven bombers, flew in at 2,000 ft and dropped ninety-seven tons of high explosive. The resulting fires devastated a great part of the old, wooden city, the antiquated fire-brigade being quite unable to cope with them. Nine hundred people were killed, and, two hours later, Rotterdam surrendered without another shot being fired. Successful though the raid was, it was also for the Germans a matter of deep regret, and out of it the Allies made great propaganda.

On the first few days of the attack, raids were carried out on rail communications, with the aim of cutting off enemy reinforcements from the front line, especially in the area before Charleville-Sedan, where the main thrust of the German Army was to be directed. By 13th June, as soon as OKW believed effective air superiority to be established, air attacks on railways and troop movements to an average depth of forty-eight miles behind the front were commonplace. On the 13th, too, came the decisive operation of the crossing of the Meuse at Sedan by the spearheads of von Rundstedt's army group. A mistake here, and the whole basis of the German plan would be at risk. Air support from Sperrle's Luftflotte was given high priority. The orders to 1st Panzer Division emphasise the importance of the Luftwaffe's role: 'On the 13th of May the *point of main effort* of our Western Offensive lies in the sector of Group von Kleist. Almost the whole of the German air force will support this operation. By means of uninterrupted attacks lasting for eight hours the French defences along the Meuse will be smashed. This will be followed by an assault across the river by Group von Kleist at 16.00 hrs. and the establishment of bridgeheads.'[40] No fewer than 310 bomber and 200 dive-bomber sorties were made by Lörzer's Fliegerkorps II in the immediate vicinity of Sedan, and the panzers' crossing was a success. To the north of this area, von Richthofen's Fliegerkorps VIII, composed of Ju 87s, Hs 123s and fighters, was transferred from Luftflotte 2 to Luftflotte 3 in order to give further aid to the advance. As the Luftwaffe Intelligence Office reported:

> Continuous attacks by strong [air] forces within a confined space neutralized the enemy defenses, prevented the forward movement of enemy forces for a counter attack, and thereby made it possible for the spearhead units of two armoured divisions and of one infantry brigade to cross the Meuse River at two different points between Charleville and Sedan. The drive through permanent fortification systems of the enemy at Mezieres and Sedan was carried forward to a depth of twelve miles in a southward direction and our forces crossed the Ardennes Canal westward. Under the pressure of the German drive, which is supported by strong air forces, the enemy forces are retreating in disorder. . . . [41]

The next day, the 14th (known to the victorious Germans as the 'day of the fighter') the French and British threw all the aircraft they could muster against the breakthrough. By the evening, no less than eighty-nine Allied fighters and bombers lay strewn around the Sedan sector. Sixty per cent of the British bombers failed to return (the RAF was never to suffer a higher percentage loss in any operation), and the French bomber force had expended its last reserves. As the French premier, Reynaud, confessed to Churchill the following morning: 'We have lost the battle'.[42]

Over the following days, Luftflotte 3 sealed off the battle area in which Army Group A was operating. Continuous attacks supported the ground troops in the Fumay, Chalons-sur-Marne, Revigny-sur-Dorrain, Metz, Longuyon area. A further sixty-nine enemy aircraft were shot down on 15th and 16th May in the Sedan-Charleville area, and any significant movement of enemy troops to counter the developing thrust towards the Channel was prevented. Luftflotte 2 was also drawn into the decisive battle to the south. Particularly successful was the Luftwaffe's attack on the French railways. On 19th May, for example, no less than 33 transport trains were halted between Revingy-sur-Ornain and Bar le Duc. The routes leading to the rear of the German spearheads were bombed incessantly, and the Allies rendered quite unable to mount any counter-attack. On the 19th, the one occasion when the French managed to pose any threat to the advance, when an armoured force under Colonel Charles de Gaulle struck Army Group A's flank from the plains of Laon and penetrated to a considerable depth, the Luftwaffe's dive-bombers destroyed most of the French tanks. Further Allied attempts to mount armoured counter-attacks on the German southern advance, at Cambrai, Arras and Amiens on the 22nd, met with effective resistance from the air, as well as from anti-aircraft guns used in an anti-tank role. Successful anti-tank missions were not the speciality only of Luftflotte 2; to the north, Luftflotte 3 had been smashing French armoured assaults since the 14th.

However, at the point when the Wehrmacht was on the verge of a great success – the capture of all the Allied forces in the north of France, including the British Expeditionary Force (amounting to some 250,000 men) – the Luftwaffe was to experience its first failure. On the 24th, just as the armoured spearheads of Army Group A were about to move into Dunkirk and so seal the last port of escape for the almost-encircled enemy, came the order to halt the ground troops. No further advance would be made; the closing of the port of Dunkirk would be the task of the Luftwaffe. The cause of this decision has been hotly debated since the war. It is argued by some that Hitler wished to give the glory of inflicting the final blow against the enemy to the Luftwaffe, the creation of the National Socialists; it is suggested by others that it was Hitler's intention to allow the BEF to escape, to avoid inflicting a humiliating defeat on the British and give them the opportunity to negotiate an honourable peace. However, the halt of the panzer divisions outside Dunkirk should be seen not in isolation but as the culmination of fears and hesitations that had been exhibited by the German military ledership, including Hitler, over the previous nine days, since the break-out from Sedan. Halts in order to consolidate the ground won, to secure the flanks and to allow the infantry to catch up with, and relieve, the mechanised units, had been imposed before, and by the 24th it was considered that the situation again demanded a respite. Von Rundstedt and his senior commanders feared that their forces were over extended, that their mechanised divisions were too widely spaced, and that their flanks were vulnerable to enemy counter-attacks from both north and south. Furthermore, their troops were exhausted, and their mechanised formations were suffering from a high rate of breakdown; rest and repair was essential before the Army was in a fit state to embark upon Operation Red, the occupation of central and southern France. Thus, on the 23rd von Rundstedt issued an order that the advanced formations were to consolidate their hold on the Aa canal, fifteen miles from Dunkirk, but advance no further.

Far from the front, on the 23rd one other development was to have immense significance for the future. For the first time in the campaign, the Luftwaffe commander was to exert his influence. General Warlimont remembered:

> . . . late in the afternoon of 23 May, Göring was sitting at a heavy oak table beside his train . . . when the news arrived that the enemy in Flanders was almost surrounded. Göring reacted in a flash. Banging his great fist on the table, he shouted: 'This is a wonderful opportunity for the Luftwaffe. I must speak to the Führer at once. . . .' In the telephone conversation that followed, he used every sort of language to persuade Hitler that this was a unique opportunity for his Air Force. If the Führer would give the order that this operation was to be left to the Luftwaffe alone, he would give an unconditional assurance that he would annihilate the remnants of the enemy; all he wanted, he said, was a free run; in other words, the tanks must be withdrawn sufficiently far from the western side of the pocket to ensure that they were not in danger from our own bombing. Hitler was as quick as Göring to approve this plan without further consideration. Jeschonnek and Jodl rapidly fixed the details, including the withdrawal of certain armoured units and the exact timing for the start of the air attack.[43]

General Schmid was with Göring when he had the idea to destroy the British Expeditonary Force from the air. He wrote:

> I happened to be present when Göring learned, through normal communication channels, that the German tanks approaching from both east and west had reached the outskirts of Dunkirk. Thereupon, without even stopping to think, he decided that the British Expeditionary Corps had to be conquered from the air. I heard the telephone conversation which he subsequently had with Hitler. Göring described the situation at Dunkirk in such a way as to suggest that there was no alternative but to destroy, by an attack from the air, those elements of the British Expeditionary Corps trapped at Dunkirk. He described this mission as being a speciality of the Luftwaffe, and pointed out that the advance elements of the German Army, already battle weary, could hardly expect to succeed in preventing the British withdrawal.[44]

He even requested that the German tanks which had reached the outskirts of the city, be withdrawn a few miles in order to leave the field free for the Luftwaffe. Hitler, stopping no longer to think than Göring had before making his suggestion, agreed to the proposal.

At Führer Headquarters, Jodl was opposed to the plan, but his lack of enthusiasm had no effect upon Göring. who exclaimed to Milch: 'We have done it! The Luftwaffe is to wipe out the British on the beaches. . . . The Führer wants them taught a lesson they will never forget'.[45] Indeed, Hitler did. He was also relieved that the Air Force's intervention would allow Army Group A a respite in the advance. The Führer had been as worried as anyone about extended flanks and Allied counter-attacks, and, on a visit to von Rundstedt's headquarters on the 24th, concurred with the decision to halt. Later that day, in his War Directive No. 13, Hitler ordered: 'The task of the Luftwaffe will be to break all enemy resistance on the part of the surrounded forces, to prevent the escape of the English forces across the Channel. . . . '[46]

However, while Göring might have been ecstatic at the prospect, others in senior positions of the Luftwaffe were not. Milch was highly dubious of the whole matter, and Kesselring, to whose Luftflotte was given the task of annihilating the enemy, was dismayed. As he wrote after the war:

> The Commander-in-Chief of the Luftwaffe must have been suf-
> ficiently aware of the effect of almost three weeks of ceaseless
> operations on my airmen not to order an operation which could
> hardly be carried out successfully by fresh forces. I expressed this view
> very clearly to Göring and told him it could not be done even with the
> support of Fliegerkorps VIII. Jeschonnek told me he thought the
> same, but that Göring for some incomprehensible reason had pledged
> himself to the Führer to wipe out the English with his Luftwaffe. It is
> easier to excuse Hitler with so many operational tasks to occupy his
> mind for agreeing, than Göring for making this unrealistic offer. I
> pointed out to Göring that the modern Spitfires had recently
> appeared, making our air operations difficult and costly – and in the
> end it was the Spitfires which enabled the British and French to
> evacuate across the water.[47]

Although the Luftwaffe began operations against Dunkirk immediately, it was severely hampered in their execution. The necessary conditions for success – advanced airfields, fresh units, the ability to achieve pin-point accuracy, good weather – were all lacking. During the nine days of the evacuation of the British from Dunkirk, the Air Force was able to operate at full strength for only two and a half days, and then were subject to heavy attack from RAF fighters operating from their home bases in south-east England (some 177 British aircraft were lost during the battle). The Germans had their first encounter with the Spitfire. Aerial superiority was, at times, minimal. Furthermore, air units were constantly diverted to deal with the threats to the German flanks that were continually developing, as the trapped enemy troops attempted to break out. Attacks, also, had to be made on the enemy in Calais, Lille and Amiens. Not until the afternoon of the 26th, did the Luftwaffe nominate Dunkirk as its main target, at about the same time as the British Admiralty ordered Operation Dynamo, the rescue of the BEF, to begin. The first day of the evacuation, the 27th, was disastrous for the British. Suffering heavy air attacks all day, they managed to save only 7,669 soldiers. For the next thirty-six hours, however, poor weather over the target was to bring a lull in the fight, and on the 28th and 29th respectively, 17,804 and 47,310 Allied soldiers were evacuated. Following a fine afternoon on the 29th, during which the Luftwaffe had resumed its pounding, the 30th saw the return of poor weather; the Luftwaffe was unable to operate, and 58,823 more troops were embarked. Moreover, the ground advance, which had been resumed late on the 26th, was making little progress in face of the stiff resistance that the Allies were by then capable of mounting. Time lost to the advance had been time well used by the enemy. The 1st June saw the resumption of good weather, but, despite the heavy air raids, 64,429 soldiers were saved. The toll was high, however. Fourteen ships were sunk, including four destroyers, and the decision was made to continue the evacuation only at night. Thus, when German aircraft flew over Dunkirk the following day, not a ship was to be seen. The night embarkation continued until dawn on the 4th, when Operation Dynamo was ended. Some 50,000 abandoned vehicles littered the streets and beaches of Dunkirk, and 235 vessels lay submerged beneath the sea. Around 40,000 French troops were left behind to defend the approaches to the port, and were made prisoners. However, it was not the victory that the Germans had hoped for. No less than 338,226 British and French soldiers had reached safety in England. Although it had lost 2,700 guns and 120,000 motor vehicles in France and Belgium, the BEF had survived to form the nucleus of a new army. The Luftwaffe, impeded by the weather, had failed, and, in the course of its failure, had lost some 200 aircraft.

After the conclusion to the campaign in the north, the Wehrmacht turned its attention to the south. As Army Groups A and B regrouped to undertake Operation Red, the invasion of the centre and south of France, the Luftwaffe prepared to act as their support. In the four days before the opening of the offensive, on 5th June, it undertook missions against the French Air Force in the south. On the 3rd, for example, according to OKW it destroyed 72 aircraft in the air and between 300 and 400 on the ground. The aircraft industry in Paris and fuel depots in Marseilles were also attacked, so as to prepare the way for the forthcoming attack. On the 14th, Paris was occupied by the Germans, and the Luftwaffe began to turn its attention to the ports, from which British and French forces were being evacuated. By the 25th, the campaign had been won.

In the attack on the West, the Luftwaffe had performed well. Mastery of the air and constant support for the ground forces had been achieved for the loss of 1,389 aircraft (521 bombers, 122 Ju 87s, 367 fighters, 213 transports, and 166 reconnaissance aeroplanes). According to OKW, no less than 4,233 enemy aircraft had been destroyed, 1,850 of them on the ground. A notable characteristic of the campaign had been the close co-operation between the air and ground forces. Although the material damage done by the bombers and dive-bombers was not great, the effect on the morale of the enemy troops and headquarters was considerable. As the OKW report on the operation stated, without the aid of the Luftwaffe, success on the ground might not have been so complete and would certainly not have been so quick. In celebration of victory, Hitler gave out honours and ranks in profusion. On 19th July, he made Göring the Reichsmarschall des Grossdeutschen Reiches, a new rank which placed him above serving officers of all three services, and awarded him the Grosskreuz of the Iron Cross, also a unique distinction. Three Luftwaffe generals, Milch, Kesselring and Sperrle, became Field Marshals, and others were promoted to Generaloberst and lesser ranks of General. The glory that accrued to the Luftwaffe, in common with the Army, was never to be greater.

V

The Onslaught Against Britain

Before 1938, the Luftwaffe had no thought of embarking upon a war with Britain. However, in the middle of February of that year, the RLM instructed General Felmy's Luftwaffengruppenkommando 2, whose territory covered the Reich's North Sea coast, to draw up proposals for action in the event of Britain's intervention in a war in the West. Two memoranda were produced the following autumn, which made clear that any air war against Britain could have nuisance value only, and under no circumstances would it exercise any decisive effect. They pointed out that the limited range of Germany's existing bombers would not permit effective action against Britain from their Friesian bases; airfields in Holland and Belgium would be essential. At the same time, the Operations Staff of the Luftwaffe General Staff made its own evaluation, which concluded that, in existing circumstances there could be no hope whatever of securing a decisive victory in a combined attack on the British war economy by the Luftwaffe and the Navy. The essential task of the Luftwaffe was to guarantee freedom of action for the ground forces.

In May 1939, a further study, carried out by the Operations Staff, made it clear that the strength, equipment and training of Luftflotte 2 would not enable it to secure a quick decision against Britain in the air. At the same time, it was pointed out that no result could be obtained by any attack on Britain's overseas supplies, since all her important western and south-western ports were out of range. Because of the increasing strength of her air defences, no decision could be arrived at through terror attacks on London; on the contrary, such attacks were more likely to strengthen the national will to resist. The study also held out little hope of success in an onslaught against Britain's fighter force as a preliminary to a general attack at a later date. Conditions favoured the defence, and it was considered that losses suffered by the attacking forces would be prohibitively high. This form of air warfare was generally regarded with distrust and misgiving; it would play into the hands of the enemy, and distract the attention of the Luftwaffe from the bombing of objectives more vital to Britain's existence. The most favourable target for air attack on the mainland was the aircraft industry; port and harbour installations and oil storage tanks could also be bombed with profit. On 9th July 1939, Luftflotte 2 was given instructions in accordance with this study. The main targets listed were war industries and supply centres.

Finally, in July 1939, 'Beppo' Schmid, Chief of Intelligence of the

Luftwaffe Operations Staff, presented Göring with a detailed study of Britain's air strength. It pointed out that, given further development, the RAF could be as strong as the Luftwaffe by 1940. The preliminary condition for any successful air war against Britain was the destruction of the Royal Air Force and the aircraft industry which supplied it; only then would it be possible to attack Britain's ports, harbours and shipping. Furthermore, such large objectives would require powerful forces, and the task would be so arduous that it would not be possible to fix any date by which the campaign could be concluded. The study pointed out that, because of the well-known ability of the British to improvise, and their general moral toughness, air attack alone might not secure their surrender. In that case, the British Isles would have to be invaded and occupied.

Before the invasion of Poland, the Luftwaffe had held a very realistic view as to its capabilities against Britain. However, from the beginning of the war, it found itself, on Hitler's orders, engaged in precisely the task which it had believed impossible to fulfil: the economic blockade of Britain. Although preparations for this had never played a part in the Luftwaffe's development, in May 1939 it became an element of German policy in the event of a European war. Then, on the 23rd, Hitler held a conference with his service chiefs, at which Göring, Milch, Jeschonnek, and Bodenschatz were present, to inform them of his decision to invade Poland. This act, the Führer recognised, might well bring about war with France and Britain. The former, he argued, could be dealt with by conventional military means (i.e. the defeat of her armies and the occupation of part, or all, of her territory), but the latter, because of her geographical position, could best be subdued by a combined air and sea blockade of her ocean lanes. As Hitler said: 'The moment England's food supply routes are cut, she is forced to capitulate'.[1] That would be achieved by daily attacks by the Navy and the Air Force (the latter operating from bases in occupied Holland, Flanders and northern France) to cut Britain's life-lines; there would then be no need for an invasion.

This strategy was confirmed on 31st April 1939, when Hitler issued his Directive No.1 for the Conduct of the War. In the East, Poland would be invaded; in the West, the Wehrmacht was to remain on the defensive, until such time as the British and French might attack. Its task would then be to damage 'enemy forces and war potential . . . as much as possible'. The Luftwaffe would 'take measures to dislocate English imports, the armaments industry, and the transport of troops to France'. The Royal Navy would be attacked at every opportunity. Hitler concluded by declaring that 'Attacks on the English homeland are to be prepared, bearing in mind that inconclusive results with insufficient forces are to be avoided in all circumstances.'[2] Any decision to bomb London would be taken by him alone. All this was reaffirmed in Directives Nos.2, 3 and 4 dated 3rd, 9th and 30th September respectively. Thus, while any marine target was to be considered fair game, provided it was not a passenger carrier, no attacks were to be made on the mainland of Britain itself.

After the conquest of Poland, Hitler again addressed himself to the matter of Britain's resistance. On 9th October he produced his War Directive No.6, which reaffirmed his intention to defeat the French, and occupy 'as large an area as possible in Holland, Belgium and northern France as a basis for conducting a promising air and sea war against England'.[3] In an accompanying memorandum, he elaborated this argument:

> The Luftwaffe cannot succeed in efficient operations against the industrial centre of England and her southern and south-western ports, which have increased in importance in wartime, until it is no longer compelled to operate offensively from our present small North Sea coast, by extremely devious routes involving long flights. If the Dutch-Belgian area were to fall into the hands of the English and French, then the enemy forces would be able to strike at the industrial heart of Germany and would need to cover barely a sixth of the distance required by the German bomber to reach really important targets. If we were in possession of Holland, Belgium, or even the Straits of Dover as jumping-off bases for German aircraft, then, without a doubt, Great Britain could be struck a mortal blow, even if the strongest reprisals were attempted. Such a shortening of air routes would be all the more important to Germany because of our difficulties in fuel supply. Every 1,000 kg of fuel saved is not only an asset to our national economy, but means that 1,000 kg more of explosives can be carried in the aircraft; that is to say, 1,000 kg of fuel would become 1,000 kg of bombs. And this also leads to economy in aircraft, in mechanical wear-and-tear of the machine, and above all in valuable airmen's lives. These very facts are reasons for England and France to secure for themselves these regions under all circumstances, just as they compel us, on the other hand, to prevent such an occupation on the part of France and England.[4]

On 29th November, Hitler transformed his thoughts into orders in his Directive No.9 entitled 'Instructions for Warfare Against the Economy of the Enemy'. The defeat of Britain was declared 'essential to full victory', and the 'most effective means of ensuring this is to cripple the British economy by attacking it at decisive points'. Once the Army had occupied Holland, Belgium and northern France, 'the task of the Navy and Air Force to carry the war to British industry becomes paramount.'[5] In order of importance, the following targets were to be attacked: ports (either by mining their approaches or bombing their installations), merchant-shipping and its naval protection, storage depots, transport conveying British troops to the Continent, and vital military industries such as aircraft and munition factories. However, until the campaign in the West had been carried out successfully, the trade war was to remain limited to the high seas and coastal waters around Britain.

The German air offensive against the United Kingdom began in the second week of the war, when, on 10th September, the Luftwaffe was given permission to attack British naval forces if they ventured into the neighbourhood of German naval bases or German minefields. On 18th October, this permission was extended to attacks on the Royal Navy in its anchorages, and, on 1st November, to attacks on merchant convoys. However, the Luftwaffe was ill-equipped for these tasks. Before the opening of hostilities, it had shown little interest in such operations. Trials had taken place in the laying of minefields, and, in 1939, training courses for bombing ships were held, but both with little effect. Experiments were made with torpedo-attacks by seaplanes, but, owing to the opposition of Udet and the unsuitability of naval torpedoes, development was slow. Navigation over the deep sea was, likewise, largely unpractised by the Luftwaffe, except by fleet reconnaissance units. The main forces allocated to maritime duty came under the control of the Navy and the direct command of the General der Luftwaffe beim Oberkommando der Kriegsmarine (Luftwaffe General with the Naval High Command). At the outbreak of war, they comprised 228 aircraft – the obsolete He 59 twin-engined biplane with floats used for mine-laying and torpedo attack, and the elderly He 60 seaplane needed for close-range reconnaissance. There were also a few Ar 95 and He 114 floatplanes. For longer reconnaissance sorties, the German coastal units had the Do 18 flying boats, also outdated by 1939; of the sixty-three operational on 1 September 1939, only thirty-six were in the North Sea area. However, a few more advanced types were on the way: deliveries of the first He 115 floatplane torpedo bombers had begun in August 1939, and the promising BV 138 long-range flying boat was already undergoing flight tests. There was also a small number of the fast and well-armed Ar 196 floatplanes, at that time reserved exclusively as shipboard aircraft on the major German warships. In addition, specially adapted Bf 109 fighters and Ju 87 dive-bombers, together with Fi 167 biplane torpedo-bombers, were intended for service aboard the planned aircraft carriers. The first, *Graf Zeppelin*, had been launched in December 1938, by which time work was also begun on the second, but in the event neither were ever completed.

In the first few months of the war, most of these units were under the command of General Coeler (Führer der Seeluftstreitkräfte), and were given permission by the Navy to conduct minelaying operations against British ports and coastal waters. The He 59s sowed their mines in the Thames estuary, the Downs, the Clyde, Firth of Forth, Plymouth, Liverpool, Belfast, and off Sheerness, waters which were often out of reach of naval units. By September, the He 59s had already begun to be replaced by He 111s, an indication of the importance that was beginning to be attached to the maritime air service, and, although losses of aircraft were high, success was considerable. In the first four months of the war, direct attacks by aircraft sank 2,200 gross tons of British shipping, and mines (many of which were laid by the Navy) some 99,400 tons. In mid-December, Coeler reported the results to Göring, and, in February 1940, the RLM, convinced of the efficacy of mine-laying, created a special command for such operations – Fliegerdivision 9, which was under the control of the Luftwaffe, the first evidence of the withdrawal of the air maritime forces from the control of the Kriegsmarine.

Although the forces initially allocated to maritime duty were indeed meagre, plans were afoot for greater things even before the war began. In April 1939, General Hans Geisler had been appointed General zur besonderen Verwendung (General for special duties) with Luftflotte 2 at Kiel, and was charged with organising anti-shipping forces which would be under the direction of the Air Force and not of the Navy. The General Staff wanted bombers to be available to attack enemy naval forces both in German waters and in their own anchorages, where the Kriegsmarine might not be able to penetrate. In 1938, Göring promised that, by 1942, no less than thirteen bomber Geschwader would be available for this role. However, war came earlier than expected, and by its outbreak only two Geschwader, both under strength, had been designated to undertake shipping attacks: one with sixty-five He 111 bombers and the other with eighteen Ju 88s (the first unit to be equipped with this aircraft). Operations began as soon as war was declared. Attacks were made on the guarantors of the British sea lanes, the British fleet, at Scapa Flow, the Firth of Forth, and in the North Sea; during one of these, on 28th October, the Luftwaffe had its first aircraft brought down on British soil, an He 111. By the end of the year, the Luftwaffe had lost forty-six aircraft in engagements with the RAF. The first operational employment of Ju 88s in the war took place on 26th September, when they attacked the aircraft carrier, HMS *Ark Royal*, the battleship, HMS *Hood*, and a number of other warships. Little damage was done, although it was believed for a time that HMS *Ark Royal* had been sunk. Indeed, it soon became clear that attacks on the Royal Navy were not nearly so effective as those on the Merchant Navy. The successes against the convoys impressed the General Staff, and, in December 1939, General Geisler's command was up-graded, to become Fliegerdivision 10, and more aircraft were given to it. In February 1940, the division became known as Fliegerkorps X.

In the spring of 1940, the anti-shipping forces were strengthened by the addition of the Focke-Wulf 200 Condor, which began to enter service as a long-range maritime reconnaissance-bomber. The lack of such a machine at the outbreak of the war had prompted Fliegerkorps X to suggest to Jeschonnek that the four-engined civilian transport FW 200 be converted to a military role as a stop-gap until the He 177 came into service. Capable of a radius of action of 1,000 miles with 2,000 lb of bombs, or of 1,400 miles with a single 550 lb bomb, the initial maritime version could remain in the air from fourteen to sixteen hours. However, the FW 200 was slow, with a maximum speed of only 224 mph, vulnerable to anti-aircraft fire, and possessed a weak structure which made it prone, among other things, to break its back. It had, however, some success, and established a formidable reputation for itself as 'the Scourge of the Atlantic'. By September, fifteen FW 200s were operating in a Gruppe based near Bordeaux. Not only were they invaluable as the 'eyes' of the U-boats, guiding them to their prey, they also proved effective in attacking merchantmen. Between 1st August 1940 and 9th February 1941, for example, the FW 200 Gruppe sank eighty-five merchant ships totalling 363,000 tons. Unfortunately for the German maritime forces, few Condors were produced. No more than sixty were in front-line units at any one time, a low figure made worse by the fact that the serviceability of the aircraft seldom rose above twenty-five per cent.

During the campaigns in Norway, for which Fliegerkorps X was the combat command, and in the West, specialised shipping attacks were kept up against the British Navy at its bases and on merchant shipping. After the fall of France, minelaying was stepped up and another Kampfgeschwader with 100 He 111s was added to Fliegerdivision 9. Successes claimed were high. However, such operations could only be pinpricks in the side of the British Lion. It was recognised in the RLM that, with existing forces, the Luftwaffe on its own lacked the necessary strength to gain a decisive victory over Britain. This was in line with Hitler's own views, expressed on 23rd May 1939, when he told service chiefs that a country could not 'be brought to defeat by an air force', and that a war against the British would be long and require 'the unrestricted use of all resources'.[6] There is no reason to think that Hitler had ceased to believe this when he issued his War Directives Nos.6 and 9. In both, he envisaged a long-term struggle, one that would be shared by both the Navy and the Air Force, and he stipulated that a necessary precondition for its success would be the occupation of the Channel Coast, thereby bringing Luftwaffe aircraft to within less than thirty-minutes flying time of London. This policy was reiterated on 17th January 1940, when OKW ordered certain measures in connection with the coming offensive in the West: 'In the interests of the conduct of the war as a whole, it is not desirable that anything should be done to step up the war against Britain to the full until suitable bases have been obtained and until strong forces are available for the purpose.'[7] However, on 24th May, when it had become apparent that Germany was victorious in the West, Hitler announced in his War Directive No.13 that, as soon as enough units became available, the Air Force should embark upon its independent mission against the British homeland. The targets were to be those laid down in War Directive No.9, and the operation would begin 'with a crushing attack in retaliation for British raids on the Ruhr area'.[8] Hitler required only to be informed of the timing and planning of the attack on the British mainland; his permission for the extension of the war had been given. On the 26th, OKW issued a supplement to War Directive No.9, stating that the primary target should be the British aircraft industry, 'the last potent weapon which could be employed directly against us'.[9]

On the night of 5th June, twelve hours after German armies had begun the second phase of the campaign in France, the Luftwaffe launched its first attack against land targets in Britain. About fifty He 111s ranged across the countryside, dropping bombs on airfields and other military installations. Accuracy was low, and little damage done. This raid was followed by others on the next two nights, and then by a pause until the 18th, when bombing was resumed. On that night the first bomb of the war to be dropped, albeit accidently, on London fell on Addington, some ten miles from the centre. The forces engaged never amounted to more than seventy bombers (there were, in any case, few crews in the Luftwaffe trained to undertake night operations), and damage was negligible. In the course of the months, thirteen airfields, sixteen industrial plants and fourteen ports were bombed, at a cost of eleven bombers. In addition 54,700 tons of shipping was sunk, roughly equivalent to the total sunk by direct air action since the war began. Effective though the attacks on shipping were becoming, those on British industrial sites were less promising. An indication of the futility of such raids was the decision to allow factories to continue full working even after air raid warning sirens had sounded. The disruption of output caused by men going to their shelters was far greater than that resulting from German bombing itself, and few lives were lost.

The aim of these German raids has never been clear. They were, however, used to test methods of navigation which would enable the bombers to find their targets irrespective of weather conditions and visibility. In particular, the Germans experimented with a new navigational device, Knickebein (crooked-leg), whereby aircraft were guided by two radio navigational beams intersecting over the target area. In July, with the campaign in France over, the pilots having rested, and units moved to airfields nearer their targets, a new vigour became apparent in Luftwaffe operations against Britain. However, doubts were expressed as to their efficacy. The Luftwaffe's senior legal officer, Dr Christian von Hammerstein, recalled:

> At the end of the French campaign, we were sitting in the dining car of Göring's special train and were discussing the forthcoming air attacks against England. Göring turned to Jeschonnek and asked him whether he believed that these attacks would be successful. Jeschonnek replied firmly, 'Yes, of course I do!' Later we heard him say to Göring, 'I don't think it will take over six weeks at the most!' Göring doubted this and pointed out that if we assumed that the Germans would continue to fight even if Berlin should be destroyed, we ought not to consider the British to be softer than the Germans and simply assume that they would stop fighting once London had been destroyed.[10]

At the time, even the Luftwaffe crews themselves were aware of their own limitations. For example, Werner Baumbach, who was later to become General of Bombers, wrote:

> We know that England is the hardest nut to be cracked in this war. Our experience at the front has shown us that final victory against England can only be attained by the systematic co-operation of all arms of the service and ruthless application of the elementary

principle of concentrating all one's strength and effort at the vital strategic point. This vital point is not necessarily the same as the enemy's strongest point. Even if the air arm is the most important weapon in total war, it cannot by itself ensure the decisive, final and total victory.[11]

To reach Britain, pilots had to fly over water for fifteen minutes or more (giving rise to 'Channel sickness') and this, added to poor weather and the strength of the RAF, were all major obstacles that had to be overcome before the targets could be located and destroyed, in itself a difficult enough task even on a clear day. The euphoria of previous victories lingered, but it was tempered by realism as to the difficulties of the struggle which lay ahead.

On the 30th June, Göring issued his 'General Directive for the Operation of the Luftwaffe against England,' to the three Luftflotten that were to carry out the assault: Luftflotte 5 in Norway, by then under General Stumpff, Luftflotte 2 in the area north of Le Havre, and Luftflotte 3 in the south. The aims were identical with those contained in the Führer's Directives. The prime mission of the Luftwaffe was, in co-operation with the Navy, to attack merchant shipping, naval escorts, ports and harbours in order to cut Britain off from her overseas supplies. To achieve this, the RAF would have to be destroyed, as would Britain's aircraft factories. Both tasks were to be pursued concurrently. But the Directive made clear that 'So long as the enemy air force remains in being, the supreme principle of air warfare must be to attack it at every possible opportunity by day and by night, in the air and on the ground with priority over other tasks.' However, until the air units had regrouped in their new bases, and arrangements completed to ensure uninterrupted supplies and replacements, operations against Britain were 'to be confined to nuisance raids by relatively minor forces on industrial and RAF targets'.[12] During that time, heavy civilian casualties were to be avoided. These orders were confirmed on 11th July with the issue of the General Staff's 'Directive for the Intensified Air War Against England'. The RAF was to be destroyed as soon as practicable, as a precondition to a successful conclusion to the blockade of Britain.

The preliminary skirmishings lasted throughout July and into August. Night raids continued, light but widely scattered, causing considerable inconvenience. The bomber units, learning from the experience of the previous month, flew higher over their targets, thus minimising the danger from anti-aircraft fire and fighter interception, but with some detriment to accuracy. The heaviest casualties were inflicted on 12th August, when over fifty people were killed or seriously injured in Aberdeen. More damaging, however, was the new series of daylight raids, which began on 1st August. They were of two varieties: either single bombers or small formations would penetrate inland using cloud cover to avoid detection, or larger formations of up to twenty bombers, together with an escort of fighters, would undertake heavier attacks on ports. In the first nine days, no fewer than five ports were bombed in daylight, and seven Channel convoys attacked. On the 2nd, Luftflotte 2 instituted a new command – Kanalkampfführer (Channel Battle Leader), whose primary task was to close the Channel to enemy shipping. Colonel Johannes Fink, commander of a Kampfgeschwader (with seventy-five Do 17s), was given this post. His headquarters were on the cliffs at Cap Blanc Nez, directly opposite Folkestone and Dover, some twenty-five miles distant. He was given two Ju 87 Gruppen (sixty-five aircraft) and one Bf 110 Geschwader (with 100 fighters). To the south-west, near Le Havre, some 105 miles from Portsmouth, Luftflotte 3 gave the same task to von Richthofen's Fliegerkorps VIII, composed mainly of Ju 87s. In addition, Coeler's Flieger-korps X made repeated attacks on shipping, and claimed to have sunk 950,000 tons by 31st July.

In accordance with the Luftwaffe's overall strategy, the attacking forma-tions of bombers were also given the task of drawing the RAF fighters into the battle, so that they could be attacked by the escorts of BF 109s and Bf 110s. Toward the end of July, the Germans initiated a series of sweeps by fighters over south-east England, in an attempt to draw their counterparts into action. But RAF Fighter Command did not accept that challenge; the Luftwaffe was left quite free to raid British air-space. As Kesselring was to write after the war:

> After costly initial engagements the English fighters kept out of the way of the superior German forces. By the employment of small bomber units to bait the English fighters we managed to bring them up again, until even this chance of a battle became so rare that no decision could be forced, as they were expressly ordered to avoid any engagement. Our difficulty was not to bring down enemy fighters – in Galland, Mölders, Oesau, Balthasar, etc., we had real aces, while the huge figures of aircraft shot down are further proof – but to get the enemy to fight.[13]

Only when targets on the mainland were threatened, or convoys under attack, would the RAF give combat, and then its pilots took care only to engage enemy bombers, and to avoid the fighters whenever possible. Otherwise, RAF Fighter Command preferred to conserve its strength for the great onslaught which was believed to be coming. However, the material damage inflicted by the Luftwaffe during this phase of operations, known as the Kanalkampf, was not inconsiderable. In the six weeks beginning 1st July, it mounted some 7,000 bomber sorties, dropped some 1,900 tons of high explosive, and attacked numerous ships, ports and industries. Roughly 70,000 tons of shipping was sunk, most of it between Land's End and the Nore. As for the RAF, the Luftwaffe succeeded in destroying 142 of its fighters in aerial combat, and damaging another fifty-one, for the loss of 279 with seventy-one damaged. Of the 142 RAF machines destroyed, only fourteen could be positively claimed by bombers, seaplanes and Bf 110s, leaving the Bf 109s with the remaining 128 for the loss of eighty-five of their own number.

Just as the Luftwaffe was getting under way its campaign against the RAF and the British supply lines, which, together with the operations of the Navy, was designed to defeat 'perfidious Albion', Hitler gave it a new task. On 25th June, he quite unexpectedly asked OKW to prepare a study for a seaborne assault. This done, Hitler came to the conclusion that a successful invasion was possible, and on 2nd July OKW asked the three services to draw up plans accordingly. On the 13th, the Army presented its proposals to the Führer, who thereupon decided to undertake the operation. On the 11th, he issued his Directive No.16, which opened with the words: 'Since England, in spite of her hopeless military situation, shows no sign of being ready to come to an understanding, I have decided to prepare a landing operation against England, and, if necessary, to carry it out.'[14] Hitler was no longer willing to rely upon economic blockade; he wanted the quicker result which a military solution would bring. In pursuance of that, the Luftwaffe was to abandon its mission of economic blockade before it was even properly begun, and revert to its traditional role: that of support for the ground forces.

Hitler's Directive No.16 made it clear that the role of the Air Force in the invasion (code-named 'Sealion') was 'to prevent interference by the enemy air force', and to mount attacks on British strong-points, especially landing places, troop concentrations, as well as on the Royal Navy. In other words, the Luftwaffe was to provide the 'umbrella' under which the seaborne assault could be undertaken without serious interference from the enemy, either by air or by sea. In this there was nothing that differed from the operational basis for the campaigns in Poland, Norway and the West, except that enemy ships became a major target for the first time. For this, all concerned in the planning thought that the Luftwaffe was sufficiently equipped, its successes against the Royal Navy in Norway and the losses it had inflicted on the marine force during the evacuation from Dunkirk, were seen as proof of the efficacy of air power over sea forces. The weather was considered to be the most serious uncertain factor. By the middle of August, the Luftwaffe was to render the RAF incapable of delivering 'any significant attack against the German crossing'. In previous campaigns, the aerial onslaught against the enemy air forces had taken place simultaneously with the Army's advance across the border; for Operation 'Sealion', it was to be a precondition to military action. Until the Luftwaffe's air superiority had been established, the Army would not move. For the Luftwaffe, however, this was not important, for, in previous campaigns, the gaining of initial command of the air over enemy territory had not been dependent on any advance by the ground forces. Permanent command of the air over all the British Isles would, it was recognised, have to wait for the physical occupation of the country. That, however, was not considered crucial. Given the limited range and bomb-loads of the Luftwaffe's aircraft, only superiority over the Channel and the south-east could be assured, but that was all that was required for the landings to be attempted with a reasonable hope of success.

On 21st July, in accordance with Hitler's new objective, Göring added attacks on the British fleet when not escorting merchantmen to the list of the Luftwaffe's priority targets. On 1st August, Hitler issued his Directive No.17, 'For the Conduct of Air and Sea Warfare against England'; in it, the task of the Luftwaffe was further elaborated: 'In order to establish the necessary conditions for the final conquest of England, I intend to intensify air and sea warfare against the English homeland. . . . The Luftwaffe is to overpower the English Air Force with all the forces at its command, in the shortest possible time. The attacks are to be directed primarily against flying units, their ground installations, and their supply organisations, but also against the aircraft industry, including that manufacturing anti-aircraft equipment.'[15] Having attained command of the air, the Luftwaffe could then return to its economic blockade of the country, but it had to be ready at any moment to assist the Navy and Army in Operation Sealion, should it be launched. With the invasion in prospect, Hitler ordered that the south coast ports, the main landing sites for the German Army, should be spared as far as possible. The intensification of the air war was to begin on 5th August, or as soon thereafter as the Air Force was ready. It was clear from this Directive that Hitler had still not committed himself irrevocably to invade Britain. Indeed, the day before it was issued, he was talking about first attacking the Soviet Union, since, with Russia defeated, Britain's last hope would be gone. The decision to attempt to destroy the RAF was for him an easy matter; its destruction had always been a part of his plan to blockade Britain – indeed, it was essential for the success of the operation. Should the Luftwaffe gain its expected victory, he could then decide which course finally to adopt: economic blockade or invasion. For both, a successful assault on Britain's air defences over south-east England was essential.

On 2nd August, the RLM issued its plan for Adlerangriff (Eagle Attack), the destruction of the RAF. The target for Luftflotten 2 and 3 was to be RAF Fighter Command in south-east England: its aeroplanes, aerodromes, radar stations, and entire ground organisation. This would be achieved in three phases; during the first five days, attacks would be made in a semi-circle starting in the west and proceeding south and then east, within a radius of ninety to sixty miles of London; in the following three days, the radius would shorten to between sixty to thirty miles; and during the last five days the attack would be in a thirty-mile circle around London. As General Otto Stapf, the Army Liaison Officer to the RLM, reported to Halder, the Luftwaffe believed the entire operation would take between two to four weeks. The limited range of the Bf 109s, which could spend at most only ninety minutes in the air, meant that they never had more than half an hour over British soil. This restricted the daylight operations to a relatively small area over south-east England, including London, for without fighter cover any bomber sorties further afield would occasion unacceptably high losses. However, this was not regarded as too severe a handicap. Not only would the extensive RAF ground organisation covering the British capital in the south of England be dislocated, but the fighting, especially that around London, would draw in RAF fighter units from throughout the country, there to be destroyed by the Bf 109s. According to Kesselring, it was recognised that 'permanent air supremacy was impossible without the occupation of the island, for the simple reason that a considerable number of British air bases, aircraft and engine factories were out of range of our bombers [in fact, they were within range, but would be without fighter escort], it was believed that temporary air supremacy over the invasion area would be possible.'[16] That would be sufficient to allow Operation Sealion to proceed. No date was set for the beginning of the attack, and, until it was undertaken, the Luftwaffe would continue with its Kanalkampf.

Such was the aim of Adlerangriff. No-one disagreed with its practicability. The plan of operation, however, was another matter. During the fighting, the bombers would be used not only to knock out the RAF's ground organisation and aircraft factories, but also to act as bait for the RAF fighters. As experience had shown, the presence of Bf 109s alone in British air space was not enough to tempt RAF Fighter Command into action; what was required was a direct threat to military, industrial or civilian targets, and this only the bombers could provide. Once the defenders had risen to give battle, the German fighters could meet them in the element of their own choice. However fine this theory was, however, its practice gave rise to doubts, and these were expressed by both Sperrle and Kesselring. According to the fighter commander, Theo Osterkamp, on 1st August, when Göring held a meeting at The Hague to discuss the forthcoming operation, the Luftflotten commanders 'hesitated to stage [daylight] bomber attacks before the destruction of the British fighter force. They proposed, with reason, first to destroy, with continuous night bomber attacks, the ground organisation, the airfields etc. of the fighters, as well as the fighter producing industry centres. Only after the British fighter force had been decisively weakened should mass [day] attacks on the fighter fields around London take place'.[17] Göring, however, would have none of this, believing, as did many in the RLM, that not only had RAF Fighter Command already been substantially weakened, but that the Luftwaffe was quite capable of defeating it in daylight operations.

Thus, Göring's decision determined the tactics to be adopted during Adlerangriff. The short range of the Bf 109s meant that they would only be able to spend, at most, twenty minutes over the bombers' targets in south-east England, and then only if they flew straight across the Channel, instead of zig-zagging to match the slower speed of cruising bombers which they were supposed to support. That would give little enough time either to provide an adequate escort for the bombers or to engage the Hurricanes and Spitfires in combat. Moreover, escorting fighters were always at a disadvantage when meeting the enemy. As Osterkamp noted: '. . . they could neither determine the time of the attack nor exploit the advantages of height or the sun'.[18] The bombers usually kept to altitudes of between 13,000 and 15,000 ft., whereas the Bf 109s were at their best at altitudes above 20,000 ft., where their superiority over the Spitfire told. Moreover, the slow speeds of the bombers, which cruised at 190 mph, caused the fighters to be vulnerable until they had accelerated to their fighting speed of some 300 mph. But if the fighters operated independently, the bombers would be liable to suffer high losses, and that, apart from being unacceptable, would cause them to withdraw from the battle and leave the fighters without their bait. By the middle of August, the Luftwaffe had evolved a compromise. A bomber Geschwader would be given a fighter escort of one Gruppe, which would accompany it during the entire operation. In addition, another Gruppe would operate as an indirect escort, meeting the main bombers near the British defences, and then flying higher and ahead of the main body, so being able to attack the enemy whenever possible.

The force committed to Adlerangriff was composed of Luftflotten 2, 3 and 5. Luftflotte 5, under Stumpff, based in Norway, was formed of only Geisler's Fliegerkorps X (four Geschwader, one each of Ju 88s, He 111s, Bf 110s and Bf 109s, and coastal and reconnaissance units). Luftflotte 3, under Sperrle whose headquarters were in Paris, was made up of von Richthofen's Fliegerkorps VIII (three Ju 87 Geschwader, one Bf 109 Geschwader and reconnaissance units), von Greim's Fliegerkorps V (two Geschwader of Ju 88s and one of the He 111s), Pflugbeil's Fliegerkorps IV (three Geschwader, each of Ju 88s, He 111s, and Ju 87s, a Gruppe of Ju 88s and a reconnaissance Staffel), and Werner Junck's Jagdfliegerführer 3, (Fighter Commander 3 – a new tactical grouping of three Geschwader of Bf 109s, and one of Bf 110s). Kesselring's Luftflotte 2, with headquarters at Brussels, was to bear the main attack, and was composed of Grauert's Fliegerkorps I (two Geschwader of He 111s, Ju 88s and Do 17s and two long-range reconnaissance Staffeln), Lörzer's Fliegerkorps II (two Geschwader of Do 17s, one of He 111s, two Gruppen of Ju 87s, and an experimental Gruppe of Bf 109s and Bf 110s), Coeler's Fliegerdivision 9 (one Geschwader of He 111s and Ju 88s, one Gruppe of FW 200s in formation, various coastal detachments, and one Gruppe of He 111s used as 'Pathfinders'), Kurt von Döring's Jagdflieger-führer 2 (five Geschwader and one Gruppe, both of Bf 109s and two Geschwader of Bf 110s), and Kammhuber's Night-Fighter Division (one Geschwader of Bf 110s). On 10th August, this force comprised a total of 3,196 aircraft, of which 2,485 were serviceable. Of combat aircraft capable of taking part in Adlerangriff, Luftflotte 5, whose Bf 109s could only be used for defence, possessed 138 He 111s and Ju 88s (of which 123 were serviceable) and 37 Bf 110s (34), while Luftflotten 2 and 3 had between them 1,232 He 111s Ju 88s and Do 17s (875), 406 Ju 87s (316), 282 Bf 110s (227) and 813 Bf 109s (702). It was a formidable force.

Despite its mauling in Belgium and France, the Luftwaffe's opponent, RAF Fighter Command, was still a tough opponent. Its commander, the fifty-nine-year-old Air Chief Marshal Sir Hugh C.T. Dowding, was a highly respected officer, behind whose reserved manner lay an ability to command of the highest order. RAF Fighter Command, the headquarters of which were at Bentley Priory near Stanmore in north-west London, possessed fifty-nine squadrons, distributed over Britain in four Groups, each of which was subdivided into sectors, the main operational units. Of these, the most important was 11 Group, commanded by Air Vice Marshal Keith Park, which covered south-east England, including London, and contained some forty per cent of RAF Fighter Command's strength. On 1st August, there were 570 Hurricanes and Spitfires in the squadrons (two-thirds of which were Hurricanes) 203 being unserviceable, together with a further eight second-rate machines such as Fulmars and Defiants (the latter with no forward armament), two-thirds of which were unserviceable. Thus, in numbers of first-class fighters capable of operation, the Bf 109s of Luftflotten 2 and 3 outnumbered the Spitfires and Hurricanes of RAF Fighter Command by two to one, and the entire operational aircraft strength of the Luftwaffe in the West (not including Luftflotte 5) outnumbered the RAF defenders by over six to one. For the further defence of Britain, some 1,200 heavy and 650 light anti-aircraft guns were deployed, a negligible number when it is realised that, for the defence of the Reich, at least 2,000 heavy and 4,500 light guns were in action. However, during the forthcoming battle, anti-aircraft fire was to account for roughly twelve per cent of the Luftwaffe's casualties.

But if the amount of equipment available for the air defence of Britain was not impressive, its quality has often been the subject of some remark. Both the Hurricane and the Spitfire were excellent aircraft, significantly superior in aerial combat to anything possessed by the Germans, except for the Bf 109, its main opponent. Both were more manoeuvrable than the German fighter, in part because of the Bf 109s relatively weak wings, and were able to execute tighter turns, but there their advantages ended. The Bf 109 was capable of higher altitudes than both (up to 34,000 ft), and had a higher speed than the Hurricane at all altitudes (as did the Bf 110), and than the Spitfire at above 20,000 ft, and a diving performance better than either of theirs. Its armament, too, was superior, being heavier. Moreover, its pilots had developed tactics that were considerably more effective than those of the RAF, both in flexibility and protection. By contrast, the RAF pilots were instructed to place manoeuvre second to keeping formation. Moreover, RAF pre-war training had laid great stress on the defensive fire-power of bombers, with the result that fighter attacks were often broken off before it was necessary, and before they had been effective.

However, the RAF did possess two unique advantages. First, there was the benefit of fighting over its own territory, thereby minimising losses of aircrew and damaged aircraft and increasing the amount of time fighters could stay over the combat area. Secondly, there was the possession of a chain of twenty-nine radar stations, known as Radio Directional Finders (RDFs), along the southern and eastern coasts of England and Scotland. These were able to detect and track incoming aircraft flying from distances between forty to 100 miles. The help this gave to RAF Fighter Command was considerable. German-occupied Europe was no more than twenty minutes' flying time away from any target in south-east England, and it took a fighter half that time merely to reach an operational height at which interception of bombers was possible. Standing fighter patrols were extremely extravagant in terms of flying hours, men, and resources of all types, and RAF Fighter Command was too small to maintain enough of them at the necessary height for a sufficient time in every area to be protected. With the RDFs, however, this problem was largely solved, and RAF Fighter Command was enabled to use its scarce resources to their fullest extent. Not only was it informed of the direction and strength of the attacks well in advance, but it was able to keep its squadrons on the ground until the enemy was approaching and then direct them, through their sector stations, to the enemy formations.

At the time, the Germans knew little about the British radar system. However, they suspected its true purpose, so that, by September, the Luftwaffe had jamming devices ready to be put into operation, devices that were to give the British radar operators considerable difficulties. In the event, they were not used until the outcome of the Battle of Britain had been decided. That the Germans did not understand the full importance of the RDFs is evidenced by an intelligence summary, dated 7th August, which stated that the RAF fighters were 'controlled from the ground [and] are tied to their respective ground stations and are thereby restricted in mobility. . . . Consequently, the assembly of strong fighter forces at determined points and at short notice is not to be expected.'[19] However, it was precisely this the RDFs facilitated.

But RAF Fighter Command's system of air control, while it had strength, was also a potential weakness, because of its vulnerability. Certainly, owing to their construction, the RDF masts were difficult to destroy, but the vital receiver huts around them were not, nor were the operations rooms of the various sectors, situated at the most important airfields, nor, indeed, any of the airfield installations. Communications were by telephone cable, powered by electricity generated at the various stations or headquarters, and these were also vulnerable to bomb damage. A concentrated effort by the Germans against this system would have paid handsome dividends. Moreover, the air control had other severe defects. The RDFs could neither determine the height of incoming aircraft nor detect them at either very low or very high altitudes, and they were useless after the raiders had passed the coast. Then, the only means of detection lay in the eyes and ears of the Royal Observer Corps, whose ability to determine accurately the extent and direction of a raid was limited, especially during periods of cloudy weather. By a stratagem of feints and high or low altitude attacks, it would not have been impossible for the Luftwaffe to severely limit the effectiveness of even an intact RDF system. That the Luftwaffe failed to make any significant attempt to overcome the enemy radar has been regarded as its cardinal error of the Battle. As will be shown later, however, this is something of an over-simplification.

In addition to the fighters, the RAF also mustered some 500 bombers, mostly the twin-engined Hampdens, Wellingtons, and Whitleys, but all were below the performance of their German counterparts. They could not, of course, intercept the enemy's aircraft, but they did pose a threat to the airfields on the Continent, a threat which inhibited the Luftwaffe from committing all its forces to the attack at any one time. The Luftflotten commanders were always mindful of the security of their bases, and made sure that they held in reserve sufficient fighters for their protection. In the event, RAF Bomber Command did not undertake any such missions during the main part of the fighting, although in September it mounted attacks on the German naval preparations for Operation Sealion. However, the threat caused Bf 109s to be kept in Norway and prevented Luftflotten 2 and 3 from putting all their fighters in the air at once. Continual, if light, bombing of targets in the Reich caused a further 300 fighters to be withheld from the battle and committed to home defence.

In its appreciation of the enemy, the Luftwaffe both over- and under-estimated the fighting power of the RAF. In an intelligence summary dated 16th July, it was stated that RAF Fighter Command possessed some 900 Hurricanes and Spitfires (of which 675 were serviceable), and that RAF Bomber Command had 1,150 front-line bombers (of which seventy-five per cent were fit to fly). These figures exaggerated Britain's fighter strength by more than one-third, and her bomber strength by more than double. In other matters, the Luftwaffe's Intelligence underrated its enemy. While Britain's fighter pilots were highly regarded, their command structure was considered inflexible and their aircraft inferior to those possessed by the Germans (indeed, by implication, the Bf 110 was regarded as equal to, if not superior to, the Hurricane). It was believed that the aircraft industry was producing between 180 to 300 front-line fighters a month, and that output would decrease owing to difficulties in the supply of raw materials, disruption by air attack, and the like. As a result, any intensification of the air war would, it was alleged, cause the strength of the RAF to fall rapidly. In fact, in the month of July, British factories produced no less than 448 Hurricanes, Spitfires, Blenheims and Defiants. Only in the number of anti-aircraft guns, did the Intelligence appreciation come near to the truth; they were regarded as 'by no means adequate to ensure the protection of the island'. The conclusion drawn was that 'The Luftwaffe is clearly superior to the RAF as regards strength, equipment, training, command, and location of bases. In the event of an intensification of air warfare, the Luftwaffe, unlike the RAF, will be in a position, in every respect, to achieve a decisive effect this year. . . .'[20]

In numerical and qualitative terms, this conclusion was not so far from the truth as historians have suggested. Facing some 467 operational Spitfires and Hurricanes, supported by twenty-five operational Blenheims, Defiants and Gladiators (all second-rate aircraft) were 702 operational Bf 109s, which were, at the very least, their equals in performance and their superiors in use, supported, however ineffectively, by 261 operational Bf 110s and the defensive fire-power and bomb-loads of 998 operational bombers and 316 operational dive-bombers. It was a not inconsiderable superiority. With

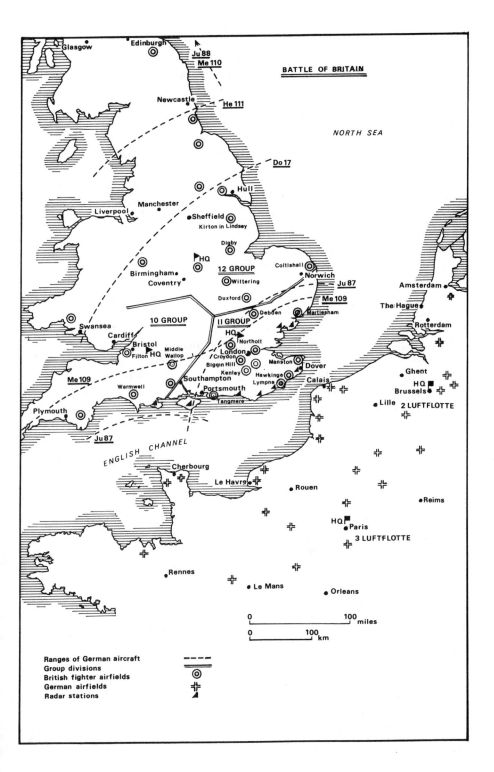

BATTLE OF BRITAIN

NORTH SEA

Glasgow
Edinburgh
Ju 88
Me 110
Newcastle
He 111
Do 17
Hull
Manchester
Liverpool
Sheffield
Kirton in Lindsey
Digby
HQ
Birmingham
Coventry
12 GROUP
Wittering
Coltishall
Norwich
Ju 87
Me 109
Amsterdam
The Hague
Duxford
Debden
Martlesham
Rotterdam
Swansea
10 GROUP
II GROUP
HQ
Cardiff
Northolt
Ghent
Bristol
Middle
London
Manston
Dover
HQ
Filton HQ
Wallop
Croydon
Brussels
Warmwell
Biggin Hill
Kenley
Hawkinge
Calais
Lille
2 LUFTFLOTTE
Me 109
Southampton
Lympne
Portsmouth
Tangmere
Plymouth
Ju 87
ENGLISH CHANNEL
Cherbourg
Le Havre
Rouen
Reims
HQ
Paris
3 LUFTFLOTTE
Rennes
Le Mans
Orleans

0   100 miles

0   100 km

Ranges of German aircraft
Group divisions
British fighter airfields
German airfields
Radar stations

roughly the same difference in reserves and replacements between the Luftwaffe and the RAF, and with the operation designed to last no more than a month at the outside, confidence was understandably high in the senior circles of the Luftwaffe. As General Stapf reported to Halder on 29th July: 'Our Luftwaffe on the whole feels that they have the edge on the British in equipment, leadership, staff and with respect to the geographical factors. Decisive results will be forthcoming before the close of the year'.[21]

On 6th August, Göring set the 10th as the date for the opening of Adlerangriff. The following day, the 7th, however, poor weather prospects caused a postponement of the offensive, which, on the 12th, was finally fixed for the following day, Tuesday the 13th. Until then, however, the Luftwaffe maintained its attacks on the British defences, and these had been considerably increased in intensity even though the weather was deemed unfavourable for Adlerangriff. After a lull in operations that had begun on 30th July, the Luftwaffe returned to the Kanalkampf with a vengeance on 8th August, when it shattered convoy CW9, seven of the twenty ships being sunk and six critically damaged, as well as four escort and rescue vessels. Although the Luftwaffe lost thirty-one aircraft in combat that day, the losses suffered by the RAF were appreciably higher in the all-important fighter battles, with sixteen Hurricanes and Spitfires shot down, whereas only eleven Bf 109s were destroyed, and three damaged. Three days later, on the 11th, further major battles took place over the Channel, the RAF losing twenty-nine fighters and seven damaged, and the Luftwaffe thirty-five aircraft, of which fifteen were Bf 109s, together with ten damaged. On the 12th, a new departure in Luftwaffe tactics was evident, although it was entirely in accord with the strategy of 'economic warfare' that was still in operation: the targets were RAF airfields and radar stations, along with the more traditional objectives of Portsmouth and shipping in the Thames estuary. The German bombers, heavily escorted, undertook six major operations, attacks in one area being timed to coincide with, or closely follow upon, raids or decoy threats elsewhere, thus stretching the reserves of RAF Fighter Command beyond their limit. The forward daytime landing airfields of Manston, Hawkinge, and Lympne, all on the coast of the Straits of Dover, were badly damaged (although serviceable by the next day), and six radar stations were attacked; five of them suffered little damage, (although at one every building was destroyed except the three that were vital to its operation), but the sixth, Ventnor on the Isle of Wight, was put out of action for some days, chiefly because of delayed-action bombs. This attack on the RAF radar system was the first, and the heaviest, of the entire air war against Britain, and was undertaken as a preliminary for Adlerangriff, scheduled for the next day. By the time darkness descended on the 12th, the Luftwaffe had lost twenty-six aircraft in combat, eleven of which were Bf 109s, and eight damaged. By comparison, the RAF had suffered a loss of twenty-two fighters, with a further four damaged. The balance of the fighter conflict, the most important aspect of the forthcoming offensive, was already unfavourable to the RAF.

The morning of the 13th, the day known as Adlertag, was dull and overcast. As a result, the early attack of Luftflotte 2 was called off, although Fink's Kampfgeschwader, not having received the cancellation, bombed the RAF Coastal Command airfield at Eastchurch. The same morning, units of Luftflotte 3 set out to attack RAF ground installations (unrelated to RAF Fighter Command), but failed to reach their targets. However, the purpose of the raids was not so much to inflict damage as to test the British defences in the south-east. In the afternoon, the weather improved, and the two Luftflotten mounted heavy attacks, this time bombing two airfields, the RAF Coastal Command station at Detling and the RAF Bomber Command base at Andover, together with the port of Southampton. Channel shipping was also attacked. Other bombs were dropped indiscriminately on the English countryside. Three of the main objectives, the RAF bases at Odiham, Farnborough and Rochford, were not even reached. That night, a raid was mounted on the Spitfire factory at Castle Bromwich, Birmingham, but only four of the nine He 111s involved found their target, and the damage inflicted was not sufficient to disrupt production. Bombs were also dropped on Bristol, Cardiff, Swansea, Liverpool, Sheffield, Norwich, Edinburgh, Aberdeen and Belfast. Only at the Short Brothers factory, where the new four-engined Stirling bombers were made, was any significant damage inflicted. Total civilian casualties throughout the night amounted to just over 100. In the twenty-four hours of Adlertag, the Luftwaffe had flown no less than 1,485 sorties against Britain, two-thirds of them by fighters, as against 727 by RAF Fighter Command. It lost in combat twenty bombers destroyed and fourteen badly damaged, fifteen Bf 110s shot down and six damaged, and nine Bf 109s destroyed. Apart from the loss of fourteen fighters destroyed and six damaged, RAF Fighter Command suffered no other damage during Adlertag.

The course of the fighting on the 13th high-lighted the significant error of judgement on the part of the Luftwaffe during the period that has come to be known as the Battle of Britain: the failure to concentrate fully upon the major enemy – RAF Fighter Command. At the beginning of its onslaught, the Luftwaffe's choice of targets indicated a lack of knowledge of the precise nature of its enemy's ground organisation, with its dependence on an elaborate network of operations rooms, sector airfields, observer posts and direction-finding posts, all of them linked by telephone cables. Thus, the Luftflotten, responsible for the choice of their targets, included airfields such as Eastchurch, Worthy Down and Upavon among their objectives, airfields which had not accommodated regularly-based fighters for almost ten years (although Eastchurch was at that time the temporary home of one fighter squadron). Moreover, ignorance of the factories producing fighters led it to regard the Woolston factory at Southampton as a manufacturer of bombers rather than the parent factor making Spitfires. Thus, the devastation of the only two targets listed for attention on Adlertag which were part of the enemy's fighter defence (RAF stations Rochford and Middle Wallop), had they in fact been bombed, would not have significantly impaired the operations of RAF Fighter Command for one moment. Certainly, none of the damage to those airfields actually hit caused any disruption to Dowding's operations. Moreover, not only did the Luftwaffe lack any clear idea of the precise nature of the RAF's dispositions, but it also dissipated its resources on targets such as Southampton and Channel shipping, targets that, it knew, played no part in Britain's air defence. For the future, in order to eliminate Park's 11 Group as an effective defensive organisation for south-east England, the Luftwaffe would have to put out of action a high proportion of its sector stations (Northolt, Tangmere, Debden, North Weald, Biggin Hill, Kenley and Hornchurch) controlling the fighters, and a number of its most important secondary airfields (such as Manston, Croydon, Westhampnett, Hawkinge, Gravesend, Rochford and Martlesham). In addition, two airfields in 10 Group, covering south-west England, Middle Wallop and Warmwell, were important targets. Much had to be done.

The Luftwaffe, however, was far from unimpressed by its own activities; on the 13th, it estimated that it had destroyed 134 British aircraft for the loss of thirty-four of its own, and on the next day, the 14th, an RLM report stated that, for the four days of heavy combat on the 8th, 11th, 12th and 13th, the 'primary objective of reducing enemy fighter strength in southern England' was meeting success: 'Ratio of own to enemy losses, 1:3 . . . lost three per cent of our first-class bombers and fighters, the enemy fifteen per cent. Fighters: Ratio of losses 1:5 in our favour . . . British will probably not be able to replace losses . . . Eight major air bases have been virtually destroyed.'[22] The RLM was wildly inaccurate, however. The numbers of aircraft destroyed in combat between the Luftwaffe and RAF Fighter Command were 136:96, while the ratio of losses in single-engined fighters was only 1:2 in the Luftwaffe's favour (forty-six Bf 109's to ninety-three Spitfires and Hurricanes), and significantly less than this if the thirty-five Bf 110s destroyed is added.

Over the next five days, the Luftwaffe maintained the pattern of operations it had begun on Adlertag. On the 14th, a day of poor weather, 489 sorties were flown, but on the 15th, when for the first and only time Luftflotte 5 joined the battle, there were 2,000 sorties, followed by 1,715 the following day. Little activity was shown on Saturday the 17th, but intense aerial operations on the 18th marked the last day of the first phase of the Battle. In combat, from the 13th to the 18th, inclusive, the Luftwaffe lost 247 aircraft, and RAF Fighter Command just over half that figure, 131. Vital RAF Fighter Command bases were attacked (Biggin Hill, Tangmere and Kenley, each once) as were other important aerodromes (Manston and Middle Wallop (thrice) and Croydon (twice), together with a number of lesser airfields such as Lympne, Hawkinge and Martlesham and two maintenance units at Sealand and Colerne. The damage inflicted was for the most part light, and repairable after a few hours, although a few stations suffered fairly considerable disruption. At West Malling, for example, the only airfield to be put out of action for more than twenty-four hours, the damage took several days to make good. At Croydon, the operations room suffered a significant attack on the 15th; at Tangmere on the 16th, many buildings and fourteen aircraft on the ground were destroyed or damaged and electricity and water services temporarily cut; and at Kenley, the Luftwaffe inflicted such a severe mauling on the 18th, that, thereafter, it could accommodate only two squadrons instead of three. In addition, raids were mounted on two radar stations, at Ventnor, on the 16th, where further delay caused to its repair prevented it operating again until the 23rd), and at Poling, in West Sussex, on the 18th, which was temporarily put out of action.

However, raids on RAF Fighter Command bases formed but a small part of the Luftwaffe's activity over England. On the 15th, the day of heaviest activity during the entire Battle, and known as 'Black Thursday' by the Luftwaffe because never again in the war against Britain was it to suffer such high losses in one day, nearly fifty of the seventy aircraft lost in operations (with eight heavily damaged) fell in raids on targets quite irrelevant to the operations of RAF Fighter Command; fortunately for the defenders, cloudy weather prevented German bombers from finding a number of the fighter bases. On that day, for the loss of one-eighth of its bomber force (fifteen He 111s and Ju 88s, with three heavily damaged) and one fifth of its Bf 110s (seven machines), Luftflotte 5 destroyed ten Whitley bombers at Driffield aerodrome, an ammunition dump and some thirty houses in Sunderland and Bridlington, for the loss to RAF Fighter Command of only one damaged Hurricane. Throughout these four August days, other airfields quite unrelated to the immediate air defence of the United Kingdom were attacked, such as Lee-on-Solent (Coastal Command), Harwell, Brize Norton, Farnborough, Ford, Gosport (both naval air stations) Thorney Island, (Coastal Command), Worthy Down, Eastchurch, Linton-upon-Ouse, Dishforth, and Andover. Airfields of great value to RAF Fighter Command were left untouched, Hornchurch and Northolt being the two most important; others were Debden, North Weald, Gravesend, and West-hampnett, all within Park's 11 Group. In addition, the Luftwaffe aimed some of its raids against the British aircraft industry in an attempt to destroy the RAF's life-blood. Factories at Filton, Rochester, and Croydon were damaged, the last fairly severely, but others escaped scot free. Nine attempts to bomb the Westland, Rolls-Royce and Gloster works were made, but only twice did the bombs fall within five miles of the target. Nothing approaching even a partial dislocation of the aviation industry was achieved; attacks on the factories proved almost as wasteful as the raids on shipping, railways, and military targets ranging from Southampton to Birmingham. Even the Varne Lightship was not considered to be beneath the attentions of Luftflotte 2.

At the end of the first phase of the Battle, the Germans had little to show for their effort. Losses and damage from all causes (including bad landings and other mishaps) from 13th to 18th August amounted to 350 aircraft for the Luftwaffe and 171 for RAF Fighter Command (or approaching 250 if all RAF losses are taken into account, such as the forty-six trainers destroyed at Brize Norton). The ability of the British to put their fighters up in the air in sufficient numbers to prove dangerous remained unimpaired. The Luftwaffe clearly needed to reconsider its strategy. Indeed, during this first phase, some attempt had been made to restrict the attacks to certain, well-defined, targets. On the night of the 13th, Göring had ordered that the offensive should concentrate on RAF ground installations, an instruction he repeated on the 15th, when he held a conference with the senior commanders of the three Luftflotten. It was laid down: 'Until further orders, operations are to be directed exclusively against the enemy air force, including the targets of the enemy aircraft industry . . .'[23] Göring also added that it was deemed doubtful whether further attacks on the radio-directional masts would be worth while, since the Germans believed that none had been put out of action by the onslaught on the 11th.

Göring's instructions were put into action, and the radars were subjected to only two further, minor, attacks; in future, the Luftwaffe concentrated almost exclusively on the Royal Air Force, but this still did not enable them to achieve victory. By the 18th, an Intelligence report estimated that the British had lost 770 fighters in the period from 1st July to 16th August and that only 300 were still operational, whereas in reality 214 had been destroyed and seventy-one damaged in combat, and more than 600 were still operational. But to the German pilots in the air, it was clear that RAF Fighter Command was far from incapable of defending British airspace. On the 18th, the highest total casualties of the Battle were experienced, with sixty-eight British and sixty-nine German aircraft being shot down. On the next day, the 19th, at another conference at Karinhall, a further narrowing of the Luftwaffe's objectives was ordered. Göring announced: 'We have reached the decisive period of the air war against England. The vital task is to turn all means at our disposal to the defeat of the enemy air force. Our first aim is the destruction of the enemy's fighters. If they no longer take to the air, we shall attack them on the ground, or force them into battle by directing bomber attacks against targets within range of air fighters.'[24] So far so good; the main objective had been clearly defined. The destruction of RAF Fighter Command would be the object of the daylight raids, and the bombers would be used primarily to tempt the RAF interceptors into action with the Bf 109s, and to destroy their airfields. Luftflotte 2, with its bases nearer south-east England, would take on the brunt of the daylight fighting, while Luftflotte 3 would undertake night raids. Park's II Group, with its bases ringing London in a protective screen, would be made the prime target. Over this most vital corner of England, the resources of RAF Fighter Command would be drawn in to meet destruction at the hands of Luftflotte 2, which, henceforth, would employ three or four fighters to every bomber. Victory here, dominance of the airspace over the greatest capital city of the world, would mean that in the air the Battle of Britain had been won, however temporarily, and that the invasion could proceed.

At the meeting on the 19th, certain tactical changes were also decided upon. In the previous six days, no less than forty-four Ju 87s had been destroyed, and seven damaged, (twelve per cent of the total in Luftflotten 2 and 3). Henceforth, they would be conserved to give close support to the Army when the invasion took place; only two Staffeln would be retained for operations against the RAF when pin-point accuracy was required, and they would be used only when local air supremacy had been assured. The poor manoeuvrability of the heavy Bf 110s had ensured that the elite Zerstörer units had suffered severely, no less than sixty-seven being lost, and eleven damaged, (twenty-four per cent of the total in Luftflotte 2, 3 and 5), but Göring would not hear of their being withdrawn. Instead, he instructed the Bf 109 fighter units to add the Bf 110s, some of which would be used as light bombers, to their escort responsibilities.

The Reichsmarschall then proceeded to place much of the blame for the Luftwaffe's failings on the Bf 109 pilots. Despite the fact that they had accounted for the great majority of the RAF's fighter losses, and that they themselves had had only fifty-four machines shot down and seven damaged (seven per cent of the total of Luftflotte 2 and 3), he insisted on ascribing to them a lack of aggression. This, he asserted, had brought about a high casualty rate among the bombers (eighty-two destroyed and twenty-eight damaged, eight per cent of the total of the three Luftflotten) and dive-bombers. Paying no attention to the difficulties experienced by the fighters in effecting rendezvous with the bombers, in remaining long over the target area, and in escorting closely the slower aircraft (thus giving the enemy fighters the advantage of speed and surprise), Göring insisted that, henceforth, they must do all they could to fulfil their task of protection, quite unaware that escort duty was not compatible with the destruction of the enemy. Over the forthcoming weeks, several of the older fighter commanders were replaced by younger men, who, it was hoped, would instil the élan that was thought to be so lacking among the Jagdgeschwader. Osterkamp, for example, left his Jagdgeschwader to become Jagdführer in Luftflotte 2, his command being taken by the younger Werner Mölders. Adolf Galland also took command of another Geschwader. Young though such men were, they soon proved themselves worthy of their new responsibilities. The resentment of the fighter force, however, at its treatment by the Luftwaffe high command was considerable. As Galland wrote after the war, at its inception, 'The fighter arm was not regarded as part of the strategic air arm. It was looked upon as a tactical weapon. When the German fighter pilots were given strategical tasks during the course of the Battle of Britain, there was surprise that they were not equal to them, and people spoke of a "let-down". . . . We felt like the Cinderellas of the German Luftwaffe, and that is what we were.'[25]

Finally, at the meeting of the 19th, it was reaffirmed that the British radio directional-finding masts, difficult to destroy because of their construction, would not be a target for the Luftwaffe. Göring concluded that it was doubtful whether there was any point in continuing the attacks on radar sites, 'in view of the fact that not one of those attacked has so far been put out of action'.[26] Factually, he was wrong, since the RDF on the Isle of Wight had been made inoperable. His order, however, was carried out; with the exception of two raids on separate stations, no attempt was made to put the British radar system out of action until jamming was begun. For the Luftwaffe's conduct of operations in the first stage of the Battle, this was a major mistake. Detection by radar, in conjunction with the forewarning of German moves given by British intelligence (who had broken the German code by a system known as Ultra), was to prove valuable to RAF Fighter Command. Despite all the deceptions practiced by the Germans, which included feints and screening raids, the British fighters were more often than not in the air at the right place and height to meet the invaders, thus making unescorted bomber attacks quite impossible. However, ironically, in the second phase, when the Luftwaffe pursued the only strategy that could have gained its victory, radar and Ultra were more of an aid to the attackers than a disadvantage. Then, the destruction of the British fighters, whether on the ground or in the air, was paramount, and the bombers were in large part used as bait to tempt them into combat, when the Spitfires and Hurricanes would be outclassed by the Bf 109s. Deichmann, then chief of staff to Fliegerkorps II, argued that, since the object of the Battle was to destroy RAF Fighter Command, every warning the latter received as to an approaching attack would be beneficial. In a gladiatorial contest, as phase two (and, in part, phase three) undoubtedly was, it did not help to have one of the participants missing.

The second phase of the Battle of Britain did not immediately follow the first. From 19th to 23rd August there was a lull in the fighting due both to poor weather and to the Luftwaffe's reorganisation of its fighter forces facing England, the majority of which were concentrated under the command of Luftflotte 2 in the Pas de Calais, the point nearest to their target. However, it was deemed important to give the RAF as little respite as possible, and bombers were therefore sent in small, scattered, raids the length and breadth of Britain. RAF Fighter Command did not escape attention, Manston and Tangmere, for example, were attacked. In the five-day 'lull', the RAF lost fifteen fighters destroyed and seventeen damaged in combat, and the Luftwaffe twenty-seven destroyed (of which only one was a Bf 109) and seven damaged. On the 24th, the Luftwaffe began the second phase of operations, with 1,030 day-time sorties over the south of England. Manston suffered two attacks, which damaged it so severely that its aircraft had to be withdrawn, and Hornchurch and North Weald were also bombed, the latter quite heavily. However, the Luftwaffe's attention was still not wholly concentrated on RAF Fighter Command; Southampton was attacked during the day, and at night over 170 bombers were sent to targets around England, which included aircraft factories and oil storage tanks as well as aerodromes, but to little effect. At the close of the day's operations, RAF Fighter Command had lost twenty-three aircraft destroyed and six damaged in combat, and the Luftwaffe thirty-five destroyed and four damaged. Both sides were aware of changes in their opponent's tactics. The defenders noted that the German formations contained fewer bombers and more fighters (as shown by the casualties – fourteen bombers shot down as against seventeen Bf 109s), and that greater attention was being paid to escort work, while the attackers noticed that the British were even more reluctant to do battle with their fighters, searching instead for their bombers. Indeed, this was Park's new strategy, designed to preserve his force; only if RAF Fighter Command's vital sector stations were threatened, would the pilots be allowed to accept combat with fighter and bomber alike.

However, the new German targets meant that the RAF fighters would soon find themselves in conflict with the large formations sent over daily by Luftflotte 2. On the 25th, Warmwell aerodrome was attacked, its communications being disrupted for eighteen hours; on the 26th, Debden was badly damaged, and Luftflotte 3 undertook its last daylight raid, once again on Southampton; on the 27th, Rochford suffered slight damage, but Eastchurch was severely bombed; and on the 29th Biggin Hill was attacked twice, and sustained some of the worst destruction yet experienced. On the 31st, Luftflotte 2 launched its heaviest attack of phase two; 1,450 daylight sorties aimed primarily at five aerodromes, Biggin Hill, Debden, Hornchurch, Croydon and Eastchurch. The following day, 1st September, Biggin Hill suffered its sixth raid in three days; on the 2nd, Lympne and Hornchurch were attacked; on the 3rd, North Weald and West Malling; on the 4th, Lympne and Eastchurch, and on the 5th, Biggin Hill once again. As a result of these raids, Biggin Hill was left fit for use by only one of its three squadrons, and joined Kenley, Manston, Lympne and Hawkinge as aerodromes that had been rendered incapable of functioning adequately (as also was Eastchurch, an RAF Coastal Command station used by fighter units). The RAF was losing the war in the air. The sector stations that were daily the targets of the Luftwaffe were vital to RAF Fighter Command, serving as its nerve centres, through which higher command was exercised, and from which the aircraft assigned to meet the enemy were controlled. Many were the times that the pilots of the Spitfires and Hurricanes managed to deflect the raiders from their stations (the most memorable day was the 26th, when the Luftwaffe was prevented from reaching Hornchurch, North Weald and Manston), but that was not so important to the Germans. The threat that they posed to these sector stations was enough to cause the RAF fighters to engage in combat, and it was this that really mattered.

From 24th August to 6th September, the last day of phase two of the Battle of Britain, the Luftwaffe came near to achieving its aim. During this period, RAF Fighter Command lost 273 fighters in combat, with a further forty-nine damaged, whereas the Germans lost 308 aircraft, and sixty-six damaged. The margin of losses between the two sides was significantly narrower than in the previous phase. Indeed, for the final eight days, from 30th August to 6th September, equal numbers of aircraft were destroyed in combat on both sides (the Germans had rather more damaged), and, for the first three days in September, the Luftwaffe actually suffered significantly fewer combat losses: forty-three destroyed and thirteen damaged compared with sixty-two and thirteen respectively for RAF Fighter Command. In fighter combat, the Germans were, as always, markedly superior despite all the disadvantages which came from operating over enemy territory, losing to the RAF fighters only 146 Bf 109s destroyed and twenty-seven damaged; whereas the Bf 109s destroyed 208 Spitfires and Hurricanes, and damaged thirty-one.

By the end of the first week in September, then, RAF Fighter Command was facing defeat both in the air and on the ground; von Döring, co-commander of Jafü 2 with Osterkamp, claimed on 29th August that the Luftwaffe possessed 'unlimited fighter superiority'.[27] Indeed, the RAF was faced with the prospect of disappearing from the sky altogether. Losses of fighters, averaging nineteen and a half shot down each day, were too high to be sustained for long. From all causes, including such mundane ones as bad landings, the RAF had lost 657 fighters in the period 8th August to 6th September, of which some eighteen per cent were classified as 'damaged'. Until then, sufficient replacements had been available; on 1st September, the front-line strength of RAF Fighter Command was similar to what it had been a month previously: 650 machines (244 of which were unserviceable), including 358 serviceable Spitfires and Hurricanes. Reserves, however, were dwindling. In the week ending 6th July, there had been no less than 518 Spitfires and Hurricanes in maintenance and storage units; in the week ending 7th September, this figure had shrunk to 292, and was destined to go down to 254 by the 14th. Losses, therefore, were exceeding production at a considerable rate; in the week ending 31st August, for example, only 91 Spitfires and Hurricanes had been turned out of the factories, while 137 had been destroyed completely and a further 11 had suffered significant or serious damage. Thus, it was reckoned that, should losses continue at the same rate as they had been during the preceding weeks, the reserves of fighters would be exhausted in three weeks, after which a steady depletion in the front-line strength of RAF Fighter Command would be experienced (it would take some four weeks to destroy all the serviceable Hurricanes and Spitfires, although well before then the squadrons would have ceased to be effective fighting units). Should the Luftwaffe be fortunate enough to damage severely a fighter-producing factory as well, the end would be hastened. As it was, given continuous production at the current rate, and the ability of the Luftwaffe to maintain its onslaught, effective air superiority would go to the Germans in four to five weeks. Before that had come to pass, should RAF Fighter Command come to the conclusion that it had no alternative but to withdraw 11 Group from south-east England altogether, the essential precondition for an invasion could be fulfilled far sooner.

The RAF also faced defeat from another cause: the loss of fighter pilots. A shortage in trained fliers had been experienced for some time, about 300 having been lost during the campaign for France and Flanders in May. A steady, though small, drain had continued since then, although it was more than compensated for by the new pilots coming from the training schools. The first phase of the Battle, however, had taken a further, significant toll.

Between 8th and 18th August, 154 pilots had been killed, severely wounded or listed as 'missing'; in the same period, only sixty-three new fighter pilots had left their schools. At the end of the first phase, it was reckoned that, just to bring the existing squadrons up to their full establishment, 350 new pilots were required; the number due to complete their training in the next nine days was less than eighty. In the second phase, the situation worsened; from 24th August to 1st September, 231 pilots were killed, wounded, or missing, a wastage in one week of more than twenty per cent of RAF Fighter Command's combat strength. At the end of August, the number of pilots in RAF Fighter Command was 1,023, roughly one third less than the previous month (1,434). By the first week of September, Dowding's squadrons had, on average, only sixteen operational pilots out of their full complement of twenty-six. As Dowding himself recalled: '. . . the incidence of casualties became so serious that a fresh squadron would become depleted and exhausted before any of the resting and reforming squadrons were ready to take its place.'[28] Just as worrying as this numerical depletion, was the diminution in combat experience of the average fighter pilot. In July and August, no less than eleven of the forty-six squadron commanders and thirty-nine of the ninety-seven flight commanders had been killed or seriously wounded, while seven flight commanders had been promoted to take charge of squadrons. This loss of experienced leadership was placing intolerable burdens on the surviving 'old hands', of whom there were no more than 500. The rest of the pilots were young men, often having flown no more than twenty hours in fighters before they joined their squadrons. Even volunteer pilots who came from other units in the RAF were quite inexperienced in fighter tactics and manoeuvres. Nor was it uncommon for the men of 11 and 10 Groups to go into action three or even four times a day; the physical and psychological stress was intolerable. One squadron, No.85, based at Croydon, had fourteen of its eighteen pilots shot down in two weeks, two of them twice. In the first week of September, RAF Fighter Command was near to breaking point.

It was on the ground, however, that RAF Fighter Command faced its most immediate danger. The attacks on the airfields were, at last, having their effect. Difficult though it was to prevent 11 Group from operating (squadrons could be moved to new airfields; cratered runways could usually be mended fairly easily; emergency airfields could be activated, and so on), the continual hammering of the sector stations around London which controlled their operations could not but have severe consequences. Manston was out of use except for emergency landings; West Malling, Lympne, and Hawkinge were more or less untenable; Biggin Hill was on the verge of becoming completely inoperable, and Hornchurch and Debden would soon be so. It only needed concentrated attacks to be made on Kenley and Tangmere, with additional attacks on Croydon, Westhampnett and Gravesend, to put them out of action as alternative sector stations, and it would then be impossible for 11 Group to carry on the defence of south-east England from stations south of London.

As Park wrote:

> The enemy's bombing attacks by day did extensive damage to five of
> our forward aerodromes, and also to six of our seven sector stations.
> By 5th September the damage was having a serious effect on fighting
> efficiency. . . . The absence of many telephone lines, the use of scratch
> equipment in emergency operations rooms, and the general dislo-
> cation of ground organisation was seriously felt in the handling of
> squadrons. . . . Had the enemy continued his heavy attacks against
> Biggin Hill and the adjacent sectors, and destroyed their operations
> rooms or telephone communications, the fighter defences of London
> would have been in a perilous state. . . . [29]

Withdrawal north of London was near to being forced on the RAF, taking its
bases as far from the English Channel and intended German landing areas as
were those of the Luftwaffe. Air superiority over Kent and Essex, at least for a
week or two, was in the Luftwaffe's grasp; the aim of Adlerangriff was near to
being realised.

What of the Luftwaffe at this point? Certainly, it was experiencing
difficulties. The fatigue of the crews was considerable. They had not been
rotated as the RAF pilots had been, and the need for bomber escorts in
particular had caused the fighter pilots to undertake two sorties daily over
many weeks. Losses in aircrew had been high, five for every one lost by the
enemy, so that Göring was forced to give an order that no more than one
officer be allowed in each aircraft. The fighter arm was short of three per cent
of its pilots to fly the serviceable Bf 109s, although the bomber arm had an
eighteen per cent surplus. Material losses, too, were high. In the fortnight
beginning 24th August, the Air Force lost in the West, from all causes, 545
aircraft of all types destroyed or damaged, some two hundred more than the
total RAF losses. However, the offensive of the Luftwaffe had not be blunted.
By the end of the second phase on 7th September, Luftflotten 2 and 3 between
them possessed 1,158 bombers (772 operational), 232 Bf 110s, (129 operational) and 787 Bf 110s (623 operational). Apart from the almost total
withdrawal of the Ju 87 units (together with a Bf 110 Gruppe that had been
converted for use in ground-attack in preparation for the invasion), the past
month had seen a diminution in the serviceable combat strength of the two
Luftflotten by roughly one seventh of its bombers and only one eighth of its
Bf 109s. The supply of both machines and pilots, although strained, was
proving sufficient, but the low production of Bf 109s, which was averaging
some 190 a month (just about one half that of Spitfires and Hurricanes) was
giving rise to some concern. In the month from 8th August to 6th September,
the losses of Bf 109s from all causes amounted to 289, about one and a half
times the output from the factories, together with eight damaged, of which a
quarter would be repaired. However, reserves were, for the time being
adequate, and bomber units were eighty six per cent of their establishment
and single-engine fighter units eighty per cent. Not only had the two

Luftflotten some 620 operational Bf 109s to face their 350 serviceable counterparts in the RAF, but they also possessed 891 bombers and Bf 110s, which, while no match for the enemy's fighters, had, between them, succeeded in destroying some sixty in the previous fortnight (i.e. one for every five destroyed by the Bf 109s). As the inexperience of the RAF squadrons increased, so also would the success of the German bombers and twin-engined fighters, whose crews were, thus far at least, more easily replaced with experienced personnel.

Indeed, during the operations of the previous fortnight, despite the fatigue felt by the pilots and aircrews, matters had never been better for the Germans. In the first phase of the Battle, they had lost an average of forty-one aircraft a day in combat, whereas in the second phase the number fell to just twenty-two (in terms of aircraft loss per sortie, there was a corresponding fall, from roughly one in every fifty-eight in the first phase to one in seventy-six in the second). Bomber losses had decreased significantly; only ninety-four had been destroyed and twenty-five damaged in the fourteen days ending on the 6th. Only in the employment of Bf 110s were the Germans still sadly deficient, with no lesss than fifty-nine destroyed and seventeen damaged in combat between 24th August and 6th September. The losses of Bf 109s, while large, were nevertheless little higher than in the first phase (an average of eleven a day compared to nine), and were certainly less than the number of enemy fighters they themselves destroyed (a ratio of almost 1:1.5). Reports from the front-line indicated that, for the first time, the strength of the British defence was failing, and that was confirmed by Luftwaffe Intelligence. On 3rd September, the RLM gave OKW a report dealing with the results of the battle from 5th August to 1st September, in which it noted that, in addition to significant damage to the RAF's ground organisation, RAF Fighter Command had only 600 aircraft left, of which 420 were operational, a reserve of 100, and a monthly output from the factories of 300. These figures, although inaccurate, were not entirely misleading; RAF Fighter Command had, in fact, significantly fewer machines operational than the Luftwaffe believed: 404, which, if the Defiants and Blenheims are discounted as of little or no value in operations, left just 358. However, the number of reserves (including those under maintenance and repair, which the RLM report had not taken into account), was larger by almost two hundred, and the manufacture of Spitfires and Hurricanes was higher by some ninety machines a month. Nevertheless, given the state of RAF Fighter Command in the first week of September, it is difficult to disagree with the conclusions of the report: 'The British fighter defence is severely crippled. In case the German attacks on British fighters were to continue in September, and if the weather is favourable, the British fighter defence is likely to be so weakened that air attacks on British production centres and, port installations can be increased, with the result that British supplies will suffer seriously'.[30] The report could have added that, in the circumstances of an aerial victory, the invasion might be undertaken. However, just as it was on the verge of victory, the Luftwaffe turned its attention to pastures new.

During the second phase of the Battle, RAF Fighter Command, while it had been the Germans prime target, had not been the only one. Indeed, Göring's orders on 19th August had stipulated that: 'At the same time [as the destruction of the enemy's fighters], and on a growing scale, we must continue our activities against the ground organisation of the bomber units. Surprise attacks on the enemy aircraft industry must be made by day and by night'.[31] In addition, port installations were to receive attention. There were two reasons for this: the Luftwaffe was concerned both to prepare the ground for the invasion of Britain (or for economic blockade if there were to be no invasion), and to deny to the RAF the means to continue the fight. Thus, Luftflotte 3 made its last major daylight raid on Portsmouth on 24th August, but undertook night raids on Liverpool, Sheffield, Bristol, Birmingham, Exeter, Coventry, and numerous other towns and cities throughout Britain. Its targets included such places as on the Spitfire factory at Castle Bromwich (Birmingham), and the Merseyside docks area, which on the night of 28th-29th August, was bombed for the first time in the heaviest night raid up to that time, the beginning of an ordeal that was to last for four consecutive nights. During the fortnight ending on the 6th, some 2,500 sorties were made by the Luftflotte (roughly one fifth of all sorties made between 18th August and 6th September), causing much discomfort but little disruption. As the Allies themselves were to find later in the war, it was difficult enough for a horizontal attack bomber flying above effective anti-aircraft artillery range (25,000 ft) to hit a factory by day, let alone by night. Even if the target were to be hit, it was quite another matter for it to be destroyed. For example, in a later period of the air war, on 26th September, the factories producing Spitfires at Woolston and Itchin at Southampton were hit; but, although the buildings were seriously damaged, the machine-tools and jigs inside were not. Production was continued under canvas, with little detriment to final output for the month; the work was later dispersed to thirty-five smaller factories within a fifty-five mile radius of Southampton, which made the whole process almost invulnerable to air attack. Certainly, the German night attacks in the second phase had no effect on RAF Fighter Command's capacity to continue the Battle, and did very little damage to the British war economy.

However, although the night bombing may not have done much good to the Luftwaffe's cause, neither did it do much harm. Undertaken by bombers and involving no fighter escort, it came at a time when German daytime tactics relied upon the Bf 109s rather than the He 111s, Do 17s and Ju 88s. Of these, Luftflotte 2 had sufficient for its prime task of bombing RAF airfields and of acting as bait to attract the RAF fighters by day, while Luftflotte 3 could take responsibility for operations by night. But it was not long before the attention of the German bombers was diverted during the day from the RAF stations to targets that were more properly the province of the night-raiders. On 30th August, thirty He 111s penetrated the RAF fighter screen as far as Luton, where they bombed the town and civil airport, as well as the Vauxhall

Reichsmarschall Hermann Göring

Hitler and Göring together, 1938

Field Marshal Erhard Milch

General Walther Wever

General Hans Jeschonnek

General Ernst Udet

General Hans Jurgen Stumpff

Field Marshal Albert Kesselring

Field Marshal Hugo Sperrle

General Otto Rüdel

Milch with a visiting Italian Air Marshal, 1938

Göring hands a Luftwaffe standard to a unit of the former Austrian Air Force, 1938

The standard-bearer of the Condor Legion, 1939

Field Marshal Wolfram von Richthofen

General Hans Keller

General Otto Dessloch

General Alexander Löhr

General Bruno Lörzer

General Kurt Student

General Hans Grauert

General Joachim Coehler

A Ju 86 bomber

An He 51 fighter

He 111 bomber

Do 17 bomber

An Hs 123 ground attack aircraft

Ju 88 bomber

Ju 87 dive bombers

Bf 110 fighters

Bf 109 fighter

Do 217 bomber

FW 190 fighter

Ju 388 bomber

He 177 bomber

W 200 bomber-reconnaissance aircraft

Me 210 multi-purpose aircraft

Hs 129 ground attack aircraft

Me 262 jet fighter

aircraft works, inflicting 113 casualties. On 1st September, Tilbury docks were attacked, and over the following days aircraft factories in the Medway towns and at Weybridge were included among German targets. Raids on RAF stations declined in number, and after the 3rd did no significant damage. Finally, on 6th September, the oil storage installations at Thameshaven were heavily bombed. The Luftwaffe was embarking upon a new plan of attack.

London had always been a favourite target among several senior Luftwaffe commanders, including Jeschonnek. In submitting its plans for Adlertag, for example, the command of Fliegerkorps II had proposed that the British capital be made the main objective. It had recognised the impossibility of sending the bombers into the interior of England in daylight without fighter escort, and had understood that the British fighter defence would be primarily destroyed by the German Bf 109s. An attack on London would force RAF Fighter Command to defend the city with all the reserves at its disposal; it was here that air superiority could be won, a superiority that would then allow the German bombers free range in whatever task was assigned them. As the fighter ace, Adolf Galland, wrote in his memoirs: 'The fact that London was within the range of day-bombing attacks with fighter cover . . . must be regarded as one of the positive aspects of our offensive. We fighter pilots, discouraged by a task which was beyond our strength, were looking forward impatiently and excitedly to the start of the bomber attacks [on London]. We believed that only then would the English fighters leave their bases and be forced to give us open battle'.[32] The General Staff had proposed such a course of action in its initial plans for Adlerangriff, but was unable to carry it out owing to Hitler's prohibition of attacks on London. Indeed, the idea of concentrating on a vital target to lure the enemy fighters into action had lain behind the introduction of a new pattern of operations on 19th August, although instead of London it would be London's RAF defenders themselves (primarily 11 Group) that would form the target.

However, by the first week of September, there was considerable dissatisfaction with the outcome of phase two. Still, the reluctance of the RAF fighters to give combat with the Bf 109s was noticeable, and the German pilots, believing victory was within their grasp, were becoming exasperated by the constant appearance of RAF Fighter Command in strength, an appearance facilitated not by any great numbers of fighters, but by the operation of the RDFs. The higher command recognised that their opponents were weakening, and probably realised that it was only a matter of time before victory was theirs. But time was of the essence; in mid-August, OKW had specified 15th September as the beginning of the invasion, a date which, on 3rd September, was postponed to the 21st. Air superiority, which, it was recognised, had still to be gained must be assured by then. With this in mind, Göring told Kesselring and Sperrle on 3rd September: 'We have no chance of destroying the English fighters on the ground. We must force their last reserves . . . into combat in the air'.[33] Certainly, the British were giving battle to defend their sector stations, and were prepared to suffer heavily for it. But, it was argued, they would commit themselves to the utmost only in defence of their capital. Moreover, that battle would be over a far smaller area than hitherto, an area in which the German fighters could make sure of their prey. Sperrle, however, disagreed, fearing that the British fighters still remained a formidable force, as, indeed, for a few weeks longer they would have been. He wanted the offensive against their installations to continue. Kesselring, however, agreed with Göring and the matter was decided in favour of the proposed change. Henceforth, the aim would be to destroy not only the enemy's fighter defence, but also the London docks, one of his vital economic centres, a target the elimination of which would, it was considered, 'hasten the end of the war.'[34] It was, for the Luftwaffe, a fortunate combination of objectives – or so it was thought.

Whether the decision to attack London was militarily sound or not, it would have remained academic had not Hitler supported it. In all his Directives concerning the air war, the Führer had stipulated that he, and he alone, would decide when to attack the British capital from the air. His ban on such action was inspired by political and military reasons; he had no wish either to outrage international opinion, inflame the British against Germany at a time when he still wanted an honourable peace, or court retaliation by RAF Bomber Command. But in allowing his Luftwaffe to range over Britain at night, Hitler was playing with fire. One night, the inevitable happened; on 24th August, some bombers overshot their targets, the oil installations at Rochester and Thameshaven, east of London, and dropped their loads over the centre of the capital. It was a mistake, but this the British were not to know. In retaliation, eighty-one aircraft of RAF Bomber Command took off for Berlin the next night, ten of them dropping their loads on the target. It was an operation that was repeated on three further nights that month. The damage inflicted was insignificant, but the Führer's anger great. Not only was he affronted by the enemy's deliberate attack on the Reich's capital, and outraged by the indiscriminate bombing practised, but he was also fearful for his own popularity. The Berliners were stunned; they had been assured that no bombs would land on them. Retaliation was imperative. On 31st August, Hitler gave his permission for reprisal attacks with strong forces against London, and on 3rd September he asked for an increase in the output of 2,200lb bombs, designed for use against built-up areas; on the 4th, he announced in public: 'When they declare that they will attack our cities in great strength, then we will erase theirs'.[35] On the night of 5th-6th September the first raid on London took place. The 'Blitz' had begun.

Even without the element of retaliation in Hitler's decision to bomb London, it is probable that he would have allowed the Luftwaffe to embark upon such a course in any case. For the Führer, in common with many of the military and naval leaders, had always had his doubts as to the feasibility of a full-scale invasion. This was in large part because of the Navy's inability to transport sufficient forces and to keep them supplied during the vital weeks of the build-up of the bridge-head, which, initially, was to have a frontage of 150 miles. By the end of August, the plans for Operation Sealion had been substantially revised. Not only was it to take place over a far smaller area, but it was to be viewed simply as the means to finish off the British once they had been already defeated by air power. Hitler, fearful of strong enemy resistance to an invasion, saw the Luftwaffe as the instrument which would bring the island race to the brink of collapse. By the beginning of September, therefore, both the Führer and the Luftwaffe high command believed that the time was ripe for the adoption of a 'Douhetian' policy of bombing designed to bring about victory independently of the other two services. Only in the targetting was there any disagreement; the Air Force commanders wanted to attack residential areas in order to induce mass panic, but Hitler would have none of it. The only civilians to suffer would be those who lived near military targets in the middle of cities. Only once the invasion was under way, would the Führer countenance the bombing of the capital with the intent of terrorising its population, and then only to cause them to leave the city and so block the roads to enemy military movement. However, such disagreement aside, from the end of the first week in September London was to be the prime target of the Luftwaffe in its attempt to reduce Britain's defences by air attack alone.

Late in the afternoon of Saturday, 7th September, Göring having temporarily assumed direct command of air operations, the Luftwaffe launched its first daylight raid on the London docks, with 650 bomber and well over 1,000 fighter sorties, a bombardment that was kept up throughout the night. With this, the third phase of the Battle had begun. That the Germans were prepared to allocate daytime attacks to London indicates the importance they attached to their newly adopted 'Douhetian' attempt to bring about the defeat of Britain by air power alone. In the eleven hours of operations, 660 tons of high explosive and many thousands of incendiaries were dropped, and no less than 448 Londoners were killed and over 1,500 seriously wounded. Material damage was substantial in the dockland area on both sides of the Thames below Tower Bridge, at Woolwich Arsenal and among oil installations and factories further down the river, and huge fires remained burning to serve as beacons for the bombing attack the following night. In the defence of the capital, no less than twenty-eight RAF fighters had been destroyed, and a further eleven damaged, for the loss, in combat, of thirty-six Luftwaffe aircraft destroyed and eleven damaged. Again, the Bf 109s had had the better of the fighter duel, destroying twenty-five Hurricanes and Spitfires and damaging a further ten, in return for fourteen and two respectively of their number. But in the new strategic environment, that mattered little.

After the war, Churchill commented on the turn of events thus:

> If the enemy had persisted in heavy attacks against the adjacent sectors and damaged their operations rooms or telephone communications, the whole intricate organisation of Fighter Command might

have broken down . . . It was, therefore, with a sense of relief that Fighter Command felt the German attack turn on to London on September 7th, and concluded that the enemy had changed his plan. Göring should certainly have persevered against the airfields . . . By departing from the classic principles of war, . . . he made a foolish mistake.[36]

However, the Luftwaffe had not forfeited all its hopes of success. While RAF Fighter Command had been saved from defeat on the ground, it could still be destroyed in the air. For that, two conditions had to be fulfilled: sufficient determination to do so on the part of the Germans, and good flying weather, both to last for at least a month. With autumn less than three weeks away, the latter at least was problematical.

In the following days, two major daylight raids (more than 200 bombers each) were undertaken against London on the 9th and 15th September, and two minor ones on the 11th and 14th. Attacks by day also took place on Southampton (twice), Portland, Brighton, Eastbourne, Canterbury, Great Yarmouth and Norwich. London was also attacked every night, and from the 8th to the 15th over 1,000 tons of high explosive and thousands of incendiaries were dropped on the capital (not counting daylight raids, which added a further 500 tons). Indeed, on the 9th, the Luftwaffe General Staff, confident that the demise of RAF Fighter Command was near, had issued new instructions for the attack, calling for a systematic destruction of London. Luftflotte 2 would undertake daylight raids against key military and commercial targets in Greater London, while Luftflotte 3 would bomb the areas of government and docks. The capital, rather than just its docklands, was now the target (although attacks were not to be aimed specifically at the civilian population). In Göring's eyes at least, London seemed to be taking on an importance far greater than either the destruction of the RAF defences or the preparation for Operation Sealion. Indication of this came on the 9th, when it was ordered that the first duty of the fighters was to protect the bombers, not to attack the enemy, and that if substantial enemy opposition was met, the German aircraft should disengage rather than risk loss.

RAF Fighter Command received less attention than it had had for some time. Its ground organisation was hardly touched, the only action of note taking place on the 14th, when the south coast radar stations were attacked by Ju 88s. The number of RAF fighters destroyed during the nine days of phase three of the Battle of Britain, which ended on 15th September, was 131, with a further thirty-seven damaged. This was an average daily rate of fourteen and a half destroyed, one which equalled the output from the factories, and which was partly aided by mistakes made by the RAF command, allowing raids to get through to their targets unmolested. It was markedly less than the loss experienced in phase two, when an average of nineteen and a half Spitfires and Hurricanes were destroyed every day. In terms of fighter combat, the Bf 109 was still dominant, but total combat casualties for the Luftwaffe remained higher than the RAF's, with 174 destroyed and sixty-nine damaged. Total losses from all causes increased the disparity still further: 321 destroyed or damaged in Luftflotten 2 and 3 compared with 178 in RAF Fighter Command. Moreover, Dowding's units were being allowed some respite. Despite the intense attack on London in the late afternoon, 8th September was the first occasion in ten days that Park's 11 Group had not been kept in a state of 'readiness' throughout the daylight hours. German pressure had clearly shifted. Indeed, until the 15th, the RAF fighter pilots were at no time extended to the degree they had been in phase two; on four of the nine days, thanks in large part to cloudy weather which inhibited German operations, combat losses of aircraft amounted to four or less, something that had occurred only once in the previous fourteen days. For the first time since mid-July, there were no exhausted squadrons in 11 Group, and most of the units were able to enjoy day-long rests without being called into action. Training sorties to acclimatise newly arrived pilots were even being organised. A new vigour was evident in RAF Fighter Command during its actions, a vigour that was to be put to the test on 15th September, the day that is now celebrated every year as Battle of Britain Day.

The Luftwaffe's assault on London on the 15th September was designed to be decisive. On its eve, Hitler, Göring, Kesselring, and the RLM chiefs were optimistic. They believed that RAF Fighter Command was broken. Its resistance to the attacks on the 11th and 14th had been poor, in the main owing to mistakes by the RAF, and it was clear that significant numbers of its fighters were still being destroyed in aerial combat. Indeed, the Luftwaffe's air attacks were considered to be on the verge of success. It was believed that the British were being defeated by the Luftwaffe alone. On 5th September, Göring declared that an invasion was probably no longer necessary, while on the following day Hitler voiced himself of the opinion that 'Britain's defeat will be achieved even without the landing'.[37] On the 10th, the Naval Staff, dubious about the new aims of the air war, recorded in its diary: '. . . the Führer thinks the major attack on London may be decisive'.[38] By this time, Hitler was convinced of the necessity of an invasion, something he had not been either in July or August, but only as the means to conclude the victory already won by the Luftwaffe. By the 10th, Hitler was as certain as he could be that Sealion should take place on the 24th, and he let it be known that he would make his final decision on the 14th. Reports coming in from the United States indicated that British morale was low and that physical damage was considerable. On the 14th, for example, OKH produced a memorandum which quoted a highly placed source in Washington to the effect that British aircraft production was in a critical state, while that same day the military attaché at the embassy reported that leading members of the US General Staff believed that 'England will not be able to hold out against the German attacks.'[39] On the 14th, the Führer told his military chiefs that '. . . the operations of the Luftwaffe are beyond all praise. Four to five days of good weather are required to achieve decisive results. . . . There is a great chance of totally defeating the British.'[40] In prospect of that aerial victory, Hitler postponed his decision concerning the date of Sealion. As Jodl wrote that night: '. . . the Channel crossing would only come into question, as before, if it is a matter of finishing off a country already defeated by the air war.'[41] Whether or not Britain was in such a parlous state is not of such importance here; what is of interest is that the Germans believed it to be so. The next few days were to be decisive. Success was not in doubt, and with it would come invasion.

On the 15th, the Luftwaffe undertook nearly 1,300 sorties against London, 300 of them by bombers, the rest by fighters, together with thirty against Portland and aircraft works outside Southampton. A failure by Luftflotte 2 to undertake the usual diversionary flights and feints to cover the direction of its main thrusts, itself a sign of overweening confidence, ensured that 11 Group could commit its squadrons in good time and in the right places, and, in addition, call upon 12 Group for support. The Germans were met with the formidable opposition of some 170 Spitfires and Hurricanes in the air, operating with all the advantages of being near, or over, their own bases – bases, moreover, which were not under attack. By the end of the day, for the loss of twenty-six fighters destroyed and eight damaged, the RAF had shot down fifty-eight German aircraft and damaged a further twenty-five. It was the third most damaging day to the Luftwaffe during the Battle and, as matters were to turn out, the last. The Germans were shattered by the outcome of the 15th. While it could cope with the material losses, psychologically it was unable to come to terms with the strength and vitality shown by RAF Fighter Command, which it had previously considered near its demise. In particular, the Luftwaffe was disturbed by the high loss of bombers, thirty-five destroyed and twenty-two damaged, losses that exceeded by five and sixteen respectively even those experienced on 'Black Thursday', 15th August. During the past month of the Battle, the average daily loss of bombers had been less than eight destroyed and three damaged. As the RLM admitted to OKW, the day's operation had been 'unusually disadvantageous'.[42] Lack of adequate fighter protection was the cry of the bomber crews, and it found receptive ears at RLM. The next day, the 16th, Göring gave vent to his feelings: 'The fighters have let us down'.[43] Time and again, despite their best efforts, the Bf 109s had allowed the British fighters to get through their protective screen to attack the bomber formations, causing the aircraft to break formation and scatter, often jettisoning their bomb loads well short of their targets. In vain did Osterkamp and Milch, the fighter pilots' only ally in the RLM, remonstrate. To give close support to slow, heavily laden bombers was not a suitable operation for Bf 109s because they became disadvantaged vis à vis their British counterparts. Moreover, they had not the fuel to put up an effective cover over the target area for long; any mishap in scheduling link-ups between fighters and bombers might cause the former to run short of fuel before their task had been fulfilled, and set course for home.

But wherever the blame lay, and posterity will show it lay more with the higher commanders than with the pilots, the effect of the 15th on the Luftwaffe's morale was significant. After so many days and weeks of hard fighting, its enemy was, clearly, far from defeated; indeed, he had never been seen in greater numbers. RAF Fighter Command's victory was further reinforced by the activities of RAF Bomber Command, which, for some time had been actively engaged in hitting the channel ports where the invasion fleet was assembling. By the end of September, no less than twenty per cent of the assembled barges had been sunk or seriously damaged, and, on the 10th, RAF bombers had even destroyed nine He 111s and damaged two others on their airfield in Holland. All this served to emphasise the importance of air superiority to the success of Operation Sealion. But it was just that which, on the 15th, the Luftwaffe realised it was still far from achieving. At his conference on the 16th, Göring might affirm that, with conventional attacks, RAF Fighter Command would be shattered in four or five days, but it was an empty promise. If he did not realise that, his senior commanders and pilots certainly did. So did Hitler. On the 17th, after two days of little activity in the air owing to poor weather, during which the RAF lost eight fighters and the Germans twelve aircraft in combat, with a further three and six respectively damaged, the Führer made the decision to postpone Operation Sealion indefinitely. As the entry in the diary of the German Naval Staff for the 17th puts it: 'The enemy air force is still by no means defeated; on the contrary, it shows increasing activity. The weather situation as a whole does not permit us to expect a period of calm. The Führer has, therefore, decided to postpone operation Sealion indefinitely'.[44] Thereby the Battle designed to gain air superiority as a prerequisite for the invasion of Britain, was concluded.

Although fatigue, unstable weather and the change in priorities scaled down operations after the 15th, numerous daytime sorties were made over the south of England in a vain attempt, decided upon at Göring's meeting on the 16th, to wear down the enemy, in particular by shooting down his fighters. Major raids took place by day on the 18th, 25th, 26th, 27th and 30th. On the 18th, London was bombed. On the 25th, some seventy bombers strongly escorted by fighters, dropped their loads on Plymouth, Portland, and the Bristol aeroplane factory at Filton, the main target for the day, where serious damage was inflicted, causing a curtailment of production for many weeks. The next day, the Spitfire factory at Woolaston was badly bombed. Emboldened by their successes, on the 27th, Luftflotte 2 sent fifty-five Ju 88s over London and Luftflotte 3 attacked Bristol with thirty He 111s. It was, however, a disastrous day for the Luftwaffe, which, in twenty-four hours, lost fifty-two aircraft in combat, with another six damaged; in comparison, the RAF lost twenty-eight fighters and a further thirteen damaged. On the 30th, the last major daylight raid over England of the war took place, when the Luftwaffe flew 173 bomber and 1,000 fighter sorties. London and the Westland aircraft factory at Yeovil were the main targets (the latter escaping damage), at a total cost to the Luftwaffe of forty-three aircraft lost and eleven damaged, whereas the RAF lost only sixteen fighters, with seventeen damaged. On this day, for the first time, the Spitfires and Hurricanes showed a marked ascendancy over the Bf 109s, shooting down no less than twenty-seven, and damaging a further four of the German machines for a loss of seven destroyed and nine damaged.

Since 15th September, the fighting had proved that RAF Fighter Command was not only intact, but was increasing its combat capabilities. At the beginning of the month, the Luftwaffe had been able to launch massive raids with relative impunity against almost any target within range of the Bf 109s; at the end, it could no longer do so. Air superiority lay with the RAF. As Galland, who had just shot down his fortieth British aeroplane, told Göring on the 27th, '. . . in spite of the heavy losses we were inflicting on the enemy fighters, no decisive decrease in their number or fighting efficiency was noticeable. . . . Even if the German figures of enemy aircraft destroyed were perhaps overestimated, the fact that their fighter strength obviously did not diminish could only be accounted for in this way: England, by a great concentration of energy, was making up her losses. . . .'[45] Although on four days, the 20th, 26th, 28th and 29th, the RAF lost a total of thirteen more aircraft in daytime combat than did the Germans, the total combat casualties for the last half of the month showed a decisive advantage in favour of the defenders. In the period from the 16th to 30th September, RAF Fighter Command lost 115 fighters, with a further fifty-one damaged, compared with the Luftwaffe's 199 destroyed and forty-six damaged. Losses and damage from all causes were 202 aircraft for RAF Fighter Command and 362 for Luftflotte 2 and 3. The rate of attrition of experienced leaders was also high; in the thirty days of September, the Luftwaffe lost four Geschwader commanders, thirteen Gruppe commanders, and twenty-eight Staffel leaders killed, missing, or made prisoner. One Kampfgeschwader had lost forty (thirty per cent) of its Ju 88s in just fifteen days, with 160 trained crewmen. What had this carnage achieved? Certainly not the depletion of the RAF, nor the destruction of the vital British war industries. As Hitler was to remember in April 1942: '. . . the munitions industry . . . cannot be interfered with effectively by air raids. We learnt that lesson during our raids on English armament centres in the autumn of 1940. Usually, the prescribed targets are not hit; often the fliers unload their bombs on fields camouflaged as plants; and . . . the armaments industry is so decentralised that the armament potential cannot be really interfered with'.[46] Clearly, if daylight operations were to be continued, new tactics would be needed.

From the middle of August onward, the Luftwaffe had been experimenting with fighter-bombers (Jagdbombern or Jabos), both Bf 110s and Bf 109s. In October, when the bombers were virtually phased out of daylight operations, the main burden of the fighting was taken over by the Bf 109s, either fighters or fighter-bombers. Some 250 were used in this new role, each carrying either one 110 lb bomb or, for a new version of the fighter the Bf 109 E-4, a bomb load of up to 500 lb. Occasionally, a few Ju 88s were included in the attacking formations, and, on 29th October, even Ju 87s were used over Portsmouth.

Two daytime attacks by the Italian Air Force were also mounted against coastal targets on 29th October and 11th November, but they accomplished virtually nothing.

During this period, the German daylight tactics achieved little except to cause annoyance and fatigue to RAF Fighter Command. The Jabos, flying between 25,000 ft and 32,000 ft, were effectively out of reach of the Hurricanes and they caused the Spitfires to venture to heights at which their inferiority to the Bf 109 escorts, unencumbered by bombs, was most marked. At these altitudes, too, it was easy for the invading formations to escape detection by radar and observer; but even were they noticed, the speed of their attack gave the defenders, at most, just twenty minutes' warning before the Jabos reached London. By the middle of October, the German formations were on the verge of gaining virtual immunity in the air. Indeed, in six days, they managed to inflict more losses on their enemy than they themselves suffered. RAF Fighter Command was again stretched to the limit; on the 27th, it had to fly a total of 1,007 sorties, to bring down nine German aircraft, in comparison with 974 sorties on 15th August, the Luftwaffe's 'Black Thursday', when it had brought down sixty-seven. The average of fourteen sorties to account for one enemy aeroplane in mid-August had degenerated by late October to roughly 112 sorties. During the thirty-one days of October, the Luftwaffe lost only 200 aircraft in daylight raids, just over half of which were Bf 109s, compared to 133 by RAF Fighter Command (seven of which were destroyed in a bombing raid). Sixty German and thirty-six British fighters were damaged in combat, while those lost and damaged from all causes by both day and night were 603 of the Luftwaffe and 272 of RAF Fighter Command.

However, relative ease of operation in the air for the fighters by day, and strain on the RAF, in itself counted for little. Bombs fell on numerous targets, ranging from the capital to airfields, but to small overall effect; the bomb-load of one Jabo was, at most, but one quarter than that of an He 111, and was delivered from a great height with no more accuracy than that which the larger, slower bombers were capable. No significant material damage was inflicted. Moreover, operating the Jabos (nicknamed 'Light Kesselrings' after the official title of 'light bombers'), which formed roughly one third of all available Bf 109s in the West, was highly unpopular with the fighter pilots, who believed that they were being used simply as scapegoats and stopgaps. The losses of the slower-moving, less manoeuvrable fighter-bombers rose, so that, in desperation, Osterkamp told Jeschonnek that they would have to be grounded 'thanks to these senseless operations'.[44] Thus, in October, when the number of operational sorties was well below those of the previous two months, no less than 103 Bf 109s were destroyed in combat, with a further twenty-three damaged. At the same time, the pilots could see that RAF Fighter Command had continued to build up its strength. During October it lost just half as many pilots killed or wounded as it had done in September, and half the aircraft. By the end of the month, reserves of Spitfires and

Hurricanes were larger than at any time since August, and more pilots available. Indeed, by the beginning of November matters had so much improved for the RAF that there were twelve new fighter squadrons in existence to meet the invader. Göring's bombast on 18th October in an address to his airmen, was devoid of any connection with the truth: 'In the past few days and nights you have caused the British world enemy disastrous losses by your constant destructive blows. . . . These losses which you have inflicted upon the much-vaunted Royal Air Force with your determined fighter combat are irreplaceable'.[47] The reality was very different, and had been indicated six days previously, on the 12th, when Hitler issued a War Directive renouncing all idea of an invasion in 1940. Far from achieving air superiority over south-east England, or bringing the British nation to the verge of defeat by bombing, all that the Luftwaffe had proved capable of undertaking by daylight after almost three months of heavy aerial combat was to send small groups of Bf 109s, flying high through gaps in the British fighter defences, to bomb one or two buildings, kill a few people, annoy and exhaust RAF pilots, but otherwise achieve nothing whatsoever. Certainly the raids could neither destroy Britain's defences nor damage her capacity to continue the war. There was little point in their continuance; in November only a few attacks took place, mostly on targets along the coast, and at the beginning of December they were stopped altogether. In such a manner did the daylight operations over England simply peter out.

Where lay the reason for the Luftwaffe's defeat, and the consequent retention by the RAF of effective command of the air over Britain by day? It has generally been ascribed to the valiant efforts of RAF Fighter Command, to the genius and determination of its leaders, especially Dowding and Park, to the skill and heroism of its young pilots, to its first-class aircraft, the Spitfires and Hurricanes, to its ground crews, and to its 'hidden weapons', radar and British intelligence. In the words of Winston Churchill, uttered on 20th August: 'Never in the field of human conflict has so much been owed by so many to so few'.[48] Certainly, this was so. Arguments over the tactical policies pursued by its leaders (whether, for example, Wing or Squadron formations should have been used) will no doubt continue, but the exploits of the British fighters have already gone down in history as one of the finest examples of military achievement, and rightly so. Without their valour and perseverance the Luftwaffe would have had an easy victory. But this should not obscure the final truth about the Battle of Britain: that, heroism and leadership apart, RAF Fighter Command was not a sufficient force to prevent the Luftwaffe from achieving its goal of air superiority over at least south-east England in support of a seaborne invasion. It was weaknesses in the Luftwaffe's own conduct of the Battle that ultimately prevented it from gaining the victory within its grasp .

The achievements of the German pilots during the Battle were as remarkable as those of their enemy, and deserve the highest praise. However, without doubt there were mistakes in the tactical employment of the

Luftwaffe during the Battle. Among these, General Deichmann has pointed to the initial division of the German fighter units into three groups, so that only those under Jafü 2 in the Pas de Calais could reach the combat area over London. Moreover, the nature of the equipment with which the Luftwaffe undertook the Battle was deficient. The bombers were vulnerable to fighter interception and carried only relatively light bomb-loads; the dive-bombers and heavy fighters were quite incapable of protecting themselves from the ravages of the enemy; and the Bf 109s lacked an effective range and were ill-suited to their role as escorts for the bombers. The Germans also had the disability of having to fight across the Channel and over enemy territory. However, the Luftwaffe did have advantages. It possessed an overwhelming numerical superiority over the RAF defence; its bombers were available in sufficient numbers to drop fairly heavy concentrations of bombs; and, in combat, its single-engined fighters, though numerically streched to the limit by their dual role of escorting and hunting, were superior to those of the RAF. But perhaps most important of all, it had the advantage of the location of London, the RAF's main concern in defence, which, by happy conjunction, came within range of the Bf 109s. Without London, RAF Fighter Command could have withdrawn the few miles necessary into the interior of England to place itself out of range of the Bf 109s, and thereby preserve its strength to destroy the German bombers that strayed beyond the limits of their fighter escort and strike at the German invasion fleet should it ever set sail. This, the location of the capital prevented. London had to be protected, and thus Park's 11 Group was forced to remain within range of the German fighters, thereby acting as a vortex that would suck in the strength of RAF Fighter Command, there to be destroyed, or forced to retire, beaten. Thus, with the Battle confined to this small area of south-east England, which, by further fortunate coincidence, was the main area for the projected invasion, and with its attacks concentrated against the enemy's air defences, the Luftwaffe's disadvantages were reduced to the minimum, and its resources sufficient for the task it set itself. Even the enemy's radar proved its ally.

However, in the first week of September, just as the Germans, concentrating on RAF Fighter Command both in the air and on the ground, were on the verge of victory over south-east England, the Luftwaffe's high command took the decision to transfer the attack to London. By so doing, not only was the RAF enabled to preserve the command and ground organisation of 11 Group, then on the point of disintegration, and thereby ensure its continued presence south of London, but also its operational requirements were significantly eased. Although fighting remained heavy, as it was bound to while London was under attack, the casualties inflicted upon the fighter pilots and the losses of their aircraft also significantly diminished. RAF Fighter Command was revitalised, and on 15th September proved able to inflict a severe defeat on the Luftwaffe, both material and psychological. Thereafter, the Luftwaffe's disinclination to commit bombers in large numbers during daylight, ensured that their fighters alone, though able to preserve for themselves the use of the sky over south-east England, achieved nothing.

What would have happened had the Luftwaffe continued its offensive solely against RAF Fighter Command and not switched the brunt of its attacks to London and industrial targets, is a matter for conjecture. Any conclusion must be purely hypothetical. Certainly, at the decisive point in the Battle, the Luftwaffe's losses were high, and, whatever course it pursued, they were destined to get higher. Even had the rate of RAF Fighter Command's losses continued as they had been in the second phase of the Battle, the British defences had, at the least, three weeks fight left in them. But, provided that the weather did not curtail air operations (which, in September at least, it did not) the Luftwaffe could have continued its major onslaught for that length of time. In the month from 13th August to 15th September, German losses (those of RAF Fighter Command are given in brackets) amounted to 1,216 (688) aircraft, of which 729 (535) were destroyed in combat, and 185 (120) damaged. This was roughly half the loss for the four-month period from 1st July to 31st October, during which no less than 2,848 (1,486) German aircraft were put out of action from all causes, of which 1,446 (935) were destroyed and a further 370 (261) damaged in combat. For each RAF fighter shot down, the Luftwaffe lost one and a half aircraft, a proportion which, during the month of the Battle, decreased to one and a third. Aircraft lost or damaged for all reasons showed a greater disparity, RAF Fighter Command losing one fighter during the four months for one and nine-tenths German aircraft, although this decreased to one and seven-tenths during the month of the Battle. However, in early September the Luftwaffe had proved itself as capable as the RAF of sustaining such losses, certainly in the short term. Moreover, in the all-important fighter combat, the Germans were shooting down two enemy aircraft for the loss of one of theirs.

Despite the fatigue of the aircrews there was no material reason, apart from the possibility of poor weather, why the assault against RAF Fighter Command should have been slackened off. That it was, however, is a matter of history; that, thereby, air superiority over south-east England was forfeited is, at least, a reasonable inference. In conclusion, then, it may be said that the strategy finally pursued by the Luftwaffe during the Battle of Britain allowed RAF Fighter Command both to avoid defeat and, after only a short loss, to regain control of the air over south-east England, thereby frustrating the plan to invade Britain in the autumn of 1940. Success or failure in the sky was in the gift of the German Air Force, a gift which one wrong decision gave to the RAF.

With hindsight, it is possible to see that failure over south-east England in the summer of 1940, and, with it, the decision to turn eastwards to attack Russia before Britain was defeated, was the turning point in the fortunes of the Luftwaffe. Indeed, it was the turning point in the fortunes of the Third Reich. With command of the air over the Channel and the landing areas in England, an invasion, had it been attempted, might well have been successful. Once the German Army was on British soil, and advanced Luftwaffe bases were established near to the front-line, it is at least a distinct possibility that victory would have belonged to the Germans. Even if it had not, failure could not have resulted in a reciprocal invasion by the British on the Continent of occupied Europe, and it would probably have prevented Hitler from embarking upon an invasion of the Soviet Union. If, on the other hand, victory had been gained, the Germans could then have turned East with all their available forces, free of all diversion in the West and the Mediterranean. In such an event, if total success had not been won against the Soviet Union, at least a stalemate could have been guaranteed. As it was, matters turned out very differently. A defiant Britain was left in the Germans' rear and on their flank. With the entry of the USA into the war at the end of 1941, this menace became even greater, as the island served as a base for a heavy bomber offensive as well as for an invasion. With all this, the Luftwaffe proved quite unable to deal. So, too, did Germany. Defeat in all theatres of the war was the result. Such were the probable consequences of one failure in the summer of 1940. With hindsight those few weeks in August and September may be considered the most important in the entire war.

VI

Blitz and Counter-Attack

While the German daylight offensive ceased to have any relevance after 15th September, the Luftwaffe's night raids not only continued, but greatly increased in their intensity, to bear the main brunt of the war against Britain. Lacking any effective long-range escort fighter, or command of the air over south-east England, attacks under the cover of darkness was the only method of offence open to the Germans. To be sure, night bombing had been a constant part of the Luftwaffe's operations since 5th June, but until late August their objectives had been scattered, their bomb-loads light (rarely had more than sixty or seventy bombers a night been involved, and often less), and their results poor. On 24th August, the number of sorties had been significantly increased, and from then until 6th September, German bombers flew an average of 190 sorties nightly, and on several occasions Luftflotte 3 concentrated more than 150 bombers over Liverpool and Birkenhead. However, results were singularly unimpressive, few bombs hitting their intended targets. Such raids had little relation to the strategic purpose of the Battle then being waged by day, except that aircraft factories would be included in the targets to be destroyed. However, on 7th September a new phase of operations began, and for a brief period the purpose of both day and night raids was the same: the destruction of London's military and economic life, and a reduction in the civilian population's will to resist.

After the debacle of the 15th, which put an end to effective heavy bombing attacks by day, the Luftwaffe's night offensive took on a life of its own. By the end of October, during which month the tonnage of bombs dropped by night was nearly six times as great as that dropped by day, all but four bomber Gruppen (100 aircraft, mostly Ju 88s) had been withdrawn from the daylight battle, and ten bomber Geschwader and ten Gruppen, amounting to more than 1,150 bombers, based in Holland, Belgium and France, were made available for the night offensive. For a period in October and November, eighty medium bombers from the Italian Air Force aided the Luftwaffe's offensive by mounting daylight attacks on south-east England, but to little effect.

From 7th September onwards, London was the major target, accounting for roughly half the sorties flown. In the sixty-eight nights between 7th-8th September to 12th-13th November, there were only ten on which the Luftwaffe did not mount what it regarded as a 'major raid' (i.e., one in which at least 100 tons of high explosive were dropped), and there was only one when no bombers at all appeared over the capital. In this period, no less than 11,117 bomber sorties (an average of 163 a night) were made over London, 13,651 tons of high explosive were dropped (201 tons nightly) and 12,586 incendiary canisters (an average of 182 a night), each containing seventy-two incendiary devices. This was an ordeal that, for its continuity (though not for the severity of the destruction) was never to be approached by either side for the rest of the war. Indeed, the ordeal was to last, with far less regularity, until the night of 10th-11th May 1941, by which time London had been bombed on no less than eighty-six nights, and a grand total of 15,744 bomber sorties had deposited 19,141 tons of high explosive and 36,568 incendiary canisters on the British capital, a total of 21,774 tons of bombs.

There were several reasons why the Luftwaffe was prepared to continue with this major operation after the failure of the day air offensive. First, and this alone may well have been sufficient, neither Hitler, having publicly committed himself to heavy bomber raids, nor the Luftwaffe high command was prepared to lose face by withdrawing from the air battle. Defeat in the sky by day was to be compensated by victory over the enemy's cities by night. It was a matter of prestige, both for Führer and Luftwaffe. Second, it was believed that a concentrated aerial bombardment on London would destroy the economic framework of the capital, which lay at the heart of Britain's war effort. Third, it was hoped that a heavy bombardment would destroy its citizens' will to resist, and that this, together with the economic blockade, would induce the Government to sue for peace. Not that the Luftwaffe had taken to deliberately bombing civilians, a policy which Hitler had expressly forbidden on 14th September. Such attacks were, he argued, the 'ultimate reprisal'. Bombing 'to create mass panic must be left to the last'.[2] Indeed, over the coming months the targets assigned to the bomber formations did not suggest that indiscriminate bombing of civilians was intended. However, when they included factories, docks, the government quarter of Whitehall, and the economic and financial centre of the City of London, it was inevitable that a large proportion of the population would be killed and their houses destroyed, simply because it was impossible to drop a bomb, either by day or night, with accuracy on a legitimate military target without harming or hitting the surrounding residential area. This, Hitler and the Luftwaffe leaders knew, and were quite prepared to tolerate. Indeed, because of the impact they hoped it would have upon the British people, they positively welcomed it. Göring revealed this in his order of the day on 18th October, when he praised his crews by stating: 'Your indefatigable, courageous attacks on the heart of the British Empire, the City of London, with its eight and a half million inhabitants, have reduced British plutocracy to fear and terror'.[3]

However, by early November, the Germans were forced to recognise that Göring's confidence was misplaced. In September and October, over 13,000 enemy civilians had been killed, nearly 20,000 injured, and many more made homeless, but morale had not suffered significantly. To be sure, there was some consternation in official circles as to how the population in the East End, London's dockland, would react. Here, the slums and unemployment had bred dissatisfaction before the war, a dissatisfaction that would be fuelled by continual bombardment which received no effective counter-attack. Rumours of excessive death tolls, of anti-aircraft guns running out of shells, of government ineptitude were rife, and intense human misery no doubt exacerbated dislike of the British social system. However, morale did not break, although the Ministry of Home Security's allegation that it received only good reports concerning the attitude of Londoners must be treated with scepticism. However, despite individual incidents, there is no doubt that, overall, the will to resist shown by the eight million inhabitants of the capital was hardened rather than weakened by the German attacks, and a significant improvement in morale was noticed in the rest of Britain. 'If London can take it, so can we' was the attitude that the first stage of the Blitz fostered among the people, one which was to be of great value in the forthcoming months.

While London's population weathered the bombing, its buildings did not. Damage was widespread, especially in districts near the river Thames. However, the capital was a huge target, and the Luftwaffe could not hope to destroy it completely with the resources at its disposal. As Churchill told Parliament on 8th October: 'Statisticians may amuse themselves by calculating that, after diminishing returns, through the same house being struck twice or three times over, it would take ten years, at the present rate, for half the houses of London to be demolished. After that, of course, progress would be much slower'.[4] Houses, however, were not the Luftwaffe's prime target; it would be long enough before their destruction brought London's economic life to a standstill. The docks and railway communications were a different matter, but, although they had taken a severe hammering, their continued operation was not rendered impossible. Of the docks, the Ministry of Home Security noted that the damage was 'serious but not crippling',[5] and the basins, quays, equipment and railway lines which served them remained substantially intact. Buildings suffered most, but these were not vital to the docks' operations. The ability of the Port of London to deal with the trade necessary to keep the capital and the country alive was not significantly impaired. Damage to power stations and public utilities was, likewise, disruptive but seldom long-lasting. Repairs were undertaken under the supervision of a Special Commissioner, and proceeded with creditable speed. The menace of non-exploded or delayed-action bombs was well dealt with by the bomb-disposal units. Only in the bombing of railway communications did the Luftwaffe achieve any significant, if temporary, result. At one stage, just four of the usual fifty or sixty trains a day could pass from the northern to the southern region, and, in September, no less than five to six thousand goods-wagons stood idle because of the menace of unexploded bombs. Outside the capital, the railway system was also subject to attack, and in September alone it was hit on no less than 667 occasions. Clever re-routing, immediate repair, and reliance on motor transport, however, minimised the disruption of the nation's war effort.

While, night after night, London suffered considerable material damage, the Luftwaffe itself escaped any severe injury. It was soon realised that night attacks represented a safe way of proceeding with the war against Britain. Owing to the paucity and ineffective nature of Britain's night-time defences, the Germans had lost from all causes roughly 100 aircraft in the two months from 7th September to 13th November, a rate, which, with an average output of 333 bombers a month in 1940, could be sustained indefinitely. The reasons for this were several. Once the raiders were over the Channel coast, there existed no radar which could chart their course; it was, as Churchill later noted, a transition from the twentieth century to the stone age. The anti-aircraft artillery depended on sound-location to determine the whereabouts of the enemy forces, and an aircraft flying at 300 mph at 20,000 ft would be one and a half miles further on before its sound reached the ground, and five or six miles further before the burst of the first shells, during which time the pilot may well not have maintained a constant course. Even were the aircraft located, the limitations of the anti-aircraft units were considerable. Their searchlights could neither hold an aircraft for a satisfactory length of time nor illuminate effectively above 12,000 ft, a height above which the Germans took care to operate. The guns themselves were few in number (on 11th September, for example, there were only 235 heavy guns in and around London), and only the heavies could deal with aircraft above 6,000 ft, and even then their effective limit was 25,000 ft. Thus, in September and October, the anti-aircraft guns were able only to shoot down fifty-four bombers over Britain.

Lamentable though the British anti-aircraft artillery screen was, the night-fighter force was in an even poorer state. The Blenheims were slower than the bombers they were supposed to intercept, and by September there were still too few of their replacements, the Beaufighters, to have any influence on the course of the battle. Nor did the use of Hurricane and Spitfire squadrons, which had neither the training nor equipment for night-flying, have any success. The few aircraft that were equipped with airborne radar sets were, similarly, of little use; the early AI (Air Interception radar), could track at distances of only between two miles and 800 ft, and the newer set, the AI Mk IV, which could track between four miles and 600 ft, was only just completing its development. Indeed, so ineffective was the night-fighter force, that, in the first phase of the Blitz, it shot down just eight enemy aircraft. This figure, when added to those destroyed by the guns, the four brought down by barrage balloons and the fifteen by other means, represents a total claim of only eighty-one German aircraft destroyed in darkness by the British defences in September and October. The Luftwaffe's bombers, which by day were so vulnerable, had, in the autumn of 1940, little to fear by night.

If attack after dark provided almost total security from interception, however, it made the location of targets considerably more difficult, especially as the British did their best to hamper this. Indeed, it is estimated that only one quarter of the bombs dropped by the Germans during the Blitz came near to hitting their targets. Dummy airfields and factories were constructed, even towns, and, by January, decoy fires were in action, all of which misled the Germans into bombing empty fields. On one occasion, some 400 tons of bombs were deposited on moors and fields in a raid which the Germans claimed the next day had been successfully carried out on Derby and Nottingham. To improve the chances of hitting the target, the Germans employed radio beams for guidance. The first, using medium-frequency direction-finding beacons to plot position during flight, was discovered by the British early in the war, and counter-measures were devised which rendered it ineffective. The second, however, was potentially far more dangerous to the defenders. Called Knickebein (Crooked Leg), it consisted of a band of signals, less than half a mile wide, transmitted from a station on the Continent, down which a pilot could fly; at the appropriate point, the signals would change their tone as they were intersected by those of another beam transmitted from a different station. This system was accurate to within roughly one square mile, and, although impracticable for the destruction of a single factory, was well-suited to bombardment of an industrial area.

Had the Luftwaffe begun its night offensive using Knickebein to the full, its bombing accuracy would have been considerably improved. However, thanks to the efforts of British Intelligence which was deciphering German code messages, and the perspicacity of the RAF's Scientific Intelligence, the existence of these beams had been established as early as 21st June, while the Germans had been testing their efficacy in small night raids over Britain. Counter-measures were developed, whereby the Knickebein signals were either jammed, 'bent' (broadened until they lost their original accuracy), or interfered with by the insertion of a cross beam short of the planned point of intersection. By such measures, the British hoped either to deny to the Germans the use of the beams, or, more cleverly, to induce them to drop their bombs harmlessly away from the target. This was not an easy matter, however, since the beams themselves had to be located before they could be interfered with; but it was not impossible, especially with the aid of Ultra. Certainly, interference was a trump card which the British were to play with such skill that, by the end of the first phase of operations in mid-November, the Germans had become reluctant to use Knickebein. But they had a replacement at hand, a sophisticated piece of equipment known as X-Gerät. To use it, the aircraft flew along a fine beam in the centre of a coarser one, passing through no less than three intersecting beams before the target was reached: the first beam served as a warning, the second as a preliminary signal, and the third as the main signal, upon receipt of which a device was set in motion which released the bombs at a predetermined distance. However, unlike Knickebein, X-Gerät required a special apparatus that was not generally available to be fitted to the bombers. It was therefore decided to equip only selected units, to be used as 'pathfinders', who would fly ahead and mark the target for the main force by means of fire attacks. With such equipment, the Luftwaffe was ready to proceed with the Blitz.

The problem which confronted the Luftwaffe's leaders in early November was not whether to continue the attack on Britain by night, but on what targets to concentrate. The RLM's estimates of the material and moral damage done to London were more optimistic than realistic, but, nonetheless, conceded that the Luftwaffe's efforts were not meeting their desired reward. The enthusiasm of the high command was somewhat diminished; a new strategy was clearly needed. After the war, Göring remembered the change:

> During the night air offensive, I finally secured the Führer's permission to attack other objectives besides London, because it was always my contention that attacks on the British war industries would be much more valuable. I argued that it was no use to us to have another hundred houses go up in flames. I wished for attacks on the aircraft plants in the south of England and around Coventry, the shipping yards, Glasgow, Birmingham and the ports. . . . I told the Führer again and again that, in as much as I knew the British people as well as I did my own, we should never force them to their knees by bombing London.[6]

Indeed, before the introduction of this new policy, there had been fairly widespread harassing activity by single bombers as well as relatively strong attacks on major economic centres such as Birmingham (on which the Germans dropped 217 tons of high-explosive), Liverpool and Manchester (220 tons), and Coventry (17 tons). Aerodromes up and down the country received some 190 tons of high explosive in October, the aircraft industry sixty-three tons, and ports and shipping a total of 352 tons. By November, Yarmouth in East Anglia had suffered seventy-two raids, and Falmouth in Cornwall thirty-three. On such targets, incendiary canisters were also dropped. In October, a long-range night fighter unit began raids on British aerodromes with the purpose of hampering the ever-increasing efforts of RAF Bomber Command, a practice which, in December, the RAF began to copy in raids against the bases of Luftflotten 2 and 3. However, these activities were as nothing compared with what was to come. In early November, the Luftwaffe General Staff issued new instructions to the Luftflotten Commanders. London was to remain the main target, but industrial centres such as Birmingham and Coventry were not to be excluded, nor was the aircraft industry throughout the country. The mining of the Thames, the Bristol Channel, the Mersey and the Manchester Ship Canal was assigned to Fliegerkorps IX. Shipping in the Channel and the Thames was also to be attacked. Economic warfare was to be pursued by bombing the twin objectives of Britain's war industries and seaborne supplies.

The new phase of the Blitz began on the night of 14th-15th November, when 449 German bombers flew over Coventry depositing 503 tons of high-explosive and 881 canisters of incendiaries in an attack which lasted ten hours. One third of the city's houses were made uninhabitable; its medieval centre was gutted; and all the main railway lines were blocked. No less than 554 people were killed, and 865 seriously wounded. Twelve important aircraft plants and nine other major industrial works, the targets assigned to the bombers, were severely damaged by fire or direct hits, while damage to water and gas supplies in particular caused disruption to most other factories. The raid was devastating, and aircraft production suffered a bad setback. Nevertheless, recovery was surprisingly quick, and, even at the worst-hit factories, production was resumed within two weeks. It was recognised by the British that further heavy raids would curtail output over a much longer period, but, surprisingly, the next night the Luftwaffe made no use of its opportunity, and less than half the sixteen bombers dispatched to the city reached their target. Instead, the main effort was diverted back to London, which, over the next three nights received a total of 578 tons of high-explosive and 1,274 incendiary canisters. Indeed, not until 8th April was Coventry again to experience a major raid, by which time its vital war industries had been dispersed. Coventry, which assumed such importance in British propaganda, represented in reality an opportunity wasted.

However, the raid marked the beginning of the new phase in the Luftwaffe's strategy, which was to last until the latter part of February. During that time, port installations and war industries in fourteen major locations were heavily bombed. Of the forty-eight raids (thirty-one of which were 'major'), twelve were on London, six on Birmingham, five each on Southampton and Bristol, three each on Liverpool, Manchester and Swansea, two each on Plymouth, Portsmouth, Sheffield, and Avonmouth, and one each on Coventry, Cardiff and Derby. A total of 7,760 tons of high-explosive was dropped, and many thousands of incendiary canisters to the total of 10,500 tons of bombs. The Germans concentrated their effort on a single target each night, and, perhaps learning from their failure to follow up the attack on Coventry, began bombing the same city two or three times at brief intervals in the hope of impeding either recovery or dispersal. However, the weight of the onslaught was much reduced by the weather, so that the number of sorties declined from over 6,000 in November 1940 to just 1,200 in February 1941, a month during which no major raids were made. This was just as well for the Luftwaffe, since the strain imposed on Luftflotte 2 and 3 by continual operations was considerable. At the beginning of the New Year, their combined serviceable strength was 551 bombers (with a total strength of 1,291), some 250 fewer than in September. In four months, the ratio of serviceable bombers to total strength had fallen from sixty-one per cent to forty-three per cent. The quiet month of February was made good use of by the Luftwaffe ground services.

Until this point in the Blitz, German casualties from action had remained low. In the four months from the beginning of November to the end of February, the British defences destroyed no more than seventy-five aircraft out of a total of over 12,000 sorties. Of these, approximately two thirds were claimed by the guns, and one third by the night-fighters. Such losses could not have occasioned anxiety in the Luftwaffe, but the jamming of X-Gerät had caused the Germans considerable annoyance, so much so that they no longer directed their beams before the attack, thereby risking inaccuracies when the bombers set out on their missions. However, although the British defences could still be discounted except for their nuisance and diversionary value, doubts about the efficacy of the night bombing offensive remained, and not only within the RLM. Keitel and Jodl voiced their scepticism, as did Raeder, who, on 4th February, pointed out to Hitler that the Luftwaffe's attacks had neither crippled British production nor shaken morale. He urged that the Air Force should return to its primary targets in the air war before the demands of Operation Sealion had to be met; by this he meant that it should co-operate with the Navy in exploiting the main weaknesses of the enemy: their dependence on imports and their shortage of shipping. Hitler's War Directive No. 23, dated 6th February 1941, admitted that 'Contrary to our former view, the heaviest effect of our operations against the English war economy has lain in the high losses in merchant shipping inflicted by sea and air warfare. This effect has been increased by the destruction of port installations, the elimination of large quantities of supplies, and by the diminished use of ships when compelled to sail in convoy'. It was, Hitler stated, difficult to estimate the effect of air attacks on British industry, although there must have been a considerable fall in production, and there seemed to be little reason to think that bombing had made any significant impact on the morale of the British people. Indeed, it was recognised that 'No decisive success can be expected from terror attacks on residential areas'. For these reasons, and because other theatres of war (in the Mediterranean and, in the future, the East) compelled a reduction in the units available for operations against Britain, it was desirable 'to concentrate air attacks more closely and to deliver them chiefly against targets whose destruction supplements our naval war. Only by these means can we expect a decisive end to the war within the foreseeable future'.[7] In accordance with this principle, Hitler laid down that the Luftwaffe was to make every effort both to limit British imports, and at the same time to inflict more damage on the British aircraft industry. The blockade of Britain became once again the priority target for the Luftwaffe. The wheel had turned full circle, and victory was once more to be achieved by economic blockade in which the Air Force partnered the Navy.

With the advent of spring and better weather, the Luftwaffe embarked on its new campaign. Between the night of 19th-20th February and 12th May, it undertook no less than sixty-one attacks each involving more than fifty aircraft, of which forty-six were directed against ports – in particular, those most used in the vital traffic across the Atlantic. Portsmouth, Plymouth, Bristol, Avonmouth, Swansea, Merseyside, Belfast, and Clydeside were all heavily and repeatedly bombed, as were the aircraft producing centres of Nottingham, Coventry and Birmingham, with one, two and five raids respectively. Plymouth was very heavily attacked; major raids like those of 20th and 21st March, when 18,000 houses were destroyed or damaged, being repeated a month later on 21st, 22nd, 23rd, 28th and 29th April, by which time the housing casualty figures had exceeded the total number of houses, as many had been hit more than once. London, as a port and centre for war industries, was subjected to seven attacks, the last three of which were the heaviest ever to be suffered by any British city. Great damage was done, especially to the riverside areas. On 16th and 19th April, the capital received two poundings, known as 'The Wednesday' and 'The Saturday', in which well over 1,000 people were killed on each night, and 148,000 houses were damaged or destroyed (in the previous September and October the average weekly rate had been 40,000). The heavier raid of the two, and the heaviest to be mounted on any target in Britain during the war, was that of the 19th, when 712 raiders had dropped 1,026 tons of high-explosive and 4,252 incendiary canisters in their attempt to make London unusable as a supply centre. On 10th May, however, London experienced its worst night, when 1,436 people were killed and 1,792 seriously wounded. One third of the streets in Greater London were rendered impassable, and every main railway station except one was blocked for weeks. Some of the fires were not put out for eleven days. In these three attacks, the Luftwaffe had flown 1,904 sorties dropping 2,627 tons of high explosive and 10,845 incendiary canisters.

However, as the full fury of night bombing was being felt in Britain, the Luftwaffe was preparing to bring the campaign to an end. In April, some 150 bombers were withdrawn from the West for employment in the Balkans. In May, the move East began, when Luftflotte 2 and many units previously assigned to Luftflotte 3 (such as Fliegerkorps IV and V) were redeployed in preparation for the invasion of the Soviet Union. On the 21st, Sperrle became the sole air commander in the West; of the forty-four bomber Gruppen that had been operating against Britain during the Blitz, only four were left. Attempts to conceal this run-down were made by means of dummy signals traffic and by increased activity on behalf of those units remaining. Indeed, Hitler stipulated that all efforts were to be made 'in order to give the impression that an attack on the British Isles is planned for this year'.[8] However, after the raid on London on 10th May, only four attacks of over a hundred tons each were made, and, by the end of June, Britain's ordeal was over, and it faced with equanimity the occasional 'tip and run' raids.

The Luftwaffe withdrew from the West just at the time when the British night defences were beginning to find an answer to the challenge presented them. A successor to X-Gerät, Y-Gerät, depending on a single beam in conjunction with a range system, had been deduced by the RAF even before it was used operationally, and it was jammed on its first application in early 1941. The six squadrons of night fighters, by then composed mostly of Beaufighters, many of which were equipped with the Mk IV AI radars, were supported by ground radars for long-distance inland tracking (which could put a fighter to within a thousand yards of a bomber), and eight squadrons of ordinary Hurricanes and Defiants and two of Havocs. In addition the pilots and ground-controllers were rapidly gaining in skill and experience. The results were impressive. In May, 196 combats were recorded (a ratio of one for every twenty enemy bombing missions, which compares with the January ratio of one to 218), and no less than ninety-six raiders were destroyed. The guns, too, were increasing in efficiency; the 20,000 rounds expended for every bomber shot down in September had dropped to less than 3,000 in February. Batteries of rockets, too, were coming into action. Thus, in April, British anti-aircraft artillery claimed thirty-nine aircraft, and in May, when German aerial activity was less, thirty-one. In the last month of the Blitz, then, a total of 138 bombers went missing over Britain, representing some three and a half per cent of the sorties made. One in every thirty bombers that flew over Britain was destroyed, compared with one in every 326 in December. As Air Vice-Marshal W. S. Douglas, a member of the Air Staff whose duties were largely concerned with air defence, remarked: 'If the enemy had not chosen that moment to pull out, we should soon have been inflicting such casualties on his night-bombers that the continuance of his night offensive on a similar scale would have been impossible'.[9]

The damage left behind by the Luftwaffe when it turned towards the Soviet Union was considerable. By 19th June, over two million houses had been destroyed or damaged, sixty per cent of them in London, or one out of every six and a half in all Britain. Of these, one in fifteen were beyond repair. One in five of the nation's schools had been damaged. Over 40,000 civilians had been killed, 86,000 seriously injured and over 150,000 slightly injured. It was not until three years of war had passed that the casualties inflicted by the Germans on the British armed forces exceeded those on civilians. However, these figures are mainly incidental to the Luftwaffe's purpose in the Blitz. Only for a short time, from September to mid-November, did it hope to shatter civilian morale, and then only as a by-product of the bombing of 'military' targets such as aircraft factories and ports. The destruction of the British war economy remained always the prime purpose of the Luftwaffe's attacks. But this it came nowhere near to achieving. To be sure, there were individual successes, such as a short-term decline in aircraft production by some twenty per cent as a result of the raid on Coventry on 14th November (for the loss of one German bomber), which pointed to the possibility of ultimate victory, but, overall, the effect of eight months' bombing was small. Production of aircraft and other essential war materials was never seriously hampered; the steady increase in the output of military aircraft continued, with 2,381 being turned out in the first quarter of 1940, and 4,515 in the corresponding period of 1941. There were problems: for example, as a result of the bombing of the British Thomson-Houston Works, production of magnetos, and with it of engines, was retarded for several months, and the repercussions continued for nearly a year; but these were not vital, in large part owing to the policy of dispersal which had been carried out in the early autumn of 1940. The arrival of shipping reaching the ports, which had been falling since the beginning of the war, was not significantly affected; indeed, in the second quarter of 1941, when ports were a particular target of the

Luftwaffe, the total tonnage of ships passing through the docks actually increased, from an all-time low of 5,886,000 tons in the first quarter, to 6,270,000 tons, marking a rise that was to continue until the end of the year. In five months of raids on docks and ports in 1941, only 70,000 tons of food stocks were completely destroyed, and half of one per cent of oil stocks. Vital imports continued to arrive in the country. Internally, railway traffic suffered continual dislocation, but never sufficiently prolonged or widespread as to inhibit the war economy to any significant degree. This was true also of the damage to the public utilities of water, gas and electricity. The hardship and inconvenience caused by the Blitz no doubt had their consequences, but despite them London never ceased to be the administrative and economic capital of the Empire; Portsmouth and Plymouth still served the Royal Navy, Liverpool's docks remained open, as did all others under attack, and even Coventry continued to be a vital centre of British war production.

In nine months, from 7th September 1940 to the end of May 1941, the Luftwaffe dropped some 46,500 tons of high explosive and 110,000 incendiary canisters on Britain, a total of 54,420 tons of bombs, for the cost of some 600 aircraft lost from all causes, whether through enemy action or bad landings on rough airfields at night. It had been a cheap campaign, but one that had achieved little of any permanence. Whether the Germans could have made a decisive impact on Britain's war effort if, from the beginning, their bombs had been aimed at one or two sensitive targets (such as those laid down in Hitler's War Directive of 6th February 1941) is open to doubt. Certainly, later in the war, at a time when, in the third quarter of 1944, the Allies were able to deposit in a month an average of two and a half more bombs on the Reich than was dropped on Britain in the entire Blitz, it was shown how difficult it was to achieve a decisive victory by aerial bombardment alone. It seems clear that, even if such a victory was within the reach of any of the belligerents during the Second World War, the Luftwaffe was singularly ill-equipped to achieve it. During the nine months of the Blitz, it mounted some 40,000 bomber sorties against Britain, each carrying, on average, 1.1 tons of high explosive and 2.75 incendiary canisters, an average of 6,046 tons of bombs each month. In contrast, in twenty-eight months from January 1943 to the end of the war, the Allied heavy bombers dropped 1,888,871 tons of bombs on targets in Germany and occupied Europe, an average of 67,459 tons a month largely delivered by aircraft capable of carrying up to eleven tons of bombs to their targets. At the peak of their offensive, the Allies possessed 3,500 operational bombers; during the Blitz, the Germans had at most 700, each carrying only one ton of bombs to their targets. Thus, all that such a force could be expected to achieve was a slight reduction in the growth of the British war economy, a reduction, moreover, that could only be as temporary as the offensive.

With Germany's attention firmly concentrated on the East for the latter half of 1941 and 1942, and, increasingly occupied by events in the Mediterranean, it was inevitable that the West should become a mere side-show, and an unwanted one at that. For the next few years, the Luftwaffe grudgingly maintained a presence in Norway and Western Europe that was designed to be little more than of nuisance value to the British, a reminder of what lay ahead once the Soviet Union had been conquered. By the end of June 1941, with only 780 combat aircraft in Luftflotten 3 and 5, of which just fifty per cent were operational at any one time, there was little that could be achieved where a force four times that number had failed. Nevertheless, the Luftwaffe continued, in a half-hearted and indiscriminate fashion, to attempt the economic blockade of Britain, attacking her shipping lanes both by day and night, and a few ports and key industries by night. Such was the low level of importance placed on these operations, that whenever a crisis arose on any of the other two fronts (as it did in the East at the end of both 1941 and 1942, and in the Mediterranean in November 1942) it was the West that was raided for reserves. As a result, at the end of 1942, the proportion of the Luftwaffe's combat strength employed there was significantly lower than it had been eighteen months earlier: sixteen per cent as compared to twenty-three. Perhaps the most that can be said of the Luftwaffe's effort against Britain in this period, is that, for relatively little effort, it tied down large defensive forces that would otherwise have been available for employment in the Mediterranean theatre. During 1942, for example, the RAF's fighters based in Britain flew no less than 73,000 sorties in purely defensive work, such as the protection of shipping, a high level of activity imposed by the relatively few aircraft possessed by the Germans in the West.

After the failure of the Blitz, the onslaught on Britain's economy returned to its shipping lanes. There were also occasional small night raids on ports such as Hull or Portsmouth, and industrial centres such as Birmingham, and, on the night 28th July, no less than sixty bombers were sent over London in retaliation for the bombing of Berlin; but these were expected to achieve little. More was to be gained by attacking the shipping lanes, an activity that had continued even through the Battle of Britain. In this, the Luftwaffe had a vital role to play, providing for the U-boats accurate information as to where their prey lay. The submarines were restricted to a maximum circle of vision of twenty miles; only by use of the FW 200 reconnaissance aircraft flying above 15,000 ft for a maximum of sixteen hours, could the battle for control of the Atlantic sea lanes be won. As the Naval High Command stated in January 1941: 'To enable our naval command centres to prosecute the war in the Atlantic, systematic reconnaissance is essential'.[10] But the Air Force was not used solely as the 'eyes' of the Navy. By 30th August 1940, the Luftwaffe itself had claimed the sinking of no less than 1,376,813 tons since the beginning of the war (British figures are somewhat lower, showing 201,300 tons lost through enemy air action, though this does not take into account the tonnage sunk by mines, a proportion of which had been laid by aircraft). Fliegerkorps X in Norway and Fliegerdivision 9 (elevated in October to a Fliegerkorps) in Holland had continued their activities, although some of their units had been used to bomb the British mainland. Indeed, the withdrawal of units from the blockade was to become standard practice, and at the end of 1940 Fliegerkorps X was removed to the Mediterranean theatre. In March 1941, there was a reorganisation of the maritime forces. In Norway, tactical control of Luftflotte 5's forces was divided between two commands, Fliegerführer Nord (later to be divided into Nord and Nord-Ost) and Fliegerführer Lofoten, whose duties were not only to attack shipping but to undertake wide-ranging reconnaissance missions. Luftflotte 5 had control of operations north of latitude 58° North, while Luftflotte 3 controlled the area southwards to latitude 52° North. It deployed both Fliegerkorps IX, which continued to lay mines around the British coast, and Fliegerführer Atlantik, based in Brittany, responsible for reconnaissance and attack in the Western Approaches as far as the east coast of Britain. Independent of Luftflotte 3, was the Führer fur Seeluftstreitkrafte, responsible to the Navy, whose reconnaissance seaplanes were based on the west coast of Jutland, available to undertake missions over the North Sea.

Although there had been a struggle between the Luftwaffe and the Navy as to who should control the maritime air forces, with the Luftwaffe emerging as the winner by Hitler's final decision in March 1941, the fact that the command of maritime operations was divided between air and sea forces does not seem to have affected co-operation between the two services, which was good, at least at the beginning. A far more important factor, however, was the lack of sufficient aircraft not only for attacks on shipping but also, and more important, to provide effective reconnaissance for the U-boats. After the removal of the bulk of the Luftwaffe to the East, there were few aircraft left for the blockade of Britain. Luftflotte 5 disposed of only a small offensive force of some twenty He 111s and twenty-four Ju 88s, and otherwise was primarily engaged in providing reconnaissance for U-boats; Fliegerkorps IX, with some 250 aircraft, continued its mine-laying, while Fliegerführer Atlantik, under Colonel Martin Harlinghausen (a pioneer of shipping attack) was left to undertake the main offensive operations on the convoy routes from the United States, the south Atlantic and Gibraltar, so vital to Britain's continued existence. Based in Western France, in April 1941 this command consisted of only twenty-one long-range reconnaissance FW 200s, of low serviceability (of which eight were in Norway), twenty-six He 111s, twenty-four He 115 seaplanes, carrying bombs or torpedoes, and twelve Bf 110 and Ju 88 short-range reconnaissance aircraft. After six weeks of operations resulting in heavy losses, the He 111s were withdrawn and replaced by improved versions. By July, the number of aircraft at Harlinghausen's disposal had increased from eighty-three to 155 – twenty-nine FW 200s, thirty-one He 111s, forty-five Ju 88s and twenty Do 217 bomber-recon-naissance aircraft, eighteen He 115s, and twelve short-range reconnaissance machines. With their serviceability so low, this meant that at any one time there were seldom more than eight FW 200s available to operate over the Atlantic. Admiral Dönitz, the U-boat commander, had requested twenty. However, the aircraft was never forthcoming in such numbers, the RLM

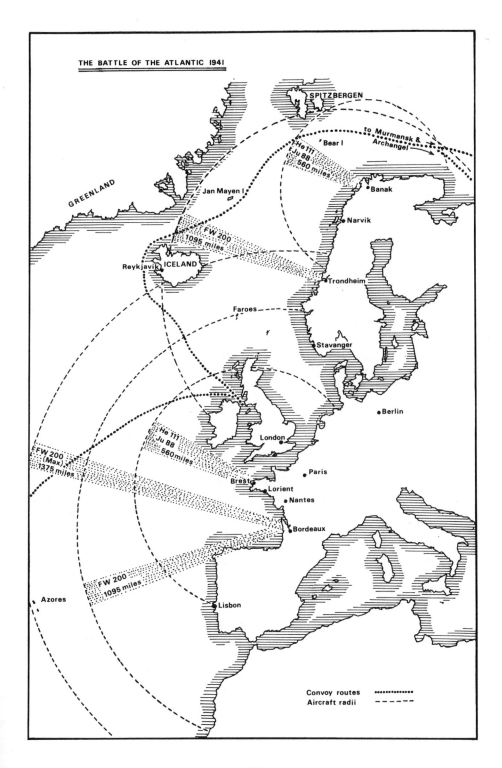

THE BATTLE OF THE ATLANTIC 1941

SPITZBERGEN

to Murmansk &
Archangel

He 111
Ju 88
560 miles

Bear I

GREENLAND

Jan Mayen I

Banak

Narvik

FW 200
1095 miles

Reykjavik ICELAND

Trondheim

Faroes

Stavanger

Berlin

He 111
Ju 88
560miles

London

FW 200
(Max)
1375 miles

Paris

Brest

Lorient

Nantes

Bordeaux

FW 200
1095 miles

Azores

Lisbon

Convoy routes   •••••••••••••••
Aircraft radii   — — — —

having decided that, in view of its role as a stop-gap until the He 177 could be brought into service, no extensive, and expensive, production facilities would be made available for it. In 1941, just four or five Condors were produced each month.

However, it was ironical that, in 1941, at the time when the Luftwaffe was making a particular effort to organise its few available aircraft into an effective force to blockade Britain, the conditions that would make such an operation successful had passed. By mid-1941, the defensive armament on both deep-sea and coastal merchantmen (which included catapult-launched fighters) had increased considerably, so much so that in the late summer the FW 200s were forced to discontinue their attacks for fear of suffering dangerous losses. Convoy protection, too, had improved, and Fliegerführer Atlantik simply had not sufficient serviceable aircraft to carry out major attacks on massed shipping. In addition, coastal waters were rendered distinctly unsafe for German aircraft by the patrols undertaken by RAF Fighter Command, which, in the latter half of 1941, undertook no less than 28,000 sorties in operations to protect shipping. The number of ships sunk off British coasts was reduced from ninety-eight in the first half of 1941 to just thirty-four in the second half. In December, one He 111 Gruppe began to convert to FW 200s for a reconnaissance role as anti-shipping missions near the British coast were regarded as too dangerous to continue. At this time, a new version of the FW 200 was coming into operation, the C-3, capable of carrying 4,626 lb of bombs and possessing more effective defensive weapons. The He 177, however, was still awaited eagerly. By mid-1941, the capabilities of the existing long-range units had been brought into question. Patrols against U-boats mounted by the RAF caused many of the submarines to operate outside the radius of the FW 200s, thus severely reducing their effectiveness. Employment of serviceable He 177s, on the other hand, would have given the reconnaissance units an extension in their radius of action of over 300 miles, together with faster aircraft, better armed aircraft, more able to take care of themselves against RAF Coastal Command. Friction arose between the Luftwaffe and Navy, and the Fliegerführer Atlantik angrily stated that his forces were being ignored. Meanwhile, the increasing enemy air activity over the Atlantic was making the patrols of the slow FW 200s more risky as time went on, so that, in December, they made only twenty-three sorties, roughly a third of what they had been capable of a few months earlier.

By the end of 1941, it was clear that Fliegerführer Atlantik was losing the battle to blockade Britain. At the beginning of its operations, it had been estimated that one aircraft would be lost for every 30,000 tons of enemy shipping sunk; by the end of the year, this figure was more accurately one for every 10,000 tons. Between July 1940 and December 1941, when the Germans sank some 4,986,000 tons of Allied and neutral shipping in the Atlantic, the Luftwaffe's aircraft accounted for only 287,500. An indication of the low regard with which the Luftwaffe's High Command viewed the activities of Fliegerführer Atlantik is revealed by the fact that, after

Harlinghausen's removal to take control of aircraft-launched torpedo development, he was replaced in early 1942 by a General Kessler, who, until then, had held only obscure posts and had had no experience of maritime operations. At about the same time, one of the two Gruppen of FW 200s was sent to Norway to engage shipping bound for Russia. Fliegerkorps IX, too, had received cursory treatment from the RLM, being forced either to relinquish many of its units to the Eastern and Mediterranean theatres, or to divert its efforts to bombing the British mainland. All protests that such a mis-employment of specialised units did nothing to help the war effort, were ignored. The West was no longer considered the decisive theatre of operations.

In 1942, the economic blockade of Britain continued very much as it had done in the latter half of 1941. Some improvement was experienced with the introduction of an effective torpedo for the bomber units (its development by the Luftwaffe having been strenuously resisted by the Navy), which allowed aircraft to attack ships without getting too near the anti-aircraft artillery. Its application in the West, however, was minimal. By the end of April, the first crews trained in their use were based in northern Norway, and by June one Gruppe of forty-two He 111s was capable of mounting torpedo attacks. By July, some thirty Ju 88s based in France were also trained; and on 3rd August, after having been misused in bombing raids on Birmingham, they were sent in the first massed attack on a convoy off the Scilly Isles. But their employment under Fliegerführer Atlantik was to be short-lived, and by September the Ju 88s were being deployed, together with units of Luftflotte 5, against Allied convoys in the Arctic carrying supplies to the Soviet Union (an operation which had been occupying the attention of Stumpff's command since the spring). In November, after the Allied landings in North Africa on the 8th, the torpedo units in Norway were moved down to the Mediterranean. Flieger-führer Atlantik, therefore, was deprived of an effective weapon, which, had more attention been devoted to its earlier development, could have been used to great effect during 1941 in the Battle of the Atlantic.

Indeed, by the end of 1942, Fliegerführer Atlantik and Fliegerkorps IX had very little to show for their efforts. Sinkings of enemy ships had declined to half that of the previous year, owing as much to the effective defence put up by the enemy as to the withdrawal of units to the East and the Mediterranean. In November, when the Mediterranean became a decisive theatre of war, no less than five bomber Gruppen were transferred, temporarily, to the South of France and one Staffel of FW 200s had gone to Italy. A few weeks later, at the beginning of 1943, a further eighteen FW 200s were also sent to assist in the Stalingrad air lift. Only one Staffel of Condors remained available for the Atlantic. The Führer der Seeluftstreitkräfte was dissolved in July 1942, and Fliegerkorps IX added shipping attack to its mine-laying duties. In the summer, the offensive force of Fliegerführer Atlantik stood at some forty Ju 88s, and of Fliegerkorps IX at some ninety Do 217s, aircraft that were as likely to be used in bombing missions over England as against shipping. The most important operational task during the year was the battle to maintain FW 200 reconnaissance over the Bay of Biscay, in order to warn the surfaced U-boats of enemy presence as they went to and from their bases on the French Atlantic coast. For their part, the British were anxious to control the air over this area so as to inflict a decisive defeat on the German U-boats. In June, the Germans managed to bring down only three RAF aircraft over the Bay, but in July, with the arrival of twenty-four Ju 88C heavy-fighters, their opposition increased. In October, no less than sixteen RAF aircraft were shot down, for the loss of twelve of the Luftwaffe's. However, the importance of the operation for the German Air Force, although not for the Navy, ended at the end of the year with the withdrawal of the FW 200s to the Mediterranean and the East. The desultory battle continued, but to little end. The U-boats had lost their greatest ally.

As has been made clear from the record of events, after the conclusion of the Blitz the Luftwaffe High Command adopted no definite or consistent policy regarding the blockade of Britain's vital shipping lanes. After the removal of the effective area of submarine operations out of the range of the FW 200s, the Luftwaffe played no decisive part in the Battle of the Atlantic. This is revealed by the British figures for British merchant shipping sunk by U-boats in all seas in 1941 and 1942 (4,323,000 tons) compared with that by aircraft (973,000 tons, with, perhaps, an extra 50,000 tons sunk through mines dropped by aircraft), and is confirmed by the fact that 574,600 tons of British ships in all seas were sunk by direct aircraft attack in 1941, compared with 398,700 in 1942, a drop of sixty-nine per cent. Indeed, by the end of 1942, the level of shipping attack was back to that which it had been in the first few months of 1940. Only in the Arctic did the Luftwaffe conduct a determined anti-shipping effort, and even this was to prove short-lived, and only indirectly formed a part of the war against Britain.

In the West, what had begun for the Germans as primarily an offensive campaign had, by 1942, become a defensive one. On 4th September 1939, the RAF had undertaken its first raid on Germany, when it attacked, by day, warships in the Kiel Canal. In the subsequent months, missions to drop propaganda leaflets on civilians greatly predominated over those designed to drop bombs on military targets. For the rest of 1939, in which just eight tons of bombs were dropped on the Reich, only three other main raids were undertaken, all on naval bases. Damage was minimal, and the Luftwaffe's fighters and Flak succeeded in bringing down twenty-four aircraft, one third of the total force engaged. Clearly, a daylight offensive was out of the question for the RAF, a conclusion that, later, was to be reaffirmed by the German failure in the Battle of Britain. The theory that the well-armed bomber flying in formation always got through the defences, was shown to be false. Henceforth attacks would have to be made over Germany by night. On the night of 15th/16th May, while the German armies were moving towards the

Channel, the first targets within the Reich that were not of a purely military nature were bombed, when ninety-nine bombers attacked oil and railway targets in the Ruhr. This was the beginning of a bombing offensive in which the Western Allies were to drop 1,899,979 tons of bombs over Europe in five years, of which sixty-three per cent, 1,206,022 tons, were on Germany. By contrast, the Soviet Air Force, designed primarily for ground-support, dropped just 7,394 tons on the Reich.

The bombing offensive over Europe began on a small scale compared with what was to come. In 1940, 13,547 tons of bombs were dropped over Germany and the occupied countries, followed by 37,106 tons in 1941, in all just ninety-three per cent of the total dropped by the Luftwaffe in the nine months of the Blitz. The damage done was slight. In 1940, the targets selected by the RAF were oil, aluminium and aero-engine plants, but by the end of the year it was realised that the poor results obtained necessitated a change. Already, marshalling yards in the Ruhr had been attacked repeatedly, and in the summer of 1941 they were made the prime target. Again, minimal success was recorded. The precision required for such operations was impossible to obtain. Navigation aids were primitive, relying on the mathematical calculations of 'dead reckoning', the stars, and signals from radio beacons. Raiders were fortunate if they arrived over their target area at all, let alone if they actually hit their objectives. In 1941, only one in three bombers placed their bombs within five miles of their targets, while over the Ruhr, the industrial heartland of the Reich, only one in ten had done so. In all, just one quarter of the bombs dropped actually came near their targets. Such an offensive gave little cause for alarm to the Luftwaffe.

However, the German Air Force could not allow the RAF's challenge to go unheeded. It was obviously vital that the Luftwaffe retained complete command of the air space over Europe. Production of anti-aircraft guns was increased, and by 1942 there were some 3,500 heavy and 8,000 medium and light guns in the West, an increase of twenty-three per cent of the total with which the Luftwaffe had begun the war. Of more significance, however, was the development of the night-fighter arm, which, at the beginning of the war had consisted of just thirty aircraft. Between February and June 1939, the RLM had formed eleven experimental night-fighter Staffeln, equipped with Bf 109s and Ar 68s, but by mid-July nine of these had been incorporated into the day-fighting arm, leaving only two Staffeln of the Ar 68 biplanes for night duties. Shortly after the commencement of hostilities, three more night-fighter Staffeln (two of Bf 109s and one of Bf 110s) were created, but it was not until June 1940, after the first British raids on the German war economy, that the RLM ordered the first night-fighter Geschwader (Nachtjagdgeschwader) to be formed. By the end of November, three Geschwader had been raised, although they consisted of only five Gruppen and one Staffel between them. These units came under the control of the Nachtjagddivision, formed in July under General Josef Kammhuber, who, a year later, was made 'General of Night Fighters'. By the end of 1940, his command had an effective strength of 164 aircraft, mostly Bf 110s, with a few Ju 88s, of which some sixty per cent were serviceable. These aircraft differed from their daytime counterparts only in their black camouflage paint and their extra radio equipment. No purpose-built night fighter was available, and none was seriously contemplated. The greatest problem that faced the night-fighters lay in finding the enemy bombers, which flew at heights between 13,000 and 20,000 ft in pitch dark across hundreds of square miles of sky. At first, it was thought that only by searchlight illumination could this be achieved, and a special 'fighter zone' some 13 miles wide was established, west of Münster, free of anti-aircraft fire but packed with searchlights. The British, realising what the Germans were about, learnt either to avoid the known fighter zone, or to cross it at full speed in three minutes. The success rate of the interceptors was not good, and Kammhuber realised that a more comprehensive solution to air defence in the West was required. From this, there grew what became known by the British as the 'Kammhuber Line', begun in late 1940 and completed by the end of the following year.

An important element of the new German defence system was radar, and Freya stations came to cover the approaches to German air space from Denmark to the Swiss border. But these alone were not sufficient. While the Freya had been able to provide advanced warning of an enemy raid, a shorter-range device was required to allow Flak batteries to locate aircraft within their range, and by mid-1940 there had appeared the Würzburg, a small, reliable, mobile set on a 5.3 m wavelength, with a range of between six and thirty-one miles. The first Würzburg-guided night kill was made by a Flak battery in September 1940. The new radar was of considerable value, too, to the night-fighters; a co-ordinated defence system was now possible, and in October Kammhuber set up three night-fighter zones in the path of RAF bombers flying to the Ruhr. They were contained in an area fifty-six miles in length, and twelve in width, and each was occupied by a searchlight battalion and two Würzburg radars. The night-fighters could be placed, individually, anywhere in the zones to within fifty-five yards of their prey, by being linked to the Würzburgs through their ground control while the searchlights were used to pick out the target for the kill. This method was known as Helle Nachtjagd (Henaja). Zones were also established along the coast in which searchlights were not used; this form of fighting was known as Dunkel Nachtjagd (Dunaja).

The new system had many deficiencies; even six-tenths cloud cover presented considerable difficulties for the defenders. The short range of the Würzburg, too, was a problem, as was its inability to distinguish between friend and foe. It was not unknown for radar and listening posts to identify a German night fighter as a target, and for ground control to bring in another Bf 110 to chase it. Furthermore, there was no central command system in Germany as there was in Britain, to receive and evaluate the data coming from the various radars, and to issue the necessary orders to the fighters and Flak units accordingly. Information from the Freya sets was sent to both the

Navy and the Luftwaffe, and to the latter it went partly to the Luftflotten (in charge of air units) and partly to the Luftgaue (directing Flak), as well as to the RLM in Berlin. However, despite such deficiencies and the criticisms of unit commanders and pilots, many of whom disliked 'controlled' interception, Kammhuber was satisfied with the results of his experiment. By the end of 1940, the night-fighter force had shot down forty-two bombers using his method, and the Flak units thirty. An extension of the system was undertaken. Late in 1940, a line of illuminated night-fighter zones (Henajas), each some 20 miles wide, was established, and by March 1941 it stretched from the Danish Border to Maubeuge in France, a distance of some 430 miles. An additional belt between Frankfurt and Mannheim (forty-five miles) was brought into operation in the late autumn. Three Würzburgs were allocated to each searchlight site, which made it possible to locate bombers and night-fighters as they entered the zone. In addition, Kammhuber increased the circular zones in which individual fighters were guided to their targets in darkness (Dunajas), and these were extended not only along the coast of northern France and the Low Countries, but also around Berlin. The Flak units, out of Kammhuber's control, were distributed, as before, throughout the Reich and occupied territories at important targets.

In the autumn of 1941, came the first deliveries of an improved Würzburg radar, with a range of almost 50 miles, together with the new Seeburg plotting table, a glass screen which dealt with plots to a radius of 22 miles, using different colours for raider and interceptor. With the arrival of this equipment, Kammhuber was able to undertake considerable changes in his organisation. The width of the illuminated zones was increased from 25 to 60 miles, and Dunajas, 22 miles in radius, were provided in front. It was also planned to introduce Dunajas behind the line, while Freyas would be placed in front and behind the Henajas for early warning, together with a number of 'master' searchlights to complement the new radars. This procedure often, but wrongly, referred to as Himmelbett ('Four-poster bed') became operational in September, but was so complicated that the number of enemy aircraft shot down decreased. After certain changes, such as reducing the depth of the searchlight belt to six miles and then widening it to over twelve, it only began to work effectively in the spring of 1942. In addition to the Henaja and Dunaja methods of interception, there was one other, the Konaja (combined method), which was seen as the answer to the new four-engined bombers introduced by the RAF in early 1941, and which outpaced the Bf 110s. As they approached their targets, the bombers were forced to fly at a fixed height (usually not over 18,000 ft) in a straight line. There, they were most vulnerable to attack, and fighters would co-operate with Flak and searchlights in a tightly controlled operation. Six Konajas were set up over large towns, including Berlin, but the danger of night-fighters being shot down by their own anti-aircraft artillery was too great for the system to be successful.

Despite all problems, 1941 had been fairly satisfactory for the German defenders. RAF bombers destroyed over Europe rose from just under three per cent of aircraft despatched in 1940 to 3.6 per cent, with a promise of a further increase. In one raid on 7th-8th November, for example, no less than 12.4 per cent of the attacking force of 169 bombers were destroyed in a raid over Berlin. In all operations, bombers made inoperable owing to damage from poor landings, as well as bullets and shells, were higher, averaging eleven per cent. The efficiency of the night-fighters was fast improving; in the West they had accounted for 422 enemy aircraft (including one by day). By November, there were nine Gruppen and one Staffel of night-fighters in existence. On 10th August, the Nachtjagddivision was retitled Fliegerkorps XII, composed of a new Nachtjagddivision, under General von Döring, two searchlight divisions, three signals regiments, and the few day fighters then in the Reich. The command of air defence in the West had undergone some change, although the results were far from ideal. In the occupied territories, Luftflotte 2 had left for the East in April, leaving Luftflotte 3 in sole charge of operations against the British. Sperrle retained command of all fighter units in the occupied territories, although supervision of the night-fighters within his territory lay with Kammhuber. In Norway, Stumpff's Luftflotte 5 remained responsible for air defence. In the Reich, a new command was formed on 21st March, that of Luftwaffenbefehlshaber Mitte (Luftwaffe Commander Centre), under General Hubert Weise, an anti-aircraft gunner who was responsible for the air defence of the Reich. Under him, came the fighters stationed in the Reich (Kammhuber's command) and the Flak units (the responsibility of the Luftgaue), with the exception of those in the Luftgaue at Munich and Wiesbaden, which remained subordinate to Luftflotte 3, and in East Prussia, which remained under Luftflotte 1.

Despite the build-up of the Reich's air defences in the first two years of the war, there was much complacency within the Luftwaffe high command about the enemy's offensive capacity, a complacency which, however understandable in view of the poor results achieved by the RAF, nevertheless boded ill for the future. Even the entry of the United States into the war in December 1941, with her vast resources and her long-range bombers, did nothing to alter this. In the early autumn of 1941, Udet had given voice to his fears: 'If we cannot considerably increase the fighter forces and cannot go off the defensive by 1942, the war is lost.'[11] However, his was a lone voice within the RLM at that time. Jeschonnek, according to Schmid, worked most 'unwillingly on air defence', and his management of the subject was 'dragging'.[12] The prevailing attitude was summed up by Göring in the autumn, when, in reply to the urgings of Galland to increase the Reich's defences, he said: 'This whole phoney business won't be necessary any more once I get my squadrons back to the West'.[13] As if to confirm this attitude, the winter months of 1941, when the weather was unsuitable for sustained operations, saw a decrease in enemy activity over Western Europe. The final quarter of the year saw a reduction from 13,550 tons of bombs dropped in the previous quarter, to just under 7,600 tons, a trend which continued into the first quarter of 1942, when the figure was 6,753 tons. However, this was the lull before the storm, a storm with which the over-stretched night defences were in poor condition to deal.

Until 1942, the British air offensive against Germany had consisted of a few attacks by day on military targets in the occupied territories, and by night many more on the war economy of the Reich. However, in attacks on targets as small as factories and rail junctions, the RAF did not possess the ability to achieve the pin-point accuracy required of it even by daylight, let alone by darkness. Of the 10,000 high explosive and 5,900 incendiary bombs which were dropped in October and December 1941, almost half fell on open ground and another seventeen per cent on decoy installations. The RAF was well aware of its failings; area bombardment was seen as the only solution, especially with the introduction into service of heavier bombers. It was argued that a major impact on German war production would be achieved by destroying the social fabric on which it was based – the workers' homes, towns, and cities. The first indication of this change in strategy came on the night of 16th-17th December 1941, when the built-up areas of Mannheim were bombed by 134 aircraft. On 14th February 1942, the British War Cabinet ordered an intensified bombing offensive, initially to last six months, and, on the 20th, Air Marshal Sir Arthur Harris was made Commander-in-Chief of RAF Bomber Command. His brief, with which he readily concurred, was contained in Bombing Directive No. 22, issued on 14th February, which stated '. . . the primary object of your operations should now be focussed on the morale of the enemy civil population, in particular, of the industrial workers'.[14] In 1942, of the 50,456 tons of bombs dropped on Europe (over a third more than the previous year), no less than seventy-seven per cent were in 'area raids' over Germany.

The first major operation following the adoption of this new strategy was undertaken on the night of 28th-29th March 1942, when 191 bombers dropped 300 tons of bombs, half of them incendiaries, on the ancient Baltic port of Lübeck. Over 1,000 houses were destroyed, and another 4,000 damaged. The inner city, largely made of wood, was left a smouldering heap of ruins, and no goods could be sent through the town or port for the next three weeks. Some 320 people lost their lives, and 785 were severely wounded. This, the first of what the Germans called 'Terrorangriffen' (Terror Attacks), was but an indication of the death and destruction that would soon fall on the Reich from the sky. The second major operation was aimed at Rostock, where the Heinkel works were situated; on four consecutive nights between 24th-27th April, it received the attention of 468 bombers, a large number of which were the new Lancasters capable of carrying six tons of bombs. Sixty per cent of the old city was burnt down. As a final indication of what was intended, on the night of 30th-31st May 1,042 bombers took off from Britain for Cologne, and 900 reached their target (in all operations, an average ten per cent of the bomber force would turn back due to technical failures). There, they dropped 1,455 tons of bombs, of which two-thirds were incendiaries. Some 12,000 fires linked up to form one inferno, in which 18,432 flats, houses, workshops and public buildings were destroyed, 9,516 heavily damaged, and 31,070 damaged less severely. No fewer than 486 civilians were killed, 5,027 injured and 59,100 rendered homeless. The pattern had been established, and during 1942, the enemy deposited over 50,000 tons of bombs in roughly 100 raids, seventeen of which involved more than 500 tons each. Of the total, seventy-seven per cent was in area bombardment, as compared with thirty-nine per cent of 37,000 tons the year previously. The German leadership was, understandably, worried by this new turn of events. After the second night of the Rostock raid, Goebbels recorded in his diary: 'It has been, it must be admitted, pretty disastrous. . . . The Führer is in extremely bad humour about the poor anti-aircraft defence. . . . The Luftwaffe wasn't prepared.'[15]

Indeed, the Luftwaffe's defences were insufficient to meet both the increased enemy activity and the new tactics adopted by RAF Bomber Command. The commitment of fighter units to the West had been much reduced as a result of the Luftwaffe's diversion to the East. By the summer of 1941, Luftflotte 3 had been left with just two under-strength fighter Geschwader to guard the coast, and, in December, two Gruppen of night-fighters were taken from Fliegerkorps XII and sent to the Russian front as ordinary Bf 110 'destroyer' units. In May 1941, one Staffel had been sent to the Mediterranean, followed in November by the Ju 88 Gruppe. Thus, by January 1942, Kammhuber possessed only six Gruppen in the West. Moreover, not only were existing units taken away from air defence, but, because of the drain on resources caused by the intense fighting in the East, and, to an increasing extent, in the Mediterranean, it proved impossible to keep the remaining units in the West up to strength. Thus, at the beginning of February 1942, out of an established strength of 367 aircraft, Germany's night-fighters numbered just 265, of which only fifty per cent were operational, and ten per cent stationed elsewhere than in the West.

A further weakening of the Luftwaffe's defensive capabilities in the West had come in October 1941, with Hitler's order prohibiting night intruder operations over England. When the Nachtjagddivision was set up in 1940, one of its Gruppen consisted of Ju 88C heavy fighters, whose task it was to inflict damage on RAF Bomber Command at its bases, before even its aircraft had taken off to attack Germany. In December, Göring gave Kammhuber permission to raise three Geschwader of long-range night-fighters, so impressed was he by the arguments of the General of Night Fighters: 'if you want to render a swarm of wasps harmless, it is better to destroy the nest rather than to wait until the swarm flies out and then chase each individual wasp'.[16] However, this policy ran into many difficulties, foremost among them being that there were simply insufficient machines suitable for the task. In 1940, the output of Ju 88Cs was just sixty machines, quite inadequate even to keep pace with the attrition suffered by the existing long-range Gruppe, let alone to raise three Geschwader. At the beginning of 1941, there were but twenty-four aircraft in service with the Gruppe, of which just seven were ready for action. In the following months, this position improved, so that, by the end of July, it possessed fifty-seven aircraft, of which twenty-nine were serviceable. This total, however, included a Staffel of Do 17Z-10 Kauz's (Screech Owls), which had been used in the same role as the Ju 88Cs since October 1940, and which, although their performance was inadequate for chasing enemy bombers over the Reich, was quite sufficient for night intrusion when they could lie in wait for their prey.

The effectiveness of this intruder force was considerable, and by November 1941 it had claimed 144 kills, thirty 'probables', and 222 air combats the outcome of which was not known. In addition, fifty-two bombers had been destroyed on the ground, together with another fifty-eight 'probables', and 440 tons of bombs had been deposited on targets. Just as important as this material destruction, which amounted to over a quarter of the 'kills' claimed by the night-fighter force, was the psychological impact on the RAF crews. They were made particularly nervous by the German technique of mixing with the returning bombers and then shooting down the unsuspecting enemy over their bases. Many British pilots crash-landed because they brought their aircraft down at too high a speed or with insufficient caution, in order to avoid a possible attack by an unknown intruder. Night flying training was even ended in East Anglia, Yorkshire and Lincolnshire, the areas most affected by the intruders. But, however successful this form of defence might be, it had its critics. Jeschonnek, for example, disliked the allocation of all the Ju 88Cs to this role, while Sperrle was resentful that there was a unit engaged in operations over Britain which did not come under his control. Hitler himself was extremely sceptical, pointing to the fact that, during the Gruppe's operation, the RAF's offensive had grown rather than declined. The German people, he argued, wanted the raiders to be brought down over Germany, not far away in their country of origin. On 13th October, after a night-fighter ace had been lost over East Anglia, the Führer gave his order for the intruding missions to be ended. The following month, the Ju 88 Gruppe was sent to the Mediterranean. Thus was brought to a conclusion a method of defence which, had it been expanded, might well have caused insuperable difficulties for RAF Bomber Command. As it was, the enemy was allowed to operate for over three years with its bases undisturbed. This, according to the RAF, was 'an important factor which contributed to the final crippling of Germany'.[17] General Walter Grabmann, one of the Reich's defenders, was more specific: 'In view of the highly complicated and weather-sensitive take-off and landing manoeuvres practised by the Royal Air Force in its steadily increasing nocturnal bombardment activity, a well-developed system of German long-range fighter pursuit would have had an excellent chance of success. The fact that Germany neglected to develop this weapon as long as she had the chance to do so must be counted as one of the gravest sins of omission on the part of the night-fighter command.'[18]

Apart from its shortage of aircraft, in the spring of 1942 Fliegerkorps XII also suffered from a change in the RAF tactics, a change facilitated by the advent of the 'GEE' navigation system, whereby the bombers were guided to the target by pulse signals received from three gound stations on the east coast of England. Although relatively inaccurate, it did allow a third of the bombs to fall near to their targets. Moreover, it enabled the RAF to improve its tactics. Previously, bombers had made their own way to their targets, using different routes and staging the attack over several hours; indeed, it was this independence of action which many pilots believed was the main reason for their survival. It was now possible to concentrate the raiders in streams, guided by 'GEE', which would punch through the Kammhuber line in places where only one or two fighters could be brought to bear, and drop their loads in a far shorter time than ever before. Thus, in the '1,000 Bomber Raid' over Cologne, the period of attack (and therefore of vulnerability) was cut to two and a half hours, while German airspace was penetrated on a front barely eighteen miles wide. Only twenty-five night-fighters were directed towards the enemy, one ninth of the total force available. Thus, the central weakness of the German night defence system was exploited; the allocation of one fighter to each defensive box, in which only one bomber could be engaged at a time. If all the raiders were to be pushed through a small area at one time, only two or three unfortunates would have to deal with the attentions of the German fighters. Once through, the raiders would be able to fly over northern and central Germany unhindered by interceptors, their only hazard being the German Flak. Thus, the percentage of RAF bombers shot down in operations, which had been averaging some 3.6 per cent during 1941, were suddenly reduced to three per cent. In the Cologne raid, for example, only forty-four bombers failed to return to base, just 4.2 per cent of the total. Overall, owing to combat damage and poor landings, the RAF was losing some 12 per cent of its aircraft on each mission, a third of which were repairable, a rate of attrition that could be endured almost indefinitely.

The Germans, however, were to prove themselves equal to the threat. By the end of the year, Fliegerkorps XII had been reorganised (on 1st May, its unwieldy Nachtjagddivision was divided into three Jagddivisionen), and, in mid-February 1943, the strength of the Reich's night-fighters lay at 477 aircraft (out of an establishment of 653), of which 330 were serviceable, double the number at the beginning of 1942. Of these, ninety per cent were in the West. Moreover, ninety-five per cent of these aircraft were equipped with the airborne radar, Lichtenstein, which had a maximum range of 3,000 yards and a minimum of 20 yards, and allowed the fighters to close to firing range of their prey once the ground radar had taken them to within two miles. The main drawback of the Lichtenstein was that the height of its antennae caused a loss of speed, of at least 25 mph for the Bf 110. However, this was more than compensated for by the advantages which accrued from being able to locate the target for the final attack, and the success rate soon grew considerably. Indeed, the night fighters were deemed to be able to operate without the support of searchlights, and these were released from the illuminated zones to aid the Flak units guarding Germany's cities. In addition, the German scientists found a way to jam the GEE signals, and by August it was impossible

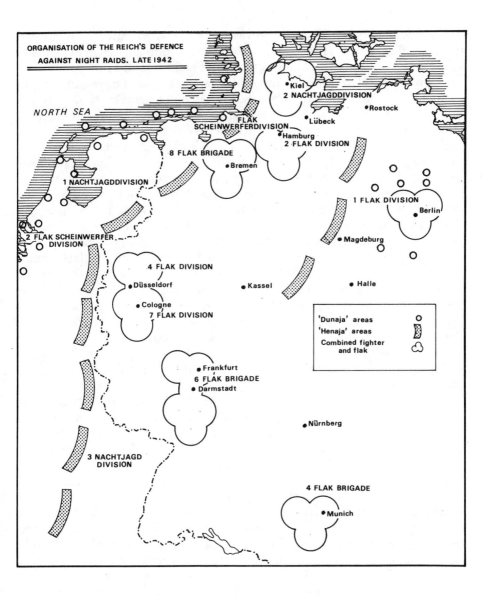

ORGANISATION OF THE REICH'S DEFENCE
AGAINST NIGHT RAIDS. LATE 1942

NORTH SEA

• Kiel
2 NACHTJAGDDIVISION

• Rostock

FLAK
SCHEINWERFERDIVISION

• Lübeck

• Hamburg
2 FLAK DIVISION

8 FLAK BRIGADE

• Bremen

1 NACHTJAGDDIVISION

1 FLAK DIVISION

• Berlin

2 FLAK SCHEINWERFER
DIVISION

• Magdeburg

4 FLAK DIVISION

• Düsseldorf

• Kassel

• Halle

• Cologne
7 FLAK DIVISION

'Dunaja' areas   O
'Henaja' areas
Combined fighter
and flak

• Frankfurt
6 FLAK BRIGADE
• Darmstadt

• Nürnberg

3 NACHTJAGD
DIVISION

4 FLAK BRIGADE

• Munich

for the RAF to use the system far beyond the coast.

The organisation of Germany's night air defence was also adapted to meet
changing circumstances. By June, the Kammhuber line had been extended
south towards Paris and northwards to the tip of Denmark, and a further
extension to southern Norway was in preparation. Kammhuber rejected any
idea of 'free' night fighting, or the forming of main defence points, as was
possible during the day, but nevertheless made the defence line far more
flexible. Before the illuminated barrier was ended, he extended the Dunaja
zones to a depth of 124 miles in front and behind the Henajas, using to the full

the improved ranges of both the Freyas and Würzburgs. After the removal of the searchlights, the Himmelbett method was adopted, whereby, in each sector, one Würzburg would chart the course of the intruder, and another the interceptor. This fighter was controlled, as always, from the ground until the Lichtenstein would allow the pilot of the interceptor to make the final attack. Still, each zone was capable of handling only one fighter, but they were made to overlap by fifty per cent, so that it was possible to send three fighters into one zone, provided that the halves of the two outer zones could be left unattended. However, this reorganisation still left the major problems unsolved: huge areas of Germany remained devoid of night-fighters, and streams of enemy bombers on a narrow front would still be faced by only a very few of the night-fighters under Kammhuber's command. Such restrictions made it impossible to raise the number of kills above a certain percentage, estimated to be around six per cent of enemy sorties.

However, by a greater commitment to night defence in 1942, the Germans had managed to redress the balance against the RAF. In that year, sixty-five per cent of all intercepts resulted in kills, and in the West 687 enemy aircraft were brought down (an increase of sixty-three per cent over the previous year's total) for the loss of ninety-seven night-fighters, with a further 189 damaged. On 10th September, Fliergerkorps XII celebrated its 1,000th victory, comprising 648 bombers in 'dark' night fighting, 200 in illuminated night-fighting, 141 shot down by intruders, and eleven that crashed by being blinded by searchlights. Indeed, together with Flak, the night-fighters were, by the autumn of 1942, shooting down some 5.6 per cent of the British aircraft over Germany. The anti-aircraft guns were even more effective. In the period July to August, the RAF reported 696 bombers missing, of which 169 were probably shot down by fighters, 193 by Flak, and 334 crashed due to unknown causes. Of the 1,394 damaged in the same period, 153 were by fighters, 941 by Flak, and the rest by causes other than enemy action.

But defensive measures were not the only method by which the Luftwaffe sought to combat the RAF's offensive. In 1942, therefore, apart from its somewhat inadequate attempt at economic blockade, the Luftwaffe undertook one other type of mission against Britain: the reprisal raid. This was an entirely new departure, and one made necessary only by their loss of total command of the air over Europe. When, on the night of 28th-29th March 1942, the RAF made its first concentrated bombing attack on a German city, Lübeck, and razed its centre to the ground, Hitler and his advisers were confronted with a dilemma. Should they continue to wage war against the British homeland as if nothing had happened, or should they copy the action and retaliate with the few forces they had at their disposal, perhaps with the hope that the British might abandon their policy? Reprisal was decided upon, and on 14th April Hitler sanctioned raids on targets 'where attacks are likely to have the greatest possible effect on civilian life. Besides raids on ports and industry, terror attacks of a retaliatory nature are to be carried out on towns other than London. Minelaying is to be scaled down in favour of these attacks'.[19] As an indication of the importance that Hitler attached to these raids, the Luftwaffe brought back its pathfinder Kampfgeschwader from the East, and two Gruppen from Sicily, where they were bombing Malta, and these, together with units assigned to maritime duties, composed a force of some 450 bombers.

The 'Baedeker' raids, as both sides came to call them after the famous guide book from which it was presumed the targets were selected, began on the night of 25th April with an attack on Exeter. In the following seven months, a further thirty-eight raids took place, directed at such non-military towns as Bath (twice) Norwich (six times) and Canterbury (four times) as well as the old targets such as Birmingham and Southampton. The impact of these attacks, however, was very small, as the number of aircraft made available for them dwindled, either through losses in action (which amounted to some 80 machines) or transfers to other fronts. Over half the total tonnage delivered (2,979 tons) was dropped within the first two months. The heaviest attack was on Bath on the night of 25th April (210 tons), and the smallest on Colchester on the 26th August (six tons). An average of seventy-six tons was dropped in each raid, of which only twenty-six per cent actually landed on its target. The number of German bombers lost to the British air defences was around eighty.

As the 'Baedeker' raids continued in desultory fashion, Luftflotte 3 made greater use of daylight fighter-bomber attacks. These had begun again on Christmas Day in 1941, and early in 1942 a special Jabo Gruppe, of two Staffeln, was added to the Luftflotte's order of battle. From March, small numbers of bomb-carrying Bf 109s, delivering surprise attacks on Channel ports and towns, became a regular occurrence, at the rate of two or three a week. In July, the Bf 109s were replaced by the new FW 190s, and operations were stepped up. From March to August, just ten Jabos were shot down by the defences, and an operational level of thirty fighter-bombers was maintained. In October, the Germans even undertook a massed Jabo raid against Canterbury, with sixty-two Bf 109s escorting a further sixty-eight bomb-carrying machines; thirty-one bombs struck the target, for the loss of only three aircraft. Single bombers and small formations also made daylight raids over England; one day in July, for example, when clouds were low, as many as thirty such raiders roamed the country, damaging four factories, two airfields, and four railway targets. Fortunately for the British, a scarcity of trained crews kept these missions to a minimum. For example, in January 1942, one Kampfgeschwader had eighty-eight crews; by September, it had only twenty-three. In the summer, too, a handful of Ju 86Rs, a specially developed high-altitude reconnaissance version of the Luftwaffe's former bomber, made several sorties over Britain, each dropping 550 lb of explosive from 40,000 ft to little effect. At the end of August, a handful of Me 210s made their first appearance over England as fighter-bombers, but within a short space of time four had been shot down, thus confirming their failure as combat machines. Such were the missions in which, together with the 'Baedeker' raids, the Luftwaffe deposited some 6,500 tons of bombs on Britain in 1942, the equivalent of one month's bombing at the height of the Blitz. The deterrent value was nil.

At the same time as night bombing was wreaking destruction over Germany, day raids by British fighters and light bombers against objectives in France and the Low Countries continued. Begun originally in order to inhibit German preparations for Operation Sealion, they continued as a means to inflict casualties on Luftflotte 3's fighters, to maintain and improve battle-readiness on the part of RAF Fighter Command, and to show the people of the occupied countries that Britain was still capable of fighting. For example, from March to June 1942, no less than 22,000 fighter and 700 light bomber sorties penetrated across the Channel; 303 fighters and eleven bombers did not return. It was an unequal struggle, as the Germans lost only ninety of their fighters, which belonged to the two Geschwader and one Gruppe allocated to Luftflotte 3. Indeed from May 1941 to the end of 1942, the Germans lost some 350 fighters in combat, and 450 from all causes, in the West. Of particular interest during the period of air operations over Luftflotte 3 territory, were the two attempts to protect naval battleships and the repulse of the enemy raid on Dieppe. Between 26th and 28th May 1941, Luftflotte 3's bombers made a vain bid to rescue the *Bismarck* from pursuit by the British fleet, while on 12th February 1942, its fighters successfully aided the *Scharnhorst, Gneisenau* and *Prinz Eugen* to break through the Channel. Later, on 19th August 1942, however, came a major battle, when British and Canadian troops attempted a full-scale landing at Dieppe. One of the enemy's aims was to draw the strength of Luftflotte 3 over the area, there to destroy it. However, both on the land and in the air, the invaders failed. Their troops proved unable to capture some of the commanding points, or to overcome all resistance in the town, and the RAF, for the loss of 108 machines, succeeded in shooting down only forty-eight German aircraft and inflicting damage on another twenty-four, just nine per cent of Sperrle's combat force. In the fight over occupied Europe, the Luftwaffe was the clear victor.

By the end of 1942, therefore, the Luftwaffe had some reason to be satisfied with its performance in the defence of the West. In 77,500 enemy sorties made at night, since the war had begun, 2,859 aircraft had been destroyed (3.6 per cent), and many more damaged. In attacks upon certain targets, the RAF was suffering losses of twelve per cent or more. In raids by day over Europe, the enemy had lost 627 bombers (4.2 per cent of their sorties), and the percentage lost was increasing with time. In 1940, one bomber was lost, or crashed in England after a raid, for every thirty-two sorties undertaken; in 1942, one was lost in every twenty. Moreover, the scale of the enemy's offensive had been fairly modest, a modesty that could be ascribed as much to the activity of the Luftwaffe as to the limited resources of RAF Bomber Command. Whereas, up to the beginning of 1943, the Germans had deposited some 67,000 tons of bombs on Britain, the enemy had dropped 78,579 tons over the Reich and a further 22,537 on occupied Europe.

The disruption suffered by the German economy and armed services by the bomber offensive had been minimal. Post-war calculations by the Allies, for example, put the loss of output in 1942 at between 0.7 per cent and 2.5 per cent of the total. Britain, on the other hand, had committed roughly a third of her war economy to the prosecution of the air offensive. Nor was the effect upon German morale significant; if anything, the hardships suffered by the civilians served to unite the country behind the war effort, and to make the transition to a total war economy that much the easier. During this initial period of the Allied bombing offensive, the Reich continued to take up the slack in its economy and increase production. The achievements of the aircraft manufacturers, a special target of the RAF, is a case in point; between September 1939 and December 1942 the number of aircraft produced monthly rose from 700 to 1,548. Some small reduction in potential output was caused at the Heinkel works at Rostock and the Focke-Wulf works at Bremen. However, the dispersal of manufacturing processes brought about by the bombing of the factories put the industry in a better position to face any fiercer onslaught which might come in the future.

By its reaction to the enemy's bomber offensive, the Luftwaffe had shown that it was not complacent. By the end of 1942, immeasurably greater resources in men and material were committed to the defence of the Reich than there had been at the beginning of the war. However, what was lacking to an alarming degree was any particular concern for the future. Few precautions were taken. Even as late as December 1942, no less than 150 Flak batteries had been transferred from the Reich to Italy, to improve the Italian anti-aircraft defences. The neglect of fighter production was of more significance. In July 1942 when listening to a lecture on the potential of the Allied bomber force, Jeschonnek remarked: 'Every four-engine bomber the Western Allies build makes me happy, for we will bring these . . . down just as we brought down the two-engine ones, and the destruction of a four-engine bomber constitutes a much greater loss to the enemy'.[20]

Milch, alone among the chiefs of the RLM, was concerned by developments. 1942 had, after all, seen as many tons of bombs dropped by the enemy in the West as in the previous two years combined. He realised that the advent of the four-engine bomber was greatly improving the efficacy of the enemy bomber force, which by the end of 1942 had increased the bomb-load it carried by seventy per cent. Milch saw the emphasis being placed by the Allies on their strategic air offensive, and understood what resources the United States was bringing to the air war, resources which, when combined with those of the RAF, would overwhelm the German defences as then constituted. He was aware that the 1,000 bomber raids over the Reich (of which there were three in 1942) were a precursor of the great destruction to come, which, he feared, would paralyse the German war economy and thus end the fighting capabilities of the German Armed Forces. The twenty-seven daylight raids undertaken by the US 8th Air Force over France and the Low

Countries with their B-24s and B-17s carrying between two and four tons of bombs respectively, he viewed with concern, not for the damage which they achieved, which was slight, but for what they presaged. The raid by 108 American bombers on Lille on 9th October, in which they deposited some 300 tons of bombs for the loss of just four of their number, should have served as a dreadful warning to the Germans. But Milch was, however, a prophet whose words went unheeded. On 21st March 1942, he advocated to Göring and Jeschonnek the formation of a fighter 'umbrella' over Germany. Addressing the Reichsmarschall, he said 'Your total demand is for 360 new fighter aircraft per month. I fail to understand. If you were to say 3,600 fighters, then I would be bound to state that, against America and Britain combined, even 3,600 are too few!' Jeschonnek, however, unable to see how the enemy's air offensive would grow in 1943, objected vehemently: 'I do not know what I should do with more than 360 fighters'.[21] And so the matter was closed for the time being. After the war, Milch was to refer to 'One hundred and forty thousand unbuilt fighter aircraft'[22] as the cardinal error of the Luftwaffe.

VII

The Mediterranean

In mid-1940, except for some vague notions about a thrust to the Persian Gulf, and an occupation of Gibraltar, Hitler had no plans to add the Mediterranean to his conquests. Yet, in 1943, no less than nine German divisions and 1,200 aircraft were committed there, a sizeable force that would have been of immense value on the Eastern Front, where the war was being won or lost. The cause of such a change lay with the Italian dictator, Benito Mussolini, whose military resources bore no relation to his grandiose foreign policy. On 10th June 1940, Italy declared war on France and Britain, and sent troops into southern France to participate in the final victory. On 17th September, the Italians moved over the border of their North-African colony of Cyrenaica (Libya) into Egypt, and occupied Sidi Barrani, 400 miles from Cairo. On 28th October, the Italians began their third military action of the war: the invasion of Greece. But before the end of the year, they were in trouble. Their forces had become bogged down in Greece, and, with the Greeks pushing into Albania, were suffering reverses. Crete was occupied by the British, who, at the same time, had forced the Italians out of Egypt and were advancing into Cyrenaica, to reach within four hundred miles of its capital, Tripoli, by early January 1941. The loss of the Italian North-African colony was in sight.

Hitler was in a dilemma. Although not wishing to become embroiled in another campaign, the Italian action in Greece, taken without his prior knowledge, had created a threat to the German southern flank which could not be ignored. British bases in Greece had placed the Romanian oil-fields at Ploesti, so vital to the German war effort, within range of RAF bombers. In particular, Crete, had to be conquered, or, at the very least, neutralised. This could best be done by the German occupation of the Greek mainland north of the Aegean Sea, which would enable the Luftwaffe to attack any British airfield whose aircraft threatened Romania. If necessary, all Greece would be conquered. On 13th December, Hitler issued his War Directive No. 20, which declared his intentions. Three days earlier, in an attempt to aid the Italians in North Africa, Hitler had undertaken to send German air units to southern Italy, for a limited period only, to attack British ships in the Mediterranean or, if required, the Ionian and Aegean seas. On 11th January 1941, Hitler's War Directive No. 22 also committed German troops to North Africa in the defence of Tripolitania; by June there were two

German armoured divisions, together with a number of anti-tank and other units, in the Deutsches Afrikakorps under the command of General Erwin Rommel, and subordinated to the Italian Army.

The presence of the Luftwaffe in the Mediterranean had begun as early as June 1940, when a Liaison staff, known as Italuft, was instituted in Rome under the command of General Maximilian Ritter von Pohl. Although initially confined mainly to intelligence work, it was later to represent the Luftwaffe in the Mediterranean. In early December, as the Blitz against Britain was under way, the first flying unit appeared, consisting of Ju 52s, whose task it was to ferry Italian troops to Albania to halt the Greek offensive. In fifty days they were to ferry no less than 30,000 troops and 4,700 tons of supplies, for a loss of not a single aircraft. At the end of the year, Fliegerkorps X, under Geisler, with Colonel Harlinghausen as Chief of Staff, was moved from Norway to Southern Italy. On 9th January 1941, the first attack on British shipping was mounted, by nine Ju 87s on Scirocco Bay, Malta. By the middle of January, there were some 330 front-line operational aircraft based in Sicily, consisting of 120 bombers, 150 Ju 87s, forty Bf 110s, and twenty reconnaissance machines. According to War Directive No. 22, the main task of Fliegerkorps X was 'to attack British naval forces and British sea communications between the Western and Eastern Mediterranean. In addition, by the use of intermediate airfields in Tripolitania, conditions will be achieved for the immediate support of the [Italian Army] . . . by means of attack on British port facilities and bases on the coast of Western Egypt and in Cyrenaica.'[1] The Mediterranean between Sicily and North Africa was declared a 'closed area' to neutral shiping, so as to help Fliegerkorps X in its task.

While the Luftwaffe was becoming embroiled in a new theatre of operations in the Mediterranean, it was also busily infiltrating the Balkans. In September 1940, before the Italian invasion of Greece, a German Air Mission was set up in Bucharest, the capital of Romania, ostensibly with the task of training the Romanian Air Force. This move was, however, taken as part of Hitler's intention to move against Russia. By December, a number of air and anti-aircraft units had also entered the country, with the primary object of protecting the Romanian oilfields. Preparations for the forthcoming offensive against Greece and the Soviet Union were also undertaken, and the constancy of Romania to the German cause assured. In Bulgaria, a similar development took place; in December, the first Luftwaffe personnel entered the country, as civilians, and, after March 1941, when Bulgaria formally joined Germany and Italy in the Axis, Luftwaffe units were openly transferred there. By the end of March, a total of 490 German aircraft were in the two countries, the majority based in Bulgaria in preparation for the attack on Greece which was to take place in April. Of the 490, forty were bombers, 120 Ju 87s (all in Bulgaria), 120 Bf 109s, forty Bf 110s, and fifty long-range and 120 short-range reconnaissance aircraft. For the forthcoming operation, control would be exercised by von Richthofen's Fliegerkorps VIII, transferred from the West, under the overall supervision of Löhr's Luftflotte 4. The tasks of the Luftwaffe units were, as usual, to obtain command of the air and to support the ground force, in this case 12th Army.

But just as Hitler was to launch his invasion of Greece, the unexpected happened. On 26th March, a revolution in Jugoslavia, which had just recently joined the Axis powers, brought a government to power which was mistrustful of the Third Reich's ambitions. The German right flank being uncovered, Hitler declared that the unreliability of the new Jugoslav government would jeopardise the invasions of both Greece and Russia. There was no alternative but to occupy Jugoslavia. On the 26th, the day of the revolution in Belgrade, new Luftwaffe units were ordered to the Balkans under Löhr's command: five bomber Gruppen (three from France, one from north-west Germany, and one from North Africa), six Bf 109 Gruppen (from France) and one Bf 110 Gruppe (from north-west Germany), a total of some 600 aircraft. On 6th April, the attack on Jugoslavia and Greece began, with most of the aircraft of these units in action. It had been a considerable administrative achievement, which had involved moving a force comparable to a large Fliegerkorps over an average of 1,000 miles in twelve days from bases as far apart as Ardorf in North Germany to El Machina in North Africa.

On 6th April, the invasion of Greece and Jugoslavia began. At no time did the overwhelming strength of Luftflotte 4, with 1,090 aircraft, together with a further 660 Italian machines, meet any determined opposition. In the air, they were faced by only 400 Jugoslav and eighty Greek aircraft, mostly of inferior quality. The OKW report on the campaign in Jugoslavia noted: 'Through continuous combat action against the enemy communication and supply routes . . . the Luftwaffe did much to bring about the disintegration of the Serbian Army.'[2] On operations in Greece, OKW judged that:

> . . . the Luftwaffe, through its speedy defeat of the enemy air forces and through action which maintained air supremacy throughout the campaign, made it impossible for the enemy to take air action planned to interrupt the progress of the operations. In exemplary co-operation, the Luftwaffe supported the Army through constant close and long-range reconnaissance operations; through combat action by dive-bomber forces, it facilitated the breaching of the enemy main lines of resistance; and through day and night attacks against the withdrawing enemy forces and their rear communications speeded up their disintegration. . . . Particularly good successes were achieved by the bomber and dive-bomber forces in continuous attacks against enemy transport ships in the coastal waters around Greece. This prevented the planned withdrawal of the British forces and very seriously damaged British shipping.[3]

During the campaign, the Luftwaffe added yet one more controversial act to the bombing of Warsaw, Rotterdam, and London: the bombing of Belgrade, which was attacked in the first three days of the invasion of

Jugoslavia, causing the death of 17,000 civilians. Once again, the Germans were accused of aiming to terrorise innocent civilians, and there is no doubt that such was one of the results of their action. However, it was not their aim; as with the attacks on both Warsaw and Rotterdam, the operation was undertaken only because of the aid it would give to the offensive on the ground, in which speed was considered to be vital. Foregone conclusion though the outcome might be, it was imperative that the campaign be ended as soon as possible, so that the forces that had been diverted from the attack on Greece, where British troops were arriving, could be returned to their main task. Moreover, it was important to avoid any possibility of a delay, or a reverse, in the invasion of the Balkans, so that the Germans could turn with all their forces to the attack on Russia, scheduled to start in a few weeks time, in full confidence that their southern flank was secure. It was against this background that the Germans viewed Belgrade as a military objective. The Jugoslav capital formed an important military target, which, should it be rendered inoperable, would cause severe dislocation to the Jugoslav deployment and thus aid the German advance. In five heavy raids, the German bombers were directed against the Ministry of War and the General Staff buildings, the operational headquarters of the enemy forces, the railway station, a particularly important element of the somewhat limited Jugoslav railway system, as well as several other ministries. Such targets fell within the definition of indirect support for the Army, and the fact that they were distributed throughout a heavily populated capital city, many of whose buildings were constructed of wood, was a matter of coincidence rather than planning. The attack was carried out; the military objective was secured; and the world once again condemned the Luftwaffe.

On 15th April, when the Balkan campaign was at its height, Löhr suggested to Göring that the conquest of Greece be concluded with an airborne invasion of Crete by the paratroop and air-landing units of General Student's Fliegerkorps XI, which consisted of an air-landing assault regiment of four battalions, Fliegerdivision 7 (three parachute regiments) and 22nd Air Landing Division, together with various corps and divisional troops. On 20th April, Student himself, together with Jeschonnek, were sent to the Führer by Göring to explain what had by then become the Luftwaffe's plan. The OKW chiefs argued that Fliegerkorps XI would be better employed in occupying Malta, a British base which they considered to be more dangerous to Axis prospects in North Africa than Crete, lying, as it did, astride the communications to southern Europe. The Luftwaffe generals, however, pointed out that not only was Crete a base for British air operations, but that the island itself would prove a useful stepping stone to Cyprus and the Suez canal. This appealed to Hitler, who had some time previously expressed the view that Crete might be susceptible to occupation from the air. After consultation with Mussolini, the Führer issued his War Directive No. 28 on 25th April, approving 'Operation Mercury'. The date set for the attack was 16th May. Fliegerkorps XI immediately began the move from its bases in central

Germany to Athens, where it came under the command of Luftflotte 4. However, because of the great difficulties involved in the move, especially due to the destruction of road and rail communications in Greece, the date of the attack was postponed to 20th May. Transport problems brought 22 Air Landing Division to a halt in Romania, and, with the Army heavily involved in preparing for the invasion of the Soviet Union on 22nd June, it proved impossible to move it further south. In its place, the 5th Mountain Division, already in Greece, was substituted for the operation. In addition to Fliegerkorps XI, the Luftwaffe had detailed Fliegerkorps VIII with 650 operational aircraft to support the invasion of Crete: 280 bombers, 150 Ju 87s, 90 Bf 109s, 90 Bf 110s, and 40 reconnaissance machines, to face twenty-four Hurricanes, Gladiators and Fulmars, of which only twelve were serviceable with reinforcements being flown in from Egypt in twos and threes. No less than 700 Ju 52s and 80 gliders were assembled to ferry the airborne troops to their targets. As a preliminary, bombing attacks were made on British vessels in the Suda Bay anchorage of Crete, and on the British air bases. A blockade of the island was maintained by air, so that of the 27,000 tons of supplies sent from Egypt to Crete between 1st and 20th May, only ten per cent were delivered.

At 0600 hours on 20th May, the invasion of Crete began, with heavy air attacks on the British positions at Maleme airfield and Canea, the capital, the main object of which was to silence the anti-aircraft batteries. By then, there were no enemy fighters left on Crete, thirty-eight having been destroyed and the few remaining withdrawn to Egypt. At 0715 hours, the first airborne forces arrived, to land near Maleme. By the end of the morning, some 5,000 Germans were on Crete, meeting strong opposition from larger British and Empire forces than had been expected (some 28,000 men in all, under General Freyberg), forces, moreover, that had been prepared for just such an operation. The fighting was hard. By the end of the 20th, Freyberg wrote: 'Today has been a hard one. We have been hard pressed. So far, I believe, we hold aerodromes at Rethimnon, Heraklion, and Maleme, and the two harbours. The margin by which we hold them is a bare one, and it would be wrong of me to paint an optimistic picture. . . .'[4] On the 21st, the 5th Mountain Division was flown into Crete, and the scales tipped in the Germans' favour. All that was required were the extra men and heavy equipment that were to arrive by sea, reinforcements that were indispensable to victory. However, this, the Royal Navy was determined to prevent.

On the night of 21st-22nd May, the first German reinforcements were sent by sea to Crete, to be met by fourteen British cruisers and destroyers off the north coast of the island. The transports were blown out of the water, and some 4,000 much-needed men, together with their equipment and heavy guns were prevented from reaching their destination. To stop such a fiasco happening again, Fliegerkorps VIII began the first major air-sea battle in history. It was to last several days, and ended with a clear victory for the Luftwaffe. Early in the morning of the 23rd, despite all exhortations from the

Chiefs of Staff in London, the British fleet was forced to return to Alexandria, two cruisers and four destroyers having been sunk and several damaged. German reinforcements were free to cross the Aegean, and the fate of the British on Crete was sealed. By the 27th, some 27,000 troops had been landed on the island, 4,000 of them Italian. On 28th May, the enemy's evacuation was begun, to be completed by 1st June with 14,500 soldiers taken back to Egypt, during which time the British Mediterranean Fleet was again bombarded. A number of cruisers and destroyers laden with troops were sunk or damaged, bringing the total losses during the battle of Crete to three cruisers and six destroyers sunk, with a battleship, an aircraft carrier, a special service ship, six cruisers and eight destroyers damaged. The Royal Navy's experiences at the hand of Fliegerkorps VIII can only lead to speculation as to what would have been the impact of the Luftwaffe during Operation Sealion, had it been mounted following a successful conclusion to Adlerangriff.

The cost to the German Air Force of victory in Crete was considerable. In the ten-day struggle, the paratroops had lost some 5,140 men dead, wounded or missing out of a force of 13,000. Between 14th May and 1st June, no less than 220 aircraft were lost, of which 119 were Ju 52s, and a further 148 damaged, of which 119 were Ju 52s. The losses in transport aircraft particularly worried the Luftwaffe high command, as they had a considerable impact on the training programme. However, although the taking of Crete proved to be the last major airborne operation undertaken by the Luftwaffe, it was not without its importance for the course of the war in the Mediterranean. The loss of this strategic position was a severe blow for the British, as they could have used it as a base from which to menace the 'soft underbelly' of Axis-dominated Europe. By its occupation, the Germans had laid open the whole of the Eastern Mediterranean to the Luftwaffe. The taking of Crete had, however, left Malta untouched. The consequences of that for the Germans were to be dire.

Moreover, the victory in Crete came too late for the Germans to be able to exploit the pro-German uprising in Iraq, which had brought Raschid Ali to power on 3rd April. By that rebellion, British interests in the Middle East were directly threatened. Had the Germans been able to go to Raschid Ali's assistance, not only would the enemy have found their access to oil from Iraq and Persia barred, but also they would have been confronted with the possibility of an Axis advance on Egypt from an entirely new direction. As it was, Hitler, unable to send strong forces, sent a military mission, Sonderstab F, under General Felmy, to advise and support the Iraqi forces and to prepare for any German forces that might in the future be dispatched. In addition, the Luftwaffe gave some slight support to Raschid Ali's soldiers, who were under British attack. But only a few He 111s and Bf 110s were used in action, the latter from a base, Msul, inside Iraq. By 30th May, British forces had occupied Baghdad and Raschid Ali fled abroad. The occupation of Iraq was followed by that of Syria, then a colony of Vichy France, which was completed by 14th July, an act made necessary because its aerodromes were being used by the few Luftwaffe aircraft supporting the Iraqi rebels. But just as the operation against Crete prevented any significant aid to Raschid Ali, so the invasion of Russia, begun on 22nd June, prevented assistance being given to the Vichy French in Syria. Even before the conclusion of the battle for Crete, Fliegerkorps VIII had received orders to transfer to the East, to begin what was for it, and the Luftwaffe, the fifth campaign of the war.

The successful conclusion to the campaign in the Balkans (the last complete German victory of the war), did not mean the end of a Luftwaffe presence in the Mediterranean. Geisler's Fliegerkorps X, the operational command covering southern Italy, Sicily, part of Sardinia, Greece and part of North Africa, had gained the effective status of a Luftflotte. Comprising some 390 combat aircraft by July 1941, it operated directly under the orders of the RLM. In January 1941, it was given three tasks: the neutralisation of Malta as a British air and naval base in order to secure the Axis supply route from Italy to North Africa; the interference of the British supply route to Egypt; and the support of Axis ground troops in North Africa. Of particular importance was Malta, the symbol of Britain's mastery of the Mediterranean. Situated fifty-six miles south of Sicily, and 225 miles east of Tunis, with an area only ninety-two square miles, it provided refuge and sustenance for the British fleet and air force, from which they could not only protect the convoys taking men and equipment to Egypt, but also threaten the continuance of the Axis supply lines to North Africa. Its neutralisation would have a major impact on the desert war, and tip the scales significantly in favour of the Axis. A victory there might well allow the Germans to gain access, via the desert, to the unlimited reserves of oil from the Near East, and relieve the Wehrmacht from any long-term involvement in the Mediterranean theatre of operations. Totally reliant upon its sea communications for food, men and munitions, possessing only limited air defence, and only a few minutes' flying time away from German and Italian bases, Malta was particularly vulnerable to air attack. Here, at least, the Luftwaffe could prove capable of acting independently from the other two services, in a role that would have a significant impact on the course of the war. The campaign in North Africa would be won or lost by the battle for command of the air over the Mediterranean.

Fliegerkorps X began its onslaught in January 1941. The first action came on the 9th, when shipping in Malta's Marsa Scirocco Bay was bombed. The next day, a convoy bound for Malta from Gibraltar was attacked by sixty Ju 87s and He 111s, and the aircraft carrier, HMS *Illustrious*, was badly damaged. On the 11th, two cruisers were also severely hit, one of them, HMS *Southampton*, having to be abandoned. On the 16th, after two nights of RAF bomber raids on German airfields in Sicily, Malta's Grand Harbour at Valetta came under concentrated attack, HMS *Illustrious* being hit again, a merchant vessel damaged, and a dock temporarily put out of action. Heavy damage was suffered by civilian property. On the 18th, the Luftwaffe's attack

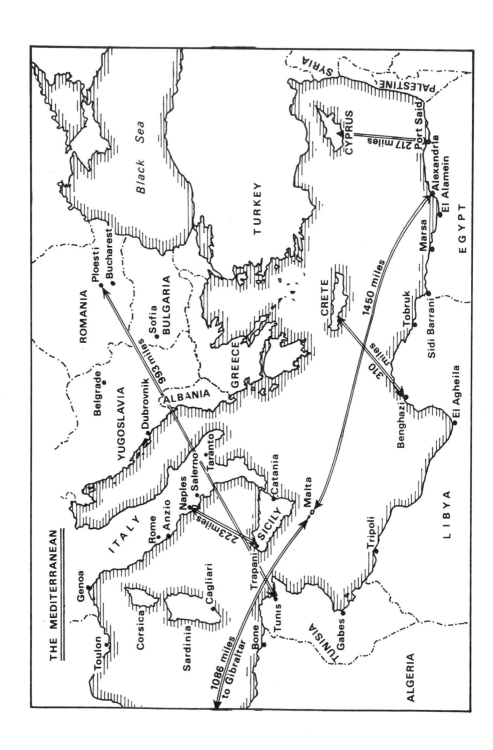

THE MEDITERRANEAN

concentrated on Malta's airfields, and by so doing established a pattern that was to last, weather permitting, throughout January, February and March. In May, the withdrawal from Sicily began in preparation for the campaign in the Balkans, and Malta was given its first respite.

Fliegerkorps X's failure to subdue Malta with some 250 bomb-carriers and the services of a number of Italian aircraft, was ascribed to the limited supplies and inadequate ground organisation that were then available in Sicily. Not only was that island at the end of a long line of communications, but the Luftwaffe was deeply involved both in the Blitz against Britain, and with its redeployment for the invasion of Greece. Fliegerkorps X was also forced to despatch a large number of its aircraft to North Africa to bolster the Italian forces there, which had suffered severe setbacks. At the end of May, after the conclusion of the Balkan campaign, and the restoration of the Axis' position in North Africa by Rommel's small force, the air situation in the Mediterranean was reviewed. Geisler proposed that, since the natural German supply route to North Africa was via Greece and Crete, it was the eastern half of the Mediterranean that required the attention of Fliegerkorps X. The Italians, however, argued that the main effort should revert back to the supply routes from Italy to Cyrenaica, the protection of which was quite impossible for the Italian Air Force alone. Geisler's advocacy won the day in the RLM and OKW, however, and by July the last units based on Sicily had moved eastwards. Of the 390 aircraft belonging to Fliegerkorps X, 240 were in Greece, Rhodes and Crete, and 150 in North Africa, mainly Ju 87s and Bf 109s, coming under the tactical control of an ad hoc subordinate command known as Fliegerführer Afrika, under General Stefan Fröhlich.

During the remainder of the summer and autumn of 1941, the Luftwaffe's attention was directed mainly on the desert, the Suez Canal and the Red Sea. Minelaying and torpedo-bomber operations were mounted from Greece and Crete, and sorties in support of the ground forces were made almost daily. However, it was becoming increasingly clear that these activities were quite insufficient to significantly aid the Axis cause in North Africa, and would not prevent the enemy from building up his strength; by the end of the year, the British had thrown back the German and Italian army to Marsa el Brega, where it had been at the beginning of the year. The enemy air force had proved a formidable weapon. During the British advance, the RAF and anti-aircraft gunners had destroyed 326 German and a similar number of Italian aircraft, for the loss of 575 machines. The Italian Regia Aeronautica had been virtually eliminated as an effective force in North Africa. It was clear that not only were more aircraft required in the desert, but also the British presence in Malta had to be ended.

Since May, the island had been the base for strong naval attacks on the Axis shipping lanes, to such an extent that by November no less than seventy-seven per cent of the total tonnage shipped was sunk. In the last six months of 1941 more than 280,000 tons of military cargo had been sent to the bottom of the Mediterranean. The resulting shortages in men, equipment and munitions suffered by the Axis forces in the desert were particularly severe, and were a significant factor in the reverses suffered at the hands of the British and Empire forces. Accordingly, in October, Hitler concluded that he should reinforce Fliegerkorps X, a decision embodied in his War Directive No. 38, dated 2nd December. This came at a time when conditions on the Eastern Front appeared to allow some redisposition of forces; Lörzer's Fliegerkorps II was moved from there to Sicily, and Kesselring's Luftflotte 2 command was transferred from the central front before Moscow to Italy in December, to take control of the increased air activity in the Mediterranean theatre. Fliegerkorps X lost its independence, and was subordinated to Luftflotte 2, as was Fliegerführer Afrika. The reorganisation was completed by January 1942, when Kesselring had some 650 front-line aircraft at his disposal, of which 260 were in Africa. In order to fulfil his three-fold mission (to neutralise Malta and restore communications with North Africa; to support the Axis ground forces; and to paralyse enemy communications in the Mediterranean), Kesselring was also made Commander-in-Chief South, and empowered to issue orders to German naval units in the area.

Kesselring, with his customary energy, immediately set about his task, and in mid-January 1942 air operations against Malta were resumed. At first, they were on a modest scale, with some sixty-five sorties being flown daily by aircraft of all types, but they increased steadily. In February, almost 1,000 tons of bombs were dropped on the island, mainly on or around RAF airfields. By the middle of March, preparations for a major onslaught were complete. By this time, Fliegerkorps II had some 425 aircraft based on Sicily, of which 190 were bombers and 115 Bf 109s. A new plan of operations was adopted. Previously, military targets had been bombed indiscriminately, but henceforth a concentrated programme of attack would aim at reducing the island's defences and then at rendering it ineffective as a base for naval operation. Pinpoint accuracy by dive-bombing would not be required, and reliance was placed on massed 'carpet' bombing to destroy the targets. First, the British fighters would be destroyed on the ground by a surprise attack on their airfield at Ta'Qali. That would be followed by an attack on the bomber and torpedo-planes at Luqa, Hal Far, and Kalafrana, and then attention would be concentrated on the major dock and harbour installations.

On the night of 20th March, a massed bomber raid took place against the RAF fighter airfield at Ta'Qali, in which special 2,000 lb rocket bombs were used against suspected underground hangars, followed by a day-time attack on the 21st. Success was considerable, and command of the air over Malta was won. On the 22nd, the offensive was switched to the island's other airfields, a process which was designed to take several days before the attacks were finally turned on Malta's sea-communications. On the 23rd, the attention of Fliegerkorps II was temporarily distracted by the arrival of a convoy, which it proceeded to bomb so effectively that it sank four-fifths of its cargo. After a few more days attacking the bomber airfields, the Fliegerkorps began the pounding of Valetta harbour and the naval installations. By the end of the month, it had deposited some 2,200 tons of bombs on the island, in over 2,800 sorties, for the loss of sixty aircraft. In April, the offensive intensified, and the British were forced to vacate Malta as an air and naval base. Some 4,900 sorties were flown against the island, and 6,700 tons of bombs dropped, and on two days, the 7th and 20th, the number of sorties rose above 300. The efficacy of German operations was revealed on 20th April, when a reinforcement of forty-seven new Spitfires were flown into Malta, and within twenty minutes of their arrival, Fliegerkorps II attacked, leaving only twenty-seven still serviceable, a number that was to diminish still further over the next few days.

By the end of April, the Germans were confident of success. In an order of the day, Lörzer announced: 'During the period 20th March to 28th April 1942, the naval and air bases of Malta were put completely out of action. In the course of 5,807 sorties by bombers, 5,667 by fighters, and 345 by reconnaissance aircraft, 6,454 tons of bombs were dropped. . . .'[5] Indeed, from the beginning of 1942 to the end of April, no less than 10,000 tons of bombs had been dropped on Malta, half the amount deposited on London during the Blitz over a much longer period. This had its effect. By May, there were no more submarines or warships based at Malta, and the sea-lanes to the Axis troops in North Africa became virtually free of interference. Sinkings steadily diminished. As Rommel noted, the air raids on Malta 'made possible an increased flow of material . . . [and] the reinforcement and refitting of the German-Italian forces thereupon proceeded with all speed'.[6] By July the situation had improved so much that Rommel's Chief of Staff could record that, for the first time, the minimal requirements of the troops had been met. All the aircraft remaining on the island had been destroyed, and the anti-aircraft batteries were in a poor condition. Only the island's troops had remained virtually free of casualties, as they had been able to take refuge in huge limestone caves. Conditions for the defenders, however, were severe. The RAF Commander, Air Vice-Marshal Lloyd, wrote: 'our diet was a slice and a half of very poor bread, with jam for breakfast, bully beef for lunch with one slice of bread, and . . . the same fare for dinner. . . . Even the drinking water, lighting and heating were rationed. . . . Malta was faced with the unpleasant fact of being starved and forced into surrender from lack of equipment'.[7]

Successful though this offensive had been, however, the Luftwaffe proved unable to continue it beyond the middle of May. The intensity of effort had meant that aircraft were forced to fly up to three sorties a day, and, although losses from enemy action were extremely low (Kesselring boasted, falsely, that only eleven aircraft had been shot down), the wastage rate was high, amounting to no less than 250-300 in April alone. By the middle of May, some 500 aircraft had been rendered inoperable owing to bad landings on poor airfields, collisions, and general wear and tear. In May, too, came the almost inevitable orders from RLM moving Lörzer's units to other theatres of war. Their very success had brought this about, for, with its over-stretched resources, the Luftwaffe could not afford to keep its formations in areas where they were not continually employed to maximum effect. With Malta subdued, Fliegerkorps II was an obvious choice for redeployment. One bomber Geschwader and two fighter Gruppen were sent to Russia, where preparations for a major offensive were under way; one bomber Gruppe was sent to Greece to reinforce Fliegerkorps X in controlling the eastern Mediterranean, and four Gruppen, one each of Ju 87s, Bf 110s, Bf 109s and night-fighters, were allocated to Fliegerführer Afrika. Lörzer was left with but 150 aircraft to deal with Malta. As Kesselring wrote: 'Naturally, enough units remained in the Mediterranean to keep Malta under surveillance, to harass enemy convoys, and to protect our own convoys . . . without having to draw upon the units assigned to the Fliegerführer Afrika. In the long run, however, these units were too weak to prevent the recovery of Malta and to keep supplies from reaching the island fortress indefinitely.'[8]

Air attack against Malta and its life-lines across the Mediterranean continued after mid-May, with less intensity but still to great effect. German air superiority had been aided by Rommel's advance in the desert at the end of January, which had won back Cyrenaica as far as Gazala, thus bringing the Luftwaffe presence in North Africa to the edge of the eastern Mediterranean, opposite Crete. Fliegerkorps II and X, between them, rendered the Mediterranean quite unfit even for British warships, as evidenced by the attack on four destroyers on 11th May, in which three were sunk by a small force of Ju 88s in 'Bomb Alley' (the shipping lane, 200 miles wide, between Crete and North Africa). The Malta convoys, struggling to preserve the strategically-placed island still in British hands, suffered greatly. When British supply ships did manage to reach Malta during the first four months of 1942, their unloading operations were subject to constant harassment. Often cargoes were redeemed from Valetta harbour after the ship had been sunk. The Royal Navy was forced to provide massive protection for the convoys; for example, in March it took no less than four cruisers, eighteen destroyers, and an anti-aircraft ship to escort four merchantmen from Alexandria to Malta. This was the last large scale attempt at supplying the island for some time. Some supplies were brought in by submarine, but not until June was another major effort made. Six merchant ships from Gibraltar and eleven from Egypt were sent, with considerable escort, in an attempt to divide the enemy's attention. However, in the end, the convoy from Alexandria was forced to return whence it came, while only two cargo vessels from Gibraltar managed to complete the run. The next convoy was sent in August from Britain, consisting of fourteen merchantmen with an escort of three aircraft carriers (seventy-two fighters), two battleships, six cruisers, twenty-four destroyers and an anti-aircraft ship. Once past the Straits of Gibraltar, the convoy faced the attention of no less than 700 Axis aircraft based on Sicily and Sardinia, 270 of which were German. Between the 10th and 15th, the convoy was subjected to constant air attack, and, by the time it had reached Malta, only five of the fourteen merchantmen remained. The rest had been sunk.

However, despite this success (which, once again, proved the potential superiority of air power over warships), Malta was not subdued. Indeed, even during their darkest days in early May, the resourceful defenders had managed to indicate their continuing ability to cling to the island. On the 9th, sixty-one Spitfires landed on Malta, to be immediately placed in splinter-proof shelters, and on the 10th, a fast minelayer arrived in Valetta bringing much-needed anti-aircraft ammunition. The Luftwaffe missed these targets, and on the 10th, the day that Kesselring signalled Führer Headquarters with the message 'Enemy naval and air bases in Malta eliminated',[9] Fliegerkorps II's raiders suffered their highest casualties in the offensive. In the attacks of 10th-12th May, the Axis air forces lost more bombers than they had during the previous five weeks. With the dissipation of Lörzer's command that shortly followed, British air presence over Malta resumed, never again to be ended. It was clear that, for the menace of Malta to be ended, the bombardment of the island was not sufficient; it had to be occupied.

This was no new realisation, although events no doubt highlighted its truth. Kesselring's immediate reaction to his new task at the end of 1941 had been that Malta must be invaded before the Axis could proceed with confidence to dominate the Near and Middle East. At a conference in February, he persuaded Hitler and Mussolini to give their approval in principle to such a project. On 11th March, Kesselring submitted his feasibility study to OKW, stating that the capture of Malta by Italian troops would be significantly easier than the invasion of Crete ten months previously. The Italians, however, were dubious, and, a few days later, Marshal Cavallero, the Italian Chief of Staff, announced that the invasion could not possibly be launched before August. After some hard bargaining, the Italians agreed to an earlier date for the assault, but with the proviso that the Luftwaffe should have previously neutralised the island's defences. A special Staff was established under the command of the Italian general, Gaudin, to undertake the planning of the operation, and preparations proceeded. On 29th April, at a conference in the Führer's mountain retreat in Obersalzberg, Hitler, Mussolini, Cavallero and Kesselring made the final decision to invade. The Commander-in-Chief, South, stipulated that the operation should take place after Rommel's planned attack had reached the Egyptian border, where it would halt to allow a redisposition of air units for the invasion of Malta. Luftflotte 2 was simply not strong enough to support both assaults simultaneously. The plan was agreed, and the date for the invasion was fixed for no later than 18th July.

Operation Hercules, as the invasion of Malta was code-named, was primarily the responsibility of the Luftwaffe. Not only was the Air Force to render the island's air, sea and land defences inoperable, but it was also to provide the bulk of the transport (500 Ju 52s and 500 gliders) for the most important troops – the men of Student's Fliegerkorps XI, and two Italian paratroop divisions, some 30,000 soldiers (equivalent in number to the British garrison) who would be reinforced by 70,000 Italian troops carried by sea. In

Student's view, 'it was an impressive force, five times as strong as we had against Crete'.[10] To ward off the British fleet that might be sent to help the defenders, Luftflotte 2 would deploy all its available forces in the Mediterranean, amounting to some 510 combat aircraft (of which 240 were bombers), together with a similar number of Italian machines. The success of von Richthofen's Fliegerkorps VIII against the Royal Navy at Crete provided an assurance that the Luftwaffe was likely to succeed in this mission.

The Germans who were involved in the preparation of the invasion were convinced that it would end in victory. Some Italians, however, were sceptical. Count Ciano, Italy's Foreign Minister, noted in his diary on 28th April '. . . whether the undertaking will ever take place and, if so, when, is quite another matter. . . .'[11] On 31st May, after an interview with General Carboni, Ciano wrote: 'he is dead set against it [the operation]. He is convinced that we'll suffer very high losses and that we won't accomplish anything at all'.[12] However, it was not to be such doubts which decided against the invasion; it was to be the success of Rommel's offensive towards Tobruk, a success which, ironically, had been greatly aided by the Luftwaffe's neutralisation of Malta and command of the air over the vital supply lanes to North Africa. On 26th May, Rommel's attack began; after the brilliant victory of the Gazala battles, Tobruk was gained on 21st June. The redeployment of the air units under Fliegerführer Afrika was then begun in preparation for Operation Hercules. According to plan, Rommel, newly promoted Field-Marshal, should have halted, and allowed the Luftwaffe to undertake the attack on Malta, before resuming his offensive east to Cairo and beyond. However, he did not stop, and his tanks continued their advance towards the Egyptian frontier while he sent personal messages to both the Führer and the Duce requesting that he be allowed to proceed. The advice given to Hitler by Kesselring, the naval staff and even General von Rintelen, OKH liaison officer in Rome, was that Rommel should be halted, his army rested and refitted, and Malta invaded. Hitler, however, chose not to heed them. Condoning Rommel's action, he wrote to Mussolini: 'It is only once in a life-time that the Goddess of Victory smiles'.[13] Von Rintelen later remembered that the Italian dictator 'was extremely enthusiastic at the prospect of an immediate offensive against Egypt in order to capture the cities of Cairo and Alexandria. At this stage of operations, Mussolini still had unlimited confidence in Hitler's military genius. Cavallero and his objections were simply brushed aside. . . . He had no alternative but to alter his orders and to postpone the Malta undertaking until September.'[14]

Rommel's request was opportune for Hitler. The Führer had never been entirely happy at the prospects for the invasion, and was particularly fearful that the airborne forces would be left without reinforcement from the sea. In conversation with General Student in early June, he had voiced his worry: 'I can assure you, though, that as soon as we begin our attack, the Gibraltar squadrons will take to the air and the British fleet will set sail from Alexandria. You can imagine how the Italians will react to that. The minute they get the news on their radios, they'll all make a dash for the harbours of Sicily . . . both warships and freighters. You'll be sitting all alone on the island with your paratroopers'.[15] Göring, too, was concerned about Operation Hercules. As Kesselring wrote: 'In Göring, Hitler had a loyal supporter for his own aversion to an attack on Malta. Göring was afraid of another Crete, with its "huge" losses, although in reality the two operations had nothing whatsoever in common.'[16]

Thus, with the invasion postponed until September, all reliance was placed on Rommel's advance reaching the Nile. By 30th June, he had arrived at El Alamein, sixty miles from Alexandria and 125 miles from Cairo. But there he stopped; his troops were exhausted and he had barely twenty German tanks of the original 332 left fit for action. All effort to resume the offensive came to nothing, and at the end of October the British and Empire troops had compelled the Axis forces to begin the long retreat that was to end seven months later with their complete withdrawal from North Africa. The invasion of Malta, therefore, was destined never to take place. This was to have serious consequences. With the Luftwaffe's resources stretched to the limit in all four corners of Europe (in one of which, the Ukraine, a major offensive was underway which made events in North Africa seem a side-show), Luftflotte 2 proved quite unable to allocate sufficient force to keep Malta neutralised by continual air bombardment. This inability became more acute when the Axis was thrown on the defensive in the desert. Increasing aerial and naval activity took place from the island fortress, so that sinkings of Axis supply ships increased steadily to reach fifty-two per cent by the end of the year. Defeat in the desert was, thereby, ensured.

As Rommel's offensive drew to an end in June 1942, so did German air supremacy over the desert. Until then, Fliegerführer Afrika had possessed an average strength of some 190 combat aircraft, which, despite their numerical inferiority, had held the initiative in the air. For the second offensive in 1942, which began towards the end of May, when three German and three Italian divisions thrust 380 miles as far as El Alamein, no less than 260 aircraft were assembled, owing to reinforcements arriving from Fliegerkorps II, together with a further 240 Italian machines. Heat, dirt and sandstorms, however, continued to produce an unusually high rate of unserviceability, at times up to sixty per cent. Some 300 to 350 sorties a day were flown in the first week of the attack, which, after a reduction in the second, were exceeded in number during the third. No less than 1,400 sorties were mounted against Bir Hacheim over nine days, a vital fort held by the Free French, and these contributed significantly to its downfall on 11th June. However, the real significance of Bir Hacheim was summarised by a historian in the Luftwaffe's Historical Section: 'This meant a nine days' gain for the enemy, and, for our Army and Air Force, nine days of losses in material, personnel, armour and petrol. Those nine days were irrecoverable'.[17] The battle was immediately followed by a furious onslaught against Tobruk; in twenty-eight hours on 20th June, some 600 sorties were flown against the enemy positions, and these, together with a tank attack, resulted in the capitulation of the port. This, however, weakened the Luftwaffe still further. By the time the battle was over, the German Air Force had exhausted itself over the desert: its operational strength was down to less than 100 aircraft, fuel was dangerously low, and its forward bases lay far behind the rapidly advancing front. Kesselring was forced to inform Rommel that his units could no longer provide effective air cover during any further advance. Rest and consolidation were essential. During the final advance to El Alamein, which was reached at the end of the month, the Luftwaffe had proved unable to take part in the fighting. In the three days which it took the enemy to move back from Gazala to El Alamein, only six soldiers were killed by Axis air attack.

It was at this point in the war in North Africa, that the limitations of logistics deprived the Air Force, and indeed, the Axis armies, of success, and highlighted the extreme importance of Malta. Indeed, since the beginning of the German presence in the desert, the supply of its forces had been the major problem faced by the high command. It had two aspects: first, the Reich's military resources were stretched to the limit, and, involved as they were in a major campaign in the Soviet Union, neither the OKH nor the RLM had much to spare for its units in the Mediterranean. Second, and hence the importance of Malta, such supplies and reinforcements as could be made available, had to come across the Mediterranean, either by sea or by air. The length of this supply line, alone, was a major problem. Initially, once the men, equipment and munitions were in Italy, they would then be borne by sea round the west coast of Sicily, across to eastern Tunisia, and from there down the coast to Tripoli, an indirect route, some 600 miles in length. Once there, however, these supplies had to be brought to the front, by either lorry or coastal vessel, which, to Gazala, involved a further 1,000 miles. The neutralisation of Malta in April and May 1942 had enabled a shortening of the sea route, and once El Alamein had been reached, Benghazi was even used, being the port nearest to the front (750 miles) that was safe from air attack.

To overcome the length of time and the danger of attack involved in the seaborne supply routes, the Luftwaffe had flown in men and supplies direct from Sicily or Crete to North Africa, at any of a number of places and even as far east as Tobruk. In February 1941, Fliegerkorps X (then based in Sicily) was given a Gruppe of twenty-five Ju 52s, whose main mission was to transfer air units to North Africa, and keep them supplied; on return flights, wounded and sick personnel, unserviceable equipment and the like were ferried back to Sicily. In March and April, a second Gruppe was also allocated for these duties. It soon became the practice to fly in urgently needed supplies for the Army units as well. This small-scale operation, never involving more than sixty-five transports at any one time, was undertaken with remarkably little loss, and on only seven days, between 7th February and 10th December 1941, did the Ju 52s meet enemy air opposition. However, the increasingly high loss suffered at sea owing to enemy action emanating principally from Malta, had caused a greater air effort to be mounted at the end of 1941. As transports could not be acquired from other fronts, the training schools were, once again, raided, and 150 Ju 52s were thereby made available for the Mediterranean. Some of these, however, had a stay of short duration; in January 1942, one Gruppe was sent to the Eastern Front, where it was urgently needed. Operations continued, meeting more opposition from the enemy, and, for the first half of 1942, Luftflotte 2 disposed of some 150 Ju 52s and ten BV 222 six-engined flying boats, under the command of the Transportfliegerführer (Mediterranean) in Rome. Serviceable aircraft were often used on as many as three missions a day; but even so, the Axis troops were denied sufficient reinforcements and material. After the capture of Tobruk in June, the strength of the transport units rose to 250, of which fifty to sixty per cent were serviceable, and with that force it proved possible to transport 1,000 troops and twenty-five tons of equipment daily. In the three months of July, August and September, while the situation in the desert hung in the balance, some 46,000 men (in 2,600 sorties of eighteen men per aircraft) and 4,000 tons of supplies (in 1,900 sorties at two tons per aircraft) were transported to North Africa.

However, all this activity still proved insufficient. With the increasing dislocation of the sea lanes, both the Army and the Air Force suffered acute shortages. Particularly serious was the lack of fuel, which caused a large part of the 200 aircraft available for Rommel's final, and abortive, attack lasting from 31st August to 5th September 1942, to take place with little air support. In this battle, known as Alam Halfa, the RAF dominated the air, dropping, according to German estimates, no less than 1,300 tons of high explosive in six days. Although, previously, Rommel had achieved miracles with minimal air support, he was now confronted with a new situation, and had to face massive bombardment from the air, of an intensity never experienced before. According to Rommel, this pinned his army 'to the ground, and rendered any smooth deployment or any advance by time schedule completely impossible'. As the Field Marshal was to conclude: 'Anyone who has to fight, even with the most modern weapons against an enemy in complete control of the air, fights like a savage against modern European troops, under the same handicaps and with the same chances of success. . . . In every battle to come, the strength of the Anglo-American air force was to be the deciding factor.'[18] By the beginning of the battle of El Alamein, the Luftwaffe in the desert was outnumbered by the enemy by a factor of three to one.

Even against Malta, the Luftwaffe was henceforth outclassed. On 10th October, a new, and final, assault was undertaken by the 600 aircraft based in Sicily, when the number of sorties flown daily by the Luftwaffe against Malta rose from the average of twenty-five of the previous months to over 120, but such was the RAF's defence that not a single bomb fell on the island. The next day, the 11th, 216 sorties were made, and each day until the 19th an average of between 200 and 270 were undertaken. However, from then on the intensity of the raids decreased. Damage to the island was slight, and the defenders had been the easy victors: for the loss of thirty Spitfires, they shot down forty-six German and an equal number of Italian aircraft. Kesselring's admission of defeat came on the 18th, when he withdrew his precious Ju 88s from the battle. The subsequent fighter sweeps by Bf 109s proved no substitute for heavy bombardment. At the end of October, Göring ordered that Malta be put out of action within eight days; Kesselring replied that only invasion could achieve that. The Air Force, alone, was no longer capable of such an operation. In the Mediterranean, the Luftwaffe was a spent force, and the Axis presence there was henceforth doomed.

The responsibility for this state of affairs lay with one man: Hitler. It was he who had committed Germany to North Africa, at a time when the forces available were insufficient to ensure a successful outcome to the intervention. It was he, also, who had allowed Rommel to push ahead with his advances, without the security of a safe and adequate supply line behind him, and it was he who had decided to abandon the invasion of Malta in favour of a gamble that Rommel's exhausted force could reach Cairo. Kesselring, to whom much blame has often been attached, may have been over-optimistic as to what could be achieved in the way of supplying that force, but there is no doubt that he did all he could to provide the Axis troops with the material they required. However, he was not entrusted with overall responsibility for supplies to North Africa, his power being restricted solely to the German air transport units. The Italian Navy was responsible for all shipping, and jealously guarded their prerogative. Kesselring certainly understood the danger posed by Malta, and did all he could to bring about its downfall. He also constantly warned Rommel about over-extending the advance, and imposing strains on a supply line that was quite unable to bear them. As General Westphal, then Rommel's Chief of Operations, wrote: 'No other Air Force commander could outdo Kesselring in his efforts to support the ground troops. That his resources were often inadequate and had to be spread out, this is another story.'[19]

Certainly, the relationship between Rommel and the senior Luftwaffe commanders in the Mediterranean was not good. Tension always existed with Kesselring, who was not over-impressed with Rommel's capabilities, while the first Fliegerführer Afrika, General Fröhlich, had experienced such difficulties in dealing with the Army commander that he had taken to avoiding contact with him (strangely enough Rommel appears to have found Fröhlich always amiable and helpful). In March 1942, Fröhlich was replaced by Hoffman von Waldau, Jeschonnek's former deputy, whose forthright manner and fresh approach had not endeared him to either Göring or the Chief of General Staff. He proved an able field commander, and ensured that co-operation between the two services proceeded smoothly. He was also particularly effective at preventing any dissipation of the forces at his disposal by not reacting to all the Army's demands. The successful air support during the advances in May and June testified to his ability. However, even von Waldau could not withstand the powerful reality of logistics, which, by the end of June, rendered his force quite unfit for further large-scale operations. Once the Axis forces had failed to regain the initiative at Alam Halfa in early September, there began a race against time to build up men and material to face the inevitable enemy onslaught. The air transport units were particularly busy, especially since, with the resumption of British naval activity in the Mediterranean and the sinkings of tankers, the fuel shortage in North Africa became acute. Further limited reinforcements of transport aircraft were made available, including FW 200s from the Atlantic. However, only an average of 250 to 275 tons of supplies could be brought over daily, quite insufficient to build up any reserves to meet operational requirements. The enemy offensive, known as the Battle of El Alamein, opened on 24th October. The British and Empire forces possessed massive material superiority. Heavy air attacks on the Luftwaffe's forward airfields, which had for some days been receiving the unwelcome attention of the RAF, signalled the beginning of the onslaught. These attacks reduced serviceability and the operational efficiency of the units, already crippled by a fuel shortage, so that the 290 aircraft available to von Waldau could provide neither effective opposition nor support. The position of the ground forces was equally serious. On 4th November, the retreat began. The battle of attrition had been won decisively by the enemy.

The Luftwaffe's effort in North Africa was far from over, however. Towards the end of October, the Germans had noticed a considerable increase in shipping and air activity at Gibraltar, which indicated that the Allies might have the intention of spreading the war to the western Mediterranean, either in the south of France, in the Gulf of Sirte, in the rear of the Axis troops in the desert, or in Tunisia. Partly for that reason, and partly because of the reverses suffered by Rommel, the Luftwaffe's strength in the Mediterranean was increased, and by early November, amounted to some 940 combat aircraft (an increase of 220 over the previous month). Of these, 375 were in the desert, two thirds of them Bf 109s. On 8th November, Anglo-American forces landed quite unexpectedly in Algeria, and began moving on Tunisia. In the four weeks that followed, the Luftwaffe's strength was increased to reach 1,220 machines by 12th December, 850 of which were in Sicily, Sardinia, and Tunisia and 120 in the south of France. In mid-November, 250 combat aircraft had been moved there to preclude any landings. Their bases also made it possible for the Luftwaffe to undertake more anti-shipping operations in the Western Mediterranean than formerly. By December, when it became clear that the south of France was not to see any enemy landings, 130 of these aircraft returned to their former bases.

On 15th November, a new command under General Harlinghausen, Fliegerführer Tunisia, was instituted to take control of the fighter and dive-bomber units that had been in the area since the day after the Allied landings. His task was to co-operate with the German ground forces that were being assembled under General von Arnim. After the first week, no less than 100 combat aircraft were in Tunisia, and by the end of the third up to 120 daily sorties were undertaken. However, Harlinghausen was hampered by a shortage of supplies, a lack of good airfields and poor weather (though that had even greater effect upon the enemy), so that his efforts were mainly restricted to the defence of harbours and shipping and air transport. No attempt was made to establish bomber units in Tunisia, an indication not only of their shortage but also of the defensive nature of the German position; but some bomber support was acquired from the bases in Sardinia and Sicily. Instead, fighters and ground-attack aircraft predominated in Tunisia, together with the inevitable reconnaissance machines.

With this force, equality in the air was maintained with the Allies, whose units were suffering considerable problems with supply. Not only was their line of communications long, it was also vulnerable to attack from the air. The German bomber force in the Mediterranean had come to include any units with experience in anti-shipping operations that could be spared. Initially, attacks were directed against shipping at Algiers and convoys in that area; but, owing to the extreme range of these targets from Sicily (some 675 miles) and the inadequacy of facilities in Sardinia (275 miles nearer Algeria) which prevented it from being used as a major base for operations, the activities of the Luftwaffe were severely handicapped. However, as the Allies advanced and began to use ports, such as Phillipeville, Bougie and Bône, which were nearer their front, the Germans took every opportunity to dislocate their supply services. Much success was recorded, but at high loss. By the end of the year, the average strength of the bomber units had fallen to seventy-five per cent of their establishment, and of these aircraft, only fifty per cent were serviceable. Moreover, the Germans themselves were suffering from severe logistic difficulties. The importance of Malta was again high-lighted, and the failure to capture it in the summer of 1942 resulted in high losses of the men and material transported to Tunisia. If Malta had been taken in Operation Hercules as planned, it is quite possible that not only would Rommel have gained victory, but that the Allied landings in North Africa, if ever attempted, would have failed in the mountains of Algeria.

By the end of 1942, the position of the Luftwaffe in the Mediterranean was dire. In Cyrenaica, it had provided poor air cover for Rommel's retreat, and, despite all efforts, had proved unable to transport by air the supplies his army required. Matters were not helped by the high attrition rate experienced during the race to build up supplies in the four months before the battle of El Alamein, by the use of air transport to ferry supplies to Tunisia, and by the loss to the enemy of landing places along the North African coast, which prevented the use of the eastern route via Crete. However, without the fuel flown in, it is doubtful whether Rommel's force would have succeeded in withdrawing the 1,400 miles from El Alamein to the Mareth line, which was reached by 15th February 1943. Von Waldau's command was seriously depleted; he had only 150 aircraft by 1st January, of which 100 were Bf 109s (thirty of them Jabos). However, by then they were able to operate, not from second-rate desert landing grounds, but from well-maintained airfields in the Tripoli area. Moreover, the shortening of the overland supply line produced beneficial results. On the other hand, the British Desert Air Force found itself operating at the end of extended supply lines and having to use poor airfields. Similarly with von Harlinghausen's command, consisting of 140 aircraft, 105 of which were fighters. The Allies, whose initial thrust towards Tunis had failed, were building up a ground organisation on unfavourable terrain with inadequate communications, whereas the Germans were well-established and able to operate their latest fighter, the FW 190, which gave them a decisive advantage in the air. On the periphery, the Fliegerführer Afrika and Tunisia had the support of 390 combat aircraft of Fliegerkorps II based in Sicily and Sardinia (of which 270 were bombers), and some 400 transports. Despite the removal of numbers of Ju 52s to the Eastern Front in December, where 6th Army was fighting for its survival, and despite heavy operational losses, largely due to increasing RAF attacks, an additional 170 had been found from training units in Germany. As well as the Ju 52s, there were also twenty Me 323s, which each carried a load of ten tons. This force proved capable of air-lifting to Tunisia alone no less than 19,000 soldiers and 4,500 tons of supplies in December 1942 and January 1943. In addition, there were a further 120 combat aircraft under Fliegerkorps X in the eastern Mediterranean, bringing the total for the whole area to 800 combat machines and 400 transports.

The disposition of aircraft around the Mediterranean indicates the strategy pursued by Kesselring and his senior air commanders. In North Africa, he stationed an air defence and close-support force, equipped mainly with single-engined fighters and possessing no bombers (just 40 Ju 87s between them, and 35 Jabos). This force, clearly, could not effect a decision, it could only, at best, help to bring about a stalemate. The units upon which Axis hopes in North Africa were based were those belonging to Fliegerkorps II and X, whose task it was to attack enemy maritime transports and to protect friendly sea traffic. The battle centred around the control of the supply routes; the issue in North Africa would, as it always had been, be decided by command of the air over the Mediterranean.

Events in Africa, remarkable though they were from the point of view of the Luftwaffe's achievement, were of secondary importance. The numbers of combat aircraft there remained between 300-330 to the middle of April 1943, and serviceability, except during retreats, was high. Not until the second week of April, when air units were restricted to the few remaining airfields east and south-east of Tunis, were the Allies able to re-establish the complete air supremacy over the desert that they had enjoyed in the latter half of 1942. An improvement in the Luftwaffe's ability to react to the enemy advances on German positions, from both east and west, came in January when, with the loss of Tripolitania, Fliegerführer Afrika was abolished, and Fliegerführer Tunis became the only operational command in North Africa. This permitted greater flexibility in the employment of forces on either flank, an advantage which became clear in mid-February. Then, an Allied break-through from central Tunisia threatened to divide the armies of von Arnim and Rommel. A counter-attack was ordered, and, in support, Fliegerführer Tunis was able to fly 375 sorties on the first day. Indeed, throughout the remainder of the campaign, the units of Fliegerführer Tunis provided the most efficient support for the hard-pressed ground troops that could be hoped for, and were a classic example of what a small, compact force of high morale and efficiency, even though outnumbered, could achieve. Only at the very end of the campaign in North Africa, at the beginning of May, when the total number of aircraft available to Fliegerführer Tunis had fallen to 200 (with a continual decline to be experienced over the following days) was it unable to influence the battle.

Unfortunately, the level of the Luftwaffe's effort in North Africa was not matched elsewhere in the Mediterranean. The vital bomber force on which all hopes rested was in a poor condition. Having suffered severe losses in the intensive operations mounted at the end of 1942, on 1st January 1943 its strength was down from a peak of 310 to 270 aircraft, of which only fifty-five per cent were serviceable. A further diminution was unavoidable. Because of the withdrawal of so many Ju 52s from training schools, there was a severe reduction in the availability of the highly trained torpedo-bomber crews. This, together with a high rate of unserviceability, caused the operational strength of the torpedo-bombers, the main weapon for attacking the enemy convoys, to fall from 90 or 100 machines to just five or ten by early April. The rest of the bomber force suffered scarcely less severely. In addition, a shortage of convoy-escort aircraft (primarily Bf 110s and Me 210s, of which there were only forty-five on 1st January) meant that bombers had to be employed in that role, to the extent of one-third of their total sorties. Attacks on ground targets in North Africa were also required, especially in March and April, owing in large part to the vulnerability of the Ju 87s and Hs 129s in the face of heavy enemy opposition. Moreover, at the end of March, the Allies mounted heavy air attacks on the Luftwaffe's bases in Sardinia, inflicting considerable losses; an appreciable decline in serviceability, and a withdrawal of units to the Italian mainland was the result. The combination of these factors had a considerable impact on the level of operations that could be sustained. Attacks on convoys by both Fliegerkorps IX and X fell from an average of eleven sorties a day in January to two in April. The number of sorties against ports was uneven and low, averaging five per day in January, two in February, four in March and five again in April. Indeed, of the average of thirty-nine sorties a day flown by the bombers in the first four months of 1943 (in itself a low number), only twelve were against the enemy supply lines. But the number of sorties does not tell the whole story. Because of high losses among aircrews, especially during the last month of 1942, and the deterior-ation in training, the effectiveness of the bomber attacks dropped appreci-ably. Indeed, it often happened that the inexperienced crews completely failed even to locate their targets. Against this background, no appreciable dislocation of the enemy's supply lines was achieved.

Just as Luftflotte 2's offensive action against the enemy's supplies was quite inadequate, so was the defence of its own. The few Bf 110s and Me 210s available proved unable to protect the Axis shipping crossing to Tunis, and the bombers were too few in number and so ill-equipped for the task, that they afforded little help. With the British fleet and Allied air forces in command of the Mediterranean, the sinking of Axis shipping rose from forty-one per cent at the beginning of 1943 to over seventy-five per cent by April. The efforts of the air transports, prodigious though they were, proved quite unable to make up the difference, and as time went on and as unserviceability and enemy action took their toll, their effectiveness was to diminish considerably. The condition of the Axis forces deteriorated to such a degree that, by 25th April, von Arnim reckoned that there was sufficient ammunition for only three days fighting, and fuel to move all his vehicles seventeen miles. With the Luftwaffe's complete failure to dominate the Mediterranean and so win the battle of supplies, the German position in North Africa was made quite untenable. The Allied advance continued inexorably, and on 13th May the Axis forces, cornered around Tunis, capitulated.

VIII

The Attack on the Soviet Union

In the middle of July 1940, even before the Luftwaffe had begun its attempt to win command of the air over south-east England, Hitler's thoughts were turning eastwards, towards the Soviet Union. On 28th September, when the Battle of Britain had clearly failed and the Blitz was in its initial stages, OKW issued a directive which ordered preparations to be made for an attack on Russia, and on 18th December, at a time when the Luftwaffe was heavily engaged in its night offensive in the West, Hitler signed his War Directive No. 21, entitled 'Operation Barbarossa'. It opened with the words: 'The Wehrmacht must be prepared, even before the conclusion of the war against England, to crush Soviet Russia in a rapid campaign'.[1] The aim was to defeat the Red Army in the western part of the Soviet Union, and occupy an area up to the line Volga-Archangel, some 1,000 miles from the border as it then existed. There, a barrier would be erected against 'Asiatic Russia', and the area occupied would be exploited for German gain. The campaign, scheduled to begin in May 1941, would be short, and victory gained by the onset of winter; once over, the Air Force would be free to return in strength to the air war against Britain's supplies, a conflict which War Directive No. 18 had stipulated would not be allowed to lapse.

The Luftwaffe's leaders were strong in their rejection of the idea of a campaign in the East. The offensive required the raising of forty new divisions for the Army, which, together with the stocks of munitions and equipment needed for such a major extension of the war, placed an extremely heavy burden on Germany's industries. There was, therefore, little possibility of any expansion of the Luftwaffe; output from the factories was essentially limited to the replacement of the losses entailed in the air war against Britain, in both the West and the Mediterranean. At a time when, following upon the campaigns in Poland, Norway, France and Flanders, and over Britain, rest and reinforcement were required, the Luftwaffe was faced with the prospect of a war on two, if not three, fronts without any commensurate increase in its strength. Nowhere could sufficient force be concentrated. Moreover, any relaxation of the pressure on Britain would allow a major air offensive to be waged by the RAF against the Reich. Göring, Milch and Udet, were united in their opposition, and were supported by men such as Schmid and von Seidel. Jeschonnek's attitude is uncertain, but his deputy, von Waldau, was aghast at the implications of failure. Milch, when he heard that the campaign in Russia was expected to be over before winter, predicted that it would last for four years, and ordered winter clothing and equipment for all the Luftwaffe units likely to be operating in the East, an action that was not taken by the Army.

For the first time, Göring found himself in open conflict with his Führer, a position he did not enjoy. But so much opposed was he to the campaign, that he was left with little alternative. He told Hitler that the invasion would entail the transfer of two-thirds of the Luftwaffe's strength to the East, with the result that 'The sacrifices we have made thus far will have been in vain. England will have time to reorganize and rebuild her air armament industry undisturbed. . . . We would be giving up a comparatively certain victory in the Mediterranean in favour of a far less certain alternative. . . . On the other hand, a German success in the Mediterranean would be far more likely to lead to a satisfactory compromise with England'.[2] On another occasion, Göring attempted to show the Führer that his economic reasons for occupying the rich agricultural areas of the East were fallacious. He concluded his argument thus: 'My Führer, the final decision rests with you. May God guide you and help you to prove your rightness in the face of opposition! I, myself, am forced to oppose your point of view in this respect. May God protect you! But please remember that I cannot be blamed if I am unable to carry out our plans for expanding the Luftwaffe'. To this, Hitler replied, 'In six weeks you will be able to resume the war against England'. In conclusion, his Air Force Commander stated: 'My Führer, the Luftwaffe is the only branch of the Wehrmacht which has not had a breathing spell since the war began. Before the outbreak of the war I told you that I was going into battle with my training groups, and now these are practically all gone. I'm not at all sure that you will be able to subdue the Russians within six weeks. The ground forces can't fight any more without Luftwaffe support. They're always screaming for the Luftwaffe. There's nothing I'd like better than to have you proven right, but, frankly, I doubt that you will be'. But coming up against the intransigence of Hitler, Göring had no alternative but to resign himself to the inevitable. To Milch, he said: 'The rest of us, we lesser mortals, can only march behind him [Hitler] with complete faith in his ability. Then we cannot go wrong'. On being told that it was his duty to Germany to bring Hitler to see sense, Göring replied: 'The Führer has made up his mind. There is no power on earth that can change it for him now'.[3]

The Luftwaffe, charged by Hitler in his War Directive No. 21 with making available 'supporting forces of such strength that the Army will be able to bring land operations to a speedy conclusion . . .',[4] proved incapable of fulfilling the task. Out of a total front-line strength of 3,340 combat aircraft in June 1941 (thirty-four less than on 1st September 1939), the air war in the West accounted for 780 machines (660 with Luftflotte 3 and 120 with Luftflotte 5 in Norway), operations in the Mediterranean for some 370 (Fliegerkorps X and Fliegerführer Afrika), and the air defence of the Reich another 190. This left for the Eastern Front fifty-eight per cent of the

Luftwaffe's total, just 1,945 combat aircraft, together with 150 transports, eighty liaison aircraft, and, under the control of the Army, 700 reconnaissance aircraft, 2,875 machines in all. The combat aircraft were composed of 880 medium bombers (mainly Ju 88s, some He 111s and a few Do 17s), 280 Ju 87s, 600 Bf 109s, 60 Bf 110s, and 120 long-range bomber-reconnaissance aircraft. Of these, one-third were unserviceable. Sixty Hs 123s were to arrive from the Balkans later. In addition, units of the Romanian, Hungarian, Finnish, Italian and Croatian Air Forces were arrayed against the Soviets, some 980 machines of all types, many of indifferent quality, thus bringing the grand total of aircraft to 3,915. This force was to support an Army whose initial front was 995 miles, to be increased to 1,240 miles as the attack proceeded, together with a further front of 620 miles along the Finnish border. By the time the ground troops had ended their advance in 1941, the Luftwaffe's combat zone was over a territory of 579,150 square miles, thus allowing one serviceable combat aircraft (either fighter or bomber) to every 445 square miles. In the campaign against France and Flanders in May 1940, over a far smaller geographical area, the Luftwaffe had at its disposal 2,750 bombers and fighters, 600 reconnaissance aircraft and 500 transports, a total force of 3,850, as many as were sent into the Soviet Union a year later.

Concerning the operational employment of the Luftwaffe during Operation Barbarossa, Hitler's War Directive No. 21 was clear: 'It will be the duty of the Air Force to paralyse and eliminate the effectiveness of the Russian Air Force as far as possible. It will also support the main operations of the Army. . . . Russian railways will either be destroyed or, in accordance with operational requirements, captured at their most important points (river crossings) by the bold employment of parachute and airborne troops'.[5] In short, the Luftwaffe was to follow the course of operations which had proved so successful in Poland and the West. With the exception of airborne assaults, which the heavy losses sustained at Crete rendered impossible, the German Air Force carried out these tasks as well as its limited resources allowed. To ensure the necessary concentration of effort, Hitler, with the agreement of the RLM, forbade attacks on the Soviet armaments industry during the advance. All reliance was placed on the ground forces gaining their objectives within four months. To this end, the Air Force was to give all the support within its power. It was a gamble, but, given Hitler's decision to invade, one which had to be taken; there was no other choice.

To support the Army, which itself was divided into three Army Groups, the air units were divided among three Luftflotten: Luftflotte 1, under General Keller, was attached to Army Group North under von Leeb; Luftflotte 2, under Field-Marshal Kesselring, was given to Army Group Centre under von Bock; and Luftflotte 4, under General Löhr, was assigned to Army Group South under von Rundstedt. In addition, a number of units from Luftflotte 5 were grouped under Fliegerführer Kirkenes, commanded by Colonel Nielsen, and were detailed to support operations on the Karelian front. Of the three Luftflotten, Kesselring's command was by far the strongest (it was supporting the largest Army Group) with 910 combat aircraft and ninety transports and liaison aircraft, divided among Fliegerkorps II (Lörzer) and VIII (von Richthofen), over an initial front of 186 miles. Luftflotte 4 in the south, composed of Fliegerkorps IV (Pflugbeil) and V (von Greim), came next, with 600 combat and ninety auxiliary aircraft over a front of 685 miles, followed by Luftflotte 1, half the size of 2, with 430 combat and 50 auxiliary aircraft in Fliegerkorps I (Förster) and Fliegerführer Baltic (Wild), over 125 miles. Fliegerführer Kirkenes possessed 60 combat aircraft. These commands possessed anti-aircraft units, also used to support the ground forces; each Luftflotte had a Flakkorps, and Fliegerführer Kirkenes had an anti-aircraft battalion.

Against this force, the Germans estimated that the Soviets possessed some 7,500 aircraft in the West, with a further 2,500 in the Far East. But, although large in numbers, over eighty per cent of the aircraft of the Red Army Air Force were considered obsolete, and the introduction of new types begun in 1940 was slow. It was known that the heavy bomber elements were equipped with the four-engined TB-3, flying no faster than 160 mph, and a small number of the more modern Pe-8, having a maximum speed of 270 mph. Most of the medium bomber force consisted of SB-2 variants and some DB-3s which could reach about 280 and 250 mph, while the light reconnaissance bombers were represented by the R-5 (R-Z) biplanes and a limited number of the new 280 mph Su-2 and 330 mph Yak-4 monoplanes. The standard fighter was the I-16, generally known as the Rata, with a maximum speed of about 330 mph, backed by I-15*bis* and I-153 biplanes capable of only 230 and 265 mph. Although more manoeuvrable, all these fighters were outstripped by the Bf 109s and Bf 110s.

The several hundred new fighters already in service in June 1941, the 365 mph Yak-1 and the 390 mph MiG-3, were potentially on the same level as their German counterparts, but not quite trouble-free and still in the process of assimilation. Only the new twin-engined Pe-2 multi-purpose aircraft with a maximum speed of over 340 mph then coming into service, seemed on the same level as German combat aircraft. A type, of which the Germans had no counterpart, was the heavily-armoured BSh(Il-2) Shturmovik ground attack aircraft, the early version being vulnerable in that it lacked any rear defence. In addition, there was the Soviet naval aviation force of about 1,400 dated seaplanes and the land-based DB-3F long-range bombers, distributed between the Arctic, Baltic and Black Seas. Of all these aircraft types, the R-5, SB-2, DB-3, I-15 and I-16 were already known from the Spanish Civil War and the Finnish War, and the more modern aircraft were not considered to pose a threat. The new Bf 109F version with a top speed of 390 mph at 19,680 ft and a normal combat radius of 220 miles, represented a significant improvement over the Bf 109E series, and was a match for all known Soviet designs – especially since the German pilots also possessed better training and combat tactics.

By June 1941, the Luftwaffe's preparations for the invasion were complete.

The ground organisation had been under development since October 1940, and by May it was ready to receive the combat units. In three weeks, the bulk of the air units were moved from the West to take up their new positions. Because of operations in the Mediterranean, elements of Luftflotte 4 could not move to the East until 17th June, just four days before the invasion began. However, the unexpected campaign in the Balkans did not cause any significant delay to the invasion, as, owing to an unusually late thaw in the East, the ground was so soft that it was quite unsuitable for operations, including the establishment and use of airfields.

On 22nd June 1941, the Wehrmacht advanced upon Soviet Russia. The Luftwaffe, acting upon information gained in high-altitude photographic reconnaissance missions, concentrated its strength on the Red Air Force, in an attack that was to last three days. The first missions to aid the ground forces were flown at 0330 on the 22nd, a time set by OKW. In the north, it was light enough for Luftflotte 1 to attack with all its strength, but, further south where it was darker, the Luftwaffe feared that the Army's offensive would give the Soviet Air Force at least forty minutes warning before the visibility would be good enough for them to mount the first air attack. To prevent the enemy from exploiting this, however, Luftflotte 2 attacked each Soviet airfield where fighters were based, with three bombers flown by crews used to night flying over Britain. This, it was hoped, would cause such confusion as to delay the take-off of the enemy machines, and thus prevent their intercepting the main attack which, perforce, would come later. The attacks were a complete success; at the only field where enemy fighters were ready to take off, they were destroyed just before doing so.

After the preliminary skirmish, the main attack began. Over the next few days, He 111s, Ju 88s and Do 17s each flew as many as four to six missions every twenty-four hours, Ju 87s seven to eight, and Bf 109s and Bf 110s five to eight, according to the distances of their bases to their targets. Between 22nd and 25th June, Fliegerkorps I alone attacked seventy-seven airfields in 1,600 sorties. The first bombers found the enemy machines on the ground, unprotected, often drawn up in long rows, extremely vulnerable to the new fragmentation bombs, the four lb SD 2s, carried by the bombers and Jabos in large numbers. The success gained thereby appeared to paralyse the Red Air Force for days. Only a few units appeared over German lines, to participate in unco-ordinated and unsystematic raids, and these fell easy prey to the aggressive German fighter pilots. In the first attack, by 637 bombers (including Ju 87s) and 231 fighters, many carrying bombs, for the loss of only two aircraft, thirty-one airfields were hit, three high level command posts, two barracks, two artillery positions, a bunker system and an oil depot, as well as installations at the port of Sevastopol. During the day, 1,800 enemy machines were destroyed, and by 29th June, OKW could report the destruction of 4,017 Soviet aeroplanes for the loss of 150 German destroyed or significantly damaged (a ratio of 1:27). The Luftwaffe's command of the air was complete, and ground operations could continue unhampered by the

Red Air Force. It had been a decisive victory. Indeed, so staggering were the claims of the Luftflotten, that the Luftwaffe high command had difficulty in believing them. Göring, for example, would not credit Kesselring's claim that 2,500 aircraft had been destroyed in the central sector alone, and ordered an investigation. His check, however, showed that, far from exaggerating, Kesselring had understated the successes of his pilots, and the true figure was between two and three hundred higher than claimed. Indeed, the German victory in the air was so devastating that the Soviet bomber force never fully recovered, and in later campaigns seldom put in an appearance over German lines.

However, although decisively defeated in the first seventy-two hours of the campaign, the presence of Soviet aeroplanes over the front was not ended. Many pilots remained alive, largely because their machines had been destroyed on the ground, and the factories continued to turn out new aircraft for them to fly. As if to signal its defiance, single aircraft or small formations of the Red Air Force flew over East Prussia and occupied Poland in the first few days, but they were so effectively met by Bf 109s and anti-aircraft fire that significant operations ceased after the first four days. Losses amounted to some seventy per cent of the sorties undertaken, and on several occasions entire formations of up to forty bombers were shot down. On the night of 8th-9th August, the Red Air Force sent three bombers to the outskirts of Berlin, but heavy anti-aircraft fire forced them to turn away from their target. As early as 30th June, large daylight battles were waged over the Bobruisk area, when Soviet aircraft attempted to prevent the Germans from crossing the Berezina river. In this action, however, as in all others, they were turned back by the Luftwaffe fighters, with the loss of 110 of their number. But the German air units, especially the fighters, were kept constantly aware of the existence of the Red Air Force. In the first three days, for example, Fliegerkorps I shot down some 400 enemy aircraft, and destroyed a further 1,100 on the ground; in the next sixty, it accounted for a further 1,000. Bomber units, too, were used continually against Soviet airfields, but however much they might pound the enemy air force, more aircraft appeared in the sky to take the place of those destroyed. In the period 22nd June to 10th July, the Red Air Force flew no fewer than 47,000 sorties, and dropped 10,000 tons of bombs on the advancing German units.

The fact that the enemy air force continued to operate provided some annoyance to the Luftwaffe's command, and prevented it from concentrating solely upon the support of the ground troops. Losses inflicted by the Red Air Force were minimal, but the number of sorties undertaken against it was not inconsiderable, at times reaching one quarter of the total. Despite the large number of enemy aircraft destroyed (by 30th August, Fliegerkorps II alone had accounted for 1,380 shot down and 1,280 destroyed on the ground) there were always Soviet pilots who remained alive to fly the new machines from the factories. Never could the Luftwaffe end the threat of low-level ground-attack aircraft travelling singly or in pairs, which would drop their bombs and immediately turn for home before the defenders were aware of their presence. Nor, because of their lack of fighters, could the Germans deal adequately with all the major incursions into the airspace over their vast front. If this was true at the beginning of the campaign, how much more so was it after several months, when exhaustion induced by constant combat had taken its toll. By mid-August, for example, von Greim's Fliegerkorps V had only forty-four fighters left fit for action, to cover an area that was some 500 miles in length. On some days in late September, after almost all its fighters had been transferred to the central front, Fliegerkorps V possessed fewer than ten operational Bf 109s. With these, there was no hope of containing the Soviet Air Force, or even of gaining local superiority over certain areas of its own front. Only the weakness of the enemy prevented this from becoming serious.

For, thanks to the Luftwaffe's efforts in the first seventy-two hours of the campaign, the Red Air Force posed no real menace during 1941. Over vast tracts of Russia, no Soviet aeroplanes would be seen for days, and even when they did appear, they provided relatively little danger. The Ju 87s and Bf 110s, so vulnerable in the Battle of Britain, were easily a match for the opposition, and the Ju 88s and He 111s were superior to most of the fighters that, in 1941, came their way. Whenever it was essential the Germans could always achieve air superiority over any sector of the Eastern Front they chose; it was only superiority over all sectors simultaneously which eluded them for lack of aircraft. This is well illustrated by the situation in the area of operations of Pflugbeil's Fliegerkorps IV in the Crimea. There, in October, 11th Army struggled to gain control of the peninsula in face of what its commander, von Manstein, was to call Soviet domination of the sky. Enemy bombers and fighters were able to attack any ground target they wished, until the fighter ace and General of Fighters, Werner Mölders, was assigned from his Jagdgeschwader on the central front to take control of fighters in the south. After a week of his fighter sweeps, command of the air by day was won by the Germans; only by night did the enemy bombers dare to continue their attacks.

Despite the continued existence of the Soviet Air Force, then, German air superiority had been effectively achieved within the first three days. Lörzer's Fliegerkorps II, for example, could report that all enemy aircraft had been destroyed on fields within a 185 mile radius. German air activity was never seriously threatened for the rest of 1941. Thus, between 22nd June and 26th July, of 1,574 sorties mounted by Bf 110s of a Schnellkampfgeschwader (fast bombers) in Fliegerkorps II, only twelve were destroyed in combat, a loss of one aircraft in every 131 sorties. By 25th June, the Luftwaffe was so assured of victory in the air, that it could turn the majority of its aircraft to the support of the ground forces. There can be no doubt that in this, as in the air, the Luftwaffe was extremely successful, the only inhibition to its actions being the limited number of aircraft at its disposal.

In the first phase of operations, which lasted until early August, the German Army made considerable gains. In the north, the Baltic States were occupied, and Leningrad approached to within sixty miles; in the south, the west bank of the Dnepr river was cleared, and a major encirclement at Uman resulted in the capture of 103,000 enemy soldiers. In the centre, where the most important fighting took place, two encirclements, Bialystock-Minsk and Smolensk, between them resulted in the capture of some 630,000 Soviet soldiers, and numerous tanks and guns. In these operations, the Luftwaffe played a significant part. Not only did it ensure that the advance of the German troops would be unhampered by enemy air attack, but it also provided assistance in the fighting on the ground, mounting attacks against strong-points, tank formations and the like. More important, by a systematic onslaught against Soviet communications, it impeded enemy reaction to their advance.

The efforts of the Luftwaffe were divided equally between direct and indirect support. As General Hermann Plocher wrote: 'The campaign in the West, in 1940, had brought about another shift in emphasis in the mission. Direct air support for the Army on the field of battle had become just as important as indirect support . . . which, in the past, had been considered the primary mission of the Air Force'.[6] In the vast expanses of the Soviet Union, where there were usually several points of major effort in the German advance and frequent shifts in concentration, it proved no longer possible simply to assign a special formation, such as von Richthofen's, to close support operations. As a result, all the Fliegerkorps had to be as capable of providing 'direct' as 'indirect' support. At the same time, Fliegerkorps VIII, with one bomber Geschwader, in addition to its two Ju 87 Geschwader and one Geschwader each of Bf 110s and Bf 109s, became capable of longer-range, 'indirect', missions. The relative weakness of the German Army (it possessed only fifteen divisions more for the attack on the Soviet Union than for the invasion of the West), and its shortage of effective anti-tank guns and other weapons, meant that it had to call on the Luftwaffe to intervene on the battle-field with ever increasing frequency. In such manner, did the Air Force depart from the principles of air power laid down in *Luftkriegführung*, which placed far greater emphasis on indirect missions than direct. Whereas, in previous campaigns, only twenty-five per cent of sorties flown were in direct support of the ground forces, from the outset of the campaign in Russia this figure rose to sixty per cent. Not all senior Luftwaffe commanders were happy at this change, although, given the circumstances in which the Wehrmacht found itself in the war in the East, they perhaps recognised that it was inevitable. Kesselring remembered: 'I instructed my air force and Flak generals to consider the wishes of the Army as my orders. . . . All my commanding officers and I prided ourselves in anticipating the wishes of the Army and on carrying out any reasonable requests as quickly and completely as we could'.[7] So vital was direct air support thought to be, that Army commanders began to plan their attacks relying on the Luftwaffe's presence. This process was taken to its logical conclusion by Hitler, who, in the autumn of 1941, ruled that large-scale offensive operations should only begin after extensive support by the Luftwaffe had been ensured.

Important though direct support had come to be, the Luftwaffe began the campaign in the East equipped primarily for 'indirect' missions. With no less than 880 twin-engined bombers for attacks on the enemy's rear and communications, and the only aircraft suitable for close support being 340 Ju 87s and Bf 110s together with some thirty Jabos and the promise of sixty He 123s within weeks, it was inevitable that the Ju 88s, He 111s and Do 17s would become involved in missions for which they were ill-suited. The dense concentration of weapons on the battlefield posed great problems for the twin-engined aircraft, which presented large targets to the defenders. While the losses were not too unbearable, damage was great, causing aircraft to be out of action and under repair for some considerable time. Before June 1941, medium bombers would be used in the battle zone only when cloud ceiling below 2,600 feet prevented dive-bombers from operating, or at the beginning of a major offensive; after the initial onslaught in the East, their use there became a regular occurrence.

However, in 1941 the distinction between 'direct' and 'indirect' support units had not yet become completely blurred. Still, as far as circumstances would allow, there was a division in the type of missions flown by twin- and single-engine bombers. Between 22nd June and 9th September, for example, in 'indirect' operations the Ju 88s of one Kampfgeschwader in Fliegerkorps II, destroyed no less than 356 trains (seven of which were armoured) and fourteen bridges, interrupted rail traffic 332 times, and flew 200 sorties against troop concentrations, barracks and supply depots, and in 'direct' support of the Army, it destroyed thirty tanks and 488 motor and other vehicles and flew some ninety sorties against twenty-seven artillery and field positions. Clearly, indirect missions predominated. This was in contrast with the afore-mentioned Schnellkampfgeschwader, whose Bf 110s, between 22nd June and 27th September, destroyed only fifty trains (one being armoured) and four bridges, compared with 148 tanks, 166 guns, and 3,280 motor and other vehicles. Even Bf 109s, whose principal concern was with the Soviet Air Force, were used to attack ground targets. By 10th September, for example, one Jagdgeschwader on the central front had destroyed 1,655 aircraft in the air and on the ground, but had also destroyed 142 tanks and armoured cars, sixteen guns, thirty-four locomotives, 432 trucks and one armoured train. In the campaign in the East, the units of the Luftwaffe were involved in many tasks other than their designated roles.

The interdiction of Soviet communications was a mission which Hitler and the high commands were unanimous in believing to be vitally important to the conduct of ground operations in the East; paralysis, or even temporary inhibition of movement on the roads and railways, would not only hinder the Soviets from bringing up their reinforcements to the front, but would also prevent them from deploying their existing forces to meet the German thrusts. Despite the vast extent of the zone of operations in the Soviet Union, the Luftwaffe was aided in this task by the primitive nature of Russian communications. Just three per cent of Russian roads possessed any type of stone surfacing, so that the railways became the only reliable means of transport, especially during periods of rain or thaw. Throughout the entire Soviet Union, which covers 8,354,393 square miles (approximately one-seventh of the earth's surface), there were only 52,000 miles of track in 1941; thus, disruption of the few lines that ran through the western part of the country, posed no insuperable problem, and, by preventing the enemy from moving troops and equipment at will, offered one of the most effective ways of aiding the progress of the ground troops. From 26th June onwards, units of Luftflotte 2 made successful attacks on the railways in, and leading to, the zone of operations on the central front, particularly the railway junctions. In the Bryansk area alone, the Luftwaffe penetrated to a distance 420 miles east of the spearhead units of the German advance. By 9th July, rail traffic west of the Dnepr was effectively blocked, and Soviet troops were suffering greatly from lack of supplies. On the 11th, Halder, Chief of the Army General Staff noted that 'The number of track sections occupied with standing trains is increasing satisfactorily. . . . The Luftwaffe now appears to have succeeded in cutting the Russian railroads, even in the far rear area'.[8] The next day, Halder wrote that there were large traffic jams on the railroads south of Kiev, in the region south of Orsha-Smolensk, and between Vitebsk and Smolensk. On the 13th, OKW reported that the Luftwaffe had already prevented any possibility of a large-scale counter attack by destroying the enemy railway system. But not only this; such action also hindered the enemy troops from withdrawing in time to escape certain encirclement.

However, the destruction of railways and bridges was no easy matter. For example, in early July, despite forty-two hits on six bridges over the Dnepr, the complete destruction of even one of them was not achieved, a task made more difficult by the efforts of the Soviet engineers and workers. On one occasion when the vital railway bridge at Bobruysk over the Dnepr was destroyed, it took 1,000 labourers only thirty-six hours to restore the structure so that traffic could move again. Similarly with rail track; because of the efforts of the Russian repair teams, the average period of disruption to traffic was only five hours and forty-eight minutes for each break. Many attacks, therefore, were required, and by the end of the year no less than 5,939 had been made on railways adjacent to the front. Attacks on the main roads, too, had their difficulties. These had been successful in previous campaigns, especially in May 1940, but they were not, however, effective in the East. Villages and even towns in the Soviet Union were laid out in unplanned and dispersed fashion, generally consisting of wooden or mud houses. It proved useless to block the roads, as the advancing troops could simply march or drive round the debris. Only at river crossings were attacks worthwhile, and these the Luftwaffe pursued with vigour. Other 'indirect' targets were troop concentrations and supply depots in the enemy's rear. For example, on 27th June a supply depot at Orsha, then 180 miles behind the front, was attacked by twenty bombers in the belief that it contained 2,000 tanks and combat vehicles. When, however, Orsha was occupied later, it turned out that all that had been destroyed were items for cavalry and horse-drawn vehicles.

Even before the Red Air Force had been rendered harmless, units of the Luftwaffe were ordered to support the Army, so crucial was their assistance thought to be. At daybreak on the 22nd, on the central front, Lörzer's Fliegerkorps II, which had been detailed to work closely with 4th Army (and, more especially, with its spearhead, Guderian's Panzer Group 2), was sent to destroy the enemy batteries in the area around Brest-Litovsk, commanding the principal crossings over the river Bug which formed the border between Soviet and German occupied Poland. At Guderian's request, Ju 87s were kept constantly in the air, ready to attack any battery that opened fire. As a result, the enemy guns remained silent and the German troops could proceed unhindered. The citadel at Brest-Litovsk, however, was another matter; it held out for several days after the Bug had been successfully crossed, inhibiting supplies from reaching units which were advancing eastwards. Ju 87s, each carrying one 1,100 lb bomb, proved incapable of destroying the fortifications, and so, on the 28th, Ju 88s had to be brought in, one of them loaded with a special 'block-busting' bomb weighing nearly two tons. After this attack, the garrison was forced to capitulate. Fliegerkorps II and VIII continued to give support to the advance, and were especially useful during the closing of the first pincers around Bialystock and the second around Minsk. Indeed, in an order of the day, von Bock commented that the encirclement had only been possible through the support of Luftflotte 2. On numerous occasions, critical situations that developed as the trapped Soviet units attempted to break out of the, at first, weakly-held ring, were saved by the Luftwaffe's intervention. For example, on 24th and 25th June, Flieger-korps VIII, supporting 9th Army and Panzer Group 3, halted an enemy breakthrough near Grodno and Kuznica, destroying 105 tanks and dispers-ing cavalry units. In order to improve still further the co-ordination of the needs of the ground troops with the resources of Fliegerkorps II, a close-support air command (Nahkampfführer) was instituted, which directed the light units in support of Panzer Group 2. Von Richthofen's Fliegerkorps VIII, which had from its inception been a close-support formation, did not require such a command. Despite initial problems, such as breakdowns in communi-cations, it was Kesselring's opinion that the Nahkampfführer, Martin Fiebig, 'developed into a close-support air commander comparable to von Richt-hofen'.[9] A few weeks later, Luftflotte 4 organised two similar commands, Nahkampfführer Nord and Nahkampfführer Süd.

As with the Bialystok-Minsk pockets, so with the Smolensk operation. Luftflotte 2's operations in close support proved invaluable to the Army. However, at the beginning of August, Fliegerkorps VIII was transferred to the north, to support the attack upon Leningrad, and Fliegerkorps II was left to carry on alone during the last days of the battle for Smolensk. In the forthcoming weeks, the casualties and wear-and-tear inflicted in the previous two months of constant fighting, and the burden of undertaking the brunt of the air war in the central sector, caused Fliegerkorps II to be seriously overstrained. Its resources were quite insufficient to carry out all the tasks required. It was able to support the southern wing of Army Group Centre in the Roslavl-Rogachev area, west of Gomel, a vital base for forthcoming operations, but only at the cost of severely limiting the support of troops in the Yelna bridgehead on the road to Moscow. On 5th September, this salient was evacuated. The Germans, however, withstood the attacks of the Russians west of Gomel and consolidated their front, in preparation for the next major movement in the East: the encirclement of Kiev.

Without the Luftwaffe's close support operations, the German lines would have been breached on numerous occasions, and the vital battles of encirclement rendered less effective. On their own, the air units were too few to be able to prevent troops of the Red Army from escaping, particularly during the Smolensk battles; but in conjunction with ground attacks, they proved invaluable. The successes on the central front were repeated in the north and south, despite the fact that the Luftflotten there were, initially, lacking any Ju 87s or ground-attack Bf 110s. Apart from regularly attacking the enemy, Luftflotte 1 in the north found itself as early as 23rd June flying in supplies to German troops at the front. The only road which led to 16th Army was repeatedly closed by Soviet units operating from almost impenetrable forests, with the result that, until mid-August, all supplies were brought up by Ju 52s or Ju 88s. To the south, air support was more spectacular. On the 26th June, for example, von Greim's Fliegerkorps V mounted low-level attacks with its bombers against a strong Soviet tank attack that was threatening Panzer Group 1's open flank. Von Kleist, the commander of the armoured force, was unequivocal in ascribing to this action the fact that an entire Soviet motorised corps was halted, and Panzer Group 1 allowed to continue its advance unhindered. On 1st July, there was a similar occurrence; the danger that a strong counter-attack in the rear of Panzer Group 1 would encircle that formation was only averted when the Ju 88s and He 111s of Fliegerkorps V destroyed forty tanks and 180 other vehicles, and put out of commission numerous others, thereby bringing the enemy's advance to a halt. However, as many requests for direct air support had to be refused as were granted. Luftflotte 4, with only two-thirds the strength of its neighbour, simply did not possess anything approaching sufficient aircraft to cover the entire front. Paulus' 6th Army, in particular, felt hard done by when Löhr decided to commit his units to 17th Army and Panzer Group 1 in the Uman encirclement. There, air attacks proved their worth; breakout attempts were frustrated, and, in the progress, fifty-eight tanks, 420 motor vehicles, and twenty-two batteries were destroyed.

After Uman, Panzer Group 1 drove on to Dnepropetrovsk and Nikolayev to seize bridges over the Dnepr, from whence a new encirclement could be mounted in conjunction with Army Group Centre around Kiev, the largest battle of encirclement in history. However, before this could be achieved, a major Soviet counter-attack began south of the city at the junction of 6th

Army and the Panzer Group, which threatened to dislocate the entire German advance. Emergency units, including a bakery and veterinary companies, were thrown in the way of the Red Army, but to little avail. Into the breach, however, flew Fliegerkorps V. Told only to destroy the strong tank and cavalry forces in the Kanev-Boguslav area (which, in fact, comprised a whole army), the air units carried out numerous, and continual, low-level sorties, despite severe weather on 7th August. In the first three days, ninety-four tanks and 148 motor vehicles were destroyed, and bridges over the Dnepr were put out of use. Ground reinforcements arrived in strength after the second day, but still the German air attacks continued, made even more effective by the advent of better weather. On the 13th, when the Soviet command began to withdraw, its troops were harassed from the air, suffering particularly heavy losses as they attempted to cross the Dnepr to the east. According to von Schwedler, the general who was most involved in the operation on the ground, the commitment of Fliegerkorps V during the two days before reinforcements arrived had, alone, averted a crisis which might otherwise have had serious consequences for the entire southern front.

Moreover, by its efforts, Fliegerkorps V had made possible the vast encirclement of Kiev, covering some 15,440 square miles, the outer pincers of which were to close 100 miles behind the Dnepr. Begun on 25th August, this operation was undertaken by 2nd Army and Panzer Group 2 of Army Group Centre with Fliegerkorps II, and by 6th Army, 17th Army and Panzer Group 1 of Army Group South with Fliegerkorps V. By the time it finally ended, around 26th September, the Germans had taken 665,000 prisoners, 884 tanks, and 3,718 guns. In this significant victory, the Luftwaffe had played a prominent part. By continuous and effective attacks against railways, roads and bridges, it had managed both to isolate the battlefield from outside interference, and also to prevent the marshalling of a sizeable counter-attack within the pocket. With air support, local attempts to break through the encirclement were contained, and with total air superiority over the whole area being established early in the attack, the German troops suffered no interference from the Red Air Force. From 12th to 21st September, Fliegerkorps V flew 1,422 sorties for the loss of just seventeen aircraft, with another nine severely and five lightly damaged. It deposited over 558 tons of high explosive, destroying forty-two aircraft on the ground, with a further sixty-five in the air, twenty-three tanks, 2,171 motor vehicles, fifty-two trains, twenty-eight locomotives and one bridge, and damaging a further 355 vehicles and thirty-six trains. The activity of Fliegerkorps II was of a similar nature.

After the encirclement of Kiev, the German Army in the East had three objectives. In the centre, the main attack was to take place: the encirclement of the main Soviet forces left in the west, followed by the final advance on Moscow. On the flanks, which were of less importance, Leningrad was to be taken and, in the south, the Caucasus occupied, with Kharkov as the immediate objective. As before, air support was of great importance. Of events in the north, little need be said, for the Germans failed in their objective, and the Luftwaffe's activity was limited. Neither the bombardment of Leningrad nor the disruption of its supply lines had any significant impact. Attacks on the enemy's route to the city over the frozen Lake Ladoga between 25th November and 3rd December, although they inflicted great losses, did not permanently interrupt communications, since holes blasted by bombs soon froze over again. Ultimately, the severe weather brought the activity of Luftflotte 1 to an end.

In the south, the disruption of the Soviet railways around and to the south-east of Kharkov to a depth of 180 miles was to be, initially, the main task of Fliegerkorps V. From 23rd September to 12th October, ninety-five trains were destroyed, 288 others heavily damaged, and rail traffic cut in sixty-four places, with the result that the Soviet command was unable to respond as it wished to the German advance. In addition, by a concentrated effort, the Fliegerkorps succeeded in gaining air superiority over Kharkov. On the 23rd, immediately after a heavy bombing attack, advanced units of 6th Army entered the city, and had it firmly in its hands by the following day. The Luftwaffe then turned to the next major objective, Rostov-on-Don, the gateway to the Caucasus, and, again, attacked its rail communications. Movement of traffic was severely disrupted and, when the Germans entered the city on 20th November, seventy-nine trains were destroyed and 148 others damaged. However, the German advance had overreached itself; to the rear of 1st Panzer Army (as von Kleist's command was then named), the Soviets were attacking the 6th and 17th Armies, and by so doing threatened the co-ordination of the weakly held front. After much hesitation, Hitler sanctioned a withdrawal from Rostov. Fliegerkorps V, with some assistance from Fliegerkorps IV, which was mainly occupied by 11th Army's fight for the Crimea, kept up so incessant an attack on the Soviet forces, that it was the belief of von Reichenau, the new commander of Army Group South, that they had thwarted the enemy's primary objective, a breakthrough towards Taganrog, and had also denied him his secondary objective, the isolation of the Rostov salient. The orderly withdrawal of the German troops was ascribed to the audacious and ceaseless sorties of the fliers.

While such dramatic events were taking place in the Ukraine, the Germans were concentrating all their available forces on the central front, 400 miles in length for the final advance on Moscow. In the north, 9th Army and Panzer Group 3 were to meet 4th Army and Panzer Group 2 at Vyazma, eighty miles in the Soviet rear and 100 from Moscow. To the south, 2nd Army and a part of Panzer Army 2 were to undertake a subsidiary encirclement, its pincers meeting at Bryansk. These operations once completed would result, it was hoped, in the destruction of the Soviet forces defending Moscow and allow the subsequent envelopment of the capital to take place. In support of the ground troops, the Luftwaffe high command allocated a large portion of the units in Luftflotte 1, including Fliegerkorps VIII, to Luftflotte 2, which was re-inforced also by a few units from Luftflotte 4. Kesselring was given the task of concentrating on the flanks of the attack, and, with his dive-bombers, of giving close support to the motorised units. For this, he was allotted over half the available aircraft in the East, amounting to some 600 bombers, 120 Ju 87s, 100 Bf 110s, 400 Bf 109s and 100 long-range reconnaissance aircraft, a total of 1,320, of which well over one-third were unserviceable.

On 30th September, the advance began, and by 14th October the two encirclements had been completed, yielding to the Germans a haul of 673,000 prisoners. Optimism was high; the RLM reported on the 15th that the enemy's final destruction was imminent. The Luftwaffe, while giving its usual support to the ground forces, had fought some fairly brisk battles in the air with the Red Air Force, which was showing more activity than ever before, and was even repeatedly raiding German airfields. Poor road conditions necessitated the flying of supplies to the forward troops, and no less than 132,100 gallons of fuel were sent to 2nd Panzer Army alone. The RLM's report of activity on the central front on 4th October is descriptive of the operations that the Luftwaffe was undertaking. On that day, 402 sorties were flown by dive-bombers and 479 by bombers; these destroyed twenty-two tanks, 450 motor vehicles, and other military equipment, and damaged or destroyed thirty-seven trains and ten railway depots. Personnel losses were also deemed to be high, although they could not be quantified. Forces escaping from the encirclements were actively pursued.

But however elated the Germans were after the Vyazma-Bryansk encirclements, their high hopes were destined to come to nought. On 7th October, the weather began to break, and conditions degenerated throughout the month to such an extent that the operations of Army Group Centre were brought to a standstill. Armoured units could no longer move, and even horse-drawn vehicles were immobilised by the mud, which was three feet deep in places. On 16th October, the Chief of Operations in the General Staff, von Waldau, noted that 'The boldest hopes are disappearing under rain and snow. . . . Everything remains stuck in bottomless roads'.[10] A shortage of supplies and replacements, which could not be transported to units, and the muddy conditions of advanced airfields both curtailed the operations of Luftflotte 2, and at times rendered them impossible. Temperatures fell as low as 17.6° Fahrenheit, and, while the Luftwaffe's personnel were relatively well-provided with warm winter clothing, a lack of heating equipment further reduced the serviceability of aircraft. On the night of 20th-21st October, except in south-east Ukraine, conditions were unsuitable for air operations along the entire front for the first time in the campaign. Thereafter, the level of activity fluctuated considerably. On the 25th, for example, over six hundred sorties were mounted over the areas of Mtsensk, Mozhaisk, Kalinin, and Volokolamsk, and yet two days later only one sortie there was possible.

On 30th October, with Moscow still fifty miles away, ground operations came to a halt. However, a period of mild frost and clear weather, which hardened the ground, soon occurred, and on 17th November the advance was resumed. After only a few days, the weather again changed, but this time for the worse. Fog, snow, and temperatures of -22° Fahrenheit considerably reduced the effectiveness of the troops, who were meeting with increasingly strong Soviet resistance both on the ground and in the air. By the 27th, the most advanced German spearheads were only nineteen miles from Moscow, but they were destined to get no nearer. On the 22nd, Halder had noted that the troops had reached the limit of their endurance, and on the 30th he wrote that Hitler and his advisers 'have no idea of the condition of our troops, and move about with their thoughts in a vacuum'.[11] On 4th December, a last desperate attempt was made to gain the objective, but to no avail. In the air, the 500 serviceable aircraft left to the Luftwaffe found strong opposition from the 1,000-odd possessed by its opponent, while on the ground similar odds halted the German troops. On the 8th, Hitler officially recognised failure in his War Directive No. 39, which opened with the words: 'The severe winter weather which has come surprisingly early in the East, and the consequent difficulties in bringing up supplies, compels us to abandon immediately all major offensive operations, and go over to the defensive'.[12]

The German's first offensive in the East was over. Throughout more than six months of campaigning, the Luftwaffe had performed well. Mistakes there had been. Bombs, for example, were not always in sufficient supply or of the correct type, and, occasionally, German troops were attacked in mistake for the enemy; but such failings occur in all wars, and they pale into insignificance when compared with the expertise and endurance of both fliers and ground personnel. Within an area bounded in the south by the mouth of the Danube river, the Black Sea and the Sea of Azov, in the East by a line running from Rostov-on-Don to Moscow and up to Lake Ladoga, near Leningrad, and in the north by the Gulf of Finland and the Baltic, they had operated in temperatures which ranged from 120° Fahrenheit to -49° Fahrenheit, over seas, mountains, swamps, impenetrable forests, and wide steppeland. In this vast space of nearly 580,000 square miles, they had kept up with the advancing armies and had attacked a wide range of targets, from gun emplacements to the Soviet capital, from troop trains to battleships, while at the same time supporting divergent advances to Moscow, Leningrad and Rostov, the gateway to the Caucasus. Never operating with more than 1,400 serviceable aircraft, and often with considerably less, they managed to maintain an average of 1,200 sorties a day for over 130 days until the end of October, rising on some occasions to 2,000 or more. Despite the many difficulties in transport – the muddy or non-existent roads, the congestion, the breakdowns and shortages of vehicles, the low availability of Ju 52s – and the occasions when vital supplies of fuel, ammunition and even food were delayed, the ground organisation had managed to move the Luftwaffe's bases at creditable speed behind the Army's advance, so as to maintain close co-operation between troops and aircraft (especially dive-bombers and fighters). There had been mistakes and delays, but, overall, the Luftgaue organisation enabled the air units to achieve the maximum efficiency possible for their low numbers. Indicative of their dedication was that officers with sub-machine guns would sometimes ride on open trucks on Luftwaffe supply trains in order to prevent interference from Army authorities who believed that the Air Force was getting more than its fair share of transport.

The exploits of the flying units were remarkable. Lörzer's Fliegerkorps II, which began the campaign with some 450 combat aircraft, of which one-third were unserviceable, may be taken as an example. In 144 days between 22nd June and 12th November, it flew over 40,000 day and night sorties (an average of 277.7 daily) depositing more than 23,150 tons of high explosive. It destroyed 3,826 Soviet aircraft (2,169 in aerial combat, and the rest on the ground, with a further 'probable' 281 aircraft destroyed and 811 damaged), 789 tanks, 614 guns, and 14,339 vehicles of all types. In addition, 240 field positions, machine-gun nests, and artillery emplacements were attacked, and thirty-three bunkers put out of action. Troop concentrations also came in for much attention. Rail lines were attacked on 3,579 occasions, resulting in the severing of 1,736 tracks, the destruction of 159 trains and 304 locomotives and damage to a further 1,584 trains and 304 locomotives. Anti-aircraft units attached shot down 100 enemy aircraft, with a further twenty-three 'probables'. Lörzer's command had put up a creditable performance, and when it is remembered that it was but one Fliegerkorps among five on the Eastern Front (albeit, with Fliegerkorps VIII, one of the strongest), together with other commands such as Fliegerführer Kirkenes and Fliegerführer Baltic, as well as the various combat units subordinate to Luftflotten headquarters, some estimate of the damage inflicted upon the enemy by the Luftwaffe in the campaign can be arrived at. The following figures of equipment destroyed cannot be far wrong: 15,500 aircraft (in fact, the Germans claimed 20,000 up to the end of October), 3,200 tanks, 57,600 vehicles of all kinds, 2,450 guns, 650 trains (with damage to 6,300 others), 1,200 locomotives (with damage to 1,200 others), and rail lines cut in some 7,000 places.

The Luftwaffe had destroyed the equivalent equipment as in one major encirclement operation by the Army, an achievement of considerable value to the German ground forces, and, its contribution to victory was even more significant than that. Despite frequent, and sometimes bitter, complaints by military commanders that air support was not always forthcoming when requested (itself a sign of how much they relied upon it), the flying units on a number of occasions not only helped to strengthen the ring around a pocket of Soviet soldiers, but actually prevented severe dislocation to the over-stretched German front by halting Soviet counter-attacks. Of this, Army Group South was a particular beneficiary. In addition, the Luftwaffe prevented any significant enemy aerial bombardment of the German troops. Away from the immediate front, and far more difficult to quantify in terms of results, the action by the Luftwaffe against Soviet communications, especially railways, had its impact on the enemy's ability to resist the German advances. In view of its achievements, the Luftwaffe's losses in battle were remarkably small; they amounted to some 900 aircraft for the whole campaign up to 8th

December. Losses from all causes (bad landings on poor airfields and the like) were as high as 2,093, of which 758 were bombers and 568 fighters (with a further 1,361 damaged), but replacements had not been slow in arriving, so that the overall strength in the East had never fallen below 1,800 combat aircraft, and, in fact, was usually higher. On 6th September, for example, the four Luftflotten operating in the East possessed a total of 1,916 machines, 1,175 (sixty-one per cent) of which were capable of immediate action.

Since the war, there has been a tendency to belittle the magnitude of the Luftwaffe's achievements in the Soviet Union. In particular, two related criticisms have been levelled against the Air Force: first, that it needlessly dissipated its bomber strength in close-support operations; second, and more important, that it failed to undertake any attacks against the enemy's sources of supply. It is argued that the Air Force was ill-equipped to undertake its role in close support of the Army, for which it should have increased production of Ju 87s at the expense of bombers, and have had a far greater proportion of these machines in the attacking force; on the other hand, it is said that it was not sufficient merely to destroy Soviet equipment at the front; it was necessary to destroy it at the source – in the factories. The initial blow against the Soviet Air Force should have been followed by bomber attacks on the Soviet centres of aircraft production. As it was, only during July and October were a very few raids, often by a single aircraft, mounted against such targets, and then, except at Moscow, at only one, Voronezh, was any significant success recorded. The Soviet capital was the only target of importance to the enemy's war production that was bombed repeatedly, and between 21st July 1941 and 5th April 1942 it received only seventy-six daytime and eleven night raids. But even here, most of the attacks were carried out by a force ranging from between three and ten bombers. The Luftwaffe's presence over the city had a political as much as a military aim, and achieved little in the way of economic disruption.

As a result, it is argued, factories were able to move away, unhindered, from the fighting, the output of the Soviet war industries was uninhibited by German air action, and production was quadrupled. In the second half of 1941, losses at the front were replaced with little difficulty, by late summer, for example, the Red Air Force had regained its strength to an extent whereby it was becoming troublesome to the German ground forces on certain sectors of the front. In addition, material was coming to the Soviet Union from abroad, through the ports of Murmansk, Archangel, and from certain others on the Black Sea, all of which merited the attention of the Luftwaffe but received none. Each aircraft, tank or gun destroyed in the factory, or not produced, would have saved the German Armed Forces losses at the front. But, in 1941, the Luftwaffe made no attempt to bomb the sources of supply. With very few exceptions, all effort was reserved for the support of the forces in the field, a support which entailed the unacceptably high destruction of its bombers. In short, it is argued, the German Air Force was operated only as an ill-equipped appendage of the German Army, and failed to prepare itself either to undertake properly both close support and independent missions, either of which might well have proved of value to the war effort.

Such criticisms, however, are unfair, and take little account of the realities of the position in which the Luftwaffe found itself when planning the campaign. Bombers were still required for indirect support missions which had proved so successful in Poland, the West and the Balkans, and, in any case, production of such machines could not be switched in favour of the output of dive-bombers quite so easily, especially since, once the Soviet Union had been defeated, it was the intention to return to the attack against England in 1942, for which Ju 87s were quite useless. Rather than a change in production, an increase in the output of Ju 87s and even of Bf 110s would have been desirable since the appearance of the Me 210 was long delayed. This, however, given the nature of the Luftwaffe's procurement and supply policies, was true not just of the dive-bomber, but of all aircraft types. That it was not forthcoming, and, instead, a reduction in their production occurred, is not a criticism that can be levelled at the preparations for Barbarossa; rather it is a criticism of a failure in the procurement policies of all aircraft, the causes of which go back to the origins of the Luftwaffe and the beginnings of German rearmament.

As for independent operations, they were simply not feasible. With units fighting the British in both the West and the Mediterranean, the maximum force that the Luftwaffe high command could deploy against the Soviets was some 2,000 combat aircraft, consisting of twenty-nine bomber Gruppen, nine Ju 87 Gruppen, four Bf 110 Gruppen and twenty Bf 109 Gruppen; these were inadequate for the related tasks of achieving air superiority and supporting, both directly and indirectly, the ground forces, let alone for penetrating deep into the Soviet Union to bomb its widely dispersed war economy. As had been shown in the air war against Britain, a large force of bombers was required to mount a sustained campaign over many months to achieve anything approaching a significant reduction in the output of war production. Against Britain, a force of 1,200 bombers had been employed, for the greater part of the Blitz, which had lasted roughly eight months; against the Soviet Union, however, only 880 bombers were deployed, of which, at most, fifty-five per cent were serviceable. These could not have been expected to produce any significant results, especially since a large part of the Soviet war industry was either already in, or was being moved to, the Urals, where, until late in 1941, it was beyond the effective range of the Ju 88s.

Moreover, the Soviet war economy was by no means easy to destroy. By the end of October, the German Army had succeeded in occupying an area which deprived the Soviet Union of forty-five per cent of her total population, and almost one half of her pre-war production (more than two-thirds of pig-iron output, for example), the attainment of which objective would have been quite beyond the capabilities of the heavy bomber fleets of the Allies even two years later, let alone those of the relatively few medium bombers possessed by the Luftwaffe in 1941. As subsequent events were to show, the Soviet Union proved capable of withstanding such a high loss. The movement of vital war industries to the East had already begun before the war (although in a desultory fashion), and by 1941, for example, the output of aircraft from the factories in the Urals amounted to more than half that in the western areas. This movement was accelerated considerably after the German invasion, and between August and October, eighty per cent of Soviet war industry was 'on wheels' to the East. That this movement eastwards, involving no less than one and a half million truck journeys, presented a vulnerable target for German bombers is clear; however, many of the journeys were undertaken at night, or at distances far from German bomber airfields, and, as experience was to show at the front, the Soviets were adept at overcoming obstacles to the movement of trains, including bombed bridges and destroyed locomotives. In the first three months of the war, the Soviet railways managed to transport two and a half million troops with their equipment to the west. German effort to inhibit such a movement of men, while it significantly delayed many, succeeded in preventing only a relatively small percentage from ultimately reaching the front. It is doubtful whether attacks on the industry-bearing sectors of the railway far from the battle zone would have had more than a temporary and limited success.

Even had the Luftwaffe's existing bombers concentrated solely upon one industry (say, the aircraft industry), it is probable that no decisive result would have been achieved, and, even if it had been, it alone would have gained little for the Germans in 1941 without the elimination of other war industries. Furthermore, there were also the ports to be taken care of, through which the Allies were to send large amounts of war material to the Russians, targets which would have been extremely difficult to destroy. Thus, in pursuit of the unobtainable, the withdrawal of 880 bombers from the support of the Army would have left just 1,000 aircraft, well over half of them fighters, for operations to aid the advance. This would have been woefully inadequate. But had a force of less than the 880 bombers been deployed on independent missions (as small a force as 200 has been suggested by some, which, with a high rate of unserviceability, would have meant only 110 or less operational), then certainly no results of any relevance could have been expected. Furthermore, to obtain the necessary accuracy, the bombers would have had to operate over long distances by day unescorted by fighters over ranges beyond 220 miles, which, in the face of Soviet opposition, however inadequate, may have resulted in not insignificant casualties.

All this, the Luftwaffe high command no doubt realised. With the lesson of the campaign against Britain in mind, and the realisation that, even if such a bombing policy would have been successful, it had not the resources to make the necessary allocations without seriously diminishing the support given to the ground forces, the Luftwaffe's leaders did not seriously consider such a strategy. Certainly, if they had done so, the indirect support which was the main task of the bombers would have had to be significantly reduced or ended altogether, with detrimental effect on the conduct of operations. Thus, the

RLM had no alternative but to rely on the strategy which they had practised to such effect in the past. Because of their overstretched resources which were quite inadequate even at the outset of the campaign (let alone after August 1941, when Hitler sent his forces in pursuit of three, widely separated, objectives over a front that was to extend over 1,000 miles), the Luftwaffe, correctly, based its contribution to victory on making every effort to help the Army to inflict a decisive defeat on the enemy, occupy the main economic areas of the Soviet Union, and enable the air units to establish bases from where they could attack the Soviet industries in the Urals. Alone, with only 2,000 combat aircraft, the Luftwaffe had no hope of defeating the enemy; and, certainly, with only 500 serviceable medium bombers it could not hope to reduce significantly the output of Soviet armament. Only by supporting the Army to gain victory by the winter of 1941, could the Air Force prove its effectiveness. It was a gamble, but, given Hitler's decision to invade the Soviet Union with limited military forces, it had to be taken. Indeed, this was fully understood by the Führer. When, on 5th December 1940, the Army Commander-in-Chief, Walther von Brauchitsch, had told him that he did not believe the Luftwaffe to be strong enough to undertake a war on two fronts, the Führer replied that its force was sufficient, but only if the campaign in the East was not prolonged. In the event, the Army, bedevilled by having too few men and vehicles and insufficient time to fulfil Hitler's operational demands, failed. The consequences for the Air Force, as indeed for the entire Wehrmacht, were dire indeed; but, for this, its commanders were not to blame. They had done all that they possibly could to give Germany victory in the East. The causes of defeat lay not with them, but with their Führer.

ByBy early December 1941, it was clear that Hitler's gamble had not paid off, and that the German Armed Forces would be committed to the East for at least another year. For the Luftwaffe, this was to prove an unbearable strain. In October, when victory still seemed to be within German grasp, OKW had ordered the withdrawal of the mass of the Luftwaffe's forces by the following spring. Only eight bomber, three dive-bomber and ten and a half fighter Gruppen, together with anti-aircraft and reconnaissance units, were to be left, distributed along the length of the Eastern Front, facing the defeated and demoralised Asiatic horde. Some redeployment actually took place. In late November, the command of Luftflotte 2, together with Fliegerkorps II, were transferred to the Mediterranean, leaving Fliegerkorps VIII as an independent command on the central front. In addition, the command of Fliegerkorps V was moved to Brussels, with the intention of forming a special mine-laying air corps for use against England, although its aircraft were made over to Fliegerkorps IV. However, this was the sole extent of the transfer. By late December, OKW was requesting the Luftwaffe to withdraw units from operations against Britain (which was to have been the main enemy in 1942), and send them back to support Army Groups North and Centre. The command staff of Fliegerkorps V was returned, half in January 1942, to form Sonderstab Krim (Special Staff, Crimea), a short-lived command under von

Greim, the rest in February, to the central front, where on 1st April 1942 it prepared to assume control of air operations in place of Luftflotte 2 as Luftwaffenkommando Ost (Luftwaffe Command East) under von Greim, prior to the transfer of Fliegerkorps VIII to the Crimea. Whether it wished it or not, the Luftwaffe, however ill-equipped, was to remain fully committed to the East.

The overall combat strength of the German Air Force on 27th December was 1,332 bombers, 1,472 fighters and 326 dive-bombers, only 144 more aircraft than on 22nd June, to be proportioned between three theatres of war – the West, the Mediterranean and the East – all of which were growing in importance as the strength of the enemy increased. In the East, of the 1,700 combat aircraft, 250 less than the number with which the invasion had begun, only forty-three per cent were serviceable (in bomber units, the figure was as low as thirty-four). This was due to the high level of operations that had been sustained in the campaign (amounting to around 180,000 sorties in six months), to the poor weather conditions and rough nature of the landing strips, and to the failings in the supply and servicing facilities (in large part due to factors out of the Luftwaffe's control). Some bomber Geschwader on the Eastern Front had but six aircraft operational. The state of the ground organisation was similarly depressed; by January 1942, for example, of the 100,000 vehicles available to the Luftwaffe in the East, only fifteen per cent were still functioning. In order to supplement its strength, the Luftwaffe made increasing use of the small air forces of Germany's allies in the East: the Romanians, Bulgarians, Hungarians, Finns and Italians, equipped to some extent with German aircraft, a large percentage of them obsolescent. In addition, use was made of personnel in conquered territories in establishing the Slovakian and Croatian Air Forces in 1941, and Spanish volunteers were also incorporated into the Luftwaffe. Although they deployed between them no more than 900 aircraft at any one time, many of doubtful quality, they did perform a useful role for the Germans. In the defence of Hungary, for example, which came later in the war, Hungarian fighters made about forty per cent of the sorties which opposed the enemy. In the whole course of the conflict, the Finns destroyed 1,567 Soviet aircraft in combat, for the loss of 209 of their own machines. However, such a small accrual of force was by no means sufficient to offset the Luftwaffe's insufficiency in aircraft.

On such a sadly depleted force, Hitler's War Directive No. 39 of 8th December 1941 placed two major tasks: first, to mount independent operations to prevent the rehabilitation of the Soviet forces, by launching attacks on training and armament centres such as Moscow, Leningrad, Gorky, Stalingrad, Rostov, and Krasnodar, and, secondly, at the same time to support the Army 'by all available means against enemy attacks on the ground and in the air'. In pursuit of both roles, Soviet communications were to be continuously attacked. However, it was clear from the outset that the Air Force was quite unable to undertake properly one of the tasks, let alone the two simultaneously. Indeed, even before the issue of the Directive, the

Soviet counter-offensive, begun on the central front on the 5th and followed by attacks in the north and south in early January 1942, ensured that the Luftwaffe's attentions would have to remain concentrated on activities immediately affecting the battle at the front. Despite Hitler's insistence that there was to be no withdrawal, and that units should fight to the last man, the German front was forced back between 100 and 200 miles by the end of March 1942, with the loss of roughly a quarter of a million men, in battles which General Halder was to describe as 'absolutely grotesque'.[13]

The climatic conditions under which the Luftwaffe was forced to operate were extremely hard. Snow had continually to be cleared from runways; warming ovens and other expedients were introduced to warm the engines of the aircraft; special hydraulic fluids were developed that did not freeze in temperatures as low as -60° Fahrenheit; and tools used by ground personnel had to be heated and reheated to ensure their effectiveness and to prevent the user from suffering flesh burns. Serviceability dropped to alarmingly low levels, so that by mid-March there were only 646 combat aircraft ready at any moment to support the ground forces in the East. Nevertheless, the fury of the Soviet onslaught, and the acute danger in which the German Army found itself, made it necessary that the Luftwaffe's aircraft, however few, were kept continually in the air. In the centre, von Richthofen's Fliegerkorps VIII (which was reinforced with four bomber Gruppen, one Bf 110 Gruppe, and transport units) quickly became no more than a 'fire brigade', expected to extinguish the countless conflagrations that broke out simultaneously along the front. It was employed exclusively on the daily, even hourly, tactical developments within the operational area of Army Group Centre, and was, in effect, nothing more than an auxiliary weapon of the ground forces. Air support was particularly effective in defending German troops against dangerous incursions towards Yukhnov on the boundary between 4th Army and 4th Panzer Army, and in slowing the enemy breakthrough towards Rzhev, between Ostashkov and Kalinin. In addition, the Luftwaffe began the practice of air lifting and dropping vital supplies to isolated or encircled ground forces, such as to the units temporarily enveloped at Velizh and Demidov, or to the 9th Army between Vyazma and Rzhev. Typical were the activities of the units of Nahkampfführer Nord, under General Otto Dessloch, which, between 6th January and 21st March 1942, flew 5,087 sorties in fifty-six days, destroyed 158 enemy aircraft (seventy-six of them on the ground), 838 motor vehicles, forty-four tanks, and seventy-three guns.

The situation to the north and south of the Eastern Front was similar; close air support was the major preoccupation of Luftwaffe units, so much so that Luftflotte 1 could not even find sufficient aircraft to attack the Soviet supply columns crossing Lake Ladoga on the ice roads, the effective dislocation of which might well have resulted in the capitulation of Leningrad. Of particular note in the north, was the Luftwaffe's support for the two pockets of Kholm and Demyansk, the first containing 3,500 men and the second around 100,000. The German defenders at Kholm managed to hold out for 103 days against very heavy Soviet attacks, solely through the efforts of the Luftwaffe, which not only kept them supplied with essentials but also harried the enemy. Between 6th and 9th March, for example, no less than 1,024 tons of bombs were dropped in an attempt to gain contact with the garrison, which, in the event, was not to be relieved until 5th May. At Demyansk, where the German troops held out for ninety-one days until relieved by ground forces on 18th May, Luftflotte 1 mounted a major airlift for the loss of 265 aircraft, mostly Ju 52s. No less than 24,303 tons of supplies, 692,106 gallons of fuel and 15,446 soldiers were flown into Demyansk, and 22,093 wounded evacuated. The partial supply to Demyansk by air was to continue until 1943 (the German troops there although remained connected to the main front), by which time no less than 64,800 tons had been transported by aircraft. The speed with which the Luftwaffe assembled over 300 transport aircraft was remarkable, and within days the necessary Ju 52s were brought together from other parts of the Eastern Front, from training units in Germany and even from the Mediterranean. The feats of the pilots were considerable. At Demyansk, for example, one of the two airstrips was only thirty yards wide, and loads had to be restricted to one and a half tons in case the surface of the snow gave way. At Kholm, where there was no airstrip, the Ju 52s initially had to land in no-man's land, drop the supplies while taxiing, and take off before Soviet artillery could open fire; casualties, however, became so high that supplies were either dropped by He 111s or flown in by glider. Soviet air attack, too, took its toll on the transports, although, fortunately for the Germans, their home bases were seldom raided.

With the arrival of spring, the German Army began a series of counter-attacks along the length of the Eastern Front, designed both to recover its equilibrium and also to prepare for a major offensive to be mounted deep into the Ukraine and the Caucasus later in the year. In the north, Army Groups North and Centre undertook operations to eliminate Soviet salients, and in the south in May a major attack was aimed at the enemy's Balakleya-Izyum salient near Kharkov. In all these operations, the Luftwaffe took part, its presence before an attack could be mounted being regarded as indispensable. Air superiority, although not general throughout the East, could always be achieved over any area on which the Luftwaffe decided to concentrate, and effective ground support for specific operations proved quite possible, provided that those operations were not simultaneous and widespread. During the Kharkov battle, for example, air support from Pflugbeil's Fliegerkorps IV would often arrive less than twenty minutes after the request had been made. However, it was in the fight for the Crimea that the value of the Luftwaffe's support was, once again, proved beyond all doubt. There, the Soviet threat to the German right flank was considerable; since the end of 1941, when a Soviet counter-attack recaptured the Kerch peninsula, the Red Army had been attempting to break out of the junction of the Kerch and Crimean peninsulas, and from there attack the flank of Army Group South. In addition, the enemy held Sevastopol, and presented a threat to the rear of von Manstein's 11th Army which was occupying the main part of the Crimea.

Clearly, before any offensive in the Ukraine could be mounted, a major effort was required to eliminate this threat to the German flank. Air support was regarded as essential and, for that purpose, in early May Fliegerkorps VIII, a command whose experience of close-support operations was un-rivalled in the Luftwaffe, was transferred from the central front. Although technically under Luftflotte 4, von Richthofen received his instructions direct from the Commander-in-Chief of the Luftwaffe, and was ordered to collaborate closely with 11th Army. On 8th May, after several days of air attacks on Soviet airfields and ports in the area, the first phase of the final conquest of the Crimea began, with the assault on the heavily defended Parpach Line defending the Kerch peninsula. Over 2,000 sorties were flown on the first day, and, by the 12th, victory was certain. By the 19th, the Kerch peninsula was in German hands, together with more than 150,000 Soviet troops. The role of Fliegerkorps VIII in this operation was fully recognised by von Manstein, when he wrote after the war:

> Fliegerkorps VIII, which also included strong Flak artillery forces, was, by virtue of its composition, the most effective and powerful Luftwaffe force available for close-support operations. Its command-ing general, Freiherr von Richthofen, was certainly the most prominent Luftwaffe commander we had in World War II. He demanded terrific performances from the units under his command, and he personally supervised from the air every important action in which they were engaged. He was to be found at all times with the foremost Army units at the front, where he gained personal impressions on existing possibilities for the support of Army oper-ations. Collaboration was always excellent with him, both during my assignment in command of 11th Army and later in my assignments in command of Army Groups Don and South. I recall with most sincere admiration and gratitude his performances and those of his air corps.[14]

Success in the Crimea was not complete, however, without the seizure of the fortress of Sevastopol, which had often been described as the strongest in the world. On 7th June, the ground attack began, with the 600 aircraft of Fliegerkorps VIII, which had been in action against the target for the previous six days, much in evidence. Between 2nd June and 4th July, von Richthofen's units flew a total of 23,751 sorties, and dropped 20,529 tons of bombs. The decisive factor of the whole operation was the co-operation between the air and ground forces; a constant series of attacks was maintained against the Soviet positions in front of the advancing infantry. For the loss of thirty-one aircraft, Fliegerkorps VIII achieved total air superiority, destroyed 141 Soviet aircraft, ten tanks, twenty bunkers, and thirty-eight guns, silenced forty-eight artillery batteries, and partially destroyed forty-three more. Without air support, von Manstein's troops could not have achieved their goal. As the OKW report on the operation stated: 'In the attacks, the Luftwaffe struck the first breaches against permanent and reinforced field fortifications by bombing attacks, dive-bombing attacks, and fighter-bomber attacks, and then by destructive bombing effects made it possible [for ground units] to push through the fortified zones.'[15]

As the operations cited above indicate, the Luftwaffe in the East in 1942 had become primarily a close-support weapon. The Luftwaffe General Staff admitted in 1944:

> The further course of the war in the air, after 1941, was characterized by the fact that the Luftwaffe was no longer as in the past employed in concentration on only one front against only one enemy within the overall pattern of the whole war. Through its employment in a number of theatres simultaneously, it was compelled to dispatch its forces against the enemy in widely separated areas. This necessarily resulted in a reduction of the operable strength available in the individual segments of the fronts. This made the departure from the past principles of operational warfare in favour of direct support for the Army and the Navy an accomplished fact.[16]

Thus, in mid-1942, with the resumption of a major offensive in the East, but this time confined to the south, Luftflotte 1 in the north was left with only 375 combat aircraft instead of the 600 it had had the year previously, and Luftwaffenkommando Ost, in the centre, with just 600 (Luftflotte 2 had had 910). Throughout the year, eighty per cent of the Luftwaffe's sorties were undertaken in close support of the ground forces. Certainly, indirect support continued (in April, for example, the main preoccupation of air units on the central front was the interdiction of the railway lines in the Kalinin-Bologoye-Toropets area, vital to the Red Army), but such operations became increasingly rare. During 1942, attacks against railways came to be usually mounted by night and in areas near to the front. Special units were even activated to carry out such tasks. Towards the end of the year, too, effective night harassing attacks on the Soviet pattern were undertaken near to the front lines, using obsolete aircraft quite unfit for use by daylight. These were known as Störkampfstaffeln (harassing units), and after their effectiveness had been established, were retitled Nachtschlachtgruppen (night attack groups). Such missions were new, but originated from the indirect support that had previously been carried out by day against troop concentrations and command posts in the enemy's rear. They aimed as much at undermining morale as at physical destruction. By 1942, day attacks of a similar nature were largely a thing of the past.

Because of a shortage of aircraft, it remained impossible for the Luftwaffe to mount independent operations on any appreciable scale. In January, three small raids had been made against Moscow; in February, an attack was made on aircraft factories at Voronezh and on a factory at Gorky believed to be manufacturing tanks (in fact, it was producing soft-skinned vehicles). In March, Voronezh and Moscow were again bombed, the latter three times, together with an aircraft engine factory in Rybinsk and an oil refinery at Kalinin. In April, Moscow and Rybinsk received further attention, and in May Gorky was again bombed. These raids, however, did not represent a major onslaught against the Soviet war economy, and can hardly be described as even of nuisance value, so few, small and infrequent were they. In the summer months, it proved impossible to continue them, and not until October were such attacks resumed.

Indeed, the only significant operations the Luftwaffe were to mount against the Soviet war economy, took place not over the land but over the sea, and were aimed at the Anglo-American convoys shipping vital supplies and munitions to the ports of Murmansk and Archangel. A little over half the tonnage imported into the Soviet Union in 1942 (1,200,000 tons out of 2,300,000 tons) came through the White Sea ports, the rest being brought through Persia and Far Eastern and Arctic ports. Responsibility for operations against these convoys was given to Stumpff's Luftflotte 5 in the extreme north, which, throughout 1942, also continued to attack the Red Air Force and the Soviet communications much as it had done in the previous year. However, its main effort, together with the Navy, was directed at the closing of the Atlantic route to Russia. Three local air commands were responsible for the operations – Fliegerführer Nord (Ost) which had replaced Fliegerführer Kirkenes in December 1941, Fliegerführer Lofoten Islands, specially organised in the spring of 1942 for anti-convoy tasks, and Fliegerführer Nord (West), whose area of responsibility covered an area south of a line from Trondheim to the Shetland Islands and Iceland. In February 1942, the forces available for anti-convoy operations comprised sixty bombers, thirty Ju 87s, thirty Bf 109s, and fifteen He 115 seaplane torpedo-carriers; by June, the numbers had risen substantially, to 103 Ju 88s, forty-two He 111s (torpedo bombers), fifteen He 115s, thirty Ju 87s, eight FW 200s, twenty-two reconnaissance Ju 88s, and forty-four BV 138 reconnaissance seaplanes. Such a three-fold increase in strength was indicative of the importance placed on the operations.

During March and April, four Allied convoys (PQ 12, 13, 14, and 15) passed through Arctic waters into White Sea ports, sustaining little damage, only five merchantmen being sunk by air action. In the middle of May, however, a more notable success was gained in sustained operations against PQ 16; the Germans believed that the whole convoy was destroyed, although in fact, only seven of the thirty-four ships were lost, and all were scattered partly as a result of weather and partly by the attack. Against the next convoy, PQ 17, which was attacked in July, the Germans secured even greater success. Helped enormously by a mistake on the part of the British Admiralty, which gave the convoy an untimely order to scatter, thereby depriving it of its main protection, they destroyed twenty-four of the thirty-four ships, though

Stumpff again believed that all had been accounted for. Eight had been sunk by air attack alone, and seven 'shared' with the U-boats, for the loss of seven aircraft and the expenditure of sixty-one torpedoes and 212 tons of bombs.

However, despite the reinforcements of Ju 88s, which brought the number of torpedo-bombers to ninety-two, the Luftwaffe's successes were not to continue; had they done so, it would almost surely have meant the end of the Anglo-American supplies to Russia by this route. The next convoy to pass through the Arctic waters, PQ 18, was in October; it was heavily escorted by cruisers, destroyers and an aircraft carrier. The British fighters and the anti-aircraft fire put up by the naval ships, made the launching of torpedoes and bombs against the inner ring of merchantmen an extremely hazardous undertaking. The Germans lost a large number of aircraft, and managed only to sink thirteen out of forty ships by air and submarine attack. What would have happened in future attacks is only a matter for conjecture, for, with the Allied landings in North Africa in November, the four Gruppen of bomber and torpedo-bombers were transferred to the Mediterranean. The remaining forces in Luftflotte 5 consisted of He 115s (which, because of their low speed, were of use only in attacking stragglers), Ju 87s, vulnerable to British fighters, and reconnaissance aircraft. The failure in the Battle of the Atlantic and Western Approaches in 1941 was repeated in the Arctic.

But all this was a side-show compared with the main effort of the Luftwaffe in the East in 1942: the support of the offensive into the Caucasus and the Ukraine, culminating in the battle of Stalingrad. Hitler's War Directive No. 41, dated 5th April, had laid down the operational premises on which the attack, code-named Operation Blue, was to be based: 'Our aim is to wipe out the entire defence potential remaining to the Soviets, and to cut them off, as far as possible, from their most important centres of war industry'.[17] To achieve this, an operation would be mounted to the south, where the main enemy forces would be destroyed west of the Don, and the advance into the Ukraine pursued as far as Stalingrad, thereby allowing the Caucasus, and its oilfields, to be occupied. After this had been successfully undertaken, Leningrad in the north would be captured. The armies on the central front would stand fast, and make no attempt to capture Moscow.

The Luftwaffe was barely strong enough to undertake the role required of it in carrying out these plans: the acquisition of air superiority over the area of operations, and the provision of direct and indirect support of the Army. By the beginning of the offensive in June, it possessed 2,750 combat aircraft in the East (sixty-four per cent of the total front-line strength available to the Air Force of 4,262 aircraft), which were outnumbered by 3:1 by the Red Air Force. Only by reducing its allocations to other sectors of the front, could the Luftwaffe provide 1,593 for the southern offensive (just over fifty-four per cent of the total in Russia), of which 1,155 were ready for action. These came under the control of Luftflotte 4 commanded by Löhr until 19th July, when he became Commander-in-Chief South-East in charge of all Wehrmacht units in the Balkans and was succeeded by the forty-seven-year-old von

Richthofen, one of the most able of Luftwaffe field commanders. Their task was to support Field Marshal von Bock's Army Group South (to be divided and renamed Army Groups A and B after the beginning of the campaign), and were allocated to Fliegerkorps IV under Pflugbeil and Fliegerkorps VIII under von Richthofen, who was succeeded by General Martin Fiebig on 3rd July. With Fliegerkorps VIII heavily engaged in the Crimea, it was not until the end of the first week of operations that it was fully employed in Operation Blue. An additional command, Luftwaffen-Gefechtsverband Nord (Tactical Air Command North), had been instituted on 10th June under Colonel Alfred Bülowius, to take control of the Voronezh front once Fliegerkorps VIII had moved, south-eastwards, in support of the advancing ground units.

It could be expected that the operational aircraft available to Luftflotte 4 would be around 900 after a week of operations, unless substantial reinforcements were forthcoming (but from where?), with the prospect of far less should the rate of serviceability fall to below sixty per cent, as it could easily do during continued fighting. Such a force would be sufficient, although barely so, provided that the objectives in the south were pursued successively: first, the destruction of the Soviet armies east of the Don and the capture of Stalingrad on the Volga and then, secondly, the occupation of the Caucasus. However, should both objectives be pursued concurrently, with Army Group B attacking eastwards to Stalingrad at the same time as Army Group A moved south south-east deep into the Caucasus (diverging lines of advance that would take the two spearheads more than 700 miles apart), then Luftflotte 4 would find itself quite incapable of providing sufficient air support. On Hitler's appreciation of the order of priorities once the offensive had begun, therefore, lay the Luftwaffe's ability or otherwise to conduct the campaign.

The offensive opened on 28th June, and met with initial success. By 2nd July, the first envelopment of Soviet forces had been achieved, and by the 6th the Don river had been crossed and Voronezh, more than 100 miles from the original front line, had been seized. The German Army proceeded to destroy the Soviet forces west of the Don as planned. In this, the Luftwaffe's role was significant. Until the end of July, Luftflotte 4 performed tasks similar to those undertaken so successfully in the East the year before. Fighters dominated the air, bombers attacked enemy troop concentrations, supply columns and railways, and close-support units destroyed Soviet strong-points and played their part in halting enemy breakthroughs. Constant air support had become indispensable to the Army, and many were the instances of troops refusing to move forward without it. An example of the efficacy of the air units was given by von Richthofen, who wrote of one action undertaken by his old command, Fliegerkorps VIII: 'The attack completely paralyzed the Russians and enabled von Wietersheim's panzer forces to advance thirty-six miles practically unopposed. At 1600 hours these units reached the Volga River. A very narrow wedge was driven forward, which will undoubtedly be under Soviet attack from the right and the left from tomorrow on. During this time, units of

Fliegerkorps VIII flew a total of 1,600 sorties, delivered 1,000 tons of bombs on targets, and downed ninety-one Soviet aircraft, losing only three German planes. . . .'[18] In addition to combat support, the Luftwaffe provided a considerable supply service for Army units in the field, beginning in the first few days of the campaign. As the armies thrust further into enemy territory, the transport units were called on to an increasing extent; over the whole Eastern Front, between 1st August and 30th October, no less than 21,500 transport sorties were flown, covering over 10,500,000 miles and delivering some 42-43,000 tons of fuel and equipment. Two-thirds of this activity took place on the southern sector.

However, the level of air support was not to be maintained at such an intense level for more than the first month of operations. On 23rd July, Hitler issued the fatal order that the offensive should be continued in two widely divergent directions: Army Group B (with Fliegerkorps VIII), would advance east to Stalingrad, while, simultaneously, Army Group A (with Fliegerkorps IV) would proceed south down into the Caucasus. Both the Army and the Air Force leaders were unhappy with this plan, realising that they possessed insufficient strength to pursue both advances simultaneously. The Führer also placed extra tasks on the Air Force, requiring it to attack Astrakhan, and shipping on the lower Volga and the Black Sea, as well as to cut enemy supplies of oil from the Caucasus by destroying railways, pipelines, and shipping on the Caspian Sea. Luftflotte 4, instead of operating over a front of some 1,000 miles as it would have done if Stalingrad had remained the prime and initial objective, was faced with the prospect of a front of more than 2,700 miles, comprising the Black Sea, the Caucasus, the Kuban, the Caspian coastline, the Kalmyk Steppe, the Ural river, the Volga river from Saratov to its estuary, and almost the entire length of the Don river. For this, it possessed 1,359 aircraft on 20th July, of which just 763 were operational. This number was quite inadequate, and von Richthofen could make no pretence that he would, henceforth, be able to provide the Army with the level of support on which it had come to rely.

The difficulties arising from the divergent direction of the two advances became increasingly apparent the further the Army's spearheads moved eastwards and southwards. Not only were there too few aircraft to support them, but the existing ground organisation was inadequate to allow the full concentration of air units in the areas of main effort. No concerted attack, for example, could be made against Soviet communications to the vital Stalingrad front, thus allowing an uninterrupted supply of men and material to be brought up to check the German offensive and to prepare for a major counter-attack. Moreover, each move of air units over a long distance to new bases, resulted in a considerable reduction in operational strength. The numbers of aircraft available to Luftflotte 4 fell from 1,600 in June to 975 on 20th October, of which 594 were fit for operations at any one time. Moreover, there was no possibility of any reinforcement from other theatres, or even from other sectors of the Eastern Front. In the Mediterranean, Germany was having to make an ever-deepening commitment, and, in the West, bomber units had already been reduced to a minimum, while fighter units were having to cope with an increasing scale of enemy attacks. On the rest of the Eastern Front, Luftflotte 5's forces were committed to anti-convoy operations, Luftflotte 1 (reinforced in preparation for the final onslaught on Leningrad) had already given up Fliegerkorps I and was heavily engaged in fierce fighting around Demyansk, along the Volkhov river, and at Leningrad, while Luftwaffenkommando Ost was also involved in defending the line in areas such as the Yukhov bulge, Rzhev, and Toropets. The newly established Luftwaffenkommando Don (which had been formed out of Fliegerkorps I (minus most of its aircraft) and Luftwaffen-Gefechtsverbard Nord, and was made an independent command under General Günther Korten) held the line between Luftflotte 4 and Luftwaffenkommando Ost, but had only some sixty aircraft at its disposal, and none to spare. Thus, with the Luftwaffe fully extended throughout Europe, the Mediterranean and in the East, and with no possibility of change in the distribution of its units, at any rate in the East owing to increasing enemy pressure, no further concentration of force was possible in the southern sector.

Von Richthofen did all he could to alleviate the consequences of his shortage of air units, but with little success. Especially annoying to him were the operations that Hitler had ordered should take place far behind the front line, such as the bombing of oil-lines in the Caucasus, which could not possibly have an immediate impact on the position at the front, and which in any case, because of the few aircraft involved, could have nothing more than a nuisance value. Von Richthofen argued that his Luftflotte would have to concentrate its efforts in accordance with its resources, and not only establish priorities but also confine its missions to the support of the ground forces. Dissipation over large areas and against many targets was to be avoided, even though this would deliberately leave large areas of the front with no air cover at all. However, Hitler's desire to do everything all at once, which was supported (although not willingly agreed with) by the Luftwaffe high command, ensured that von Richthofen's proposals went unheeded.

Nevertheless, despite the lack of adequate air support, the German Army made significant advances. In the attack into the Caucasus, Rostov fell on 29th July. By 9th August the oil centre of Maykop, 200 miles distant, was captured, and by 2nd November, Ordzhonikidze was gained, over 400 miles from Rostov. Away to the north, on 23rd November, the outskirts of Stalingrad had been penetrated by 6th Army under General Paulus. However, except for the occupation of most of that city, German forces were destined to advance no further eastwards. Quite simply, they had insufficient strength for their dual tasks. Victory was soon to turn into defeat. By 6th September, the Germans had become bogged down in Stalingrad; on 19th November, the Soviets counter-attacked, and by the 21st the 6th Army had been encircled and 280,000 men trapped in a pocket measuring thirty miles by twenty-five. Only then, when forced to do so by enemy action, did the

German high command decide upon a main point of concentration in the south. The three remaining bomber Gruppen in Fliegerkorps IV were withdrawn, and transferred to Fliegerkorps VIII at Stalingrad, and at the end of November even Pflugbeil's headquarters were moved to a location nearer the beleaguered city, so as to give more active support to the forces that were to relieve 6th Army. The few air units remaining in the Caucasus, mainly reconnaissance and close-support, were combined with Dessloch's Flakkorps I, to form a new command, Fliegerführer Kaukasus.

The strain on Luftflotten 4's resources had been evident in its reaction to the increasing Soviet threat to the flanks of the 6th Army at Stalingrad before 19th November. Aerial reconnaissance had shown a build up of strong enemy forces at vital points along the Don, and von Richthofen had expressed his fear that a counter-attack would take place. This fear was shared by the new Chief of the Army General Staff, Kurt Zeitzler, and even by Hitler. However, there was little that could be done about it; both the Army and the Air Force were so overstretched that few units could be found to bolster the flanks or to provide Fliegerkorps VIII with additional aircraft. Although several bomber Gruppen were brought from the Caucasus before 19th November, one bomber Geschwader was lost to North Africa after the Allied landings in Tunisia on the 8th. Indeed, as the invasion there made it necessary for other units to be moved from the East (to a total of 240 combat aircraft from the central and southern fronts), there were none available for von Richthofen as large areas of the Eastern Front were left without any air support at all. Thus, with but 300 serviceable combat aircraft, Fliegerkorps VIII proved quite unable to mount a significant blow against the Soviet movements and concentrations for the counter-offensive, let alone to halt it once it had begun. The Luftwaffe simply did not possess enough units to cater for emergencies on more than two fronts. For the Germans, it was extremely unfortunate that the landings in North Africa took place twelve days before the Soviet counter-offensive at Stalingrad – but such was war.

The enemy attack began on 19th November under the protection of poor weather conditions, which were the worst possible for flying: freezing temperatures and dense fog alternating with sleet and snow. Ice on the ground immobilised many aircraft. The war diary of Luftflotte 4 noted:

> Rain, snow, and ice-forming have completely prevented air operations, and Fliegerkorps VIII, from its command post at Oblivskaya, can direct only a few single aircraft to the attack. It is impossible to close the Don River bridges by bombing. It is not even possible to gain an insight into the situation by aerial reconnaissance. We can only hope that the Russians will not reach our rail route, our main supply artery. ... Urgently needed transfers [of air units] are as yet impossible because of the miserable weather. We must have good weather soon, otherwise there is no longer any hope.[19]

Only a handful of sorties were made on the 19th, and, in addition, airfields between the Don and Chir rivers, from which close-support units were operating, had to be evacuated, in some cases the last aircraft leaving as the Soviet tanks arrived. On the 20th, the situation was little better, and poor weather restricted Fliegerkorps VIII and the few Romanian units available to only 120 sorties. Von Richthofen noted: 'Once again, the Russians have exploited the weather situation in masterly fashion. To save anything from the rot, we must have good flying conditions'.[20] On the 21st, the Soviet flanking attacks met in the rear of 6th Army, and their spearheads continued to move west. By the evening of the 23rd, they had no less than thirty-four divisions over the Don.

On the evening of 22nd November, General Paulus, Commander of the encircled 6th Army, sent the following message to his superior, General von Weichs, commander of Army Group B: 'Army completely encircled. . . . Ammunition situation critical; food supplies on hand for six days; the Army intends to hold the territory between Stalingrad and the Don river, and has made the necessary preparations. Success depends upon closing the gap on the southern front, and on whether or not adequate food supplies can be delivered by air'.[21] Von Weichs was highly sceptical, and that same evening, in a message to OKH, stated: 'It is not possible to keep an army made up of twenty divisions supplied from the air. Even assuming weather conditions are favourable, the available air transport space is not sufficient to provide the encircled force with more than one-tenth of its actual daily requirements in supplies'.[22] Von Weichs was confirmed in his opinion by the Luftwaffe commanders at the front, von Richthofen, Fiebig, and Pickert (commanding the Flak units in Stalingrad), as well as the five corps commanders of 6th Army, and von Manstein, who on 21st November was nominated to command the new Army Group Don, which included 6th Army. The newly appointed Chief of the Army General Staff, Kurt Zeitzler, also believed that air supply would prove impossible, as also, it appears, did his counterpart in the Luftwaffe, Jeschonnek. There are many conflicting views as to the attitude of the Chief of the Air Force's General Staff; but, according to Fiebig, he was in agreement with the field commanders as to the impossibility of air supply, and this view is corroborated by members of the General Staff such as General Kurt Kleinrath and Colonel Werner Leuchtenberg, who, then as a Major, was Jeschonnek's Adjutant.

What advice Hitler received from the Luftwaffe on the possibility of an air-lift is difficult to ascertain. Certainly, from the beginning of the Soviet counter-offensive, he was against any idea of a withdrawal by 6th Army. In line with his previous insistence on not voluntarily yielding an inch of ground to the enemy, he dismissed any proposal for a retreat even as early as 19th November. Supply from the air was in his mind from the beginning, the impressive operations at Demyansk and Kholm no doubt being uppermost in his thoughts. His creation of Army Group Don on the 21st was motivated by a wish to create a formation whose immediate task was to bring the enemy attacks to a standstill and recapture the positions previously held. On the 21st, too, Jeschonnek had an interview with Hitler at which he appears to have attempted to dissuade him from pursuing with his plan for an air-lift; but, according to Zeitzler, he was unconvincing, and was not sufficiently vehement in pronouncing the operation impossible. Matters were not helped during the meeting by a telephone call from Göring, who forbade Jeschonnek to displease the Führer. On the 24th, after several telephone conversations with Hitler, Göring arrived at the Führer's headquarters to assure him that an air-lift was possible. According to Zeitzler, who was present, the Reichsmarschall said: 'My Führer, I report to you that the Luftwaffe will supply the 6th Army by air', to which Zeitzler retorted 'That the Luftwaffe cannot do'. After further heated exchanges between the two men, Hitler concluded the discussion by saying: 'The Reichsmarschall has reported to me that the air supply movement will work. I must believe his reports. My decision remains unchanged'.[23] However, even had Göring advised against the operation, it is likely that Hitler would have ordered it to go ahead anyway, so determined was he that not an inch of ground should be lost to the enemy, certainly not at a place with a name as symbolic as 'Stalingrad'. Moreover, by this time in the war, it had become the established pattern of Hitler's leadership not to heed the advice of his subordinates if it conflicted with his own wishes, nor to be bothered overmuch with the dictates of military reality. It would, therefore, have been surprising had the air-lift to 6th Army not proceeded, whatever the reactions of the senior Luftwaffe commanders.

Whether or not Göring realised the full implications of what he was promising, is debatable. Lörzer, his close associate, remembered after the war that the Commander-in-Chief of the Luftwaffe was subjected to great pressure from Hitler, who had insisted that the Luftwaffe should support 6th Army. It was the Führer's only hope; the evacuation of Stalingrad would, he feared, entail an unacceptable loss of face. Göring, fearful of his position in Hitler's eyes, probably felt he simply could not refuse this request and lay himself open to further condemnation after failure in the skies over Britain, and, increasingly, over the Reich itself. Jeschonnek, too, after his first expression of doubt, refrained from arguing against his Führer's wishes, and his concept of unswerving obedience prevented him from following the dictates of his own commonsense. The dominance of the Führer in operational decisions was, by this point in the war, total. Even von Richthofen, when hearing of the final decision to mount an air-lift, had resignedly commented: 'We have only once chance to cling to; so far, the Führer has always been right, even when none of us could understand his actions and most of us had strongly advised against them'.[24]

Preparations for an air-lift to 6th Army had begun as early as 20th November, when Luftflotte 4 anticipated that, whether Paulus was instructed to stay out or withdraw, supplies would have to be sent to the beleaguered force for a short period at least. General Fiebig was appointed to take command of the operations, and, on the 25th, the first supplies were air-lifted into Stalingrad. On the 29th, Fliegerkorps VIII was relieved of its combat mission and given the responsibility for the air supply operations. Control of the combat units went to the ad-hoc command, Fliegerdivision Donetz, under General Alfred Mahnke, who was made responsible to von Richthofen. The Fliegerdivision took over the previous task of Fliegerkorps VIII of attacking the Soviet forces on the Chir front that were threatening to push even further westwards and render any re-establishment of land communication with 6th Army quite impossible. On 12th December, the German counter-attack began, under von Manstein's direction, and by the 17th the spearhead had reached to within thirty-five miles of Stalingrad. However, the Germans were destined to get no further; on the 18th, the left flank of Army Group Don broke, and relief of 6th Army became impossible. Despite the earnest entreaties of his generals, Hitler still refused to countenance a breakout, and Paulus, without such orders, stayed put. The Soviet offensive continued with ferocity, and by the 23rd Stalingrad had ceased to become the primary concern of Army Group Don, which was by then fighting for its own existence. On the 27th, 4th Panzer Army began its withdrawal, and by the last day of the year more than 100 miles separated 6th Army from the nearest German units.

Relief by ground attack had failed, and thereafter all hope for the survival of 6th Army relied on the operations of the Luftwaffe. Success was dependent on four conditions being fulfilled: first, that sufficient transport aircraft be made available; second, that the weather remain good enough to allow them to fly when necessary; third, that there be adequate airfields both outside and inside the pocket to support the operations; and, fourth, that enemy action, either from the air or the ground, should not inflict unacceptable losses on the transport units. At Demyansk, earlier in the year, sufficient aircraft had been made available to lift a daily average of 300 tons to meet the needs of 100,000 men (less than half the number in Stalingrad); the weather was reasonable and improving; the front was stabilised and the approach and return routes to serviceable bases were relatively short; and sufficient fighter aircraft were available for escort duty over an area that was relatively free from enemy air and anti-aircraft units. At Stalingrad, six months later, none of these conditions pertained.

The supply needs of 6th Army were estimated at 750 tons a day (later, this figure was reduced to 500 tons), the transport of which required a total of 375 sorties daily by Ju 52s, each carrying two tons. With serviceability of transport units then as low as thirty to thirty-five per cent, this meant that over 1,000 aircraft would have to be assembled, and even then many of them would have to undertake two sorties a day. The Luftwaffe, however, possessed only some 750 Ju 52s, and even if they were all brought together, which would entail denuding the flying schools, the Mediterranean theatre and the rest of the Eastern Front, it would have meant that 500 tons a day, at most, could be delivered. However, although the Chief of Training was deprived of his Ju 52s, the requirements of the Mediterranean theatre, where supply problems in North Africa rendered the transports vital to continued German presence there, meant that only 500 could be spared for the Stalingrad airlift. Even these, moreover, could not be sent at once, and it immediately became clear that old Ju 86s and He 111s would have to be used. By the beginning of December, Fliegerkorps VIII had only 320 transports under its command. This was quite insufficient, so von Richthofen committed his He 111s to carrying supplies, and they were first used in this role on 30th November; they were also be to be used in combat whenever the situation demanded, as during 4th Panzer Army's advance towards Stalingrad. In addition, eighteen FW 200s were taken from their duties over the Atlantic and made available for the Stalingrad operation, their first sorties taking place on 9th January. They were followed a few days later by two giant Ju 290s, carrying ten tons, several Ju 90s, and seven He 177s. Except for the FW 200s, the other aircraft proved quite unsuitable for their transport tasks; both the Ju 290s were quickly put out of action, and the He 177s, originally intended for operations over the Atlantic, were used in only one mission. At no time, were there more than 500 machines under the control of Fliegerkorps VIII, just half the requisite number. Moreover, their serviceability occasionally dropped to as low as twenty-five per cent owing to the acute weather conditions. Thus, at no time would it be possible for the Fliegerkorps to send more than 350 tons daily to 6th Army, and on many occasions it would be less, only 250 tons, depending on serviceability. Only if each serviceable aircraft flew two missions a day, 6th Army would have received the supplies required to continue the fight. However, that would have been possible only under ideal conditions: good weather, adequate airfields, and negligible enemy opposition. In the event, none of these conditions was fulfilled.

Between mid-November and February 1943, there was scarcely a day of clear weather with good visibility in Fliegerkorps VIII's area. Either the snow on airfields was so thick that aircraft could not take off, or the cold so intense that the engines seized up, or fog shrouded the airstrips in the pocket and prevented landings. Operations were restricted or even stopped for days on end. The most frequent source of difficulty came from rising thick layers of cloud, in which ice formation between the layers presented considerable danger to aircraft. Sometimes, entire units were lost while trying to get through areas of bad weather, and such losses far exceeded those from enemy action. Not only did poor weather hamper operations, but also the continual Soviet advance westwards caused Fliegerkorps VIII to move back from airfield to airfield. The closer the bases were to Stalingrad, the greater were the number of sorties that could be flown, and the more certain the possibility of fulfilling 6th Army's demands. At the outset of the operation, the Luftwaffe was fairly well served, having its Ju 52s and Ju 86s based at Tazinskaya, and its He 111s at Morozovskaya, 160 and 130 miles respectively (sixty and fifty minutes' flying time) from the pocket; but, on 24th December, enemy tanks forced the Ju 52s to move further back to Salsk, 250 miles away from Stalingrad (Tazinskaya was later reoccupied, but only for a short period), and on 2nd January 1943 the He 111s also were forced to move back to Novocherkassk, 210 miles from 6th Army. These moves meant that the aircraft were capable of only one sortie a day. The Soviet advance continued, and, after 10th January, the He 111s were forced to operate from Taganrog, 250 miles from Stalingrad. On 16th January, the Ju 52s had to retire to Cherekovo, thus leaving the pocket barely within their operating range. In addition, the airfields at Stalingrad were lost; on the 16th, Pitomnik, the most important, fell to the Russians, and on the 21st, Gumrak was also captured. On the 22nd, it was clear that landings were impossible on the few strips left available, and supplies had henceforth to be dropped from the air.

As if these obstacles were not sufficient, Fliegerkorps VIII also had to contend with ever-increasing Soviet opposition. Powerful enemy anti-aircraft forces were deployed around Stalingrad, especially along the approach routes to the airfields in the pocket, and fighter attacks grew daily. The Ju 52s and Ju 86s, weakly armed and slow, were particularly vulnerable to interception, although the He 111s could usually hold their own. Attacks were made on the German bases, with some effect. For example, on 17th January, no less than fifty transports were lost at Cherekovo during bombing attacks. German fighter cover in Fliegerkorps VIII's area was meagre, owing to the heavy demands from elsewhere that were made on the 375 single-engined fighters, all that, by the end of December, were available along the whole of the Eastern Front. Moreover, as the German line was pushed further back from Stalingrad, so the city came outside the effective range of the fighter units. Matters were made still worse by the loss of Pitomnik airfield at Stalingrad, which caused the six Bf 109s that had been operating there since the beginning of December to move to Gumrak, where five were destroyed by bad landings in snow drifts, craters and the like. As a result of all this, air superiority could not be maintained over Stalingrad and its approaches. It was fortunate for the Luftwaffe pilots that bad weather was as much the enemy of the Red Air Force as it was of theirs.

Nor were these difficulties the only ones with which Fliegerkorps VIII had to contend. There were problems in supplying the airfields with sufficient equipment in general, including vital spares and heating machines, which, once it arrived, might well be lost as the enemy advanced. The severe cold reduced the efficiency of the air crews and ground personnel, and morale was so low that some pilots turned back before Stalingrad was reached, pleading engine failure upon their return. Other, similar, incidents were suspected. Hitler's interference, too, had its impact. Owing to his having forbidden Luftflotte 4 to evacuate any airfield until the first enemy shells had landed on it, Tazinkaya was not left until it was clear that its Soviet attackers would capture it. The Ju 52s and Ju 86s took off as Russian tanks moved onto the airfield; 109 Ju 52s and sixteen Ju 86s were saved, but sixty aircraft were lost, and nearly all the spare parts and ground equipment had to be left behind. Such were the straits to which Hitler's orders had reduced even Luftwaffe field commands.

While such senseless waste took place, the soldiers of 6th Army starved. In temperatures as low as –50° Fahrenheit, men were even reduced to eating the brains of their dead colleagues to remain alive. One by one the heavy weapons and tanks of the defenders became immobilised, either having broken down or lacking ammunition. On 22nd January, Paulus asked Hitler for permission to open negotiations for surrender. The Führer refused. On the 31st, by which time even the wounded were not receiving rations, Paulus and his staff surrendered. In the next forty-eight hours, the fighting ended. An army of 250,000 men had been totally destroyed. Only 34,000 (specialists and wounded) had been evacuated, the rest had been left to die either in defence of Stalingrad or in Soviet captivity. Just a few thousand men of 6th Army were to return to Germany after the war.

It is not surprising that, even early in its operations, the Luftwaffe was accused of betrayal by Paulus and others in 6th Army. Such allegations, however, were unfair. From the outset, the field commanders of Luftflotte 4 did their best to persuade the commander of 6th Army that to supply 250,000 men by air was impossible, and they undertook their mission only with the greatest reluctance, hoping against hope that the ground attack by 4th Panzer Army would bring relief to the defenders at Stalingrad. This having failed by the end of December, there was no alternative but to continue the unequal fight against both the elements and Soviet opposition until the inevitable material and physical exhaustion of 6th Army brought matters to an end. Everything possible that could be done with the resources at hand, was done. As General Fiebig wrote on 13th January: 'I believe that no heart was more filled with concern over the fate of 6th Army than the hearts of the men assigned to organise and carry out the air supply operation for the Army. We have done our best. When I examine my actions, I find nothing that I have done wrong, nothing that could have been done otherwise'.[25]

In the seventy days of the airlift, from 25th November 1942 to 2nd February 1943, Fliegerkorps VIII mounted some 3,500 transport sorties to the beleaguered 6th Army, and delivered 6,591 tons of food and equipment, of which it is estimated some 400 tons did not reach the troops, being dropped in no-man's land or even onto the enemy's lines during the last days of the operation. An average of ninety-four tons a day reached 6th Army, whose initial requirements were put as high as 750 tons. On three days, no supply missions were flown at all owing to the weather (24th and 25th December, and 2nd January), and the highest tonnage transported on any one day was 290 tons, on 19th December. In the period 12th to 21st December, the Fliegerkorps reached the peak of its activity, supplying a daily average of 137.7 tons, but in subsequent periods this fell off considerably, owing in large part to the loss of the two airfields of Tazinskaya and Morozovskaya on 24th December and 2nd January.

Fiebig's verdict on his own operations was more or less confirmed by Milch when he arrived at Luftflotte 4's headquarters on 16th January, with the task, entrusted to him by Hitler, of ensuring that 6th Army received its supplies. He found that aircraft availability on the 16th was 140 Ju 52s, of which just fifteen were operable, 140 He 111s, of which forty-one were serviceable, and twenty FW 200s, only one of which could fly. Thus, of a total strength of just 300 transports, Fliegerkorps VIII possessed only fifty-seven, nineteen per cent, that could actually ferry supplies to Paulus' troops. Over the succeeding days, Milch did his best to solve the problem, but only by resigning himself to heavy losses of Ju 52s and He 111s (as well as of irreplaceable flying instructors who were shot down in their machines) did he succeed in increasing by only about thirty per cent the already seriously low level of supplies sent to Stalingrad. Moreover, it is probable that this increase would have come about anyway, owing to more aircraft becoming available and to an improvement in the weather. As an indication of the impact which the unfavourable conditions had upon Fliegerkorps VIII, its efforts should be compared with those of the transport units on the Eastern Front in the ninety-one days from the beginning of August to the end of October 1942. Then, in good weather and operating from secure bases in air-space largely free from Soviet interference, an average of 236 sorties a day were made by a force of some 350 aircraft with a serviceability rate of forty per cent and above. During the Stalingrad airlift, however, with more aircraft but a significantly lower operational rate, a daily average of only fifty sorties were possible. The supply of 6th Army was doomed to failure from the outset.

The fruitless operation at Stalingrad had cost the Luftwaffe dear. Fliegerkorps VIII lost, either destroyed or beyond repair, no less than 488 aircraft, of which 266 were Ju 52s, 165 He 111s, forty-two Ju 86s, nine FW 200s, five He 177s (most in a bombing mission) and one Ju 290, together with some 1,000 aircrew. The consequences of this were far-reaching. No doubt referring to the impact on the bomber training schools, as well as to the loss of He 111s, Göring later remarked: 'There died the core of the German bomber fleet'.[26] But they were but one part of the severe losses sustained by the Luftwaffe in the East during the winter of 1942-43, losses which reduced its combat strength (bombers, fighters and reconnaissance machines) to barely 1,700 aircraft by mid-January 1943, of which just forty per cent were operational. This was sixty per cent of the force which had been in the East six months previously, and was but twenty per cent of the force which the Soviets were, by then, able to put into the air. For Stalingrad was only one part of the Eastern Front, over almost all of which the Soviet forces were advancing. In the north, Leningrad was relieved on 18th January; on the central front, a Soviet attack was launched which resulted in the capture of Rzhev and Vyazma by the end of winter, and the reoccupation of Voronezh even sooner. But it was in the south that the main Soviet onslaught was mounted. By-passing 6th Army in Stalingrad, the Red Army swept forward to the Donets, reaching Rostov, Voroshilovgrad and Kharkov by mid-February, while at the same time covering their northern flank by an advance to Kursk. In the Caucasus, too, the Germans were in retreat. Mozdak was recaptured at the beginning of January, and five weeks later the Germans held only a narrow bridgehead on the Kuban peninsula. The concentration of Luftwaffe strength in the south, and especially on the Don Front, indicates the intensity of the fighting there. In mid-October, the southern sector took fifty-three per cent of all combat aircraft in the East (1,040 out of 1,950, not including those under the command of Luftflotte 5 in the far north), whereas by mid-January this had risen to sixty-six per cent (1,140 out of 1,715). The highest concentration was then in the Don-Donets area, amounting to fifty-two per cent of the Luftwaffe's strength in the East. This was achieved only by surrendering air superiority in the north (where Luftflotte 1 had only 195 combat aircraft by mid-January), and by accepting a low level of activity on the central front, where the majority of Luftwaffenkommando Ost's 380 aircraft were suitable solely for close support and reconnaissance duties.

In the south, command was divided between Luftwaffenkommando Don, under Korten, and the much larger Luftflotte 4 under von Richthofen. At the beginning of 1943, Luftflotte 4 was composed of the following units from north to south: Fliegerdivision Donetz under Mahnke, Fliegerkorps VIII under Fiebig (primarily a transport formation, but with combat units attached, which, after the fall of Stalingrad, was moved to the south to support German troops on the Kuban bridgehead), Fliegerkorps IV under Pflugbeil, and Luftwaffengruppe Kaukasus under Dessloch (on 27th January renamed Luftwaffengruppe Kuban). In addition, the Royal Romanian Air Corps was employed between the Don and the Manych rivers. However, despite the 1,140 combat aircraft allocated to Korten and von Richthofen (900 to the latter), it proved quite impossible to secure air superiority and to support the ground forces. By 1943, the Red Air Force possessed no less than 5,000 front-line aircraft, of which two-thirds were in the south, machines which were better able than those of the Luftwaffe to operate in the cold climate. Even over the Don-Rostov area, the Germans were unable to secure complete air supremacy, their lack of aircraft being aggravated by poor flying conditions, low serviceability, and a loss of forward airfields for fighter units. The Luftwaffe had been caught unawares by the strength of the Soviet counter-offensive, and had not taken preparatory measures in time. For an appreciable period, all it could do was to extricate itself to avoid total defeat.

In his support of ground operations, von Richthofen was severely hampered. From the beginning, he had to make the decision to abandon certain areas altogether. The Eliste Steppes, for example, 200 miles wide, saw no German air activity except for a few reconnaissance machines, whose bombs were the only opposition given to the advancing enemy forces. The exposed northern flank of the Stalingrad salient was provided with only meagre air cover, and lack of support for the German troops favoured the rapid Soviet advance to, and beyond, Voronezh. The Caucasus, too, was largely without aircraft (by mid-January, only 240 combat machines were stationed there and in the Crimea), its probable loss being regarded as unimportant compared with the maintenance of the German front along the Donets, destruction of which would mean the loss of the southern armies and, possibly, lead to a retreat from the whole of Russia. However, elsewhere Luftflotte 4 was able to bring its influence to bear on the ground operations. Von Richthofen did all he could to produce maximum flexibility among his units, and was therefore able to switch their operations, whenever necessary, to almost any point within his area of responsibility. Indeed, owing to the lack of Army formations, the irregular pattern of the main lines of resistance, and the poor conditions of the roads and railways in the immense area of the southern sector, Luftflotte 4 was the only mobile reserve available to the Germans. On several occasions, a Soviet breakthrough was thwarted by the bombers and close-support aircraft of von Richthofen's command. On 20th January, for example, the Red Army assaulted the Lower Manych river line, with the intention of driving through to Rostov and Bataysk. Had they been successful, the 1st and 4th Panzer Armies would have been cut off in their withdrawal to the West, and another 'Stalingrad' would have occurred. It was only by the actions of Luftflotte 4 that the Manych line was not breached.

However, despite all efforts, the German front was continually pushed back. By the last week in February, the Red Army had taken Belgorod, fifty miles north of Kharkov, and, to the south, it was threatening the Dnepr crossings. Success here, and the Soviets might encircle Army Group Don. However, the danger was more theoretical than real; the Russian forces were in no condition to continue the advance against opposition. Their communications fully extended, and the mud from the early thaw playing havoc with their supply lines, they could proceed no further. The Germans took swift advantage of this, and on 19th February von Manstein launched a daring counter-stroke. By the first week in March, he had reached the Donets, and on the 15th Kharkov was retaken, but on the 19th, when Belgorod was occupied by the Germans for the second time, his offensive came to a halt in the slush of the spring thaw. Both sides exhausted, the front stabilised along a line from Taganrog on the Sea of Azov, up the Mius to the Donets, along to Belgorod, and to Orel. Stalingrad lay 500 miles to the East.

IX

The Crisis

While the German Air Force was engaged in undertaking one major campaign after another, with scarcely a respite between them, the Luftwaffe high command was involved in providing the field commands with the men and material necessary to achieve victory. The nature of this task was two-fold: first, to ensure that sufficient aircraft were produced, and crews trained, to replace losses at the front and to provide for future commitments; and, second, to forestall the enemy in the development of new weapons or the improvement of old. For the Luftwaffe Command this was a particularly difficult task: a war machine as complex as an air force, dependent on highly intricate technology and on complicated equipment that was time-consuming and costly to develop and produce, was far less capable than an army of recovering from serious setbacks or losses. Immediate provision for, say, the opening of a new front, or the replacement of an obsolete aeroplane, was impossible; only with careful planning could such eventualities be foreseen and catered for, involving as they would the preparation of adequate reserves of well-trained men and battle-worthy machines, and the continual development of new and efficient equipment. A mistake in any one of these areas might take at least two years to rectify, by which time the battle might well have been lost. Unfortunately for the Luftwaffe, in the production of aircraft, the training of men, and the development of new equipment, its high command was sadly deficient.

The losses of aircraft in the first two years of the war are difficult to quantify, but it seems certain that, from all causes, no less than 18,000 of the Luftwaffe's combat and transport machines were rendered incapable of further operation by the end of 1942. During that period, the Reich's aircraft factories produced over 31,000 military aircraft (not including trainers). However, because some aircraft types, such as the Do 17 and the He 111, were being phased out in favour of others (in this case the Ju 88 and Do 217), and new, improved, models of existing types were replacing older ones (for example, Bf 109 F and G superseded the D and E versions), this apparent excess of production over losses did not in fact exist. Indeed, the Luftwaffe had begun the war with 3,356 front-line combat aircraft, most of which it employed in the Polish campaign. After just over three years of war at the end of 1942, it possessed only 3,950 (after reaching a peak of 4,800 in mid-1942), at a time when it was committed to one major area of activity, the Eastern Front, and two subsidiary areas of growing importance – the Mediterranean and the West. In any of these theatres of war, the commitment of the Luftwaffe's entire operational strength would not have been too much for the task in hand; a proportion was quite insufficient.

There can be little doubt that it was Hitler who must bear the greatest responsibility for the dramatic over-extension of the Luftwaffe's resources that took place after 1940. The Air Force had been committed to a general European war three years earlier than its leaders had planned for, and far too soon for it to have developed sufficiently from its birth in 1933 to become an effective war machine. The consecutive campaigns in Poland, Norway and the West had been within its capabilities, as indeed, had the battle to achieve air supremacy over south-east England. However, when, on Hitler's orders, the Luftwaffe turned against the Soviet Union in 1941, with less strength than it had when it attacked France the year before, it was imperative that a decisive victory be gained before the close of the year. Already, the Air Force was embroiled in two other campaigns against Britain in both the West and the Mediterranean. With its limited resources, the Luftwaffe could not afford to get involved in another major commitment while the enemy remained active in its rear, especially since he was becoming ever more capable of unleashing a major onslaught against Germany's war industries, including those which produced its aeroplanes. But despite Göring's reluctance, Hitler insisted on launching the invasion of the East, cognisant though he was of the need for a quick victory. His gamble, however, did not pay off; operations against the Soviet Union were of a very different order of magnitude from those in which the German Armed Forces had been engaged hitherto. Their resources were insufficient to enable them to meet the challenge, and failure outside Moscow in the winter of 1941 was the result, a failure ensured (perhaps, even, directly brought about) by Hitler's decisions affecting the strategic employment of the Army during the campaign. From this time on, the Luftwaffe's incapacity to wage war effectively on three fronts simultaneously was obvious, an incapacity that prior planning, even had the eventuality been envisaged, would have been unable to preclude. The combined might of the British, American, and Soviet Air Forces was to prove insuperable. Thus, by overburdening the Luftwaffe (and, indeed, the other two armed services) with tasks quite beyond its capacity, Hitler ensured its ultimate downfall.

Against this background, the manufacture of aircraft in the first three years of the war must be viewed. That there was no complacency among the Luftwaffe's leadership is revealed by the changed nature of aircraft production during that period. In the pursuit of quick victory, the Luftwaffe abandoned the concept of a 'balanced' air force. A concentration of limited resources on the manufacture of aircraft capable of combat rather than on those used for other roles, such as training, was regarded as the best way of ensuring success; indeed, because the Luftwaffe had been committed to war before its planned development was complete, it was seen to be the only way.

Therefore, the ratio of the output of combat aircraft to that of trainers, transports, reconnaissance machines and such-like rose from 57:43 in 1939 (a ratio which, it was planned, would remain substantially unchanged until the expansion of the Luftwaffe was complete three years later), to 75:25 in 1942, to reach 88:12 in 1944. Training and transport, in particular, were relegated to secondary roles in an attempt to win the war with fire power in as short a time as possible. This, however, was a gamble (and, probably, a necessary one) which, in the event, was lost, with dire results. Failure in the Soviet Union was the stumbling block. By 1943, the consequences were well in evidence.

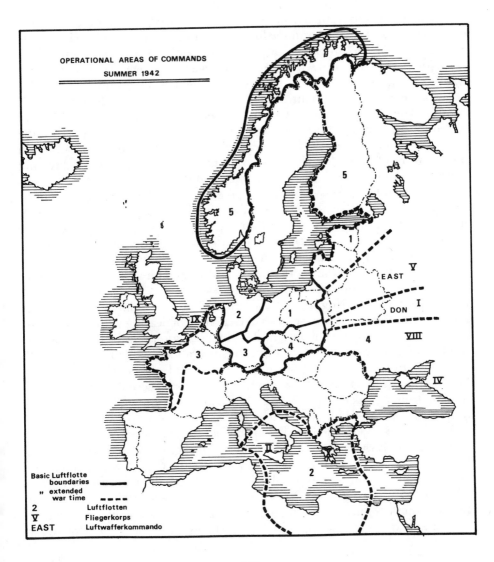

OPERATIONAL AREAS OF COMMANDS
SUMMER 1942

Basic Luftflotte
boundaries
„ extended
war time
2 Luftflotten
V Fliegerkorps
EAST Luftwafferkommando

However, the change in the composition of aircraft manufacture was but one aspect of the Luftwaffe's adaptation to the demands of war. The others were the quantity and quality of aircraft produced. In 1939, the output from Germany's aircraft factories was 8,295 military aircraft, of which 4,733 were front-line combat machines. In 1940, these totals increased to 10,826 and 7,103 respectively, in 1941 to 11,776 and 8,082, and in 1942 15,556 and 11,752. (These figures would be higher if conversion of older models and major repairs were taken into account, the total of 10,826 in 1940, for example, would be 11,376). Overall production in 1940 was over thirty per cent higher than in 1939, in 1941 nearly forty-two per cent, and in 1942 over eighty-two per cent, whereas in combat aircraft the ratios were even higher, fifty, seventy and 148 per cent respectively.

The increase in output was not spectacular; indeed, no attempt was made even to carry out the programme for the five-fold expansion of the Luftwaffe announced in 1938, an expansion which might have been out of touch with reality in peace-time, but which cannot be regarded as over-indulgent during war (at least, not with hindsight), especially when the occupation of large areas of Europe had brought untold economic potential under the Reich's control. The final plans of the Generalluftzeugmeisteramt in peace-time had called for a monthly output of 1,553 aircraft by the summer of 1941; in the event, it reached only 981. Little shift work was introduced, although mobilisation plans had envisaged two shifts of eight to ten hours a day, and workers continued with a forty-hour week and the observance of all holidays. The considerable excess capacity that existed in the factories remained substantially unused, and some of it was even diverted to the production of items such as landing craft and scaling ladders. However, the relatively low level of output compared with what was to come later (by July 1944, monthly production was over half that in all of 1939) was quite sufficient to keep pace with events, provided that Hitler did not overreach himself. The conquest of the West, for example, cost only the equivalent of six weeks' output from the aircraft factories. During the Battle of Britain, losses did out-run production, especially in fighters, but reserves were capable of dealing with the situation for as long as the operation lasted. By mid-1941, after relatively low losses in the Balkan campaign, the total front-line aircraft available to the Luftwaffe had risen to as many as 4,300, with reserves still at twenty-five per cent. During the campaign in Russia, monthly production actually fell, according to plan, from a peak of 1,174 in March to 895 in November, but, despite this, output managed to balance combat losses.

Thus far, so good. The flaw lay in the fact that no provision was made for failure in the East. A deepening commitment there (which, had it been the only one, the Luftwaffe might well have been able to deal with adequately) ensured that no solution was possible in either the Mediterranean or the West, where enemy strength was daily increasing. A vicious circle was begun; because no decision was forthcoming, the Luftwaffe's involvement became deeper as the enemy's strength grew. Shortages and crises in one theatre, or even one sector, had their repercussions on the others, and, within a short time, losses were out-running production and rates of serviceability were dropping to dangerously low levels. By the end of 1942, the Luftwaffe, which had begun the war with a surplus on established unit strength of three per cent, was short on establishment of forty-three per cent of its combat aircraft. While there had been an increase in total combat strength of twenty-four per cent, from 2,761 bombers, dive-bombers, ground-attack aircraft and fighters on 1st September 1939 to 3,440 on 30th December 1942, this was accompanied by a considerable decrease in serviceability, from seventy-five per cent to fifty-nine per cent. As a result, the number of operational combat aircraft available to the Luftwaffe dropped from 2,070 to 2,030, at a time when its commitments had undergone a considerable extension. The loss of the initiative was the result, and, with that, the Luftwaffe was brought to face defeat.

By the end of 1942, the Luftwaffe had failed not only to produce sufficient aircraft to meet its requirements, but also to re-equip the majority of its hard-pressed units with models significantly better than those with which they had entered the war. Changes in the relative numbers of the various types of aircraft had certainly taken place, but few obsolete machines had disappeared, as had been planned. The one exception among the main combat aircraft was the Do 17, which had been phased out as a bomber although it was still retained, in diminishing numbers, for long-range reconnaissance. Only three new models had been introduced in appreciable numbers, the Ju 88, FW 189, and FW 190. Of these, the Ju 88 had been on the verge of entering service when war began, while the short-range reconnaissance FW 189 was in prototype as early as 1937. Of the He 177 and Me 210, on which the Luftwaffe's equipment plans depended, only a handful of unserviceable machines were to be seen in operational units, despite the fact that it had been intended to build 8,000 and 4,500 respectively by March 1943.

The successor to the medium bombers, 'Bomber B', was nowhere to be seen, although in anticipation of its introduction the He 111 had been reduced in numbers from 780 on 1st September 1939 to 310 on 31st December 1942, while the total of Ju 88 bombers had reached 520 machines (it was also employed in long-range reconnaissance units). The only new aircraft in the bomber force was the Do 217, of which there were 190 in service. But their performance was in some respects unsatisfactory, and they equipped only one Geschwader and several Staffeln. The number of Ju 87s had declined, from 335 to 270, while the numbers of Bf 110s had risen from 195 to 365. The only appreciable change lay in single-engined fighters; while the Bf 109 remained the dominant type (660 in all), the new FW 190 had been introduced in sizable numbers, to reach 580 by 31st December 1942.

To compensate for the non-appearance of the He 177, the Me 210, and the 'Bomber B', it had proved necessary to resort to certain expedients. The production of He 111s, originally intended to be phased out in 1940, was extended to 1942, when it was expected that it would be ended, and production of the Ju 88 decreased, in order to make way for their successors. In the event, however, production of the Heinkel aircraft was increased despite its rapidly approaching obsolescence, and continued until the autumn of 1944. The machine itself was progressively improved, so that by the end of 1942 the H-16 version was capable of a radius of action of 640 miles with its maximum bomb-load of 5,500 lb, and a top speed of 252 mph at 19,685 ft. This marked a significant improvement on the P-2 and H-1 versions of the He 111 which entered the war. Similarly, with the Ju 88, whose A-4 variant, free from most of the teething troubles that had made the A-1 so unpopular with its crews, possessed a normal radius of action of 556 miles with a bomb-load of 4,400 lb and a top speed of 292 mph at 17,390 ft. Defensive armament on both machines, too, was markedly superior. However, neither proved any substitute for a serviceable bomber with the specifications required of 'Bomber B' or, more important, of the He 177, with its radius of 1,200 miles with 2,000 lb of bombs (less with its maximum of 6,000 lb) and a top speed of 303 mph at 19,030 ft. Dietrich Peltz, General of Bombers, was of the opinion that it had been a mistake to chose an aircraft like the Ju 88, with its compromise between range, bomb-load and dive-bombing capability, while Colonel Edgar Petersen, commander of the Luftwaffe's experimental station at Rechlin, was forthright in his hope that 'the days of the medium bomber are numbered'.[1] In addition, the inadequacies of the FW 200, principally its high rate of unserviceability, made the appearance of the He 177 over the oceans as a long-range reconnaissance bomber in sufficient numbers a matter of some importance to those concerned with the conduct of maritime war.

As with the bomber, so with the dive-bomber, ground-attack, and heavy fighter aircraft, the Ju 87 and Bf 110. The former some believed to have been obsolete in 1939, while the latter had revealed its glaring inadequacies as a day-fighter as early as the summer of 1940. Both types were in the process of being phased out of production in 1941 in favour of the Me 210; in November of that year, only two Ju 87s were delivered, and by the end of December output of the Bf 110 had ceased completely. However, the non-appearance of the Me 210 caused both to be resurrected in early 1942, and, by the end of the year, 917 Ju 87s and 577 Bf 110s (as both a heavy and night fighter and a ground-attack aircraft) had been accepted by the Luftwaffe. Production of the Ju 87 was to continue until September 1944, and of the Bf 110 until March 1945. The specifications of the two updated versions, both with improved armament, were as follows: the Ju 87D-1 was capable of a top speed of 255 mph at 13,500 ft with a bomb load of 2,205 lb (its maximum was 4,000 lb), while the Bf 110 F-2 had a maximum speed of 352 mph at 17,700 ft and a radius of action of 370 miles. In addition, the long obsolete Hs 123 was still in action, despite the fact that production had ended in 1938, and was not to be finally discontinued in front-line service with the Schlachtgruppen until mid-1944. Even small numbers of the old He 45 reconnaissance aircraft, production of which had ended in 1936, were being used in night-attack. A variant of the Ju 88, the C-6, had been introduced into service during 1941 as a heavy fighter and 'destroyer'. The heaviest fighter of the war, it had a top speed of 343 mph at 15,600 ft, a radius of action of 615 miles, and better armament than its partner, the Bf 110. Other stop-gaps were the specially equipped older versions of the Bf 109 and the new FW 190 which were used as Jabos or ground-attack aircraft, the latter being found to be particularly effective.

The only new, purpose-built aeroplane used in close support was the Hs 129 ground-attack aircraft. Well armed, its performance was disappointing as its airframe was not strong enough to be fitted with any but relatively low-powered engines. As a result, the maximum speed of the aircraft, without bombs, was only 253 mph, and its radius of action just 174 miles. Serviceability of the machine was low, too, owing to the vulnerability of the engines to dust, and their propensity to catch fire. For these reasons, by the end of 1942 the Hs 129 only equipped only one Gruppe. Clearly, neither the Ju 87, nor the Bf 110, the Ju 88, the FW 190, the Bf 109, or the Hs 129 matched up to the theoretical specifications of their intended successor, the Me 210: a maximum speed of 350 mph at 17,820 ft, a maximum radius of action of 565 miles, and a maximum bomb load of 2,200 lb, as well as excellent manoeuvrability. The Me 210 also possessed significantly better armament than all but the Ju 88 and the Hs 129.

The night fighter arm in particular found itself in trouble. Its reliance on the Bf 110 was almost total, and severe shortages in front-line strength were experienced when production was phased down. A compensatory increase in the output of the Ju 88 heavy fighter was not undertaken, as it was considered that it was too expensive for controlled night fighting, which did not call for an aircraft with a rapid rate of climb, high speed or long range. No purpose-built night fighter was available, and none designed. Kammhuber called for a twin-engined aircraft, with two seats, good visibility and cannon armament positioned so that no dazzle would result from firing. The He 219, which Heinkel had originally designed in 1940 as a heavy-fighter/reconnaissance aircraft, might have been suitable, but this project was given low priority by the Generalluftzeugmeister, who was anxious that the number of specialised aircraft types should be strictly limited in the interests of mass production. He ordered that it was not to enter service before early 1945. As a stop-gap, the Do 217 J-1 arrived in March 1942, but any high expectation of its performance was soon dashed, the aircraft exhibiting poor manoeuvrability, an insufficient reserve of power, and problems in take-off and landing. The Do 217 N, which entered service in early 1943, was little better, and came into being simply because the bomber force could absorb only a limited number of Do 217 bombers. Reliance was, in the end, placed on the updated versions of the Bf 110, the F-4, and the Ju 88, the C-6, which began to appear in the summer 1942. However, they were by no means the ideal solution, the only significant modifications for their night fighter role being exhaust flame dampeners and more space for extra radio and radar equipment. All hope for the future was placed on the special night fighter versions of the Bf 110 and Ju 88 that were being planned in early 1943 to enter service in 1944.

The only success enjoyed by the Luftwaffe in significantly improving the quality of its aircraft came in its day-fighter arm. From the spring of 1941 onwards, the Bf 109 E had been progressively replaced by the F version, an unsatisfactory machine. Within a year however, a further, improved, model of the Bf 109 was produced, the G, a machine significantly better than any possessed by Germany's opponents. The Bf 109 G-2 was capable of a top speed of 398 mph at 20,670 ft (or 406 mph for a very short period of time), and a radius of 170 miles (264 miles with a drop tank attached). Some pilots felt that, in this version, the qualities of manoeuvre and good handling suffered in pursuit of higher speed, but this could not be said of the new fighter, the FW 190, that by the end of July 1941 had begun to equip front-line units in accordance with a decision taken in early 1940. The A-3 version was capable of a maximum speed of 382 mph at 19,685 ft (and, for one minute only, with override boost, 418 mph at 21,000 ft), and possessed a radius of action of 248 miles. In speed and handling characteristics it was superior to the Spitfire V then in service, and closely comparable with the new Spitfire IX which began to appear in 1943. More manoeuvrable than both, the FW 190 failed only to match the tighter turning circle of the British machine.

It was decided to keep both the Bf 109 and the FW 190 in production together, for, although Focke-Wulf's machine was sturdier, more manoeuvrable, and better armed, its performance deteriorated rapidly above 20,000 ft, at altitudes where the enemy heavy bombers were operating. Fighter combat here was dangerous for the FW 190s; reliance had to be placed on the Bf 109. However, as a team the two machines were formidable. But even their effectiveness was reduced by the delayed appearance of the powerful armament which had been displayed to Hitler at Rechlin as early as the summer of 1939: the 30 mm MK 108 cannon, which fired novel HE 'mine shells' that could destroy a bomber with one round (an average of three were usually required for a B-17). Development had been slow, and it was not until 1943 that they were used to arm the Bf 109s and FW 190s. Till then, an average of twenty hits from a 20 mm cannon was required to bring down one four-engined bomber, a difficult enough process since the average Luftwaffe pilot, who hit his target with just two per cent of the rounds fired, would have to shoot for twenty-three seconds, during which he would be on the receiving end of heavy defensive fire. The introduction of the MK 108 was none too soon.

To sum up, by the beginning of the fourth year of the war, eighty per cent of the Luftwaffe's front-line aircraft consisted of six main types: the Ju 88, He 111, Ju 87, Bf 110, Bf 109, and FW 190. Of these, the He 111, Ju 87 and Bf 110, amounting to a quarter of the Luftwaffe's combat strength, were obsolete, and could be used to effect only on the Russian front where the enemy's air defences were less formidable. Only the Luftwaffe's day fighters had been maintained at a level comparable with the developments of their enemies, and even these were soon to be outclassed; the rest of their aircraft, nearly seventy per cent of the total, if not obsolete themselves, were awaiting successors that failed to materialise.

Just why the Luftwaffe had reached such a dismal situation in both the quantity and quality of its aircraft is difficult to ascertain. Certainly, the optimism of the first year of the war, understandable but, in the event, misplaced, had some influence. An almost effortless victory in Poland had been followed by spectacular successes in Scandinavia and the West, successes which must rank high in the annals of military endeavour. After the defeat of France in June 1940, an exultant Udet summed up the feelings of many within the RLM when he declared to his staff: 'The war is over! All our plans can be tossed into the waste-basket. We don't need them any longer!'[2] How far Udet and his officials were responsible for the sad state of affairs into which the Luftwaffe's aircraft had been reduced, is difficult to assess. A top-level legal investigation undertaken later during the war arrived at the conclusion that the individuals involved would be able to exonerate themselves since there was no incontrovertible evidence of inefficiency. Moreover, as the Air Force's Judge-Advocate pointed out to Göring, none of the Luftwaffe's leaders could be absolved from responsibility. Continuing the lamentable state of affairs that existed before the war, Jeschonnek had shown a distinct lack of interest in air armament, even though he had a responsibility for it, while Göring had displayed even less. The General Staff, in the Judge-Advocate's opinion, had failed to control tactical-technical development and requirements, and thereby co-ordinate the activities of the Generalluftzeugmeisteramt. Thus: 'Neither the General Staff nor the Technical Office Chief had, since 1939, set specific requirements for performance characteristics of aircraft, but had contented themselves with generalities.'[3]

Nor did Milch, Udet's nominal superior, exercise any significant control over the business of the Generalluftzeugmeisteramt. The relationship, both personal and organisational, already tenuous before the war, had been further weakened after 1939, when Udet's relations with Göring took a turn for the better. The closer the Generalluftzeugmeister drew to the Commander-in-Chief, the less the Secretary of State could interfere. Ploch, Udet's Chief of Staff, remembered: 'While Milch was away in Norway. . . . Udet got along splendidly with Göring. When Milch got back, he saw immediately that his position of influence had been usurped. He realized right away that Udet had dropped him. This was quite possibly true, for our own inclinations (mine, Tschersich's, Lucht's, and Reidenbach's) tended in this direction. We felt that Milch's habit of interfering everywhere was not beneficial and we were against his personal tendencies and his efforts to gain power'.[4] This was the impression gained by Kesselring, who wrote: 'The relationship between the engineers and Milch was antipodal. Udet was in their hands, and it was chiefly Lucht who was responsible for driving Udet into a position of isolation'.[5]

Such was the position of the Generalluftzeugmeisteramt in the early years of the war, one of isolation, self-sought as much as imposed. No-one in the Luftwaffe exercised any overall supervision to ensure that aircraft procurement coincided with the Luftwaffe's strategic needs. Matters were not helped by the loss of Colonel Max von Pohle over Britain in October 1939, shortly before he was to return to the General Staff to advise Jeschonnek on tactical-technical requirements for aircraft. After his capture, no one man, or agency, made any effort to co-ordinate operational needs with production and development. Nor is there any evidence to suggest that, even after the great losses inflicted in the Battle of Britain, anyone outside the Generalluftzeug-meisteramt drew the attention of Udet to the need to increase aircraft production in preparation for the campaign in the East.

Apart from there being no clear realisation that a significant increase in output was required, the lack of co-ordination resulted in a continual dislocation of the Luftwaffe's procurement programme. No less than sixteen thorough revisions were undertaken between September 1939 and November 1941, an average of one every six weeks. Not a single programme was carried through as planned, and the frequent changes served only to confuse the industry and hinder output. According to the engineer general, Walter Hertel, the reasons for the frequent alterations lay in the fundamental changes in the conduct of operations; changes in the targets of military operations, affecting the employment of aircraft and equipment; the failure of the General Staff to inform the technical agencies well in advance of the operations that were planned, thus disrupting the production process; the inadequate allocation of materials necessary for production both before and during the war; and, finally, the drafting of skilled workers from industry to serve in the Armed Forces. All this serves to emphasise the distinct division that existed between the operational employment of the Luftwaffe and that aspect of an air force on which that operational employment so greatly depended: aircraft development and production. For this, the blame must go not only to Udet but to Milch, Jeschonnek, and, above all, Göring.

By default, then, almost all the responsibility for the Luftwaffe's aircraft fell on Udet's shoulders, which were particularly ill-suited to bear it. He had, moreover, an exceedingly difficult task to perform. In such a complex activity as the production programme of an air force, in which plans exist not in isolation but within an environment as volatile as a nation at war, and subject to immense economic and political pressures, Udet was far from being his own master. He had, perforce, to accept the consequences that arose from the political leadership's organisation of the economy, and its allocation of resources. The most remarkable feature of their decisions was the low priority given to the output of armaments for all three services in the first three years of the war, an output determined not so much by economic potential (which, with the occupation of much of Europe, considerably increased, especially in the availability of raw materials), as by political judgement – ultimately, that of one man, Hitler. For various reasons, foremost amongst which was the leadership's desire not to become unpopular with the German people, the output of consumer goods did not fall during the first few years of the war; indeed, in some sectors it actually rose. The allocation of steel to the civil sector increased from 732,000 metric tons in the fourth quarter of 1939 to 908,000 tons a year later, and, as a percentage of the whole, dropped only from 41.5 per cent to 40.8 per cent. Mobilisation for total war was, therefore, not a feature of Germany in the early war years as it was in Britain or the Soviet Union.

Moreover, the Luftwaffe's leaders had to continue the somewhat unseemly scramble for the material resources allocated to the Armed Forces as a whole. To a similar extent as the Air Force, both the Army and Navy were unprepared for the major war into which they were plunged by Hitler in 1939, and they clamoured with as much justification as the Luftwaffe for as large a portion of the economic resources as they could get. Had the Army been able fully to mechanise its forces instead of being reliant upon half a million horses, or had the Navy built sufficient U-boats, how different might have been the outcome of the war? Thus, while the Army claimed 446,000 tons of finished steel a month in the first quarter of 1940, and was allocated just 342,000 and the Navy requested 195,000 and received 140,000, the Luftwaffe, after calling for 337,000 tons, was left with just 195,000.

On the few occasions in the early war years when Hitler laid down definite priorities in the armament programme, the Luftwaffe did not necessarily benefit. On 13th July 1940, at a time when he regarded the subjection of Britain as the Reich's main war aim, the Führer ordered that substantial war production be diverted from the Army to the Navy and Air Force. Output of the Ju 88, in particular, was to be increased, and the level of aircraft production in general raised so that it required an extra 110,000 men for work in the factories. However, a few weeks later, Hitler's attention turned towards the East, and, on 28th September, he ordered that production should concentrate on the Army in preparation for a major land campaign. Despite the fact that the Führer had not altered the programme targets set in July, aircraft were made fifth in order of the Reich's priorities, and a sharp fall in the production of aeroplanes was the inevitable result. The material resources allocated to the war were not sufficient to expand the Army, build more tanks, guns and vehicles, and at the same time continue with the plans for increasing the size of the Luftwaffe.

Matters were made worse for Udet by the alienation of the Luftwaffe high command from the command system of the German Armed Forces as a whole. Göring would have nothing to do with a unified approach to the prosecution of the war as represented by the High Command of the Armed Forces (OKW), should his authority over the Luftwaffe thereby be weakened. No-one but he, or his Führer, was to have command over a single man in the Air Force. His attitude was clearly revealed at the Nuremberg war trials:

> ... the Commanders in Chief of the three Armed Forces branches

were directly subordinate and responsible to the Führer. They were in no way whatsoever . . . sub-ordinate to the Armed Forces High Command. . . . For example, an order or directive from the Armed Forces High Command to me as Commander in Chief, Luftwaffe, would be inconceivable unless it began with the words 'The Führer has ordered . . . ' or 'In the name of the Führer you are informed that . . .' To put it drastically, I once told General Keitel that the only orders I considered binding were those from the Führer. I explained that the only original orders I ever saw were those bearing the signature Adolf Hitler. All those beginning with 'At the Führer's orders . . .' or 'In the name of the Führer . . .' went to my General Staff Chief, and the important points were then summarized for me at the staff conferences. Under these circumstances . . . and this is what I meant by putting it drastically. . . I told Keitel that it was completely irrelevant as far as I was concerned whether the signature 'By order of the Führer, Keitel, Generaloberst' or 'By order of the Führer, Meier, Private First Class.' I told Keitel that if he was considering sending me direct orders signed by himself, he might just as well save himself the time and paper, because I wouldn't consider them binding anyway. . . . I was Commander-in-Chief and as such responsible only to the Führer.[6]

While Göring's attitude had little effect on the harmonious and co-operative relations that existed between the Luftwaffe's General Staff and those of the Army and the Navy during the war, it did have the effect of alienating the OKW. This served as the executive arm in Hitler's general approach to the war, and, among other things, was responsible for the allocation of priorities in armaments between the three services. Its importance grew as Hitler concentrated more military power within his own hands. Although the dictator would ignore the advice of his OKW chiefs, Keitel and Jodl, as much as he would that of anybody else, they were nevertheless responsible for carrying out many of his decisions, which, in the complex business of conducting a war, left them with considerable influence. This, Göring did not recognise. His favoured position in the Reich before the war did not continue long after the Air Force's failure in the Battle of Britain, and by his opposition to the plan to invade the Soviet Union. By 1942, when the Luftwaffe was about to face its hardest years, the Reichsmarschall's influence with his Führer was negligible. But with his personal dominance over, Göring still failed to understand the paramount importance of co-operation with Hitler's command staff. This is exemplified by the fact that he allowed very few Air Force officers to be employed in OKW: in March 1942, for example, the Army outnumbered them by five to one; they possessed no officer above the rank of colonel, whereas the other two services had nine generals between them; and the Luftwaffe representative on the important Operations Staff held only the rank of major.

To neglect or abuse the OKW, as Göring did, had serious consequences. General Koller, the last Chief of the Luftwaffe General Staff, recalled a meeting with Keitel and others late in the war:

> In June 1944, in order to counter the many recent attacks on Luftwaffe policy, I took advantage of a small conference at the Obersalzberg to point out the weakness of Luftwaffe armament resources, and voiced my feelings that the Armed Forces High Command, which ought to have supported the Luftwaffe armament programme in the interests of the Armed Forces and the nation as a whole, had limited itself to negative criticism. I stated frankly that our top military leaders had simply neglected their duty in this connection. And with this I had stumbled into a wasp's nest! They refused to consider my arguments and tried to persuade me that Göring would not have countenanced any participation by the Armed Forces High Command in the affairs of the Luftwaffe, that he would have termed it interference and forbidden it. There can be no doubt of the inaccuracy of this contention. To be sure, Göring was not a man to countenance interference, but he would certainly have welcomed constructive support and assistance from the Armed Forces High Command in improving the Luftwaffe's armament situation.[7]

It was the consequences of this alienation which, by 1944, were to cause Milch, by no means a man to yield responsibility voluntarily, to bring about the end of the Luftwaffe's independent procurement policy, for so long insisted upon by Göring, in the hope that, thereby, more resources would be allocated to aircraft production.

Over such matters, Udet had no control whatsoever, and there can be no doubt that they significantly affected the output of aircraft. However, over the introduction of new aircraft types, he had sole responsibility, and in this area his failings, and those of his Department, are clearly evident. The bringing into service of aircraft is a finely balanced process between service requirements, industrial capacity, and technological potential. A failure, or change of goal, in any one of these would have repercussions on the other two. Unfortunately for Udet, the results of mistakes made in the selection of aircraft replacements in 1938 (at a time when the operational requirement for dive-bombing did not match up to the technological capabilities of the aircraft manufacturers) became obvious in 1940 and 1941. Because of the pre-war decision to base the Luftwaffe's offensive capability in the early 1940s on four main combat types, the Bf 109, Ju 88, Me 210 and He 177, to the extent that they would have composed some seventy per cent of the Luftwaffe's front-line strength, the whole development programme was particularly susceptible to delays or changes affecting any one of these aircraft. In the event, two of them, the Me 210 and He 177, were total failures, and thus had a considerable effect on the Luftwaffe's capacity to wage war.

By mid-1940, there is no doubt that Udet was worried by the situation of the Reich's aircraft industry, not through any fear that it was incapable of producing the numbers of aircraft required, but that it would not produce the right types. As early as March, he had spoken in desperate terms to Heinkel: 'I hope there won't be any trouble with the He 177. The Ju 88 has caused enough difficulty for my taste. The He 177 has got to get into operation. We don't have any other large bomber that we can use against England. The He 177 has got to fly! . . . It must!'[8] The easing of his conscience which the victory in France in May and June gave him, was only temporary, and foreboding descended upon him with greater force in September and October, with the failure of the air attack on Britain. In June, he had delayed planned production of the He 177 by three months at the request of Koppenberg, who wanted the resources saved thereby to be allocated to his Ju 88 programme. By October, when the strategic outlook for the Luftwaffe had altered dramatically, and a long-term bombing offensive against Britain was likely, Udet suddenly decided to rush the new bomber into production, occasioning considerable reorganisation in the aircraft factories concerned. Heinkel remembered:

> . . . production had to be stopped until the plants had had time to retool for the large aircraft. All this was bound to take months. . . . The long-range, heavily-armed big bomber seemed to be the only hope. Yet, it was precisely in this respect that catastrophe struck. Now produced for the first time in quantity and subject to thorough testing, the He 177 with its parallel-coupled engines did not measure up to the military requirements for which it had been designed. Many of them went down in flames when their engines caught fire, or crashed when their wings cracked for apparently inexplicable reasons. Thus, as suddenly as it had been released for production, the He 177 had to be withdrawn once more. Time had been wasted, comprehensive preparations had been made in vain, and precious raw materials had been consumed to no avail.[9]

Udet's concern over the He 177, originally scheduled to see service in mid-1940, was equalled, if not surpassed, by his dissatisfaction over the delay in the appearance of the Me 210, destined to reach front-line units in the spring of 1941. On 28th June 1941, when the much-needed successor to the Bf 110 and Ju 87 had failed to arrive, he wrote to Messerschmitt in terms which reveal to what extent the development of new aircraft was outside his control:

> As highly as I esteem the performance of your creations, which are making a decisive contribution to our operations at the front, I feel it imperative to point out to you with the greatest emphasis that you are, in my opinion, moving in the wrong direction. Military aircraft, especially in time of war, must be designed on the basis of tried and true ideas; we cannot afford the luxury of making subsequent, time-consuming alterations. Proper design would also make the coordi-

nation between development and series production more harmonious. In this connection, may I remind you of the necessary strengthening of the wings on the Bf 109 and the Me 210, and the delay in finding a solution to the tail assembly defect in the Bf 110. Not only in my capacity as Chief of Supply and Procurement, with responsibility for ensuring that production-deadlines on new models are met and that their performance meets the standards set for them, but precisely in my capacity as your friend, I consider it my duty to inform you clearly that the path you are following is dangerous and capable of getting us all into serious difficulties.[10]

A month later, Udet composed, but did not send, another letter to Messerschmitt:

This month once again we have received no Me 210s for battle tests, so that the employment of the model has to be postponed for another month. I also have the impression that since the first prototype was built you have made far too many changes. The prototype and the proposed machines in the series are so different that the results of testing are of no use for the practical question of behaviour in action. One thing, dear Messerschmitt, must be made quite clear between us, and that is that there must be no more losses of machines in normal ground landings as the result of a faulty undercarriage; this can hardly be described as a technical novelty in aircraft construction. All these unnecessary scandals and this waste of time, call for higher standards in the testing of your new aircraft, and I shall report in that sense to my Department.[11]

Udet was also extremely worried by the new radial, air-cooled, engine, the BMW 801, which was to power the FW 190 and Do 217. Production figures were only one third of the agreed delivery schedule. Of this, Udet said 'This breakdown in air armament at the decisive point in the war is catastrophic and indefensible. It is particularly painful for me, inasmuch as I was the one who spoke up most warmly for the air-cooled engine and who ordered the development of the twin-row radial engine in the face of nearly unanimous opposition'.[12] Further delay in production schedules was the inevitable result.

Against this background, the manufacture of the Luftwaffe's aircraft must be viewed. Production in 1940 had increased by thirty per cent over its level in 1939, a not unhealthy rise carried out with very little strain on the industry. This, had it been continued as Udet hoped, would have brought production in 1943 to 23,700 aircraft, some two thousand more than actually was the case. However, the modest but heartening expansion of the first full year did not continue in 1941, when the increase was less than nine per cent. Indeed, there was an actual decrease in output after March, 279 fewer aircraft being produced in November than eight months previously. Not until March the following year was output back to its former highest level. Indeed, it was reckoned that, through changes in production schedules alone, some twenty per cent of output was lost in 1941. Had there been no resumption of the Luftwaffe's priority in armaments production in June, the final output for aircraft in 1941 might well have been lower than in 1940. Moreover, not a single battle-worthy Me 210 or He 177 was near to entering service.

Despite the disintegration of the RLM and the indolence of Göring, which, by 1941 was greater than ever before, the Luftwaffe's leadership could not remain unmoved when faced with a drop in production and the non-appearance of long-awaited aircraft. In February 1941, Milch was heard to exclaim 'Everything turns to dust in Udet's hands',[13] and in April Jeschonnek pointed to discrepancies in the figures for aircraft production. The following month, when Milch was alone in the RLM during one of Göring's prolonged absences, he told Udet to improve upon his performance. He even tried to get him to reorganise his rambling Department, but with no success. Not long afterwards, Göring also strongly criticised the Generalluftzeugmeister. Udet was beginning to feel the strain, and vented his feelings to Heinkel: 'They're all against me! The "Big Man" has just gone on leave and left me at Milch's mercy. Milch deputises for him at the Führer's Headquarters, and will see that every error I have ever made is served up for the Führer's edification!'[14]

Dissatisfaction with Udet and his Department was widespread when Hitler, on 20th June, anticipating the success of the forthcoming invasion of the Soviet Union, ordered that priority in armaments be switched from the Army back to the Luftwaffe in preparation for the air war against Britain. That same day, Göring gave orders for the quadrupling of the Air Force's front-line strength within the shortest possible time. However, he realised that Udet was not the man to undertake that responsibility, and, instead, gave the commission to Milch, thereby bringing the State Secretary back to the very centre of the Luftwaffe: the business of its procurement and supply. It was a strange decision, one worthy of a man like Göring whose weakness when dealing with subordinates was notable. Clearly not trusting Udet to undertake the tasks given him, Göring could not bring himself to take the logical step and remove his old war-time comrade to a new post, perhaps even something more to Udet's taste. Thus, although Milch was to have effective responsibility for aircraft production, Udet still remained at his post. He continued to run his Department, and his signature was required for any production changes decided upon by Milch in order for them to become valid.

However, the Secretary of State was given advantages incomparably greater than those of the Generalluftzeugmeister. The day after his appointment, Göring allowed him full plenipotentiary powers to reorganise the aircraft industry in any way he thought necessary to gain the quadrupling of production. Milch was empowered to close or requisition factories, to erect temporary buildings irrespective of regulations, to seize and distribute equipment, to draft workers, to acquire raw materials, to remove key personnel from office, or transfer them, regardless of contracts, to break agreements, create companies, abolish inadequate plants, and even to force payment. The final paragraph of the order read: 'Any such decisions made or orders issued by my representative [Milch], are to be given precedence over all other official orders and decisions insofar as the latter may be deemed to stand in the way of the earliest possible realization of an increase in industrial capacity'.[15]

Armed with such powers, the like of which Udet had never possessed, and with complete authority over the aircraft industry, Milch set to work with his customary vigour. Given the potential that existed within the industry, and the fact that the Luftwaffe once again had top-priority in the allocation of raw materials, it was impossible that Milch's endeavours would not meet with greater success than Udet's had done. On 23rd June, he ordered the erection of three huge aircraft factories, which were completed in eight months. On the 24th, he began a reorganisation of the industry, with the object of encouraging factories to work more on their own initiative as well as in conjunction with the needs of other plants producing the same type of aircraft. He also began to rationalise production methods and to increase efficiency by merging the smaller factories into a few large complexes. On the 26th, he announced his aims to the major industrialists, and urged their cooperation. The Reich's aircraft production was to be doubled by the late spring of 1942, the first target in a programme aimed at a four-fold expansion, which he later called the 'Göring Programme'.

However, even Milch, with all the advantages at his disposal, could not fly in the face of the realities with which Udet had struggled for so long. Production did increase, so that by May 1942 it had reached 1,315 aircraft a month, but this was not the quadrupling that had been called for in June 1941 which would have taken output to over 4,000 machines. The old difficulties still pertained: a lack of material resources and problems in production schedules mainly stemming from the non-appearance of new aircraft. Despite strict savings in aluminium and copper (the introduction of better machining techniques, for example, saved no less than 1,500 lb of aluminium on one aero-engine alone), it was evident even as early as July that the quadrupling of the Air Force was impossible under the existing economic regime. Indeed, rather than an increase in output, there was an actual decrease. On orders from Milch, a new production plan, No 17a, was drawn up by Udet's Department, with a target for doubling front-line strength, beginning in the summer of 1942. Production continued to fall in the latter half of 1941, and by November it was nearly twenty-four per cent lower than it had been in March. The situation was further exacerbated by the increasing requirements of the Army, whose battles on the Eastern Front were costly in both men and equipment. Manpower could not be demobilised to work in the aircraft factories, as had been planned, and new tanks, guns and equipment in general made further demands on the limited resources of raw materials.

Milch called for the adoption of total war measures before it was too late, but his warnings went unheeded. The OKW Office for the War Economy held similar views, and was of the opinion that the new priorities announced by Hitler in the summer of 1941 (his decision of 20th June was reaffirmed by Decrees on 10th July and 11th September), were only possible if all 'the mobilisable strength in the Greater German area is mobilised as quickly and as fully as possible'.[16] However, as the Chief of OKW, Field Marshal Keitel, made clear, this would not take place. On 16th August, he defined the principles on which the Reich's war economy would be based: the capacity to produce armaments would not be increased; there would be no greater utilisation of raw materials; and the labour strength of the armaments industry would not be increased. A quick victory in the East was still foreseen.

Faced with such a hindrance to expansion beyond his control, it is doubtful whether Milch managed the overall production of aircraft significantly better than Udet had done. However, in one area he proved of immense value, and averted a situation that might well have resulted in a severe shortage of bombers in 1942. Udet had planned to run down the production of all existing bomber types other than the Do 217 (which had entered service in late 1940) in favour of their successors, 'Bomber B' and the He 177. Of the problems attending the appearance of the latter, the Generalluftzeugmeisteramt was apprised, but of 'Bomber B' there was nothing but vagueness. Although it was destined to enter service in late 1942, no decision had been taken as to which of the two contenders, the Ju 288 or FW 191, it would be. Since the development of the FW 191 was a year behind its Junkers counterpart, it was not difficult for Milch to decide. Unfortunately, however, the engines which were to propel the Ju 288 not only lacked sufficient power but were also too unreliable to be used. Despite assurances from Koppenberg, Milch realised that the aircraft would not be ready by 1944; in the event, it was never to be serviceable. The Generalluftzeugmeisteramt, however, had programmed for an output of 300 a month by the end of 1942, and planned to phase out the He 111 and Ju 88 altogether and to produce only 100 Do 217s a month. Milch feared that the non-appearance of the Ju 288 would cause a significant decrease in bomber production before the mistake was recognised (as was then taking place with the Ju 87s and Bf 110s in respect of the Me 210). He therefore proposed to Göring that it be cancelled altogether. On 1st November, the order for production of the Ju 288 was rescinded and, pending the entry of the He 177 into service the next year, the manufacture of the bombers already in operation continued.

While Milch scrutinised the production plans, he also turned his attention to the organisation of the office that produced them, the Generalluftzeug-meisteramt. It was a veritable empire, composed of twenty-six departmental heads and four thousand staff. Göring became almost paranoid about it. In 1943 he stated: 'There's still many a scoundrel there. . . . You'll find people there who have been thrown out on their ears three times already, and they come to light in some other department again, only bigger and stronger than ever'.[17] Milch, too, remembered: 'What they dished up there was just rubbish. Nobody understood it, least of all the people who had prepared the figures'.[18] Göring's verdict was straight forward: 'Never have I been so deceived, so bamboozled and so cheated as by that office. It has no equal in history'.[19] He did not add, however, that it was he who had allowed such a situation to come about.

Milch was not a man to allow such an unwieldy organisation that had come under his close purview to continue. However, he could enforce nothing; it all had to be done with Udet's consent, or by Göring's decree. At one point, Udet reluctantly gave his approval to the State Secretary's proposal to reduce the departmental heads to four, but later withdrew it. Göring, however, was more easily persuaded, and, on 7th September, he gave Milch the necessary authority required to undertake organisational changes. The axe soon began to fall. On the 9th, Engineer-General Tschersich was fired, with the words: 'As the Reichsmarschall's representative, I have asked you to come to see me. He is not satisfied with your work. Your plans are inaccurate. Your attitude is one of constant negativism. I have been ordered to inform you of these facts and to let you know of his displeasure. You are herewith relieved of your assignment, and you are expected to tender your resignation.'[20] Reidenbach was dismissed, Ploch, Udet's Chief of Staff, was sent to the Eastern Front, and Koppenberg was removed from the supervision of the Ju 88 programme. On the 14th September, Udet agreed to a reorganisation of his office, and, on 3rd October, approved Milch's nominations for the four new departmental chiefs: Colonel Wolfgang Vorwald for the Technical Office, General (retired) Karl-August Freiherr von Gablenz for the Air Force Equipment Office, Ministerial-Director Hugo Geyer for Supply, and Ministerial Director Alois Czeijka for the Industrial Office.

Udet was, by this time, a broken man. Indeed, he had been suffering from considerable strain and depression for a year, ever since German failure in the Battle of Britain. Heinkel remembered:

> I met Udet in the Hotel Bristol in Berlin late in October 1940, after the first phase of the Battle of Britain. I hardly recognized him. He looked bloated and sallow, as if he were being torn to pieces inside, in short, as if he were heading for a nervous breakdown. He was suffering from an apparently irremedial buzzing in his ears and bleeding from the lungs and gums, which certainly must have been due in part to his unsound eating habits . . . his diet consisted almost exclusively of meat . . . coupled with over-indulgence in alcohol and nicotine. Primarily, though, these symptoms were probably the results of the terrible disappointment in connection with the war against England and worry over the technological catastrophe it was bound to unleash. Udet drank a good deal more on this occasion than I had been accustomed to seeing him. 'The Iron Man wants to shove me off to Behlerhoen' said Udet, referring to a well-known sanatorium in the Black Forest, 'but I refuse to go!' A few days later, however, he did go after all, but soon returned to Berlin on his own initiative, just as ill

and worn as he had been before, apparently because he was afraid of Milch gaining too much influence in his office during his absence. When he moved into his recently completed house in the Stall-upoener Allee in Berlin, he stopped short in the garden and cried out, 'There's a cross on the door. I won't move in here!'[21]

Udet's premonitions of his death were becoming increasingly frequent. His relations with Milch worsened, and Udet became quite convinced that the Secretary of State was plotting his downfall. By October 1941, he certainly must have realised that his presence in the highest counsels of the Luftwaffe was achieving nothing. Reliant to an ever-increasing extent on alcohol and narcotic stimulants, by November he was openly hinting at suicide. On the 17th, he telephoned his mistress, and said hurriedly: 'Inge, I can't stand it any longer. I'm going to shoot myself. I wanted to say goodbye to you. They're after me.'[22] She pleaded with him not to do so, but in vain. While talking, she heard the shot which put an end to his life.

His own high office had destroyed Udet. His last words, scrawled in red crayon on the grey wall over his bed, indicated the total despair to which he had been reduced. ' "Iron Man", you left me',[23] he had lamented, and asked why he had surrendered to 'those Jews' Milch and von Gablenz. Both Göring and Milch, indeed all who had known and, despite all friction, liked Udet, were profoundly upset by his death. No public mention was made of his suicide, however, the RLM announcing that the Generalluftzeugmeister had died after receiving severe injuries while testing a new weapon. At the state funeral a few days later, Göring gave a deeply emotional speech, in which he referred to Udet as his 'best friend'. He continued:

> In Ernst Udet the German people have lost one of the most victorious fighter pilots of the World War, one whose record was second only to that of von Richthofen, a shining example to our youthful fliers, and for the German Luftwaffe a bold and single-minded mentor. . . . In the sombre years that followed Versailles, and especially since his re-entry into our ranks, General Udet paved the way for rearmament and victory. As Chief of Supply and Procurement, he looked after the developing of equipment which the German Luftwaffe has forged into a mighty shield to protect the homeland and a powerful sword to smite the enemy.[24]

Whether or not Göring believed these words at the time, is unknown. Certainly, he was giving vent to his true feelings in October 1943, when he said: 'If I could only understand what Udet was thinking of. He made a complete chaos out of our entire Luftwaffe programme. If he were alive today, I would have no choice but to say to him, "You are responsible for the destruction of the German Air Force".'[25] This is a harsh, and misplaced, judgement, but it is one that history has accepted. Unfitted for his position, Udet most certainly was; that his Department was responsible for mistakes

A Do 335 fighter

Ju 52 transport, with Me 323 in background

Göring and Jeschonnek at a conference, 1941

Professor Claude Dornier

Dr Ernst Heinkel

Professor Willi Messerschmitt

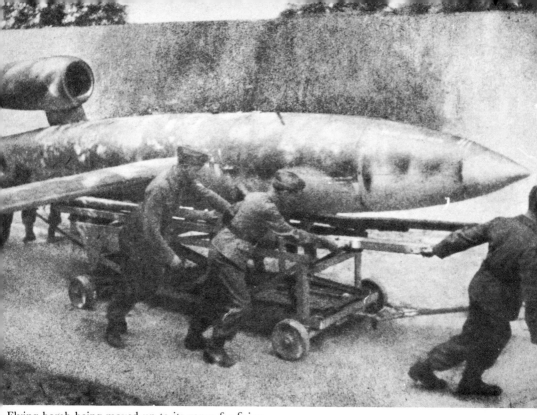
Flying bomb being moved up to its ramp for firing

Fritz X radio-controlled bomb

8.8 cm anti-aircraft gun

2 cm anti-aircraft gun

Udet with the fighter aces Galland and Mölders

Field Marshal Robert Ritter von Greim

General Karl Koller

General Werner Kreipe

General Günther Korten

Göring, Kesselring and Jeschonnek during the Battle of Britain

Göring surveys the coast of England during the Battle

Bf 109s off the coast of southern England, summer 1940

Heinkel 111s on their way across the English Channel

German fighter pilots relaxing before an engagement, May 1940

Hitler being presented with a trophy by a Luftwaffe aircraftsman, September 1939

The nose cone of an He 111

A Heinkel over London, September 1940

A Ju 87 waits on an airstrip in Poland, 1939

A death in Russia for a Luftwaffe crew

An airborne supply canister dropped by the Luftwaffe for the defenders of Kholm, 1941

A Ju 87 night-attack aircraft in Russia, 1943

An aircraft graveyard in Stalingrad, 1943

The Luftwaffe attacking a Malta convoy, 1942

Civilians killed by the RAF bombing attack on Hamburg, July 1943

3.7 cm anti-aircraft gun in ground role

Paratroops in action, Crete 1941

that were to have major consequences for the Luftwaffe is also beyond dispute. That Udet should bear the main responsibility is unfair. Their disengagement from the problems with which he wrestled provides no absolution for Milch, Jeschonnek and Göring; indeed, it serves only to condemn them further. The 'Iron Man's' verdict in 1943 should have been more properly reserved for himself, for it was he who insisted on maintaining Udet in an office for which he knew he was ill-equipped, and, while doing so, made no attempt to oversee his subordinate's activities or to ensure there was proper co-ordination between policy, technology and production. This was a default of leadership for which there was no excuse.

Milch succeeded Udet as Generalluftzeugmeister. Certainly, as the events of the previous four months had shown, he brought more energy, ability and ruthless determination to the task than his predecessor had done, but still he remained unable to obtain the considerable increase in production that was required. Output in 1942 was only thirty-two per cent above that in 1941, an increase similar to that achieved by Udet in the first full year of war. Nor was it a steady progression, for, after reaching a peak of 1,400 aircraft in March 1942, production fell to 1,282 in June, and only rose to its previous level in October. Indeed, aware of the difficulties, Milch produced a plan in March 1942 which called for an output of only 1,650 aircraft a month by the end of the year; but even that modest target was not reached, the December production being only 1,548 machines. The old problems remained. Despite more realism being injected into the organisation of the war economy at the beginning of 1942, and the creation of a new Ministry for Armaments and War Production under the able and energetic leadership of Albert Speer, the Luftwaffe continued to suffer from the same lack of resources. In January 1942, after failure in the East, Hitler cancelled the top priority allocated to aircraft production, and placed emphasis on the development of a total war economy, with the Army as the most favoured of the three services. Although consumer expenditure fell below its 1939 level, the Luftwaffe was only one of many beneficiaries. A letter from Milch, dated 11th March, indicated that the Luftwaffe's problems had not changed: 'The Luftwaffe accepts the Flak programme which has been laid down. The main difficulty is the allocation of copper, as in the first quarter of 1942 the Luftwaffe is receiving only half the copper allocated to it in the last quarter of 1941. The whole of the copper allocation of the Luftwaffe would only cover seventy-five per cent of the Flak programme, assuming, of course, that all aircraft production ceases.'[26] A shortage of labour was particularly acute, so that only ten per cent of the aircraft industry could operate two shifts. The pressures from the Armed Forces, together with the requirements of the factories producing armaments for the Army and the Navy, resulted in workers being switched from the aircraft industry, so that foreign workers and inmates of concentration camps had to take their place. However, the aircraft industry was not the only sector to suffer during 1942, despite greater activity on the part of the Reich's economic leaders, and from July to October the overall output of armaments showed no increase.

During 1942, too, the problems of the Me 210 and He 177 continued to upset all planning. At the end of 1941, the Me 210 had been pronounced totally unsuitable for issue to operational units, but, because of its crucial importance to the Luftwaffe's future, and the fact that output of the aircraft it was intended to replace had already been discontinued, Milch decided to push ahead with its further development. Series production began at the end of 1941, and during January 1942 sixty-four Me 210s were accepted into the Luftwaffe. Meanwhile a Generalluftzeugmeisteramt commission had recommended that production of the aircraft be stopped altogether, and it ceased at the end of January. On 14th April, the RLM officially cancelled its order for the Me 210 after further disastrous events; in one week in March, no less than seventeen lives had been lost owing to the aircraft's poor performance. Milch forced Willi Messerschmitt's resignation as Chairman and Managing Director of the company, but that did nothing to compensate for the failure of the Me 210, which had cost the Luftwaffe the equivalent of 600 aircraft in raw materials and production facilities alone. The gap in the Luftwaffe's armaments caused by the non-appearance of the aeroplane, however, was disastrous.

But not all was lost. Shortly before the RLM had officially decided to end production of the Me 210, a solution to its poor stability had been found, which called for a totally redesigned rear fuselage. It had come just too late, however, to be of use to the Me 210, which was on the production line. The revised project was submitted to Milch's Department in March, and was accepted, being given the designation Me 410. Production was promised by early 1943. Although the aircraft was quite incapable of dive-bombing, it was deemed suitable to be the long-awaited successor to the Bf 110, which, like the Me 210, could undertake the roles of both heavy-fighter and ground-attack. Although its handling characteristics were uninspiring, they were sound; the fatal spins of the Me 210 were a thing of the past. The specifications of the Me 410A-1 were considerably better than those of the Bf 110; it was capable of a top speed of 388 mph at 21,980 ft, a maximum radius of 525 miles, and possessed more powerful armament. However, it was not to be until January 1943 that the first few Me 410s were accepted by the Luftwaffe, and by May there were only forty-eight with the operational units. Owing to the failure of the Me 210, there was no successor to the long obsolete types in service until well into 1943.

Unlike the Me 210 project which, as the Me 410, was at least to result in perfectly serviceable aeroplanes in operational roles, however late, the He 177 programme continued throughout 1942 with little prospect of eventual success. Because of its importance, Milch could not bring himself to abandon it, and continued to believe that the coupling arrangement of the aircraft's engines could be made to work. To revert to four separate engines would involve redesigning the whole machine and, according to the experts, take four years before full-scale production could begin. There was no alternative but to live with the mistakes of 1938. Urgently required on both the Eastern and the Western Fronts, Milch planned a production of 200 He 177s a month. By September, 1942, however, only thirty-three had been accepted for service. Of the delay, which was, by then, of the order of two years, Milch said 'one can only weep', while Göring pronounced: 'It really is the saddest chapter. I do not have one single long-range bomber. . . . I look at those four-engined aircraft of the British and Americans with truly enormous envy; they are far ahead of us here. I have never been so furious as when I saw this engine. Surely it must be as clear as daylight. How is such an engine to be serviced on the airfields? I believe I am right in saying that you cannot even take out all the sparking plugs without pulling the whole engine apart.'[27]

Milch's disillusionment with Heinkel grew. In early 1942, when he was committed to producing five He 177s a month until the solution to its problems had been found, it was shown that he had devoted little attention to the aircraft, preferring instead to concentrate on the profitable He 111 series. Throughout the summer, crashes continued, and by September only two He 177s were operational. In that month, the RLM ended its requirement that the aircraft be able to dive, but to little effect. Early in October, the testing station at Rechlin produced a report which showed that the strength of the wings was one-third that estimated by Heinkel, a fatal mistake in any aircraft, but especially so in one as heavy as the He 177. Milch described this as no minor fault but 'a major foul-up'.[28] The commander of one Gruppe to which He 177s were allocated refused to take responsibility for sending the aircraft out on operations. Hitler's urgent request, transmitted through Jeschonnek, that the bomber be used in combat in the East at the earliest opportunity, was in vain. By February 1943, only thirteen bombing missions had been flown by He 177s in the East, during which seven of the aircraft (one third of the total) had crashed in flames without a shot being fired by the enemy. But still development of the aircraft was continued. In mid-November, Heinrich Hertel, former technical director of Heinkel, was made responsible to the RLM for producing the He 177 as soon as possible, and was given full powers to reorganise its development. As 1943 began, the Luftwaffe still hoped for a solution to the problem.

Not only was the Luftwaffe denied a heavy bomber in 1942, but also a new medium bomber as a much needed replacement for the He 111 and, to a lesser but growing extent, the Ju 88. In February, the Ju 288, production of which had already been delayed, was reaffirmed as the successor, but by the summer it had become clear that difficulties in its development would take a long time before they could be solved. Milch looked towards an advanced version of the Ju 88, known as the Ju 188, to fill the gap. Although the performance of this aircraft was known to be less effective than the Ju 288, which was designed to have a longer range (840 miles with 6,614 lb of bombs instead of 745 miles with 3,307 lb), a higher speed (387 mph instead of 323 mph) and be able to fly at higher altitudes, the Ju 188 A-2 had one considerable advantage: it had been under development since 1940, and was proven to be a serviceable aircraft. The General Staff, however, would have none of it, and insisted on the 'Bomber B' project continuing, arguing that it was expected to see service in 1943. No decision, therefore, was made to discontinue with the Ju 288 and concentrate resources on the Ju 188; instead, development of both was continued simultaneously, and yet another year passed without an alternative to the Luftwaffe's existing medium bombers appearing. Thus, while Milch made plans for a fourth generation of Luftwaffe aircraft, bombers which would fly at altitudes above 45,000 ft carrying guided missiles, and fighters capable of supersonic speeds, the long-awaited third generation of bombers, ground-attack aircraft and heavy fighters still had not appeared. By 1943, they were, on average, two years late.

In the first three years of the war, then, aircraft production and development had failed to keep pace with operational demands. Not until mid-1944 was the quadrupling of output, decided upon in mid-1941, achieved, by which time losses at the front and general unserviceability had risen so high that it proved quite impossible even to double the Luftwaffe's combat strength. At the end of 1942, it was clear to Milch that the Luftwaffe had failed to maintain the lead with which it had begun the war. According to intelligence estimates, whereas Germany had averaged an output of 367 fighters and 349 bombers a month in 1942, her Western enemies alone had averaged four times that amount, with 1,959 and 1,378 respectively. Moreover many of the bombers were of a significantly better quality than those produced by the Reich. When Göring was presented with these figures, he dismissed them with the words: 'I don't want to be bothered with such rubbish'.[29] However, if the output of Soviet aircraft was taken into account, Germany was being out-produced by its enemies by a ratio of 1:8.

Even had Milch been able to make prodigious strides in aircraft production, it is doubtful whether the Luftwaffe could have found sufficient crews to fly them. Although the Air Force had begun the war with a large body of fully-trained pilots and aircrew, losses had been great. In the Battle of Britain, between 3rd August and 28th September 1940, no less than 400 bomber and sixty-one dive-bomber crews had been lost. In the forty months of war up to 1943, 34,500 flying personnel had been killed, and 14,000 wounded, during operations and training. Had the training schools been allowed to continue their courses uninterrupted, there is no reason to suppose that they could not have coped with this rate of loss and, at the same time, increased the total number of pilots and crews available to the Luftwaffe; but there was an acute shortage of Ju 52s in which the advanced bomber training was undertaken. These aircraft were required not only for the airborne attacks in Belgium and Holland in May 1940, for the attack on Crete in June 1941, and in preparation for the invasion of Malta in June 1942, but also to ferry supplies to Luftwaffe units in the field, and, in ever increasing numbers, to the Army, whether in particular situations such as Demyansk, Kholm and Stalingrad, or in a whole theatre of operations such as North Africa and, increasingly, the Eastern Front. Between 1st August and 30th October 1942, no less than 21,500 transport sorties were flown in the East alone, covering 10,500,000 miles and delivering some 43,000 tons of equipment. No increase in the production of Ju 52s, however, was forthcoming, nor was any replacement, although one had been requested by the RLM in the autumn of 1939, when the aircraft was already regarded obsolete. Resources were, however, insufficient and priorities were placed elsewhere. Beginning the war with just 550 Ju 52s, then the only aircraft capable of transport in the Luftwaffe, by the end of 1942 their number had risen to only 800, quite insufficient to take account of their deepening involvement in the Wehrmacht's operations. Even He 111s and He 177s had to be used in a transport role as well as a few Me 323s and FW 200s. Losses of the Ju 52, the main workhorse of the transport units, had reached a point in 1942 where they were twice as many as were produced.

At the outbreak of the war, the Training Command possessed two-thirds of the available Ju 52s, for use in its bomber, blind-flying, instrument flying and bomber-observer schools. For major operations, there was no alternative but to allocate them and their crews on a temporary basis to the front. For the campaign in the West, for example, no less than 380 Ju 52s were made available, for a period of roughly ten weeks away from their training bases; in the event, over 150 did not return. The flying schools suffered considerably. In December 1941, for example, Hitler ordered the creation of five new Transportgruppen for the Eastern Front, aircraft and personnel for which were to be drawn from the bomber and instrument-flying schools, thereby almost denuding them of machines, instructors and advanced pupils.

As General Deichmann noted, 'It is a well-known fact that the practice of requisitioning Ju 52s from the training schools continued unabated and, in fact, became more and more common as the war progressed. As a result, of course, the schools were simply unable to fulfil their mission of providing trained replacement personnel for the bomber and long-range reconnaissance forces'.[30] Indeed, the effects were felt as early as January 1941, when the Quartermaster General's reports first began to emphasise a lack of crews (the initial impact fell most heavily on the Ju 88 formations). Nor, indeed, was the raiding of the training formations restricted merely to Ju 52s. Other aircraft in short supply, such as bombers, and, during the Battle of Britain, fighters were also taken. During the final months in the campaign in North Africa, the Luftwaffe was to find itself particularly short of crews trained in torpedo bombing operations, a result of the closure of the specialised schools during the crisis at Stalingrad. Even the lack of ground-attack aircraft was felt, when, in the autumn of 1942, old He 45 reconnaissance aircraft were taken from the pilot schools and sent to the East to undertake harassing raids by night. Such were the expedients to which the shortage of aircraft had reduced the Luftwaffe.

Since the schools were under the control not of the Chief of Training, who was responsible only for the methods employed, but of the Luftflotten commanders, there was little he could do to prevent the ravaging of his training programmes every three or four months. The fact that, from October 1941 to April 1942, the Chief of Air Transport was also the Chief of Instrument Flight Schools, and therefore subordinate to the Chief of Training, was of little benefit; the operational requirements of the Air Force at the front always came first. Complaints were made to Jeschonnek and Milch, but both of them, in the interests of bringing the war to as quick a conclusion as possible, refused to assist the Training Command. By the time the war was won, it was reckoned, the fall in trained personnel would be an inconvenience that could be dealt with during peace. Even a proposal to replace the Ju 52s in the training units with Ju 86s of the same vintage, was turned down, in the interests of concentrating upon the production of combat aircraft. Deichmann remembered:

> In 1940, while I was Chief of Staff to the Chief of Training, I took advantage of a conference with Göring to suggest to him that the Ju 86 be adopted to replace the Ju 52 as a training aircraft. . . . It would have taken only a few man-hours to adapt the Ju 86 as a trainer by installing double controls and a second instrument panel. By replacing the crude oil engine with a gasoline engine, the Ju 86 with its highly satisfactory flight characteristics . . . could be made into an ideal training machine. There was one disadvantage involved in the conversion from crude oil to gasoline: the fuel tanks, of course, had been constructed for crude oil and would hold only enough gasoline to keep the aircraft aloft for one and a half hours; however, I did not feel that this was a serious obstacle to its use as a trainer. Moreover, auxiliary fuel tanks could be installed in the wings without any difficulty. Another thing in its favour was the fact that large supplies of the necessary raw materials were available since its removal from the armament programme had come as a surprise. A single small aircraft plant could easily have produced the quantity needed for the C (Bomber) Schools. Field Marshal Milch, who was also present at the conference, objected strongly to my recommendation, ostensibly on the grounds that the Ju 88 programme required every bit of available industrial capacity. He explained that the new aircraft procurement programme called for the production of eight Ju 52's per month, which would easily be enough to meet front requirements for transport aircraft as well as the needs of the schools. He brushed aside my objection that the needs of the front in transport aircraft were practically unlimited. Göring decided against my suggestion.[31]

Indeed, in the interest of combat machines, even the production of purpose-built single-engined training aircraft was reduced from thirteen per cent of total aircraft output in 1939 (1,112 machines) to seven and a half per cent in 1942 (1,170). Further limitation on training came in the summer of 1942 with a temporary shortage of aircraft fuel. A considerable curtailment of flying hours in the Training Command was ordered, which Jeschonnek justified:

'First we have got to beat Russia, then we can start training'.[32] By 1943, pressures from all sources had resulted in a drastically curtailed and insufficient training programme for all categories of flying personnel in the Luftwaffe. By March 1943, the bomber force was short of 364 crews to fly their serviceable machines, and the night fighters lacked fifty-one. The dive-bomber and single-engined fighter formations were dangerously low on their establishments, while only the twin-engined fighters had sufficient crews to overcome any problems arising from sickness or battle.

By this point in the war, too, the Luftwaffe's organisation had become bloated by the growth of formations which many believed had no place in an air force. First among these were the mobile Flak units which accompanied the Army in the field. Certainly, they had rendered sterling service. In the campaign in the West, for example, the two Flakkorps which were assigned to Army Groups A and B accounted for 854 of the 2,379 enemy aircraft shot down, and also destroyed over 300 armoured vehicles. During the invasion of Russia, they performed similar work. Flakkorps I with Army Group Centre, for example, shot down no less than 259 enemy aircraft between 22nd June and 30th August 1941. Indeed, by 31st October 1941, the Luftwaffe's Flak had destroyed no less than 5,381 aircraft since the war began, together with 1,930 armoured vehicles, 1,253 bunkers and fortifications, 279 artillery positions, 2,901 guns of all calibres, 5,631 machine-gun nests, 5,024 vehicles, fifty-five trains and so on. The list is impressive, and yet at the same time reveals in what non-aerial activities the Luftwaffe's Flak units were engaged. In the front-line, their employment as anti-tank units, when their 8.8 cm guns proved extremely effective, was widespread, and by 1942 they had come to be considered as of more value in this role than in shooting down aircraft. By mid-1943, some 200,000 men were in the Flak units in the field.

In addition to these, there were some 240,000 who served as fighting men in the same way as soldiers in the Army. To be sure, 20,000 of them were trained to be able to drop into battle wearing parachutes, but this was no reason why they should be part of the Air Force; indeed until 1939, the Army had had its own battalion of paratroops. The rest consisted of some 20,000 men in the Hermann Göring Division, an élite panzer-grenadier unit, and 200,000 men in the twenty-two Luftwaffe Field Divisions, formed from late 1942 as part of the Luftwaffe's contribution to the heavy fighting in the East. Created by exacting a ten per cent cut in many of the Air Force's branches, such as the signals units, the drain on trained manpower brought about by the formation of these Field Divisions had a deleterious effect on the operational efficiency of air units. The divisions themselves were generally of low quality, of inadequate training, equipment and strength, and their formation was highly controversial – Göring, however, would have his way; he wished to show his Führer that the Luftwaffe, too, was capable of immense sacrifices in the desperate fight in the East. The loss of trained manpower to the ground organisation which sustained the air units he regarded as of little importance. Thus, of the 2,100,000 men in the Luftwaffe by the spring of 1943, no fewer than 240,000 would have been more properly employed in the Army, where the resources existed to train and employ them more effectively. As it was, they were all used under the operational command of the Army, the logical consequences of which, however, Göring refused to accept.

At the beginning of 1943, then, the Luftwaffe's position may be summarised as follows: having relied on a series of rapid campaigns, dealing with one enemy after another, to mitigate against the defects with which it began the war, the Air Force had become involved in a conflict whose nature was the very antithesis of the conditions which it regarded as a precondition to success. Without an operational reserve of any kind, the Luftwaffe was, within a period of six months in 1941, forced to undertake a prolonged war on three major fronts simultaneously. Sudden requirements for reinforcements at individual sectors could only be met by withdrawing units from others, and thereby creating dangerous gaps. Resources were so overstretched that, henceforth, a solution in the air over one front was impossible. This was the turning point in the fortunes of the Luftwaffe, and in the nature of the air war.

The new situation was marked by the launching of the El Alamein offensive and the Anglo-American landings in North Africa. During November, it became necessary to withdraw 400 operational aircraft from the East, of which seventy-five per cent were bombers, to send to the Mediterranean, which, for the first time, had become a major theatre of war, absorbing almost twenty-five per cent of the Luftwaffe's strength compared to eight per cent a year earlier. In spite of this, the 1,000-odd combat aircraft there proved quite insufficient to command success, while the depletion of air strength on the Eastern Front, to some 2,000 front-line aircraft by December, ensured that, there too, the German Air Force was unable to meet the demands placed on it. At the same time, a third major operational commitment arose: the defence of the West, and of the Reich itself, from the ravages of Allied bombers. This was beyond the power of the Luftwaffe to undertake successfully without causing serious detriment to its other operations. During 1942 it had been necessary to increase the night-fighters by ninety-five per cent, from 180 to 350 aircraft, and by the end of the year it was clear that a similar expansion of the day-fighters was necessary. By February 1943, almost seventy per cent of the German fighter force was engaged in the West and the Mediterranean, and the expansion in the West was only just beginning. Never again would the Luftwaffe's strength in the East rise for long above the level of 1,600-1,800 front-line aircraft to which it had sunk at the beginning of 1943. Confronted by three major commitments, for which it possessed aircraft neither in sufficient quantity nor adequate quality, the Luftwaffe was faced with the spectre of almost certain defeat. The initiative was gone. German air superiority was a thing of the past. Continual attrition and ultimate collapse was all that lay ahead.

X

1943 – Year of Defeat

The spring of 1943 found the Luftwaffe heavily involved in three major fronts: the East, the West and the Mediterranean. Any one of them would have required its full strength to force a decision, and, with hindsight, it seems clear that the continued dissipation of its limited resources between the three would ensure failure. However, the withdrawing from one or more of these theatres of war was, by then, beyond the power of the German Armed Forces. The only choice they, or rather Hitler, possessed was in which of the three areas to concentrate the main effort. Each had its claim to pre-eminence: the East, where the Russian colossus was growing in strength and the German invader was weakening, and where no water separated the enemy from German soil; the West, where the Allied bomber forces were preparing to bomb the heart out of the Reich; or the Mediterranean, where an enemy landing on the 'soft under-belly' of Europe, anywhere from the south of France to Greece, could result in the establishment of a major second front, the invasion of territories bordering the Reich, and, perhaps, the loss of Romanian oil, followed by an advance on Germany itself. Indeed, in a conference held at the RLM at the end of January 1943, the General of Fighters, Adolf Galland, predicted that the centre of gravity for the German Air Force would have shifted from the East to the Mediterranean by the end of the year.

The loss of North Africa in May 1943 posed the Luftwaffe high command with two major problems. First, it had to restore the strength of the fighter and ground-attack units mauled in Tunisia, as well as the bomber formations operating from Sicily and Sardinia which had been exhausted by constant action over the Mediterranean. Second, it had to redispose its existing forces, and reinforce them where possible, to meet an Allied invasion which might be launched anywhere between the south of France and the Aegean islands. To guard against this threat, Kesselring's Luftflotte 2 was responsible for Italy and the Central Mediterranean, while another command, Luftwaffen-kommando Südost under Hoffmann von Waldau (instituted on 1st January), covered Greece, Crete, and the Balkans. By this organisation, it was hoped that the Luftwaffe would be in a better position to react to an enemy invasion in either area. Cooperation with the Italian Air Force was minimal, and relations far from cordial, the Italians showing a marked distrust for their northern ally. The arrival of able and experienced officers from the Eastern Front was of considerable importance. Foremost among them was von

Richthofen, who took command of Luftflotte 2 on 12th June. Kesselring remained Commander-in-Chief South, and was therefore responsible for all military units, Army, Navy and Air Force, in the Western Mediterranean. General Bülowius arrived to take charge of Fliegerkorps II in place of Lörzer, while General Malincke, who had proved his ability as commander of Fliegerdivision Donetz during the Kharkov counter-offensive earlier in the year, was given tactical control of Sicily. Harlinghausen was replaced by Peltz as commander of bomber units, and Galland arrived to speed up the arrival of pilots and aircraft and restore the efficiency and morale of the fighter units.

By 3rd July, the total commitment to the Mediterranean theatre was 1,280 combat aircraft (975 in Luftflotte 2 and 305 in Luftwaffenkommando Südost), no fewer than 460 more than there had been one and a half months earlier, when North Africa was lost. This represented an increase of fifty-six per cent, which was matched also by a corresponding improvement in serviceability. The paramount importance of fighter defence had been recognised during the final stages of the North African campaign, and sixty per cent of the increase consisted of Bf 109s and FW190s. Luftflotte 2 possessed 380 single and 100 twin engined fighters, and Luftwaffen-kommando Südost had seventy and ten respectively. The allocation of fighters to the Mediterranean between 1st May and 15th July took some forty per cent of total production from the factories and, although no units were removed from other fronts, two newly formed formations intended for the air defence of Germany were sent to Luftflotte 2. The Ju 87, which had shown itself in the desert to be, once again, vulnerable to enemy interceptors, was confined to the Eastern Mediterranean, beyond the range of the Allied fighters. For its ground-attack aircraft, Luftflotte 2 relied on 150 FW 190s, many of which had come from Luftflotte 3 conducting the air war against Britain. Only the 300 Ju 88s and He 111s, the great majority of which were under Luftflotte 2, remained without reinforcement. Upon an improvement in their efficiency, however, the Luftwaffe based its hopes of seriously damaging the Allied invasion fleet.

But at no time were the Germans able to concentrate their resources against the Allied preparations. Through a skilful use of cover plans and diversionary tactics, the Allies kept the German High Command uncertain as to where the landings would take place. An unacceptable dispersal of strength was the result. For some time, it was believed that the enemy would invade Greece or Crete, and the Luftwaffe more than doubled its strength there by the end of June. Similarly, fears for Sardinia led to forces on the island being increased considerably. Ironically, the area where the Allies' blow was to fall-Sicily – saw a reduction in the number of German aircraft, from 415 in mid-May to 175 by the time of the assault eight weeks later. Although this was due in part to the heavy Allied air attacks on the island, which made its bases untenable for bombers, no such reduction would have been allowed had its importance as a probable site for the invasion been recognised. Reinforcements, however, were near at hand in central and southern Italy, where, by the second week of July, no less than 460 aircraft were based. This brought the number of combat machines immediately available to face the invasion of Sicily to 635 by the second week of July.

However, in part because of the necessary dispersal of force that was occasioned by German ignorance of Allied intentions, the Luftwaffe failed to make any serious attempt to interfere with the enemy's preparations for the invasion. Heavy air attacks caused the Germans to evacuate their bombers from bases within range of the North African ports to airfields in northern Italy and southern France, and although Sicily and Sardinia were still used as advanced landing grounds, the scale of effort that was possible at such a distance was limited. Moreover, the enemy's command of the air over the Mediterranean made the bombers extremely reluctant to undertake raids by day, and even at night the Luftwaffe failed to maintain any consistent effort. The ineffectiveness of the German bomber force, which had been so evident in the closing stages of the North African campaign, remained the outstanding weakness of the Luftwaffe in the South. Of the 300 bombers available, only a daily average of fifty-five per cent were serviceable, and, owing to the severe shortage of trained crews, only just fifty per cent of those could be used at any one time. Furthermore, the ill-trained crews often proved incapable of finding their targets, and losses on operations, due often to faulty navigation, were disproportionately high, amounting regularly to between ten and fifteen per cent of the force engaged. The Allies, then, were left to their preparations undisturbed. During the fortnight preceding the invasion of Sicily, only two bomber attacks were undertaken against North African ports, with negligible results.

On 10th July, the Allies landed in Sicily after a week of intense bombing, during which the German defenders lost 100 aircraft. All serviceable FW 190s had to be withdrawn from Sicily to Naples, some 200 miles away, and by the 10th only fifty combat aircraft were based on the island to meet the invasion. Of the attack, Colonel Christ, Chief of Luftflotte 2's Operations Staff, recorded: 'In the last few weeks before the landing, all the aerodromes, operational airfields and landing grounds in Sicily were so destroyed in continuous attacks by massed forces that it was only possible to get this or that airfield in running order again for a short time. . . .'[1] A similar reduction in the Luftwaffe's strength had taken place in Sardinia, where, in the course of the week, the serviceability of Jabo's based there dropped from fifty-five to thirty-five per cent, thereby weakening the forces available for transfer to Sicily as soon as the invasions began. The attack on Sardinia also prevented the German bombers from using the island's airfields as advanced landing grounds. Under these circumstances, the Luftwaffe's reaction to the Allied assault was hesitant and lacked coordination. Moreover, the continued attack on the Sicilian airfields caused the Germans to divert a large proportion of their resources to defence. Between 10th and 12th July, an average of only 275 to 300 sorties were maintained every twenty-four hours, fifty per cent by night, falling off to 150 after the 12th. For their part, the Allies maintained an average of 1,500.

The Luftwaffe had shown itself powerless to interfere with the landings; in the first twenty-four hours, the Allies lost only twelve vessels, although the plan of invasion had allowed for 300 before matters would become critical. By 16th July, the Luftwaffe had only 120 aircraft left in Sicily, of which forty were serviceable. There was no alternative but to withdraw. By the 18th, there were just thirty-five German aircraft on the island, together with 600 destroyed or damaged lying broken on the ground. The Italians had lost a further 500. On the 22nd, the last Axis aircraft left Sicily. The only air support for the German troops came from the Italian mainland, but here the sixty fighters and fifty Jabos available were operating at extreme range, with limited airfield facilities and vulnerable to Allied air attack. An average of sixty sorties every twenty-four hours was all that the Luftwaffe could maintain. Only in the last phase of operations, from 14th to 17th August, when it was necessary to provide some air cover for the evacuation of German troops, did the number of sorties rise to around 150 a day. Compared with this, the Allies undertook an average of 1,200 sorties. In the battle, the Axis had lost 1,850 aircraft, and the Allies fewer than 400. Command of the air in the Mediterranean was, for the Luftwaffe, simply a memory.

The losses suffered by the Luftwaffe in the Mediterranean between 3rd July and 17th August were compounded by demands from the western theatre of war. During August, units representing an establishment of 210 aircraft were withdrawn, and all but one sent to the West. By 3rd September, when the British 8th Army crossed the Straits of Messina and landed at Reggio on the tip of the Italian peninsula, the strength of the German Air Force in southern Europe had fallen to 880 aircraft, of which 625 were in the western and central Mediterranean area. To meet the invasion, there were only about 120 single-engine fighters and fifty Jabos in central and southern Italy, operating from heavily-bombed airfields, and these flew a total of 150 sorties on the first day. The bombers, based as far north as Foggia, played no part in combating the landings. However, five days later, on the 8th, when the Americans and British sailed into the Gulf of Salerno, 150 miles south of Rome, the Luftwaffe mounted an operation stronger than anything seen in that theatre since the attack on Malta in March 1942. On the 8th, 170 sorties were flown by ground-attack aircraft, rising to 250 on the 13th, in support of a counter-attack by the German ground forces which seriously threatened the bridgehead. On the night of the 8th-9th, the bombers joined the battle, flying a total of 150 sorties against the Allied positions and ships, followed by 100 on the night of the 10th-11th. In daylight, the new radio-controlled bomb, the FX1400, and the rocket-powered glider-bomb, the Hs 293, were used against shipping by specially equipped Do 217s, and these attained an average of one hit for every fifteen sorties undertaken.

All the Luftwaffe's efforts at Salerno were to little avail, as the advance of the 8th Army, virtually free from Luftwaffe opposition, eventually ended the threat to the Salerno bridgehead. By the 17th September, the Germans were forced to begin the evacuation of the airfields at Foggia. On the 21st, fighter and Jabo units were withdrawn to the Rome and Viterbo areas, and thereafter German air activity against Salerno fell rapidly. Half the air units were moved north to Pisa, to cover the evacuations of Sardinia and Corsica made necessary because of the Italian capitulation on the 8th. With the occupation of Naples on 1st October, the Allies confirmed their hold on southern Italy, for by then they were provided with the necessary facilities for supply. Such was their control of the air, that the Luftwaffe gave little thought to disrupting this important port. The Allies, on the other hand, with their occupation of the Foggia airfields, found themselves in a position from which they could attack southern Germany.

Elsewhere in the Mediterranean, the Allied landings at Salerno and the capitulation of Italy on 8th September had caused the Germans much concern. In the area of Luftwaffenkommando Südost under General Fiebig (Hoffmann von Waldau had been killed on 17th March), the German position in the Balkans, the Ionian Islands, and the Aegean was compromised by the defection of the Italian garrisons that were of prime importance in the defence of key points from which an invasion of the Balkan mainland might be launched. The German preoccupation with Italy was transferred to the Balkans, where their primary concern was to restore their position in the Ionian islands and the Dodecanese, garrisoned by Italians. During the period between the Italian capitulation and 3rd October, Luftwaffenkommando Südost was reinforced by 110 aircraft from the West and Russia, to reach a strength of 345 combat machines. Operations began on 21st September, with an invasion of the island of Cephalonia, covering the entrance to the Gulf of Corinth, and ended two months later with the invasion of Leros, on which 500 paratroops were dropped, and the occupation of Syros and Samos without a fight. The German position was established in the Eastern Mediterranean until the end of the war.

While Luftwaffenkommando Südost was busily on the offensive, Luftflotte 2 virtually ceased to operate. After the occupation of Naples at the beginning of October, the front-line stabilised and ground operations became so limited and local in character that they would scarcely be assisted by air support, even were it possible in the face of massive enemy aerial superiority. A need to conserve forces, and an inability to fly in periods of bad weather, limited the fighters and Jabos to a daily average of thirty to thirty-five sorties over the battle area every twenty-four hours. Nor did the bombers take much action against the Allied supply lines, and between 15th October and 5th December only 400 sorties were made, most of which achieved nothing. In a raid on Naples, for example, on the night of 23rd/24th October, only twenty out of the ninety aircraft involved were reported to have reached the target. Better results were achieved by the anti-shipping forces based in Southern France, but only at the cost of high losses, amounting on occasion to twenty per cent of the aircraft engaged. Consequently, after four operations in October and

November, no further sorties were mounted until 10th January 1944.

In the autumn and winter of 1943, then, with the front in Italy stabilised and the situation in the Balkans secured, the Mediterranean came to be regarded as a secondary theatre of the air war, where henceforth defence would rely on the difficult terrain rather than on air support. Units were withdrawn to the West and the East; in December, for example the bomber force in northern Italy, amounting to some 110 aircraft, was sent to Luftflotte 3 in preparation for reprisal raids on Britain. Thus, by 1st January 1944, the strength of the Luftwaffe in the Mediterranean was down to just 575 aircraft, forty-five per cent of its total in July. Galland, who had prophesied that the Mediterranean would be the major centre of the Luftwaffe's operations in 1943, was proved wrong. With more pressing engagements elsewhere, the Germans were forced to accept inferiority in the air over southern Europe.

By 1943, with Germany on the defensive, the Luftwaffe had become firmly established as the 'fire-brigade' on the Eastern Front. In critical situations, its use was the only way the High Command could compensate for the Army's shortage of heavy weapons and lack of reserves. The Air Force's flexibility, which allowed it to deploy aircraft at short notice to threatened areas of the front, became a vital element in German strategy. According to the General Staff, the close support of ground forces accounted for at least eighty per cent of air operations in Russia in 1943. As an indication of their importance, direct radio communications were even established between tanks and their supporting aircraft. However, for its task the Luftwaffe was ill-equipped. At most, it deployed only 2,500 aircraft over a front 1,800 miles long, and of these machines normally only sixty per cent were operational. There were insufficient aircraft either to form a reserve or to mount substantial indirect-support operations, the value of which had been proved during the years of victory. Over vast areas of the front, the sight of a German aircraft was a rarity. A crisis on one sector meant denuding another, while the perpetual struggle of the German soldiers to hold their ground against mounting odds called for continued close support and ensured that an effective interdiction of the Soviet communications, command structures and war industries was impossible. Indeed, during the year the Red Army's attacks grew to such a level that the Luftwaffe proved unable even to maintain a clearly defined concentration of power at any single point in the East. Command of the air, even only over certain selected sectors of the front, for so long a German prerogative, had become a thing of the past.

By 1943, the Soviets possessed five times the number of aircraft than the Germans, the quality of which had significantly improved. The Yak-9, which entered service at the end of 1942, was a capable factor, with a top speed of 368 mph at 16,400 ft, while the La-5FN, mainly of wooden construction, entered service in the summer of 1943. It had a maximum speed of 402 mph and carried two 20mm cannon. In addition, combat aircraft were sent from

Britain and the USA, to a total of 22,000 during the war. With such machines, the Soviets were able to mount effective attacks on positions whenever necessary, and to intercept successfully the Luftwaffe's bomb-carriers, especially the slow Ju 87s. Losses suffered by the Red Air Force remained high, but the vast industrial and manpower resources of the Soviet Union proved quite capable of keeping pace with them. Above all, a shortage of fighters was felt especially severely by the Germans, who, by the end of 1943, had been forced to commit nearly two-thirds of their Bf 109s and FW 190s to the war in the West.

But however ill-equipped the Luftwaffe was for its task, its superior training and leadership ensured that, in the East at least, its units could still prove formidable. The operations of Luftflotte 4 during von Manstein's counter-offensive to Kharkov in February and March 1943 indicated that, even after the disastrous defeats of the winter, the German Air Force was by no means done for. In the first three weeks of February, a major rehabilitation of von Richthofen's command was undertaken in the face of continued Soviet pressure. The He 111s, which had been used as transports, returned to their proper duties as bombers; weak units were withdrawn and rehabilitated and their aircraft redistributed among those remaining; while the enforced return to old, established airfields, constructed on a permament basis twelve to eighteen months previously, with good communications to major supply depots such as Poltava, also proved of great benefit. As a result, Luftflotte 4 was able to increase its rate of sorties from a daily average of 350 in January to just under 1,000, with a peak of 1,250 on 23rd February. The extreme flexibility and co-ordination manifested by all units under von Richthofen (who, on 16th February, had been promoted to Field Marshal in recognition of his valuable services), allowed swift switches of concentration during the counter-offensive, which proved of immense value to the ground troops. Particular emphasis was also placed on destroying the enemy's rail communications, which, in view of the thaw, were the only reliable way of bringing up supplies and reinforcements to the front.

In the extreme south, however, Luftflotte 4 was less successful. In February, it had taken control of the air defence of the Crimea, and Fliegerkorps VIII was moved there after the capitulation of 6th Army at Stalingrad. Its main task was to support 17th Army in the Kuban bridgehead, which, Hitler insisted, was to be held in order that it might form a spring-board for a resumption of the German offensive into the Caucasus. It also served the purpose of preventing a Soviet invasion of the Crimea, which would threaten the entire German southern flank and the vital Romanian oilfields. The most immediate problem was to supply the troops from the air, and on 4th February the first transport missions were flown, by FW 200s. By the middle of February, the 'Condors' had returned to the West where they were urgently required, and some 180 Ju 52s were made available for the operation, together with limited numbers of gliders. They were to continue a high level of sorties until the end of March, by which time communications over the Straits of Kerch, separating Kuban from the Crimea, had been established. In the fifty days of the operation, a daily average of 182 tons of supplies were transported to 17th Army (5,418 tons in all), compared with the daily average of ninety-four tons that had been sent to 6th Army by a far larger force a few months earlier. However, both the weather and tactical conditions were favourable to the Kuban airlift, and, once again, the Luftwaffe was able to maintain an army in the field in fulfillment of Hitler's strategy.

In the rest of its operations over the Kuban peninsula, however, the Luftwaffe was less successful. After the termination of the air-lift, Fliegerkorps VIII was transferred to support Armeegruppe Kempf on the north flank of Luftflotte 4, and its bases were taken over by Fliegerkorps I under General Korten, which also assumed control over the naval Air Command Black Sea, equipped mainly with BV 138 seaplanes. In order to consolidate the position of 17th Army, and, in particular, to eliminate the Soviet bridgehead at Novorossiks which was particularly threatening, the Luftwaffe concentrated some 550 aircraft in the Crimea. On 17th April, a heavy attack was mounted, the first operation in a major effort that was to reach a peak of 950 sorties in one day in April, and achieve a daily average of 400 throughout May. It was insufficient, however, either to maintain control of the air or to support effectively the activities of the ground troops, and did not meet with success.

During May, many of the units at the disposal of Fliegerkorps VIII were dispersed to other areas of the Eastern Front, where the available forces were distributed fairly evenly over all sectors from Smolensk southwards. On 11th May, Luftwaffenkommando Ost, under von Greim, was retitled Luftflotte 6. Command of Luftflotte 4 passed to General Dessloch upon von Richthofen's removal to command Luftflotte 2 in Italy at Kesselring's urgent request, and much to the regret of the soldiers in the East. During June, a further redistribution of units began, and two concentrations were established on both sides of the Soviet salient at Kursk, where Hitler had determined to mount a major offensive, code-named 'Citadel'. It was the Wehrmacht's main effort of 1943, and it is evidence of the sorry state to which German arms had sunk that the attack was to take place over a frontage of only 120 miles and have a territorial objective just ninety miles distant. Its aim was to encircle and destroy the strong enemy forces in the salient and, thereby, inhibit any enemy offensive. Two army groups would be involved, Army Groups Centre and South, with forty-three divisions, 1,850 tanks and 530 assault guns between them, to destroy the Soviet line which consisted of six defended belts with 3,500 miles of trenches, 20,220 guns and 3,306 tanks. It was to be a battle of attribution the like of which had not been seen since the First World War.

To support the ground forces, the Luftwaffe committed Fliegerkorps I under the command of Luftflotte 6, and Fliegerkorps VIII under Luftflotte 4. At the end of June, Fliegerkorps VIII, under the newly appointed General Hans Seidemann, had been brought up to a strength of 1,100 front-line aircraft (including those of the Hungarian Air Force, equipped with German machines) and Fliegerkorps I, then under General Paul Deichmann, to 730. These, together with other aircraft belonging to certain night-fighter and reconnaissance units, comprised an attacking force of some 1,900 machines, of which sixty-five per cent were operational. But the German onslaught at Kursk, begun on 5th July, although powerful in terms of men and material, was a failure. On the 12th, when the Germans were still sixty miles from their objective, the Russians launched their counterstroke north and east of the German salient at Orel, immediately to the north of Kursk. The Wehrmacht's offensive gave way to a defensive battle to save the Orel position, and aircraft from Fliegerkorps VIII were transferred north, to Fliegerkorps I, for the purpose. During these days, the Luftwaffe maintained an effort seldom experienced before. At the beginning of the Kursk offensive, a daily average of 3,000 sorties were undertaken, with ground-attack aircraft each flying five or six missions in twenty-four hours. That the Luftwaffe proved of immense value to the ground forces, is revealed by the report of 9th Army on the results of Fliegerkorp I's actions during the battle for Orel:

> The Fliegerkorps, which through its action decided the issue in many highly critical situations, dispatched its units in the execution of a total of 37,421 sorties, shooting down 1,735 enemy aircraft . . . 1,671 of them by fighter units alone . . . against a loss of only 64 of its own planes. In addition, the air units put out of action 1,100 tanks, 1,300 wheeled and tracked motor trucks and other vehicles, and numerous artillery batteries. Delivering more than 20,000 tons of bombs on targets, the air units also inflicted heavy losses on the enemy in personnel, railway rolling stock, and supplies. During the Battle of the Orel River Bend area, units of the Fliegerkorps at times flew as many as five or six missions on a single day.[2]

In individual actions, the Luftwaffe proved decisive. On 8th July, for example, a Gruppe of Hs 129s stopped a Soviet tank attack on the left wing of the German advance. This success was repeated on the three days from the 19th to 21st, when Ju 87s and Hs 129s of Fliegerkorps I frustrated an armoured breakthrough which threatened the rear of two armies (9th Army and 2nd Panzer Army), and thereby prevented a second 'Stalingrad'.

However, despite its successes, the Luftwaffe proved quite incapable of meeting all the tasks required of it. By the end of the first week of the Kursk offensive, its sorties had dropped by a half, and for the rest of July a daily average of 1,000 were undertaken by Luftflotten 4 and 6, just half those of the Soviet Air Force. The opening of a secondary offensive by the Red Army to the south, on the Lower Donets front, immediately after the attack on Orel, proved to be the final blow to the Luftwaffe in the East. Luftflotte 4 was again forced to transfer units from Seidemann's command to the threatened sector. Thus, the concentration of force that had existed around the Kharkov-Belgorod area at the beginning of July, was, by the middle of the month, dissipated over three main areas: Orel, Belgorod, and Stalino. Losses mounted, rising from 487 in June to 911 in July, and serviceability declined, while the strength of the Red Air Force appeared undiminished.

During the remaining months of 1943, the Soviets maintained their offensive in the south, so that, by the end of the year, the German line had been pushed back behind the Dnepr, to within 200 miles of the Romanian border. Since November 1942, the Red Army had advanced between 310 and 800 miles along the whole front. A German army lay isolated in the Crimea, having been cut off from the main front since the end of October. Of the 1,750 combat aircraft in the East, sixty-four per cent (1,150) were positioned south of Kiev; yet, even here, operations were dominated by German numerical inferiority, and the Soviets held the strategic initiative. With no reserve, Luftflotte 4 was forced to switch its forces from one sector to another in response to Russian pressure. Command of the air, even locally, was over. Pleas to the high command for more fighters were continual, but in vain; at the end of the year, there were only 425 along the length of the Eastern Front, twenty less than at the beginning of the year when enemy superiority had been marginal, and of these just sixty-five per cent were serviceable. Yet during the year, the monthly output of fighters had risen by one hundred per cent. The Eastern Front, however, was not to be a beneficiary; nor, indeed, was the Mediterranean. By the autumn, every fighter that the factories could produce were needed for the defence of the Reich. It was here, in the West, that during 1943 the Luftwaffe's main effort came to be.

But even in the West, the offensive capability of the Luftwaffe was but a shadow of its former self. Throughout 1943, as in 1942, it proved quite incapable of mounting a serious threat to the British. Command of the air over the Atlantic was in the hands of the enemy. As Admiral Dönitz reported to Hitler on 8th July:

> The course of the war to date had made it clear that, in the operations at sea the Luftwaffe is destined to play an outstanding part. While control of the open sea is now unthinkable without simultaneous control of the air, the Luftwaffe has become of decisive importance in the fight in coastal waters. Yet most serious of all has been the failure of the maritime air force in connection with the Navy's critical task: the submarine war. As the greatest difficulty facing our U-boats has been not in attacking their targets but in finding them, there can be no doubt that wide-ranging reconnaissance from the air could increase the success of the submarine operations many times over. The influence of the enemy's air force in fighting the U-boats has been very marked; in fact it can be said that the crisis in the submarine war is the result of the enemy's control of the air over the Atlantic.[3]

Not only did Fliegerführer Atlantik prove incapable of assisting the German Navy, but also it failed in its other task of destroying enemy shipping. At the end of the year, a Gruppe of He 177s were allocated to Fliegerführer Atlantik, but within five days ten of the seventeen machines had been lost due to heavy enemy opposition. The Gruppe, trained for operations with the radio-controlled anti-shipping bombs, was withdrawn from service by day and used only at night, with little success. British figures for the tonnage of merchant shipping lost owing to air action in 1943 (273,300 tons including the Mediterranean theatre as well as the Far East) show a decline of thirty-one per cent over 1942, and fifty-two per cent over 1941. As General Kessler reported in August 1943, only if the entire resources of the Luftwaffe were made available for the attack on enemy sea-lanes would there be any prospect of success in the blockade.

In attacks on the British mainland, too, the Luftwaffe proved itself to be quite inadequate either to affect the enemy's will to resist, to inhibit his war economy, or even to deter him from continuing his bombing offensive against the Reich. On the night of 17th January 1943, the Germans made their first major raid on London since 1941, in retaliation for an attack on Berlin, and dropped 115 tons of bombs for the loss of six of the 188 bombers involved. This was followed on the 20th by a Jabo daylight raid by twenty-eight bomb-carrying FW 190s, for the loss of three fighter-bombers and six fighter escorts. In February, two small raids were undertaken by night on Plymouth and Swansea, but none by day, and on the night of 3rd March London was again attacked. On that occasion, the Luftwaffe's bombers were extremely inefficient, and deposited only eleven per cent of their 108 tons of bombs on the target. Hitler was furious at the mishandling of the offensive, especially since it was designed to meet terror with terror to deter the British from continuing their onslaught on the Reich. He therefore ordered greater resources to be committed to the fight. On 30th April, there were only 135 bombers, of which 107 were serviceable, and 123 FW 190 fighter-bombers, of which ninety-seven were serviceable with Luftflotte 3. A steady increase in strength was made throughout the year, so that, by the end of December, General Dietrich Peltz, General of Bombers and Angriffsführer England, possessed some 450 bombers and fifty fighter-bombers (twenty-seven of them Me 410s), of which over eighty per cent were operational. However, the force allocated to the West had proved quite insufficient for a major campaign. During the year, the Germans undertook attacks by bombers on only thirty-one nights, and Jabos on just twenty-two days. For 1,975 sorties, the bombers dropped 1,906 tons of bombs, of which only twenty per cent fell on the target, while the Jabos, whose activities were temporarily cut short in June when they were sent to the Mediterranean, dropped just 425 bombs in 434 sorties, seventy per cent of which reached their targets. Losses had been high, one bomber and one Jabo each being lost for every eighteen sorties made, not including the fighter escorts for the FW 190s. This amounted to 5.4 per cent of the force engaged. In these raids, the Germans dropped less than one per cent of the tonnage deposited by the Allies on the Reich and occupied Europe in the same year.

For the Luftwaffe, the most significant development in 1943 came with the increased Allied bomber offensive in the West. No less than 206,188 tons of bombs were dropped by the strategic air forces (which comprised RAF Bomber Command and the US 8th and 15th Air Forces), an increase of more than 300 per cent over the total dropped in 1942. In January 1943, the British and American leaders met at Casablanca, and there decided upon an intensification of the air war, the object of which was 'the progressive destruction and dislocation of the German military, industrial and economic system, and the undermining of the morale of the German people to a point where their capacity for armed resistance is fatally weakened'.[4] According to Sir Arthur Harris, the RAF was thereby allowed to attack 'any German industrial city of 100,000 inhabitants and above'.[5] In pursuance of this policy, over 131,000 tons of bombs were dropped in 'area raids' in 1943, and by the end of the year some 180,000 German civilians had lost their lives. By the end of the war, a third of all bombs dropped by the Allied strategic bomber forces had been in area raids.

In fulfillment of the Casablanca directive, which placed the destruction of the German submarine yards first on its list of priorities, the Allies opened their attack in 1943 with raids on the main U-boats bases. These continued for the first six months of the year, but to little effect. RAF Bomber Command, in particular, was dissatisfied with the results, and, even as early as February, began returning to its favourite target: cities. After two fairly heavy attacks on Cologne, the night offensive concentrated its efforts on the Ruhr, the centre of the German armaments industry. On the night of 5th/6th March, Essen received 1,014 tons of bombs in the beginning of a series of raids which were to last until the end of June. In forty-three major attacks, RAF Bomber Command made 18,506 sorties, many of them led by 'Pathfinders' equipped with the new 'Oboe' target direction beam which guaranteed a high degree of accuracy to within 200 yards even on the darkest night and through the thickest cloud. Some 34,000 tons of bombs were dropped on the Ruhr, which came within the 270 mile range of 'Oboe', and the damage in some areas was considerable; nine-tenths of Wuppertal-Barman, for example, lay devastated after an operation lasting just fifteen minutes, and 2,450 of its inhabitants lost their lives.

The reaction among the German leadership to this night offensive was considerable. On 10th April, after surveying the damage done to Essen, Goebbels wrote in his diary 'the damage . . . is colossal and, indeed, ghastly. . . . The city's building experts estimate that it will take twelve years to repair the damage,' He referred to the negligence of Göring and Udet, whose sins of ommission had been committed 'on a scale deserving to be commemorated by history.'[6] On 8th May, Hitler told Milch that 'There's something wrong with the Luftwaffe, and its either with its tactics or its technology'.[7] On the same day, after an interview with the Führer, Goebbels wrote: 'The technical failure of the Luftwaffe results mainly from useless aircraft designs. It is here that Udet bears the fullest measure of blame. . . . The public shows its commonsense when they rumour that it is Göring himself who is to blame.'[8] On 4th June, Milch, who was doing all he could to increase fighter production, warned his subordinates: 'The German people have become accustomed to the fact, as far as one can be accustomed to such a thing, that each night one town or other is heavily bombarded. But it will not understand it. . . . The attack on Jena has struck deeply at public morale and at faith in the Luftwaffe. . . .'[9]

Indeed, the reaction of the German Air Force in the first half of 1943 to the increase in enemy night bombing had been quite inadequate. Although, by June, there were eighteen Gruppen of night fighters in the Reich, five more than at the end of 1942, their use was limited by the tactics employed by Kammhuber. These meant, for example, that just thirty-six fighters could be employed over the Ruhr. Only in the reorganisation of the Flak was any significant action taken by the Germans in the first half of 1943. Anti-aircraft artillery that had been sent to Italy, and units in the East, were recalled, and 'Grossbatterien', composed of two or three batteries, were placed at all important targets to counter the RAF's tactics of saturation bombing. The defences in the Ruhr, which, at the end of 1942, comprised 200 heavy batteries, were almost doubled, to take forty per cent of the Reich's Flak units, and increasing numbers of 10.5 cm and 12.8 cm guns were employed.

Kammhuber, however, was not idle. In May 1943, at a time when the night fighter arm possessed only 500 operable machines, of which a third were in the East or the Mediterranean, he presented a long memorandum to Göring, which called for his command to be increased to 2,160 aircraft. He was particularly fearful that the US bombers, which at that time were engaged in fairly light daylight raids, would be committed to the night offensive. Göring agreed with his General of Night Fighters, and on 24th May took him to present his views to Hitler. The Führer, however, was far less receptive than his Reichsmarschall, and was particularly critical of Kammhuber's figures of American aircraft production, which, in fact, came from the OKW. 'It's absolute nonsense', Hitler shouted. 'If the figures of 5,000 a month were right, you would be right too. In that case I would have to withdraw from the Eastern Front forthwith, and apply all resources to air defence. But they are not right! I will not stand for such nonsense.'[10] The interview was over. Göring felt humiliated, and later rounded on Kammhuber: 'You are a megalomaniac. You want to have the whole Luftwaffe. Why don't you sit right down in my chair?'[11] Kammhuber's days as General of Night Fighters were numbered. Hitler remained convinced that the only effective response to enemy bombing was to attack British cities. 'You can only smash terror with terror. You have to counter-attack. Anything else is useless',[12] he told Göring and Milch in July. However, on 6th July, after finally heeding the evidence of the repeated bombing raids on the Ruhr, and the warnings of men such as Milch, the Reichsmarschall agreed to a significant increase in the Reich's fighter defences. But it came too late.

On the night of 24th/25th July, the RAF attacked Hamburg, the second largest city in the Reich, in the first of four raids ending on the night of 2nd/3rd August. Together, they represented the highest point of destruction to be reached in the war in Europe, with the exception of the attack on Dresden in 1945. In all, 8,621 tons of bombs were dropped, of which half were incendiaries. Some 50,000 civilians were killed, almost as many as Britain was to suffer from bombing throughout the entire war. Sixty-one per cent of Hamburg's living accommodation was destroyed or rendered uninhabitable, 183 out of 524 large factories were destroyed, and 4,118 out of 9,068 smaller ones, together with 180,000 tons of shipping sunk in the port. A new phenomenon had taken place in these raids: the fire storm. On the night of 27th/28th July, after half an hour of bombardment, a single fire covered an area of twenty-two square kilometres, the heat from which was at times estimated to approach 1,000 degrees centigrade. A vast suction was created which, according to Hamburg's Police President, caused the air to storm 'through the streets with immense force, bearing upon it sparks, timber and roof beams and thus spreading the fire still further and further until it became a typhoon.' Winds exceeding 150 miles an hour were experienced, which flung humans into the fire, and even sucked in young babes from their mothers' arms. After the raid, the scene was gruesome. As the Police President wrote:

> The streets were covered with hundreds of corpses. Mothers with their children, youths, old men, burnt, charred, untouched and clothed, naked with a waxen pallor like dummies in a shop window, they lay in every posture, quiet and peaceful or cramped, the death-struggle shown in the expression on their faces. The shelters showed the same picture, even more horrible in its effect, as it showed in many cases the final distracted struggle against a merciless fate. Although in some places shelterers sat quietly, peacefully and untouched as if sleeping in their chairs, killed without realization or pain by carbon monoxide poisoning, in other shelters position of remains of bones and skulls showed how the occupants had fought to escape from their buried prison. No flight of imagination will ever succeed in measuring and describing the gruesome scenes of horror in the many buried air raid shelters.[13]

Not only was the intensity of the raid disturbing to the Germans, so were the methods by which it was undertaken. Greater accuracy was achieved by the bombers' use of the new H_2S air-to-ground radar to identify the target, and considerable immunity from German defences was gained by the use of 'Window' to jam German radar. This consisted of bundles of silver-strips, each cut to half the wave-length of the Würzburg radars, which, when dropped from aircraft, produced millions of tiny echoes on the German plotting screens. Thus, although Hamburg was ringed by fifty-four heavy Flak batteries and twenty-two searchlight batteries, and its approaches were covered by twenty night-fighter 'boxes', its defences were rendered effectively impotent. Neither the night fighters nor the Flak could be directed to the enemy. Thus, RAF losses due to enemy action were reduced to 2.8 of the bombers despatched, and 3.4 of those that actually reached Hamburg. Ironically, the Germans, as well as their enemy, had known about the effect of silver strips on radar as long ago as the spring of 1942, but, like the British, had not used it for fear of courting similar reaction from the enemy. However, unlike the RAF, the Luftwaffe had not developed any counter-measures. Indeed, Göring had actually prohibited any further research on the matter, fearing it would enable the enemy to get to know of the vulnerability of the German radars.

At the same time as RAF Bomber Command had shown the Germans the full extent of its potential over Hamburg by night, the USAAF was beginning to pose a major threat by day, its B-17 bombers flying at heights of up to 36,000 ft, the limit of the German fighter's endurance, to their targets. During the first six months of 1943, American activity had been largely experimental. Of the forty bomber raids in that period, twenty-seven were directed against U-boat bases and supply-depots, and the remainder against miscellaneous military and industrial targets. Fighter escorts had been provided for the bombers, although the P-47 Thunderbolt, one of the first fighters faster than 400 mph, was able to reach only the coastal area of Belgium and Holland, while the twin-engined P-38 Lightning, with a longer range which reached to beyond the Reich's borders, was no match for the single-engined German fighters. Some attacks were undertaken on objectives on the fringes of the Reich, but most were in the occupied territories, and all were on a modest scale, until mid-July averaging only 80-100 sorties. Thus, by mid-1943, the Luftwaffe General Staff was content to leave the day-time defence of the West to the Flak and some 300 fighters spread out in a weak defensive screen from the Heligoland Bight to Biarritz. Interceptors suffered high losses and met with little success, but, in face of the heavy commitments in Russia and the Mediterranean, the Luftwaffe had no alternative but to leave the West's daytime fighter defences in such a weak state. The Allies, however, were in no mood for a continuation of half-hearted measures any longer than was necessary. Once it was believed that the USAAF was capable of bombing targets deep in enemy territory by day, beyond the range of fighter escort, and with minimal loss, it was decided to make greater use of the 300 B-17 Fortresses and B-24 Liberators of 8th Air Force. In June, the 'Pointblank' Directive was agreed among the Allies, making the German fighter aircraft industry the main, and most urgent, target for destruction. Having experienced the efficacy of the FW 190s, and noted the increase in fighter production, the Allies had no wish to jeopardise their position by allowing the Luftwaffe's defence to develop to a point where the continuance of air operations would be placed in doubt. On 28th July, therefore, B-17s of the 8th Air Force undertook their deepest thrust into Germany of the war till then, beyond the range of their escorts with, as their targets, Oschersleben. It was the beginning of a phase of operations that was to cost them dear.

The RAF's operation against Hamburg had caused consternation among the German leadership. Goebbels, rightly, referred to the destruction of the city as 'a catastrophe, the extent of which simply staggers the imagination'. Milch, too, was aghast: 'It is one minute to twelve. It is a matter of trying to turn back the clock of Germany's destiny, no less.'[15] The question was, would it provide the final catalyst for some decisive action to be taken in the defence of the Reich? To begin with, the signs were beneficial. On 28th July, Göring conceded Milch's oft-repeated request that aircraft manufacture be concentrated on fighters. On the same day, also, Milch ordered the production of an airborne radar, already under development, that would not be subject to jamming by 'Window', and would allow the interceptors to inflict losses on enemy night bombers amounting to at least twenty to twenty-five per cent. On the 30th, it was decided that night fighters be allowed to undertake unfettered pursuit, leaving their zones and mingling with the bomber streams, and that an experimental unit of Bf 109s be enlarged, and allowed to patrol freely over threatened cities, as 'Wilde Saue' – wild boars. On 1st August, Göring announced: 'The provision of day and night fighter defence will take priority over all other tasks.'[16]

However, this determination was not to last long in the face of Hitler's intransigence. At a conference held in late August, attended by the Reichsmarschall, the Chief of the General Staff, the Secretary of State, the Commander of Luftwaffenkommando Mitte, the General of Bombers, the General of Fighters and many others, it was decided that the Luftwaffe would have to concentrate its resources on the defence of the West. After the raiders had been defeated, the Air Force would then be able to recover its strength and resume the offensive. Of this meeting, Galland wrote in glowing terms:

> Never before and never again did I witness such determination and agreement among the circle of those responsible for the leadership of the Luftwaffe. It was as though under the impact of the Hamburg catastrophe everyone had put aside either personal or departmental ambitions. There was no conflict between General Staff and war industry, no rivalry between bombers and fighters; only the one common will to do everything in this critical hour for the defence of the Reich and to leave nothing undone to prevent a second national misfortune of this dimension.[17]

Straightway after the meeting, Göring left to seek Hitler's permission for the Luftwaffe's new defensive strategy, which the Luftwaffe high command was unanimous in regarding as the only way the Third Reich would avoid defeat. After a while, the Reichsmarschall returned. Galland wrote:

> Göring had completely broken down. With his head buried in his arms on the table, he moaned some indistinguishable words. We stood there for some time in embarrassment until at last he pulled himself together and said we were witnessing his deepest moments of

despair. The Führer had lost faith in him. All the suggestions from which he had expected a radical change in the situation of the war in the air had been rejected; the Führer had announced that the Luftwaffe had disappointed him too often, and a changeover from offensive to defensive in the air against the West was out of the question. He would give the Luftwaffe a last chance to rehabilitate itself by a resumption of air attacks against England, but this time on a bigger scale. Now as before, the motto was still – attack. Terror could only be smashed by counter-terror. This was the way the Führer had dealt with his political enemies. Göring had realised his mistake. The Führer was always right. All our strength was now to be concentrated on dealing the enemy in the west such mighty retaliation blows from the air that he would not risk a second Hamburg. As a first measure in the execution of his plan, the Führer had ordered the creation of a leader of the attacks on England [Angriffsführer England].[18]

Thus, the determination to change the whole basis of the Luftwaffe's strategy before it was too late came to nothing.

One of the few Luftwaffe leaders to continue to press for the needs of defence was Milch. In response to the Allied bombing, he called for a significant increase in the output of fighters. Whereas production plan No.223-1 of 15th April 1943 called for an increase of sixty-five per cent in fighter production between October 1943 and June 1944, Plan No.223-11 of 15th August, known as the Reich Defence Plan, counted on a 120 per cent increase. Finally, Plan No.224-1 of 1st October 1943 called for a monthly production by June 1944 of 3,038 single-engine fighters and a further 1,304 twin-engined ones, an increase of 168 per cent over the total produced in June 1943. The production of all other aircraft types would suffer accordingly. In the circumstances in which the Reich was to find itself, such a rearrangement of priorities could not come about soon enough. His proposals, however, met with considerable opposition from Hitler and the RLM chiefs determined to carry out the Führer's orders. In addition, Milch was also forced to argue against Speer and his staff, who declared in August that the Reich Defence Programme was an impossibility. Speer stated that the limits of aircraft production had already been reached because of a bottleneck in the output of engine crank-shafts, and he refused to place fighters on a level with other top priority armaments. In October, came Hitler's demand to draft 60,000 workers from the aviation industry into the Armed Forces, which the Luftwaffe unsuccessfully resisted.

In October, too, a month when the Allies dropped some 20,000 tons of bombs on the Reich, the Reichsmarschall requested that, in line with Hitler's wishes, bomber production should be increased to 900 a month as soon as possible (in October just 410 He 111s, Ju 88s, and He 177s were manufactured). The Führer was particularly concerned to see the He 177 in operation in large numbers on the Eastern Front, where he wanted it to carry out nocturnal attacks on targets beyond the range of the existing bombers, and over the Atlantic. On the 14th, Milch remonstrated: 'It is precisely in these coming months that we must avoid weakening the Reich Defence Programme. Otherwise the enemy will smash our bomber production anyway, and that's an end to your Junkers 188 and 388 production'.[19] Indeed, at that very time, the German aircraft manufacturers, especially those producing fighters, were under Allied attack, and this was a major factor in bringing down total output from a peak of 2,475 aircraft in July to 1,734 in December, a decrease of thirty per cent. A new production programme, put forward in early November, called for a monthly production of some 5,700 fighters by 1945, together with 930 long-range bombers, but it was rejected by Speer as 'Utopian'. He refused even to discuss it. Milch, however, would not be deterred, and pushed ahead with his policy of rationalising the aircraft industry, reducing the number of aircraft types that were built and increasing by every possible method the production of fighters. However, there was a limit to what he could do, and his plans had to be tapered to meet the opposition. On 1st December, therefore, Milch issued a new production programme which called for an output of only 2,933 fighters of all types by mid-1944.

Although, thanks to Milch, production of fighters more than doubled from 521 in January 1943 to 1,263 in July, representing thirty-three per cent of total aircraft weight produced, this was to be short-lived. Owing to a shortage of raw materials for aero-engine manufacture and to Allied bombing, which not only destroyed factories but also caused a reduction in output because of the dispersal of assembly lines to less vulnerable areas, production dropped to just 687 fighters in December. Moreover, the extraordinarily heavy wastage incurred in the Mediterranean, and, to a lesser extent, in the East, absorbed a large part of new production. In addition, the ground-attack units found that a modified version of the FW 190 was ideal for their role, and this called for ever greater numbers of the aircraft to be made over to them, requests to which Göring and Jeschonnek readily acceded. Only by a far-reaching redisposition of its fighter forces, would the Luftwaffe high command be able to deal adequately with the enemy's threat in the West. The East and the Mediterranean were raided for fighter units, and by the end of the year there were no less than 1,650 single and twin-engine fighters in the West, of which three-quarters were in the Reich. This represented sixty-eight per cent of the Luftwaffe's front-line fighter strength of 2,440, compared with fifty-nine per cent of the total of 1,770 at the beginning of the year. The Eastern Front, which suffered very severely by the transfer, was left with just 425 fighters to defend a front of 1,650 miles. Had the Luftwaffe not suffered such a severe drain on its resources during the invasion of Sicily in July, there is no doubt that its capacity to defend the Reich against the bombers would have been greatly enhanced. In July, a month when losses of aircraft on the Eastern Front had risen to 911, those in the Mediterranean had amounted to 850, of which no fewer than 600 were Bf 109s and FW 190s. Some 350 fighters were sent to that area, representing almost twenty-eight per cent of July's production, and this slowed down the formation of new units. In such a way did events in the Mediterranean have their effect upon the Luftwaffe in the West.

The 975 day-fighters that had been assembled in the West by the beginning of October (an increase of 175 over 1st July) were barely sufficient for their task, and use had to be made on occasions of the night fighters. By the end of the year, the latter had destroyed no less than 110 American bombers by daylight, although at high cost to themselves. By night, the Luftwaffe was in no better position to meet the invader than at the beginning of the year – indeed, it was somewhat worse. On 15th September, after a period of little success, Kammhuber was relieved of his command of Fliegerkorps XII, and was succeeded by 'Beppo' Schmid. In mid-October, the Fliegerkorps itself was disbanded, being replaced by a new command, Jagdkorps I with authority over three Jagddivisionen. Like its predecessor, it combined units within both Luftflotte 3 and Luftwaffenkommando Mitte, but, in contrast, it had both night and day formations under its command. This advantage, however, was partly offset by the merging of the functions of General of Night Fighters with those of General of Fighters, much to the consternation of Galland, who felt himself quite unable to take over Kammhuber's responsibilities. Moreover, the operational strength of the night fighters in the West fell over the period, from some 420 on 20th September to just 240 by the end of the year. In addition, there was a shortage of trained pilots, which would not be overcome until the training courses ended in the spring of 1944, by which time new 'jamming proof' airborne radars would also be available in considerable numbers. The number of guns at the disposal of the anti-aircraft commands in the Reich, however, increased, as most of those newly produced were made over to them. In 1943, output of all types of Flak increased by forty-eight per cent. Extra manpower to service the guns was taken from the Reich Labour Service, Hitler Youth, and even female personnel.

In addition to more aircraft, new tactics were also required to meet the Allied onslaught. By day, the Germans instituted a system, introduced in June, whereby fighters could fly two or three sorties against one raid, using a number of fully equipped and well-stocked airfields within occupied Europe and the Reich. Closely linked with this, was the adoption of large attack-formations, in which anything from fifty to 150 fighters were coordinated by centralised ground control through divisional and corps headquarters and directed to meet the raiders at fixed assembly points at pre-determined altitudes. An intricate and flexible ground organisation was quickly built up which allowed this tactic to function well.

By night, the fighters made every effort to overcome the effects of 'Window'. Controlled night-fighting was retained, but great emphasis was placed on the 'Wild Boar' tactics undertaken by Bf 109s transferred from day-fighter formations. Once a bomber stream was identified, fighters might fly as much as 300 miles to attack it, guided by information from ground observers which was relayed over the radio. To help them, Flak would refrain from shooting above pre-determined altitudes; visual aids were used to great effect, searchlights acting as guiding beacons, and flares being dropped at the estimated height of the bombers. In addition, another method, 'Zahme Sau', Tame Boar, was introduced, whereby fighters were infiltrated into the bomber streams well before they reached their target, remaining among them even back to their bases to exact what retribution they could.

In addition, the armament of the interceptors was increased. In place of one 15 mm and two 7.9 mm machine guns, the Bf 109 was re-equipped with two 13 mm machine guns and one 20 mm cannon, while the FW 190 exchanged its 7.9 mm machine guns for 13 mm, retaining its four 20 mm wing cannons, and was capable of delivering twenty-six lb of shells in a three second burst, exactly double that fired by the Bf 109 E-3 in 1939. By such measures, the fire-power of the German fighters was more than doubled. New weapons were used, one of the most effective being a 21 cm rocket mortar, which fired 90 lb shells into the bomber formations. Twin-engine fighters were also used in day combat, and by the end of October there were some 17 Bf 110 and Me 410s available, whose task was to break up the formations of unescorted bombers to allow the Bf 109s and FW 190s to press home their attacks on individual raiders. They were both heavily armed, the Bf 110s carrying two 30 mm cannon, four 20 mm cannon and four 21 cm rockets, and the Me 410 a 50 mm cannon, the BK 5, of extremely high destructive power. Formidable weapons though these aircraft were, events were soon to overtake them.

During the day-time fighting, the new resources and tactics of the Luftwaffe's defences proved highly successful, despite the formidable nature of their new opponents. As Galland wrote of the American bombers: '. . . the defensive firing power of a formation of Flying Fortresses as well as the invulnerability of each individual bomber were very real facts. One can reckon that a formation of twenty-seven B-17s can bring to bear at least 200 heavy machine guns, with an effective range of 1,000 yards to stern, i.e. in the direction from which fighters usually attack. On the other hand, according to experience it took about twenty to twenty-five hits with 20-mm shells to shoot down a Flying Fortress.'[20] But, devoid of any fighter escort over the Reich, the raiders were to fall prey to the German defenders, and by June the interceptors were hitting over eighteen per cent of the American bombers with their cannon fire. On 28th July, as Hamburg was still blazing, the Americans were given a foretaste of what was to come when the German fighters shot down twenty-two B-17s out of seventy-seven, for the loss of just seven of their number. This was followed on 1st August by the loss of forty-eight of the 178 B-24s sent from North Africa to the Romanian oilfield of Ploesti (another fifty-five were severely damaged). And so it continued. A most notable success was achieved by the German fighters on 17th August, when 500 sorties were flown against 376 American bombers operating against Schweinfurt and Regensburg. For just twenty-five Bf 109s and FW 190s shot down, sixty enemy machines were destroyed, approximately sixteen per cent of those taking part, and a further hundred damaged.

Such high battle casualties could not be sustained for long, and the Americans revised their bombing policy. Reliance was placed on the P-47 Thunderbolt which, fitted with new auxiliary fuel tanks, could reach as far as Hanover and Frankfurt. Henceforth raids would only be undertaken with full fighter escort, even though this meant that only the fringes of the Reich could be touched. Thus, in the period from 18th August to 7th October, only three of the fifteen USAAF attacks were against targets in Germany, and those three were confined to the periphery. A systematic onslaught against the German war economy by day was rendered impossible. On 8th October, long-range, unescorted raids were resumed, after a series of attacks had been undertaken on German fighter bases in occupied countries. Again, the Americans met disaster. In one week, from 8th to 14th October, in which Bremen, Marienburg, Danzig, Münster and Schweinfurt were bombed, the Americans lost 148 bombers, eleven per cent of the force engaged. On the 14th, when well over 500 sorties were flown against the 294 B-17s raiding Schweinfurt, no less than sixty enemy machines were shot down, more than twenty per cent of the force engaged. A further seventeen bombers reached England so severely damaged that they were beyond repair. Another 121 aircraft had been damaged. In their turn, the Luftwaffe lost thirty-eight fighters, with a further fifty-one badly damaged. It was the climax to a campaign in which one third of 8th Air Force's B-17s and B-24s had been put out of action, for an average loss in combat of four per cent of the German fighters. The importance of effective long-range fighter escorts, not to be possessed by the Luftwaffe, was never more clearly illustrated.

No air force could continue to suffer such losses. Not only was it expensive in aircraft, but also in crews, ten men being lost with every B-17 that was destroyed. Therefore, the 8th Air Force was again forced to limit its activities over the Reich. Instrument bombing through thick cloud which inhibited the activities of the German defenders, and the development of continuous escort by relays of fighters, were no substitute for a properly escorted bomber force able to operate in clear visibility. A more serious threat to Germany came from the bombers of 15th Air Force based in Italy, which were capable of bombing Austria and southern Germany. However, although this caused a dissipation of the Reich's air defence forces, the Luftwaffe high command was not seriously disturbed by its level of activity, and, being capable of inflicting losses of up to ten per cent of the enemy aircraft engaged, saw no reason why stronger forces should be committed to meet the attacks. By the end of 1943, the Germans were in effective command of the air over the Reich by day. Before the American campaign had begun, both Galland and Milch had predicted that, to inflict decisive losses, the fighters would have to outnumber the bombers by four to one. In the event, actions were fought with less than half that superiority, and yet a decisive success was won.

By night, however, matters were very different. The British estimated that, for their bomber force to be rendered ineffective, it would have to suffer operational losses of more than seven per cent over a period of three months of intensive operations. Effectiveness might become unacceptably low if losses were more than five per cent over the same period. Such were the targets for the Reich's defenders. In individual operations, they certainly met them. For example, in the first three major raids on Berlin on the nights of 23rd August and 1st and 4th September, RAF Bomber Command lost 7.2 per cent of its force, with another 6.8 per cent damaged. In August, when the impact of 'Window' was at its greatest, the night fighter force claimed 250 victories, a monthly record, of which 202 went to the 'Wild Boar' tacticians. However, the RAF soon adjusted its tactics to the new defensive methods. For example, the bombers operated for preference in bad weather, when the uncontrolled Wilde Saue operations were more difficult or even impossible; they concealed their intentions by diversionary raids with sky and ground markers; and they spent even less time over the target. In addition, the RAF began to employ night fighters, at first Beaufighters and then the far more formidable Mosquitoes, to attack the interceptors and raid their airfields. Losses from these, anti-aircraft fire, technical faults and fuel running out meant a high wastage rate for the night fighters; in the first half of August, for example, one night fighter was destroyed for every two enemy bombers brought down. This, together with faulty coordination between the various means of air raid tracking, the inadequacy of electronic and other equipment, and difficulties in communications, led Milch to declare on 8th October: '. . . the system is not in order. It is all the same to me whose fault it is. . . . I am fighting against the system. It is wrong'.[21]

In November, when the Germans were particularly inhibited by poor weather, British losses sank to only two per cent, while German night-fighter losses in combat rose to three per cent. The year, however, closed on a better note for the Luftwaffe. Owing to the increasing availability of the Lichtenstein SN-2 which was, as yet, impervious to jamming, and the Naxos and Flensburg sets, which homed onto the British H_2S radar and Monica tail-warning radar, respectively, the number of kills increased, further aided by the spread of Y and Egon radar control stations, which were also capable of withstanding the effects of 'Window'. In December, then, losses inflicted upon RAF Bomber Command amounted to 4.1 per cent, or 0.6 per cent higher than the average for night operations in 1943 and 0.2 per cent higher than in 1942. There was hope for the future. Despite the activities of the RAF and its own inadequate resources, the Luftwaffe night fighter force had improved its performance, raising its tally of one bomber destroyed for every forty-seven bomber sorties in 1942, to one in thirty-four in 1943. Milch's promise, made in August, had some hope of coming true: that when, by the spring of 1944 the Reich would be producing 2,000 fighters a month, the night attacks would cease altogether. There were, at least, grounds for optimism. However, this could not obscure the fact that, in the past year, the Allies had dropped 206,188 tons of bombs in the West, mostly by night, four times as much as in

1942, destroying some 173,000 buildings in Germany and damaging 212,000 others. As Milch lamented: 'If we had had enough day and night fighters before, all this would never have happened. Then, we would not now be having to disperse our factories. Then, no enemy bombers would be coming over.'[22]

The year 1943 had been one of disaster: Stalingrad, Tunis, Hamburg, Sicily, the East. No less than 151,366 tons of bombs had been dropped on Germany by the enemy. On all fronts, the Reich was on the defensive and the Luftwaffe had suffered significant setbacks. Losses were averaging 1,700 aircraft a month. To those who had any understanding of military reality, the situation in which the German Air Force found itself was dire. There seemed little hope that it could keep the Reich from defeat. Small wonder, then, that tensions within the Luftwaffe high command reached breaking point, and that, in the culmination of the strain suffered after four years of war, Jeschonnek should have put a bullet through his head.

The Luftwaffe high command began the war fragmented, and neither victory nor defeat succeeded in bringing unity. As was evident in Udet's tragic suicide in 1941, the man most responsible for this state of affairs was the Commander-in-Chief of the Air Force and Minister of Aviation – Göring. Providing little in the way of effective leadership in the pre-war years, he withdrew almost completely from the heavy responsibilities of a war-time commander. His aversion to work increased in direct proportion to his acquisitions of works of art and estates, a process greatly aided by Germany's victories. After the fall of France, his life became almost wholly concerned with hunting, for either wild beasts or paintings, and he took to taking prolonged leaves at his estates of Karinhall, Romintern, or Veldenstein. He almost completely lost interest in the war after the Luftwaffe's failure in the Battle of Britain, and only really became concerned once again when the enemy bombers were laying waste large areas of the Reich. His attitude to work was indicated by Stumpff: 'I recall one occasion in which he had retired to Karinhall for a month after having given strict orders that he was not to be disturbed. I had to see him, however, and he finally agreed to give me an hour of his time. He listened to what I had to say and made a number of decisions which hit the nail on the head. But then . . . the hour was not yet up and I was not finished . . . he jumped up and said, "That's enough! Now I'll show you Karinhall!" As time went on, these distractions gradually gained the upper hand, until he no longer had firm control over the Luftwaffe.'[23]

There was also evident a perceptible weakening of Göring's influence with Hitler after he had made his outspoken, and brave, warning against the invasion of Russia. From this time, Göring attempted to offset Hitler's growing disillusion with the Luftwaffe by submitting unquestioningly to his wishes. He became, as the last Chief of the General Staff called him, 'his master's voice'.[24] Göring even took to cunning stratagems to convince Hitler that he remained a competent commander-in-chief. Raeder remembered:

The following situation is typical of Göring's eagerness to display his full agreement with the Führer. A morning conference attended by Göring's adjutant, Colonel Bodenschatz: The Führer points out a sector on the Eastern Front in the operational area of the Army Group under Field Marshal von Bock, about which he [the Führer] is concerned, since he considers it insufficiently secured, although the Field Marshal [von Bock] maintains that the line is stable. Afternoon conference on the same day, after Bodenschatz had had an opportunity to orient Göring concerning the morning's discussion: At the beginning of the discussion, Göring reports to the Führer that he has been worrying for days about a particular point along the Bock sector of the Eastern Front. The Führer views this as a substantiation of his own acuteness, and is delighted that Göring is always of the same opinion as himself.[25]

But Hitler was no fool. He was aware of the true nature of his Reichsmarschall, an awareness which had prevented him from making Göring Commander-in-Chief of the Wehrmacht in 1938, when von Blomberg had been dismissed. As Hitler then confided, there was 'no question of it. That fellow Göring does not understand even how to carry out a Luftwaffe inspection.'[26] On more than one occasion, Hitler referred to Milch as the real commander-in-chief of the Luftwaffe. Nevertheless, out of the strong sense of loyalty which he showed towards old, faithful political comrades, the Führer did nothing that would diminish the Reichsmarschall's prestige. As he argued in early 1943: 'What happened at Stalingrad is my fault, and mine alone. I could perhaps say that I was inadequately informed by Göring regarding the prospects of success of an air supply action by the Luftwaffe and thus pass on at least a part of the responsibility. But the fact remains that Göring is my successor by my own designation, and I therefore have no right to burden him with the responsibility for Stalingrad.'[27]

However, Stalingrad had been a great blow to the Luftwaffe's prestige, and from then on Hitler subjected the Air Force to increasingly sharp criticism. Bodenschatz noticed that it was not only Hitler who had changed; Göring, too, began for the first time to criticise the Führer to his own circle. Bodenschatz added: 'the former long discussions between Adolf Hitler and Hermann Göring became shorter, rarer, and finally stopped altogether. The Reichsmarschall was no longer called to participate in important conferences.'[28] The destruction of Hamburg placed a further heavy strain on the relationship. Hitler had suffered a severe shock with the raid. Warlimont remembered:

Up to August 1943, German Supreme Headquarters had treated the air offensive more or less as a routine matter, but since the attack on Hamburg at the beginning of that month more attention was paid to it. When the first news of this attack arrived, Hitler unexpectedly appeared during the night in Jodl's hut and, obviously more shaken than he had been since the time of the Norwegian campaign, gave vent to bitter reproaches. Jodl and his staff, however, had always been designedly excluded from the strategy of the war in the air, and did not even know the background of the steady deterioration of the Luftwaffe; they were therefore hardly the correct target for Hitler's complaints. Subsequently the air attacks became far more devastating and Hitler – not without reason – began to direct his criticism at Göring; the staff were only spectators, but on occasions the atmosphere in the map room became such that they felt it best to leave quietly.[29]

Matters were not helped by the reports from Party leaders which were continually brought to Hitler's attention by Martin Bormann, head of the Party Chancery, the Führer's Secretary and Hitler's closest aide after 1941. As such, he was a natural enemy of the Reichsmarschall. The reports were highly critical of Göring and the Luftwaffe leaders for allowing such a wholesale destruction to be unleashed on the Reich. The Gauleiters (regional Party leaders) were particularly prone to vicious abuse, and wrote detailed, often inaccurate, accounts of the raids in their areas. Every effort was made to make the Air Force a scapegoat in order to avoid odium being heaped upon the National Socialist Party. Allegations of treason became common, and served only to heighten the growing suspicion in which Hitler held the Luftwaffe high command. This led him to taking a growing interest in the operations of his Air Force. Using his unfettered power as Commander-in-Chief of the Wehrmacht, he gradually began to take over the tactical, technical, and organisational command of the Luftwaffe, making its General Staff as much an instrument of his will as he had done that of the Army. Even by the winter of 1942, Hitler's influence had had its deadening effect on operations at the front. During the Stalingrad battle, von Richthofen noted that 'As things are at present, one is, from the operational point of view, nothing more than an overpaid non-commissioned officer'.[30]

Faced by disaster at the front and disillusion at home, Göring increasingly withdrew into a world of fantasy. He only wished to hear what was favourable, and was unable to face sobering reports dealing with reality. As 'Beppo' Schmid, in charge of Luftwaffe Intelligence until late 1943, remembered:

> As soon as the tide began to turn against Germany . . . with the crisis in the East, America's entry into the war, and the increased bombardment of German cities by the Royal Air Force . . . Göring's relationship to his General Staff Chief and his Chief of Intelligence [Branch V] became more and more tense. The reason for this was the unwillingness of Branch V to depart from its tradition of objective evaluation of information. . . . Unfavourable reports submitted by intelligence officers at the front were simply dismissed as inaccurate. On the other hand it was rather embarrassing for us to have to correct

the exaggerated reports of successes sent in by certain corps. . . . Our reports on the development and expansion of the Russian Air Force during the campaign in the East were interpreted as an expression of a 'defeatist attitude on the part of Branch V.' We were unable to convince Luftwaffe leaders of the tremendous capacity or the significance for Russia of the supply routes via Archangel, the Far East, and the Persian Gulf was brushed aside as inconsequential. The recovery of the British aircraft industry and the establishment of a four-engine bomber fleet in England were considered unimportant. Countless oral reports and written memoranda dealing with the American armament programme went entirely unnoticed. Our reports on the establishment of a huge American fleet of four-engine bombers, on the first appearance of American aircraft in England and Africa, and on the construction of a large number of airfields in Great Britain (air reconnaissance over Britain had been all but discontinued because of the efficacy of the British fighter aircraft defence; thus we had no aerial photographs to present in support of the last contention) . . . all of which were of the greatest importance in planning the future conduct of the war . . . were not only doubted but held up to ridicule. Our reports regarding the number of British aircraft appearing over Germany at night were not believed. The importance which the Chief of Intelligence had attributed to the attaché service was dismissed as grossly exaggerated, and the traditional attaché conferences, which admittedly took these people away from their posts temporarily, were severely criticised. Those memoranda submitted by the attachés and reporting on the dissatisfaction of Bulgaria, Romania, Hungary and Turkey at the small amount of German support they were receiving wandered into the wastebasket, and the attachés were told to omit all references to political matters from their reports in the future. Finally, when the Chief of Intelligence dared to confirm . . . by means of a detailed report and several diagrams . . . a statement made by Churchill to the Lower House to the effect that England had employed a force of 1,000 aircraft in a night raid on Cologne, his 'defeatist attitude and tendency to theorize' were proved beyond any doubt. The Führer and his immediate staff arbitrarily termed all reports coming from Branch V 'reports of lies'. By this time none of us really enjoyed our work any longer.

Even Jeschonnek was not immune to the ostrich-like manner adopted by his Commander-in-Chief. As Schmid noted: 'In addition, the Chief of the General Staff ordered that the personnel strength of the Intelligence Branch to be reduced to a minimum in order to cut down the "pointless evaluations of conditions abroad" and to do away with the reports "which made such unpleasant reading." '[31]

Göring further alienated himself from the Luftwaffe's leaders by his tendency to surround himself with younger men, who acted as unnofficial advisers. Together with the old group of personal friends such as Bodenschatz, Keller, and Lörzer, there grew up a 'Kindergarten' of young, highly decorated officers under the leadership of Göring's chief adjutant, Colonel Bernd von Brauchitsch. The influence of this circle was well summed up by General Koller:

> It was extremely unfortunate that the Reichsmarschall preferred to fill his personal staff with such young officers, men from the flying forces, anti-aircraft artillery units, or signal troops who had had only a few years' experience as soldiers. Most of them had had no really thorough training . . . at least no all-round training . . . and at most only a few weeks of General Staff experience. It is no wonder that their views were immature and their professional and personal experience painfully limited. Their training was spotty and incomplete; they tended to be conceited and the heady atmosphere into which they came often had the effect of turning them into megalomaniacs and spinners of intrigues. They were taken into the General Staff even before they had had any basic training, and given the right to wear the coveted crimson stripe on their trousers; they were promoted with astonishing rapidity . . . over the heads of their comrades; and they were accorded a position of influence which they were totally unqualified to fill. These youngsters were infuriatingly quick to pass judgement on anything and anyone . . . commanders-in-chief, generals to whom they were abysmally inferior in professional knowledge and personal savoir faire, men who could have been their fathers. They were just as quick to pass judgement on technical matters or on questions pertaining to the employment of forces. That Göring's 'court clique' came in for a great deal of adverse criticism from troops and commanders as well as from leaders in the top echelons of the Luftwaffe itself is a well-known fact.[32]

As the war progressed, and the Luftwaffe's failures became apparent, Göring became disillusioned with his Chief of the General Staff, and often vented his frustrations on him. By mid-1943, it was clear that the Reichsmarschall was dissatisfied by Jeschonnek's performance, and wanted somebody else, preferably von Richthofen, to fill his place. Matters were not helped by Hitler's tendency to ignore the Reichsmarschall and deal directly with the Chief of the General Staff. The 'Kindergarten', or 'Little General Staff', under von Brauchitsch, took to issuing orders in Göring's name, without consulting Jeschonnek. Often, he was unable even to secure an appointment with his master, while the members of the 'Little General Staff' walked in and out of Göring's office with impunity. General Deichmann later wrote about their relationship: 'If Göring appeared before his troops in the company of his Chief of General Staff, one could observe how the latter played the role of a recipient of orders. "Write this down! . . . See to that!" Such was the usual tone used by the Reichsmarschall with his Chief of General Staff. [Jeschonnek] . . . who had much work to do, found his time taken up with social affairs and waiting around in outer offices in a way which was disrespectful to his rank. If Göring was with Hitler, the Chief of the General Staff would have to wait for hours on end in a room at Führer Headquarters on the possibility that information concerning some matter might be needed.'[33] Because he jealously guarded his own popularity with the troops, and because he desired to keep Jeschonnek close at hand, Göring even refused to allow him to visit the front.

Göring's working methods soon degenerated to such a level that the atmosphere within the RLM became almost impossible. As Koller remembered:

> The Reichsmarschall must also be blamed for the frequency with which conferences and orientation periods were simply broken off before a decision had been reached. He talked things over with anyone he felt like, the Chief of Supply and Procurement, the Secretary of State, a Luftflotte commander or two, or with young Staffel captains or Gruppe commanders with fantastic, completely immature ideas and concepts, but always apart from the others. No one knew what he had been discussing with anyone else, and the Chief of the General Staff was usually the last to find out (and then only by chance) what was actually going on. Then, too, the Reichsmarschall was hopelessly under the influence of his none too reliable intimates and his totally incompetent friends who had absolutely no ideas of the functioning of the Luftwaffe. The Reichsmarschall delighted in playing one man off against the other, and it gave him malicious pleasure when the two protagonists were at each other's throats. He would stand nearby and make scornful comments to those around him. He often impressed me, and others as well, as being pleased with the disharmony reigning among his own most important staff members. One had the feeling that he had no interest in bringing about an atmosphere of smooth co-operation, that he was almost afraid that this would lead to the establishment of a united phalanx against himself.[34]

In that assumption Göring may well have been correct.

The Reichsmarschall's abnegation of his responsibilities and his method of conducting business placed considerable burdens on his subordinates. In theory, a unifying influence should have been exerted by Milch, who, as Secretary of State and Inspector-General, was Göring's nominal deputy. This, the Reichsmarschall would not allow. As Milch recalled: 'The only time I took Göring's place during the war was in the winter of 1940-41, when he went on leave. At that time I spent about two months at his headquarters near Beauvais in France.'[35] Indeed, even on that one occasion, Milch failed to provide the strong leadership that was required, for the simple reason that

Jeschonnek would not accept it. The day he arrived at Göring's headquarters, the Chief of the General Staff left, and, until the end of Milch's stay of duty, transmitted all his orders by telephone to the Chief of Operations. Friction between the men most closely concerned with the fortunes of the Air Force, Milch, Jeschonnek, and, while he was alive, Udet, worsened to a considerable extent. The effect of the almost complete break between operations and aircraft development and procurement was, as has been seen, considerable, and may be regarded as the most significant factor in the Luftwaffe's final defeat. Matters within the high command were not improved after Udet's death. The rift between those responsible for the operational deployment of the Air Force and those in charge of design and production of its aircraft, remained as wide as ever.

The problems within the gigantic edifice known as the Generalluftzeug-meisteramt have already been noted, but not so those within the General Staff. These, too, were great, and largely revolved round the personality of its Chief, Jeschonnek. His difficulties in maintaining good relations with those around him was evident from the beginning of his tenure of that office. In 1940, he appointed General Otto Hoffman von Waldau to become Chief of the Operations Staff. Von Waldau was a brilliant staff officer, of quick mind and outspoken views, and a long-standing friend of Jeschonnek. However, his appointment as Jeschonnek's deputy was to end their close relationship. General von Seidel remembered: 'Von Waldau, originally a good friend of Jeschonnek's, was a General Staff officer of greater than average ability. A man of sound and sensible views, he evaluated the potential development and employment of the Luftwaffe objectively and was well aware of the dangers of military involvement with the Western Powers. . . . Waldau's clarity of vision, his objective evaluation of Germany's top leaders, the military situation, and the inevitable outcome of the war, and his unconcealed impatience with Jeschonnek's role as "yes-man" to Hitler and Göring, gradually led him into the disfavour of Jeschonnek and Göring.'[36] Early in 1942, Jeschonnek decided to rid himself of von Waldau, and sent him to North Africa. In May 1943 when von Waldau was killed in an air crash in the Balkans, the Chief of the General Staff refused to attend his funeral.

For a time, Jeschonnek undertook the duties of Chief of Operations, but, finding this task too onerous in addition to his others, appointed General Rudolf Meister to the post in mid-1942. Lacking such a strong personality as von Waldau, Meister nevertheless failed to work as harmoniously with Jeschonnek, as, ideally, a deputy should have done. After the war, he noted: 'Jeschonnek never reported any of the details to me. Jeschonnek generally didn't allow his Operations Staff to advise him. Decisions were made during the morning in the Command Post, so that the Operations Staff was usually faced with a *fait accompli*.'[37] Meister found Jeschonnek difficult to approach, and thus was unable to exercise much influence over his decisions. They met little outside duty, and according to Meister, when they had to confer, Jeschonnek 'was cool, polite, but abrupt.'[38]

Relations were poor, too, between Jeschonnek and his second most important assistant, Georg von Seidel, the Luftwaffe's Quartermaster-General, an astute, if caustic, man. General Kurt Kleinrath, one-time chief of Branch VI (Armament) in the General Staff, wrote after the war: '. . . the relations between Jeschonnek and von Seidel were extremely bad. All direct co-operation between the two was interrupted for months at a time. In all Quartermaster-General matters, Jeschonnek got in direct touch with the chiefs of Branches'.[39] Of Jeschonnek, von Seidel remembered:

> Although his name is justly associated with the victories enjoyed by the Luftwaffe during the early blitz campaigns, no objective appraisal of his career can ignore the fact that his abject acceptance of Hitler's leadership and the awkward position he occupied between the latter and Göring after 1941 (largely his own fault) were factors which contributed much to the defeat and final collapse of the Luftwaffe. Moreover, the young aides and advisors (particularly in connection with technological matters) with whom he surrounded himself. . . all of them were as immature as Jeschonnek and most of them were far less scrupulous than he in their all-consuming ambition . . . had no qualms about indulging in behind-the-scenes intrigues, and were certainly much to blame for the final catastrophe. The names Christian, Diesing, and Storp [all of whom were later to gain high positions] stand out particularly in this connection.[40]

In addition, Jeschonnek was aware of the growing disillusion the men in the field had for his General Staff. As General Nielsen wrote:

> It was not until the war began, or, more precisely, during its early stages, that the relationship between the General Staff officers and the troops began to change perceptibly. One of the main reasons for this change lay in Göring's refusal to let his General Staff Chief visit the troop units during wartime lest they be tempted to give the major part of their personal allegiance to the General Staff Chief rather than to Göring himself. Inevitably, of course, this made it difficult for the Chief of the General Staff to procure an accurate picture of the conditions obtaining among the troop units, and also gradually decreased the feeling of closeness between the Staff and the troops. Moreover, the burden of work within the Luftwaffe General Staff itself and within the higher-level field staffs was so great, and the available staff so limited in number, that there was no longer time to maintain the close relationship which had prevailed during peace-time. As a result, the gap between the two finally became so great that the General Staff occasionally issued orders so unrealistic as to cause the troops to doubt the military ability of that body.[41]

The situation was made worse by a shortage of General Staff officers, which rendered it impossible to assign them to alternate periods of duty between headquarters and the front, and by a shortening of the training they received, made necessary by a critical shortage of instructors. By the middle of the war, Hitler's demands had brought about a situation whereby the General Staff had to issue orders demanding more than the field commands could accomplish. Objectives became ever more divorced from reality, with results that were exacerbated by the extreme inflexibility which characterised Hitler's decisions, an inflexibility which, alas, Jeschonnek was willing to comply with. As von Richthofen wrote in his diary at the end of 1942, during the height of the crisis at Stalingrad:

> No matter what I do, I can reach no one! On the whole I haven't telephoned Jeschonnek since 16th December because all of the recommendations submitted by me have been either tacitly rejected or, after oral assurances, have been given [to me], different orders have been issued. Furthermore, I now have irrefutable evidence that certain statements of mine have been reported in the opposite way. I now send only teletype messages – one four-page communication was sent today concerning the situation. In my messages I request directives for the conduct of operations because in the recent past I have heard only futile complaints instead of orders or directives. Probably they were, themselves, at a loss what to do. . . . [42]

Against this background, Jeschonnek's position in 1943 must be viewed. Responsible for the operational employment of an air force in three theatres of war, bearing the consequences of one defeat after another, alienated both from his chief and the field commanders, and isolated from all other centres of power within the Luftwaffe high command, by the fourth year of the war he had come to feel that he had lost the confidence of his beloved Führer. Whether this was so, is a matter for conjecture. Certainly the Chief of the General Staff was experiencing all Hitler's bitterness towards the Air Force for its failures. Every enemy raid on a German city filled the Führer with anger, and occasionally he reacted with outbursts of temper. This was made worse by Jeschonnek's loss of confidence in himself. As von Seidel recalled: 'In my own opinion (which is based chiefly on the first and only long conversation I ever had with Jeschonnek (in July 1943), during which he dropped the rigid mask of a soldier and revealed the more personal aspects of his character) . . ., Jeschonnek had come to the clear realisation that he himself was in part responsible for the defeat of the Luftwaffe, and he knew that the war was already lost.'[43]

Jeschonnek was in a difficult position. Resignation he considered outside the ethics of his military code, and his request to be allowed to take over a Luftflotte was rejected by Hitler. He also deemed it incompatible with his soldier's honour to tell his Führer of Göring's shortcomings. By the beginning of August, this vulnerable, shy, even timid man could no longer find it within himself to continue hiding behind his cool, slightly sarcastic public façade. He was no stranger to periods of depression, even of emotional breakdowns, and his few intimates realised that he was near complete collapse. As early as April, Guderian had judged Jeschonnek to be 'burned out'.[44] On 13th August, after a raid by the USAAF on Wiener Neustadt, Hitler berated him for over an hour, after which the Chief of the General Staff asked of Meister pathetically, 'Why does the Führer say all this to me, and not to the Reichsmarschall?'[45] Four days later, on the 17th, the Americans raided Schweinfurt and Regensburg, and again the Führer sent for Jeschonnek and shouted at him unmercifully. Early the next morning, the Chief of the General Staff learnt that, on the previous night, the RAF had heavily bombed Peenemünde, the rocket research station. Because of orders he had issued, the night fighters had assembled over Berlin instead, induced there by an RAF feint attack, and they had been fired upon by their own Flak. Jeschonnek could take no more. The two rocks on which he had built his life – his military competence and his Führer – appeared to be crumbling beyond repair. Suicide, which he had come close to attempting once before, seemed the only answer. He went to his room, locked the door, and shot himself.

By the side of Jeschonnek's body was found a slip of paper on which was written: 'I can no longer work together with the Reichsmarschall. Long live the Führer!'[46] When Göring arrived, he shut himself in the room with the dead body for ten minutes, and then called for Major Leuchtenberg, Jeschonnek's adjutant, and asked why the Chief of the General Staff had shot himself. Leuchtenberg told him that the General had wished to emphasise the terrible shortcomings of the Luftwaffe's leadership. He then elaborated on the impossible position in which Jeschonnek had found himself. 'Why' Göring demanded of Generals Meister, Martini and Schmid who were waiting outside the door 'has no-one ever told me the truth as this young man has done?'[47] The Reichsmarschall then had Jeschonnek's safe opened. Meister remembered: 'He personally studied Jeschonnek's reference files and found among them a study, the only other copy of which belonged to Below, Hitler's adjutant. He didn't give it to me to read, but I believe it recommended that Göring have a deputy, something which had first been planned with Pflugbeil in mind, later von Greim. Göring said to me, "You see, the man was working against me!"'... Göring read both of the slips of paper which had been found by Jeschonnek, then gave them back to me, keeping the study for himself.'[48] The study has never come to light. The next day, the world was told that Jeschonnek had died of a haemorrhage of the stomach, and the date was falsified to the 19th to avoid any connection with the Peenemünde raid.

Jeschonnek's successor as Chief of the General Staff was not, as some had expected, von Richthofen (perhaps because he was too forceful a man for Göring's taste), but General Günther Korten. Born in 1898, the same year as Jeschonnek, he had entered the Army in 1914 as an artillery cadet. After service in the First World War and in the Reichsherr, he transferred to the secret Air Force in April 1934, acting as Milch's General Staff Officer until October 1936. After that, he was chief of staff to the commanders of, successively, the Austrian Air Force after the *Anschluss*, Luftflotte 3 and

Luftflotte 4. In August 1942, he was given charge of Luftwaffenkommando Don, and in June 1943 was made commander of Luftflotte 1. On 25th August, he took up his new duties in control of the Luftwaffe's operations. A gifted staff officer, intuitive and with a winning personality, Korten was not unsuited to his post. His first act was to make his close friend, General Karl Koller, the new Chief of Operations, much to the latter's reluctance. Between themselves they arranged that, from the beginning, Korten's main task would be to keep Göring in good humour, while Koller would be the 'hard man', presenting the objective, uncompromising facts to the Reichsmarschall.

The new team held much promise for the Luftwaffe. Both Göring and Hitler were happy with Korten, as indeed, was Milch, whose ideas were very similar to those of the new Chief of the General Staff. Korten recognised that the days of conquest were over, and that Germany's Armed Forces should adapt themselves to the defensive. He realised that there was no alternative for the Luftwaffe; it had to reduce its operations in support of the Army to the minimum, and concentrate its resources to inhibiting the onslaught of the Reich's enemies. The Mediterranean, he felt, might be left quite safely to the ground forces, as, with more adept generalship than had yet been shown on Hitler's part, could operations in the East. There, he reasoned, the best assistance that could be given by the Luftwaffe lay in independent, long-range, operations against the Soviet war economy, where the armaments that kept the Red Army and Air Force in the field could be destroyed before they were used against German troops. In the West, Korten believed, every effort should be made to build up the Reich's air defences to bring Allied bombing to an end. Otherwise, the Luftwaffe would surely be destroyed. There lay the main task for 1944. It remained to be seen whether the new Chief of the General Staff could achieve it.

XI

1944 – The Beginning of the End

At the beginning of 1944, there were grounds for believing that the Luftwaffe would manage to see the year out as an effective fighting force. Its ranks had never been larger; almost 2,000,000 men and women wore the Air Force blue-grey, and were assisted by a further 900,000 civilians and Luftwaffenhelfer, (Air Force 'helpers') most of them manning Flak units and consisting of a large number of foreigners. The material position, too, was impressive. During 1943, no less than 25,527 aircraft had been produced by the Reich's factories, representing an increase of sixty-four per cent over the previous year, and a further 18,600 had been returned to the front-line after repairs. On 1st January 1944, the Luftwaffe's front-line combat strength stood at 5,585 aircraft, an increase of forty-one per cent over the total on 1st January 1943 (3,955 machines). The rate of serviceability had improved over the past year, and stood at seventy per cent overall.

There were other grounds for satisfaction. Training during 1943 had shown a marked improvement, and the output of new crews had not only been increased to meet existing deficiencies, but had at the same time catered for the anticipated expansion of front-line strength. In 1942, only 4,591 crews had been trained; in 1943, 9,593 passed through the schools, an increase of 108 per cent. Although the bomber formations were still short of over 270 crews, and the night fighter arm roughly sixty, it was not to be long before newly qualified personnel gave them a surplus. Moreover, the stocks of aviation fuel had shown a marked improvement in the last months of 1943, and reserves had been built up to a level higher than any since the summer of 1941. At the same time, the composition of the Luftwaffe's aircraft had changed in order to fulfil its developing defensive role. In 1943, a total of 15,151 fighters had been produced (a number of which were used in ground attack), and this represented an increase of 125 per cent over 1942, when 7,128 fighters had come off the production line. Compared with 1939, when the output of fighters represented only twenty-two per cent of total aircraft production, manufacture of these, primarily defensive, machines had increased to forty-six per cent in 1943.

But a closer inspection of the Luftwaffe's order of battle reveals its weaknesses. Still, a large percentage of the Luftwaffe's personnel more properly belonged to the Army. Some 100,000 men were in the anti-aircraft units remaining in the field, while a further 240,000 fought as soldiers in the front-line. Although, in September 1943, Hitler had ordered that the Luftwaffe Field Divisions be made over to the Army, their loss was compensated by a considerable growth in the strength of the paratroops, to reach 200,000 by mid-1944 (most not trained to parachute), and an expansion of the Hermann Göring Division into a Corps in October 1944. Many of these men were drafted from the Luftwaffe's ground organisation which, with the loss of territory and the considerable reduction in the bomber force, had a surplus of personnel. To have transferred them to the Army, however, would have been a more satisfactory way of dealing with the problem; but that Göring would not hear of.

Far more important, however, was the state of the Luftwaffe's flying units. The greater emphasis that had been placed on fighters in 1943 had not, as yet, been undertaken at the expense of the bombers, production of which had fallen from thirty-five per cent of the total in 1939 to thirty-four per cent in 1943, but of the transports, trainers and other aircraft which had fallen from forty-three per cent of the total in 1939 to just twenty per cent. Had the Air Force been waging a short war, such a reduction in 'ancillary' aircraft might not have mattered; as it was, however, in a prolonged war the lack of transports and trainers, especially, had considerable impact on the training programme, and that, in its turn, seriously affected the operational efficiency of the Luftwaffe. A closer analysis of the figures for front-line strength at the beginning of 1943, compared with those at the beginning of 1944, show that both bombers and fighters remained constant as a percentage of the whole, at twenty-eight (1,135 and 1,580) and forty-three per cent (1,740 and 2,400) respectively. In single engine fighters, the Bf 109 and FW 190, used for interception, there was a decrease, of from thirty-one per cent (1,245) of the Luftwaffe's order of battle in 1943 to twenty-seven per cent (1,535) in 1944. In twin-engine fighters, there was an increase, from twelve (495) to sixteen per cent (905). In ground-attack aircraft, many of which were FW 190s, there was an increase from almost seven (270) to over ten per cent (610). The night fighter arm was in a particularly serious position, output of their fighters having fallen from a peak of 190 in August 1943 to just 116 in January 1944, and because of the destruction of the Bf 110 factory facilities, it was to be further reduced to only seventy in February. Day-fighter units were thirty per cent below establishment. To offset the numerous losses that the fighter arm was experiencing, it was necessary to raise fighter production to far higher levels, and at the expense of other aircraft types.

Moreover, the increase in production of aircraft in 1943 was more than surpassed by Germany's enemies. In Britain and the USA alone, no less than 102,000 military aircraft had been manufactured in 1943, four times the number produced by the Reich. Of the Luftwaffe's front-line strength of 5,585 on 1st January 1944, some 735 were regarded as 'non operational', i.e. in units undergoing retraining, rest and re-equipment, compared to 125 the previous year. This left 4,850 aircraft for distribution over three fronts, just over forty per cent more than at the outbreak of war in 1939. Their deployment was as follows: 1,710 were committed to the East, 505 to the Mediterranean, and 2,635 to the West, of which 1,225 were within the Reich. In none of these theatres did the Luftwaffe have sufficient aircraft to give it air superiority. Indeed, only in the sky over the Reich was the enemy outmatched by the German Air Force, and then just by day. Elsewhere, the Germans were inferior to greater and lesser degrees.

By 1944, too, the quality of the Luftwaffe's aircraft was little better than it had been a year earlier; indeed, in some respects the outlook was considerably worse. Despite all attempts at rationalisation, by 1944 there were twenty-seven different types of combat aircraft being built, with eleven variations (compared to eleven types in 1939, with seven distinct variations). However, despite this embarrassment of riches, the Germans had improved the quality of their combat aircraft only in one area of activity: ground-attack. In the autumn of 1943, there had been a complete reorganisation of the Luftwaffe's ground-attack units. Until then, the dive bomber Gruppen (Ju 87s) had come under the control of the General of Bombers, and the ground-attack units (FW 190s, Bf 110s, Ju 88s, and Hs 129s) under the General of Fighters, and were regarded as appendages of the arms they belonged to. However, in September Korten set up a new organisation under the General of Close-Support Aircraft, which united both forces, and represented the Luftwaffe's final acceptance of the importance of ground-attack. The aircraft allocated to this role was around 600, prominent among which was a substantial anti-tank force, consisting of Ju 87s and Hs 129s armed with 3.7 mm anti-tank guns. In late 1944, this was supplemented by a 7.5 mm gun for the Hs 129s and anti-tank rockets for the FW 190s, both weapons of dubious value. Conversion from the obsolete Ju 87s to the new FW 190s was accelerated, and by the autumn of 1944, only one Gruppe and two Staffeln of tank-destroyers would be flying the old dive-bombers by day, the remaining Ju 87s being retained by night attack units. The Hs 129, whose serviceability rate was improving, equipped five Staffeln, but the main burden of ground attack fell on the FW 190s, whose special variants, the F and G, were relatively easy to service and proved extremely formidable, both in speed, manoeuvrability and armament. They were highly effective in their support of the troops in the field.

However, the Luftwaffe's bomber force had received no such renewal of its aircraft types. The He 177 had still failed to appear in appreciable numbers; only 261 had been completed in 1943, and they, because of their high rate of attrition, were ordered to be scrapped (an order tacitly ignored). Although production of this unsatisfactory machine continued throughout 1944, only about 200 of the 1,094 produced by April 1945 were ever delivered to combat units. The two Gruppen and several other Staffeln which were equipped with them achieved nothing of significance. The 'Bomber B' programme had been cancelled in June 1943 owing to the shortage of raw materials and failure of the Jumo 222 engine, while, by the beginning of 1944, the Ju 188 was available only in small numbers and equipped just one bomber Gruppe.

Production of this highly regarded machine was to continue throughout the year, so that by the time production ceased the Luftwaffe had accepted a total of 1,076. Over half, however, were reconnaissance types, and only five bomber Gruppen and several other Staffeln were equipped with them. Thus, at the beginning of 1944, the Luftwaffe still relied on the Ju 88 for offensive purposes, an aircraft that it had wished to supplant in 1943. Do 217s and He 111s were in service, although the latter were coming to be used more often than not as transports, together with a handful of Me 410s, used as 'Schellbombern'. Thus, with such machines, the great majority of which could carry only just over one ton of bombs to their target, the Air Force was to undertake the bombing of Britain and the USSR. By contrast, in 1944 the British Lancasters were each capable of dropping an average of just over four tons on the Reich by night, and the American B-17s almost two tons by day.

However, it was in the quality of its fighters that the Luftwaffe faced its greatest problem. What, in 1943, had been adequate to meet the best possessed by the enemy in the West, in 1944 was to be insufficient. By day, the Luftwaffe still relied on the Bf 109 and FW 190, the former equipping almost twice as many fighter units as the latter. Improved models of both had been produced during 1943, which made the new basic version of the FW 190, the A-8, faster than its predecessor, the A-5, by twenty to thirty miles an hour at 18,700 ft, and gave the new Bf 109 G-6 and G-10 a similar advantage over the G-2 version. This ensured that the two fighters had comparability with the British Spitfire IX and the Tempest V then in service, and superiority to the American Lightning and Thunderbolt. However, these developments were by no means sufficient to meet the challenge of the new American escort fighter, the P-51B Mustang, which made its first appearance over the Reich on 11th January 1944. It had a top speed of 440 mph at 30,000 ft, which made the FW 190 slower by between forty to sixty mph at all heights and the Bf 109 by thirty to fifty. The three aircraft had similar rates of climb, but the American machine was able to operate at higher altitudes than both. It had the edge on the FW 190 in manoeuvrability and was significantly superior to the Bf 109. These were remarkable qualities when it is considered that, with external drop tanks introduced in March, the Mustang carried sufficient fuel to give it a radius of action of 840 miles (a flight endurance of seven hours), which allowed it to range freely over almost the entire Reich.

The problem with the German fighters was that, loaded down with the heavy armament required to destroy the bombers, their performance was reduced to such an extent that they could not hope to equal the Mustang. The Bf 110s and Me 410s were hopelessly outmatched, and had to be withdrawn from service by day. The Bf 109s and FW 190s were forced to change their tactics. Separate 'heavy' and 'light' Gruppen were introduced, the former for attacking the enemy bombers with their heavy guns while the latter dealt with the enemy fighters. The 'Sturmgruppen' and 'Begleitgruppen' worked together in a grouping of around 100 aircraft. However, the Americans soon learnt to counter these tactics by mounting large-scale fighter sweeps across the flanks of the bombers' route, to catch the unwieldy German formations before they could attack. Whatever they did, the Luftwaffe pilots were always faced with one inescapable fact: the superiority of the Mustang, a superiority which was to be repeated later in the year with the appearance of the Spitfire XIV.

In night-fighting, too, the Luftwaffe lacked a fighter designed for the demanding role of combating the British bombers and Mosquitoes in the dark. The machines with which the Luftwaffe began 1944 were old, and their performance had been adversely affected by the additional equipment that they were forced to carry. Greater reliance was placed on the Ju 88 as a night fighter. In June 1943, it had been used to equip only four Gruppen, but by August it was in service with eight, and by July 1944 with twelve, as well as being on the strength of almost every other night-fighting unit. Moreover, in January 1944 the first Ju 88 G-1 was delivered, and it was clearly superior to all other German night fighters that were operational. It possessed a top speed of 402 mph at 29,800 ft and a maximum endurance of 5.2 hours. In addition, the night-fighting equipment that was becoming available in ever-increasing amounts was of high quality. In 1944, for example, the fully equipped night fighter was provided with the Lichtenstein SN-2, Flensburg and Naxos sets, three radios, a tail warning radar, a radio altimeter, a blind landing-navigation set, and an identification set for ground radars, in addition to a heavy armament, which, in the Ju 88 G-1, amounted to six 20 mm cannon, and one 13 mm machine gun. Part of this armament was positioned in the top of the aircraft's fuselage, to fire obliquely at enemy bombers, which with no armour plating, presented much larger and more vulnerable targets. Known as 'schräge Musik' (slanting music), this was first fitted to new and existing types of night fighter in the autumn of 1943, and was an immediate success. However, all this equipment and armament placed a considerable burden on aircraft that were not designed with it in mind. Performance was bound to suffer, and did not match up to that possessed by the He 219, which had been planned as long ago as 1941, let alone to that of the British night-fighter hunter, the much-feared Mosquito, which, in 1944, was capable of a top speed of 407 mph.

The Luftwaffe's failure to employ a fighter comparable or superior to the best possessed by its enemies, was not due to any German failure to produce the high technology involved; in five years of war, the aircraft designers increased the speed of the fighters by fifty-eight per cent, from 342 mph to 540 mph, their altitude by twenty per cent, from 34,000 ft to 41,000 ft, and their fire-power by seven hundred per cent, from twelve pounds in a three seconds burst, to ninety-six pounds. Rather, it was the result of a carefully considered policy, one which was summed up by Milch in a speech in August 1943. At that time, he was particularly concerned with night fighting, a concern which he was to extend to day fighting in early 1944:

We must definitely decide on priorities. That means the Bf 109, the

FW 190 and the Bf 110, which bears the brunt of night fighting. That is why I have said, in the case of the Do 217, for instance, that all aircraft requiring considerable outlay were to be put further down the list. Everything must be staked on the Bf 110. Only the Bf 110 in sufficient numbers can give us the necessary relief at night. Moreover, the Bf 110 can also be used by day. Compared with other fighter types it has the great advantage of considerably longer range. . . . It has yet another advantage in that it is perhaps the most easy aircraft to adapt to high altitude work. We are very much afraid that enemy bombers will be appearing at very great altitudes above the effective ceiling of the Bf 109 and FW 190. These types could reach such heights, but only for a very short time, just because their endurance is so limited. We are making every effort to develop a high-altitude type of Bf 110 with the same basic engine.[1]

Milch's policy was clear: the production and further development of a few existing types of multi-role aircraft in order to equip the Luftwaffe with reliable machines in sufficient numbers. He rejected any reliance upon new, more sophisticated aircraft which might prove difficult to develop and unreliable in service, and which would certainly involve, for a time at least, a reduction in output. For example, Milch refused to allow mass production of the He 219 night fighter, a machine considerably better than the Ju 88 and Bf 110; not only was it unable to perform any role other than night fighting, but production of the initial machines would take 90,000 man hours for each, three times as many as for a Ju 88.

The Luftwaffe's design and procurement policy was one that had been in force since early 1940, when severe restrictions on technical research and development had been introduced. On 7th February of that year, Udet had been forced to request from Göring that he be allowed to introduce certain curtailments in production plans. He wrote:

The present shortage of aluminium as well as of other non-ferrous metals such as copper, tin, molybdenum, and chromium, leaves me no choice but to recommend the following: I consider it imperative that everything possible be done to increase the production of those aircraft models which are in active use at the front. It is my opinion that a decrease in the production of aircraft models not in use at the front (i.e. training aircraft and reconnaissance machines), which could be replaced by converted single-engine and twin-engine fighters, can be justified for the near future. This change in our production programme would result in a shift within the overall production to those models chiefly in use at the front.[2]

Göring approved this policy, and two days later he confirmed it at a meeting with Keitel, Milch, and the Economics Minister, Funk. The minutes read:

The Reichsmarschall announced as policy new instructions to the effect that the material resources presently on hand will be utilized to the maximum in order to produce as much armament equipment as possible. This takes precedence over previous instructions to conserve our available stocks of raw materials. Those projects slated for completion in 1940 or 1941 at the latest will receive priority. Projects of longer range than this will be approved only within the framework of the Krauch Plan, designed to insure our ultimate independence of the necessity of importing material from abroad. All other long-range programmes will be re-evaluated carefully. Re-assessment of our present areas of main effort in the armament programme, such as has already been carried out by the Luftwaffe in its recommendation to discontinue the production of certain aircraft models, will be of paramount importance.[3]

In 1942, after a Führer Directive dated 11th September 1941 in similar vein, and instructions issued by OKW on 10th October 1941, the RLM made a further order concerning development projects. Milch was required 'to evaluate all development projects in terms of their feasibility as regards the current status of raw materials and production capacity.'

Such then, was the Luftwaffe's policy. It did not stop all development, and indeed, most projects were allowed to continue until well into 1944; it did, however, seriously inhibit many programmes. Apart from the He 219 already mentioned, most important among these were the Me 209; the Me 309, another fighter, begun in 1941; the Ta 152 and Ta 154, both begun in 1942 by Focke-Wulf at the request of the RLM, the former being a high-performance, high-altitude interceptor, a prototype of which was capable of 472 mph at 41,000 ft, and the latter a night and bad weather fighter with a top speed of 404 mph at 23,000 ft; the He 280, the Me 262 and Ar 234, the former two jet fighters and the latter a jet reconnaissance bomber, which were begun in 1936, 1938 and 1941 respectively, and whose performances were well beyond those of conventional aircraft; and the Me 163, a rocket propelled fighter begun in 1938. Development of these machines was undertaken, but with little sense of urgency. The Luftwaffe's priorities lay elsewhere. Of them all, only the Me 262 and Ar 234 was to see service in anything more than handfuls, and then only in pitifully small numbers. This was the inevitable result of the policy introduced in 1940, a policy which many have criticised since the war. And yet, in the circumstances of the time when it was made, it was sensible. Indeed, it was probably inescapable. It was brought about by the acute shortages of raw materials and the need to concentrate resources on producing as many aircraft as possible to meet the ever-deepening commitments of an air force that had been thrown into a major war three years before it was properly equipped. The policy was one of the few about which all the chiefs of the RLM, Göring, Udet, Milch and Jeschonnek were in agreement, although each might have had different ideas as to which projects should be maintained. It had, however, of necessity, one major flaw: it gambled on the fact that Germany would win the war before the enemy had developed aircraft superior in performance and greater in number than those possessed by the Luftwaffe. By 1944, this had been shown not to be.

Apart from the defence of the Reich, the theatre of operations which involved the Luftwaffe most heavily in the first half of 1944 was still the East. By the beginning of the year, however, only 1,710 combat aircraft (thirty-eight per cent less than in June 1941), could be made available for a front of 2,000 miles, and of these 1,150 (sixty-four per cent) were south of Kiev, under Luftflotte 4. This concentration in the south had been deemed necessary by the overriding need to hold the enemy far away from the oil installations in Romania, but it prevented any effective intervention in the battle elsewhere in the East. Nor did it achieve its object, for, by the spring of 1944, the Germans had been pushed back to within 200 miles of that target. Outnumbered in the air, the intervention of the Luftwaffe in the ground operations was no longer on a scale formidable enough to delay the advance of the Red Army. This became obvious during January 1944, when the Soviets ended their policy of concentrating on the southern flank, and began to exert pressure along the entire front. The Luftwaffe proved ill equipped to meet the simultaneous offensives which took place on the Leningrad, Rovno, Smela, and Nikopol sectors and in the eastern Crimea. The 345 Bf 109s and FW 190s along the front, together with a further eighty twin-engine fighters (half of which were used at night), proved incapable of wresting the command of the air from the enemy, who had skilfully begun to harass the smaller German Air Force by constant and ever-shifting pressure up and down the front.

Matters had not been helped by the decision made in the autumn of 1943 to form a long-range bomber force to carry out independent missions against the Soviet war economy. Until then, few raids had been made on the factories producing the guns and aeroplanes which were being used, in overwhelming numbers, by the Soviets at the front. In early June 1943 several raids had been undertaken by Luftflotte 4 on the tank works at Gorky, in which 684 tons of bombs had been dropped with some success. The action provided the spur for a reconsideration of long-range bombing independent of the Army's operations in the field. It was a policy that had for long been advocated in certain sections of the Luftwaffe. In particular, Colonel Fritz Kless, chief of staff of Luftflotte 6, had been untiring in his proposals to convince the General Staff that only by a clear distinction between 'tactical' (close-support) and 'strategic' (long-range) units could the Luftwaffe meet its responsibilities. Until the middle of 1943, these proposals had been rejected by Jeschonnek, but, with the succession of Korten as Chief of the General Staff, and the failure of the Kursk offensive, the climate of opinion within the highest counsels of the Air Force changed. Korten, a member of the so-called 'Defensive Clique', wished to place the Luftwaffe on a footing that would make the utmost use of his forces in the defence of Germany. An emphasis on fighters in the West and on long-range bombers in the East were the main operational features of his policy. Göring, too, became convinced of the need to employ bombers against the Soviet war industry. On 24th November, he instituted such a force in a directive which stated: 'In order to carry out systematic bombardment of Russian armament industries, I intend to unite the majority of the heavy bomber units assigned in the East – together with other special duty bomber units – under the command of the Headquarters of Fliegerkorps IV. These units will be assigned the mission of conducting air attacks against the Russian armaments industry with a view to destroying Soviet material resources . . . tanks, artillery, and aircraft . . . before they can be put to use at the front. In this way, the Luftwaffe will be able to provide greater relief for our hard-pressed Eastern armies than by its commitment in ground-support operations alone.'[4]

For this purpose, Fliegerkorps IV, under Jeschonnek's former deputy, General Meister, was made independent of Luftflotte 4, and subordinated directly to the Luftwaffe high command. The eight bomber Gruppen (250 aircraft on establishment) allocated to it were withdrawn from the front and began training in their new mission in December. At the same time, plans were drawn up whereby as much as fifty to eighty per cent of the Soviet Union's manufacturing capacity could be destroyed. It was proposed that the offensive would begin in February 1944. In the event, this experiment with long-range bombing proved a complete failure. By the time preparations were complete, at the end of March, the continued Soviet advance had placed many of the more important targets, such as Gorky, out of range of the He 111s, which equipped six of the eight Gruppen. The planned replacements of He 177 had not arrived, and were not destined to do so on the Eastern front until several months later, and then in far smaller numbers than had been hoped, and with poor success. Deprived of its targets, and never able to shake itself free of the requirements of the front-line, Fliegerkorps IV concentrated mainly upon the enemy's rail communications, a well-tried and effective method of 'indirect support'. Between 27th March and 22nd July, when the last independent mission was flown by Meister's command, the Fliegerkorps attacked important Russian rail depots in twenty major raids. The number of other missions were innumerable; for example, one Geschwader in the Fliegerkorps, with three Gruppen equipped with He 111s, flew no less than 3,164 sorties against railways between 27th March and 5th May. Only in its attack on the Soviet airfield at Poltava on the night of 21/22 June did Fliegerkorps IV achieve any significant success. Then it destroyed forty-four B-17s and fifteen Mustangs of 8th US Air Force which had landed there several hours earlier, together with 300,000 gallons of fuel.

Throughout the winter campaign of 1943/44 and the spring of 1944, Korten's new strategy had seriously affected the capacity of the German Air Force in the East. First, the withdrawal of fighters for the defence of the Reich resulted in fifty less Bf 109s and FW 190s at the opening of 1944 than there had been a year previously to meet an enemy who was numerically more superior than ever before. On 1st January 1944, of the 385 day fighters on a front extending from the Black Sea to the Arctic Coast, only 306 were operational, plus a further twenty-five in Romanian, Hungarian or Croatian units. In June 1941, there had been 462 serviceable. Secondly, Fliegerkorps IV was out of action completely from the end of November 1943 to the end of March 1944, and, although it was occasionally thrown into the ground battles on Hitler's instructions, it contributed little to German efforts at the front. The withdrawal of its 200 bombers, almost twelve per cent of the Luftwaffe's combat aircraft in the East, from the front-line for such a period was of benefit only to the enemy. Only 165 serviceable bombers were left to support the ground forces along the entire Russian front.

At the beginning of April, when the Soviet advance came to a temporary halt in the mud of the spring thaw, a lull descended on the Eastern front. In the Baltic region in January, the Germans had been forced back from Leningrad to Lake Peipus, a distance of 100 miles; from there, the front line ran for 1,650 miles due south, via Vitebsk and Bobruysk to the Pripyat Marshes, where it turned abruptly westwards to beyond Kovel, thence to the Carpathians at Kolomiya, then south-east to Jassy and west of Odessa. The Red Army was only fifty miles from the part of the river Bug from which Hitler had launched his invasion three years before. In the south, the front lay just fifty miles from the Hungarian border, and 200 miles from the Romanian oilfields. The German presence in the Soviet Union was almost at an end. Moreover, the Reich itself was threatened, and two new air commands were instituted accordingly: Jagdkommando Ostpreussen and Jagdkommando Oberschlesien (Upper Silesia). To the south, the Balkans had also come within the scope of operations on the Eastern front. In May, Anglo-American air attacks, made from bases in Italy against Danube ports and shipping in support of the Soviets in the Crimea, illustrated the need for the unitary control of air defence in the South-East. As a consequence, Luftflotte 4 took over control of the units in many of the Balkan states, and Luftwaffen-kommando Südost was confined to Jugoslavia, Albania and Greece. The shrinkage of the battle fronts was graphically illustrated on 2nd June, with the inauguration of 'shuttle' bombing by the USAAF, from Italy to Russia and back.

However, there were occasions when the Luftwaffe was still able to make an important contribution in the East. In addition to the usual close-support missions and the interception of enemy aircraft, it mounted several major air supply operations. In mid-January, it supported seven divisions that had been encircled at Cherkassy, keeping them supplied with 2,026 tons of arms and food until they reached the relative safety of the main German front on 19th February. In the Crimea, too, the Luftwaffe, together with the Navy, had supported the 6th Army, which remained cut off from 5th November 1943 to 8th May 1944, by which time the peninsula had finally been evacuated. In the Ukraine, a major air operation was mounted from 26th March to 10th April to supply 1st Panzer Army which had also been cut off by the Soviet advance. Some 3,500 to 4,000 tons were flown in from airfields which were over 125 miles away, in an operation which was one of the most successful of its type. However, the supplying of Cherkassy, the Crimea and 1st Panzer Army took heavy toll on the German Air Force, which lost some 650 transports in the first five months of 1944. But the sacrifice and the success of these operations did not restore the confidence of the ground troops in the Luftwaffe which had long been lost. The soldiers were unable and unwilling to understand that it was no longer possible to keep the skies free of enemy aricraft, or that air support during operations was seldom forthcoming. But in the face of Soviet air superiority of six to one, there was nothing the Luftwaffe could do about it.

That the Luftwaffe's weakness in the East had contributed to the successive German defeats since the winter of 1942, was clearly understood by the high command. Once the front had stabilised in April 1944, every attempt was made to strengthen its commitment there, especially in close-support aircraft. By June, the rest and re-equipping of all units in the East had been undertaken. Strengths were well up to establishment and serviceability was high. On 1st June, there were 1,980 combat machines divided between the three Luftflotten on the main Eastern front, together with a further 105 in Luftflotte 5 in the far north, making a grand total of 2,085. Of these, 580 (almost twenty-eight per cent) were ground-attack aircraft, mainly FW 190s, 405 (nineteen per cent) were Ju 88s and He 111s, with a handful of He 177s, and 225 (ten per cent) were aircraft belonging to night-harassing units. These, then, together with the 345 reconnaissance machines, were the aircraft that were to provide support for the Army. For air defence, 395 single and 105 twin engine fighters had been assembled. Thirty coastal aircraft made up the total. The greatest concentration of force still lay in the south, where the majority of ground-attack aircraft were based, waiting for what was believed to be the forthcoming major offensive by the enemy, designed to seize the Romanian oilfields. To this end, Dessloch's Luftflotte 4 was given 845 aircraft to cover the front from Lvov, just above the Carpathians, to the Black Sea along the line of the river Pruth. On the central front, in Poland, von Greim's Luftflotte 6 was left with 775 aircraft to cover the approaches to Germany, almost half of them being He 111s and Ju 88s. It had only 100 ground-attack aircraft. In the north, along a relatively small front, Keller's Luftflotte 1 had 360 aircraft, which included no bombers and only seventy ground-attack machines. With this small, ill-equipped force, the Luftwaffe awaited the expected Soviet onslaught.

In the Mediterranean, 1944 opened with the Luftwaffe at its lowest ebb since 1941, with just 575 combat aircraft. To face the enemy in Italy, Luftflotte 2 had 370 machines, made up of two hundred single-engine fighters, eighty-five bombers, fifteen ground-attack aircraft, fifty-five reconnaissance machines, and ten coastal aircraft. Operations were confined to reconnaissance missions over the static front and to the interception of enemy bombers attacking targets in north Italy. However, on 21st January came the Allied attempt to resolve the deadlock on the ground by a landing in the enemy rear at Anzio, thirty miles from Rome. The Luftwaffe reaction was prompt. Between 23rd January and 3rd February, 140 bombers were moved from Greece, France and north-west Germany, anti-shipping units in the South of France were reinforced by some sixty radio-controlled bomb carrying Do 217s and He 177s, and fifty fighters were moved south from their bases in northern Italy. In late February, forty fighters were moved from the West to support a counter-attack (the third) on the Anzio positions, bringing the overall increase in strength by 1st March to nearly thirty-five per cent. By then, Luftflotte 2 possessed some 600 aircraft, of which 475 were available for operations in the Anzio area.

However, as in Sicily and in southern Italy, the Luftwaffe's efforts at Anzio were quite insufficient to redress the balance against the enemy. The Allied air forces mounted five or six times as many sorties as the Germans, and at no time were the latter able to fly more than 200 missions a day in support of their ground forces. The radio-controlled bombs, the Hs 293 and Fritz X, were effectively jammed by the enemy, and the aircraft carrying them suffered heavy losses from the Allied fighters who dominated the sky. Fortunately for the Germans, however, the landings failed in their objective; a stalemate ensued, so that in March a number of air units could be redeployed, either in northern Italy or in the West. Indeed, after its failure to achieve any significant results at Anzio, the Luftwaffe ended any substantial commitment to Italy. In fact, this decision appears to have been taken even before the battle at the beach-head had been decided, when, in February, Fliegerkorps II was transferred to the West. A month later, the anti-shipping units in southern France, temporarily under the control of Luftflotte 2, returned to their independent status before coming under the command of Luftflotte 3 in preparation for the expected enemy invasion in the West. By the time the Allies entered Rome on 4th June, the German Air Force had practically ceased to intervene in the fighting. Only in the air defence of northern Italy was the Luftwaffe prepared to make any effort, although by the end of June it could spare just sixty-five Bf 109s for this task. Von Richthofen, perhaps the Luftwaffe's most successful field commander, was left with a force that was merely the shadow of its former strength. In the Balkans, too, there was a considerable withdrawal of forces, with Fliegerkorps X being moved to the West in March and large parts of Luftwaffenkommando Südost's area of responsibility being incorporated into Luftflotte 4. By the middle of 1944, there were just 240 German aircraft in the Mediterranean – 115 in the Balkans and 125 in Italy. The Luftwaffe had ceased to play any part in events in the South.

However, although the Air Force had relieved itself of a heavy commitment in one theatre of war, at the same time it became more deeply embroiled in another. From the beginning of 1944, the Luftwaffe had begun preparing for an Allied invasion of Europe which the German High Command believed would come in that year. Sperrle's Luftflotte 3, covering the occupied Low Countries and France, was, therefore, steadily reinforced. Already, in August 1943, General Peltz had returned from Italy, with the bomber units from that theatre of operations, to take command of Fliegerkorps IX in preparation for an aerial offensive against Britain. In February 1944, an even more significant move was made with the transfer from Italy of Bülowius' Fliegerkorps II, one of the Luftwaffe's most experienced close-support commands. In the middle of March, Fliegerkorps X, an anti-shipping command under General Holle, was moved from the Balkans to the West, and incorporated the units of Fliegerführer Atlantik, which ceased to exist. At the same time, the torpedo-bomber units based in the south-west of France came under Fliegerdivision 2, which was put under Holle's command. Although the Luftwaffe's commanders recognised that they could not hope to rival the enemy's numerical superiority, they hoped that their advantage of fighting near to their bases would to some extent offset it. In order to allow for a quick concentration of force over the invasion area, which might be anywhere from the German/Dutch border in the north to the French/Italian frontier in the south, a distance of 3,000 miles, preparations were made to allow for the fast transfer of units. Even training formations were kept prepared to operate in an emergency, and all fighters were equipped to enable them to assume the role of fighter bombers.

The Luftwaffe's efforts against the Allies in the West in the first half of 1944, however, were not totally defensive. Still, Hitler continued with the policy of bombing Britain, as much in the hope that it would deter the RAF from attacking Germany as in the belief that it would retard the enemy's war economy. On 3rd December 1943, Göring told the Angriffsführer England, General Peltz, that 'To avenge the terror attacks of the enemy, I have decided to intensify the air war over the British Isles, by means of concentrated attacks on cities, especially industrial centres and ports.'[5] The operation was given the code-name 'Steinbock'. By the end of the third week in January, the force under Peltz consisted of 525 bombers, of which 462 were serviceable. Nearly four fifths were Ju 88s (270) and Do 217s (121), while He 177s (47), Ju 188s (35), Me 410s (27), and FW 190s (25) comprised the rest. The general standard of training was poor, and Peltz based his hopes on the few 'pathfinder' crews at his disposal, who would find the target by special radar-radio control and mark it by an elaborate system of flares and ground markers. However, his worst fears were realised in the night of 21st January, the first attack of the so-called 'Baby Blitz', when 447 sorties were made (thirty-five by He 177s) carrying a load of some 500 tons of bombs to drop on London. Only half this amount fell on land (268 tons), and of that only thirty-two tons hit the capital. The poor training and inadequate navigational aids of the German bomber force were clearly demonstrated, even though the Luftwaffe was not aware of the full extent of its failure. Furthermore, in the future, British jamming of the pathfinder procedure on which all was based, was to prove highly effective.

This raid on London, the first in 1944, was indicative of what was to come. By the end of May, when the offensive ended, attacks had taken place on twenty-nine nights. In 4,251 sorties, carrying 2,812 tons of bombs, of which just twenty-seven per cent had reached their target, at a cost of 329 bombers. The missing rate averaged 7.7 per cent of the sorties made. The intensity of the offensive had fallen considerably over this period, as the numbers and serviceability of the aircraft available to Peltz declined. By the end of April, only 170 remained available, of which fifty per cent were unserviceable. The He 177s had, once again, shown their unsuitability. In a raid during February, for example, eight of the thirteen He 177s returned to base almost immediately with overheating, or flaming, engines. When they did manage to drop their bombs while in shallow dives to reach a speed of 430 mph, they were scattered far and wide because of the method of delivery. For the rest, with the current emphasis being placed on the manufacture of fighters, there were insufficient reserves or new machines to replace those lost in operations over Britain and in the East. As a result, Luftflotte 3 was left with just 130 serviceable bombers in Fliegerkorps IX with which to meet the invasion. Such was the significance of the 'Baby Blitz': by it, the German bomber force did more damage to itself than to the enemy.

Active measures by the bombers to inhibit the build-up of the enemy invasion forces were few. Not until 25th April was the first attack mounted, when 193 bombers were sent against shipping at Portsmouth. This was followed by raids on the succeeding four nights on either Portsmouth or Plymouth, all part of the 'Baby Blitz'. Only three attacks were made in May, and to little avail. The inaccuracy of the bombers and the strength of the defences proved too great. Indeed, the efficiency of Britain's fighters and anti-aircraft guns was such that they prevented the Luftwaffe from carrying out any proper photographic reconnaissance of the invasion forces in their bases, a major cause of the inability of OKW to arrive at an accurate idea as to where the landings would come. This was particularly unfortunate as, by June, Luftflotte 3, despite all its preparations, was poorly equipped to meet an invasion. As Jodl had commented in his diary earlier that year: 'How *is* the air defence against the invasion to be carried out? Major action against the enemy air forces is not possible. Fighters can carry out minor attacks against shipping and targets at sea. We must not accept battle with the enemy air force.'[6]

Because of the Luftwaffe's heavy commitments elsewhere, Sperrle possessed only 815 combat aircraft to face the 7,000 marshalled by the Allies across the Channel. Moreover, his was an unbalanced force, quite unsuited to the close-support operations that were required to repel an invasion. No fewer than 325 of his aircraft (nearly forty per cent) were bombers, quite unable to

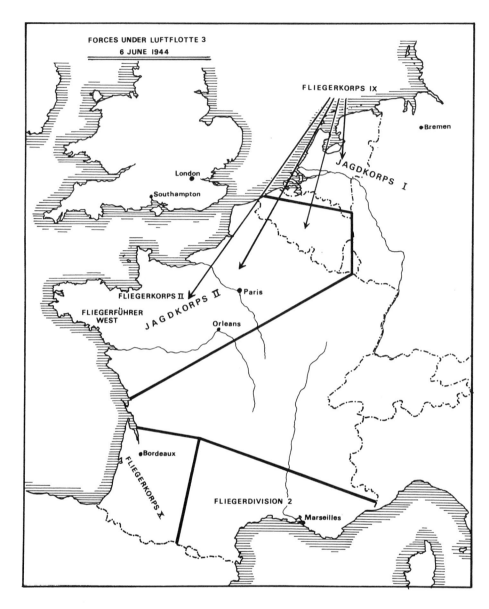

undertake operations by day in face of enemy air superiority, 170 (twenty per cent) were single-engine fighters, 145 (seventeen per cent) were twin-engine fighters (ninety of which were for use only by night), and only 75 (nine per cent) were ground-attack aircraft (FW 190s). In addition, there were ninety-five reconnaissance machines and five coastal aircraft. Moreover, the units suffered an average rate of unserviceability of thirty-five per cent. The weakness of the ground-attack units of Fliegerkorps II was particularly serious, as was the shortage of reconnaissance aircraft. However, despite urgent and repeated demands from Luftflotte 3, no reinforcements were forthcoming; all available close support units were already committed to the East in preparation for the expected Soviet summer offensive. Because of the importance of the Romanian oilfields, no diminution of the forces in Luftflotte 4 covering them was even countenanced by the high command. The single-engine fighter force under Jagdkorps II, too, was insignificant. The anti-shipping aircraft of Fliegerkorps X, amounting to some 200, suffered from a deep seated weakness in the inexperience of a high proportion of its crews, while the bombers of Fliegerkorps IX, 130 in all, suffered from an inordinately high rate of unserviceability. The ability of both Peltz's and Holle's commands to maintain sustained operations was much in doubt. Finally, although preparations had been made for a quick redeployment of units should this prove necessary, when the Allies did land the forces of Luftflotte 3 were dissipated across a front which extended from Holland to the south of France. The anti-shipping units, for example, were based as far away as Bordeaux, Toulouse, and Marseilles. In the face of massive enemy superiority in the air, a concentration of these forces to meet the enemy landings, which, in the event, came forty miles west of the Seine estuary, was bound to be highly difficult, if not impossible to achieve in the first twenty-four hours – the most vital part of the whole operation.

In the event, Luftflotte 3 proved quite unable to make any significant impact on the course of events on the day of the invasion, 6th June. The British and American tactical and strategic air forces flew no less than 14,674 sorties in the first twenty-four hours, against which the Germans managed just 319, just over two per cent of the enemy's total. By day, most of the sorties were flown by fighters, and by night the great majority by the bombers of Fliegerkops IX. Of the anti-shipping unit of Fliegerkorps X, which Göring had called the spearhead of the anti-invasion forces, nothing had been seen by day, and it managed only forty sorties by night. In the subsequent weeks, during which the Allies consolidated their position, built up their forces, and broke out of the bridgehead to liberate Paris by 15th August, the pattern of aerial activity begun on the first day continued. On the 6th, no less than 10,395 tons of bombs were dropped by the Allies on military targets in support of the invasion, and by the 12th around 42,000 tons had fallen. In achieving this, the enemy air forces had flown 49,000 sorties for the loss of 532 aircraft, just over one per cent of the total.

Clearly the Luftwaffe high command had to reinforce Luftflotte 3. During the first thirty-six hours, over 200 fighters arrived from Germany, and a further 100 followed by 10th June, while Fliegerkorps X was given forty-five torpedo-carrying Ju 88s and Fliegerkorps IX a further ninety bombers. But this was only achieved with high losses during the transfer due to enemy air action and bad weather. An increase in air operations however, was possible. On 8th June, for example, over 500 close-support sorties were flown, after a night's activity of over 200 sorties evenly divided between anti-shipping and bomber units. By the end of June, a level of 300-350 sorties by day and fifty by night was being maintained, and in July the average of 450 serviceable aircraft in Luftflotte 3 managed a rate of between 350 to 400 missions by day and seventy to eighty by night. However, these never amounted to more than ten per cent of the missions flown by the enemy. The Luftwaffe, like the Army, was subjected to continual attack from the air, and the dislocation caused thereby to the airfields, communications, supplies and reinforcements together with high losses, reduced the strength of many units to only sixty-four per cent of establishment within a week. After only ten days of action, five fighter Gruppen had to be withdrawn for re-equipment. Serviceability, too, fell to a low level. On 12 June, the Luftwaffe high command ordered that, henceforth, fighters should not be used in a ground-attack role, but, instead, concentrate upon weakening the enemy air forces.

To emphasise the importance then placed upon defence, Fliegerkorps II was removed from the West, and command of its units was taken over by Jagdkorps II, under General Junck (he was to be replaced by Bülowius on 1st July). However, even a concentration upon defensive fighter interception at the expense of ground-support could not weaken the total command of the air enjoyed by the Allies. The efficacy of the Luftwaffe was seriously affected by the withdrawal of the air units to the Paris area, necessitated by the Allied bombing of, and advance towards, the German airfields in Normandy. This forced the German aircraft to operate at a range no less than those of the enemy forces based in southern England. Even by night, the Luftwaffe had to modify its offensive operations. Effective jamming of the Hs 293 and Fritz X radio controlled bombs, together with high losses owing to the effectiveness of the enemy's night-fighters and anti-aircraft fire, caused the Luftwaffe to turn to high-level bombing missions. The accurate attack on ships and Allied positions was thus rendered impossible, and so, by 12th June, the activities of Fliegerkorps IX were almost exclusively concerned with minelaying, designed to prevent the movement of supplies to the enemy forces on the Continent. By the end of July, some 2,000 sorties had been undertaken in this task and 4,000 mines laid, to be swept up almost immediately by the Royal Navy. The operations of Fliegerkorps X were even less effective. The low serviceability of its units meant that only relatively few sorties could be undertaken. After the first two days, activities were suspended and no major effort was made until the night of the 13th, and even then the training of the crews was so poor that only six aircraft reached the invasion area. Desultory operations continued over the following weeks, but the Do 217s and He 177s achieved little success even when they had found their targets. With such forces the Luftwaffe proved quite unable to hinder significantly the reinforcement of the enemy forces ashore, so that by 29th July no less than 1,566,000 men, 332,645 vehicles and 1,603,000 tons of supplies had been landed on the Normandy beaches, a force that far outnumbered the German troops facing them.

But not only had the Luftwaffe proved incapable of inhibiting the activities of the Allies by sea or on the ground; by its loss of command of the air over the battlefield, it found itself quite unable to prevent the enemy from paralysing the movements of the German ground forces. On 18th July, for example, no less than 1,600 heavy and 350 medium Allied bombers intervened in bitter fighting around St Lo, and within minutes had deposited 7,700 tons on the battlefield. On the 25th, when a similar attack was undertaken in the same area, the commander of one élite panzer division stated that seventy per cent of his men were either dead, wounded, or had suffered a nervous breakdown. As Field-Marshal Rommel, in command of Army Group B in Normandy, reported to the High Command of the Wehrmacht as early as 11th June:

> Our operations in Normandy are . . . rendered exceptionally diffi-
> cult, and in part impossible to carry out by the following factors: the
> exceptionally strong and in some respects overwhelming superiority
> of the enemy air force. . . . The enemy has complete command of the
> air over the battle up to about 100 kilometres behind the front and
> cuts off by day . . . almost all traffic on roads or by-roads or in open
> country. Movements of our troops on the field of battle by day are
> thus almost entirely prevented, while the enemy can operate freely.[7]

This was confirmed on 31st July, while the Allied breakout was under way, when the Commander-in-Chief West, Field Marshal Günther von Kluge, informed Hitler that 'The enemy air superiority is terrific, and smothers almost every one of our movements.'[8] The domination of the battlefield, which the Luftwaffe had made its prerogative in the early years of the war, was taken over by the western enemy, as it had been by the Eastern. They both exacted due vengeance.

However, the Luftwaffe was not yet at the end of its offensive capability – not quite. Certainly, with the end of the 'Baby Blitz' in May 1944, its air units ceased all offensive operations away from the battle-front, and for the last year of their existence were capable only of defensive measures. Indeed, by September, the bomber force on which the Luftwaffe's aggressive strategy had for so long been based, had almost ceased to exist. However, the aerial bombardment of England was not a thing of the past, and on the night of 12th/13th June a new offensive began, when ten flying bombs were fired at London at the start of a campaign that was to last until March 1945. The Luftwaffe's new weapon was a pilotless aircraft, powered by a pulse-jet engine, guided by an internal giro system, and carrying 1,870 lb of high explosive. After being catapulted off the ground, it accelerated up to its cruising speed of 400 mph, too fast and too dangerous a target to fall easy prey to fighters, and, at a height of below 3,000 ft, too low for the heavy anti-aircraft guns to operate effectively, and too high for the light guns to reach. With an operational life of half an hour, the Fi 103, as it was known (or, as Hitler called it, the V1 - Vergeltungswaffe, retaliation weapon), had a range of 160 miles and the ability to hit a target of five miles by three. Launched from the Pas de Calais, therefore, London would be easy to reach by the bomb. If its operational efficiency could be assured, it was an ideal weapon, cheap to manufacture, using no aluminium, and fuelled by paraffin.

The Fi 103 made its first powered flight in December 1942, and by the middle of 1943 had flown a distance of 152 miles to land within half a mile of its target. The RLM ordered that the weapon be placed in full production and set the provisional date for its employment as December 1943. The aim of the offensive was summed up by Milch in August: 'A weapon against which the public sees there is no real defence has such a catastrophic morale effect that by itself – regardless of what the weapon is – it must have immense consequences.' With full production running at 3,500 flying bombs a month, one could be launched every twelve minutes. The Londoners, Milch reckoned, could take the bombardment for four days, but no longer. 'They will never endure it. It will be the end of any real life in the city'.[9] Capitulation, or a negotiated peace, would be the only alternative. Such was the hope which lay behind the employment of the V1. The reality, however, was very different. Production difficulties and heavy Allied bombing on the Peenemünde test centre and the launching sites in France, as well as on the road and rail communications in occupied Europe, caused delay, and it was not until June 1944 that the offensive could be undertaken. Indeed, it was only begun then because Göring insisted that a diversion be made to attract some of the enemy's air strength from the Allied bridgehead in Normandy. Thus, with inadequate preparations, the first flying bombs were launched six days after the invasion. Only four reached London. After a pause of three days, the battle was resumed with 244 bombs launched from fifty-five sites on the night of 15th/16th June. Thereafter, operations, under the command of Colonel Fritz Wachtel, continued on a scale averaging 120 to 190 bombs every twenty-four hours, and by 29th June no less than 2,000 had been sent against England, mainly to London. In July, constant enemy air attack against communications had taken its toll, and the transport of flying bombs to their launching sites was severely hampered. Largely as a result of this, and of unforeseen technical defects in launching, a planned rate of one rocket fired off every twenty-six minutes was reduced to one every ninety. By 5th September, the operation was over, and the last remnants of the flying bomb units retreated from France. They had fired 8,964 bombs against London, 143 against Portsmouth and Southampton, the main embarkation ports for the invasion, and twenty-one against Gloucester.

However, this was not the end of the offensive. The flying bomb could also be launched from an aircraft, the He 111 being found the most suitable. During the first stage of the offensive, 400 bombs had been launched in this manner, and in September a bomber unit on the Dutch-German border began operations as the sole means of delivering the V1s. Although losses owing to accidents and RAF action were high, and seventy-seven He 111s were destroyed, launchings continued until the advance of the Allied armies towards north-west Germany put a stop to them in mid-January 1945. By then, a total of 1,150 had been aimed at London, and fifty at Manchester. However, in the meantime, a new version of the Fi 103 had been produced with a range of 220 miles, thus allowing it to be fired from Holland. In March operations were resumed and continued until the evacuation of Holland was ordered at the end of the month. By that time, a further 275 bombs had been launched against the British capital.

The flying bomb offensive was a failure. Not only were the numbers fired at London small, and their effect lessened by being extended over a long period and falling over a wide area, but they were also extremely erratic and inaccurate in performance. Of the 10,942 flying bombs launched in the whole campaign, only 6,725 (sixty-four per cent) crossed the English coast, and 2,500 (twenty-three per cent) reached their targets. The British air defences were particularly active, and destroyed 3,957 of the machines, while effective intelligence work caused the Germans to set the internal navigational system of the flying bombs so that they repeatedly over-shot London. The damage caused by the flying bombs was, nevertheless, not inconsiderable, with 23,000 houses destroyed, 6,184 civilians killed, and 17,981 seriously injured. These casualties, together with those caused by the V2 rockets launched by the German Army against England (1,054 fell on Britain between September 1944 and March 1945, half on London, causing 2,754 deaths and 6,523 seriously injured), accounted for one person out of every seven killed in the United Kingdom by aerial bombardment, and two out of every seven badly injured. Had the German plans not been seriously inhibited by the enemy activity in the air, during which 117,964 tons of bombs were dropped on suspected flying bomb and rocket targets between August 1943 and September 1944, and far heavier amounts on the communications system which dislocated the supplies to the rocket sites, heavier damage would unquestionably have been inflicted on London. The Luftwaffe's failure to retain command of the air over Europe ensured that this would not be so.

However important developments in the East, the Mediterranean and the West had been for Germany during the first half of 1944 for the Luftwaffe, their significance was as nothing compared with the air war over the Reich itself. Here, the experience of the previous year was to prove no indication of the intensity of the onslaught that was to come. In 1943, some 151,366 tons of bombs had been dropped on the Reich; in 1944, 589,873 tons were to find their way onto German cities, industries, and the communications network, an increase of almost 190 per cent. In addition, another 611,661 tons were deposited on targets in occupied Europe, an increase of 1,015 per cent over the previous year. However, when the new year began, it was by no means certain that such would be the outcome. For 1943 had ended on a note of optimism for the Luftwaffe; its defences had decisively defeated the American formations by day, and, despite the British dominance of electronic warfare, seemed set fair to inflict high losses on the bombers by night.

At the beginning of the year, the Luftwaffe mustered some 9,000 heavy and 20,000 medium and light anti-aircraft guns in its defences against the Western enemy. This represented a considerable force, over three times the strength of anti-aircraft defences in the United Kingdom, and proved extremely effective. The importance which the Germans attached to the Flak arm is illustrated by a comparison of personnel employed: in November 1940, it accounted for 423,700 men, whereas by the autumn of 1944 1,110,900 people were involved, a large number of them women and foreigners. A great increase in the Flak arm had begun in August 1943, and was completed in the first half of 1944, during which time the number of guns per battery doubled (from six to twelve) and the number of batteries increased by a third. Moreover, the introduction in increasing numbers of heavier guns such as the 8.8 cm Flak 41 and the 12.5 cm Flak 40, meant that the high-flying enemy bombers could not escape the attentions of the artillery as they came in to attack. The development of Grossbatterien in 1943 had had beneficial results, allowing the artillery to put more shells into the target area, and this, together with the greater concentration of guns within the Reich instead of at the fronts, increased their success rate.

By contrast, at the beginning of 1944 the strength of the German night fighter force was low. The number of twin-engine fighters in the West was to sink to 480 by the end of the first week in February, of which 300 were operational, while the single-engine fighters engaged in 'Wild Boar' tactics amounted to fifty at most. Outnumbered by the RAF raiders by five to one, they were also outclassed by the Mosquito night fighters, which took increasing toll of their numbers. In addition, although the Germans were having some success in countering the jamming of their radars, they were confounded by the successful offensive mounted by the RAF against the night fighter radio communications. But despite this, enemy losses rose significantly during the first half of 1944, in large measure due to the development of the 'Tame Boar' tactics (which involved the fighters flying half way across the North Sea to meet the bombers), to the various radar devices coming into service with the interceptors, and to the general improvement in both the quantity and quality of both the night fighters and the Flak defences. The fighters were destroying one enemy bomber for every seven sorties they themselves flew, and, by the middle of the year, the Flak, which had been increased by some fifteen per cent, was engaged in bringing down some twenty per cent of the enemy raiders destroyed over the West by night. By 1st July, after an increase in production of Bf 110s and Ju 88s, the number of night fighters available in the Reich had risen to 830, of which 500 were serviceable, compared to the daily average of 1,300 bombers and 100 Mosquitos possessed by RAF Bomber Command. The majority of the fighters came under the command of General Stumpff, who, on 18th January, had relieved Weise, and, on the 31st, had assumed the leadership of Luftflotte Reich, as Luftwaffe Command Centre was henceforth called. The rest came under Luftflotte 3, which, by the end of April, had doubled its night-fighter

Gruppen to six, with a further three that could be used in 'Wild Boar' operations.

On 18th November 1943, RAF Bomber Command, which then had a daily availability of nearly 900 heavy bombers, had begun its offensive against Berlin, the destruction of which, Sir Arthur Harris promised, would cost Germany the war for the loss to the RAF of between 400-500 aircraft. In the event, the Third Reich did not crumble, and between mid-November and the end of March 1944, the period known as the 'Battle of Berlin', in sixteen major operations against the capital involving 9,111 sorties, 492 aircraft failed to return and a further 954 were damaged, of which ninety-five were beyond repair. This meant a missing rate of 5.4 per cent, a destruction rate of 6.4 per cent, and a loss rate (which includes those temporarily put out of action owing to damage) of 15.8 per cent. During the battle, one and a half million Berliners had been made homeless. In the same period, a further nineteen operations were undertaken against other targets in Germany, involving 11,113 sorties, in which 555 bombers failed to return and 728 were damaged, of which 73 were beyond repair, making a total of RAF bombers missing in the four and a half months of 5.1 per cent, a destruction rate of 6 per cent and a loss rate of 13.4 per cent. This meant that the RAF had had 1,047 aircraft shot down over Germany, together with a further 168 damaged beyond repair.

As if to emphasise the Luftwaffe's growing dominance in the air over its homeland by dark, on the night of 30th/31st March, no less than ninety-four of the 795 bombers sent to raid Nuremburg were brought down (11.9 per cent) by the defences, and total losses amounted to 155 (19.4 per cent). Such casualties were quite unacceptable to RAF Bomber Command, and caused it to reconsider its strategy. Partly because of the need to bomb targets in occupied France in preparation for the invasion in June, and partly because of the high losses over the Reich, the enemy drew away from central Germany by night, and directed their attacks to 'fringe targets' in Western Germany, France and the Low Countries. On 1st April, RAF Bomber Command came under the overall command of the Supreme Commander, Allied Forces Europe, Dwight D. Eisenhower, who directed its operations towards new targets. Over the following three months, the RAF deposited just seventeen per cent of its total tonnage of bombs on targets in Germany.

Losses suffered by the enemy over the Reich continued to be high; for example, in four attacks on oil installations in the Ruhr in June, the lowest missing rate was never less than 5.8 per cent and the highest was 27.8 per cent. But the new tactics adopted by the British, who usually sent over a series of small bomber formations flying simultaneously rather than in one large stream, together with the far shorter ranges of their raids which gave the fighters inadequate opportunity to intercept, and the smaller amount of Flak concentrated around the new targets in the West, resulted in a decline in missing rates to 2.8 per cent in May and to just over 2 per cent in June. But the reduction in British losses was achieved only at the expense of effectively discontinuing the offensive against Germany's war economy by night. In bringing this about, the Reich's air defences had played their part. They did not, however, succeed in ending the menace of the bombers altogether. It was only a matter of time before the major offensive over the Reich would be resumed.

By day, the Luftwaffe was far less successful. At the beginning of 1944, as if to emphasise the new vitality which the Americans brought to their offensive, a new command was established, HQ US Strategic Air Forces under General Carl Spaatz, to coordinate the activities of over 1,000 bombers and an equal number of escort fighters in England and Italy. They were faced by some 800 fighters committed to day-time defence in Luftflotten Reich and 3, the latter being of use only if the raiders crossed France and Belgium instead of using the northerly route over Denmark and North Germany. The first American attack of the year was as disastrous as those of 1943 had been; on 11th January, 238 bombers of 8th Air Force were attacked by over 200 Bf 109s and FW 190s as they made their way to and from the fighter-production region of Brunswick-Halberstadt-Aschersloben. Sixty were shot down, 25.2 per cent of the force engaged, for the loss of 16 per cent of the German interceptors. On this raid, however, a new phenomenon was encountered by the Luftwaffe: the presence of about fifty American Mustang fighter escorts all the way to and from the target, which were able to reach as far as Hamburg-Hanover, Kassel-Frankfurt from their bases in England. Their appearance shocked the Luftwaffe high command which, only a few weeks previously, had been assured by technical experts that a fighter with such a range was an impossibility.

Day raids deep into German territory were begun again, not to cease until the end of the war. From this time onwards, the German interceptors had not only to face the considerable weight of fire-power that came from the American bomber formations, which in itself accounted for high losses, but also the activities of their escorts, which were superior in aerial combat to the German machines, and were usually flown by men better trained than the average Luftwaffe fighter pilot then was. As more Mustangs were employed, the losses of American bombers fell considerably, while those of the German fighters rose to unacceptable limits. In February, the US 8th Air Force lost just 3.5 per cent of its heavy bombers in action, and a further 3.1 per cent damaged by fighters (in contrast, 26.8 per cent returned with Flak damage), rates which continued for the next few months. By comparison, the Germans lost in combat thirty-one per cent of the force employed, which, on 1st April, amounted to 850 single-engine and 110 twin-engine fighters in the Reich and a further 135 single-engine in the West. In contrast, the loss of fighters in the East amounted to just eleven per cent.

The drain on aircrew was particularly serious. In April, for example, the front-line units lost 489 fighter pilots and received only 396 reinforcements. As Galland reported to the RLM: 'Between January and April 1944 our day-time fighters lost over 1,000 pilots. They included our best Staffel, Gruppe and Geschwader commanders. Each incursion of the enemy is costing us some fifty aircrew. The time has come when our weapon is in sight of collapse'.[10] After the war, the commander of Jagddivision 3 covering western Germany, Walter Grabmann, wrote 'The Americans had reached the stage of enjoying complete air mastery over the Reich. The total number of fighters we still had left represented, at best, less than half the number of escort fighters the Americans used on a single raid.'[11] By 24th May, the Reich had but 246 operational single-engine fighters and thirty-five twin-engine fighters to counter a daily average of 1,200 bombers and 1,000 escort fighters available to the Allies for operations. Command of the air over the Reich by day lay with the enemy, a fact which was confirmed on 6th March, when 730 bombers protected by 796 fighters dropped 1,500 tons of bombs on Berlin for the loss of five per cent of the force involved.

Shooting down German aircraft, however, was not the objective of the enemy offensive, which sought to destroy the Luftwaffe's ability to continue to operate at all, by aiming, first, at its aircraft factories and, then, at its fuel production. In February, the offensive against German fighter production, which had been suspended since October 1943, reopened. It was estimated that, in 1943, the Germans had lost some 4,000 to 5,000 aircraft of their planned production programme, and in the first few months of 1944 the Allies hoped to bring production to an end altogether. In February alone, twenty-three air-frame and three engine factories were hit; ninety per cent of the Reich's fighter factories were attacked in the heavy raids from the 20th to 25th, and seventy-five per cent of their buildings damaged or destroyed by the 4,000 tons of bombs aimed at them. Production of fighters in that month decreased by twenty-three per cent. Milch announced despondently: 'In this month of February our output should have been 2,000 fighters, but there is now no hope of that figure being attained. We can be happy if we can produce 1,000-2,000 [in fact, it was 1,104]... As for the March figures, I calculate that, far from reaching 2,000, they may well sink below 800'.[12] The Generalluftzeugmeister, however, was unduly pessimistic. Reaction to the bombing offensive was immediate and effective. On 1st March, the Jägerstab (Fighter Staff) was instituted in the Ministry of War Production, with Speer and Milch as joint chairmen. Otto Saur was its energetic director. By placing the production of fighters under Speer's control, Milch hoped to end the harmful competition which had existed between the RLM and the Ministry of Armaments, and thereby increase the resources allocated to aircraft manufacture. By August, the aircraft industry possessed no less than 2,100,000 workers, compared to 1,900,000 involved with production for the Army.

The success of the Jägerstab was considerable, and it indicates the limitations under which the various strategic air offensives laboured during the war. Emphasis was placed on fighter production. Plan No.226, dated 8th July, envisaged a monthly output of 6,400 aircraft in which fighters outnumbered bombers by 5:1.3. Each month, no less than 2,600 FW 190s, 500 Bf 109s, 1,000 Me 262s, 400 Do 335s, 100 Me 163s, 180 Ju 88 fighters,

500 Ar 234s, 400 Ju 388s and just fifty He 219s. All efforts would be made to increase production. Bombing had destroyed relatively few machine tools (around five per cent), and production in damaged factories was resumed after only short intervals. The twenty-seven main manufacturing centres were dispersed among 300 different plants. While this entailed a loss in efficiency, the industry became a far less attractive objective in terms of ease of destruction. Although the Allied offensive caused loss to production of some 4,000 fighters, acceptances of Bf 109s and FW 190s in March exceeded the January level by 1,300, and were followed in May by an increase of twenty-five per cent. Thereafter, output of all fighter types continued to rise steadily, to reach a peak of 3,375 in September, an increase over output in February of 332 per cent. Indeed, this rise was reflected in the total monthly output of military aircraft, which, in June, reached 4,219 machines, an increase of 209 per cent over the February level. Certainly, air attack had taken its toll, for production plans called for an output of between 24,000 and 32,000 aircraft from February to August, whereas 22,821 were in fact delivered, of which 15,388 were fighters, but in 1944, as a whole, no less than 39,807 military aircraft were produced, 156 per cent more than in the previous year.

As a result of the efforts of the German aircraft industry, the Luftwaffe was able to survive the high material losses inflicted on it. Between 1st June and 31st August, a period which saw particularly heavy fighting on all fronts, the Air Force lost no less than 11,074 aircraft on all fronts. The losses of Jagdkorps II in the West alone amounted to an average of 600 machines a month. In addition, many aircraft were destroyed on their way from the factories to the front. Indeed, destruction was on such an immense scale that over the first half of 1944 that there was a decrease in the available number of what had become for the Luftwaffe its most important single asset: the single-engine fighter. They fell from 1,535 in front line units on 1st January to 1,435 by the end of June. However, in July the Gruppen began to receive more aircraft than they lost, so that by the end of the month the unit strength of single-engine fighters was 1,900 machines, representing a twenty-three per cent increase over the total at the beginning of the year. The night fighter force on all fronts had remained at roughly the same number (1,060), but had improved its quality by phasing out the Bf 109s and increasing its reliance on a new version of the Ju 88 fighter.

In the next two and a half months, from 1st September to mid-November, the day fighters were to undergo a further increase of almost seventy per cent, to 3,200 aircraft in front-line units. By the end of the year, the night fighters were at their highest peak, 1,355 aircraft, which represented an increase of some twenty-five per cent. Pilots, too were made available in increasing numbers, and until the end of the year there were always more aircrew ready for operation with units than there were serviceable aircraft. This was due in large part to a considerable increase in the numbers of fighters made available to the training schools, from 234 Bf 109s at the beginning of 1944 to over 1,000 Bf 109s and FW 190s by the autumn. However, these dramatic increases did not represent any whole-hearted acceptance of the need to defend the Reich at all costs from the enemy's bombardment, let alone the immediate adoption of a defensive strategy based on the recognition that command of the air was by then of paramount importance in the conduct of the war.

For the first half of 1944, at a time when the Luftwaffe's inferiority in the air over the Reich and its fronts had never been more clearly demonstrated, Hitler and certain senior Air Force leaders remained committed to bomber attack. In February, March and April, while Luftflotte 3 was engaged in its 'Baby Blitz' against Britain and Fliegerkorps IV was occupied by its new 'strategic' role in the East, the aircraft industry produced an increasing number of bombers, to a total of 1,852 using resources equal to those which would have produced some 5,500 fighters. To allow more defensive machines to be manufactured, the plans of the Jägerstab foresaw a decrease to just 284 bombers a month by the autumn. To except such a decline was hotly disputed by Korten, who was promoting long-range bombing on the Eastern front. He pronounced it to be the death of the bomber arm. In early May, Koller prepared a long memorandum which argued that the continued existence of the bombers in the Luftwaffe had been placed in jeopardy, and he followed this two weeks later by a study which called for a strong bomber force which he regarded as indispensable to the maintenance of Germany's position in Europe. Hitler read both memoranda, and found no difficulty in agreeing with them. On 23rd May, the Führer and Göring rejected the Jägerstab's plans, and looked forward to the day when the Luftwaffe would possess 14,000 aircraft, many of which would be heavy bombers.

Later that day, the Reichsmarschall called a meeting to discuss the Jägerstab's proposals, at which Milch, Speer and Saur were present. He told them of Hitler's interest in a strong bomber-force, especially one based on four-engine heavy machines such as those possessed by the Allies. Certainly, Göring continued, both he and the Führer recognised the need to have a strong fighter 'umbrella' over Germany (Hitler had argued for such before), but not at the expense of the bomber arm. A front-line bomber force of at least 2,600 aircraft, more than double that which then existed, was called for, to be achieved concurrently with an increase in fighters. The heavy bomber still remained 'the kernel of aerial rearmament',[13] and the Reichsmarschall ordered deliveries of the He 277 (the He 177 with four separate, instead of coupled, engines, prototypes of which had been flown, successfully) at a rate of 200 per month, together with 600-700 bombers of other types. As five single-engine fighters could be built for each bomber of the size of the He 277, that programme alone represented a potential loss of 1,000 fighters a month, and the total bomber output was equivalent to some 3,000 fighters. Milch was powerless to change the new turn in the Luftwaffe's procurement policy. That afternoon, when Göring, Speer, Milch and Petersen, director of research establishments, reported back to Hitler, an increase in bomber strength was incorporated in the Air Force's expansion programme for the first time in over a year.

Absurd though this new policy was, the Luftwaffe remained committed to it for six weeks, until 3rd July, when circumstances became so pressing that the 'Emergency Fighter Programme' was promulgated. The entire bomber programme was abandoned so as to concentrate production on jets, single-engine fighters and the few twin-engine fighters that could be classed as modern. By this time, even Hitler had been brought face to face with reality. On 20th June, an armada of no less than 1,500 US bombers, escorted by 1,000 fighters, had attacked the oil refineries, and threatened to deprive the Reich's armed forces of the ability to operate. The following day, the raiders had returned to drop over 2,000 tons of bombs on Berlin. On 26th June, the Führer had declared: 'In our position, all that matters is the manufacture of fighters, and still more fighters. . . . We shall just have to put up with the long term loss of a strategic air force which that will entail.'[14] The protagonists of the fighter force had, finally, won the day. It was, however, only a partial victory. Not only did it come a year too late, but it was inconclusive in its application. Before the Luftwaffe was to be fully committed to the defence of the Reich, the borders of Germany would be breached in both the West and the East, and the greater part of the Luftwaffe's aircraft grounded for lack of fuel.

Even when the importance of going over to the defensive in the air had dawned on Hitler, this was no guarantee that the defence of the Reich would receive the top priority that men such as Milch, Speer and Galland had long believed was its due. By 1st April, Stumpff's Luftflotte Reich had been allocated fifty per cent of the Luftwaffe's fighter versions of the Bf 109 and FW 190, some 850 machines. This, however was to be the highest proportion it was ever to receive. On 19th May, a proposal put forward by Galland that all fighter units in Luftflotte 3 be made over to Luftflotte Reich was rejected by Göring, who was, no doubt, mindful of Hitler's insistence that the front lines should be held at all costs. Indeed, plans had been drawn up for the transfer of strong fighter forces from the Reich to the West in the event of an enemy invasion, a transfer which, when it occurred, was to prove very costly in terms of aircraft destroyed on the journey and had a negligible impact upon events in Normandy. By 1st June, after the needs of both the Western and the Eastern fronts had been attended to, Stumpff was left with but 700 single-engined fighters, and by the end of the month with just 370, twenty-five per cent of the total available. Of these only 240 were ready for action. This was followed by an increase to 900 aircraft for day defence by the third week of October, roughly forty per cent of all operational Bf 109s and FW 190s, after which there was a decline to 400 by mid-December – just fifteen per cent of the Luftwaffe's total of such machines.

Twice, a reserve built up by Galland with the approval of Göring, designed to defeat the American bombers over Germany in a single 'Grosse Schlag' (Great Strike), was dissipated by Hitler to the front line. The first occasion was at the end of July, when over 800 fighters were sent to the West, where the German front was collapsing. As Galland wrote: 'That was absolutely irresponsible! They were bound to get into the stream of the retreat and be overrun, and they could no longer do anything to change the critical situation of the Army, even if there had been a ground organisation to receive them. One cannot throw fighter groups into gaps like infantry regiments! . . . The order to protect the German war industry from total destruction would have [been] justified. . . . But in the West they were doomed to be destroyed . . . without achieving any operational effect.'[15]

However, nothing daunted, Galland set about building up a second concentration of fighters. Throughout October, when operations were severely curtailed in order that new pilots could be trained and units schooled in the novel tactics of mass attack against the enemy formations, he built up a reserve that would allow him to commit 1,000 fighters over the Reich in a single operation, with sufficient fuel for 2,500 sorties. By this, he believed that 500 US bombers could be brought down for the loss of an equal number of German aircraft. Hitler, however, remained unimpressed by the activities of the defenders over the Reich, and believed that only a significant increase in Flak would succeed in deterring the enemy's bombers. He therefore, countermanded the orders for 'Der Grosse Schlag', and, instead, gave directions that the great concentration of fighters be used not against the Allied air forces but against their armies in the field, and in particular in the forthcoming offensive in the Ardennes.

Nor were the night fighters immune from dissipation. At the beginning of the year a third of their number were away from the West, while by the end of July this proportion had dropped only by ten per cent. Transfers to and from the fronts were relatively frequent; in mid-December, for example, no less than 140 Ju 88s and Bf 110s were sent to the Western front. Even Flak units would be moved away from Germany, as had been done in late spring in preparation for the landings in France. In such a manner was the defence of the Reich sacrificed by Hitler in favour of the front lines, and sacrificed to no effect. Nowhere was the Luftwaffe able to achieve the necessary concentration of force in sufficient strength to have any possibility of countering the massive enemy superiority in the air. By his decisions, the Führer ensured only that his Air Force was to prove incapable of defending Germany by day or by night.

However, being heavily inferior in the air in both numbers and quality was only one of the Luftwaffe's problems. Another, of considerable importance, was the shortage of well-trained pilots which the high losses and the inadequate training programme of the previous years had brought about. In July, Sperrle found that, with rare exceptions, only his Gruppe and Staffel commanders had operational experience exceeding six months; most pilots had seen active service for as little as from eight to thirty days. Although the training schools could produce sufficient men to replace those killed and wounded to fly the increasing numbers of aircraft coming off the production lines, to the extent of 900 fighter pilots in April, May and June, this could only be achieved at the expense of quality. Leaving aside the heavy losses of aircrew, which, for the whole Luftwaffe, amounted to 13,000 men in the five months from 1st June to 31st October, the doubling of single-engine front line fighters alone inflicted severe pressures on the training system. Restrictions on the use of fuel, too, reduced the flying-time available to trainees. The demands of the front had its impact also on the number of instructors, and their scarcity was a frequent cause for anxiety.

In an attempt to overcome these problems, on 1st July a new training command, Luftflotte 10, was instituted under von Seidel, designed to co-ordinate all the resources available. However, the quality of instruction was still sacrificed for quantity. Whereas, for example, British pilots were given as many as 200-220 flying hours in training for night fighting, the Luftwaffe's received only 110-115. American day fighter-pilots had almost three times as many flying hours than their German opponents before they were sent to the front. A considerable reduction in their efficiency was the inevitable result, a reduction which, in the hostile skies over Germany, could not be made good by enthusiasm or an excess of National Socialist zeal. Any technical superiority possessed by the Allied fighters was,· thereby, considerably enhanced. By mid-1944, no less than fifty per cent of the new German fighter pilots were shot down before they reached their tenth operational flight. Fighting efficiency, even against bombers, dropped alarmingly. In one action on 2nd November, for example, of the sixty-three Allied aircraft lost in an attack on Merseburg, 500 German fighters managed to destroy only fifteen. On another occasion on 21st November, of two formations of 170 and 180 fighters in visual contact with American formations, only six and thirty respectively engaged the enemy. Moreover, flying accidents owing to poor training and inexperience rose dramatically, so that in the three months, April, May and June, they accounted for a third of the 5,527 single-engined fighters destroyed or rendered inoperable.

But the shortage of aircraft at the front, their inadequate quality, and the rushed nature of the training of the pilots was as nothing compared to the damage to the Luftwaffe's operations that resulted from the Allied attack on the German oil industry, the success of which completely nullified all efforts of the Jägerstab, the Luftwaffe commands and the pilots. For aviation fuel had always been the Achilles heel of the Luftwaffe; never had it possessed sufficient to feel secure against shortages. It had begun the war with 492,000 tons of fuel, only thirty-three per cent of its planned stocks and sufficient at that time for just three months of campaigning. However, the brevity of the battles in Poland, Scandinavia and the West was such that no restrictions had been placed on the use of fuel. In the spring of 1941, measures were taken to curtail consumption in preparation for the attack on Russia, but for the first twelve months of the war in the East no further restrictions were required. However, by September 1942, with heavy fighting both in Russia and the Mediter-ranean, a critical position was reached whereby the Luftwaffe's fuel stocks fell to less than two weeks' requirement. Vigorous restrictions were placed on training programmes and transport and communications flights, as well as, to a lesser extent, on operations in the West. The fighting elsewhere, however, continued unabated. At the beginning of 1943, the position was temporarily eased by a natural reduction in operations during winter and by an increased output of fuel from the synthetic plants in Germany, which by then accounted for well over ninety per cent of aircraft fuel used by the Luftwaffe. With the resumption of good weather, and the deepening conflict on all fronts, the position again deteriorated. Once again, the activity of the operational units was maintained at the expense of the training programme. A reduction was also made in the fuel allowed to industry for flight testing and bench testing, an economy which resulted in an increase in the number of unserviceable aircraft reaching the front.

During the winter of 1943-1944, strenuous efforts were made to increase output from the synthetic fuel plants, and this, together with the usual reduction in operations at that time of year, allowed for an increase in stocks from 280,000 tons in September 1943 to 574,000 tons by April 1944, more than at any time since the summer of 1940, but sufficient then for only three months of full operational effort. In March, the production and import of aircraft fuel had also reached its highest level, at 185,000 tons. Then on 12th, 28th and 29th May, came the first enemy attacks against the German aviation fuel production facilities and stocks, when the US 8th Air Force dropped 2,500 tons of bombs on the nine main synthetic oil plants. The offensive continued by day and, to a lesser extent, by night, so that by 22nd June no less than ninety per cent of aircraft fuel production had been affected.

This successful attack on its sources of fuel crippled the Luftwaffe. The usual expediencies, such as a curtailing of training programmes and a reduction in aircraft testing, could do little to alleviate the dire consequences of the fuel shortage that faced the front-line units. In June, only 56,000 tons of aviation fuel were produced, compared to the 198,000 tons that had been planned in January. Consumption had been well in excess of production since mid-May, so that, by the end of June, stocks had declined to 410,000 tons, seventy per cent of the level on 30th April. In May, the Luftwaffe had consumed no less than 195,000 tons of aviation fuel; in June, it was allowed to use only 182,000 tons. Should the situation continue to deteriorate, the Air Force would, within a short time, be unable to operate. As Galland wrote after the war: 'The most successful operation of the entire Allied strategic air warfare was against Germany's fuel supply. Looking back, it is difficult to understand why the Allies started this undertaking so late. . . .'[16]

At this point in the war, there appeared a new phenomenon in the skies over Europe: a fighter powered by turbo-jet, the Luftwaffe's Me 262, an aircraft with four times the engine power and seven times the fire power of the Bf 109s which began the war. On 25th July, an enemy pilot reported the first engagement with the jet fighter, which took place over southern Bavaria and ended with his escape. It was an inauspicious event in what turned out to be a sorry saga which extended back as far as 1938. Then, the RLM had called for the development of a research aircraft to be powered by the BMW gas turbine engines then under development. In 1940, Messerschmitt's airframe was approved, and in March 1942 its first jet-powered test flight was made. The BMW engines, however, already two years late, proved quite unusable, and a switch was made to Junkers jet engines also under development. In July, the Me 262 made its second jet flight, and it proved to be successful. Further development was sanctioned by the Generalluftzeugmeister, but no urgency was expressed. Indeed, Milch believed, as Udet had done, that, while the Me 262 was no doubt an indication of things to come, its early use by the Luftwaffe would be premature. In mid-1942, the Bf 109 and FW 190 were quite adequate for the tasks required of them, and could, for the future, be improved upon. Moreover, much was hoped of the Ta 152 then under development as a possible successor to the Luftwaffe's current single-engine fighters. The Me 262 would have been little value at the front, where its delicate high technology and advanced handling characteristics would have been out of place. In defence of the Reich, not then a crucial area of operations, the existing types were also deemed to be all that was required. Any distraction from the production of tried and successful machines by a full-scale development of a new fighter for which no urgent need could be discerned, was regarded as indefensible at a time when all resources were being concentrated on increasing the output of aircraft to their highest possible level.

Development of the Me 262, then, continued slowly. Not until 1943 was strong interest shown in it as a potential major combat aircraft, when, in May, a prototype was flown by Galland. He was most impressed, and reported to Göring on 25th May: '1. This model is a tremendous stroke of luck for us; it puts us way out in front, provided the enemy continues to utilize piston engines. 2. As far as I could tell, the fuselage seems to be entirely satisfactory. 3. The engines are everything which has been claimed for them, except for their performance during take-off and landing. 4. The aircraft opens up entirely new possibilities as far as tactics are concerned.'[17] Galland recommended that development of the Me 209 be discontinued, especially since the FW 190D was its equal, if not its superior, and that the production of single-engine fighters be limited to Focke-Wulf's machines. He concluded by stating that the productive capacity thereby saved should be used on the Me 262. On 2nd June, Milch, while not agreeing to all Galland's recommendations, decided to end the Me 209 programme and release the Me 262 for a limited service production, almost one year after its first successful test flight. A production of only sixty machines a month by May 1944 was envisaged.

In the event, production could not begin until April 1944. Although airframes had been built, the mass production of the Junkers engines remained a problem. Not only was the technology involved new, and difficult, but the steel alloys necessary for the high temperatures generated by jet propulsion (chromium and nickel) were in very short supply, and quite inadequate for the mass production of jet engines. Sufficient priority had not been given to the Me 262 project to allow it to claim all the materials that it needed. Substitute materials had to be found, and it took nearly six months to overcome the resulting problems and to produce reasonably reliable engines. Although, on 2nd November, a special commission was established under the Technical Office to guide the development of the Me 262, no greater priority was accorded the project, despite Galland's urgings that 1,000 jet aircraft be produced a month. Instead, the Luftwaffe's efforts were still concentrated on the manufacture of as many conventional fighter aircraft as possible, a goal from which the jet fighter, costly in terms of man hours and raw materials, could not be allowed to divert it. Even as late as 22nd June 1944, the Jägerstab called for a production of only 500 a month by December, one eighth of total fighter production.

Against this background must be viewed the minor 'hiccup' which resulted from Hitler's insistence, expressed as early as the autumn of 1943, that the Me 262 be given the capacity to act as a fighter-bomber, instead of simply as an interceptor. A Jabo version of the aircraft had been envisaged, but the first few to be produced in May were not so equipped. On 23rd May, Hitler was told, in passing, that the Me 262 was being made only as an interceptor. His fury was immense, and he immediately gave orders that the Me 262 be brought into service as soon as possible as a fighter-bomber. On 8th June, a Führer Order was issued to that effect, although it allowed for the continued testing of the fighter version. Conversions were made, and the assembly line altered, but the Luftwaffe's opposition to Hitler's wish continued. On 4th November, Hitler finally gave his permission that the Me 262 could be manufactured as a fighter, with provision for one 551 lb bomb in case of emergency (a provision which was tacitly ignored).

This interruption, however, had little effect on the final outcome of the Me 262 programme. The modifications to the assembly line were relatively simple, and were undertaken with little delay to deliveries. The major factor limiting the availability of the jet remained the difficulties in mass producing the Junker's jet engine. In addition, further delay was experienced through the bombing of a factory manufacturing Me 262 components. From fifty-nine in July, deliveries in August fell to just twenty aircraft. In June 1944, there had been less than thirty Me 262s in service, none of them with operational units, and when Hitler rescinded his order in November less than sixty were in service, of which some twenty were fighter versions. By the end of the first week in April 1945, by which time production of the Me 262 had been running for eleven months, only 200 jet fighters were in service with front line units, 163 of which were day fighters, nine night fighters, twenty-one fighter-bombers, and seven reconnaissance aircraft. Because of their reliance on low-grade fuel, the Me 262s were never grounded, but their poor serviceability reduced their maximum daily effort to only fifty-five sorties. Hitler's fighter-bomber requirement had inhibited the use of the Me 262 against the enemy bomber formations hardly at all. That the jet was not a major element in the air combat over Germany was due not to Hitler, but to the Luftwaffe's attitude towards its development since 1938.

However, even had the Me 262 been available in large numbers by the middle of 1944, it is doubtful whether it could have brought about the reversal of the Luftwaffe's fortunes that has so often been claimed for it. On paper, the specifications of the Me 262A-la were certainly impressive: a top speed of 540 mph at 19,685 ft, an initial rate of climb of 3,937 ft per minute, and a radius of action of 326 miles at 29,000 ft. In addition, its armament was highly suitable for shooting down the heavy American bombers, firing a weight of ninety-six lb of shot in a three-second burst, almost three times greater than that possessed by conventional fighters. Galland was convinced of its value. At the end of April 1944, he said: 'We need higher performance to give our own fighter force a feeling of superiority even when we are much inferior in numbers. I can sum up my own feelings in a few words: at the moment I prefer one Me 262 to five Me 109s.'[18] However, much training and experience was required on the part of the pilots who flew the jets, in both of which the Luftwaffe was short. Indeed, in mid-November the one operational Me 262 fighter unit in action was withdrawn to receive further training, and not until 9th February 1945 was the first of the new Me 262 fighter units declared fit for action. In combat, too, while the jets had an ascendancy over the American bombers and British Mosquitoes which the conventional German machines lacked, they were no real threat to the all-important Mustang escort fighters, which even learnt to deal with the Me 262s without jettisoning their external fuel tanks. Hit and run tactics were the jets' speciality, and for these they possessed the speed and manoeuvrability to pierce the screen of escort fighters to reach the bombers. But even so, the success rate of the few Me 262s to be employed operationally gives no reason to believe that, even if used in sufficient numbers, the jet fighter could have won back command of the air over the Reich. Although some missions were extremely successful, others were not. In the largest, for example, on 10th April 1945, when fifty-five Me 262 sorties were mounted against 1,100 US bombers and their escorts, only ten raiders were brought down for the loss of twenty-seven jets. For the entire period of their service as fighters, it is estimated that the Me 262s destroyed 150 enemy aircraft, for the loss of 100 of their own number in aerial combat. On the basis of this, very many Me 262s would have had to have been built to achieve aerial superiority, for, by 1945, there were no less than 4,200 Allied heavy and 1,000 medium bombers and 2,800 escorts available daily to bomb the Reich, and further hundreds of bombers and fighters to support the Allied ground forces.

More could have been hoped for from the He 280 jet fighter, which could have entered service as early as the beginning of 1943. Heinkel had begun work on the development of this machine in 1936, and in March 1940 the RLM had ordered prototypes. In April 1941, the first prototype was flown successfully, and in subsequent trials it was shown that the He 280 was superior to any conventional fighter then in service. Development, however, was painfully slow, particularly of the jet engines, and it was not until early 1943 that the Luftwaffe considered ordering 300 of the aircraft. However, by then the Me 262 prototype was believed to show better potential, especially in range, and in late March the RLM ordered Heinkel to abandon all development of the He 280. Not long after, the He 280V6 prototype was flown as a test bed for jet engines; reaching a top speed of 508 mph at 19,600 ft, it also exhibited good handling characteristics, a performance which would have been improved upon in any production model. No doubt the He 280 was inferior to the Me 262, but its introduction into operation as a serviceable aircraft in sufficient numbers and in enough time to meet the menace presented by the enemy in the West had been a distinct possibility. That it was not, was simply the result of Luftwaffe policy.

The Me 262 was but one of the four types of aircraft on which the Luftwaffe intended to rely for the future, should it have one. In November 1944, it decided to concentrate production on the Me 262, the He 162, the Ar 234 and the Do 335, all of which, with the exception of the Dornier machine, were jets. As events were to turn out, however, apart from the Messerschmitt only the Ar 234 was to see action, and then in very limited numbers. The circumstances of the war were such that, by late 1944, it was quite impossible to introduce a new generation of aircraft in sufficient quantities to make any impact on operations. The Arado 234 'Blitz' was the world's first operational jet bomber. Development was begun as early as 1941, when it was intended to be used as a bomb-carrying reconnaissance aircraft. Progress was slow, as the RLM saw no urgency for its introduction. As with the Me 262, the Luftwaffe had other, more pressing, priorities, and not until June 1944 were the first twenty production models of the Ar 234 completed. By then, its potential as a bomber had been ascertained, for, with a top speed of 461 mph at 19,685 ft and good manoeuvrability, it was virtually impossible to intercept. It carried a bomb load of 3,300 lb over a maximum radius of action of 342 miles, and was therefore suited to fast, 'indirect support' missions. It was, too, an excellent reconnaissance aircraft, and it was in this role that it first saw operational service in early August 1944. Indeed, by 10th April 1945, of the thirty-eight Ar 234s in service, twenty-four were used for reconnaissance, only twelve for bombing, and two for night fighting. Time was too short for any greater numbers to be operational.

The Dornier 335 had, likewise, been long in development. An unusual aircraft, being driven by two propellers, one in front and one behind, work on its concept was begun by Dornier as early as 1937 with research into the efficacy of a pusher airscrew. In 1942, the Technical Office issued its specifications for a single-seat intruder capable of carrying a 1,100 lb bomb at 495 mph. Dornier's design was selected as the winning contender, and it proved adaptable to the new roles which the Luftwaffe required of it. In line with the desire to rationalise aircraft production to a few main types, the Do 335 was to serve as a multi-purpose fighter, capable of the roles of ground attack, fighter-bomber, reconnaissance, and two-seat interceptor and night-fighter. The first prototype was flown in October 1943, and revealed excellent characteristics. Easy to handle, the Do 335 was capable of a top speed of 474 mph at 21,325 ft and a radius of 650 miles, and carried an armament of one 30 mm cannon and two 15 mm machine guns, with one 1,100 lb bomb. Delays to the programme, however, and the exigencies of war, caused production of the Do 335 to be cancelled in December 1944, after just a handful had been completed.

Greater things were expected of the Heinkel 162, at least by Göring and Hitler, if not by the professional Luftwaffe officers. Its development was remarkable, and it was the only military aircraft ever to have been produced which was designed, built and flown in as little as ninety days. It originated from demands made by the Jägerstab for a cheap, effective fighter that could be mass-produced in a short period of time, and, by their numbers, overwhelm the mass formations of enemy bombers. On 8th September, the Technical Office issued specifications for a fighter armed with one or two 30 mm cannons capable of speeds over 466 mph, a flight duration of thirty minutes at sea level and a short take off, to be ready for mass production by 1st January 1945. The aircraft chosen was the jet powered Heinkel 162. Galland, among others, was aghast at this idea, believing that only a concentration of resources on the Me 262 would have any prospect of meeting the Luftwaffe's requirements. However, Göring was particularly enamoured of the project, seeing in it a parallel to the Volkssturm (People's Storm Troops), the formation of which was announced on 25th September 1944. In the air, his Volksjäger (People's Hunters) would drive back the enemy from the borders of the Reich just as surely as would the mobilised strength of the German people on the ground. That he was living in a world of fantasy is shown by his proposal that the fighters would be flown by Hitler Youth boys. In pursuance of this dream, he opened talks with the National Socialist Flying Corps and the Hitler Youth leaders, and a scheme was evolved whereby an entire year's intake of boys would begin training in gliders in preparation for the jet-powered Volksjäger. The He 162 was of light metal and plywood construction, and could reach a top speed of 521 mph at 19,690 ft and possessed a short term extra thrust to take it to 562 mph. Armed with two 20 mm cannon, it would have a radius of 303 miles at 36,000 ft. Fortunately for the Hitler Youth, however, the He 162, which required extremely careful handling even by experienced pilots, did not see action. By 4th May 1945, in which month plans had called for the production of 2,000 of the machines, there were only fifty in the Luftwaffe, and none were used in combat.

However, the Me 262, Ar 234, Do 335 and He 162 were not the only machines which the Luftwaffe planned to introduce in the last years of the war. There was the Me 163, the least conventional aircraft to see action, which was powered by rocket, and reached a top speed of 596 mph at heights between 13,000 and 40,000 ft. This made it the fastest aircraft of the war. Begun, like the Me 262, as a test aircraft, it was first flown in 1940. In October 1941, just before his death, Udet saw the Me 163 in flight and was deeply impressed. He ordered further development of the machine as an interceptor. Milch, however, would not agree, seeing no need for such an aircraft. The Reich's priorities lay elsewhere. Accordingly, as with the Me 262, the Me 163 was given a low priority in development, as more of an experimental aircraft than anything else. In January 1944, however, with the increasing fury of the Allied daylight raids, the Me 163 came back into favour. A Staffel was equipped with the few machines that had been produced, and the first rocket fighter saw action on 13th May. However, with a maximum endurance of only 6.5 minutes, and with many technical problems, the Me 163 was doomed to failure. Output reached ninety a month by December, but the next month it was dropped from the Luftwaffe's production programme. Only one Gruppe was ever made fully serviceable, and it claimed just nine enemy bombers for the loss of fourteen of its Me 163s. A similar failure, but one which did not see action, was the Bachem 349 Natter (Adder), a rocket-powered, vertical take-off interceptor. Cheap, involving only the use of low-grade materials, the Adder would be launched up a guiding mast towards the bomber formation, against which it would fire its rockets. Thereupon the pilot would parachute out, to allow his craft to fall to earth. Its endurance was 3.15 minutes once its ceiling height had been reached. Although, at the end of the war, ten Adders were set up ready for action, the premature arrival of enemy tanks ensured that they were never used.

More conventional were the Ju 388 and the Focke-Wulf fighters, the Ta 152 and Ta 154. The Ju 388 originated in September 1943 after the failure of the 'Bomber B' project, and was designed to be based on the Ju 188 and act as a high altitude fast reconnaissance-bomber, and bad-weather fighter. Milch was particularly enamoured of the aircraft and wished for it also to become the Luftwaffe's standard night fighter in preference to the He 219. In August 1944, the first Ju 388 was accepted by the Luftwaffe, and in October series production of the reconnaissance version began. With a top speed of 383 mph at 40,300 ft, and a range of 1,050 miles with extra tanks, the Ju 388 promised to be an excellent machine, but its production had to be halted in December 1944. The Luftwaffe's programme simply could not accommodate this extra aircraft. The Ta 152 was intended to be a high performance, high altitude interceptor with pressurised cabin, and the Ta 154 a night and bad weather fighter. However, a lack of initial urgency in both programmes, begun in 1942, and a refusal to assign to them the necessary priority led to their non-appearance in the skies over the Reich. Indeed, as part of the intense rationalisation in the final months of the war, the Ta 154 was cancelled in August 1944 after the sole factory producing the glue used for this mainly wooden aircraft was bombed, and little emphasis was placed on the Ta 152. A similar story could be told of the He 219 night fighter programme, which had never been favoured by Milch and which never recovered from the bombing of its factory at Vienna-Schwechat in April and June 1944. The salvation of the Luftwaffe was seen to lie in types other than these.

With the failure of any of the new generation of jet or propeller-driven fighters to enter service in other than extremely small numbers, the main burden of the fighting continued to fall on the Bf 109 and FW 190 until the end of the war. Production of the Bf 109 rose from 930 in January 1944 to 1,600 in September, and of the FW 190 from 380 to 1,390. In August, the FW 190 D, with a liquid-cooled engine, was introduced, capable of a top speed of 426 mph at 21,650 ft, twenty-four miles an hour faster than its predecessor, the FW 190 A-8, but still not sufficient to equal the best of the Allies. Later in 1944, the final version of the Bf 109, the K, appeared, capable of a top speed of 452 mph, no less than sixty-six miles an hour faster than the previous model, and a higher service ceiling of 41,000 ft. However, it came too late, and in too few numbers, to make any impact.

But even had the German designers developed a wonder aircraft whose performance was significantly superior to those of the enemy by mid-1944, it is improbable that it could have been made available in sufficient numbers to alter the outcome of the war. The switch from one fighter to another whose similarities with its predecessor were slight, if existent at all, would have had to be undertaken without any significant decrease in the overall output of fighters, thus necessitating the production of the two types in tandem for some time. This was a difficult enough process in peace-time, let alone in war, when Allied bombing was destroying the very fabric of the German war economy, and territorial losses were depriving the Reich of its production facilities. By mid-1944, the enemy bomber forces were well into their offensive against the Reich's aircraft production centres, on which in 1944 and 1945 some 28,600 tons of bombs were dropped. At the same time, and to far greater effect, the enemy was dropping 508,093 tons on German communications. This was greatly hindering production. With the dispersal of manufacturing centres brought about by the bombing of industry (by the autumn of 1944, there were some 300 separate centres involved in the production of military aircraft), the efficient assembly of complex machines depended on the use of road and rail transport. Should this be dislocated, as it frequently was, bottle-necks and delays would result in a loss of output. In face of these problems, the introduction of a new mass-produced aircraft in the numbers required to counter the overwhelming numerical ascendancy of the enemy, would have been difficult if not impossible.

But even if such a feat had been undertaken before the onset of winter, what could it have achieved? By that time, the production of aircraft fuel was so low that it could not support an offensive against the enemy attackers in anything approaching the required numbers. And even if, by some unforeseen miracle, air superiority could have been won over the Reich by the early spring of 1945, what would that have achieved for the Luftwaffe? By then, the frontiers of the Reich had long been breached by the enemy's ground forces in overwhelming strength and with the support of strong tactical air forces. The Luftwaffe alone would have been quite incapable of reversing that, and the relief afforded to the Armed Forces as a whole by freeing the Reich from the effects of bombing, would have been insufficient to delay significantly the final solution. Hypothetical analysis apart, the fact is that, by the middle of 1944, nothing could have saved the Luftwaffe from defeat. For it, the war had been lost from the moment the German armies failed to win the campaign in the East in 1941.

XII

The End

By September 1944, then, the air defences of the Reich by day proved incapable of inflicting losses on the enemy bomber formations of more than just one per cent. Indeed, such was the Allied command of the air over Germany, that RAF Bomber Command began day-time raids over the Reich in late August. The number of days in a month in which the missions of 8th Air Force were intercepted fell from eleven in March to five in September, four in October and November, and three in December. By the end of the year, an average of 4,000 sorties flown daily by the Allies could be matched by only 300 from the Luftwaffe, and the Germans were losing aircraft in air combat at a rate of six or seven to one. By night, matters for the Luftwaffe were just as bad. The number of night fighters in the West increased, from 685 on 1st July 1944 to 830 on 1st October, but their success rate declined rapidly, from 2.9 per cent of enemy bombers destroyed in June to 0.7 per cent in December. Apart from the shortage of fuel, they were particularly hampered by the loss of their early warning ground radars following the rapid Allied advances, and by the clear superiority of the enemy in electronic warfare. From September, the Lichtenstein SN-2 was rendered useless by jamming, and by the end of the year the rest of the German radar devices, together with their radio communications, were also effectively jammed. In addition, from July onwards Allied attacks on the fighter bases caused losses on the ground, or in transit to and from small dispersal fields where the aircraft hid by day, to exceed those in the air. This, together with the feared activities of the RAF Mosquito night fighters, turned the German night fighters from hunters into hunted.

With the failure of the fighter defences, ever increasing reliance came to be placed on the Luftwaffe's anti-aircraft guns, especially by day. In 1943, Flak had accounted for a quarter of all enemy aircraft shot down in the area of Luftflotte Reich; in 1944 this percentage rose to over a third of the 7,290 enemy aircraft brought down over Germany (2,570 machines). By day, the Flak was especially important, bringing down half the total number of aircraft, although by night this decreased to just eleven per cent. The role of anti-aircraft artillery was summed up by Speer on 1st August:

> In the last few months Flak has shown that in the massed attacks on our cities it has brought down more aircraft than was hitherto

thought possible. It will become increasingly important. In view of the shortage of aircraft fuel which we must expect we cannot say what are our prospects, both in home defence and in dealing with enemy air forces at the front. But we can at any rate say that Flak drives the enemy higher and higher and his accuracy is correspondingly diminished.

An indication of the effect of Flak was shown in the American raid on the major synthetic oil plant at Leuna on 25th November. Then, no less than twenty-seven per cent of the bombers that returned to base had suffered Flak damage, and two-thirds of those shot down were also the victims of the guns. This was not unique, but was representative of many daylight raids. Hitler was impressed by his Flak arm, and constantly requested increases in gun production. In an order dated 4th November, for example, the Führer declared:

> In his reports on his terror attacks on the Reich, the enemy is always speaking of the 'hell' of the German anti-aircraft fire. Many of his sorties have been frustrated by concentrated Flak defence. To exploit this tactical and psychological factor to the full we must step up the fire power of our Flak in every conceivable way. I therefore order the immediate intensification of the Flak and munitions programmes. This must extend to heavy, medium and light Flak, including their ammunition, ground directional apparatus, sighting and equipment. All current experimentation and developments designed to increase the efficiency of the guns and their ammunition, and any other new developments relating to Flak defence are to be relentlessly pursued.[2]

By February 1945, the Luftwaffe possessed a total of 31,569 anti-aircraft guns in and around Germany, of which over 12,000 were of 8.8 cm calibre or above. It proved a formidable force, but nowhere near sufficient to put an end to the enemy's incursions. There was a limit to what could be achieved by guns; it took an average of no fewer than 4,940 light and 3,343 heavy anti-aircraft shells to bring down a single enemy heavy bomber. Victory could only be won by sufficient numbers of modern fighter interceptors flown by well-trained pilots.

The Allied air offensive, then, continued with even greater ferocity in the latter half of 1944. In October, no less than 100,000 tons of bombs were dropped on the Reich, over sixty per cent more than had been dropped in any previous month. Lancaster bombers were capable of carrying eleven tons of bombs to their targets, equal to the weight of an entire Ju 88A-4. On one target, Duisburg, within the space of twenty-four hours, the RAF dropped about the same weight of bombs as the Luftwaffe had dropped on London in the entire war, some 9,000 tons. Indeed, in the latter half of 1944, the activity of the enemy air forces increased considerably, so that, of all the bombs dropped on the Reich during the war, seventy-two per cent fell after 1st July

1944. During the year, an estimated seventeen per cent of the Reich's war production had been lost; in addition, 146,809 German civilians were killed and 238,962 were seriously injured, 214,599 buildings were destroyed and 244,089 severely damaged. The events of 1944 were a terrible lesson to the Germans in the nature and importance of air superiority.

For the Luftwaffe, the most important result of the Allied bombing offensive was the impact the, mainly day-time, attacks had on the production of aviation fuel. Unable to protect even its own basis for survival – the synthetic oil plants – the German Air Force could only watch the production of its life blood fall away to nothing. As Speer warned Hitler on 30th August: 'If the Allies continue to gain successes in the air, we shall soon lack the materials necessary for prosecuting modern warfare.'[3] In September 1944, only 17,000 tons of aviation fuel was produced, just nine per cent of the total output in March before the enemy's oil offensive had begun (the output of motor fuel, too, had been reduced to forty per cent). Although there was a slight increase to 46,000 tons in November, output of aviation fuel fell again to 11,000 in January 1945 and to just 1,000 in February, by the end of which month stocks were at only 11,000 tons. Accordingly, the Luftwaffe's consumption of fuel fell to 60,000 tons in September, thirty per cent of what it had been in May, dropping to 41,000 tons in November 1944, and, after a small rise, declining still further to 27,000 tons in February 1945 and to 19,000 tons in April, less than ten per cent of the level a year previously. It is against this background, that the activities of the Luftwaffe in the last ten months of the war must be viewed.

On 10th June, the long-awaited Soviet attack opened on the Eastern front, and, contrary to expectations, it took place at first on the Finnish-Karelian front. There, a daily sortie rate of 1,000 by the Red Air Force quite overwhelmed the German and Finnish units, who were capable of only around 150. Within a week, fifty Ju 87s and Bf 109s were sent from Luftflotte 6 to reinforce the 105 German combat aircraft available to Luftflotte 5 (since November 1943 under the command of Kammhuber), but to little avail. On the 23rd, however, events in the far north ceased to concern the Germans, who were faced by the main Soviet onslaught on the central front. The Red Army was supported in the air by 6,000 aircraft, including the new La-7 fighter, capable of a top speed of 413 mph, and the Yak-3 fighter and ground-attack aircraft, which, with a top speed of 403 mph, was superior to the Bf 109 and FW 190 at all altitudes below 11,000 ft (although it became progressively inferior the higher it went). Luftflotte 6's 725 combat aircraft were outnumbered by a factor of over six to one. Reinforcements from other fronts were straightway rushed to the battle area, so that von Greim was provided with another 270 by the end of June. No less than forty single-engined fighters came from the defence of the Reich; eighty-five FW 190 ground-attack aircraft were withdrawn from Luftflotte 2's already depleted forces in Italy, together with forty from Luftflotte 3, which was struggling for its continued survival in the West. For fear of a new enemy onslaught on the south of the Eastern front, only seventy aircraft were initially moved from Luftflotte 4, although far more were later to be sent northwards. These machines, however, achieved little in the face of overwhelming Soviet superiority. By 8th July, it was clear that Army Group Centre had been destroyed, and a breach 250 miles wide exposed East Prussia and the Baltic States to the enemy's advance. By the end of the month, the Red Army had advanced 500 miles, and by the end of the first week in August the front line had stabilised, along the border of East Prussia. The Luftwaffe had suffered great losses, and, despite reinforcements and replacements, the combined strength available to Luftflotten 1, 4 and 6 had fallen from 1,980 at the beginning of June, to 1,760, the great majority of which were in von Greim's command. However, on the central front, although there were no less than 1,160 combat aircraft, serviceability had declined to such a low level, and fuel was becoming so much scarcer, that a daily effort of no more than 600 sorties was achieved, quite inadequate to relieve the hard-pressed ground forces.

The Luftwaffe was to receive no respite from the lull in the battle on the central front. On 20th August, an enemy offensive across the River Pruth in the south took the Germans completely by surprise, as did a coup d'état in Romania on the 23rd. By that time, Luftflotte 4 had been reduced to only 200 combat aircraft, none of which were ground-attack machines, and was therefore quite unable to deal with the enemy. Reinforcements were immediately sent down from the north, but to little effect. The worsening fuel situation, together with high unserviceability, rendered Luftflotte 4 a broken reed. By the 31st, the Romanian capital was in Soviet hands. The enemy had covered 250 miles in twelve days, and in the next six was to cross a further 200 to the Jugoslav border. On 8th September, Bulgaria declared war on Germany, and by the 24th the south-west salient of Hungary had been taken. The Jugoslav capital was occupied by the Red Army on 20th October, and by 4th November the suburbs of the Hungarian capital were reached. The German position in the Balkans had disintegrated. By the end of the year, the fighting in the East had brought the Germans dangerously near their own frontiers. In the north, Army Group North, together with Luftflotte 1 and its 245 aircraft, was encircled in Courland, some eighty miles from the rest of the German front which ran from East Prussia down along the river Vistula south-south west to Budapest, then to Lake Balaton and down into northern Jugoslavia. The Luftwaffe lay crippled; by 31st December, its 1,875 aircraft were unable to fly more than 500 sorties a day along the entire Eastern front even in good weather, and often very many fewer. Numerically, the Red Air Force outnumbered the Luftwaffe by six to one in aircraft, and ten to one in the number of sorties undertaken. The German Air Force in the East was no longer a factor that had to be seriously reckoned with.

In Italy, the Luftwaffe's presence in the latter half of 1944 was negligible. In May, Göring had been forced to admit that 'at the moment, the situation is such that not a single Luftwaffe aircraft dares show itself'. Matters did not improve. By the end of July, when the enemy was capable of mounting 1,000 sorties daily against the German rear areas alone, Luftflotte 2 had been reduced to just fifty single-engined fighters, forty Ju 87 night harassing bombers, and thirty-five miscellaneous reconnaissance machines. The Allied landings in the south of France on 15th August caused the transfer of the fighters to the Rhone valley, but they were returned after a week, to remain in Italy until the third week of September, when they were finally transferred to the Western front. In October, a handful of FW 190 ground attack aircraft were committed to Italy, but these left in early December, also for the West. A few jet reconnaissance aircraft and FW 190 night-harassing aircraft were sent to Italy in the New Year, but, otherwise, nothing was done to redress the balance against the enemy air forces. Even the total strength of the Luftwaffe on all fronts, had it been combined in Italy, would have been insufficient to counter the Allied aircraft in the Mediterranean, which were sufficiently strong to achieve an average daily number of sorties of 5,000 in the final offensive. This opened on 9th April, and ended on 2nd May with the surrender of the German forces in Italy. General Vietinghof, the Army commander, said of the Allied aircraft: 'They hindered essential movement. Tanks could not move. Their very presence over the battlefield paralysed movement.'[4] General von Senger und Etterlin, a corps commander, ascribed the disintegration of the ground forces to the Allied air attacks. Such was the condition to which, from as early as August 1942, the German Armed Forces had been reduced to an ever increasing extent whenever it faced the Western Allies, and, to a lesser extent, from the end of 1943 on the Eastern front.

In the West, the Luftwaffe was rendered as impotent as elsewhere. In the headlong retreat from France in August, Luftflotte 3 proved quite unable to affect the course of the fighting on the ground. On 23rd August, Sperrle was removed from his command, and his successor, Dessloch, was left to make the best he could of the situation. On the 29th, the 420 remaining Bf 109s and FW 190s left French territory to escape the attentions of the enemy air forces, and were positioned between 120 and 170 miles from the fighting in the Seine area, at the limit of their range. A number were transferred to Luftflotte Reich, so that by the end of September it had no less than 1,260 single-engined fighters, as compared with the 300 in the West and the 415 in the East. In late August, too, the bomber and night fighter forces, hitherto based in Belgium and north-west France, were moved back to Holland and Germany. In the south of France, where the Allies had landed on 15th August, and had 5,000 aircraft to meet the 220 of the Luftwaffe, all German air units were withdrawn by the 21st, the fighters being transferred to the Metz area while the anti-shipping force, of some 100 bombers, returned to Germany and oblivion. Moreover, the operability of the transport aircraft was also affected. Since July, they had been undertaking supply missions to German units cut off along the coast of France. Beginning with Cherbourg, operations were extended to Dunkirk, Boulogne, Le Havre, St. Malo, Brest,

Lorient, La Baule, St. Nazaire, La Rochelle, Verdon, Bordeaux, Bayonne and Biarritz. An average of fifty tons a night were delivered up to the end of August, but thereafter, with declining numbers of transports available and approach routes becoming longer owing to the withdrawal, this fell to twenty tons or below. By the end of 1944, there were just fifteen serviceable Ju 52s left to ferry the much needed supplies to the German troops in the West. Such were among the final operations of a force which, throughout the war had ferried no fewer than 1,199,291 troops to the front, together with 886,262 tons of supplies and 1,910,320 gallons of fuel, as well as evacuating 1,004,652 troops, wounded or whole, from the battle zone. But by the end of 1944, the German transport arm had almost ceased to exist.

By September, the German Air Force in the West was spent. The 175 bombers of Fliegerkorps IX were grounded for lack of fuel (their use in one operation would have taken two days' fuel production in August), and the 420 Bf 109s and FW 190s of Jagdkorps II were capable of a full scale daily effort of at most 300 sorties. On 21st September, the contraction of Luftflotte 3's area of responsibility was recognised, and it was degraded to the status of Luftwaffenkommando West, and made subordinate to Stumpff's Luftflotte Reich. Dessloch thereupon returned to command Luftflotte 4 in the East, leaving the remnants of his force to General Holle. At the time of this reorganisation, the few aircraft still operational were being used against the Allied airborne landings in Holland, the spearhead of which was at Arnhem. On the first day of the operation, 17th September, only seventy-five German sorties had been put up against those of the enemy, which comprised some 1,200 by fighters, 1,100 by bombers and 212 by fighter-bombers, together with numerous transport missions. During the week from 18th until 25th September, when the British finally evacuated Arnhem, almost all Luftflotte Reich's fighters were sent against the enemy attack, which was threatening to lay the way open for a thrust into north-west Germany. However, even then, only a daily average of 250 fighter sorties could be mounted. Although the enemy was forced to withdraw, it was not induced to do so by the actions of the Luftwaffe. During this operation, the bomber force in the West was used for the first time since the beginning of the month; about 100 sorties were undertaken on two nights, but to small effect. This proved to be the last occasion on which they flew in the West, and on 22nd September Peltz's Fliegerkorps IX was withdrawn from front-line duty. Much to the consternation of the fighter arm, instead of being disbanded, the Fliegerkorps was transformed into a training command for the conversion of its pilots to flying fighters as a temporary measure until it reverted to its traditional mission. This left just sixty torpedo-carrying Ju 88s and Ju 188s in Fliegerkorps X equipped for anti-shipping operations being held in reserve in anticipation of enemy landings on the Dutch coast, and sixty Ju 88s used for minelaying, while a further sixty He 111s were being converted to launch flying bombs in the air. The few remaining He 177s and FW 200s had been moved to Norway, where they were withdrawn from operations. Indeed, by the end of

September, throughout the Luftwaffe commands on all fronts there were only some 500 bombers (including those converted to an anti-shipping role), of which just fifty per cent were serviceable and even fewer actually operating on a regular basis. The Reich's bomber force was at the end of its life.

Although the increase in the strength of the Luftwaffe's day-time fighters had availed it little in the defence of Germany, it did allow Hitler to contemplate a major offensive. In October, the Führer had decided to strike a serious blow against the British and American forces in the West by counter-attacking through the Ardennes towards Antwerp. This objective once gained, the Allied forces would be divided and a large proportion cut off from their supplies, thus rendering them easy prey for final destruction. This would, at the least, delay the enemy's advance by six months, and allow the concentration of a large enough force on the Eastern front to defeat the Soviet foe. Such was Hitler's dream. In reality, however, he had insufficient force at his disposal to achieve the desired result. On 16th December, when the Ardennes offensive began, Luftwaffenkommando West had a total of 2,300 aircraft, of which 1,770 were Bf 109s and FW 190s (over 270 of them ground-attack machines). Thick fog, however, hampered operations, and in the first week a daily average of only some 600 sorties by day, and 300 by night, were flown. However, on the 24th, Christmas Eve, the fog lifted, and the enemy air forces fought back with over 600 sorties, rising to 1,200 a few days later. The Germans proved unable to cope with this onslaught, which was in large part directed against the Luftwaffe's air operations and ground organisation. Serviceability fell, and fuel, so carefully husbanded for the attack, became scarce, so that, by the 31st, the number of German sorties undertaken by day was down to 300. The ill-trained pilots suffered a crisis of nerve in the face of Allied superiority, which occasioned an order by Göring which stated: 'No pilot is to turn back except for damage to the undercarriage; flights are to be continued even with misfiring engines. Failure of auxiliary tanks will not be accepted as an excuse for turning back. The shirkers who do not realise the decisiveness of the hour are to be removed from the ranks of fighter pilots.' On New Year's Day, 1st January 1945, a major air attack, the last in the war, code-named Operation Bodenplatte (Ground Plate) was carried out against the Allied airfields, with considerable success. It was, however, costly. Some 800 fighters were used, and accounted for 465 enemy aircraft destroyed or damaged, but only for the loss of over 400 machines and their pilots. Fuel stocks were almost exhausted. It was a pyrrhic victory. The attack brought no measure of relief to the German armies, and had come too late to be of any use to the offensive. As early as 26th December, the German advance units, at most sixty miles from their starting positions, had begun to fall back. On that day, too, troops were forbidden to make any large moves by day, so complete was the enemy's command of the air. By 3rd January, when some 400 ground-support aircraft had been sent to the south in support of an abortive offensive in Alsace, the German commander, von Rundstedt, had come to the conclusion that the only course left open was to withdraw, and on the 8th

Hitler sanctioned a partial withdrawal to the rear. By this date, the Luftwaffe was capable of just 200 sorties daily over the Ardennes. The Wehrmacht's last offensive of the war was over.

Thereafter, the Luftwaffe's offensive capacity came to rely solely on the flying bombs. At the same time as the V1s were being launched against London, they were also being used against the port of Antwerp, which, in September, was supplying a large part of the enemy's armies in the West. The Luftwaffe's bomber force was quite unable to destroy this most vital of targets, and reliance was placed on the rocket bombs, at least to inhibit the supplying of the British and American troops. On 27th October, the first bomb was sent against Antwerp from a site in western Germany, and from then until 30th March 1945, 4,823 were launched on the port. Of these, only 211 landed within an eight-mile radius of the docks. The efficiency of the anti-aircraft gunners defending Antwerp was such that, at the beginning of the operation, they achieved a kill rate of sixty-seven per cent, which they improved to ninety-seven per cent by the end. Such was the nature of what was to be the Luftwaffe's last offensive.

The events of the air war in 1944 could not but have an effect on the Luftwaffe's high command. By the end of the year, its disarray was complete. By then, too, the position and influence of the two remaining survivors of the Air Force's creators, Milch and Göring, was ended. The Secretary of State was the first to go. In his single-minded and almost single-handed attempt to produce a defensive air force, Milch had contributed to his own downfall. Although his ideas were ultimately accepted, his relations with Göring, not of the best since 1936, were brought to breaking point over the question of the Reich's protection. As early as 5th March 1943, Milch had told Hitler that it was imperative that the Luftwaffe should go over to the defensive, and that as part of the process Göring should relinquish his command. This advice, Milch reported to his Commander-in-Chief. The next month, he informed Goebbels over the telephone that Göring's misdirection of the Air Force would end in disaster, firm in the knowledge that the Reichsmarschall would be informed of these sentiments through his wire-tappers. By his open questioning of Göring's fitness to command, the Secretary of State was treading on very dangerous ground. He was no longer indispensable to the Reichsmarschall, who was surrounded by his own advisers and 'Little General Staff', and he remained in his position only because of Hitler's strong respect for his capabilities. Göring's dislike of Milch became ever more apparent. On 3rd July 1943, just before the opening of the Kursk offensive, Göring had made one of his, by then usual, attacks on the Luftwaffe's pilots. Milch spoke out in defence of the aircrews, stating that he had assessed their morale very highly in his inspection report submitted in June, and had made certain proposals for improving their command structure. Thereupon, Göring rounded on his subordinate and, in front of the assembled company, sneered: 'You don't imagine that I actually read the rags you send me!'[5] At that time, the Reichsmarschall began to think of replacing Milch with Kesselring. Dissatisfaction with the Generalluftzeugmeister's performance, too, was expressed. On 3rd October 1943, the Reichsmarschall stated in a conference: 'What does the Field Marshal [Milch] think he's doing anyway? . . . Six months ago he told me not to worry, that by this time everything would be in order. What kind of a pig-sty is this? . . . Things have become worse than they were under Udet! Where is the increased production? There is none, except for the fighter planes! If the construction of bombers is stopped, then it's no trick to produce more fighters!'[6]

Göring's dissatisfaction with Milch was given concrete form with the continual transfer of responsibility from the Secretary of State to the General Staff. The battle for the command of the Luftwaffe had not been ended with the beginning of the war. As Lörzer described the process, Milch was 'organised out'[7] of the Luftwaffe. In 1940, certain of the Inspectorates, previously Milch's responsibility, were required to report directly to the Chief of the General Staff; in 1941 the most important, those of bombers, fighters and reconnaissance aircraft, were made directly subordinate to Göring (in effect, Jeschonnek); and in 1942 two new offices, the Special Commissioner for Torpedo Weapons and the Inspector for Aerial Mines, were also made subordinate to the General Staff. This process continued in 1943, when the Supply Office was abolished and replaced by the Office of the Chief of Supply in the General Staff, and a number of other offices set up in that year were also subordinated to Jeschonnek. One of them, the Office of the Chief of Personnel Armament (the old Chief of Luftwaffe Personnel) was of particular interest to Milch, who felt the loss acutely. As Lörzer, the incumbent of the office, remembered: 'Göring took from Milch all jurisdiction over legal matters, which Milch had held, as well as the right to grant pardons. Practically nothing was left to Milch. His position as State Secretary had been completely undermined. I asked Göring, "What is Milch to say to that?" He answered me, "I want to have these things close to me. Milch is always working against me".'[8]

By 1944, matters had long been at a point where a total reorganisation of the RLM was required. On 21st June, the Ministry was divided into three: the Oberkommando der Luftwaffe (the High Command), the Office of the Chief of Personnel Utilisation and Supply Planning, and the departments which came under the Reichsminister der Luftfahrt (Minister of Aviation). All three were directly subordinate to Göring. It proved an excellent opportunity to reduce Milch's authority still further. The post of Secretary of State was abolished and, with it, his position as Göring's deputy and his supervision, however nominal, over the General Staff. Milch, still Inspector General of the Luftwaffe and Generalluftzeugmeister, the authority of which post had been taken away by the Jägerstab, was left with nothing but administrative duties. Even this office, however, was taken from him on 29th July, when the post of Luftwaffe Chief of Supply and Procurement was eliminated and the Chief of Technical Air Armament was made over to the General Staff, and put under the control of one of Milch's greatest enemies, Ulrich Diesing. On the next day, the Jägerstab was disbanded and responsibility for the entire aerial armament programme was shifted to Speer's Ministry; Milch, however, still retained some influence there, and became Speer's Secretary of State. In many ways the reorganisation of the Luftwaffe's aircraft procurement and development was eminently sensible. For the first time, it gave the Chief of the General Staff the influence he needed over technological development and armament planning, although far too late to make any use of it, even if, by then, he wished to change the direction it had taken under Milch's stewardship. Moreover, the merging of the Luftwaffe's procurement with the Armament's Ministry, thereby bringing it into line with the other two armed services and confirming a position which had, in reality, pertained since the establishment of the Jägerstab on 1st March, had Milch's approval. As he told his colleagues in a speech on 29th July: 'This rearrangement is not the result of failure of any offices of the Luftwaffe or of the Chief of Supply and Procurement. . . . It was clear to me that something like that probably would develop when I, as the only one, demanded the founding of the Jägerstab. It is the child of my brain and of none other.'[9] Milch believed that, henceforth, the Luftwaffe would be allocated the resources it needed to meet the enemy's challenge in the air. For that, the loss of his office was a small price to pay.

Milch was not long to remain in any position of influence, however restricted, for on 1st October he was involved in a car accident and was immobilised until January 1945. On the 12th, he attended, uninvited, Göring's birthday party at Karinhall, where he was unpleasantly received. Three days later he received a week-old letter from Göring informing that his duties were at an end. But Milch was not the only senior Luftwaffe officer to end his career in 1944. By the summer, Korten was clearly at the end of his tether. He, like his predecessors, could no longer work with Göring, but, unlike Jeschonnek, he had no need of suicide to end his dilemma. On 20th July, as he was standing a few paces from Hitler during the daily conference, an assassin's bomb which failed to kill the Führer ended his life. The search for a successor was begun immediately, and Hitler proposed von Greim. Göring, however, would not have him and finally decided upon General Werner Kreipe, one of Milch's former staff officers. The Reichsmarschall took this opportunity, too, of ridding himself of Koller, with whom he had not got on well, and of replacing him as Chief of the Operations Staff by General Eckhardt Christian.

Kreipe, a young officer with a varied career, may have proved an excellent Chief of the General Staff had he possessed the full support of Göring. But his attempt to convince Hitler of the paramount importance of the defence of the Reich ended in a failure. He tried to persuade the Führer to reverse his decision on the Me 262, and to allocate far greater resources to Luftflotte Reich, whose commander, Stumpff, was complaining that he could not move even a single anti-aircraft gun without an order from Führer Headquarters. On 30th August, Kreipe noted in his diary of an encounter with Hitler: 'In growing temper he made short work of me. Now I was stabbing him in the back as well! Irresponsible elements in the Luftwaffe like Milch and Galland talked me into it!'[10] Hitler even seriously considered the possibility of disbanding the Air Force with the exception of jet-units, and relying instead on a greatly enlarged Flak organisation. Relations got progressively worse between Hitler, Göring and Kreipe, and the latter was forbidden to communicate with Milch. Finally, after a heated argument with the Führer on 18th September, the fourth Luftwaffe Chief of Staff was asked to submit his resignation. Kreipe's successor, Koller, fared little better, but did manage to see the war out. Chosen after some delay, and appointed on 12th November with much reluctance on Göring's part, he proved to be an excellent administrator, but his personality was not firm enough to overcome the intransigence of Hitler and the stupidities of Göring, if, indeed, anyone by that time was capable of doing so. After the war was over, he was to write of the major failure of the Luftwaffe: 'We were smothered . . . because the German High Command undertook too much . . . and because it did not direct the main weight of armament right from the beginning towards air supremacy and thereby safeguard Germany's vital zones and armament industry and ward off any attack from the West. . . . We have been beaten and eliminated. . . .'[11]

But the situation in which the successive Chiefs of the General Staff found themselves was but one aspect of the malaise which had gripped the high command of the Luftwaffe. Hitler's disillusionment with his airmen was almost total. He had long ceased to regard the opinions of the Commander-in-Chief and the Chief of the General Staff as valid, and constantly lost his temper with them. General Guderian remembered that, on one occasion, Hitler had shouted: 'Göring, your Luftwaffe isn't worth a damn! It doesn't deserve to be an independent branch of service any more! And that's your fault. You're lazy!' Tears then ran down the Reichsmarschall's cheeks. When Guderian suggested later that Göring be relieved of his command, however, that was another matter, and Hitler replied: 'That's impossible for reasons of domestic policy. The Party would never understand.'[12] Göring was, after all, Hitler's nominated successor. Instead, the Führer came to rely on the advice of others. He requested that a senior Luftwaffe general be appointed to Führer Headquarters with full authority as the Reichsmarschall's representative. The choice of man proved difficult. Kesselring was occupied by command of the forces in Italy, von Richthofen was ill, Sperrle had been dismissed, and only von Greim, commander of Luftflotte 6 in the East, was considered by Hitler to be suitable. He was a loyal, thorough, competent officer, although no highly trained strategist, and in late September he was appointed to the post. Hitler immediately gave him his full confidence. It was a position of much influence. By then, Hitler had long been used to directing almost every movement made by the Armed Forces. The Luftwaffe was no exception. As Koller recalled after the war: 'Movements of Luftwaffe units from one front to another could not usually be carried out without the approval of the Führer. He either reserved to himself the right of decision in any case, or else there was a complaint to him from the commander on a particular front, when he learnt that air units were being withdrawn from his command. Thus, in practice, the decision had always to be made by the Führer.'[13] In his new position, von Greim quickly became the executive of the Führer's will and, therefore, the most influential man in the Luftwaffe.

Almost immediately after he was appointed, von Greim attempted to define his responsibilities vis à vis the Luftwaffe High Command. On 1st October, Kreipe noted in his diary:

> Conference with von Greim in the afternoon. He showed me the outline of duties which he has worked out for himself. According to his outline, he will be Deputy Commander in Chief of the Luftwaffe, with all the duties and privileges involved, and will also take over certain tasks assigned to the Chief of the Luftwaffe General Staff. I called his attention to one or two unclear points and expressed my doubts that Göring would agree to his proposal. Von Greim replied that Hitler and Himmler were in favour of it. He indicated that Christian could easily take on the small amount of routine work normally done by the Chief of the General Staff and, if not, he would bring Koller back. He intended to obtain Göring's approval within the next few days.[14]

But Göring refused to agree to this attempt to relieve him of all responsibilities. On 3rd October, Kreipe recorded a meeting at Karinhall: 'Then I was called in; Göring was alone, completely broken. He complained that they were trying to get rid of him, that von Greim was a traitor. He was, and intended to remain, Commander-in-Chief. He wanted no more to do with von Greim.'[15] But Hitler, at the moment when he came closest to reforming the Luftwaffe's leadership, drew back, reluctant to insist on the downfall of the man who had once been one of his closest colleagues. Von Greim, however, remained at Führer Headquarters as the effective head of the Luftwaffe, a position which, unless formally ratified, he found impossible. In November, his request to return to his duties with Luftflotte 6 was granted. The new Chief of the General Staff, Koller, was allowed to attend conferences, but instead of appointing another Air Force officer to his Headquarters, Hitler turned increasingly to his personal pilot, a former Lufthansa captain named Bauer, for advice. Although an SS Gruppenführer, he was a layman in Luftwaffe affairs, but his simplistic approach to problems found a willing listener in Hitler. Such was the level of advice that the Supreme Commander was receiving about air warfare by the end of the war.

Disillusion with Göring was not confined to the higher circles of the Luftwaffe and the Reich's leadership. By mid-1944 it was becoming increasingly obvious that he had forfeited the respect of a great many officers in the middle and lower ranks of the Air Force. Once called the 'Iron Man', he had come to be referred to often as the 'Rubber Lion'. His criticisms of the fliers, and in particular of the fighter pilots, had aroused strong resentment. For example, after the failure to stem the Allied invasion of Italy, Göring sent the following message to Galland: 'During the defensive action against the bombing attack on the Straits of Messina, the fighter units failed in their task. One pilot from each of the fighter Gruppen taking part will be tried by courts martial for cowardice in the face of the enemy'.[16] On another occasion, during a conference in the autumn of 1943, Galland tore his Knight's Cross from his neck and flung it on the table in front of Göring, after the Reichsmarschall had complained that too many fighter pilots had gained decorations they did not deserve. In October, Göring instituted an organisation known as Aeropag (a version of the Greek Areopagus – a court of justice) a form of 'parliament of pilots', consisting of thirty young, front-line Luftwaffe commanders under Baumbach, who were permitted to criticise whatever and whomever they liked (with the exception of the Reichsmarschall, of course). They requested the removal of Koller, and suggested amendments to the duties of the Chief of the General Staff which would have left him little more than an office-boy. They proposed that they themselves be placed in charge of Luftwaffe operations as a kind of collective operations staff. The General Staff refused to countenance such suggestions, and Göring put an end to Aeropag's deliberations, the only result of which was to intensify the already prevalent dissatisfaction with his leadership. In the New Year, one highly decorated officer, Colonel Günther Lützow, even tried to obtain an audience with Hitler to protest at the way the Reich's fighter defences were being abused. He was refused, but at a subsequent meeting with Göring demanded, among other things, that the Reichsmarschall should desist from impugning the fighter pilots' honour. Göring regarded this as mutiny, and sent Lützow into exile on the Italian front. He even attempted to institute court martial proceedings against Galland, who, in January 1945, was removed from his post of General of Fighters. However, Hitler interceded on Galland's behalf, and he was sent to command an Me 262 unit. Dissention, as Göring bemoaned, abounded.

The Luftwaffe had suffered grievous losses in 1944, during which 13,157 aircraft had been destroyed or damaged beyond repair in battle. The bomber arm had ceased to exist, and by the end of the year, day fighter strength had decreased by twenty-nine per cent to 2,276, although the number of night fighters, 1,289, was at its highest. Manufacture of aircraft, too, had begun to fall, from 4,219 machines in July to 3,155 in December. But, far more important, production of aviation fuel had continued to deteriorate, so that in February 1945 only 1,000 tons were produced. Stocks at the end of the month were at 84,000 tons, sufficient for less than two weeks' fighting at full operability. Consumption, therefore, for all reasons (operations, training, industry, etc.) was reduced from 47,000 tons in January 1945 to just 19,000 tons in April – enough for three days of fighting at the level attained a year previously. Operating under such constraints, the numbers of aircraft available to front-line units, or the various reorganisations and redispositions made to take account of changing circumstances at the front, became almost meaningless. Luftflotte 3 had been down-graded to the status of a Luftwaffenkommando subordinate to Luftflotte Reich in September, and on 10th October Kammhuber's Luftflotte 5 was disbanded and replaced by the post of Commanding General of the Luftwaffe in Norway, under Edward von Schleich, which was also made subordinate to Luftflotte Reich. On 28th October Luftflotte 2 in Italy was likewise disbanded, its place being taken by the Luftwaffenkommando Süd, which, in December, was retitled the Commanding General of the Luftwaffe in Italy. Von Richthofen being sick, both commands were held by General Maximilian von Pohl, who was responsible only to the Commander-in-Chief of the Luftwaffe. In the Balkans, Fröhlich's Luftwaffenkommando Südost was disbanded on 18th November, and Luftflotte 4 took over its responsibilities. In February 1944, Jagdkorps II on the western front was disbanded, and its place was taken by two Fliegerdivisionen, 14 and 15, while Jagdkorps I, undertaking the defence of the Reich, was disbanded and its functions taken over by Fliegerkorps IX (J) under Peltz, by then a fighter command. Such reorganisations, however, had little impact on the course of the fighting, and merely indicated how the course of events had diminished the Luftwaffe. By the time these changes had come about, there was little that could be done; quite simply, the fuel shortage had caused the Luftwaffe to be outnumbered in the air by its enemies by a factor of fifty to one. For all practical purposes, the German Air Force had ceased to exist.

On 12th January 1945, the Soviets launched an offensive from the Vistula on the central front. On the 19th, the enemy set foot on German soil, and by the 31st they had reached the Lower Oder, barely fifty miles from Berlin. The danger had been perceived immediately the attack had begun, and, as its contribution to the battle, the Luftwaffe withdrew substantial numbers of aircraft from the West. By the 15th, 300 had arrived to reinforce the 1,000 aircraft under Luftflotte 6 bearing the brunt of the fighting, and by the 22nd a further 500 had been sent or were on their way east. However, against the overwhelming superiority of the enemy in the air as well as on the ground, where they possessed a seven to one superiority in tanks, the German withdrawal continued. The Oder was crossed and Breslau invested on 15th February, and by the 24th, when the advance was finally checked, the Red Army had reached the Neisse river. The occupation of western Poland and a large part of German Silesia caused a considerable problem for the Luftwaffe. The numerous fighter training units that had been based there, away from the ravages of British and American air power and safe from Soviet aircraft which seldom strayed far from the battle area, had to be transferred back to the Reich, where there was considerable congestion at the airfields. Room was eventually found for them in Denmark and in the Leipzig area, although the dislocation to training and the new stresses on organisation were further problems to be suffered by the ailing Luftwaffe. More important, however, was the loss of several aircraft assembly, component and repair factories, depots and dumps, in the territory either already overrun or dangerously near the front line. For example, the loss of the factories at Marienburg and Sorau caused a reduction of twenty-five per cent in the output of FW 190s, a loss, however, which the Luftwaffe's reserves proved capable of sustaining for several weeks. Serviceability was affected by the loss of spare parts, a problem that was to get worse over the following months, the inevitable result of the loss of territory and bases which, together with the enemy attack on the German communications system, seriously impaired the Luftwaffe's ground organisation.

Not all the reinforcements sent to the East in January went to Luftflotte 6. Some were assigned to Luftflotte 4, to support an abortive counter-attack to relieve the German garrison besieged in Budapest (and which was being supplied, inadequately, from the air). The 500 aircraft available between the Carpathians and the Adriatic, however, were quite insufficient for their task, as were the efforts of the ground troops, and the offensive was a failure. The attack, begun on 6th March, turned into a retreat as the Soviets counter-attacked, and by the end of the month the Germans had been pushed out of Hungary altogether. The enemy's southern offensive continued, and by the 6th April the outskirts of Vienna had been reached by the Red Army. The city fell on the 13th, by which time the Soviets were already sweeping through Czechoslovakia.

In the West, the Luftwaffe was greatly weakened by extensive withdrawals to the East, so that by the middle of March there were no more than 1,100 combat aircraft facing the enemy armies, and a further 1,000, divided equally between day and night fighters, defending the Reich from the Allied strategic air forces. Flying was so restricted, that combat was avoided whenever possible. The single-engined fighters were forbidden to operate beyond the front line, and even bomber formations were not to be attacked unless success was certain. In the second week of February, OKW ordered that all missions undertaken by Luftwaffenkommando West were to be limited to those which directly relieved the ground troops. All others were to be cancelled. Moreover, when operations were carried out, the units able to fly were used in the maximum concentration in an attempt to offset the enemy's command of the air. The West was regarded by the Luftwaffe as second in importance to the East, and even the renewal of the Allied offensive in the north in mid February did not provoke any serious reaction from the German Air Force. Only in early March, when the Allies were drawing dangerously near to the Rhine, were the units of Luftwaffenkommando West allowed to increase their scale of effort appreciably, to reach 300-400 sorties daily, weather permitting. Most of these sorties, however, were flown in defence of lines of communication and airfields, and only fifty were made against enemy spearheads. By night, harassing units, which employed some 140 Ju 87s along the Western front, put up an effort of around 150 sorties. Except for Ar 234s, bombers were not used.

Over the Reich, the scale of effort was similarly low, and dropped to negligible levels by March. Only in night intruder operations over England did the Luftwaffe achieve any significant success, when, on the night of 3rd/4th March, 100 night fighters carried out attacks on RAF Bomber Command bases and destroyed twenty-two bombers. On the following night, a similar, but smaller, raid also had good results. However, the missions resulted in the loss of many night fighters, and only one other was attempted, on the night of 17th March, by just eighteen aircraft. On that occasion, only one enemy bomber was shot down. By April, the losses suffered by the enemy formations were negligible. After the kill rate of the night defences rose to 1.3 per cent of the enemy's sorties in January, it fell to 0.5 per cent by the fourth month of the year, a decline which was matched in day-time. For example, on 19th March, when 1,250 American heavy bombers with strong escort set out to attack Berlin, the Germans managed to shoot down only twenty-four bombers and five fighters, less than two per cent of the force engaged. In April, Flak and fighters between them were accounting for an average of just 1.4 per cent of enemy daylight sorties over Germany. The last single-engine fighter action of any significance occurred on 7th April, when 120 Bf 109s and FW 190s, encouraged by martial music played over their radios, attempted a mass suicide ramming operation against American bombers, but to little effect. After 10th April, no attempts were made to intercept day bombers at all, even by the jets which, in the last few weeks, had been undertaking some fifty sorties daily. Night fighters made only twenty-five sorties a night. Fighter strength was down by 1,000 after the first two weeks of April, leaving just 400 to oppose the enemy in the West. By this time, the practice had long been established whereby the Reich was attacked by day by between 1,200 and 1,500 bombers, protected by 600 to 700 fighters, and at night by a comparable force of unescorted bombers. So powerful were the Allied raids and so ineffective the German defence, that in the four months of 1945 before Germany capitulated, no less than 386,204 tons of bombs were dropped on the Reich, over one and a half times as much as had been dropped in the first four years of the war.

The scale of enemy effort which was possible by this time is exemplified by the operation undertaken on 22nd February, when 9,000 aircraft from bases in England, France, Holland, Belgium, and Italy, were sent to deliver bombs on targets over 250,000 square miles of the Reich in an offensive designed to paralyse the German communications system. But the most terrifying example of enemy air power took place on the night of 13th/14th February, when the RAF attacked Dresden, the Reich's seventh largest city, with 2,659 tons of bombs and incendiaries, with a further 800 tons dropped by the USAAF the following day. The scale of destruction was immense. Although no figures have ever been agreed upon by British, American and German agencies, it seems that, of the 28,410 homes in the city centre, 24,866 were totally destroyed. The death toll will never be known, as the city was then filled with refugees, but compared with the 92,000 killed at Hiroshima by the atomic bomb, it was an incomparably greater tragedy, with anywhere between 100,000 and 250,000 dead (probably 130,000) and an unknown number injured. It was, without doubt, the highest rate of destruction of human life ever resulting from one military action, lasting only a few hours. To achieve this, the enemy had lost only twenty-five bombers.

On 23rd March, the British crossed the Rhine under cover of 4,900 sorties by fighters and 3,300 by bombers, undisturbed by the Luftwaffe. The 1,050 aircraft in Luftwaffenkommando West proved able to mount only 200 sorties against the crossing, and 150 against the Americans who were driving across the Rhine to the south. In the following ten days, even this low level of activity fell, and total German strength on the Western Front dropped to 850 aircraft, the activities of which were paralysed by fuel shortage and enemy attack, so that their daily sorties soon fell to just 150. The Allied air forces were left with the freedom to do as they pleased. Between 25th March and 8th May, for example, the US 9th Tactical Air Force made 29,216 fighter-bomber sorties, destroyed 13,000 vehicles, 1,600 locomotives, 8,900 railway trucks, 725 tanks and armoured vehicles, 1,495 aircraft on the ground and 240 in the air, and all for the loss of just 131 aircraft (0.4 of the total sorties). The continual retraction of the front brought about a further reorganisation of the Luftwaffe's command structure. Luftwaffenkommando West, which had withdrawn south-west into Bavaria, became responsible for air operations in southern Germany, while Luftflotte Reich took control of the north. All distinction between front support and home defence was lost, only the division between responsibilities for East and West remained, with Luftflotte 4 and 6 continuing to operate against the Soviets from German soil, and Luftflotte 1 still in action in Courland.

By the second week in April, the Anglo-American advances had confined the Luftwaffe into such a relatively small area of central Germany, that it was no longer possible to differentiate between airfields holding units engaged on the Eastern as distinct from the Western front. Clearly, there was no need for four independent commands within the Reich, and their functions were divided between von Greim's Luftflotte 6 in the south and Stumpff's Luftflotte Reich in the north. Under his command von Greim possessed Luftwaffenkommando West, Luftwaffenkommando 4 (which had evolved from Luftflotte 4 on 7th April), and Fliegerkorps VII; Stumpff had Luftwaffenkommando Nordost (which was, until 11th April, Fliegerkorps II), Fliegerdivison 14, and Jagddivisionen 1 and 2. No attempt was made to switch aircraft indiscriminately between the two fronts, and the seasoned ground attack units were kept fighting the Russians. When the final Soviet offensive was launched on the Oder on 16th April, no less than 1,000 sorties daily were flown by the Luftwaffe's 2,200 aircraft facing the invaders from the East, who possessed some 15,000 machines along the entire front. It was an effort that could not be continued for long. By the 25th Berlin had been completely encircled, and its airfields captured, so that, with the acute shortage of fuel, the number of missions flown daily were reduced to insignificance.

As the Luftwaffe came to the end of its days, there was one last upheaval in its unhappy command structure. After the return of von Greim to the front, Hitler showed his dissatisfaction with the Air Force's leadership by appointing his own special plenipotentiaries (Bevollmächtige) for certain tasks. In mid-February, he ordered that jet production be placed under the SS, and made SS Obergruppenführer Kammler his Plenipotentiary General for Jet Propelled Aircraft, an appointment that was paralleled by Göring's appointment of Kammhuber as Special Plenipotentiary for Jet and Rocket Aircraft. It was a situation that bordered on the absurd. In March, Hitler appointed Baumbach as Plenipotential General for the bombing of all enemy river crossings, his operational orders to be issued by Göring as agreed by Hitler. Since the bomber general had many other commitments at the time, the Luftwaffe substituted a Colonel Helbig to carry out his tasks, leaving to Baumbach only the duty of reporting to Hitler. In addition, plenipotentiaries in charge of defence against four-engine bombers, and of defence against enemy long-range weapons were instituted and made responsible to the Luftwaffe General Staff, in addition to a staff for 'special missions and troop recommendations'. Their appointment, at the insistence of either Hitler or Göring, seriously jeopardized the operation of the General Staff, resulting in a paralysis of the command apparatus rather than in a revitalisation of effort. As General Nielsen wrote of them: 'The special commissioners were granted unlimited authority so that they might have access to all available resources to accomplish their missions. In practice, however, the difficulties . . . bottlenecks, damaged transportation facilities, and chaos in the fields of war production and military leadership . . . had become so nearly insurmountable that they were able to accomplish little or nothing. Their intervention in the established procedures of production and of leadership only served to hasten the collapse of the entire military apparatus.'[17]

The final rupture between Hitler and his Reichsmarschall came at the very end of the Third Reich's existence, and was occasioned not by a military act but by a political one. On 20th April, the Reichsmarschall had presented his birthday wishes to Hitler in person in the Führer's underground bunker in Berlin, and had then left for southern Germany, where the Luftwaffe High Command was based. Three days later, on the 23rd, Göring sent Hitler, cornered in Berlin with Russian tanks only a few hundred yards away from his bunker, a fateful message which read: 'My Führer, in view of your decision to remain in Berlin to defend the city, do you agree to my now assuming command of the Reich with full authority in domestic and foreign policy, on the basis of the law of 29th September 1941 [making Göring Hitler's successor]? If I have not received a reply from you by 2200 hours I shall assume that you have been deprived of your freedom of action and shall act in accordance with my own best judgement. I cannot express my feeling in this hour of my life. May God protect you. I hope that you will decide to leave Berlin after all and come down here.'[18] On receipt of this, Hitler flew into a rage, and, believing Göring was betraying him, replied with the following telegram: 'What you have done warrants the death penalty. In view of your valuable past services, I shall not institute proceedings, provided you renounce all your offices and titles. Otherwise, appropriate steps will have to be taken.'[19] Later that day, Göring was arrested by the SS, and confined to his home in Obersalzburg. In his place, Hitler nominated the fifty-three-year-old General Robert Ritter von Greim to become Commander-in-Chief of the Luftwaffe, and summoned him from Bavaria to Berlin. On the 26th, von Greim, wounded in the leg after an attack by Soviet fighters on his aircraft, piloted by the famous woman aviator Hanna Reitsch, was received by Hitler. The new Commander-in-Chief told Koller afterwards: 'Just don't lose hope! Everything will still turn out all right. My contact with the Führer and his strength has strengthened me like a dip in the fountain of youth. The Führer sat at my bedside for quite a while and discussed everything with me. He retracted all of his accusations against the Luftwaffe. He is aware of what our service branch has accomplished. His reproaches are directed solely at Göring. He had the highest praise for our forces! It made me exceedingly happy.'[20]

Von Greim had been infected by Hitler's unreality. It was not to last long, however. Back in Bavaria, von Greim, now a Field Marshal but ill and on crutches, at the head of a high command with barely 120 personnel left, surveyed the remnants of a once mighty force. The strength of the Luftwaffe had dropped from its peak of 2,800,000 men in August 1944 to some 1,600,000 and its 3,500 aircraft, in units that were broken, scattered, disorganised and without supplies, were incapable of more than 150 sorties a day. On the 26th, the day he assumed command, American and Soviet forces met at Torgau, and by the end of the month all operations against the Western allies in the north had ceased. The last remnants of the Luftwaffe, some 1,500 aircraft of all types, remained in northern Austria and Bohemia, there to operate barely fifty sorties a day against the Soviet forces until the final surrender on 8th May.

Conclusion

The cost of the war to the Luftwaffe had been high. In the five years and eight months of constant battle, some 70,000 aircrew had been killed in action, and 25,000 wounded, together with some 100,000 aircraft destroyed, missing or damaged beyond repair. Of the four million men and women who passed through its ranks during the war, some 320,000 were killed and a further 230,000 seriously injured from all causes. To Germany, however, the cost of the Luftwaffe's failure was far greater than just this. Command of the air over the front-lines, so vital to the success of the Army, was lost between August 1942 and July 1943, and by the end of the year the Luftwaffe had ceased to be a factor of any significance in the outcome of ground operations. Henceforth, the German Army was to have to fight under a handicap which, in the West at least, was significantly greater than that which their enemies had suffered in the early years of the war, the years of the Luftwaffe's victories. If this, alone, did not bring about the German defeat, it most certainly hastened it, and deprived the Wehrmacht of any chance of final success.

Final defeat in the air over Germany came later, although an inability to deal effectively with the raiders had plagued the defenders from the beginning. Here, the results were disastrous. Not only did the enemy rob the Reich of some twenty per cent of its potential war production in the last sixteen months of the war, and severely inhibit the operations of the German Armed Forces by their attack on the communications network, but they denied them the means by which they could continue to operate effectively: oil. By September 1944, the German Air Force was, for all purposes, totally defeated, and, although the enemy could not completely ignore its actions, it ceased to exert any influence on the course of the war.

In human terms alone, the Luftwaffe's failure had enduring consequences. During the air war, some 3,370,000 dwellings in the Reich had been destroyed by Allied bombing, and a further 3,000,000 severely damaged. No fewer than 7,500,000 people had been made homeless. A large part of Germany's rich cultural heritage had been destroyed in a holocaust in which some 590,000 civilians were killed and 800,000 seriously injured. All this, because of the Luftwaffe's inability to maintain command of the air over its own homeland. For this, the responsibility lies not with the men and officers of the German Air Force, whose exploits during the war can only claim respect; it lies with the Luftwaffe high command, whose mode of operation disgraced

377

its profession of arms, and, above all, with Hitler, Führer and Supreme Commander. It was the actions of this War Lord, one totally unworthy of the title, that brought the Luftwaffe to defeat as surely as night follows day, and, with it, the downfall of the Third Reich.

APPENDIX

German Military Aviation, 1919-1933

In Germany from 1919 to 1933, during the republican, democratic interlude between the absolutism of Kaiser and the dictatorship of Führer, military aviation was kept alive in direct contravention of both the spirit and the letter of the Versailles Treaty. The success of the Imperial Flying Service, and the determination of the government to retain as much as possible of Germany's military potential in spite of the draconian restrictions of the Allied peace-makers, ensured that aviation was not to be neglected. Its importance is well-exemplified by the views of General Hans von Seeckt, who, from 1920 to 1926, was Chief of the Army Leadership (Heeresleitung, the Reichsheer's high command). Although he is often credited with being a great military innovator, his ideas were more in the nature of reflections, well-expressed, of prevailing contemporary beliefs within the armed services, than of any revolutionary theories. As such, his assertion that a powerful air force independent of the Army would be a valuable asset in the defence of Germany was indicative of the attitude of informed opinion within the Reichswehr. Of the future, he wrote: 'The war will begin with an air attack on both sides, because the air forces are the most immediately available for action against the enemy. It is not the chief towns and supply centres which will form the immediate object of attack, but the opposing air forces, and only after the defeat of the latter will the attack be directed against other objectives.'

Von Seeckt was particularly impressed by a memorandum drawn up by Captain Helmut Wilberg in May 1919, which argued in favour of the establishment of an air service with 1,800 aircraft manned by 8,000 men from the Army and 1,200 from the Navy. However, the imposition of the Versailles terms put an end to that project. The goal could only be pursued clandestinely. As von Seeckt announced in May 1920: 'We shall not abandon the hope of one day seeing the Flying Service come to life again. The fame of the Flying Service, engraved in the history of the German armed forces, will never fade. It is not dead, its spirit lives on!' Von Seeckt's first move was to recruit 180 specially selected former fliers into the Reichsheer's 4,000-strong officer corps. This he did in spite of considerable opposition from many officers in the Personnel Office, who argued that, to ensure that one in twenty-two of the new army's leaders was an airman, if not exactly wasteful was certainly ludicrous, since they had no aircraft to fly, nor any prospect of acquiring them. Von Seeckt's next step, in close concert with his personal chief of staff, General Ritter von Haack, a former Inspector of the Bavarian Air Force, was to create a number of agencies devoted to military aviation. On 1st March 1920, an Air Organisation and Training Office within the Truppenamt (Troop Office, the Reichsheer's general staff) was established under Wilberg; it served as the central office for the collection and dissemination of all information concerning military flying. At the same time, a special 'Foreign Aviation Department' was formed in the Foreign Armies Intelligence Office, and an Air Technical Section under Captain Kurt Student in the Department for Weapons and Equipment of the Ordnance Office, to evaluate all information about foreign aircraft industries. Nor were the field commands neglected. Teams of flying officers were assigned to the headquarters of each area command (Wehrkreis), where they co-ordinated training in aerial warfare and made the Army aware of its potential and of the importance of air defence. These 'Special-Duty Consultants' also organised emergency flying patrols with civilian flying agencies to be activated in the event of invasion. Finally, two transport companies, one in Prussia, the other in Bavaria, were instructed to continue the traditions of the Prussian and Bavarian Flying Services until a new air force emerged.

In the following years there were a number of changes, the most important of which concerned the Air Organisation and Training Office, whose commanding officers, after Wilberg, were Lieutenant Colonel Wilhelm Wimmer, Major Hugo Sperrle, and Major Helmuth Felmy. In 1925, it was upgraded and made directly subordinate to the Chief of the Army Leadership, and became the central agency for all matters pertaining to aviation. The following year, it incorporated the Foreign Air Office. However, the planning of aerial warfare remained hampered by the low rank of the officers concerned (which meant that majors had to compete with colonels and generals of other arms in the struggle for scarce resources), and, most serious of all, by administrative decentralisation, which caused disharmony between the Air Organisation Office and the Ordnance Office. The former was allowed to submit requests to the latter, but they could be rejected. Heated differences were the result. Unification was the obvious solution, but when, in 1928, Major Albert Kesselring, then the Reichswehr Commissioner for Simplification, proposed the establishment of a single Air Inspectorate, Major Wilhelm Keitel of the Army Organisation Office disagreed, saying that, although a fine idea in theory, in practice it would prove unworkable since foreign reaction would be too unfavourable. The project was shelved. The resignation of General Werner von Blomberg as Head of the Troop Office in September 1929, was a further blow, as he had been particularly sympathetic to such a reorganisation.

Not until 1931 was the time deemed correct for the realisation of Kesselring's suggestion. Then, the Air Organisation and Training Office was moved to the Reichsheer Training Inspectorate, under General Halmar Ritter von Mittelberger, and retitled Branch Inspectorate I (Air). Von Mittelberger took over the control of the air branch in addition to his other duties, with Felmy as his chief of staff. The Inspectorate was given responsibility for air strategy and tactics, personnel, technology, intelligence, air defence, training and meteorological services. Like its predecessor, it undertook its activities under strict secrecy, spending an annual budget of some ten million Reichsmarks, which had been approved by the Army Command and the Reichswehr Ministry.

The establishment of service organisations for the study and development of military aviation was only one of the four ways by which the Germans sought to circumvent the Versailles restrictions in the years 1920 to 1933. The others were: military co-operation with the Soviet Union, exploitation of civilian aviation and sport associations, and the establishment of a military aircraft industry. All four were pursued with vigour, using guile and cunning to the full. However, there was, clearly, a limit beyond which the Germans could not go without detection by the Allies, and it was this, rather than any reluctance on their part to promote aviation, which restricted development to a minimum.

Military co-operation between Germany and the Soviet Union was begun in 1922 with the signing of the Treaty of Rapallo on 16th April; for the aviators, the most important aspect was the establishment of a flying base at Lipetsk, a Russian town some 300 miles south-east of Moscow on the Voronezh river. Colonel Hermann von der Lieth-Thompson, the retired organiser and chief of staff of the Imperial Flying Service, was given control of all military collaboration in the Soviet Union, which included an armoured vehicles school at Kazan and a gas warfare school at Saratov. He and his successor, Major von Niedermayer, reported back to the office in Berlin organised to deal with all contacts with the Russians, Special Group R under Major Fischer. Lipetsk, the first operational German air training base after the war, was established in strict security in 1924 under the command of a Major Stahr (after whom it was named), and equipped mainly with fifty Dutch-built Fokker D XIII fighters. This was half the number that von Seeckt had ordered during the French re-occupation of the Ruhr in 1923; they had arrived too late to be of any use, and the other half had been sold to Romania (it is doubtful, in any case, whether the Reichswehr would have dared to be seen to possess fighter aircraft so soon after the Versailles Treaty had been signed). Every effort was made to preserve secrecy; the Lipetsk trainees had, on paper, to be discharged from military service, only to be re-engaged upon their return to Germany and their resumption of 'authorised' duties. The bodies of men who had been killed at Lipetsk were put in crates marked 'machine tools' for their return to the Fatherland, while small sailing vessels were used to smuggle bombs and other obvious military hardware across the Baltic to Russia. The base itself was cleverly camouflaged to make it look as if it belonged to the Soviet Air Force. However, the precautions were worthwhile. In Lipetsk, where the first six-month training course began in the early summer of 1925, the Reichswehr possessed a centre that was to be of value not only in testing prototypes and experimenting with the tactical employment of aircraft, in building a highly qualified group of ordnance experts, and in training future fliers and commanders, but also in stimulating interest in aviation among the military establishment. By 1930, the base held some 300 personnel, together with fifty-five fighter and reconnaissance aircraft. However, by 1933 the Lipetsk base had outlived its usefulness. Not only were there increasing difficulties in co-operating with the Russians, but also it was costly, especially at a time of depression, coming to account for some 3 million Reichsmarks annually, and much of the training could better be done in Germany, as by that time it had become possible to establish more open military bases owing to the nation's improved international status. In September 1933, the Reichswehr finally left Lipetsk after a progressive run-down that had lasted for almost three years. By that time, however, the base had trained some 150 fighter pilots and 100 observers.

Civilian airlines and sports associations offered considerable opportunity to the Reichswehr to extend its training facilities. In late 1924, von Seeckt ensured the appointment of a retired officer, Ernst Brandenburg, as chief of the Aviation Department in the Reich Transport Ministry. It was an important post, as the Department was the official representative for German aviation as a whole, and one to which Brandenburg was particularly suited. A well-known bomber commander during the war, who had pioneered the Gotha bomber raids over London and south-east England; winner of the Pour le Mérite and disabled owing to the amputation of a leg after a crash, Brandenberg had held various offices concerned with aviation as a civil servant after the war. His experience, dedication, caution, and flair for organisation proved invaluable. He organised the funding of secret military aviation projects, established flight training with civilian agencies for future officers, and provided camouflage for aerial rearmament. He was particularly keen to exploit the opportunities presented by sports flying, the restrictions on which had been lifted by the Allies in 1923. On 1st January 1924, the Reichswehr organised a civilian campaign called 'Sport Flying Ltd' (Sport-flug GmbH) with ten flying schools throughout Germany, where designated flying officers in the Army received training. It was under the control of Dr. Fritz Siebel, a war-time pilot and aircraft manufacturer. The activities of other private flying schools and clubs were also co-ordinated by the military, who provided money from the secret, or 'black', Reichswehr budget administered by the Transport Ministry. In 1925, the military aviation budget was ten million Reichsmarks, half of which was for the schools, the maintenance of disguised flying units and air raid precautions. In 1926, Allied pressure caused Germany to abolish government support for sport-flying, under the provisions of the Paris Air Agreement signed on 21st May. The company, Sports Flying Ltd, was disbanded, its assets being taken over by three commercial flying companies: the German Commercial Flying School (Deutsche Verkehrsflieger-Schule), the Academic Flying Groups (Akade-mischen Fliegergruppen) and Aviation Ltd (Luftfahrt GmbH). The last had been specially founded in 1927 as a cover for military activities.

This new development had little significance, however, and the companies remained an unofficial air reserve for the Reichswehr. Indeed, activity was, in fact, increased. The Paris Agreement allowed for seventy-two serving officers to partake in sport flying at their own expense, half of whom had had no previous experience of flying. More important, however, shortly after the signing of the agreement Wilberg prepared a comprehensive air-training programme in conjunction with the civilian schools. A system was devised, in utmost secrecy, whereby every year forty officer-candidates would receive commercial pilot instruction before formally entering the Reichswehr, and would also be sent on an annual refresher course. These young men were known as Jungmarker in contrast with the Altmarker, flying officers who had been in the service before 1926. Both groups were united in the Society of German Airmen (Ring deutschen Flieger), which, although mainly a civilian social group, kept a file on all pilots, gunners and observers who had served in the First World War. Moreover, Germany's Luftfahrt Verband (Aviation League), with its 40,000 members, represented a sizeable reserve of trained manpower.

A further development took place on 6th January 1926, with the merger, under government pressure, of the two German civil aviation companies, Deutsche-Aero-Lloyd and Junkers Luftverkehrs AG, into Deutsche Luft Hansa. Whether or not this was done at the instigation of the Reichswehr Ministry, the relationship between Luft Hansa and the military was close, in large part thanks to the work of Erhard Milch, one of its directors. Luft Hansa pilots pioneered blind-flying techniques and provided instructors for military training centres, even at Lipetsk, while Luft Hansa aeroplanes, the Ju 52 passenger and freight carriers, were capable of being converted to bombers in time of emergency. Luft Hansa thus formed part of Germany's mobilisation plans.

At the same time as motorised sport-flying flourished in Germany, so did glider-flying, the development of which can be charted by a glider competition held in the Rhön region. In 1920, twenty-four gliding enthusiasts gathered in the mountainous country north-east of Hanau, an area of abundant thermal updrafts, to hold a competition. A record flight of 1,830 metres in 142 seconds was made. The practice continued; by 1935, gliders at Röhn were flying more than 300 miles to land at Brno, Czechoslovakia, and in 1938 a record flight duration of fifty and a quarter hours was achieved. The Reichswehr was not slow to perceive the importance of gliding in training pilots and stimulating air-mindedness. Von Seeckt visited a Röhn contest; Wilberg did all he could to involve officers in the sport; and Student was an active participant. Gliding was particularly useful in furthering aeronautical research, the motorised aspect of which was prohibited by the Allies. Several of the best minds in the German aircraft industry participated in gliding, including Willy Messerschmitt, Anthony Fokker, Ludwig Prandtl, and Theodore von Kármán. Indeed, the latter asserted that glider flying advanced the science of aviation more than most of the motorised flying in the First World War had done.

The German aircraft industry had ended the war in 1918 with a production of 2,000 machines a month from thirty-five aircraft and twenty-six aero-engine companies. The Versailles Treaty, however, banned completely the design and manufacture of military aircraft, and it was not until May 1922 that the production of civil machines was allowed, and then only under strict control. To make certain that they possessed no military capability, the Allied Aviation Guarantee Committee had the task of ensuring that they could not fly at more than 105 miles an hour with a payload of more than 1,300 lb, at a height of more than 13,000 feet over a range of more than 186 miles. These 'definitions' were well below the technical capabilities of existing Allied aircraft, and effectively thwarted aeronautical advance in Germany. Although there was some slight revision of these rules in 1925, it was not until 1926 that they were lifted altogether, under the Paris Air Agreement. This was only brought about because of the German confiscation of Allied civil aeroplanes which, owing to bad weather or mechanical trouble, were forced to land on German territory and did not conform to the 'definitions'. Such action particularly hampered the French and British routes to central and eastern Europe, and, under pressure from the airlines and as part of a general rapprochement, the Allies freed German civil aircraft manufacture from all its restrictions. The ban on military aircraft, however, remained.

The Germans in the Weimar period were no strangers to subterfuge, and in that the aircraft manufacturers excelled. Before the manufacture of civilian aircraft had been made legal in 1922, firms had established offices abroad; production of Junkers, for example, took place in Sweden and Holland, and of Dornier in Switzerland and Italy. A few military machines were even built in Germany, such as those at Warnemünde, on the bay of Lübeck, for sale to the United States and Japan, as well as to the Reichswehr. In 1924, there appeared the Heinkel HD 17 and HD 21 reconnaissance aircraft, to be followed by fighters designed for the Navy, all designed in Germany. Between 1922 and 1923, while negotiations on military co-operation between the Reichswehr and the Soviets were under way, the holding company, Gesellschaft zur Förderung gewerblicher Unternehmen (Gefu), was instituted under the supervision of two retired officers, General von Borries and Major Tschunke. With offices in Berlin and Moscow, and a working capital of seventy-five million Reichsmarks, Gefu oversaw the establishment of several armament factories, including a Junkers airframe and engine plant at Fili, near Moscow. There, Junkers produced a number of models, one of which was the first all-metal passenger aircraft, but in the process, lost some 50,000 Reichsmarks for every aircraft built. Reichswehr finance was unable to meet such a deficit, and in 1927 the plant was closed.

More successful military and civil co-operation, however, was the establishment in 1926 of the 'front' company, Production Ltd (Fertigungs GmbH), which made contracts with aircraft manufacturers. Instituted by the Army Ordnance Office, it began the urgent task of standardisation among the various firms, so as to ensure continuous and inter-locking production. The scale of the problem was immense, as there were no industrial techniques, drawings, standards or numbering systems common to all firms – a recipe for chaos; one aircraft weighing only a ton could require an average of no less than 32,000 parts produced by several different manufacturers. By 1927-28, the industry was in a position to work to the specifications that emanated from Student's branch of the Ordnance Office. From Heinkel came a bomber, the He 41; from the Bavarian Aircraft Works, the Bf 22 night fighter; from Arado, the Ar SD 1 fighter; and from Albatros, the L 76/77 and L 78 reconnaissance aircraft. These were tested either at Lipetsk or at Rechlin in Mecklenburg, a facility built during the First World War, the existence of which, owing to its remoteness, was virtually unknown. However, these four prototypes failed to meet the Ordnance Office's expectations, and new specifications were issued in 1929. By 1932, these resulted in the Dornier Do 11 bomber, the Arado Ar 64 fighter, and the Heinkel He 45 and He 46 long and short range reconnaissance aeroplanes.

During the 1920s, war was never far from the minds of the Reich's military and political leaders. Having no intention of undertaking aggression themselves, they lived with the fear of invasion from the Poles and even the Czechs. Thus, in common with the soldiers, German airmen prepared contingency plans for mobilisation, which were developed each year to keep pace with changes in personnel and equipment. They were based on the Mobilisation Plan for a Wartime Armed Force (Aufstellungsplan einer Kriegswehrmacht), or 'A' Plan as it was known. In the mid-1920s, it was realised that it would be impossible to activate more than eight reconnaissance, three fighter, and three bomber Staffeln, and it was estimated that, in time of war, twenty-five per cent of the reconnaissance aeroplanes and fifty per cent of the fighters and bombers would have to be replaced every month. The Albatros L 75s and L 76s would serve in the reconnaissance role, while the Fokker D XIIIs in Lipetsk would form the fighter arm, provided that the Soviets allowed them to be returned to Germany, which was doubtful. The bombers would come from Luft Hansa, whose civil airliners could be converted for military use within a few days. As the number of qualified airmen in the Reichswehr was small, personnel would be found mainly from Luft Hansa and the German Commercial Flying School, who would be mobilised together with all their aircraft and facilities. But bombs were in short supply, and, in general, equipment was lacking to support any mobilisation.

However, greater things were planned for the future. In 1927, the Ordnance Office submitted a cost survey for a four-year programme to develop an air force to support an army of fifteen divisions. It was envisaged that the flying service would have 247 aeroplanes, sixty-four 8.8 cm anti-aircraft guns, ninety anti-aircraft machine guns, sixty searchlights and thirty directional sound-detector devices. The Reichswehr, however, already had in mind a peace-time army of twenty-one divisions; the plan was inadequate. The following year, 1928, an estimate was made that, in one year, the aircraft industry could produce 7,006 aeroplanes for the Army and 1,746 for the Navy. These figures were wildly inaccurate, and yet, on their basis, a programme was worked out whereby, in peace-time, the industry would supply the Army with 2,293 aircraft annually, and the Navy with 750. Thus, in the year 1928-29, out of a Reichswehr budget totalling 827 million Reichsmarks, twelve million went towards the expansion of the aircraft industry. However, owing to economic depression and financial stringency, the amount was reduced the following year to only nine million Reichsmarks. In fact, over the seven years, 1926 to 1932, only 150-170 million Reichsmarks were spent on secret air rearmament, quite insufficient to produce the results required. Moreover, the aircraft industry itself was reluctant to take part in any great expansion in view of the low profits. At first, orders were placed only for the manufacture of individual parts or the rebuilding of older machines, since the development of new aircraft was extremely expensive and considered too risky. Thus, although the Ordnance Office could provide specifications for aeroplanes, and the German designers could create the prototypes, the aircraft industry was in too poor a condition to mass produce for war.

By the beginning of 1929, there were eight aircraft and four aero-engine works in Germany. Albatros, Arado, Bavarian Aircraft Works, Dornier, Focke-Wulf, Heinkel, and Rohrbach produced aircraft, and Argus, Bavarian Motor Works, and Siemens made engines, and were soon to be joined by Daimler-Benz. Only Junkers combined the two. In the design and manufacture of engines, Germany was ill-equipped; most of those used in the 1920s came from abroad. By 1933, there were only three types of German engine suitable for military aircraft, and two of these were of foreign design. In the 1930s, engine development was to prove the biggest problem of the aircraft industry. Research, however important, fared poorly. The umbrella organisation instituted by private enterprise in 1928, the German Aviation Research Establishment, was extremely short of funds and lacked any overall direction, and money for aircraft design continued to be a problem. Of the 321 million Reichsmarks that were made available as a subsidy to aviation by the Ministry of Transport in the seven years from 1926 to 1932, rather less than 23 million Reichsmarks, or seven per cent, went to research. Indeed, in 1932, when the total was less than it had ever been, the amount was only five per cent.

By 1932, the German aircraft industry was in poor shape. The number employed had sunk to less than 4,000. On 4th April, the Air Inspectorate submitted a detailed report on production facilities. Among the seven airframe manufacturers (Rohrbach had succumbed to the depression) only two, Junkers and Heinkel, were able to produce aircraft in series, and these only on a limited scale; the rest were custom-built manufacturers, each with a maximum output of six aeroplanes a month. At the time of the report, Junkers had not produced a single aeroplane to the military specifications of the Ordnance Office, and its financial position was critical. Only state aid and reorganisation could save it. Of the other companies, Arado and Heinkel were solvent, Dornier was in receipt of aid, Albatros had had to amalgamate with Focke-Wulf, and even then the new firm continued to experience difficulties; Klemm, being primarily a light sport aircraft manufacturer, was unimportant. The aircraft-engine firms were faring even worse, and the Bavarian Motor Works were soon to cease business. The situation in the ancillary industry was just as bad: during a mobilisation supplies of aviation fuel would last for only three months; airborne radio equipment would not be ready for six months; and explosive for bombs would be insufficient.

However, in other fields more progress was made. A considerable impetus to aerial rearmament came with the ending of the ban on stock-piling of military aircraft on 29th November 1930. At a conference attended by the Ministers for the Reichswehr, Foreign Affairs and Transport, and the Chief of the Air Inspectorate, it was concluded that this provision of the Versailles Treaty could be ignored, and that the way would then be open for the collection of aircraft, weapons and equipment in depots ready for mobilisation. Shortly thereafter, the Army Command established three duty squadrons, each of four aeroplanes, drawing their personnel from units in Lipetsk. Although stationed and controlled by military headquarters in Berlin, Königsberg and Nuremberg-Fürth, they were given the cover title of Reklamenstaffeln (advertising squadrons) and were ostensibly owned by Luftfahrt GmbH. One Seefliegerübungstaffel (naval airmen training squadron) was also activated. By April 1932, the Reichswehr possessed 228 aircraft: thirty-six military, and 192 civilian but convertible machines (a mobilised strength of sixteen Staffeln), and over the next year it was planned to increase the number of military machines by forty-six.

At the time of the Weimar Republic the Army's interest in aviation was paralleled by that of the Navy. Under the Versailles Treaty it, like the Reichsheer, was forbidden to have aircraft but was allowed to possess heavy anti-aircraft guns at the large naval base of Königsberg. There, work was undertaken on the 8.8 cm gun, together with the 7.6 and 10.5 cm guns, all of which were to be of considerable value to the Army when it reintroduced anti-aircraft guns into service in 1930. In aviation, too, the Reichsmarine was active. It began training its own pilots at Stralsund as early as 1922, and made only limited use of the Lipetsk base. The following year, it ordered ten He I seaplanes from Heinkel, which were ostensibly built for an anonymous South American country and then shipped to Sweden, from where, after tests, they were sent back to Germany; six war-time aircraft were also used. In 1923, it set up air training and technical organisations within its Command. In 1924, training began in a manner very similar to that in the Army, the main 'civilian' firm being Severa GmbH, which, by 1928, was spending 1,350,000 Reichsmarks annually. Aircraft development was undertaken under the supervision of Captain Günther Lohmann, head of the Development Section of the Navy Transport Office, and testing facilities were based at Travemünde. In 1929, the Reichswehr Ministry ordered closer co-operation between the Army and the Navy, to avoid duplication of effort. The Navy wished to remain independent, however, and continued to develop seaplanes according to its own specifications, but nevertheless profited from co-operation in such matters as navigation and bombing aids, the conversion of land aircraft for use at sea, and in field-testing in the Soviet Union.

In 1932, considerable progress was made in planning for a German air force. The production of a purpose-built bomber and the mass-production of military aircraft were agreed upon as the aims for the next period of rearmament, stretching from 1933 to 1938. In February 1932, Felmy submitted a plan that called for the establishment of an air force of eighty Staffeln to support an army of twenty-one divisions. It would possess 750 active and 240 reserve aeroplanes by 1938 (not including 96 trainers) of which half would be bombers, whose first aim would be to destroy the enemy's air bases followed by further missions deep into enemy territory. Offence was regarded as the best means of defence. A month later, however, the Air Inspectorate Office reported that the aircraft industry was quite incapable of producing anything approaching the 300 aeroplanes a month that Felmy's plan, together with the estimates of the Ordnance Office, asserted would be required no later than after the sixth month of war; instead, they would produce only 100 single-engined aeroplanes nine months after mobilisation. In November, a further report from the Air Inspectorate concluded that, because of the depressed state of the industry and the shortage of funds, even the minimum requirements for emergency rearmament could not be completed. However, despite this gloomy prognostication, in July the Ordnance Office had issued specifications for a new generation of military aircraft, five in all, including a heavy bomber.

At the same time as the technicians were proposing and opposing various plans for the future of military aviation, the politicians and the leaders of the Reichswehr were also advocating expansion. Diplomatic sources had reported that the new French government under Eduard Herriot was sympathetic towards an increase in the German Army. In July, the Chief of the Troop Office, General Wilhelm Adam, proposed to the Minister of Defence, General Kurt von Schleicher, that an expanded Friedensheer (Peace-time Army) be created, together with a Friedensluftwaffe, which by 1938, would reach the level proposed in Felmy's study. But heavy bombers, however desirable, would not be included, at least for a while, on the grounds that the Allies would be too sensitive about Germany's deployment of such potent weapons of aggression. Reliance upon reconnaissance aircraft that could act both as bombers and civilian aeroplanes would continue for some time to come.

The planning for the Friedensluftwaffe provided impetus for the thorough reorganisation of military aviation. Within the Defence Ministry, no fewer than eight departments had responsibility for some aspect of air warfare, while the Transport Ministry was also involved. In July, the Air Inspectorate Office recommended the centralisation of Army and Navy offices for the purposes of administration, supply, weapons, research and development. Two months later, the Director of Tactics and Training in the Air Inspectorate, Captain Hans Jeschonnek, submitted a memorandum, endorsed by General von Mittelberger, which called for the concentration of all aviation agencies, including civilian, in the Reichswehr Ministry. This, he argued, was the only way to ensure that Germany's limited resources be co-ordinated to meet its defence requirements. He pointed to the fact that, in the late 1920s, only five of the forty million Reichsmarks spent by the Transport Ministry on aviation went to finance military needs. Matters were not helped by the Army and Navy pursuing different programmes. Instead of three largely unco-ordinated budgets, Jeschonnek proposed that there be one. In late October, despite some resistance to these proposals from certain Army departments, the Reichswehr Ministry submitted the scheme to the Reich Cabinet. The Army was particularly impressed by the fact that the reorganisation would place under their control all public funds for aviation, at a time when, because of economic depression, money was scarce and the aircraft industry starved of resources. The new office would have two major divisions, one for aviation, the other for air defence. which would combine all civilian and military aspects of aviation, including funding, technical development and deployment. The Troop Office began discussions with the Navy to implement the scheme. However, before the reorganisation could be put into practice, political conditions in the Reich altered dramatically, and the military leaders were forced to change their plans: Adolf Hitler was appointed Reich's Chancellor.

Notes

Chapter I *The High Command*

1. Ernst von Hoeppner, *Deutschlands Krieg in der Luft.* Leipzig, 1921, p. 179.
2. David Irving, *The Rise and Fall of the Luftwaffe.* London, 1973, p. 32.
3. US Government, *Nazi Conspiracy and Aggression.* Washington, 1946 Vol. IV, Doc. 2289 Ps.
4. Albert Kesselring, *Soldaten bis zum letzten Tag.* Bonn, 1955, p. 26.
5. Richard Suchenwirth, *Command and Leadership in the German Air Force.* 1968, p. 144.
6. Ibid., p. 19.
7. Ibid., p. 32.
8. Kesselring, p. 459.
9. Andreas Nielsen, *The German Air Force General Staff.* 1959, p. 28.
10. Suchenwirth, p. 4.
11. Ibid., p. 13.
12. Irving, p. 57.
13. Edward L. Homze, *Arming the Luftwaffe.* Nebraska, 1976, p. 238.
14. Nielsen, p. 75.
15. Suchenwirth, p. 28.
16. Nielsen, p. 24.
17. Ibid., pp. 67-8.
18. Kesselring, p. 5.
19. Karl-Heinz Völker, *Dokumente und Dokumentarfotos zur Geschichte der deutschen Luftwaffe.* Stuttgart, 1968, Doc. Nr. 48.
20. Nielsen, p. 75.
21. Suchenwirth, p. 143.
22. Richard Suchenwirth, *Historical Turning Points in the German Air Force War Effort.* 1959, p. 62.
23. Nielsen, p. 75.
24. Ibid., pp. 75-6.
25. Ibid., p. 34.
26. Ibid., pp. 160-1.
27. Irving, p. 120.
28. Suchenwirth, *Command*, p. 63.
29. Ibid., p. 72.
30. Werner Baumbach, *Broken Swastika.* London, 1960, p. 26.
31. Suchenwirth, *Command*, p. 108.
32. Ibid., p. 70.
33. Ibid., p. 71.
34. Ibid., p. 38.
35. Nielsen, p. 68.
36. Ibid., p. 51.
37. Homze, p. 235.
38. Irving, p. 55.
39. Nielsen, p. 126.

Chapter II *The Strategic Base*

1. Homze, p. 56.
2. Irving, p. 33.
3. Ibid.
4. Guilio Douhet, *Command of the Air.* London, 1936, p. 52.
5. Ibid., p. 14.
6. Ibid., p. 49.
7. Ibid., p. 22.
8. Ibid., p. 150.
9. H. A. Jones, *The War in the Air.* Oxford, 1937, Appendices pp. 8-14.
10. 'Hands Off Britain' Air League, 1934.
11. 'Miles', *The Gas War of 1940.* London, 1931, pp. 34, 72.
12. Homze, p. 34.
13. *Luftkriegführung.* Berlin, 1936, para. 9.

390

14. Ibid., para. 186.
15. Ibid., para. 174.
16. Ibid., para. 186.
17. Ibid., para. 31.
18. Anon, *The Diary of a Staff Officer.* London, 1940, p. 28.
19. B. H. Liddell Hart, *History of the Second World War.* London, 1970, p. 32.
20. B. H. Liddell Hart, *Dynamic Defence.* London, 1926, pp. 58-9.
21. Heinz Guderian, *Schnelle Truppen Einst und Jetzt.* Berlin, 1936, p. 236.
22. *Luftkriegführung*, para. 121.
23. Ibid., para. 119.
24. Ibid., 1940, para. 125.
25. Ibid., para. 130.
26. Ibid., para. 132.
27. *Luftkreigführung.* 1936, para. 26.
28. Nielsen, p. 28.
29. Suchenwirth, *Historical Turning Points*, p. 31.
30. Ibid., p. 37.
31. Suchenwirth, *Command*, p. 79.
32. Irving, pp. 65-7.
33. Suchenwirth, *Command*, p. 80.
34. Homze, p. 80.
35. Karl Bartz, *Swastika in the Air.* London, 1956, p. 47.
36. Ian Hogg, *Anti-Aircraft.* London, 1979, p. 105.
37. International Military Tribunal, *The Trial of the German Major War Criminals.* London, 1949-51, Vol. IX, pp. 280-1, hereafter cited IMT.
38. Hugh Trevor Roper ed., *Hitler's Table Talk.* London, 1953, p. 687.

Chapter III *The Onset of War*

1. Homze, p. 104.
2. Alfred Jodl, *Kriegstagebuch.* (KTB), 4 February 1937.
3. Suchenwirth, *Historical Turning Points*, p. 124.
4. Homze, p. 240.
5. Baumbach, p. 24.
6. Suchenwirth, *Command*, p. 12.

7. Neilsen, pp. 155-8.
8. Cajus Bekker, *The Luftwaffe War Diaries.* London, 1967, p. 478.
9. Nielsen, pp. 169-170.
10. Suchenwirth, *Command*, p. 82.
11. Ibid.
12. F.J. Overy, 'From "Uralbomber" to "Amerikabomber"; the Luftwaffe and Strategic Bombing', *Journal of Strategic Studies.* London, 1978.
13. NCA, Vol. VI, Doc. 3474 PS.
14. John Wheeler-Bennett, *The Nemesis of Power.* London, 1964, p. 398.
15. Alan Bullock, *Hitler, a Study in Tyranny.* London, 1953, p. 464.
16. Homze, p. 252.
17. Suchenwirth, *Historical Turning Points*, p. 23.
18. IMT, Vol. 9, p. 262.
19. Homze, p. 141.
20. Ibid., p. 166.
21. Bullock, p. 512.
22. Telford Taylor, *Munich, The Price of Peace*, New York 1979, p. 640.
23. Ibid., p. 641.
24. Ibid., p. 650.
25. Ibid., p. 834.
26. Baumbach, p. 25.
27. Homze, p. 125.
28. Suchenwirth, *Command*, p. 230.
29. Ibid.
30. Irving, p. 74.
31. Suchenwirth, *Command*, p. 231.
32. Irving, p. 74.
33. William Shirer, *The Rise and Fall of the Third Reich.* London, 1964, p. 570.
34. Ibid., p. 590.
35. Ibid., p. 645.
36. IMT, Vol. 8, p. 42.
37. Homze, p. 251.
38. Shirer, p. 554.
39. IMT, Vol. 8, p. 259.
40. IMT, Vol. 9, p. 43.
41. Irving, p. 73.
42. Paul Deichmann, *German Air Operations in Support of the Army.* 1962, p. 89.
43. Suchenwirth, *Command*, p. 226.

Chapter IV *The Early Campaigns*

1. Air Ministry, *The Rise and Fall of the German Air Force*. London, 1949, p. XVII.
2. Friedrich Heiss, *Der Sieg im Osten*. Berlin, 1940, p. 3.
3. *Luftkriegführung*. 1936 para. 103.
4. Paul Deichmann, p. 89.
5. Kesselring, p. 45.
6. Heiss, p. 4.
7. Ibid.
8. Kesselring, p. 46.
9. Bekker, p. 47.
10. Ibid., pp. 49-50.
11. Ibid.
12. Suchenwirth, *Historical Turning Points*, p. 57.
13. Deichmann, p. 105.
14. Bekker, p. 75.
15. Ibid., p. 78.
16. Air Ministry, p. 57.
17. Ibid.
18. Heiss, p. 5.
19. Herbert Mason, *The Rise of the Luftwaffe, 1918-1940*. London, 1975, p. 149.
20. Telford Taylor, *The March of Conquest*. New York, 1958, p. 57.
21. Shirer, p. 231.
22. Jodl, *KTB*. 11 January 1940.
23. Ibid., 12 January 1940.
24. B. H. Liddell Hart, *The Other Side of the Hill*. London, 1951, p. 149.
25. Ibid., p. 155.
26. Kesselring, p. 51.
27. Irving, p. 84.
28. Jodl, *KTB*. 12 January 1940.
29. Taylor, *The March of Conquest*, p. 152.
30. W. S. Churchill, *The Second World War*. London, 1949, Vol. 1, p. 440.
31. Foreign Office, *Documents on German Foreign Policy, 1918-1945*. London, 1952, Vol. 8, p. 114.
32. Jodl, *KTB*. 16 January 1940.
33. Nielsen, p. XVII.
34. Ibid., p. 199.
35. Walter Warlimont, *Inside Hitler's Headquarters, 1939-45*. London, 1964, p. 71.
36. Jodl, *KTB*. 12 June 1940.
37. Ronald Wheatley, *Operation Sealion*. London, 1958, p. 48.
38. NCA, Vol. VII, Doc. L52.
39. Bekker, p. 139.
40. Deichmann, p. 140.
41. Ibid.
42. Bekker, p. 155.
43. Warlimont, p. 41.
44. Suchenwirth, *Command*, p. 160.
45. Iriving, p. 90.
46. War Directive No. 13.
47. Kesselring, p. 59.

Chapter V *The Onslaught Against Britain*

1. NCA, Vol. VII, Doc. L-79.
2. War Directive No. 1.
3. Ibid., No. 6.
4. NCA, Vol. VII, Doc. L-52.
5. War Directive No. 9.
6. Shirer, p. 591.
7. Telford Taylor, *The March of Conquest*, p. 139.
8. War Directive No. 9.
9. Supplement to War Directive No. 9.
10. Nielsen, p. 148.
11. Baumbach, p. 77.
12. Telford Taylor, *The Breaking Wave*. London, 1967, p. 84.
13. Kesselring, p. 70.
14. War Directive No. 16.
15. War Directive No. 17.
16. Kesselring, p. 81.
17. Theo Osterkamp, *Durch Höhen und Tiefen jagt ein Herz*. Heidelberg, 1952, pp. 325-6.
18. Ibid., p. 174.
19. Air Ministry, p. 80.
20. Mason, p. 613.
21. Telford Taylor, *The Breaking Wave*, p. 107.
22. Ibid., p. 121.
23. Denis Richards and Hilary St. G Saunders, *History of The Royal Air Force, 1939-1945*. London, 1961, Vol. 1, p. 175.

24. Telford Taylor, *The Breaking Wave*, p. 138.
25. Adolf Galland, *The First and the Last*. London, 1955, pp. 58-9.
26. Richards and Saunders, Vol. 1, p. 172.
27. Wheatley, p. 73.
28. Richards and Saunders, Vol. 1, p. 192.
29. Frances Mason, *Battle over Britain*. London, 1969, p. 107.
30. Telford Taylor, *The Breaking Wave*, p. 174.
31. Ibid.
32. Galland, pp. 40-1.
33. Bekker, p. 221.
34. Telford Taylor, *The Breaking Wave*, p. 158.
35. Ibid.
36. Churchill, Vol. II, p. 292.
37. German Naval Staff War Diary, 7 September 1940.
38. Ibid., 10 September 1940.
39. Wheatley, p. 81.
40. Halder, *KTB*. 14 September 1940.
41. Jodl, *KTB*. 14 September 1940.
42. Telford Taylor, *The Breaking Wave*, p. 174.
43. Ibid.
44. Wheatley, p. 104.
45. Galland, p. 63.
46. L. Lochner, *The Goebbels Diaries*. London, 1948, p. 139.
47. Telford Taylor, *The Breaking Wave*, p. 204.
48. Mason, p. 451.

Chapter VI *Blitz and Counter-Attack*

1. Irving, p. 106.
2. Taylor, p. 163.
3. Richards and Saunders, Vol. 1, p. 205.
4. *Parliamentary Debates*. 8 October 1940.
5. Basil Collier, *The Defence of the United Kingdom*. London, 1957, p. 258.
6. Richards and Saunders, Vol. 1, p. 209.
7. War Directive No. 23.
8. Ibid.
9. Collier, p. 280.
10. Bekker, p. 370.
11. Suchenwirth, *Command*, p. 98.
12. Ibid., pp. 273-4.
13. Galland, p. 93.
14. Anthony Verrier, *The Bombing Offensive*. London, 1968, pp. 326-7.
15. Goebbels, *Diary*. 26 April 1942.
16. Gebhard Aders, *History of the German Night Fighter Force, 1917-1945*. London, 1979, p. 29.
17. Air Ministry, p. 192.
18. Suchenwirth, *Historical Turning Points*, p. 110.
19. Collier, p. 512.
20. Suchenwirth, *Command*, p. 272.
21. Irving, pp. 147-8.
22. Ibid., p. 141.

Chapter VII *The Mediterranean*

1. War Directive No. 22.
2. Deichmann, p. 107.
3. Ibid., pp. 107-8.
4. Bekker, p. 249.
5. Ibid., p. 306.
6. Erwin Rommel, *Papers*. London, 1953, p. 107.
7. Richards and Saunders, Vol. II, p. 203.
8. Suchenwirth, *Historical Turning Points*, p. 93.
9. Richards and Saunders, Vol. II, p 205.
10. Bekker, p. 312.
11. Suchenwirth, *Historical Turning Points*, p. 94.
12. Ibid.
13. F.W. von Mellenthin, *Panzer Battles, 1939-1945*. London, 1955, pp. 118-9.
14. Suchenwirth, *Historical Turning Points*, p. 95.
15. Ibid.
16. Kesselring, p. 169.
17. Richards and Saunders, Vol. II, p. 302.
18. Rommel, p. 283.

19. Siegfried Westphal, *The German Army in the West*. London, 1951, p. 128.

Chapter VIII *The Attack on the Soviet Union*
1. War Directive No. 21.
2. IMT, Vol. 12, pp. 136-7.
3. Suchenwirth, *Command*, pp. 169-170.
4. War Directive No. 21.
5. Ibid.
6. Deichmann, p. 126.
7. Kesselring, pp. 96-7.
8. Halder, 11 July 1941.
9. Hermann Plocher, *The German Air Force versus Russia, 1941-43*. 1965, Vol 1, p. 96.
10. Plocher, Vol. 1, p. 233.
11. Halder, *KTB*. 30 November 1941.
12. War Directive No. 39.
13. Halder, *KTB*. 15 December 1941.
14. Plocher, Vol. II, p. 184.
15. Ibid., p. 206.
16. Deichmann, p. 165.
17. War Directive No. 41.
18. Plocher, Vol 11, p. 231.
19. Ibid., p. 206.
20. Bekker, p. 359.
21. Plocher, Vol II, p. 238.
22. Fritz Morzik, *The German Air Force Airlift Operations*. 1961, p. 184.
23. Plocher, Vol II, p. 275.
24. Suchenwirth, *Historical Turning Points*, p. 103.
25. Plocher, Vol II, p. 316.
26. Air Ministry, p. 218.

Chapter IX *The Crisis*
1. Overy, p. 161.
2. Suchenwirth, *Command*, p. 146.
3. Ibid., p. 239.
4. Ibid., p. 90.
5. Ibid., p. 91.
6. Neilsen, p. 134.
7. Suchenwirth, *Command*, p. 136.
8. Ibid., p. 132.
9. Ibid., pp. 91-2.
10. Ibid., p. 93.

11. Baumbach, pp. 28-9.
12. Suchenwirth, *Command*, p. 96.
13. Irving, p. 120.
14. Ibid., p. 121.
15. Suchenwirth, *Command*, p. 100.
16. Shirer, p. 691.
17. Irving, p. 120.
18. Ibid., p. 122.
19. Ibid.
20. Suchenwirth, *Command*, p. 103.
21. Ibid., pp. 89-90.
22. Ibid., p. 104.
23. Ibid.
24. Ibid., p. 106.
25. Suchenwirth, p. 108.
26. Baumbach, p. 149.
27. Irving, p. 170.
28. Ibid., p. 172.
29. Neilsen, p. 160.
30. Ibid., p. 159.
31. Suchenwirth, *Command*, p. 192.

Chapter X *1943 – The Year of Defeat*
1. Richards and Saunders, Vol. II, p. 306.
2. Deichmann, p. 147.
3. Baumbach, pp. 92-3.
4. Sir Charles Webster and Noble Frankland, *The Strategic Air Offensive against Germany*. London, 1961, Vol II, p. 12.
5. Bekker, p. 393.
6. Goebbels Diary, 10 April 1943.
7. Irving, p. 216.
8. Goebbels Diary, 8 May 1943.
9. Irving, p. 221.
10. Bekker, p. 423.
11. Aders, p. 61.
12. Bekker, p. 425.
13. Webster and Frankland, Vol. IV, p. 315.
14. Irving, p. 229.
15. Bekker, p. 399.
16. Ibid.
17. Galland, p. 223.
18. Ibid., pp. 224-5.
19. Irving, p. 244.

20. Galland, p. 200.
21. Aders, p. 109.
22. Irving, p. 234.
23. Suchenwirth, *Command*, p. 145.
24. Ibid., p. 189.
25. Ibid., pp. 153-4.
26. Heinz Höhne, *The Order of the Deaths Head*. London, 1969, p. 245.
27. Suchenwirth, *Command*, p. 179.
28. Ibid., p. 181.
29. Warlimont, p. 404.
30. Plocher, Vol. II, p. 214.
31. Nielsen, p. 168.
32. Neilsen, pp. 148-9.
33. Suchenwirth, *Command*, p. 278.
34. Ibid., p. 152.
35. Nielsen, p. 161.
36. Ibid., p. 165.
37. Suchenwirth, *Command*, p. 270.
38. Ibid.
39. Ibid., p. 237.
40. Ibid., p. 164.
41. Nielsen, pp. 176-7.
42. Suchenwirth, *Command*, p. 303.
43. Ibid., pp. 164-5.
44. Ibid., p. 285.
45. Nielsen, p. 160.
46. Ibid., p. 84.
47. Bekker, p. 402.
48. Nielsen, p. 48.

Chapter XI *1944 – The Beginning of the End*

1. Webster and Frankland, Vol. IV, p. 306.
2. Suchenwirth, *Command*, p. 104.
3. NCA, Vol. 3, p. 412.
4. Suchenwirth, *Historical Turning Points*, pp. 88-9.
5. Collier, p. 503.
6. Jodl, *KTB*. 1 January 1944.

7. Matthew Cooper, *The German Army*. London, 1978, p. 503.
8. Ibid., p. 508.
9. Irving, p. 231.
10. Bekker, p. 448.
11. Ibid., p. 450.
12. Irving, p. 210.
13. William Green, *Warplanes of the Third Reich*. London, 1970, p. 360.
14. Irving, p. 287.
15. Galland, pp. 300-1.
16. Ibid., p. 279.
17. Suchenwirth, *Historical Turning Points*, p. 120.
18. Baumbach, p. 170.

Chapter XII *1944 – The End*

1. Webster and Frankland, Vol. IV, p. 104.
2. Baumbach, p. 150.
3. Webster and Frankland, Vol. IV, p. 145.
4. Cooper, p. 512.
5. Irving, p. 224.
6. Suchenwirth, *Command*, p. 46.
7. Ibid.
8. Ibid., pp. 46-7.
9. Webster and Frankland, Vol. IV, p. 210.
10. Irving, p. 289.
11. Air Ministry, p. 408.
12. Heinz Guderian, *Panzer Leader*. London, 1952, p. 197.
13. Air Ministry, p. 417.
14. Suchenwirth, *Command*, pp. 200-1.
15. Ibid., p. 201.
16. Galland, p. 368.
17. Nielsen, pp. 87-8.
18. Suchenwirth, *Command*, p. 208.
19. Ibid.
20. Ibid., p. 210.

Select Bibliography

ADDINGTON, LARRY H.: *The Blitzkrieg Era and the German General Staff, 1865-1941*. New Brunswick, N.J., 1972.
ADERS, GEBHARD: *History of the German Night Fighter Force, 1917-1945*. London, 1979.
AIR MINISTRY: *The Rise and Fall of the German Air Force*. London, 1949.

BARTZ, KARL: *Swastika in the Air: the struggle and defeat of the German Air Force, 1939-1945*. London, 1956.
BAUMBACH, WERNER: *Broken Swastika*. London, 1960.
BAUR, HANS: *Ich flog Mächtige die Erde*. Kempten, 1960.
BEKKER, CAJUS D.: *The Luftwaffe War Diaries*. London, 1967.
BERNHARDT, WALTER: *Die deutsche Aufrüstung, 1934-1939*. Frankfurt, 1969.
BEWLEY, CHARLES: *Hermann Göring and the Third Reich*. New York, 1962.
BIRKENFELD, WOLFGANG: *Der synthetische Treibstoff, 1933-1945*. Göttingen, 1964.
BOELCKE, WILLIAM: *Deutschlands Rüstung im Zweiten Weltkrieg*. Frankfurt am Main, 1969.
BRADY, ROBERT A.: *The Rationalization Movement in German Industry*. Berkeley.
BROSS, WERNER: *Gespräche mit Hermann Göring*. Flensburg, 1950.

CAIDIN, MARTIN: *Me 109: Willy Messerschmitt's Peerless Fighter*. New York, 1968.
CALDER, ANGUS: *The People's War: Britain 1939-1945*. London, 1969.
CARROLL, BERENICE A.: *Design for Total War: Arms and Economics in the Third Reich*. The Hague, 1968.
CARSTEN, F. L.: *The Reichswehr and Politics, 1918 to 1933*. Oxford, 1966.
COLLIER, BASIL: *The Defence of the United Kingdom*. London, 1957.
CONRADIS, HEINZ: *Nerven, Herz und Rechenschieber: Kurt Tank, Flieger, Forscher, Konstrukteur*. Gottingen, 1955.
COOKSLEY, PETER, G.: *Flying Bomb*. London, 1979.
CRAIG, JAMES F.: *The Messerschmitt Bf 109*. New York, 1968.

DEICHMANN, GENERAL DER FLIEGER a. D. PAUL: *German Air Operations in Support of the Army*. U.S. Historical Study No. 163, June 1962.
DOUHET, GIULIO: *Command of the Air*. London, 1936.

EARLE, EDWARD MEAD: ed. *Makers of Modern Strategy: Military Thought from Machiavelli to Hitler*. New York, 1967.
EICHOLTZ, DIETRICH: *Geschichte der deutschen Kriegswirtschaft, 1939-1945. Vol 1. 1933-1941*. Berlin, 1969.

EICHOLTZ, DIETRICH, and WOLFGANG SCHUMMANN: eds. *Anatomie des Krieges: Neue Dokumente über die Rolle des deutschen Monopolkapitalismus bei der Vorbereitung und Durchführung des Zweiten Weltkrieges.* Berlin, 1969.

ERBE, RENÉ: *Die nationalsozialistische Wirtschaftspolitik 1933-1939 im Lichte der modernen Theorie.* Zurich, 1958.

ERFURT, WALDEMAR: *Die Geschichte des deutschen Generalstabes von 1918 bis 1945.* Göttingen, 1957.

ESSENWEIN-ROTHE, INGEBORG: *Dir Wirtschaftsverbände von 1933 bis 1945.* Berlin, 1965.

ETHELL, JEFFREY, and PRICE, ALFRED: *The German Jets in Combat.* London, 1979.

FEUCHTER, GEORG WERNER: *Der Luftkrieg.* Frankfurt, 1962.

FISCHER, WOLFRAM: *Die Wirtschaftspolitik des Nationalsozialismus.* Lüneburg, 1961.

FÖRSTER, GERHARD: *Totaler Krieg und Blitzkrieg: die Theorie des Totalen Krieges und des Blitzkrieges in der Militärdoktrin des Faschistischen Deutschlands am Vorabend des Zweiten Weltkrieges.* Berlin, 1967.

FRISCHAUER, WILLI: *The Rise and Fall of Hermann Göring.* Boston, 1951.

GALLAND, ADOLF: *The First and the Last.* London, 1953.

GANDENBERGER, MOISY F. VON: *Luftkrieg – Zukunftskrieg? Aufbau, Gliederung und Kampfformen von Luftstreitkräften.* Berlin, 1935.

GIRBIG, WERNER: *Start im Morgengraven: Eine Chronik vom Untergang des deutschen Jagdwaffe im Westen, 1944-1945.* Stuttgart, 1973.

GÖRLITZ, WALTER: *History of the German General Staff, 1657-1945.* New York, 1953.

GREEN, WILLIAM: *Warplanes of the Third Reich.* London, 1970.

GREINER, HELMUT: *Die Oberste Wehrmachtführung, 1939-1945.* Wiesbaden, 1951.

GREY, C. G.: *The Luftwaffe.* London, 1944.

GUDERIAN, HEINZ: *Panzer Leader.* London, 1952.

HALDER, GENERAL FRANZ: *Kriegstagebuch.* Stuttgart, 1962.

HEIBER, HELMUT: *Hitlers Lagebesprechungen.* Stuttgart, 1962.

HEINKEL, ERNST: *Stürmisches Leben.* Stuttgart, 1953.

HENN, PETER: *The Last Battle.* London, 1954.

HERLIN, HANS: *Udet-eines Mannes Leben und die Geschichte seiner Zeit.* Hamburg, 1958.

HERMANN, HAUPTMANN (pseud): *The Luftwaffe: Its Rise and Fall.* New York, 1943.

HOEPPNER, GENERAL DER KAVALLERIE ERNST VON: *Deutschlands Krieg in der Luft: Ein Rückblick auf die Entwircklung und die Leistungen unserer Heeres-Luftstreitkräfte im Welkriege.* Leipzig, 1921.

HOMZE, EDWARD L.: *Arming the Luftwaffe.* Nebraska, 1976.

IRVING, DAVID: *Destruction of Dresden.* London, 1963.
    The Rise and Fall of the Luftwaffe: The Life of Erhard Milch. London, 1973.

JANSEN, GREGOR: *Das Ministerium Speer.* Berlin, 1968.

JODL, GENERAL ALFRED: *Diaries, 1937-1945.*

JOHNSON, BRIAN: *The Secret War.* London, 1978.

KESSELRING, GENERALFELDMARSCHALL a. D. ALBERT: *Gedanke zum Zweiten Weltkrieg*. Bonn, 1955.
   Soldaten bis zum letzten Tag. Bonn, 1953.
KILLEN, JOHN: *A History of the Luftwaffe, 1915-1945*. London, 1967.
KLEIN, BURTON H.: *Germany's Economic Preparations for War*. Cambridge, Mass, 1959.
KOCH, HORST-ADALBERT: *Flak: Die Geschichte der deutschen Flakartillerie und der Einsatz der Luftwaffenhelfer*. Bad Nauheim, 1965.
KOLLER, KARL: *Der letzte Monat. Die Tagebuchaufzeichnungen des chemaligen Chefs des Generalstabes der deutschen Luftwaffe vom 14.4 bis 27.5.1945*. Manheim, 1949.

LEE, ASHER: *Air Power*. New York, 1955.
   The German Air Force. London, 1946.
   Göring, Air Leader. London, 1972.
LEWIN, RONALD: *Ultra Goes to War*. London, 1978.
LUSAR, RUDOLF: *Die deutschen Waffen und Geheimwaffen des 2. Weltkriegs und ihre Weiterentwicklung*. Munich, 1959.

MANVELL, ROGER, AND HEINRICH FRAENKEL: *Göring*. New York, 1962.
MASON, FRANCES K.: *Battle over Britain*. London, 1969.
MASON, HERBERT MALLOY: *The Rise of the Luftwaffe, 1918-1940*. London, 1975.
MEINCK, GERHARD: *Hitler und die deutsche Aufrüstrung, 1933-1937*. Wiesbaden, 1959.
MORZIK, GENERALMAJOR a. D. FRITZ: *German Air Force Airlift Operations*. U.S. Historical Division, Study 167, June 1961.
MORZIK, FRITZ, and GERHARD HÜMMELCHEN: *Die deutschen Transportflieger im Zweiten Weltkrieg: Die Geschichte des "Fussvolkes der Luft"*. Frankfurt, 1966.
MOSLEY, LEONARD: *The Reich Marshal: A Biography of Hermann Göring*. Garden City, N.Y., 1974.

NIELSEN, GENERALLEUTNANT ANDREAS: *The German Air Force General Staff*. USAF Historical Studies, No. 173. June 1959.

ORLOVIUS, HEINZ and ERNST SCHULTZE: *Die Weltgeltung der deutschen Luftfahrt*. Stuttgart, 1938.
OSTERKAMP, THEO: *Durch Höhen und Tiefen jagt ein Herz*. Heidelberg, 1952.

PASKINS, BARRIE, and DOCKRILL, MICHAEL: *The Ethics of War*. London, 1979.
PLOCHER, HERMANN: *The German Air Force versus Russia, 1941*. Maxwell Air Force Base, Ala: Air University, 1965.
PRICE, ALFRED: *Instruments of Darkness*. London, 1967.
   Luftwaffe: birth, life and death of an air force. London, 1969.
   The Bomber in World War II. London, 1976.
   The Hardest Day, 18 August, 1940. London, 1979.
   World War II Fighter Conflict. London, 1975.

RICHARDS, DENIS and SAUNDERS, HILARY ST, G.: *History of the Royal Air Force, 1939-1945*. London, 1977.
RIECKHOFF, GENERALLEUTNANT HANS J.: *Trumpf oder Bluff? 12 Jahre deutsche Luftwaffe*. Zurich, 1945.

ROSE, ARNO: *Radikaler Luftkampf.* Stuttgart, 1976.

RUDEL, HANS: *Stuka Pilot.* Dublin, 1952.

SCHLIEPHAKE, MANFRIED: *Wie die Luftwaffe wirklich entstand.* Stuttgart, 1972.

SCHRAMM, PERCY ERNST: *Hitler: The Man and the Military Leader.* Chicago, 1971.

SCHWIFFS, WERNER: *Kleine Geschichte der deutschen Luftfahrt.* Berlin, 1968.

SEECKT, HANS VON: *Thoughts of a Soldier.* London, 1930.

SHORES, CHRISTOPHER: *Ground Attack Aircraft of World War II.* London, 1977.

SHULMAN, MILTON: *Defeat in the West.* London, 1947.

SIMON, LESLIE E.: *German Research in World War II: An Analysis of the Conduct of Research.* New York, 1947.

SMITH, JOHN R. and KAY, AL: *German Aircraft of the Second World War.* London, 1972.

SMITH, PETER, C.: *The Stuka at War.* London, 1971.

SPEER, ALBERT: *Inside the Third Reich, Memoirs.* New York, 1970.

SUCHENWIRTH, RICHARD: *Command and Leadership in the German Air Force.* USAF Historical Studies, No. 174. Air University. 1969.

    The Development of the German Air Force, 1919-1939. USAF Historical Studies, No. 160. Air University. 1968.

    Historical Turning Points in the German Air Force War Effort. USAF Historical Studies, No. 189. Air University. June 1959.

TAYLOR, TELFORD: *Sword and Swastika.* New York, 1952.

    The Breaking Wave: The Second World War in the Summer of 1940. New York, 1967.

THOMAS, GEORG: *Geschichte der deutschen Wehr-und Rüstungswirtschaft, (1918-1943/45).* Boppard am Rhein, 1966.

THORWALD, JÜRGEN: *Ernst Udet: Ein Fliegerleben.* Berlin, 1954.

TURNER, P. ST. JOHN: *Heinkel: An Aircraft Album.* New York, 1970.

UNITED STATES STRATEGIC BOMBING SURVEY: *The Effects of Strategic Bombing on the German War Economy.* Washington, 1945.

    Aircraft Division Industry Report. No.4.

    The Defeat of the German Air Force. No. 59.

    V-Weapons (Crossbow) Campaign. No. 60.

VÖLKER, KARL-HEINZ: *Die deutsche Luftwaffe, 1933-1939.* Stuttgart, 1967.

    Die Entwicklung der militärischen Luftfahrt in Deutschland, 1920-1933. Stuttgart, 1962.

    Dokumente und Dokumentarfotos zur Geschichte der deutschen Luftwaffe. Stuttgart, 1968.

WEBSTER, SIR CHARLES, and NOBLE FRANKLAND: *The Strategic Air Offensive against Germany, 1939-1945.* London, 1961.

WHEATLEY, RONALD: *Operation Sealion.* London, 1958.

Index

Adam, General Wilhelm, 35.

Adlerangriff (Eagle Attack), code name for German destruction of RAF, 131, 132-33, 138.

Adlertag – Aug. 13, 1940, 139, 140.

Air Command Office, German (Luftkommandoamt), 5, 18.

Aircraft, (see Luftwaffe, RAF, USAAF, etc.).

Aircraft Industry, German: condition between wars, 2; output 1933-36, 61; and comparison with Allies for same period, 85-6; shortages of raw materials, 61-2, 63, 75, 79, 81, 325; shortage of fuel, 68; problems with production of heavy bomber, 68, 73; layoffs, 74-5; concrete bombs because of steel shortage, 103; aircraft production 1939-42, 260-7; output vs. losses 1939-42, 262-3; types of aircraft, 263-7; rate of aircraft production, 273-4; 'Göring Programme', 275; production under Milch after 1942, 279-82, shortage of labour after 1942, 279; Milch pushes for increased production of fighters, 304; aircraft produced 1943, 320; output 1944, 343-4; development of turbo-jet (Me 262), 350; production losses 1944, 360.

Aircraft production, German (see Aircraft Industry).

Airlift (see Stalingrad, Strategy).

Air Ministry, German (see RLM).

Allies: strategic and air-strength inferiority (1939), 84-7; bombs dropped on Germany, 181; land in Sicily, 289; attack on Sardinia, 289; invasion of Europe (1944), 332ff, 362ff; bombardment of Germany and occupied Europe (1943-45), 339ff, 358ff; failure to destroy German aircraft production (1944), 344; effect of attacks on German oil industry (1944), 348; losses due to German Flak (1944), 358-9; effect of bombardment of Germany (1945), 373ff.

Armengaud, General, French Air Attaché, Warsaw, 101, 102.

von Arnim, General Jürgen, 214, 216, 217.

Aryan Paragraph, 15

Austria, seizure by Germany (1938), 75, 84.

Baby Blitz, German bombing raids on Great Britain (1944), 333, 337.

Baedeker raids, 191.

Battle of the Atlantic, 179-80.

Battle of Berlin (1943-4), 341.

Battle of Britain: 139ff; Luftwaffe failure to concentrate on destruction of RAF, 139; 'Black Thursday', 141; German detection by RAF radar, 144; lull, 144; RAF loss of fighter pilots, 146-7; Luftwaffe losses, 148-9; losses, both sides, 162; Blitz on London, 152ff; intensification of day and night raids on London, 154; 'Battle of Britain Day', 155.

Baumbach, Colonel Werner, 24; on Udet, 30; on Luftwaffe, 64, 127.

Bismarck, battleship, 192.

'Black Thursday' – Aug. 15, 1940, 141, 156, 159.

Blitz, (see Battle of Britain; Baby Blitz).

Blitzkrieg, tanks and bombing, 40, 41; 49.

von Blomberg, Field Marshal Werner, 3, 6, 15; on Milch, 19; cutback rearmament, 62; on Göring as chief of Four-Year Plan, 63.

Blomberg-Fritsch crisis, 14.

Bodenschatz, General Karl, 27; on break between Udet and Milch, 31.

Bohnstedt, General Eberhard, 3, 5, 35.

Bormann, Martin, Head, Party Chancery, 311.

von Brauchitsch, Colonel Bernd, head of Little General Staff, 313.

von Brauchitsch, Field Marshal Walther, 238.

Bulgaria, German invasion of, 196.

Bulowius, General Alfred, 246; replaces Lörzer as head Fliegerkorps II, 288.

Casualties, total, from air warfare, i.

Cavallero, Marshal, Italian Chief of Staff, 207.

Chamberlain, Neville, British Prime Minister (until 1940), 77.

Churchill, Winston, British Prime Minister (1940-45), on bombing of London (Blitz), 166; on Luftwaffe's mistakes in Blitz, 154.

Cleveland Air Races, USA (1931), 48.

Command of the Air, The, (see author, Douhet, Giulio).

Czechoslovakia, German attack on, hypothetical, 65; 70; 'Case Green', 76; Germans prepare for attack, 76, 77; Sudetenland, 77, 84-5.

Czeijka, Ministerial Director Alois, Chief of Industrial Office (RLM), 277.

Deichmann, General Paul, 6; on Göring and Milch, 14; on chaos within RLM (1937), 21; on adoption of heavy bomber by Luftwaffe, 66; on Ju 88, 69; on draining of Luftwaffe training schools, 283, 284; commander Fliegerkorps I, 295; on Göring and Jeschonnek, 313-4.

Denmark, Hitler plans to invade, 108.

Deutsche Luft Hansa, 2; (see Lufthansa).

Dive-bombing (see Strategy).

Douhet, Giulio, Italian military strategist, 37; airpower as weapon, 37; 39; 45; 64; adoption of his policy in Blitz on London, 153.

Dowding, Sir Hugh C. T., Chief, RAF Fighter Command, 133; 140; on Battle of Britain casualties, 147.

Dunkel-Nachtjagd (Dunaja), 182, 183, 188, 189.

Dunkirk, British evacuation of, 116ff.

Felmy, General Helmut, 6, 23, 35, 66; dismissed, 105.

Fiebig, General Martin, Kesselring remembers, 228; succeeds von Richthofen as head Fliegerkorps VIII,

246, 257; in Stalingrad, 250; in command of airlift operations in Stalingrad, 251, 255.

Flak (Fliegerabwehrkanone – anti-aircraft artillery), (see Luftwaffe, equipment).

Flanders, first German ground and air attack (1917, 41.

'Flying bombs': V1 & V2 – Fi 103 (Vergeltungswaffe), V1 description, 33; use against Britain, 337ff, 365; launch from aircraft, 338; V2 description, 339; use against Britain, 339; failure of offensive, 339.

Four Year Plan, (see Rearmament).

France, 65; warns Germany about attack on Czechoslovakia, 76; Dunkirk, German advance and taking of Paris, 115-120; landing of Allied troops (1944), 336; Allied invasion, 362ff.

French Air Force, aircraft, 112; final attempts against German offensive, 115-6; attacks on, by Luftwaffe, 119.

Fröhlich, General Stefan, Fliegerführer Afrika until 1942, 203; trouble with Rommel, 212.

von Gablenz, General Karl-August Freiherr, Chief Air Force Equipment Office (RLM), 277; mentioned in Udet's suicide note, 278.

Galland, General Adolf, 24, 143, 287, 288; argues for attack on London, 151; proved wrong, 292; on impact of Hamburg destruction on Luftwaffe leaders, 302; on Göring's breakdown, 302-3; added responsibilities (1943), 305; on American bombers, 306; on Hitler's dissipation of fighter defence unity (1944), 346-7; on effect of Allied attacks on German oil industry, 349; on turbo-jet (Me 262), 350, 352.

von Gantzow, Karin, wife of Hermann Göring, 7.

Gas War of 1940, The, by S. Southwold (Miles), 38-9.

Gauleiters (regional Party leaders, NSDAP), 311,

Geisler, General Hans, 6, 125.

General Staff, Luftwaffe (see Luftwaffe).

German Air Force (see Luftwaffe).

Germany, Allies attack Lübeck, 185, Rostock, 185, Cologne, 185-6, 187; bombing of Berlin (1943-45), 341, 346; bombardment by Allies (1943-45), 339ff; Soviets march into (1945), 371ff; effects of Allied bombardment and death tolls, 373ff.

Goebbels, on raids on German cities by British, 186; on damage to Essen, 298; criticises Göring and Udet, 298; on technical failure of Luftwaffe, 298; on destruction of Hamburg by RAF, 302.

Gotha bombers, 37.

Göring, Reichsmarschall Hermann, biographical, 3-8; on Germany's need of Air Force, 4-10; Chief of Four-Year Plan, 8, 63; on Wever's death, 13; relations with Milch, 13-4, 20; reorganization of RLM (1937), 20; reorganization of RLM (1938), 21-2; final reorganization of RLM (1939), 22; on Jeschonnek, 25, 26; estrangement from other chiefs, 26; relations with Udet, 31-2; rearmament, 35; on Spanish Civil War, 58; agrees with Knauss, 64; heavy bomber, 68; plans for output of aircraft, 74-7, 80-2; discusses attack on Britain with Milch, 78; on Luftwaffe (1939), 97; Kesselring remembers, 105; to Jeschonnek about onslaught on Britain, 127; believes Luftwaffe capable of destroying RAF, 132; on destruction of RAF Fighter Command, 142; decides against attacking radar in Battle of Britain, 143; on bombing of London, 165; on bombing of other targets than London, 169; on enemy's strength (1941), 184; Operation Hercules, Kesselring remembers, 209; disagreement with Hitler over Russian invasion, 219; advises Hitler on Stalin-

grad airlift, 251; on Luftwaffe losses in Stalingrad airlift, 256; refuses to co-operate with OKW high command, 269-70; criticism of Udet, 271; gives Milch responsibility for aircraft production, 274; lack of trust in Udet, 274; Udet's suicide, 278; responsibility for Luftwaffe's failure, 279; opposes loss of manpower to Army, 285-6; breakdown, Galland remembers, 302-3; ineffective leader of RLM, 309-10; loses influence with Hitler, 309-10; nears breakdown, 311-12, 313, 314; working methods, Koller remembers, 314; surrounds himself with younger men, 312-3; Jeschonnek's suicide, 318; on systematic bombing of Soviet economy, 328; Milch recommends his dismissal, 365; instituted 'Aeropag', (1944), 370; arrest, 375-6.

'Göring Programme' – expansion of German aircraft production after 1942, 275.

Great Britain, bombing of, World War I, 37; German raid on London (1917), 38; Udet on, 70; warns Germany about attack on Czechoslovakia, 76; German onslaught against, 121ff; economic blockade of, 122-3; German minelaying in ports and coastal waters, 124-5; 'Kanalkampf', 129; Luftwaffe support of ground forces in attack on Britain, 130; destruction of RAF, 122, 131, 132-3; RAF defence, 134-5; Battle of Britain (q.v.); night bombing of, 164; bombing of London: failure of day air offensive, 165; bombing civilians, 165; damage to buildings, docks and railways, 166; dummy airfields, factories and towns, 168; raid on Coventry, 169-70, 173; Germany wages economic war on, 169, 171, 175, 176, 178-9, 180; Operation Sealion, 171; flying bombs on London, 227ff; continued bombing of London (1944), 332.

Greece, Italy invades, 195; Germany invades, 197; Operation Mercury, 198-9; British on Crete, 200; Germany loses Crete, 200.

von Greim, Field Marshal Robert Ritter, 4, 19, 28, 318, 376.

Guderian, General Heinz, on air support for ground operations, 41; on Jeschonnek, 318.

Halder, General Franz, 19, 227, 233, 240; discusses invasion of West with Hitler, 104.

Hamburg, RAF raid on, 299-300, 302.

Hands Off Britain League, 38.

Harlinghausen, General, 213-4, 215.

Harris, Sir Arthur, Commander-in-Chief of RAF Bomber Command, 185, 298.

Hart, Sir Basil Liddell, on German campaign in Poland, 40-1.

Heinkel, 64; Project 1041, 70; on production of He 177, 277; on Udet, 277.

Helle Nachtjagd (Henaja), 182, 183, 188, 189.

Himmelbett, 183, 190.

Hitler, Reich's Chancellor Adolf, officially establishes Air Force, 4; belief in strong air force, 12-3, 82, 89; Jeschonnek, 24; incorporation of Sudetenland, 77; on attack on Poland, 90; decision to attack France and England, 103; draws up Plan Yellow, 103; postpones Plan Yellow, 104; on Mechelen incident, 104; Basic Order No. 1 on security, 107-8; includes Norway and Denmark in invasion of West, 108; War Directives: No. 1, 122, Nos. 2, 3, 4, 122, No. 6, 123, 126, No. 9, 123, 126, No. 13, 118, 126, No. 16, 130, No. 17, 131, No. 20, 195, No. 21 (Operation Barbarossa), 218, 219, 220, No. 22, 195, 196, No. 23, 171, No. 28 198, No. 38, 204, No. 39 (Operation Blue) 233, 239, No. 41, 245; decides to blockade Great Britain, 122-3; Blitz on

London, 152, 153; believes Britain's defeat is imminent, 155; postpones Operation Sealion indefinitely, 157; ends night flying over Britain, 187; reprisal for attack on Lübeck by Britain, 190; sanctions Rommel's Egypt offensive, 208; decision on North Africa, 212; order to split forces in Soviet Union, 247; decision re. Stalingrad airlift, 250-1; over extension of Luftwaffe's resources, 260; drains Luftwaffe training schools, 283; furious at failure of offensive against Britain, 297; criticises Luftwaffe (1943), 298; angry at figures of American aircraft production (1943), 299; rejects changeover from Luftwaffe offensive to defensive strategy in West (1943), 302-3; drafts aviation workers to armed forces, 303; attitude towards Göring, 309-310; on turbo-jet (Me 262), 351; 'hell' of Flak (1944), 359; disillusionment with Luftwaffe (1944), 368ff; rupture with Göring, 375-6.
'Hitler uber Deutschland', 12.
Holland, German occupation of, 114.
Hönmanns, Major, Mechelen incident, 105.

Iraq, German support of uprising, 200; British occupation of, 200-1.
Italian Air Force, 287; attacks on England, 164.
Italy, declares war on France and Britain, 195; invasion of Greece, 195; Luftwaffe deployment (1944), 330-1; campaign in Italy (1944), 331.

Jägerstab (Fighter Staff), 343-5, 367.
Jeschonnek, General Hans, biographical, 23-26; question of court martial, 17; conflict with Milch, 25, 26; relations with Göring, 25, 26; proposes new structure for General Staff, 26; on adoption of dive-bombing, 49; on fall in output of aircraft, 81; on Allied air strength, 88; on destruction of enemy air power, 97; to Göring on onslaught on Britain, 127; proposes London as main target for Adlertag, 151; optimistic about Allied bomber strength, 193, 194; attempt to dissuade Hitler from Stalingrad airlift, 251; lack of interest in air armament, 267; incurs Göring's dissatisfaction, 313; conflicts with others in General Staff, 315-6; gets rid of von Waldau, 315; breakdown, 317-8; suicide, 318.
Jodl, General Alfred, 19, 270; on Mechelen incident, 104; assumes Britain's defeat, 156.
Jugoslavia, German occupation of, 197; Belgrade, revolution in, 197; Belgrade, bombing of, 197-8.

Kalinowski, Major (Polish Air Force), on German attacks on Polish airfields, 99.
Kammhuber, General Josef, 6, 78, 79, 80; General of Night Fighters, 181-3; 'Kammhuber Line', 182; criticism from Göring, 299; relieved of command of Fliegerkorps VIII, 305.
Kanalkampf, 129, 138.
Kesselring, Field Marshal Albert, 6, 98; biographical, 16-7; on Milch, 11, 17, 18-9; on Milch and Wever, 16; on General Staff, 18; commander Luftkreise III, 19; replaces Wever 1936, 67; a strategic Luftwaffe, 68; on impossibility of air supremacy over Britain without occupation, 132; Malta, 204-5, 206, 207, on Operation Hercules, 209; on Milch and Udet, 267; Commander-in-Chief South, 288.
Kleiss, Col. Fritz, advocates long-range bombing, 327.
von Kluge, Field Marshal Gunther, on Allied air superiority, France (1944), 337.
Knauss, Dr. Robert, 35, 64.

Knickebein (Crooked Leg), 127, 168.
Koller, General Karl, on Göring's abuse of OKW, 271; on Göring's 'Little General Staff', 313; replaces Kreipe as Chief of General Staff, 368; on need to consult Hitler to move Luftwaffe units, 369.
Konaja, 183.
Korner, Paul, 27.
Korten, General Günther, succeeds Jeschonnek as Chief of General Staff, 318-9; end of career, 367.
Kreipe, General Werner, on Milch, 10; succeeds Jeschonnek as Chief of General Staff, 367-8; replaced by Koller, 368.
Kuban peninsula, German offensive on, 293-4.

Leuchtenberg, Major, 318.
Literature, on future of air power, British, 38; German, 39.
London, (see Battle of Britain).
Lörzer, General Bruno, 27; on Udet, 28; on Milch's removal, 366.
Lufthansa 2, 10; Spanish Civil War, 58.
Luftkriegführung, establishes Luftwaffe as offensive force, 39; Luftwaffe as support to Army, 40; indirect support preferable to direct, 42 (see also Blitzkrieg); on neutralization of enemy air power, 97.
Luftwaffe:
Organization: structure 1934, 4; structure 1935, 43; reorganization 1938, 44; reorganization 1939, 44ff.
High Command – RLM (Reichsluftfahrtministerium–Air Ministry): 3, 6; organization 1933, 5; reorganizations 1937-9, 20-22; studies possible invasion of Britain, 78; belief in peaceful settlement (1939), 91; Blitz, decides to bring about victory by air power alone, 153; decides to wage economic war against Britain, 169; orders night fighter force, 181; on strategy in East, 237; task of providing men and materials, 259; separation from OKW, 273; unpreparedness for Allied invasions in Mediterranean (1943), 288ff; tensions at breaking point, 309; loss of control of Luftwaffe to Hitler, 311; preparations for Allied invasion of Europe, 332ff; complete reorganization (1944), Oberkommando der Luftwaffe (OKL), 366ff.
General Staff: 12, 18, 20, 22, 23, 121, 267-8, 309, 311, 317.
Equipment: bombsights, 49, 219; FLAK (Fliegerabwehrkanone) anti-aircraft artillery, 56ff, 81, 181-3, 340, 358-9 (see also Strategy); radar, 57, 89, 182ff, 358; night fighting equipment, 324; radio-controlled bombs, 331, 336.
General: German Military Aviation 1919-33: Appendix 379-389; as support to Army (see Strategy); crew shortages and training, 80, 93, 95, 282, 348, 372; propaganda, 82-3; studies of possibility of attacking Britain, 88-9; strength at outbreak of war, 92ff; attack on Warsaw (1939), 101ff; Intelligence Office on Western offensive strategy 115; Battle of Britain, deficiencies and advantages, 161; Deutsche Afrikakorps and Italuft, 196; criticism of operation in Soviet Union, 236; combat strength end 1941, 239; position, 1943, 286-7; loses 60,000 men to Army, 303; regains command over Reich 1943, 307; dislocation by Allies (1944), 336ff; futility of new aircraft (1944), 356; weakening due to withdrawals to West (1945), 372; final defeat, 374ff; strength at end, 376; surrender, 376.

Aircraft: comparison with Allies (1938), 84-7; (1943), 321; choice, 44-48; heavy bombers, 64ff; jet engine experiments, 89; losses: end 1942, 25; summer 1944, 344; 1944, 370-1; Battle of Britain, 148-9; in East, 1941, 234-5; in East, 1944, 330; night-fighters, 181-7, 324ff, 340; emphasis on fighters (1943), 321; deployment at fronts (1944), 322; close support aircraft, 322; use and development of jet aircraft, 349ff, 352ff; other new types (1944), 353ff.
Ar 64: 2, 4, 36.
Ar 65: 4, 36.
Ar 68: 52, 93-4, 181.
Ar 68E: 56.
Ar 80: 52.
Ar 81: 49.
Ar 95: 124.
Ar 196: 124.
Ar 234: 326, 344, 353, 354.
Ar 240: 89.

Bf 108: 105.
Bf 109: 30, 52, 56, 60, 75-83, 94, 98, 109-12, 124, 129, 131, 133, 136, 139, 142-3, 146, 148-153, 156, 158-9, 181, 191, 196-199, 204, 206, 212-13, 220-6, 232, 236, 244, 254, 263-5, 271, 288, 293, 305-6, 321, 323, 325, 327, 328, 331, 342-6, 349-50, 355, 360, 362, 363, 373.
Bf 109B: 59.
Bf 109C: 59, 93.
Bf 109D: 59, 93.
Bf 109E: 52, 93, 112, 221, 226.
Bf 109E-1: 52.
Bf 109E-3: 52, 306.
Bf 109E-4: 158.
Bf 109F: 221, 259.
Bf 110: 30, 47, 53, 72-5, 77-80, 86-7, 94, 109-12, 129, 133, 136, 139, 143, 148-9, 158, 183, 186-8, 196-9, 206, 217, 220-9, 232, 236, 263-5, 272, 280, 306, 322, 325, 340.
Bf 110C: 93.
Bf 110D: 93.

'Bomber B': 56, 263-4, 276, 282, 322.

BV 138: 124, 244.
BV 222: 211.

Do 11: 2, 4, 36, 45, 46.
Do 13: 36.
Do 15 WaL: 2.
Do 17: 30, 36, 46-7, 50, 53, 59, 69, 75, 78, 80, 83, 86, 87, 93, 102, 112, 129, 220, 222, 226, 259, 263.
Do 17E: 93.
Do 17M: 93.
Do 17M-1: 47.
Do 17Z: 93.
Do 17Z-10: 187.
Do 18: 124.
Do 19: 30, 68, 69, 73.
Do 217: 69-70, 176, 259, 263, 265, 273, 276, 290, 323, 325, 331-2, 336.
Do 217E-2: 69.
Do 335: 343, 353-4.

Fi 98: 48.

Fi 167: 124.

FW 57: 47, 53.
FW 159: 52.
FW 187: 89.
FW 189: 82, 263.
FW 190: 89, 190, 215, 263-6, 273, 288, 293, 297, 301, 304, 306, 321-8, 332, 334, 342-6, 350, 355, 362-3, 373.
FW 190A-5: 323.
FW 190A-8: 323.
FW 191: 56, 89, 276.
FW 200: 88, 125-6, 133, 175-6, 178-80, 244, 253, 256, 264, 283, 363.
FW 200-B: 110.

Ha 137: 49.

He 45: 2, 4, 36, 45, 93, 264, 283.
He 46: 2, 4, 36, 93.
He 50: 36, 48.
He 51: 4, 36, 52, 59.
He 59: 59, 124.
He 60: 124.
He 70: 59.
He 100: 83.
He 111: 30, 36, 46, 48, 50, 59-60, 64, 69, 75, 78, 80, 84, 86, 88, 93, 102, 109, 112, 114, 124, 126, 133, 157, 176, 178, 200-1, 220-44, 226, 229, 241, 253-4, 256, 259, 263-4, 276, 281, 283, 288, 293, 323, 328, 330, 338.
He 111B-2: 46.
He 112: 52, 59, 83.
He 113: 83.
He 114: 124.
He 115: 83, 124, 176, 244, 245.
He 118: 49.
He 119: 71.
He 123: 59.
He 162: 353-4.
He 176: 89.
He 177: 70, 73, 77-82, 87-8, 91, 125, 178, 253, 256, 263-4, 271-2, 276, 281-3, 297, 322, 328, 331-2, 336, 363.
He 177A-1: 71.
He 178: 89.
He 219: 265, 324, 325, 344, 355.
He 280: 89, 326, 352.

Hs 123: 48, 93, 94, 112, 115, 220, 226, 264.
Hs 123A-1: 48, 264.
Hs 124: 47, 53.
Hs 126: 82.
Hs 129: 82, 89, 265, 295, 322.
Hs 130: 89.
Hs 293: 290.

Ju 52: 2, 4, 36, 45-6, 58-9, 82-4, 93-4, 101, 109-10, 114, 196, 199-200, 210-11, 215-6, 229, 241, 252-6, 282-3, 293.
Ju 86: 4, 30, 36, 46, 69, 84, 86, 253, 254, 256.
Ju 86R: 191.
Ju 87: 30, 49-50, 59-60, 75, 78, 82, 87, 93, 95, 105, 112, 115, 119, 124, 129, 133, 148, 158, 196, 199, 201, 206, 215, 220, 222, 224-6, 228-9, 232, 235-6, 244-5, 264, 288, 295, 322, 360, 362.

Ju 87D-1: 264.
Ju 88: 48, 50-1, 60, 70-1, 75-82, 87-91, 93-4, 112,
    125, 133, 154, 158, 176, 186, 212, 220-8, 236,
    244-5, 259, 263, 265, 271-2, 276, 281, 288,
    322-5, 330, 332, 335, 340, 343, 363.
Ju 88A-1: 51, 53, 72, 264.
Ju 88A-4: 264, 359.
Ju 88 G-1: 324.
Ju 89: 30, 68, 69, 73, 110.
Ju 90: 69, 88, 110.
Ju 188: 89, 281, 283, 304, 322, 332, 355, 363.
Ju 252: 89.
Ju 288: 56, 276, 281, 282.
Ju 290: 253, 256.

K 47: 48.

Me 109: (see Bf 109).
Me 109R: 83.
Me 110 (see Bf 110).
Me 163: 326, 343, 354, 355.
Me 209: 83, 89, 326.
Me 210: 73, 74, 77, 78, 79, 80, 82, 88, 89, 94, 191,
    217, 236, 263, 264, 265, 271, 272, 280.
Me 261: 89.
Me 262: 89, 326, 343, 349ff, 367, 370.
Me 309: 326.
Me 323: 283.
Me 410: 280, 306, 323, 332.

Ta 152: 326, 350, 355.
Ta 154: 326, 355.

Luftwaffenhelfer, 320.

Malta: German onslaught, 201-7; Marsa Scirocco Bay,
    bombing of, 201; HMS *Illustrious*, 201; British in, 204-
    5; Operation Hercules, 207-10; Operation Hercules
    postponed, 209; importance to Axis, 210, 214.
Mechelen incident, 104-9.
Mein Kampf, 65.
Meister, General Rudolf, Chief of Operations Staff, 1942,
    315; relations with Jeschonnek, 315; remembers
    Göring at Jeschonnek's suicide, 318.
Milch, Field Marshal Erhard, 3, 5, 6, 10-11; relation with
    Göring, 13-14, 20; military experience, 15; relations
    with Wever, 16; conflict with Kesselring, 17, 18-19;
    opposes General Staff, 18; conflict with Stumpff, 20,
    21; conflicts with Jeschonnek, 25; on Udet, 28, 31, 267,
    274; break with Udet, 31; on rearmament, 35; loses
    control of aerial rearmament, 64; heavy bombers, 68;
    on Germany's failure in onslaught against Britain, 72;
    discusses attack against Britain with Göring, 78; on
    training of personnel, 80; concerned by Allied bomber
    strength, 193-4; Stalingrad airlift, 255-6; ends Luft-
    waffe independent procurement policy, 271; respon-
    sible for aircraft production, 274-5, 276; dismissals,
    277; mention in Udet's suicide note, 278; responsi-
    bility for Luftwaffe's failure, 279; disillusionment with
    Heinkel, 281; ignores problem of Training Command,
    284, 299; aghast at destruction of Hamburg, 302;
    weakness of night-fighter (1944), 324-5; on V1 flying
    bomb, 338; on poor aircraft production (1944), 343;
    recommends Göring's dismissal, 365.
Mölders, Colonel Werner, 24, 143, 224.
Munich Conference 1938, 77.
Mussolini, Benito, 77; Egypt offensive, 208.

National Socialist Party (NSDAP), 8, 13, 62; attacks
    RLM, 311.
Nielsen, General Andreas, 6; on Wever, 11; on organiz-
    ational chaos within RLM, 21; on failure of Udet and
    Milch, 31; on security, 108; on strained relations in
    General Staff, 316; on special commissioners (1945),
    375.
North Africa, problems with transport of German supplies
    to, 211; acute shortages suffered by Germans in, 211;
    Battle of El Alamein, 213-4; Tunisia, 213-4.
Norway, Hitler plans to invade, 108; as base for Luftwaffe
    torpedo attackers, 179.

OKW (Oberkommando der Wehrmacht – High Com-
    mand of the Armed Forces), plan for invasion of
    Czechoslovakia, 76; on Polish Air Force, 99; on
    Poland, 102; report on Jugoslavia (1941), 197; report
    on Greece (1941), 197; directive for attack on Russia,
    218; alienated from Luftwaffe, 270-1; failure to predict
    sites of Allied invasions (1944), 333.
Operation Barbarossa, German invasion of Soviet Union,
    218; (see also Soviet Union).
Operation Bodenplatte, final air attack on Allied airfields
    (1945), 364.
Operation Dynamo, British rescue of BEF from Dunkirk
    (q.v.), 119.
Operation Hercules, German invasion of Malta, 207-10.
Operation Mercury, German invasion of Crete, 198.
Operation Red, German occupation of France (1940),
    117.
Operation Sealion, invasion of Britain, 130, 132, 153, 155-
    6, 157.
Operation Steinbock, intensification of air raids on Britain
    (1944), 332.
Outbreak of War, 92ff.

Paulus, Field Marshal Friedrich, Stalingrad, 248, 250;
    accuses Luftwaffe of betrayal, 255.
Plan Yellow (Hitler's invasion of West), 103, 104, 106, 107,
    108.
Ploch, General August, 29, 31; fired, 277.
von Pohl, Colonel Maximilian Ritter, 6, 196, 268.
Poland, invasion of, 90, 92, 97.
Polish Air Force, 97ff; attacks on airfields (1939), 99;
    aircraft, 98.

Radar, (see Luftwaffe).
Raw Materials, shortage of, (see Aircraft Industry, Re-
    armament).
Rearmament, German, 5, 17; argument for defensive air
    force, 35; Risiko Flotte, 35, 36, 37, 39; Rhineland
    Programme, 36, 45; Production Plans: No. 1, 36, 45;
    Nos. 2 and 3, 36; No. 4, 36, 74; No. 5, 74, 78; Nos. 6
    and 7, 75; No. 8, 76; No. 9, 77; Nos. 10 and 11, 80;
    No. 12, 81; Nos. 13 and 14, 82; potential of air power,
    37-9; air power as offensive force, 39; not benefiting
    from Hitler's programme, 40, 269; financing of, 61;
    shortages of weapons, 61; shortages of raw materials,
    61-3, 73; Four-Year Plan, 62-3, 73.
Red Army, extension of advance (1944), 327; offensive on
    German Eastern Front (1944), 360ff, and 1945, 371ff.
Reich Defence Plan, 303, 304 (see also Aircraft Industry).
Reinberger, Major Helmut, Mechelen incident, 104-5.
'Rhineland Programme', 36 (see also Rearmament).
von Richthofen, Field Marshal Wolfram, 6, 24, 29, 49, 60,
    287-8, 293, 294; in Stalingrad, 246-8, 250, 251; in
    South, 257-8; on Hitler's control over Luftwaffe, 311;

on inflexibility of General Staff, 317.

Risiko Flotte (Risk Fleet), 35, 64.

RLM (Reichsluftfahrtministerium), (see Luftwaffe).

Romania, German invasion of, 196; importance of oilfields to Germans (1944), 333.

Rommel, Field Marshal Erwin, 196; on Malta, 205; Tobruk offensive, 208, 210; Egypt offensive, 208-9; North Africa, 211; relationship with Luftwaffe commanders, 212; on paralyzing effect of Allied air attacks on troops in Normandy (1944), 337.

RAF (Royal Air Force), German plan to destroy, 122, 131, 132-3, 138, 139; state of air defence (1940), 134-6; anti-aircraft artillery, 167, 173; scientific intelligence, 168; bombers shot down in operations, 188; Bomber Command, 185ff; Malta, 204-5; bombs German cities, 298; Hamburg raid, 299-300; change of tactics (1943), 308; superiority of Mustangs and Spitfires, 323-4.

  Aircraft:
    Blenheim, 136, 149.
    Defiant, 136, 149.
    Gladiators, 136.
    Hurricane, 136, 138, 144-6, 149, 153, 154-6, 158, 160.
    Lancaster, 323, 359.
    Mosquito, 352, 358.
    Spitfire, 136, 138, 144-6, 149, 153-6, 158, 160, 266, Mk IX, 323, Mk XIV, 324.

Ruhr, 181; British bombing, 298ff; defences increased, 299.

Sardinia, Allied attack on, 289.

Schmid, General 'Beppo', on Göring's persuasion of Hitler to use Luftwaffe at Dunkirk, 117; report to Göring on Britain's air strength, 121-2; on Göring's breakdown, 311-2.

von Seidel, General Hans Georg, 26; relations with Jeschonnek, 316, 317.

Seidemann, General Hans, 6, 294.

Sicily, Allies attack, 289; Germans withdraw, 290; campaigns (1944), 331ff.

Simon, Sir John, 83.

Smuts, Field Marshal Jan, 38.

Soviet Air Force (Red Army Air Force), bombs dropped on Reich, 181; superiority over Germans (1944), 330; offensive on German Eastern front (1944), 360.
  Aircraft, 59, 72, 221, 292, 360.

Soviet Union, German invasion of, 218ff; military divisions for invasion, 220-1; first attack (June 1941), 222-3, initial German victory in air, 223-224; Luftwaffe support for Army, 225-6, 229, 234, 235; destruction of roads, railways, bridges, 226-7, 231; encirclement of Kiev, 229, 230; Leningrad, bombing of, 230-1; bad weather, 232-3, 240, 249, 254; damage by Luftwaffe end 1941, 234; attack on Soviet war factories, 235; attack on Soviet economy, 236-7, 244; Crimea, 241-3; Operation Blue: Battle of Stalingrad (q.v.), 248.

Spanish Civil War, Germany's reason for intervention, 58; Sonderstab W, 58; Legion Condor, 59, 83; Guernica, bombing of, 59.

Sperrle, Field Marshal Hugo, 4, 6, 24, 59, 84, 152, 172, 184, 362.

Stalingrad, Battle of, problems of split forces, 247-8; airlift, 250-5; amount of supplies dropped in airlift, 255; Luftwaffe losses result of airlift, 256; reoccupation by Soviets, 256.

Strategy:
  General: strategic base: Chapter II, pp. 34-60; 'Rhine-land Programme' – production, expansion (1934), 36; establishment of Risk Fleet and use of air power, 36ff; realization of importance of bombing, 37ff; emphasis on offence against defence, 39; dive-bombing (Blitzkrieg), 40-2, 48-51, 60; support for Army by Luftwaffe, 40-3, 99ff, 115, 225-43, 252-5, 322; general attitude of Army on Luftwaffe role (1936), 42-3; effect of Luftwaffe strategic policy on organization, 43; development of aircraft arising from strategic policies, 44ff; early view of role of fighters, 52; belief in anti-aircraft for defence of Reich (1939), 56-8; confirmation of Luftwaffe strategy by, and lessons from, Spanish experience, 58-60; opposition by Army to development of heavy bomber, 65-6; need for short-term war (1939), 96; importance of destruction of enemy air force (1939), 98; avoidance of civilian targets (1939), 101; review after Poland, 102; first failure of Luftwaffe – Dunkirk, 116; Bombing Directive No. 22, 185; Hitler ends night fighting over Britain, 187; Mediterranean strategy, 214ff; air-lifting, 240-1; attacks on Anglo-American shipping, 244-5; failure of Luftwaffe to assist Navy, 296-7; inefficient bombing of Britain (1943), 297; general state of Luftwaffe beginning 1944, 320; emphasis on ground attack, 322; reduced priority on night fighters (1944), 324ff; failure of reconnaissance (1944), 333; failures against Allied invasion, 336ff; weakness of day-fighting, 342-3; high level commitment to bomber force (1944), 345-6; defence of Germany, 345ff, 373ff; dissipation of fighter units, 346-7; fuel shortages, 348-9, 358, 360, 371; production of new aircraft types 1944, 353ff; futility of new productions 1944, 356; final failures and collapse of Luftwaffe, 358ff; disorganization of command, 369; final upheaval of command, 375; total cost to, and failure of, Luftwaffe, 377.

  Eastern front: direct and indirect support by Luftwaffe for Army, 225-6, 229, 234-5, 237-9, 241-3, 252-5; interdiction of Soviet communications, 226-7, 231, 239; independent Luftwaffe operations, 236, 243; attack on Soviet war economy, 244, 327; long-range bombing and general aircraft deployment, 327; Soviet attack on Eastern Front (1944), 360ff.

  Western Front (also Britain): Western offensive, 114ff; strategy against Dunkirk evacuation and use of Luftwaffe, 116ff; performance in Western offensive, 119-20; plan to destroy RAF, 122, 131-3; economic blockade of Britain, 122-3; techniques, onslaught against Britain, 128-30; strengthening of Western front (1933), 302-6; preparations for and strategy against Allied invasion of Europe (1944), 332ff, 335, 337, 360, 364, 372ff.

Student, General Kurt, 6, 23, 104.

Stumpff, General Hans Jurgen, biographical, 6, 19, 20, 184; conflict with Milch, 21; becomes Milch's deputy, 23; on Göring, 309.

Terrorangriffen (Terror attacks), 185.

'Trumpets of Jericho', 49.

Tscherisch, Gunther, 29, 31, 277.

Udet, General Ernst, biographical, 27-33; conflict with Jeschonnek, 30-1; relations with Milch, 31; relations with Göring, 31-2, 48, 267; replaces Wimmer (1936),

67; heavy bombers, 68, 70; anti-aircraft production, 81; fears German failure (1941), 184; sure of German victory (1940), 267; failure, 268-9, 271, 272; criticised by Milch and Göring, 274; approves Milch's dismissals in Supply and Procurement, 277; broken man, 277-8; suicide, 278; responsibility for Luftwaffe's failure, 279; criticised by Goebbels, 298; on change in production due to raw material shortage (1940), 325.

USAAF (United States Army Air Force), threat to Germany, 301; bombers, Galland remembers, 306; revision of bombing policy (1943), 307; suffers high casualties in bombing Germany (1943), 307; strength against Luftwaffe (1944), 342-3; attacks on German oil refineries (1944), 346.

Aircraft:
B-17, 72, 87, 194, 301, 306, 323, 328.
B-24, 194, 301, 306.
B-29, 72.
Curtiss Hawk, 48.
P-38 Lightning, 301.

P-47 Thunderbolt, 301, 306.
P-51B Mustang, 323-4, 328, 342, 352.

Versailles Treaty, 1, 2, 4, 41.

von Waldau, General Otto Hoffman, 6, 212, 214, 287; death, 291, 315; appointed Chief Operations Staff, 315; disfavour with Göring and Jeschonnek, 315.
Warsaw, attack on (1939), 100ff.
Western Air Defence Zone (The Zone), 56-7.
Wever, General Walther, 6, 11-12; killed, 13; relations with Milch, 16; about General Staff, 18; on selection of aircraft, 44; on importance of air force, 64-5; on heavy bombers, 66-7.
'Wilde Saue' (Wild Boars) tactics, 302, 305, 308.
Wimmer, General Wilhelm, 6, 22, 28, 39, 66.

'Zahme Saue' (Tame Boars) tactics, 306, 340.
Zeitzler, General Kurt, 349-51.
Zeppelin airships, 37.